The Encyclopedia of Native Music

Brian Wright-McLeod

The Encyclopedia of
Native Music

**More Than
a Century of
Recordings from
Wax Cylinder
to the Internet**
Illustrated with
Photographs
and Album
Covers

The University of Arizona Press   Tucson

The University of Arizona Press

© 2005 Brian Wright-McLeod

♾ This book is printed on acid-free, archival-quality paper.

Manufactured in the United States of America

10 09 08 07 06 05   6 5 4 3 2 1

Library of Congress Cataloging-in-Publication Data
Wright-McLeod, Brian, 1958–
The encyclopedia of native music : more than a
century of recordings from wax cylinder to the
Internet / illustrated with photographs and album
covers / Brian Wright-McLeod.—1st ed.
p. cm.
Includes bibliographical references (p.) and index.
ISBN 0-8165-2447-5 (cloth : alk. paper) —
ISBN 0-8165-2448-3 (pbk. : alk. paper)
1. Indians of North America—Music—Discography.
2. Indian musicians—Biography—Dictionaries.
3. Indians of North America—Music—History and
criticism. I. Title.
ML156.4.I5W75   2005
016.78162'97'00266—dc22

                                        2004023862

Publication of this book is made possible in part by the
proceeds of a permanent endowment created with the
assistance of a Challenge Grant from the National
Endowment for the Humanities, a federal agency.

Reader Note: This encyclopedia is a work in progress, and while every effort has been made to assure its accuracy and completeness, there will likely be some information that is in need of correction or revision. If you know of any corrections, updates, additions, or other changes that should be incorporated in a future edition, please send them to the University of Arizona Press, P.O. Box 210331, Tucson, Arizona 85721-0331, or via e-mail to editorial@uapress.arizona.edu. Thank you.

Contents

For Milo Walking Bird

Acknowledgments

This book is dedicated to the people, the generations who sacrificed and kept the knowledge from harm during the darkest times, the musicians and song carriers who continue to endure. And to the future generations of all nations who may come to know and appreciate the simplicity and complexity of who we are as a people with a living culture.

I thank my parents for all their encouragement; Jennifer for her love, support, and sacrifice, as well as the added determination that helped bring it all this far; and my brothers and sisters of the Red Road, the Native American Church, and the sacred pipe for giving me the strength to continue.

If it were not for my work in radio and print and for the many requests from many people seeking information on Native music, this project might never have been realized. Thanks to those who pointed the way to further research and who provided invaluable information and assistance: Agnes Patak, Rob Bowman, Norman Otis Richmond, Charlie Huiskin, and Michael Antone at CKLN 88.1 FM in Toronto; Buffy Sainte-Marie, Kevin Nadjiwon, K-9 and the Renegade Crew, Frank Dreaver and Anne Dreaver of the Leonard Peltier Defense Committee (LPDC), R. Carlos Nakai, John Running, Barry Roden, Ted Takashi Ono at Baldwin Street Music, Aztlan Underground, Casper Lomayesva, Neil Ullestad, Keith Secola, Chris Sam, David Sam, Darryl Tonemah, Sandy Scofield, George Littlechild, John Trudell, Faye Brown, Jim Boyd, Shelley Boyd, Judy Gordon, Gino Guercio, Sarge Old Horn, Steve Barr, Curtis Bailey, Ravana Black, May Yee, T. E. Salvage Inc., Marc Nadjiwan, Barbara Brown and the Canadian Broadcasting Corporation (CBC), Elaine Bomberry, Joanne Shenandoah and everyone at Silver Wave, Cordell Tulley, Leo Griep Ruiz, Brandon Friesen at Arbor Records, Martin Lea and Barbara Eigenstat at Around Again Records, George Zaragoza at Pronto Reproductions, Carrie MacPherson, Helen

Tansey, Brent Michael Davids, Robert Doyle at Canyon Records, Lisa Dowhaniuk at Makoche Records, Ted White Calf and Carol White Calf at Sweet Grass Records, Ray McCallum, Tom Bee at Sound of American Records (SOAR), Alton Walpole, Deane Cameron at EMI Music Canada, Tony Isaacs at Indian House Records, Ness Michaels at Sunshine Records, and Denise Donlon of Sony Music Canada. I am grateful to Annie Barva for her thoughtful and painstaking copyediting of the final manuscript and to Freya Godard for the index. And a very special thanks to Lynn Burns of Pro Bono Law Ontario and to Rohit Parekh and the Aboriginal Legal Department at Gowling, Lafluer, Henderson LLP. There are many, many more to thank—you know who you are. *Mitakuye-oyasin.*

The Encyclopedia of Native Music

Introduction

The need to compile and present some sort of accounting of Native music recordings has been growing. Although this volume could never possibly include every musician, group, or project, it is thoroughly researched and accurate, and it draws attention to the wealth of material that remains to be included. It is as definitive as one can hope, but an incredible amount of information remains yet to be included. I provide a representation of what exists, what has been lost, and what yet may be found.

For the most part, much of the current documentation of Native music is generally made without any critical analysis from within the Native community, combining an informed knowledge of the music and culture, and there is even less analysis of contemporary music. Although this ambitious project can never hope to present all of the information that abounds, it goes well beyond what exists now. It developed from playlists and research for several Native radio programs I created and hosted since 1985 at CKLN 88.1 FM, a community radio station in Toronto. Throughout my experience as a Native radio host and Native music columnist and reviewer, I have encountered numerous requests for information on recorded Native music of all genres. Over time it became clear to me that solid information about music by Native Americans needed to be made available. This book is a small beam of light on a massive topic that has been largely overlooked or misrepresented.

Yet the question remains: What is Native music? The answer is the foundation of this book. Is it the music or the musicians that make it Native? I suppose it's fair to say that it's a bit of both. It's the music of the people who have known the land since time immemorial, but it has also been transformed along with the people and the land to become the hybrids of modern sounds we recognize today. Identifying the roots and the source material of anything recorded by Native people serves, I hope, as a documentation of that history.

I am more concerned about cataloging the music of indigenous peoples rather than providing a massive overview of American-based folk music derived from Native origins. It is not my task to decide who is Native and who is not, especially regarding such issues as blood quantum. With respect to Chicanos, Mestizos, and Metis artists, Tex-Mex border music, fiddle music, and many other specific areas, additional volumes that focus on these topics are necessary. However, I chose the artists identified herein to represent the widest musical chasms possible, including mainstream artists of popular genres, folk artists, and activists-musicians who embrace the cultural and political identity of their indigenous roots. The area of Chicano and Mestizo music is vast in its own right and deserves several volumes.

REGIONS

Identified as North America, the geographical reach of this book recognizes the Arctic/Circumpolar region (from Greenland across northern Canada to Alaska) and the northern parameters of the U.S.–Mexico border, specifically musicians from reservations who have been recorded on commercially released albums. It's been my experience that Mexico identifies itself as being part of Latin America and contains an immense trove of musical diversity. Therefore, the majority of recordings from that region listed in this volume consists largely of traditional Native or reservation-based forms such as Yaqui ceremonial music. It would be an immense task to create a book just on Native recordings in the northern region of Mexico. I can only suggest these geographical regions with a slim margin of inclusion and without any hope of doing the topic the justice it deserves. Better some than none. The collection does not include Native music from Hawaii and the Pacific Rim at this

time. Indeed, each area of research is massive and really requires its own volume.

GENRES

This book is about recognizing the contributions made by Native recording artists in all genres. The genres *chicken scratch, contemporary, powwow, peyote,* and *traditional/archival* were developed from my own practical experience with music and through industry criteria, radio format, and historical cataloging and identification. This book traces the history of recorded Native music, specifically commercially released projects. By industry definition, traditional music relates to old songs for which the authors are unknown and, hence, for which no publishing records exist and for which ownership is often public domain, but also which continues to be recorded by contemporary artists.

ARTISTS

To manage the process, I chose a narrow but inclusive focus that represents the vast reaches of Native culture and being. I began with the recordings and labels that focused on reservation-based artists and worked my way out to the mainstream. I chose the mainstream artists by virtue of their reputation as being Native throughout their careers, such as Buffy Sainte-Marie, Redbone, Jesse Ed Davis, Rita Coolidge, and XIT, or because of the significant contributions they have made to Native music, such as Robbie Robertson and the Red Road Ensemble.

Many influential jazz and blues artists of the early twentieth century have Native ancestry and were known in their circles as Native, but were never widely acknowledged as such, including Oscar Pettiford, Mildred Bailey, Keely Smith, and many more. Time limitations prevented me from including several artists with Native roots, but who at least deserve some mention here: Kurt Winter (the Guess Who), Tommy

Bolin, Cher, Billy Ray Cyrus, Crystal Gail, Jimi Hendrix, Loretta Lynn, Holly McNarland, the Neville Brothers, Donna Summers, Hank Williams, Hank Williams Jr., Hank Williams III, and many more; some are mentioned briefly in the text here and there. In order to keep this volume manageable, I have left it to the reader to conduct research on these major artists, utilizing the abundance of widely available material derived from their immense popularity. I also focus on Native artists rather than overwhelm the text with a galaxy of mainstream stars who claim the most minuscule amount of Native ancestry in their family trees. I have found that sometimes these claims can be based on fabrication, rumor, or some kind of New Age past-life syndrome. I chose to present what some may feel is a seemingly narrow area of study in order to render this single volume somewhat manageable in its size and scope. The number of predominantly non-Native people who can trace a distant Native ancestor is, of course, quite large, and many others are self-identified as Native.

Several Native artists did not make it into the volume because of time constraints: the Isleta Poor Boys, the Wingate Valley Boys, the Fenders, the Thunders, and many more. I have them in mind for future editions, however.

I also considered including Johnny Cash for his Native-themed albums in order to represent historically important turning points. I then had to face the fact that this choice would force me to include a multitude of other non-Native musicians who deserve credit for the same reason.

HOW TO USE THIS BOOK

The book is designed to make the information accessible for quick research. The music is organized by genre with Arctic/Circumpolar first, then chicken scratch, then contemporary as a major source of current music, followed by traditional forms (flute, peyote, powwow, archival). The listings are organized alphabetically by group names or by the performer's last name or complete stage name. In the heading, this information is followed by the artist's nation (tribal affiliation), main music genre, and sometimes cross-references to other performers or projects.

Owing in part to the secretive nature of many of the older traditional recordings, specifically peyote music, singers preferred not to have their work fully revealed other than their names and nations as credited in the liner notes of albums and tapes. For contemporary groups, band members are identified under "Lineups," along with their nation(s) and their contribution to the band. If an entry is for an individual artist, the artist's biography precedes his or her band lineup; if the entry is for a band or group, then the biography follows the band's lineup. Biographies (when the information is available) include, among other things: date and place of birth, the year and place the group was formed, a brief description of the music or the recording, awards and outstanding achievements, and film/television appearances. Discographies are given next. They include album titles, labels and release dates (serial numbers are used when release dates are not available; sometimes no data were available), as well as chart appearances and record sales if the information was attainable to me. The discographies are presented beginning with the most recent project first. If a special project was recorded in collaboration with another artist, the fellow artist is mentioned accordingly: "R. Carlos Nakai: *Inside Canyon de Chelley* [Canyon 1997] w/ Paul Horn."

Recordings listed under the subheading "Appearances" provide information on an artist's session work with other performers or tracks contributed to other recordings. A listing of video singles and a filmography that includes either soundtrack work or on-camera appearances are given next.

Soundtracks for major motion pictures

are included to illustrate the extent that Native music has been used commercially and the level of involvement of Native musicians in film, video, and television. Although there are numerous films and documentaries about the various styles of Native music, I elected to focus this book on recorded music with acknowledgment to film and television as a bridge to other media. Again, this book is not about film and television, but it does mention certain film and television projects. Films about Native music or musicians are thus included in the discography or in a filmography, such as the documentary film about guitarist Don Ross. When an artist appears in a production or if the film itself is referred to, the title of the film is followed by the director's name or the film company and the year of release: *Dance Me Outside* [Bruce MacDonald, 1994]. When the soundtrack recording is referred to, the title is followed by the label and year in brackets and the abbreviation "sdtk": *Dance Me Outside* [Rez Films/Denon 1994] sdtk. Listings of video singles and music videos include the company and/or director and the year, depending on the information available. Listings of video specials, television specials, and television appearances on programs or serials contain sometimes (but not always) the title, director or company, year, episode title, and the character played, based on information acquired.

For compilation albums, the term *compilation* is used instead of *various artists*, and the term *best of* is used when referring to the compiled works of a single artist or group. In the discographies, artist appearances on compilation albums are listed under "Appearances," including the title of the compilation album with label and year in brackets and the abbreviation *comp*. If the compilation is found in a compilation section different from the current listing, a cross-reference is provided. Not all compilations listed in an artist's or group's discography are listed in the compilation sections.

In the discography and appearance lists, the spelling of names and words often varies and is given as they appear in the original recording credits. Within the listing of powwow music recordings, each drum group is identified by its members' nation or as intertribal (when group members represent various First Nations affiliations) and by its use of northern or southern style. The lineups identify original singers from a group's earliest recordings, with the lead singer named first.

All cross-references are marked by *See*: and include enough information about sections and specific subsections (as listed in the table of contents) so that a reader can locate the referenced material easily: for example, "*See*: Flute Music: R. Carlos Nakai" or "*See*: Contemporary Spoken Word: Poetry Compilations: *Aboriginal Hitch-Hike Rap*. Cross-references to artists or groups include the section name *only* if the section is different from the current section: for example, a cross-reference to Shingoose, a contemporary artist, in a contemporary entry will be "*See*: Shingoose," but a cross-reference to the Denver Indian Singers, a powwow group, in a contemporary entry will be "*See*: Powwow Music: Denver Indian Singers." Cross-references to compilation sections are given only if the compilation in question is listed in a section other than the current one: for example, if the contemporary compilation *Awakening the Spirit* is listed in the discography for a contemporary artist, no special cross-reference is given to the contemporary compilations, but if the Arctic/Circumpolar compilation *Nunavik Concert* is listed in the discography for a contemporary artist, the listing will read, "*Nunavik Concert* [Sunshine 1995] comp *See*: Arctic/Circumpolar Compilations."

NATIONS

There has been a growing debate over the use of names regarding heritage and cultural affiliation. Many times throughout history, newcomer governments and settler cultures have wrongly used many labels. In the creation of some kind of guideline for names and the use of those names, there has also been a continuing difficulty in agreeing upon what is the same culture and what is not and how the people would like to be addressed. The listing of "tribal" or nation names throughout this project is not intended to be an atlas of Native cultures, but it does draw on information related to the majority of cultures apparent in the recordings listed herein.

With the exception of album titles, Anishnabe (includes Ojibwe Potawatomi and Odawa, known as the Three Fires Confederacy) is used for Chippewa or Ojibwe and for all related spellings of the latter; Anishnabekwe for Anishnabe women; Tohono O'odham for Papago; Akimel O'odham for Pima; Wendat for Huron; Mi'kmaq for Mi'kmaw, Mic Mac, and other spellings; Inuit for Eskimo; Dineh for Navajo; and Dene (pronounced "den-ay") for the people in northern Canada: Dene, Denesoline, or Na-Dene (Chipewayan) are Athapaskan peoples—Tlicho (Dogrib), Deh Gah Got'ine (Slavey), Kashot'ine, and Dinjii Zhuh (Loucheux). The Sarcee in Alberta, belonging to the Dene, prefer to use Tsuu T'ina; their homeland, or Denendeh, stretches from the southern shores of the Beaufort Sea into northern Alberta.

The Blackfoot Confederacy includes Siksika or northern Blackfoot, whose territory lies east of Calgary, Alberta, and includes Gleichen and Cluny, Alberta; Kainah or Blood are located near Waterton National Park and Standoff, Alberta; Pikunni (Ahbut-ochsi-Pikunni) or Peigan are located near Crows Nest Pass, Fort Macleod, and Brochet, Alberta; the Pikunni (Amskapi-Pikunni), or southern Peigan or Blackfeet, reside near the foothills of the Rocky Mountains and Glacier National Park, Montana.

Onkwehonwe, or the Haudenosaunee (People of the Longhouse) or Five Nations Confederacy, now known as the Six Nations, include the Mohawk, Oneida, Onondaga, Cayuga, Seneca, and Tuscarora.

The Sioux Nation includes Lakota or Teton, Dakota or Santee, and Nakota or Yankton. The "Oceti Sakowin" or the Seven Council Fires of the Lakota include the Oglala, Minneconjou, Sihasapa, Hunkpapa, Oohenumpa, Sicagu, and Itazepco. However, many First Nations names usually translate to mean "the People."

This volume provides an overview of the abundance of recorded Native music while underlining its historical value. Performers who do not have individual biographical entries can often be found in band lineups or in a compilation album section. Information on songs, music, or performers not supplied in the introductions to each section can often be found in the biographies.

Many of the artists and labels presented herein can be contacted via the Internet. Even the finest record stores do not stock most of this music, if any of it, and if they do, they do not present it in any comprehensible manner. However, a growing number of older and rare recordings are being reissued—mostly in Europe or Japan, yet they are available. Meanwhile, a Native music industry continues to develop, gaining recognition from the numerous music associations, such as the Juno Awards in Canada and the Grammy Awards in the United States, and from industry associations and trade publications such as *Billboard Magazine*. The exact numbers of product sales remain vague, with a wide range between artists who perform and those who record.

I'm aware that I have not listed many artists and recordings because of time restraints, unavailability of subjects, or lack of information, but I see this project as the shaking of a tree to see what falls out. This single project cannot be everything to everyone. However, readers are welcome to contact us regarding the inclusion of relevant information in future editions.

Abbreviations

AFIM	Association for Independent Music (United States)
AFN	Assembly of First Nations (Canada)
AICH	American Indian Community House (United States)
AIDS	Acquired Immune Deficiency Syndrome
AIM	American Indian Movement (United States/Canada)
AMA	American Music Awards
ANDPVA	Association of Native Development in Performing and Visual Arts (Canada)
APTN	Aboriginal Peoples Television Network (Canada)
BIA	Bureau of Indian Affairs (United States)
CAMA	Canadian Aboriginal Music Awards
CARAS	Canadian Academy of Recording Arts and Sciences (Juno Awards)
cass	cassette
cassingle	a single released on cassette
CBC	Canadian Broadcasting Corporation
CBS	Columbia Broadcasting System (United States)
CCMA	Canadian Country Music Association
CD	Compact Disc
CMA	Country Music Association (United States)
CNE	Canadian National Exhibition
comp	compilation album (various artists)
CRIA	Canadian Recording Industry Association
CTVW	Children's Television Workshop (United States)
D	deleted (no longer available)
DEC	Development in Education Centre (Canada)
ECMA	East Coast Music Awards (Canada)
EP	Extended Play (a recording containing fewer than five tracks)

EZLN	Ejército Zapatista de Liberacion Nacional (Mexico: Zapatista Liberation Army)	NGO	nongovernmental organization (United Nations)
FAITA	First Americans in the Arts (United States)	NPR	National Public Radio (United States)
ICC	Inuit Circumpolar Conference (Alaska/Canada/Greenland)	NRG	dance music; e.g., Hi NRG
		NXNE	North by Northeast Music Fest (Canada)
IITC	International Indian Treaty Council (United States)	OISE	Ontario Institute for Studies in Education (Canada)
INDIE	NAIRD's award for best independent recording (United States)	OJ	Ojibwe
		o/p	out of print
		PBS	Public Broadcasting System (United States)
LCO	Lac Courte Oreilles Ojibwe Reservation, Wisconsin (United States)	PMIA	Pacific Music Industry Association (Canada)
LP	Long Play (full-length vinyl album)	R & B	rhythm and blues
		rpm	revolutions per minute
LPDC	Leonard Peltier Defense Committee (United States/Canada)	sdtk	soundtrack
		SECC	Southeastern Cherokee Confederacy of Pennsylvania (United States)
MACA	Manitoba Annual Country Awards (Canada)		
MIANL	Music Industry Association of Newfoundland and Labrador (Canada)	SICC	Saskatchewan Indian Cultural Centre (Canada)
		SOAR	Sound of America Records (United States)
MTV	Music Television Network (United States)	SRIA	Saskatchewan Recording Industry Association
NAC	Native American Church (United States/Canada)	Trad	traditional music
		UNESCO	United Nations Educational, Scientific, and Cultural Organization
NAIRD	National Association for Independent Record Labels and Distributors (United States)	w/	with
NAMA	Native American Music Awards (United States)	WCMA	West Coast Music Awards (Canada)
NCAI	National Congress of American Indians (United States)	WOMAD	World Music, Arts, and Dance (international)
NCI	Northern Communications Incorporated (Canada)	WOMEX	World Music Exposition (Europe)
NDA	no data available	YTV	Youth Television Network (Canada)
NFB	National Film Board (Canada)		
NFIC	News from Indian Country (United States)		

SECTION 1
Arctic/Circumpolar Region

The Arctic/Circumpolar region covers a vast cultural and geographical terrain that stretches from Alaska to northern Canada, Greenland, the Faroe Islands, the Scandinavian countries, northern Russia, and Siberia. For the purposes of this book, the region includes only the North American reaches of the Arctic and Greenland. Although the Inuit population is relatively small, it covers a vast region and is in a sense an extended family. The three basic music forms are throat songs, drum dance, and *a-ja-ja* songs (singing with drums).

Katajjait is the term used in the Ungava region for throat singing; the Iglulik identify these vocalizations as *kataksatuk*, the Netsilak and Caribou as *pirkusiarartuq*. Numerous forms of throat-singing styles are found in Siberia and Tuva. Often improvised, katajjait are duets performed by women who stand face to face (sometimes in groups of four) and produce rhythmic or guttural sounds through voice manipulation and breathing techniques that reach up to 240 beats a minute or more. Traditionally the katajjait was performed during the spring equinox and the winter and summer solstices, or when men were away hunting.

A throat song has three layers of expression that include the text (morphemic), melodic or intonative, and vocal quality or timbre, which includes breathing techniques with occasional diatonic pitch changes. The first (melodic) sequences are motivic, where the storyteller weaves the elements of performance into a logical saga. A good throat singer is said to be an individual who can perform with stamina and endurance and has a vast repertoire that can be rearranged through creative choices of vocal effects, timbre, and rhythm. The end of the song occurs when one or both singers become exhausted or laugh or are unable to follow a tempo or to initiate a new cycle of song.

The katajjait texts can include comprehensible words or words that have lost their meaning and vocables. Throat songs are also imitative in character, with a variety of sounds that mimic the landscape, elements of nature, and baby and animal sounds. Kettles, pans, and other objects are sometimes used as resonators to create special sound effects. In some cases, the jaw harp (or Jew's harp) is used as a solo instrument.

The total Inuit population averages little more than one hundred thousand throughout an area stretching from Tchoukotka, Siberia, to the west coast of Alaska, along the Beaufort Sea and Victoria Island, to the west and east of Hudson Bay, the shores of Baffin Island, over to Labrador, and including the southwestern shores and eastern areas of Greenland.

Some of the first recordings of Inuit music began in 1910 with the Copper (Eskimos) by Diamond Jennes, in Greenland: Thalbitzer, Thuren, and Leden. Caribou (Eskimos) were recorded by Jean Gabus in Hudson Bay from 1938 to 1939; Menovscikov were recorded in Tchoukotka, Siberia, in 1970. Since the 1960s, ethnomusicologists who have studied such music include Thomas Johnston (United States), Jean-Jacques Nattiez and Jean Malaurie (Canada), and Michel Hauser and Paul Olsen (Denmark).

The singing that accompanies drumming is called ingmerneq. Aside from the drum, a baton or piksi is held out by the singer for the duration of his performance. The songs are divided into three parts; the ending of a song can last as long as twenty to thirty minutes.

The drum (qillat) usually measures 10-by-20 centimeters in diameter, with an ellipsoidal shape, and is fitted with a handle and held in the left hand. Traditionally, the drums were made from walrus skin, which was held in place around the frame with a narwal tendon; contemporary versions are made from synthetic materials. The two lateral sides are smaller, with rectangular holes of 7.5 centimeters; the two opposite sides where the handles are fitted are the longest and serve to control the vibration and overall sound of the drum. The drum handle is approximately 8.5 centimeters long; the drumstick (traditionally made of walrus rib) is approximately 28 centimeters long. The drum is held in the left hand, and the drumstick in the right, with the palm turned toward the skin of the drum; the drum skin is always dampened with a wet cloth before use. The drum head itself is never struck, but only the exterior edge of the drum close to the frame, the drummer striking two-thirds along the length of the drum stick. The drummer stands with legs half-bent and sings solo or as a duo or in groups.

The hand drum songs known as ayaya (or ja ja) are performed with both vocable and word songs. The distinctive handle drum used predominantly throughout the region stretching from Greenland and across much of Arctic Canada to the Mackenzie River is relatively large, varies in size (approximately eighteen inches across), and is flipped from side to side and struck with a drumstick. From the Mackenzie Delta west, singers in groups use a similar drum to accompany the songs. Motion dances and drum dances use combinations of drum and voice, either vocable or word songs.

Beginning in the late 1800s, several outside music influences took root through trade with Europeans, who introduced new instruments such as squeeze-box accordions, fiddles, and jaw harps, along with new song forms. Major changes took place in the 1930s with the advent of extreme government policies of cultural eradication and repression in the wake of assimilation policies, which also employed the use of missionaries and Christian conversion. Eventually, radio introduced country–and-western music styles that flourished in popularity. Changing technologies have enabled the introduction of more outside influences such as raves, techno music, reggae, and rap or hip-hop, which have become entwined with the roots music. Several classical artists of the Inuit music scene include violinist Heidi Aklaseaq Senungetuk (*See*: Arctic/Circumpolar Compilations: *The Inuit Artist World Showcase*) and classical guitarist Jason Akearok

(*See*: Arctic/Circumpolar Compilations: *True North Concerts—Truly Something*); Deanitha Edmunds is an unrecorded opera singer; and throat singer Tanya Tagaq Gilles joined Icelandic singer Bjork on the latter's 2002 world tour.

A few artists from this region have made inroads in the larger music industry in the South, such as Susan Aglukark. The levels of technological and artistic maturity have created insulated and unique worlds of music and culture, from the techno/rave/dance scene in Greenland headed up by groups such as Nuuk Posse to the continuously popular hard-core country artists in northern Canada to inventive jazz artists such as Pamyua from Alaska. The Arctic music scene is new and evolving and is as diverse as this immense region.

Aalut—(Inuit) Reggae

Lineup: Iisaavaraq Petrussen, Jens Olsen, Mati Jensen, Niels Osterman, Holger Elias Poulsen, Lone Josefsen, Pipaluk Moller Lund, Hulda Holm, Nanna Fischer.

The Greenland-based progenitors of Polar reggae were influenced and inspired by the music of Jamaican musician Bob Marley. Complete with horn arrangements and women backup singers, their music won acclaim throughout the region for infusing Rasta music with a northern character.

DISCOGRAPHY:
Tunuartilerneq [Ulo 1990]
Aalut 4 [Ulo 1987]
Navaranaaq [Ulo 1985]
Pooq and Qiperoq [Ulo 1984]

Adams, Charlie—(Inuit) Country

From Inoucdjouac, Quebec. Adams was a founding member of a music group titled Sikumiut (the People of the Ice). Many of the early recordings he made with Johnny Inukpuk on CBC Northern Service were created for broadcast purposes only. The seven-inch vinyl records (titled *Inuit Songs*) contain album-released tracks selected specifically for high rotation on CBC Northern Service radio. The northern broadcast system laid the groundwork for the recording industry throughout the region. Adams's music reflects the perceptions and thoughts of his people, while providing an interpretion of outside influences, such as his Inuktitut version of Bob Dylan's "Blowin' in the Wind."

SELECTED DISCOGRAPHY:
Quviasupunga [Inukshuk 1997]
Piuyugit [CBC Northern Service 1988]
Minstrel on Ice [CBC/Boot 1981]
Inuit Songs [CBC Northern Service Broadcast Recording QCS-1465] four-track, seven-inch vinyl EP
Inuit Songs [CBC Northern Service Broad-

cast Recording QCS-1464] four-track, seven-inch vinyl EP

Inuit Songs [CBC Northern Service Broadcast Recording QCS-1463] four-track, seven-inch vinyl EP

Aglukark, David, and Dorothy Aglukark—(Inuit)

The parents of singer-songwriter Susan Aglukark; recorded one album of gospel songs.

DISCOGRAPHY:

Inuktitut Gospel Songs Performed by David and Dorothy Aglukark [CBC Northern Service QCS-1483]

Aglukark, Susan—(Inuit) Pop *See*: Contemporary Music: George Leach; Tara-Louise Montour

Born January 27, 1967, Churchill, Manitoba. Perhaps the only performer from the Arctic region to date to achieve international commercial success, with soda pop lounge music emulating a Marie Osmond sensibility. The daughter of a Pentecostal minister, she was raised in Arviat, Nunavut, with her seven brothers and sisters. After graduating from high school, she worked as a linguist for the Department of Indian Affairs in Ottawa and later as executive assistant for the Inuit Tapirisat, an Inuit lobby group. Her music became more important to her as a growing career began to take shape. CBC Radio featured her in its compilation of eastern Arctic performers as she prepared to release her first release "Dreams for You." Her 1990 video *Searching* received a MuchMusic Award for cinematography. Her first album, *Arctic Rose*, sold fifteen thousand copies in the Arctic and attracted immediate attention from EMI Music Canada, who signed her the following year. The 1995 release *This Child* reached number 1 on the *RPM*

Weekly charts, the *Record* AC Charts, and the *RPM Weekly* Country Charts. Her most memorable performances include two for Queen Elizabeth at Canada's 125-years celebration and two years later at the 1994 Commonwealth Games; she has also performed for Canadian prime ministers Mulroney and Chretien and appeared on many Canadian television specials, including *Solstice Rouge* [Prime 2001]. Aglukark has become a noted and respected ambassador of the North who brought deeper understanding of her people to the world.

DISCOGRAPHY:

Big Feeling [EMI 2003]
Unsung Heroes [EMI 1999]
This Child [EMI 1995] Randall Prescott, producer
Christmas Album [Aglukark Entertainment/EMI 1994]
Arctic Rose [independent 1992; reissued by EMI Canada 1994]
Dreams for You—Nitjautiit [CBC Northern Service 1991] cass

Singles:

"One Turn Deserves Another (Mokran Mix)" [EMI 1999]
"Suffer in Silence" [EMI 1996]
"O Siem" [EMI 1996]
"Hina Na Ho" [EMI 1995]
"Breakin' Down" [EMI 1995]
"Still Running" [EMI 1994]
"Song of the Land" [EMI 1994]
"Little Toy Trains" [EMI 1993]
"Searching" [independent 1990]

Appearances:

Oh What a Feeling 2 [Universal 2001] four-CD box set
True North Concerts—Truly Something [CBC North 2000] comp
Tapes for Timor [Hands Free Records 1996] comp
Here and Now: A Celebration of Canadian Music [Sony 1995] comp
Children of the World [Groupe Concept/Musicor 1994] comp

Nitjautit [CBC Northern Service 1991] comp

Videos:
One Turn Deserves Another [EMI 1999]
Casualties of War [EMI 1999]
O'Siem [EMI 1996]
Hina Na Ho/This Child [EMI 1995]
Song of the Land [EMI 1994]
Searching [independent 1990]

Awards:
2004: Juno Award, Aboriginal Recording of the Year, *Big Feeling*
2001: Juno nominations, Best Music of Aboriginal Canada Recording, Best Producer, Best Recording Engineer, *Unsung Heroes*.
1996: Juno nominations, Best Video, *O'Siem*; Chris Irschick, Producer of the Year, "O'Siem"; Female Vocalist of the Year; Single of the Year, "O'Siem"; Album of the Year, *This Child*.
1995: Canadian Country Music nominations: Female Artist of the Year; Single of the Year; Song of the Year, "O'Siem"; Album of the Year; Top-Selling Album, *This Child*. Juno Award: Best New Solo Artist; Best Music of Aboriginal Canada Recording, *Arctic Rose*.
1994: Aboriginal Achievement Award in Arts and Entertainment; Canadian Country Music Award: Rising Star and Female Video of the Year, "Song of the Land."

Aningmuiq, Etulu, and Susan— (Inuit)

From Pangnirtung, Baffin Island, Nunavut. Etulu worked as a park warden in Anyuittuq National Park, Pangnirtung.

DISCOGRAPHY:
I'm Glad in My Heart [CBC Northern Service 1989]
Aningmiuq [CBC Northern Service 1984]

Arnaituk, Juupie—(Inuit) *See:* Tumasi Quissa

From Wakeham Bay, northern Quebec. Fiddle player Juupie or Jopie, was one of the first Inuit performers to have his music recorded and broadcast on radio in the North. He is accompanied by guitarist Mark Papigatuk on the mini-album *Jigs and Reels*.

SELECTED DISCOGRAPHY:
Things around Us [CBC Northern Service 1987] twelve-inch vinyl LP of children's songs
Jigs and Reels [CBC Northern Service Broadcast Recording QC-1270] nine-track, seven-inch mini-LP
untitled [CBC Northern Service Recording QC-1235] w/ Thomassie Quissak; five-track, seven-inch vinyl EP

Ekho, Jimmy—(Inuit)

From the Northwest Territories, Ekho recorded an Inuktitut version of "Be-Bop-A-Lula" on his album produced by Dave Boileau.

DISCOGRAPHY:
Guti [Nuka Productions 1993]

Etidloiee, Etulu—(Inuit)

From Cape Dorset, Baffin Island, Nunavut. The Inuit songs composed and sung by Etidloiee received backup from bass guitarist Goo Pootoogoo.

DISCOGRAPHY:
Inuit Songs Composed and Sung by Etulu Etidloiee [CBC Northern Service QCS-1457] six-track, seven-inch vinyl EP

Hope, Beatrice—(Inuit) Country Gospel

Originally from Kammasuk and Voisey's Bay, Hope's family and community were relocated to Nain, Labrador, by the Canadian government in the 1960s. The album of cover songs written by many northern artists, including Charlie Adams, was recorded at Eagle Studios in Happy Valley–Goose Bay, Labrador.

Lineup: Richard Neville, Melvin Hamel, Ken Campbell, Chris Snelgrove, and Joan Dicker.

DISCOGRAPHY:
Panik Labradorimiuk—Daughter of Labrador [independent 2002]

Idlout, Lucy—(Inuit) Pop/Rock *See*: Contemporary Music: Leela Gilday

Born in 1973, Iqaluit, Nunavut. Her music bears similarities to P. J. Harvey and Ani DiFranco. Idlout's first three-track demo, released in 1998, raised interest in her talent. She began touring across Canada and collaborated with other musicians, including guitarist Derek Miller in 2000, and recorded a live track with Leela Gilday for the CBC album *True North Concerts—Truly Something*. She collaborated again with Miller, teaming up with rappers Tru Rez Crew (*See*: Contemporary Music) and throat singers to record the single "I'm a Lucky One." Additional session work included backup vocals on the Juno-nominated album *Standing Strong* by Chester Knight. Pursuing an interest in acting, she appeared in the 2003 Richard Sanger stage play *Two Words for Snow*.

DISCOGRAPHY:
E5700: My Mother's Name [independent 2001; Arbor 2003]

Singles:
"Aija Ja/Big Red Chair/Nunatigut" [independent 1998]

Appearances (listed alphabetically):
Chester Knight:
Standing Strong [Arbor/SOAR 2002]
Derek Miller:
Music Is the Medicine [Arbor/SOAR 2002]
Tru Rez Crew:
"I'm a Lucky One" [Trurez Productions 2002] single
Various:
Native to Canada: Showcase of Aboriginal Musicians at WOMEX 2000 [Canada Council for the Arts 2001] comp
True North Concerts—Truly Something [CBC North 2000] comp, w/ Leela Gilday

Ilaat and Peter Leibhardt—(Inuit) Rock

Lineup: Peter Leibhardt, lead guitar; Karl Leibhardt, Lars Kruse, Johannes Therkildsen, Jakob Serubabelsen, Jaaku Larsen, Fari Nielsen, Laila Moller, Paaviaaraq Lamaksen. From Uummannaq, Greenland, Ilaat's music has been described as guitar-based grandiose rock.

DISCOGRAPHY:
Oqaatsit Inorsillugit [Ulo 1997]
Inussuit [Ulo 1985]

Inneruulat—(Inuit) Rock

Lineup: Juaansi Lynge, bass/rhythm/lead guitar; Leif Immanuelsen, piano/harmonica; Kaaleeraq Reimer, lead guitar; Jaaku Larsen, drums; with Aqqaluk Alaufesen and Aqqaluu Fleischer. Inneruulat had an instant hit with their first release in 1981. They combined rock music and traditional drumming with lyrics that echoed the history and culture of Greenland. Larsen recorded a solo album in 1990.

DISCOGRAPHY:
Qaartartut [Ulo 1993]
Inummartoqaat [Ulo 1988]
Inneruulatut Naajorarpugut [Ulo 1981]

Issaluk, Anita—(Inuit) Folk

Born in Chesterfield Inlet, Nunavut. Musician, singer-songwriter, and soapstone carver, Issaluk received national airplay with her first CBC recording of country/folk music sung in Inuktitut and included throat singing in her later compositions.

DISCOGRAPHY:
Songs for the Northern Heart [Arroyo Music 1999]
Anita Issaluk [CBC Northern Service WRC8-6178]

Katuutiit—Pop

Lineup: Noah Tiktak, vocals/keyboards/harmonica/percussion; Leo Subgut, vocals/guitar/bass/percussion; Lak Angidlik, guitar/percussion; John Taipana, guitar; Norman Glowach.

DISCOGRAPHY:
Our Early Childhood [WRC8-7051]

Kristiansen, Ole—(Inupiak) Pop

DISCOGRAPHY:
Pop Uummataaruffimmi [Ulo 1991]

Loutchan, Joe—Fiddle

DISCOGRAPHY:
Fiddler on the Loose, Vol. 3 [CBC E2119]
Fiddler on the Loose Again! [CBC E2112]
Fiddler on the Loose [CBC E2119]

Mariina—(Inupiak) Pop

DISCOGRAPHY:
Utaqqivunga [Ulo 1992]

Mechanics In Ini—(Inuit) Rock

Lineup: Rasmus Rosing, vocals/acoustic/electric guitars; Lennert A. Davidsen, guitars/keyboards; Thomas K. Johansen, bass; Anders Berthelsen, drums; Laars Peter N. Pedersen, keyboards. Guest musicians include Gedion Andersen, drums; Jan De Vroede, Titken A. Jakobse, keyboards; Steen Olsen, guitar; Pilu Lynge, vocals; Nina K. Jorgensen, choir; Vandenhertz, kisima; Jorsi Sorensen, guitar/computer programming.

DISCOGRAPHY:
Inimi [Ulo 2001]

Nanivaat

Lineup: Aviaja Lumholt; Jim Milne, keyboards; Tuka Lynge, bass; Michael Hansen, guitars; Charles Gay; Ulf Fleischer, guitar; Rasmus Lyberth (*See*: Tukak).

DISCOGRAPHY:
Lyberth and Co. [Lyberth CD-2 1989]

Nanu Disco—(Inuit)

Lineup: Starman, lyrics/music; Kagutikaq Duneq, Regine Beck, vocals; Arne Heilmann, guitar/accordion.

DISCOGRAPHY:
In Search of the Roots [Ulo 1998]

Ningiuk, Charlie—Country/Folk

Born August 4, 1963, Iqaluit, Baffin Island, Nunavut. Performing since he was sixteen years old, Ningiuk toured the Arctic, playing his brand of country music.

DISCOGRAPHY:
Inuuqatik [Inukshuk 1997]

Nitjautiit—(Inuit) Folk

DISCOGRAPHY:
Nitjautiit [CBC Northern Service 1992]

Norwegian, Bertha—(Inuit) Country

DISCOGRAPHY:
Spearmaidens [independent 1992]

Appearances:
North of 60 [Alliance Communications 1994] sdtk

Nuuk Posse—(Inuit) Rap

Lineup: John Olsen, vocals; Lars Sorensen, vocals/human beat box; Henrik Pedersen, televocals; Peter Tuusi Motzfeldt, vocals/turntables/programming/samples/backup vocals. The first rap/hip-hop group from Greenland.

DISCOGRAPHY:
Kaataq [Ulo 1996, Belgium]
Annissassaqarpugut [Ulo 1993]
Sussa Appinnagu [Ulo 1992] EP

Olsen, John—(Inuit) Hip-Hop *See*: Nuuk Posse

From Sissimiut, Greenland. Part of the Nuuk Posse lineup, this turntablist supreme and extraordinary producer raises the standard of Native hip-hip to its peak with beat boxing, sampling, mixing, and turntable talents. His unparalleled debut recording features Niels Ole Nielsen, Thomas Hansen, DJ Hap, and Andreas Hojgaard.

DISCOGRAPHY:
Zero One [Arctic Boomhouse Studios 2001]

Pamyua—Jazz

Lineup: Phillip Blanchett and Stephen Blanchett (Yupik, African American); Karinna Mueller (Inupiak); Ossie Kairaiuak (Yupik).

Formed in 1995, Anchorage, Alaska. The Blanchett brothers created a synthesis of styles and cultures that reflects their diverse backgrounds. "We wanted to educate the world about our heritage and how we blended our backgrounds to create something beautiful." This education is given in their mix of gospel, blues, funk, R & B, jazz, and traditional music of Alaska and Greenland.

DISCOGRAPHY:
Verses [Arctic Voice 1999]

Panigoniak, Charlie—(Inuit) Country/Folk

Born near Chesterfield Inlet, Nunavut. A renowned figure in contemporary Inuit music, the beloved Panigoniak has headlined many showcases throughout the Arctic and southern Canadian regions with high national radio exposure through CBC Radio and CBC Northern Service, which provide specialty programming tailored for the Arctic. Influenced by contemporary country-and-western music, Panigoniak prefers to perform original Inuit-based music.

SELECTED DISCOGRAPHY:
Inuktitut Songs [CBC Northern Service QCS 1474]
Inuktitut Christmas and Gospel Songs [CBC Northern Service WRC1-1852]
Just for Kids [CBC Northern Service WRC1-3312] w/ Lorna Tasseor

Appearances:
True North Concerts—Truly Something [CBC North 2000] comp

Pitsukkut—(Inuit) Rock

Lineup: Maasi Lynge, lead vocals/bass/lyrics; Ujuwinguaq Ilinngivakeeq; Haus Peter Kleemann; Tinka Abelsen.

Lynge's lyrics express criticism of the government policy in Greenland and its historical relationships with the Inuit.

DISCOGRAPHY:
Inuiaat Naqisimaneqartugut Kattutta [Sila 7 1980]

Polar Jungle Orchestra— Experimental Jazz

Lineup: Pierre Dorge, guitar/Tibetan conch; Irene Becker, keyboards; Jesper Zeuthen, bass clarinet; Torkild Lindebjerg, iron bar; Martin Lovstrom, bass; Herluf Moller, guitar; Anda Kristiansen, Inuit drum; Petur Gretarsson, drums/percussion; Hakon Leifsson, French horn; Asa Simma, solo joik; Helene Lindholm, Esa Alanne, Hellen Willberg, vocals.

A superlative project of experimental jazz recorded in Greenland in 1992 with Inuit, Inupiak, and Saami artists. The album listed here was dedicated to the United Nations International Year of Indigenous People 1993.

DISCOGRAPHY:
Polar Jungle Orchestra [Ulo 1994]

Qimutjuit—(Inuit) Folk

Lineup: Charlie Iqaluk, acoustic guitar/vocals; Eric Atagotalook, drums/vocals; Paul Kasudluak, keyboard/vocals; Eric Gaudet, bass.

DISCOGRAPHY:
Cousin [Inukshuk 1997]

Tumasi Quissa: *Better Times* released by CBC/Boot Records, 1981. Courtesy CBC.

Quissa, Tumasi—(Inuit) Folk *See*: Juupie Arnaituk

Along with Henry Quissa and Joanasi Qaqutu.

DISCOGRAPHY:
Better Times [CBC/Boot 1981] w/ Juupie Arnaituk
Inuit Songs Composed and Sung by Tumasi Quissa [CBC Northern Service QC-1411] four-track, seven-inch vinyl EP

Quitsaq, Tumassi—(Inuit)

Musician and soapstone carver from Povungnituk, Quebec.

DISCOGRAPHY:
Tumassi Quitsaq [Inukshuk 1996]

Siissisoq—(Inuit) Rock

Lineup: Jens Samuelsen, vocals; Karl Enok Mathiassen, guitar; Villads Kristiansen, drums; Knud Mathiassen, bass.

Formed in 1998 in Uummannaq, Greenland. The group's name means "The Rhino

Is Loose." An immensely popular group throughout Greenland, Iceland, and Denmark. Their debut album sold five thousand units to a population of fifty thousand people (an equivalent of ten times platinum). For their contributions to Greenlandic music, they were awarded the Danish Music Organization KOD and the Greenland Prize in 2000.

DISCOGRAPHY:
Aammarlussuillu Live [Ulo 2001]

Appearances:
Rock from the Cold Seas [The Orchard 2000] comp

Sinuupa, Edward—(Inuit) Funk/Rock

Born November 20, 1972, eighty miles northeast of Kuujjuaq, Quebec. Raised in a traditional atmosphere, Sinuupa grew up with a sense of musical creativity stemming from early gospel influences and rock 'n' roll he heard on the radio. He recorded two well-produced albums, the first recorded in Inuktitut and the second recorded in English. His hard-edged music and honest lyrics focus on all aspects of personal, political, and cultural life, as well as on land rights and survival. He toured extensively across the Arctic and south to Toronto, Ontario. He recorded with Pat Lesyk, guitar; Pat Blonk, bass; Dave Neil, drums.

DISCOGRAPHY:
Arctic Darkness [Snowball 1998] English language
Nunaga: My Land [Snowball 1995] Inuktitut language

Tagoona, William—(Inuit) Folk/Country

Singer-songwriter and journalist. He formed his first group, the Harpoons, while in high school in Churchill, Manitoba.

DISCOGRAPHY:
Northern Man [CBC/Boot Records 1981]

Appearances:
A Northern Christmas [Inukshuk/CBC North 1995] comp
Nitjautit [CBC Northern Service 1991] comp
Children's Songs in Inuktitut [CBC Northern Service Broadcast Recording QCS-1485] comp
The Inuit (Eskimo) of Greenland and Northern Canada, Vol. 1 [Lyrichord/Ulo 1980] comp

Thompson, Mary—(Inuit) Folk

From Eskimo Point, Nunavut, on the northwest shore of Hudson's Bay. Thompson's mother, Alice Suluk, was famous for her drum dance songs, and her father, Donald Suluk, was an equally renowned traditional performer. Primarily a traditional performer herself, Thompson also recorded country music with explorations into world music and reggae with her number "My Song for the People of Africa."

DISCOGRAPHY:
My Songs for My People [CBC Northern Service 1987]

Appearances:
Nitjautit [CBC Northern Service 1991] comp

Thrasher, Willie—(Inuit) Trad/Folk

From Inuvik, Northwest Territories. One of a few Inuit performers who made an impact across North America and internationally. His music video made by CBC in 1981 in Montreal was shown across Canada and at British Columbia's EXPO '86 in Vancouver.

DISCOGRAPHY:
Indian Lady [independent 1998]

Indian/Inuit Country [Sunshine 1993]
Spirit Child [CBC/Boot 1981]

Appearances:
Sweet Grass [CBC North 1982] comp

Townley, Henoch—(Inuit)

Born 1972, St. Anthony, Newfoundland. Townley learned guitar and piano at an early age and later moved to Quebec City. He returned home and recorded an album that combined modern sounds with traditional culture and influences.

DISCOGRAPHY:
Reaching Point [Inukshuk 2001]

Tudjaat—(Inuit) Hip-Hop

Lineup: Phoebe Atagotaoluk and Madeline Allakariallak, vocals; Jon Park Wheeler, acoustic/electric guitars; Ken Post, drums/percussion; Mike Keats, lead/electric guitars; Steve O'Connor, keyboards; Charlie Grassi and Randall Prescott, keyboards/sequencing; Don Whitten, cello; John Dymond, bass; Don Reed, fiddle; Tracey Prescott, Don Paul Rogers, and Terry Tufts, backup vocals.

The project incorporated traditional throat singing mixed with producer Randall Prescott's impression of hip-hop. The album generated an initial wave of curiosity, then the group quickly faded from view. Prescott was more known for his work in the Arctic region with CBC Northern Service recordings; he also worked with CBC television for soundtrack work on the series *North of 60* (*See*: Contemporary Soundtracks). The project received a Juno nomination for Best Music of Aboriginal Canada Recording, 1997.

DISCOGRAPHY:
Tudjaat [Columbia 1996]

Appearances:
True North Concerts—Truly Something [CBC North 2000] comp
A Native American Odyssey [Putumayo 1998] *See*: Contemporary Compilations
Here and Now: A Celebration of Canadian Music [Sony 1995] *See*: Contemporary Compilations

Videos:
When My Ship Comes In [Columbia 1996]

Tukak—(Inupiak) Folk/Rock

Lineup: Makka Kleist, Otto Ignatiussen, Efa Efraimsen, Anda Kristiansen, Rassi Thygesen, Rasmus Lyberth, Naja Rosing Olsen. The 1994 album was a combination of two previously released albums.

DISCOGRAPHY:
Kiinnat and Kattutta [Ulo 1994]

Tullaugak, Laina—(Inuit) Country

Taking a modern approach to throat singing, Laina combined contemporary sounds and instruments with traditional culture.

DISCOGRAPHY:
Piaraapiuut [Inukshuk 1999]

Tuniit—(Inuit) Country/Rock

Lineup: Noah Qaqqasiq (born 1962, Arctic Bay), lead guitar/keyboards/vocals; Lucas Attagutsiak (born 1957, Arctic Bay), bass/drums/vocals; Lucy Taqtu Qaqqasiq (born 1969, Arctic Bay), percussion; Harry Iyerak (born 1966, Chesterfield Inlet), percussion/lead vocals.

Since the initial members first collaborated in 1978 as the Arctic Mukluks and later as Northwind, the addition of other players continued to transform the group.

DISCOGRAPHY:
Ikajunga! [Tuniit 1994]

Uniaqtut—(Inuit) Folk

Lineup: Arsene, Mary, and Pelagie Angalik; Doug Trineer, guitars/mandolin; Paul Gurry, bass; Richard Patterson, drums; all compositions and guitars by Arsene Angalik. Youth group from Eskimo Point; recorded in 1984.

DISCOGRAPHY:
Inusivut: Our Life [CBC Northern Service WRC1-3620]

Utatnaq, Alexis—(Inuit) Folk/ Country

From Baker Lake, Nunavut.

DISCOGRAPHY:
Igvit Kisivit: Only You [CBC Northern Service/World Records WRC1-1931]
Inuit Songs by Alexis and Victor Utatnaq [CBC Northern Service QC-1429] four-track, seven-inch vinyl EP

Uvagut—(Inuit) Folk

Lineup: Norman Ishulatuk, vocals/guitar; Noah Nowyook, bass; Susie Onalik, vocals; Serge Bougie, percussion; Paul Gurry, guitar. From Iqaluit, Baffin Island, Nunavut.

DISCOGRAPHY:
Inuusivut: Our Ways [Inukshuk 1997]
For Our Children's Future [CBC Northern Service WRC1-1484]

Zikaza—(Inuit) Rock

Lineup: Siiva Fleischer, Peter Jensen, Kaaleeraq Hansen, Anda Jeremiassen, Kristian Helmes, Ole Petersen, Per Svensson, Jakob Helmer, Ken Kragsfeidt, Aviaja Lumholt.

One of the most famous Greenlandic rock groups of the 1980s, Zikaza consisted of Greenlanders and Danes. Their albums were recorded at Feedback Studios in Aarthus, Denmark. Lead singer Siiva Fleischer was extremely popular in the region and built a substantial fan base.

DISCOGRAPHY:
Saava Mumingalu [Ulo 1992]
Miki Goes to Nuussuaq [Ulo 1988]
Zikaza [Ulo 1985]

Section 1-B
Arctic/ Circumpolar Compilation and Soundtrack Recordings

Artika—Legend [Fonovox 1998]

Inuit chants and legends.

Canada—jeux vocaux des Inuit
[Ocora C559071]

Inuit du Caribou, Netsilik, et Igloolik.

Children's Songs in Inuktitut [CBC Northern Service Broadcast Recording QCS-1485]

The Inuit teachers of Kativik, with musical arrangements by Herbert Ruff; features eleven traditional songs and one composition by William Tagoona. As with all CBC Northern Service recordings, this seven-inch vinyl, twelve-track mini-LP was made available for regional airplay only.

Erinarsoqatigiissuit, Vol. 1 [Ulo 1991]
Erinarsoqatigiissuit, Vol. 2 [Ulo 1993]

Inuit gospel. Representatives from nine choirs participated in voice-production courses with live performances over ten days. The gatherings began in 1991 in Sisimiut, Greenland.

The ICC Concerts [Ulo 1992]

Traditional and contemporary artists from Siberia, Alaska, northern Canada, and Greenland; recorded at the annual Inuit Circumpolar Conference, which was first organized in 1980.

The Inuit Artist World Showcase [Inukshuk 1996]

Lineup: Johnny Ovaut; Charlie Adams; Chuna McIntyre; Marie Meade; Nellie Echalook; Patsauq Iqaiuk; Heidi Aklaseaq Senungetuk (classical violinist); Jimmy Ekho; Anita Issaluk; Charlie Tumik; Leah Surusila; Taqurinai; Drama Group of Pond Inlet; Greenland Band; Qimutjuit; Tuniit Band. Recorded in Inukjuak, Nunavik, Quebec, Canada.

Inuit Game Songs [UNESCO]

Collection put out by Musical Sources, UNESCO, Paris.

Nitjautit [CBC Northern Service 1991]

Lineup: Susan Aglukark; Simeonie Keenainak; William Tagoona; Phillpoosie Kunilusie; Tim and the Band; Quaqtaq Gospel Group; Tommy Johanas; Kuujjuaq Band; Bob May Jr.; Mary Thompson. A wide variety of musical styles from the eastern Arctic, Keewatin, and Quebec.

North Country Ways [CBC Northern Service WRC8-6401]

Lineup: Tom Hudson; Cheryl Webster; Connie Hinchey; George Tuccaro. Country and western.

A Northern Christmas [Inukshuk/ CBC North 1995]

Lineup: Sally Taty Curley; Charlie Panigoniak; Lorna Tasseor; William Tagoona; Kenny Mianscum; Peter and Susan Aningmiuq; John Landry; Madeliene Allakariallak; Ajaaja Choir; and Jerry Alfred. Christmas carols sung in Inuktitut.

On Deadly Ground [Steven Seagal 1994] sdtk

The score features throat singers Middigak, Quanaq, and Timangiak Petaulassie.

Rock from the Seas [Tutl 1999]

A unique compilation of artists representing rock, jazz/punk fusion, samba, thrash/ death metal, hard rock joik, techno joik, and rap.

Sweet Grass [CBC North 1982; reissued on Trikont 1993, Germany]

Lineup: Morley Loon; Willie Thrasher; Willy Mitchell; Roger House. Recorded live in Val-d'Or, Quebec.

True North Concerts—Truly Something [CBC North 2000]

Lineup: Peters Dury Trio; Kashtin; Leela Gilday with Lucy Idlout; Dave Haddock; Jerry Alfred; Cyrille Fontaine; Susan Aglukark; Matthew Lien; Top of the World Fiddlers; Charlie Panagoniak; Tudjaat; Daniel Tlen; Paul Andrew; Kim Barlow; Lee Manteville with Attagtaluk; Jason Akearjuk; Tom Jackson.

Zedna [Melos Records 2001]

Lineup: Katsi Kleist; Julia Berthelsen; Stinne Jakobsen; Tupaarnaq Mathiessen; Nina K. Jorgensen; Nukaaka M. Waldau; Soorlumi Tigoqqusoq choir with Nukaaka M. Waldau, arranger; Asaneqarneq choir, Julie Berthelsen, arranger. A collection of women vocalists from Greenland and the North Sea region. Songs produced and arranged by Steen Lynge with co-producers Steffen Lynge, Mike Holm, and Soren Jakobsen.

Section 1-C
Arctic/ Circumpolar Traditional/ Archival/Spoken Word Recordings

Angaangaq

An Inuit shaman from Greenland known as "the Man Who Looks Like His Uncle."

Mountains of Ice: Eskimo Healing Chants [Four Directions Communications Group 2000]

An Anthology of North American Indian and Eskimo Music [Ethnic Folkways 1973]

Canada Inuit Games and Songs/ Chants et jeux des Inuit [UNESCO 1976, 1991, France]

Chants et tambours Inuit de Thule au Detroit de Bering [Radio France 1988]

Inuit songs from Greenland, Canada, and Alaska.

Chants Montagnais [Northern Quebec Services CBC-002]

Joachim Copeau of Bersimis, Quebec, was recorded at the Attikamek Radio Production Centre.

Day, Billy—(Inuit)

From Kitigaluit, Northwest Territories. Day's seven-track, seven-inch vinyl EP contains introductions and explanations for each song.

DISCOGRAPHY:

Inuit Drum Dances of Western Arctic [CBC Northern Service Broadcast Recording QCS-1459]

Drums across the Tundra [Wild Sanctuary]

Songs and stories from ninety-year-old Chuna McIntyre (Yupik) from Eek, Alaska (*See: The Inuit Artist World Showcase*, Arctic/Circumpolar comps).

Eskimo Songs from Alaska [Ethnic Folkways 1966]

Recorded in the villages of Savoonga and Gambell on St. Lawrence Island by Miriam Stryker, circa 1961 to 1963, with Tim Gologeren, Nathan Noonwook, Paul Jensen, John Apongalook, Nick Wonga-tilin, Thomas Apassingok, Laurence Ku-lukbon, Fred Angi. The songs are based on traditional compositions passed from generation to generation, but have contemporary subjects, such as "Eskimo Rock 'n' Roll" and the "Helicopter Song."

An Eskimo Woman Talks of Her Life [OISE 1973]

Spoken-word project recorded by Pamela Harris at the Ontario Institute for Studies in Education, Toronto.

The Eskimos of Hudson Bay and Alaska [Ethnic Folkways FE 4444]

The Eskimos of the Arctic Circle, Vol. 2 [Lyrichord 7380]

The Inuit (Eskimo) of Greenland and Northern Canada, Vol. 1 [Lyrichord/Ulo 1980]

Recorded live at the ICC, featuring William Tagoona, Qaqortoq Youth Dancers, Lars Lynge and Arnannguag, and the Arnat Tor-lussortartut Throat Singers of northern Quebec.

Inuit Fifty-five Historical Recordings [Sub Rosa SR-115]

Traditional Greenlandic music recorded between 1905 and 1987.

Inuit Singers of Nain Labrador [CBC Northern Service Broadcast Recording QC-1409]

The seven-track, seven-inch vinyl EP features Eli Merkuratsuk, Margaret Saksagiak, and Joe Tuglavina.

Inuit Throat and Harp Songs: Eskimo Women's Music of Povungnituk [Canadian Music Heritage Collection 1980]

Lineup: Alasi Alasuak; Lucy Amarualik; Alaci Tulaugak; Nellie Nungak; Mary Sivuarapik. The recording presents kataj-jait or throat songs from the village of Povungnituk, a village on the eastern shore of Hudson Bay.

Katajjait: Throat Music [Northern Service Quebec CBC-001]

Lineup: Nellie Echalook and Rebecca Nutialuk from Inukjuak, Quebec. Recorded on October 1, 1980, by the Attika-mek Montagnai radio production center, this 45 rpm, six-track vinyl recording features throat songs ranging from twenty-five seconds to a minute in length.

Komaksiutiksak

Lineup: Jamey, Nikki, Lesley, and Jessica Komaksiutiksak.

DISCOGRAPHY:
Inuit Throat Singers [Sunshine 1995]

Music of the Alaskan Kutchin Indians [Ethnic Folkways 1974]

Featuring Charlie Peter, recorded by Craig Mishler. A combination of traditional and contemporary songs features jigs, reels, medicine songs, rabbit dances, and duck dances.

Musiques de la Toundra et de la Taiga (URSS) [Maison des Cultures du Monde 1987, 1990]

Music from the Buryats, Yakuts, Tungus, Nenets, and Nganasan, Siberia.

Nganasan: Shamanic and Narrative Songs of the Siberian Arctic [Music from the World 92564-2]

Collected by Dominique Buscail and Isabelle Guillez.

Nunavik Concert [Sunshine 1995]

Lineup: Salluit Band; Charlie Tumic; Minnie Palliser; Annie Alaku and Sarah Sivuarapik; Takuginai; Rebecca Qumarluk; Charlie Iqaliuk; Kinguvaat; Andre Brassard; Charlie Takatak and Mina Arragutainaq; Charlie Ningiuk.

Songs and Dances from Yakutia [ARC 2000]

Lineup: Nicolay Petrov, accordion; Anisya Gabysheva, violin; Egor Fedotov, mandolin; Albert Popov, mandolin; Andrian Egorov, percussion; Pavel Batenev, double bass; Pyotr Kolesov, vocals; the National

Dance Theatre of the Republic of Sakha, based in northeastern Siberia. Recorded 1997.

Tradition [Inukshuk 2001]

Lineup: Chuna McIntyre and Marie Meade from the Bering Sea, Alaska; Minnie Palliser from Inukjuak, Quebec; Tagurinai puppets from Iqaluit, Nunavut; Alacie Tullaugak and Lucy Amarualik from Povugnituk, Quebec; Laina Tullaugak from Montreal, Quebec; Titus Seeteenak, Lucy Kownak and Emily Alerk with Martha Talerook, Winnie Owingayak, Jean Similiak, and James Ukpaga from Baker Lake, Nunavut.

Traditional Greenlandic Music 1905–1984 [Ulo 1992]

Fifty-five archival recordings from the four major regions of Greenland, assembled by Danish musicologist Michel Hauser.

Traditional Inuit Music [CBC Northern Service 1986] double vinyl

Lineup: Eskimo Point and Rankin Inlet from the Igloolik Workshop featuring Charlie Panigoniak, David Aglukark and Marjorie Tugak, Cathy Howmik Arnaraujak, Margaret Ujauperk, Alice and Donald Suluk, Nahaina Ulimanii, Eva Nutaraluk, Oonerk, and others.

Traditional Inuit Music [CBC Northern Service Broadcast Recording QCS-1442] nine-track, seven-inch vinyl EP

Lineup: Mary Nucktie/Mina Mikiyook; Leo Osoak; Mary Qumaluk; Povungnituk Throat Singers; Mary Sivuarapi/Nellie

Nunga; Rebecca Nuktialuk; and Anisee
Nowkawalk.

Tullaugaq, Alacie, and Lucy Amarualik

Alacie Tullaugaq, born April 20, 1935,
Povugnituk, Quebec; Lucy Amarualik,
born October 16, 1934, Povugnituk, Quebec.

DISCOGRAPHY:
Katujatut Throat Singing [Inukshuk 1996]

Appearances:
Traditions [Inukshuk 2001] comp *See*:
  Traditional/Archival Compilation
  Recordings

SECTION 2
Chicken Scratch

A hybrid of German polka, Tex-Mex, Akimel O'odham (Pima), and Tohono O'odham (Papago) music, chicken scratch is geographically specific to the Southwest region of the United States. Also known as *waila*, a term derived from the Spanish word *baile*, meaning "dance," the origins of this social music can be traced as far back as the late 1700s. The adoption of the primary instruments are a record of colonial history, beginning with the fiddle, a single snare drum usually slung over the shoulder in military fashion, the button accordion, and guitar. The instruments undoubtedly derived from contact with Spanish and American armies, trading posts, settlers, the railroad, representatives of the Catholic Church, and residential schools. These influences melded together to produce a distinctive musical form.

Scratch is instrumental music featuring *chotes* (schottisches), mazurkas, *cumbias*, and polkas, and it is often played at church feasts, weddings, birthday parties, fairs, and other social gatherings. The *pascola* and *matchini* are played at more religious gatherings, a similarity shared with other ensembles farther south. The typical band consists of two lead instruments—the saxophone and the accordion—and three rhythm instruments: the guitar, bass, and drums; the fiddle is often used for melody lines. It wasn't until the mid–twentieth century that the saxophone was introduced and later full drum kits, electric bass, lead and rhythm guitars, and upright keyboards. Female members are rare.

From the local U.S.–Mexico border towns, scratch has grown in reputation beyond its own geographical realms. Now recognized for their importance in the progression of contemporary Native music, scratch bands have been featured guests at WOMAD in Toronto, the Smithsonian Festival of American Folklife in Washington, D.C., and New York City's Carnegie Hall. The Joaquin Brothers are perhaps the genre's principal exponents, having played together for approximately thirty years prior to their retirement in the early 1990s. From the humblest of beginnings to the international stage, scratch bands have earned their place as a flourishing genre in the music industry.

Section 2-A
Chicken Scratch Recordings

American Indians

Lineup: Alex Gomez, John Manuel, Justin Francisco, Clarence Flores, Celestine Flores, Jerry Flores, Simon Cruz.

DISCOGRAPHY:
American Indians, Vol. 3 [Canyon 1985]
Waila: Social Dance Music [Canyon CR-6155]
Play Chicken Scratch [Canyon CR-6120]

Appearances:
Borderlands: Conjunto to Chicken Scratch [Canyon CR-8066] comp
Chicken Scratch Fiesta: Six Great Bands [Canyon 1981] comp

Blood Brothers

Lineup: Joe Miguel, Richard Garcia, Leo Jose, Ervin Gabriel Lopez, Layne Miguel.

DISCOGRAPHY:
Blood Brothers, Vol. 1 [Canyon 1980]

Appearances:
Borderlands: Conjunto to Chicken Scratch [Canyon CR-8066] comp
Chicken Scratch Fiesta: Six Great Bands [Canyon 1981] comp

Braves; a.k.a. Tohono O'odham Braves

DISCOGRAPHY:
Braves, Vol. 4 [Canyon 1992]
Braves, Vol. 3 [Canyon 1991]
Braves, Vol. 2 [Canyon CR-8086]
Braves, Vol. 1 [Canyon CR-8079]

Cisco Band

Lineup: Francis "Cisco" Enriquez, Frank Joaquin, Leroy Martinez, David Narcho, Mervin Enis. From Sells Tohono O'odham Reservation, Arizona.

DISCOGRAPHY:
The Cisco Band, Vol. 4 [Canyon 1990]
The Cisco Band, Vol. 3 [Canyon 1985]
The Cisco Band, Vol. 2 [Canyon 1981]
The Cisco Band [Canyon CR-6138]

Desert Suns

Lineup: Leander Miguel, percussion;
Phillip Miguel, keyboards; Sylvester
Oliver Sr.; Benedic Martinez, accordion/
saxophone; Vernon Francisco, drums;
Fidelis Manuel, saxophone/accordion/bass.

DISCOGRAPHY:
Desert Suns, Vol. 2 [Canyon CR-8108]
Desert Suns, Vol. 1 [Canyon CR-8105]
Desert Suns [Canyon CR-8105]

Appearances:
*Dancing in the Dust: The Waila Festival
Live!* [BB-00014] comp

El Conjunto Murrietta Tocando

DISCOGRAPHY:
El Conjunto Murrietta Tocando [Canyon
CR-6162]

Appearances:
Borderlands: Conjunto to Chicken Scratch
[Canyon CR-8066] comp
*Chicken Scratch: Popular Dance Music of
the Indians of Southern Arizona* [Canyon
CR-6085] comp
Chicken Scratch Fiesta: Six Great Bands
[Canyon 1981] comp

Enis and Company

Lineup: Mike, Eugene, and Gerald Enis;
Evin Garcia.

DISCOGRAPHY:
Murrietta [Canyon CR-6085]

Appearances:
Chicken Scratch: Popular Dance Music of

the Indians of Southern Arizona [Canyon
CR-6085] comp

Friends

Lineup: Ronnie Juan accordion (*See*: Thee
Express); Gilberty Jose, saxophone; Arnold
Paul, guitar; Terrence Jose, percussion;
Neal Norris, bass; Archie Miguel, drums.

DISCOGRAPHY:
His Music Lives On [Canyon 1994]
*Chicken Scratch & Friends: All 4 the Love
of Music* [independent F-109]
Back Where We Came From [independent
F-108]
Cumbias [independent F-107]
Chicken Scratch [independent F-106]
Mumsigo [independent F-105]
Friends, Vol. 4 [independent F-104]
Blast from the Past [independent F-103]
Jammin' Bar Tunes [independent F-102]
Chicken Scratch [Canyon CR-8099]

Gila River Six (Minus One) *See*: San Tan

Lineup: Elvey Whitman, Virgil Jose,
Johnnie Kisto, Guy Shurz, Leonard Harrison.

DISCOGRAPHY:
Gila River Six (Minus One), Vol. 1 [Canyon
CR-8050]

Gu-achi Fiddlers

Lineup: Gerald Leos Sr., snare; Lester
Vavages, fiddle; Tommy Lopez, bass drum;
Wil Mendoza, guitar; Elliot Johnson, fiddle.

DISCOGRAPHY:
Old Time O'odham Fiddle Music, Vol. 2
[Canyon 1990; reissued Canyon Records
Vintage Collection, vol. 7, 1997]

Joaquin Brothers

Lineup: Daniel, saxophone/accordion; Fernando, saxophone; Angelo, guitar; Leonard, bass; Jerome, drums.

DISCOGRAPHY:
. . . *Play Polkas and Chotis* [Canyon CR-6139]

Jose, Alex, and His Hickiwan Band

Lineup: Alex Jose, Willie Francisco, Lopiz Flores, James Angea.

DISCOGRAPHY:
Alex Jose and His Hickiwan Band [Canyon CR-6137]

Jose, Virgil, and Friends *See*: San Tan

Lineup: Virgil Jose, accordion; Arnold Paul, guitar; Donnie Manuel, drums; Neal Morris, bass; Lyle Reams, snare.

DISCOGRAPHY:
Virgil Jose and Friends, Vol. 3 [Canyon 1990]
Virgil Jose and Friends, Vol. 2 [Canyon 1988]
Virgil Jose and Friends, Vol. 1 [Canyon 1984]

Jose's and Gomez Band

DISCOGRAPHY:
Papago Chicken Scratch [Canyon 1985]

Legends

Lineup: Ronald Maldonado, Albert Alvarez, Dan Corella, Al and Dave Pablo.

DISCOGRAPHY:
The Legends [Canyon 1981]

Los Papagos Molinas

Lineup: Virgil and Larry Molina, Leonard Pablo, Joe Miguel, Richard Garcia.

DISCOGRAPHY:
Los Papagos Molinas, Vol. 6 [Canyon 1990]
Los Papagos Molinas, Vol. 5 [Canyon 1982]
Super Scratch [Canyon 1981]
Scratch Encores [Canyon CR-6161]
Super Scratch Kings [Canyon CR-6128]
Chicken Scratch with Los Reyes y Molinas [Canyon CR-6093]

Appearances:
Waila Fest, Vol. 4 [Rock A Bye WF4]

Los Reyes; a.k.a. Elvin Kelly y Los Reyes

Lineup: Elvin and Steve Kelly, Elmer Ray, Ken Antone.

DISCOGRAPHY:
More Chicken Scratch and Other Favorites [Canyon CR-6109]
Chicken Scratch with Los Reyes y Molinas [Canyon CR-6093]

Appearances:
Borderlands: Conjunto to Chicken Scratch [Canyon CR-8066] comp

Miguel, Joe, and the Blood Brothers *See*: Blood Brothers

Lineup: Joe Miguel, Richard Garcia, Ronnie Joaquin, Joe Velasco Jr., Layne Miguel.

DISCOGRAPHY:
Joe Miguel and the Blood Brothers, Vol. 3 [Canyon 1987]
Joe Miguel and the Blood Brothers, Vol. 2 [Canyon 1984]
Joe Miguel and the Blood Brothers, Vol. 1 [Canyon 1983]

Papago Express

Lineup: Ricardo, Isaac, Rupert, Lorenzo, and Lucius Vavages; Leon Juan.

DISCOGRAPHY:
Papago Express [Canyon 1985]

Papago Indian Band

Lineup: Phillip Celestine, guitar; Henry Juan, accordion; Nash Thomas, drums; Fedelis Manuel, saxophone/accordion; Al Jose, bass.

DISCOGRAPHY:
Papago Indian Band [Canyon 1985]

Papago Raiders

Lineup: Mark Francisco, saxophone; John Lewis Jr., accordion; Dan Corella, drums; Sylvester Oliver, guitar; Edward Corella, bass; Delvert Francisco, percussion.

DISCOGRAPHY:
Papago Raiders, Vol. 5 [Canyon CR-8090]
Papago Raiders, Vol. 4 [Canyon CR-8081]
Papago Raiders, Vol. 3 [Canyon 1984]
Papago Raiders, Vol. 2 [Canyon 1982]
Papago Raiders, Vol. 1 [Canyon 1981]

Papago Sunliners

Lineup: Andrea and Mandro Rose, Daniel Cruz, Leo Juan, Stanley Manuel.

DISCOGRAPHY:
Papago Sunliners, Vol. 2 [Canyon 1983]
Papago Sunliners, Vol. 1 [Canyon 1981]

Pima Express

Lineup: Cat Brown, drums/backup vocals; Raymond Kyyitan, bass; Lenny Thomas, bass; Lloyd Brown, guitar/vocals; Bruce Burnette, rhythm guitar/backup vocals.

DISCOGRAPHY:
Voice upon the Wind [Canyon 2002]
From the Past to the Future [Canyon 1997]
Always Be Your Friend [Canyon 1996]

Appearances:
Voices across the Canyon, Vol. 5 [Canyon 2001] comp *See*: Contemporary Compilations

Red Feather Band

Lineup: Ric Leos, lead guitar; Lester Antone, accordion; Don Manuel, drums (*See*: Renegades); Gerald Leos, rhythm guitar.

DISCOGRAPHY:
Live at Sacaton Flats (Hasan-Kek) [independent 2003]
Chicken Scratch and Specialty Songs [Canyon 1997]
Chicken Scratch and O'odham Country [Canyon 1996]
Red Feather Band, Vol. 2 [independent 2002]
Red Feather Band, Vol. 1 [independent 2001]

Appearances:
Chicken Scratch Fiesta: Six Great Bands [Canyon 1981] comp
Waila Fest, Vol. 1 [Rock A Bye WF1] comp

Renegades

Lineup: Donnie Manuel, drums (*See*: Tohono O'odham Braves); Tyson Whitman, accordion; Mike Merrietta, bass; Nicholas Narcia, guitar; Gilbert Jose, saxophone; Kevin Lewis, accordion.

DISCOGRAPHY:
Renegades [Canyon 1995]

San Tan *See*: Gila River Six (Minus One)

Lineup: Virgil Jose, Johnnie Kristo, Arnold Paul, Neal Morris, Leonard Harrison.

DISCOGRAPHY:
San Tan, Vol. 3 [Canyon 1981]
San Tan, Vol. 2 [Canyon 1980]
Pima Chicken Scratch [Canyon 1979]

Appearances:
Borderlands: Conjunto to Chicken Scratch [Canyon CR-8066] comp
Chicken Scratch Fiesta: Six Great Bands [Canyon 1981] comp

Santa Rosa Band

Lineup: Tony Moristo, Alfred Wood, Homer Marks Sr., Calvin Wilson.

DISCOGRAPHY:
Santa Rosa Band, Vol. 6 [Canyon 1995]
Santa Rosa Band, Vol. 5 [Canyon 1993]
Santa Rosa Band, Vol. 4 [Canyon 1989]
Santa Rosa Band, Vol. 3 [Canyon 1984]
Santa Rosa Band, Vol. 2 [Canyon 1981]
Santa Rosa Band, Vol. 1 [Canyon 1979]

Appearances:
Dancing in the Dust: The Waila Festival Live! [BB-00014] comp
Waila Fest, Vol. 3 [Rock A Bye WF3] comp

San Xavier Fiddle Band

Lineup: Eddie Felix, Ed Wilson, violin; Delbert Lewis, Cecil Adams, guitars; Eugene Alvarez, bass drum; Alber Nunez, snare drum.

DISCOGRAPHY:
Old Time Fiddle Music [Canyon 1989]

Appearances:
Wood That Sings: Indian Fiddle Music of the Americas [Smithsonian Folkways 1997] comp *See*: Traditional/Archival Compilations

Dancing in the Dust: The Waila Festival Live! [BB-00014] comp

Simon and Friends

Lineup: Manuel Osequeda Jr., keyboards/ vocals; Simon Enos Sr., accordion; Dennis Lopez, saxophone; Austin Reno, guitar; Jesse Diaz, drums; Gerald Leos Sr., bass.

DISCOGRAPHY:
Simon and Friends, Vol. 1 [Canyon 1995]

Southern Fiddlers

Lineup: Clarence Thomas, Eddie Felix, violin; Erwin Garcia, lead guitar; Ted Gonzalez, guitar; Ira Chavez, bass guitar.

DISCOGRAPHY:
Southern Fiddlers, Vol. 2 [Rock A Bye SF2]
Southern Fiddlers, Vol. 1 [Rock A Bye SF1]

Southern Scratch

Lineup: Alex Cruz, bass/drums/accordion; Sara Joaquin, cowbells; Ron Joaquin, saxophone/bass; Angie Joaquin, maracas; Brandis Joaquin, drums/accordion; Richard Garcia, accordion; Jesse Puentes, guitar.

DISCOGRAPHY:
Fiesta Time [Canyon 1997]
Chicken Scratch Christmas [Canyon 1994]
Em-we-hejed (For All of You) [Canyon 1994]
Southern Scratch, Vol. 2 [Canyon 1992]
Southern Scratch, Vol. 1 [Canyon 1991]

Appearances:
Voices across the Canyon, Vol. 1 [Canyon 1996] comp *See*: Contemporary Compilations

Southern Scratch became a prominent chicken scratch band. Photo by Robert Doyle, courtesy Canyon Records.

Thee Express

Lineup: Ricardo, Rupert, Isaac, Lorenzo, and Lucius Vavages; Ronnie Juan (*See*: Friends).

DISCOGRAPHY:
Thee Express, Vol. 3 [Canyon 1992]
Thee Express, Vol. 2 [Canyon 1987]

T. O. Combo

Lineup: Frederick Manuel, accordion; Michael Juan, bass; Leo Jose, guitar; Eric Lopez, drums. From Sells, Tohono O'odham Reservation, Arizona.

DISCOGRAPHY:
T.O. Forever [Canyon CR-8114]
Chicken Scratch [Canyon 1994]
T. O. Combo, Vol. 2 [Canyon 1994]
T. O. Combo, Vol. 1 [Canyon 1988]

Tohono O'odham Braves *See*: Tohono O'odham Raiders

Lineup: Alex Cruz, accordion/bass; Jason Wood, saxophone/guitar; Gilbert Jose, bass/saxophone; Donnie Manuel, drums (*See*: Renegades); Simon Cruz, guitar; Marvin Juan, percussion.

DISCOGRAPHY:
Tohono O'odham Braves, Vol. 5 [Canyon 1994]
Tohono O'odham Braves, Vol. 4 [Canyon 1993]
Tohono O'odham Braves, Vol. 3 [Canyon 1990]
Tohono O'odham Braves, Vol. 2 [Canyon 1988]
Tohono O'odham Braves, Vol. 1 [Canyon 1988]

Tohono O'odham Raiders

Lineup: John Lewis Jr., saxophone; Edward Coella, bass; Mark Francisco, saxophone; Sylvester Oliver, guitar.

DISCOGRAPHY:
Tohono O'odham Raiders, Vol. 5 [Canyon 1991]
Tohono O'odham Raiders, Vol. 4 [Canyon 1989]

Tohono O'odham Veterans

Lineup: Homer Marks Sr.; Richard Garcia; Carl Conde; Ervin Lopez; Alfred Gonzales Sr.; Cisco Antone; Phillip Miguel; Mark Assencio; Henry Juan.

DISCOGRAPHY:
Reflections Past and Present [independent NDA]

Appearances:
Waila Fest, Vol. 1 [Rock A Bye WF1] comp

T. O. Pride

Lineup: Mauel Osequeda Jr., Richard Felix, Maurice Osequeda, Jose Pilone Sr.; Richard Felix Sr.; Dennis Lopez.

DISCOGRAPHY:
Piast [independent 2002]
T.O. Pride [independent 2001]

Appearances:
Waila Fest, Vol. 3 [Rock A Bye WF3] comp

Tribesmen *See*: San Tan

Lineup: Kenny Antone, Delbert King, Johnny Kisto, Tony Leonard, Jesse Roberts.

DISCOGRAPHY:
Pima Chicken Scratch [Canyon 1984]

Verton Jackson Combo

Lineup: Verton Jackson, Leonard Harrison, Elmer Ray, Harry Ray Jr., Marvin Webster.

DISCOGRAPHY:
Verton Jackson Combo, Vol. 1 [Canyon 1983]

Warrior

Lineup: Brian Antone, accordion; Rudy Juan, saxophone; Lawrence Juan, bajo sexto; Frankie Zepeda, bass; Lou Vavages, drums.

DISCOGRAPHY:
Chicken Scratch [Rock A Bye W2]
New to Your Ears [Rock A Bye W1]

Appearances:
Waila Fest, Vol. 2 [Rock A Bye WF2]

Wilson Fiddle Combo

Lineup: Wilfred, Delbert, Clarence and Ed Wilson, fiddle.

DISCOGRAPHY:
Wilson Fiddle Combo, Vol. 1 [Rock A Bye WFC1]

Section 2-B
Chicken Scratch Compilation Recordings

Bayou Eclectico: Memories in Cababi "Old Time Chicken Scratch" [UB-27]

Borderlands: Conjunto to Chicken Scratch [Canyon CR-8066]

Lineup: American Indians; Blood Brothers; El Conjunto Murrietta; Elvin Kelly y Los Reyes; San Tan.

Chicken Scratch Fiesta: Six Great Bands [Canyon CR-8055]

Lineup: American Indians; Blood Brothers; El Conjunto Murrietta; Elvin Kelly y Los Reyes; the Molinas; San Tan.

Chicken Scratch: Popular Dance Music of the Indians of Southern Arizona [Canyon CR-6085]

Lineup: El Conjunto Murrietta; Mike Enis and Company.

Dancing in the Dust: The Waila Festival Live! [BB-00014]

Lineup: Crow Hang; Desert Suns; Group Papago; Santa Rosa Band; San Xavier Fiddle Band.

Waila Fest, Vol. 1 [Rock A Bye WF1]

Lineup: Lopez Band; Native Creed; Pisinemo and Company; Red Feather Band; T.O. Pride; T.O. Veterans; Young Waila Musicians.

Waila Fest, Vol. 2 [Rock A Bye WF2]

Lineup: Carl and Buddies; Crowhang; Group Papago; Warrior.

Waila Fest, Vol. 3 [Rock A Bye WF3]

Lineup: Group Papago; Santa Rosa Band; Too Jazzy; T.O. Pride; Wilson Fiddle Combo; Young Waila Musicians.

Waila Fest, Vol. 4 [Rock A Bye -WF4]

Lineup: Carl and Buddies; Richard Garcia; Los Papagos Molinas; Native Creed; O'odham in the Maze; Southern Fiddlers; Wilson Fiddle Combo.

Wood That Sings: Indian Fiddle Music of the Americas [Smithsonian Folkways 1997] *See*: Traditional/ Archival Compilations

SECTION 3
Contemporary Music

Cultures and civilization flourished in the Western Hemisphere prior to 1492. The European invasion had a rupturing impact on indigenous cultures, touching every part of life, including the natural world. Because Native culture is inexorably connected to nature, the music of these cultures was altered forever. Despite fervent efforts on the part of colonial governments to extinguish all traces of indigenous roots and replace them with a homogenized imitation of Eurocentric beliefs, a Native underground culture survived. Genocide, assimilation, religious conversion, relocation, residential schools, and many other policies had their culminating effects, but Native expression nevertheless continued to grow over generations and eventually had an impact on the dominant culture.

The early days of contact in the sixteenth and seventeenth centuries introduced not only harmony, found in gospel or church music, but also a variety of new instruments. Perhaps one the earliest forms of music that had a common appeal was traditional folk music. The acoustic guitar, fiddle, harmonica, and accordion made the migration to all areas because they were portable, and the simplicity of the songs accommodated any story line. By the early 1900s, many reservation-based players embraced the music and the instruments. During the 1930s, radio became accessible and brought new sounds of expression and influence.

From the residential school and relocation experiences, large numbers of trained
Native musicians emerged; some excelled
in jazz and other forms, whereas those
in the rural areas in the southern United
States found expression in the blues, derived from the influences of freed slaves.

Meanwhile, the traditional songkeepers
on the reservations kept the traditional
music hidden from destruction and per-
secution. Traditional Native and various
contemporary styles would eventually
merge and create new hybrids.

Perhaps one of the earliest contemporary Native recording artists of the
twentieth century was Louie Deer (Chief
Running Deer), a baritone who began
making records in 1920. More contemporary artists—such as Mildred Bailey, Buffy
Sainte-Marie, Peter LaFarge, Jim Pepper,
Jesse Ed Davis, Morley Loon, Link Wray,
and others—established a significant and
influential presence.

By the 1990s, there was an influx of
recordings by Native musicians in all
genres of music; only a very small percentage of these artists were actually signed
to record labels, however, which is also a
common feature in the "alternative" and
"underground" music scenes.

Native artists continue to thrive within
every possible genre and are creating new
styles by combining their Native musical
roots with contemporary sounds. Although
the diversity of Native culture can still
be observed within the context of contemporary music, the possibilities created
through combining old knowledge with
new technology continue to be indigenous
by nature. With greater accessibility and
development of media and technology,
Native music enjoys a diverse global audience. Numerous award shows acknowledge
the achievements of music makers recognized in a music scene that exists alongside
the mainstream.

This section profiles many artists who
made significant contributions in the early
days of a fledgling music industry and
those who continue to develop the music
even further. Many of the major biographies reveal the history and experiences of
this experience.

Section 3-A
Contemporary
Music Recordings

abee; a.k.a. Abigail Nahdee—
(Anishnabe) Country

From Walpole Island, Ontario. His debut
album received favorable airplay on the
local radio station CFRZ.

DISCOGRAPHY:
abee [independent 1998]

Adam, Leonard—(Dene) Country/
Rock

Born in Uranium City, Saskatchewan.
Adam was raised by his grandparents in
Fond du Lac in musical surroundings. His
first album was recorded in both the Dene
and English languages.

DISCOGRAPHY:
Spirit Flies [Turtle Island Music 1999]

Videos:
Live at Northern Lights Casino [Turtle
    Island Music TIM-50002]

Aglukark, Susan—(Inuit) Pop *See*:
Arctic/Circumpolar Contemporary

aim baby—Rock

Lineup: Philomena (Anishnabekwe) bass/
vocals; Lance (Tlingit-Haida-Yupik) acous-
tic/electric guitars/vocals; Jay (Sisseton–
Wahpeton Dakota) keyboards; Chad (Anishnabe) acoustic/electric guitar/vocals.

Formed in 1998 as musical accompaniment for poetry readings at local coffee-
houses and community events. Inspiration
for their music was derived from their involvement in the Minneapolis, Minnesota,
Native activist scene.

DISCOGRAPHY:
aim baby [independent 2000]

Alfred, Jerry—(Tutchone) Folk/Rock/ Trad

Born September 1955, Mayo, Yukon. Raised in a traditional manner and given the name Keeper of Songs.

Medicine Beat Lineup: Jerry Alfred, guitar/hand drum/vocals; Bob Hamilton, electric guitar/producer; Andrea Coleman, keyboards/accordion; Marc Paradis, percussion; Marie Gogo, backup vocals.

Juno Award nominee, Best Music of Aboriginal Canada Recording, 1997; Juno Award, Best Music of Aboriginal Canada Recording, 1996.

DISCOGRAPHY:
Kehlon [Caribou 1998]
Nendaa-Go Back [Caribou 1996]
Etsi Shon-Grandfathers Song [Caribou 1994]

Appearances:
Alcatraz Is Not an Island [James Fortier, 2002] score
20 Aboriginal Greatest Hits, Vol. 3 [Sunshine 2002] comp
Tribal Dreams [Earth Beat! 2001] comp
True North Concerts—Truly Something [CBC North 2000] comp
Festival to Go [Festival Records 1998] comp
A Native American Odyssey [Putumayo 1998] comp
Tribal Fires [Earth Beat! 1997] comp
Arctic Refuge [Soundings of the Planet 1996] comp
Tribal Voices [Earth Beat! 1996] comp
Mariposa [Ava 1996] comp
A Northern Christmas [Inukshuk/CBC Northern Service 1995] comp
Here and Now: A Celebration of Canadian Music [Sony 1995] comp
The Yukon Collection [Caribou 1995] comp

Ancestral Fire—(Mi'kmaq) Folk *See*: J. Hubert Francis and Eagle Feather

Lineup: J. Hubert Francis, rhythm guitar/vocals/percussion; J. F. (Wawa) Go-

guen, lead guitar; Christian Goguen, flute; Danny Boucher, drums; Ronaldo Richard, keyboards; Bev Theriault, Donna Augustine, Jim Augustine, vocals; Eastern Eagle Singers, Seventh Generation Singers, traditional drumming/singing (*See*: Powwow Music). This project was inspired by traditional values and political insight with the music sensibilities of veteran recording artist J. Hubert Francis. The personnel are from reserves in Nova Scotia and New Brunswick, Canada. Most of the music is original, with covers of Peter LaFarge's song "Drums" and Morley Loon's composition "Yo Ya He Yay."

DISCOGRAPHY:
Honouring Who We Are [Bear Paw Music 2002]

Ancient Brotherhood—New Age

Lineup: A. Brent Chase (Dineh) flute; Wachan Bajiyoperak (Inca); Tsa'ne Dos'e (*See*: Flute Music); Gerald J. Markoe, synthesizers.

Recorded in Thailand, Burma, Laos, and the Navajo Reservation, Arizona. The final mix was infused with dance beats and some catchy world beat riffs.

DISCOGRAPHY:
Dances for the New Millennium: Music of Native America and Asia with Tribal and Contemporary Rhythms [Astro 1997]
Where the Earth Touches the Stars [Astro 1995]

Anishnaabe Ngamwaasan—Folk

A group of Anishnabe musicians led by Cynthia Bell that combined traditional and contemporary instruments and with Anishnabe language.

DISCOGRAPHY:
Anishnaabe Ngamwaasan [Sunshine 2003]

Anishnabe—Rock

Lineup: Pascal Brazeau, Lucicien Pouca-chiche, Noel Mitchell. From Lac Simon (Abitibi), northeastern Quebec. One of several groups to use the name, this incarnation performed and recorded in their own language, Anishnabe, accompanied by rudimentary rock patterns.

DISCOGRAPHY:
Mamedenenden [SDCA Mohigan 1999]

Another Latin Timebomb—
(Chicano) Hip-Hop *See*: Haida, Litefoot

Otherwise identified as ALT, this young rapper made several appearances throughout the hip-hop scene. He worked on several projects with the Chicano group Brown and Proud and with artist-producer Litefoot.

DISCOGRAPHY:
Another Latin Timebomb [Atlantic 1993]

Appearances (listed alphabetically):
Brown and Proud:
A Lighter Shade of Brown [Pump Records 1990]
Litefoot:
The Life and Times [Red Vinyl 1998]

Apache Spirit—(Apache) Country and Western

Lineup: Matthew Ethelbah, vocals/lead guitar/keyboards/blues harp; Lee Ethelbah, vocals; Lisa Ethelbah, backup vocals; Allen Cassa, bass; Joseph Manuel, vocals/acoustic guitar; Tinker Nez, drums.

From Whiteriver, Arizona. Apache Spirit has been a long-time favorite in the Southwest, combining original songs with country standards, chicken scratch, and Tex-Mex flavors; they released their material on their own label. Best Country Artists, NAMA, 1998.

DISCOGRAPHY:
Native Country [Alta Vista 1994]
Indian Car [Alta Vista 1993]
The Spirit Is Back [Alta Vista 1989]
El Mosquito Medley [Alta Vista 1989]
Indian Cowboy [Alta Vista 1989]
Tour of Life [Alta Vista 1989]
Five in One [Alta Vista 1985]
From Me to You [Alta Vista 1984]
Now Appearing [Alta Vista 1983]
One More Friend [Alta Vista 1982]
Apache Spirit [Alta Vista 1981]
Keep Movin' On [Alta Vista 1977]

Arcand, John—(Metis) Fiddle

Born 1940, Debden–Big River, Saskatchewan. Based in Saskatoon, Saskatchewan. Regarded as the "undisputed master" of Metis fiddle music, Arcand is a ninth-generation player who specializes in preserving the traditional Metis tunes and has written more than 250 original songs. Metis fiddling, developed in western Canada, is the combination of Native rhythms and French and Scottish song brought to the area by fur traders. Arcand helped found the Emma Lake Fiddle Camp and the John Arcand Fiddle Contest in 1988. He also teaches at the Gabriel Dumont Institute of Native Studies and Applied Research, Regina, Saskatchewan.

DISCOGRAPHY:
Sugar Hill Road [independent 1999]
Traditionally Yours [independent 2001]
Whoa-Ha-Gee [independent 2000]
The Tunes of the Red River [independent 1998]
Echoes of the Prairie [independent 1994; reissued 2002]
La celebration '92 [independent 1992]

Appearances:
Drops of Brandy and Other Traditional Metis Tunes [Gabriel Dumont Institute 2002] four-CD comp

Arigon Starr—(Kickapoo-Creek) Pop/ Rock

Lineup: Arigon Starr, lead vocals/guitar; Nick Peters (Luiseno), drums; Gay Wahpecome (Kickapoo-Creek), backup vocals/flute/percussion; Bil Schnobrich, bass.

This Los Angeles–based singer-songwriter described her music as Native American alternapop mixed with Indian glam and Native pride. Peppered with sharp humor and wit, her lyrics focus on issues of cultural survival presented in a three-minute pop format via a diva persona. The Beatles were her greatest influence, but she acknowledged everything from powwow to Art Tatum and Led Zeppelin. Featured in Serle Chapman's book *Of Earth and Elders* [Bear Print/ Roundhouse 1998], she also appeared on soundtracks for feature and documentary films. NAMA Award for Best Independent Recording, 1999.

DISCOGRAPHY:
Backflip [Wacky 2002]
Wind Up [Wacky 2000] includes "The Peltier Song"
Arigon Starr [Wacky 1999] four-track cas-sampler
Meet the Diva [Wacky 1997]

Appearances:
Naturally Native [Silver Wave 2000] sdtk
Native [Wacky 1998] sdtk

Art and Soul *See*: Seventh Fire

The Atoll—Folk/World Beat *See*: Tonemah

Lineup: Cary Morin (Crow-Assiniboine), guitar/vocals; Wes Heilman, bass (replaced by Craig Fowler); Ron Plewacki, drums (replaced by Crip Erickson); James Thomas, keyboards; Peter Knudsen, percussion/ vocals.

The Atoll was Corey Morin's next group following the demise of Island. He also established the Crow Talent Agency to assist other Native musicians.

DISCOGRAPHY:
World Groove [Crow Records 2000]
Unity [Crow Records 1995]
World Dance [Crow Records 1994]
Circle of Friends [Kiva 1993] Cary Morin
Dream Marquee [Linden Street 1992] fea- tures "Peltier's Lullaby"

Atsiaktonkie—(Mohawk) Folk *See*: December Wind

This four-piece band from Akwesasne (Quebec, Ontario, and New York State) also performed under the name of the title of their only album.

DISCOGRAPHY:
December Wind [independent 1997]

Azteca—(Chicano) Jazz/Rock/R & B

Lineup: Coke Escovido, timbales; Lenny White, drums/vocals; Victor Pantoja, conga/vocals; Paul Jackson, acoustic and Fender bass; Jim Vincent, guitar; Neal Schon, guitar; Flip Nunez, organ; George DiQuatro, acoustic piano/clavinet; George Muribus, electric piano; Jules Rowell, trombone; Mel Martin, soprano, tenor, and baritone sax/flute/piccolo; Bob Ferreira, tenor sax/flute/piccolo; Tom Harrell, trumpet; Wendy Haas, Rico Reyes, Fred Knowles, Pete Escovido, vocals; Sheila Escovido, additional percussion.

A Brazil 66 with brown berets and a groove, Azteca was formed in 1970 by Pete Escovido.

DISCOGRAPHY:
Pyramid of the Moon [CBS/Columbia 1973]
Azteca [CBS/Columbia 1972; reissued GNP/Crescendo 1995]

Appearances:

Ay Califas: Raza Rock of the '70s and '80s [Rhino 1998] comp

Chicano Power [Soul Jazz Records 1998] comp

Azteca X—(Chicana) Rap

Her Spanish might not be the best, but her beats are yummy. Her single "Daddy's Crazy" addresses violence against women. The compilation album listed in the discography features twenty-eight tracks of music and poetry with a self-defense handbook and writings by Maria Mercedes, bell hooks, and others.

DISCOGRAPHY:

Appearances:

Free to Fight [Candy Ass 1995] comp

Aztlan Nation—(Chicano) Rap

DISCOGRAPHY:

Beaner Go Home [independent 1991]

Aztlan Underground—(Chicano) Heavy Metal *See*: Kalpulli, Quinto Sol

Lineup: Yaotl (pronounced "yowt," meaning "Enemy Warrior"), vocals; Bulldog, vocals; Joe Galarza, bass; Alonso Beas, guitar; Ace, drums; Bean, synthesizer/turntables.

Formed in the early 1990s, this East Los Angeles collective of musicians, artists, muralists, and filmmakers combined rap, punk, and grunge. They expressed respect for traditional values in the context of political struggle. As activists within their communities, they established Xicano Records and Film. Other projects included the Chicano Revolutionary Front, Quinto Sol (political Chicano reggae), and the Kalpulli project with rapper DJ Shane (Paiute). Aztlan Underground was invited to tour

southern Spain with Basque musicians and signed with Esan Ozenki Records; they later appeared with Rage Against the Machine and Tijuana No in the 1999 concert "Battle of Mexico City." Samples from their track "Sacred Circle" were used in the sci-fi television series *Dark Angel* [James Cameron, 2002].

DISCOGRAPHY:

Sub-Verses [Xicano Records and Film 1998]

Decolonize [Xicano Records and Film 1994; reissued in 2000 w/ bonus tracks]

Aztlan Underground [Xicano Records and Film 1992] four-track cass EP, o/p

Singles:

"Haves and Have Nots" [Xicano Records and Film 2000]

"Preachers of the Blind State" [Xicano Records and Film 1999] remix

Appearances:

Our Voice Is Our Weapon and Our Bullets Are the Truth [Red Wire Magazine 2003] comp

Peace and Dignity Journeys [Xicano Records and Film 2000] comp

Detras de nosotros estamos ustedes [Discos Armados 1999] comp

Gora Herriak [Esan Ozenki 1998, Spain] comp

Sociodad = Suciadad [BYO Records 1997] comp

Videos:

Blood on Your Hands [Smokin' Mirrors 1998]

Back, Dave—(Mohawk) Country/Folk

A project of acoustic material focusing on family values was recorded at CKON 97.3 FM, Akwesasne. Crafty wordsmithing and good melodies made this release somewhat of a delight.

DISCOGRAPHY:

Cody Flying Cloud [Akwesasne Communication Society 1989]

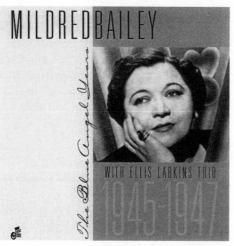

MILDRED BAILEY

The Blue Angel Years

WITH ELLIS LARKINS TRIO
1945-1947

Mildred Bailey defined the art of jazz singing.
Cover art courtesy Baldwin Street Records.

Bailey, Mildred—(Couer d'Alene–
Irish) Jazz *See*: Oscar Pettiford, Al
Rinker, Lee Wiley

1903–1951
Born Mildred Eleanor Rinker, February 27,
1903, Tekoa, Washington. Described by
many jazz historians as the greatest singer
of all time, Bailey was also directly responsible for helping Bing Crosby and Frank
Sinatra start their careers. She was also
credited for discovering Billie Holiday and
has been cited as a direct influence on
legendary singers such as Tony Bennett. A
stylistic innovator, Bailey recorded some of
the most uplifting music ever created.

Her mother nurtured the connection
with their Native roots and traditional
music with trips to the Couer d'Alene
Reservation, which inspired Bailey's natural talent for singing. The family moved
to Spokane, Washington, where they met
Crosby's family. Her brother, Al Rinker,
began singing professionally in 1921 with
Crosby in a group called the Musicaladers.

At age sixteen, Bailey landed a job playing piano at the local cinema and later
as a singer at the music counter in a department store. Bailey became her mar-

ried name after a short-lived marriage in
the early 1920s, but she kept the name
throughout her life.

Inspired and destined to sing, she headed
south to Los Angeles in the early 1920s and
found work singing in a plush speakeasy.
Her brother Al and longtime friend Bing
Crosby traveled to Los Angeles to work.
Bailey put them up in her house and got
them a gig at the Morrisey Music Hall Revue, where they were billed as Two Boys
and a Piano.

By 1929, Rinker and Crosby invited
Whiteman to Bailey's house party. He
hired her on the spot to perform on his
radio show and later to tour and perform
live. She was not only Whiteman's first
female singer, but one of the first female
singers to perform professionally with an
orchestra.

Bailey made her first professional recording in 1929 with Eddie Lang and joined
Benny Goodman's band that same year.
She became known as "the Rocking Chair
Lady" because of her signature song, written especially for her by Hoagy Carmichael
and recorded in 1932 with Whiteman.
Bailey considered traditional singing a
valuable foundation for her work in jazz.

Through the depression years, Whiteman's orchestra stayed at the top mainly
because of Bailey. She and vibraphonist
Red Norvo led their own band from 1936
to 1939, billed as Mr. and Mrs. Swing.
After their breakup in 1939, she and Benny
Goodman hosted the *Camel Caravan* radio
program. She started working solo in 1940,
performing primarily in New York, where
she worked as a headliner in many of the
best clubs; from 1944 to 1945, she hosted
her CBC program *The Mildred Bailey
Show*.

Bailey was a large woman with a beauti-
fully soft singing voice, but she also had a
reputation as a boisterous individual who
affirmed her life with plenty of good times.

Diagnosed with diabetes in 1949, she
succumbed to greater illness in the re-

maining two years of her life. Lee Wiley helped Bailey with living arrangements at this time, but she decided to return to her home in Poughkeepsie, New York. Composers Alec Wilder and Jimmy Van Heusen combined their efforts with Crosby and Sinatra to pitch in and help her out with the medical bills. She passed away on December 12, 1951, as a result of diabetes, hardening of the arteries, and a malfunctioning liver. Bailey is one of the First Ladies of Jazz through the sheer artistry of her singing. Her appearance on the U.S. twenty-nine-cent stamp (Jazz/Blues Singers series issued in 1993) secures her place as one of the foremost jazz singers of all time.

DISCOGRAPHY:

The Complete Recordings of Mildred Bailey [Mosaic 2000] CD box set
1929–1932 [CLS 1999]
All of Me [Sien 1998]
1935–1944: Thanks for the Memory [Goji 1998]
The Blue Angel Years [Baldwin Street Music 1997]
L'art vocal, Vol. 9: *1931–1939* [LVC 1997]
A Forgotten Lady [EPM 1996]
American Legends, No. 4 [DTA 1996]
Sweet Beginnings [OLD 1995]
Mildred Bailey, Vol. 2 [OLD 1995]
Rockin' Chair Lady (1931–1950) [MCA/Decca 1994]
That Rockin' Chair Lady [PEA 1994]
The Blues Singer 1929–1937 [Suisa 1991, Italy]
The Majestic Mildred Bailey [Savoy Jazz Records 1985] w/ the Eddie Sauter Orchestra and Ellis Larkins
The Uncollected Mildred Bailey with Paul Baron's Orchestra 1944 [Hindsight Records 1979]
Benny Goodman on V Disc, Vol. 1: *1941–1945* [Sunbeam 1974] w/ Perry Como
All of Me [Monmouth Evergreen MES-6814] w/ Red Norvo

Original Recordings:

Her Greatest Performances: 1929–1946 [Columbia C3L22] three-record set

All of Me [Monmouth-Evergreen MES-6814]
The Rockin' Chair Lady [Decca DL-5387]
w/ Ellis Larkin Trio:
You Started Something [Majestic/Realm 1947]
Born to Be Blue [Majestic/Realm 1947]
Can't We Be Friends [Majestic/Realm 1947]
Don't Worry 'Bout Strangers [Majestic 1947]
That Ain't Right [Victor 1947]
I Don't Want to Miss Mississippi [Victor 1947]
w/ Julian Work's Orchestra:
All of Me [Majestic/Allegro 1947]
Almost Like Being in Love [Allegro 1947]
Heather on the Hill [Allegro 1947]
w/ Ellis Larkin's Orchestra:
I'll Close My Eyes [Majestic/CBS/Realm 1946]
Me and My Blues [Majestic/CBS/Realm 1946]
At Sundown [Majestic/Realm 1946]
Lover Come Back to Me [CBS/Realm 1946]
w/ the Eddie Sauter/Ted Dale Orchestra:
All That Glitters Is Not Gold [Majestic 1946]
In Love in Vain [CBS 1946]
A Woman's Prerogative [Majestic/Allegro 1946]
Penthouse Serenade [Majestic/Allegro 1946]
Mildred Bailey and Her Orchestra:
These Foolish Things [Crown 1945]
Got the World on a String [Crown 1945]
Can't Help Lovin' the Man [Crown 1945]
Summertime [Crown 1945]
The Man I Love [Crown 1945]
The Gypsy in My Soul [Crown 1945]
I'm Glad There Is You [Crown 1945]
It's Never Too Late to Pray [Crown 1945]
Mildred Bailey's Hot Sextet:
Downhearted Blues [V-Disc-524 1944]
That Ain't Right [V-Disc-772 1944]
Love I Long For [V-Disc-879 1944]
Which Way of the Great Forty Eight [V-Disc 1944]
Just You Just Me/Bugle Call Rag [V-Disc 1944]

Mildred Bailey and Her Alley Cats:
"Willow Tree/Honeysuckle Rose/Squeeze Me/Down-Hearted Blues" [DEC 1935] 78 rpm
A Mildred Bailey Serenade [Columbia CL-6094] 78 rpm

Singles and B-Sides:
"Long about Midnight/More Than You Know" [Vocalion 378, circa 1943]
"More Than You Know" [V-Disc 1943]
"Rockin' Chair/Sunday Monday or Always" [V-Disc 1943]
"I Think of You/More Than You Know" [Decca 4267]
"Sometimes/Wherever You Are" [Decca 4252, circa 1942]
"All of Me/Almost Like Being in Love" [Majestic 1140]
"All Too Soon/Everything Depends on You" [Decca 3888]
"Fools Rush In/From Another World" [Columbia 1940]
"Prisoner of Love/There'll Be Some Changes Made" [Vocalion 5268]
"Arkansas Blues" [Vocalion 1939]
"Don't Be That Way/I Can't Face the Music" [Vocalion 4016]
"Where Are You?/You're Laughing at Me" [Vocalion 3456]
"Rockin' Chair/Little Joe" [Vocalion 3553]
"Willow Tree/Honeysuckle Rose" [Decca/Parlophone 1935]
"Someday Sweetheart/When Day Is Done" [Vocalion 1935]
"I'd Rather Listen to Your Eyes/I'd Love to Take Orders from You" [Vocalion 3056]
"Give Me Liberty or Give Me Love/Doin' the Uptown Lowdown" [Brunswick 6680]
"Lazy Bones/There's a Cabin in the Pines" [Brunswic 6587]
"Rockin' Chair/Love Me Tonight" [Victor 1932]
"Georgia On My Mind" [Victor 22891]
"Home/Too Late" [Victor 22874]

Appearances (listed alphabetically):
Louis Armstrong and the Esquire All Stars:
Metropolitan Opera House Jam Session/

January 18, 1944 [Jazz Society 1978, Sweden]
Paul Baron's Orchestra:
Hold On [V-Disc 1944]
Summertime [V-Disc 1944]
Right as Rain [V-Disc 1944]
From the End of the Sky [V-Disc 1944]
Blue Water/Accentuate the Positive [V-Disc 1944]
Sometimes I Feel Like a Motherless Child [V-Disc 1944]
Rockin' Chair [V-Disc 1944]
Hoagy Carmichael:
Stardust Melody: Hoagy Carmichael and Friends [Bluebird/RCA/BMG 2002]
Dorsey Brothers Orchestra:
But I Can't Make a Man [Brunswick-7542]
Benny Goodman:
Junk Man/Ol' Pappy [Columbia 2892-D]
Emaline [Columbia 2907-D]
Make with the Kisses/I Thought about You [Columbia 35313]
Darn That Dream/Peace, Brother [Columbia 35331]
Glen Gray:
Heat Wave [Brunswick 6679]
Tommy, Jimmy, and Eddie 1928–1929 [Parlophone 1930]
Eddie Lang:
What Kind o' Man Is You? [Parlophone E-840 1929]
Red Norvo:
Picture Me without You/It All Begins and Ends with You [Brunswick 7732]
I've Got My Love to Keep Me Warm/Slummin' on Park Avenue [Brunswick 7813]
I Was Doing All Right/Love Is Here to Stay [Brunswick 8068]
It's Wonderful/Always and Always [Brunswick 8069]
Please Be Kind/The Weekend of a Private Secretary [Brunswick 8088]
Paul Whiteman:
Dear Old Mother Dixie/There I Go Dreaming Again [Victor 1932]
Can't You See?/When It's Sleepy Time Down South [Victor 1931]

My Goodbye to You [Victor 22876]
All of Me [Victor 22879]
'Leven Pounds of Heaven [Victor 1931]
*We Just Couldn't Say Goodbye/I'll Never
  Be the Same* [Victor 24088]
Various:
Almost Like Being in Love [Regent Records
  MG-6046] comp, w/ Kay Starr
Roots of the Blues, Vol. 4 [Direct Source
  2001] comp

Bala-Sinem Choir *See*: Louis Ballard

Formed in 1970 by Mark Romancito, this
thirty-five-member choir representing
seventeen nations was also known as the
Red People of Fort Lewis College, Durango,
Colorado. The name Bala-Sinem is derived
from the Hopi language and means "Red
People." Dr. Louis Ballard transcribed and
arranged the group's songs.

DISCOGRAPHY:
Walk in Beauty My Children [Canyon
  CR-6149]
American Indian Songs and Chants
  [Canyon CR-6110]

Ballard, Louis—(Quapaw-Cherokee) Classical *See*: Bala-Sinem Choir, Five and Country Senses, Indian Chipmunks

Born 1931. Composer, musician, and educator Dr. Louis Ballard's works have been
performed by major American orchestras, bands, choral societies, chamber
ensembles, ballet companies, and soloists. In 1964, Ballard was commissioned to
compose an original score for the thirty-
minute ballet *Koshare*, with choreography
by Marjorie Tallchief (Osage) and produced
by the Harkness Ballet Company of New
York. The piece premiered in Barcelona,
Spain, and toured the United States and
Europe, sponsored by First Lady Mame
Johnson to help raise scholarships for as-

piring Native students of the genre. Ballard
wrote his second ballet, *Desert Trilogy*,
in 1967 and was nominated for a Pulitzer
Prize in music. He has created more than
fifty works, including symphonies, operas,
chorals, cantatas, songs, chamber works,
dances, concerts, and solo pieces. He has
continued to mentor new generations of
classical musicians. His album *Ballard* features the compositions "Cace'ga Ayuwi'pi"
for percussion instruments; "Music for the
Earth and Sky," performed by the Radio
Symphony Orchestra of Saarbrucken; and
"Incident at Wounded Knee" performed
by the St. Paul Chamber Orchestra, with
Dennis Russell Davies, conductor.

DISCOGRAPHY:
Native American Music for the Classroom
  [New Southwest Music Publications 101;
  reissued on CD, 1995]
Ballard [Wakan 1972]

Banks, Dennis—(Anishnabe) Folk *See*: Keith Secola, Floyd Westerman; Flute Music: George Estes

Born 1937, Leech Lake Reservation, Minnesota. This cofounder of the American
Indian Movement put together a few tracks
of traditional and contemporary songs with
poetry.
  Lineup: Narada Michael Walden, keyboards; Pony Vigil, flute; Marcus Black,
mandolin; James Fischer, bass; Gus Scherer,
acoustic guitar; Dennis Banks, Buffalo
Banks, Alice Lambert, Pony Vigil, Paul
Peralta, drumming and singing.

DISCOGRAPHY:
United We Stand—Refusing to Fall [RCR
  9770]
Still Strong [independent 1993] cass

Film:
Thunderheart [Michael Apted, 1992] as
  himself
The Last of the Mohicans [Michael Mann,
  1992] as Ongewagone

War Party [Frank Roddam, 1988] as Ben
Crowkiller

Barney, Geraldine—(Dineh) Trad/
Folk *See*: Flute Music; Traditional/
Archival Compilation Recordings

The guitar ballad "Glitter Nights" focuses
on the impacts of forced relocation. Barney
is also one of a growing number of female
traditional flute players and perhaps one of
the first to be recorded as such.

DISCOGRAPHY:

Appearances:
Heartbeat: Voices of First Nations Women
[Smithsonian Folkways 1995] comp *See*:
Traditional/Archival Compilations
*Music of New Mexico: Native American
Traditions* [Smithsonian Folkways 1992]
comp

Barrio Boyzz—(Chicano) Vocal/Dance

Lineup: Angel Ramirez Jr., David Davilla,
Hans Giraldo, Louie Marrero, Robert Var-
gas; produced by Joe Jacket, Kip Hickman,
ATN, and Mass Order.

DISCOGRAPHY:
*Piensa porque (es Navidad)/Remember
Why It's Christmas* [EMI Latin 1996]
How We Roll [SBK/EMI 1995]

Videos:
Rico [EMI 1997]

Beachey, Mark—(Anishnabe)
Classical/Folk

Born June 20, 1966, Kirkland Lake, Ontario, Matchewan First Nation. Beachey
studied at the Royal Conservatory of
Music, completing classical piano Grade
Four with honors. He worked in film production and other recording projects.

DISCOGRAPHY:
From Four Directions [Big Bear Productions
1995]

Bearpaw, Cody—(Blackfoot) Country
and Western *See*: Navajo Sundowners

A former rodeo rider and singer-songwriter
from Alberta. Bearpaw focused his ma-
terial on Indian cowboys. His work in
film includes roles in *Oklahoma Crude*
[Stanley Kramer, 1973], *The Devil and
Leroy Bassett, AKA: Pistol Packin' Leroy*
[Robert E. Pearson, 1973], and the comedy-
Western television series *Alias Smith and
Jones* [Edward Abroms, 1972] in episode
no. 3.4, October 7, 1972, "The Clementine
Incident."

DISCOGRAPHY:
Angry Mountain [Canyon 1979]
All Around Indian Cowboy [Canyon 1978]

Appearances:
Navajo Sundowners:
Navajo Sundowners, Vol. 13 [Canyon 1980]

Bearpaws—Country and Western
See: Nick Day

Lineup: Nick Day, lead vocals/guitar;
Roger Kakepetum, lead guitar/vocals; Ray-
mond Kakepetum, drums/bass; Charlie
Meekis, bass.
    From Sandy Lake First Nations. This
freewheeling foursome recorded on the
Sunshine label and gained popularity in
many Native communities throughout
Manitoba and northwestern Ontario.

DISCOGRAPHY:
Makin' Tracks [Sunshine 1990]
Kitchi-Ogamah [Sunshine SSCT-4086]
Bearpaws [Sunshine SSCT-4068]

Appearances:
20 Aboriginal Greatest Hits, Vol. 2 [Sun-
shine 1998] comp

24 Canadian Aboriginal Artists [Sunshine 1995] comp
A Northern Christmas [Sunshine SSCD-4180] comp

Bedard, Mel—(Metis) Fiddle

DISCOGRAPHY:
Metis Fiddler [Sunshine SCCT-421]

Appearances:
Drops of Brandy and Other Traditional Metis Tunes [Gabriel Dumont Institute 2002] four-CD comp

Bee, Robby—(Dakota) Hip-Hop *See*: Red Nativity

Born February 15, 1969. The son of Tom Bee gained a good start as a producer and performer. He enjoyed success with his rap group the Boyz from the Rez with tours, shows, and airplay on all the major reservation radio stations throughout North America. He marketed his music as pow-wow/hip-hop Red House swing and was one of the first contemporary Native rappers to emerge. His project *We're the Boyz* won NAIRD's Best Independent Video, 1993. He produced albums for numerous SOAR artists and recorded the *Red Nativity* Christmas album with pianist Brule.

DISCOGRAPHY:
Reservation of Education [Warrior/SOAR 1993]
Rebel Rouzer [SOAR 1989]

Singles:
"Powwow Girls/We're the Boyz" [Warrior/SOAR 1992]

Appearances (listed alphabetically):
Bryan Akipa:
Mystic Moments: Dakotah Flute Music [SOAR 1994] *See*: Flute Music
Red Nativity:

One Holy Night [Red Sea 1997]
Various:
Urban Skins, Vol. 1 [Warrior/SOAR 1999] comp

Videos:
We're the Boyz (Reservation of Education) [Warrior/SOAR 1992]

Bee, Tom—(Dakota) Rock *See*: Brule, Winter Hawk, XIT

Born November 8, 1947. A young business-minded songwriter-performer, Tom Bee founded his first label, Lance Records and Music, in the 1960s and peddled 45-rpm singles out of the back of his car. He also sold some of his songs, including "Roxanne" and "Roll It Over," recorded by Michael Edward Campbell on his self-titled 1974 Motown album, and "(We've Got) Blue Skies," recorded by the Jackson Five on their album *Maybe Tomorrow* [Motown 1971]. Bee created XIT (pronounced "exit"), one of the first all-Native rock bands of the early 1970s and signed with Motown/Rare Earth for a two-album deal. In 1990, he founded Sound of America Records (SOAR), complete with recording studios and distribution, and signed more than two hundred acts. He established several subsidiary companies, including Warrior, specializing in rap and rock; Dakotah, which distributes spoken-word projects and music for children; and Natural Visions for New Age music. Bee won several awards in recognition of his work, including a 2001 Grammy in the first Native American Music category as producer for *Gathering of Nations Pow-Wow* [SOAR 1999] (*See*: Powwow Compilations). The First Americans in the Arts recognized his accomplishments in 2003 with the Lifetime Achievement Award. He composed "Voice of the Mountain" with Kaare Whitewind (*See*: Flute Music) for the film *Windtalkers* [John Woo, 2002].

DISCOGRAPHY:
Reveal His Glory [SOAR 2004]
Color Me Red [SOAR 1988]

Appearances:
Windtalkers [RCA Victor 2002] sdtk
Urban Skins, Vol. 3 [Warrior/SOAR 2000] comp
Urban Skins, Vol. 1 [Warrior/SOAR 1999] comp
Medicine River—Man and Nature [Natural Visions/SOAR 1997] w/ Brule
Star Boy [Dakotah/SOAR 1994] spoken word *See*: Contemporary Spoken Word: Legends and Storytelling: Paul Goble
Love Flute [Dakotah/SOAR 1993] spoken word *See*: Contemporary Spoken Word: Legends and Storytelling: Paul Goble
Various Native American Artists: Solo Flights, Vol. 1 [SOAR 1991] comp, w/ Spotted Eagle
Legend of the Flute Boy [SOAR 1990] spoken word
Oyate [Nato/World 1990/1998, France] comp

Beer, Jim, and the River—(Lenape) Rock *See*: Jessie Nighthawk

Born August 30, 1975, Shreveport, Louisiana. His two biggest influences in music were Bill Miller and Lynard Skynard. He received two NAMA nominations for Best Native Debut Artist of the Year in 1998 and Best Folk-Country Artist, 1999.

DISCOGRAPHY:
Dust of Our Father's Bones [independent 1999] w/ Red Hawk Singers *See*: Powwow Music
Turtle Island [Sunshine 1997]

Appearances:
Jessie Nighthawk:
Ghost Dance the Last Hope [Sacred Fire 1998]
Various:
20 Aboriginal Greatest Hits, Vol. 2 [Sunshine 1998] comp

An Aboriginal Christmas, Vol. 1 [Sunshine 1997] comp

Belcourt, Shane Anthony—(Metis) Folk/Rock

Born December 30, 1972, Ottawa, Ontario. Founder of the Shane Anthony Band. After the initial release of *Sky Stories*, Belcourt gained attention with favorable reviews. Following his first tour in New Zealand and Australia, he became adept as both a solo acoustic act and a member of a full band.

Lineup: Shane Anthony Belcourt, guitar/vocals; Jordan O'Connor, bass/piano; Nick Fraser, drums; Sophie Raymond, vocals; Dave Draves, organ.

DISCOGRAPHY:
Hands Like Mine [independent 2000]
Fueled by Breath [independent 1999] four-track EP
Sky Stories [independent 1998] six-track EP

Bell, John Kim—(Mohawk) Classical *See*: Tara-Louise Montour

Born 1953, Kahnawake, Quebec. Bell earned renown as the first Native to become a conductor of classical music. He began taking piano lessons at the age of eight and violin at ten. At age seventeen, Bell was hired as an assistant conductor and a year later was invited to conduct the national touring company of *No No Nannette*, making him the youngest conductor in the United States. While still attending Ohio State University, he conducted the first U.S. tour for the Soviet duo the Panovs and was later appointed as an opera coach with the Chautauqua Opera Association. He graduated in 1975 with a bachelor's degree in music.

Bell continued to study piano while conducting more than thirty national tours and Broadway musicals, working with

Lauren Bacall, Vincent Price, and Juliet Prowse; he also served as conductor-pianist for the *Redd Foxx Show*, the *Sonny Bono Show*, and the Bee Gees. He later became apprentice conductor for the Toronto Symphony Orchestra for the 1980–81 season and studied in Italy a year later. He returned to New York City to become the music director of the Dance Theater of Harlem and the Aglevsky Ballet Company. Bell formed the Canadian Native Arts Foundation to provide assistance for young protégés wishing to pursue classical training. His career was the subject of the documentary *John Kim Bell: The First North American Indian Conductor* [Anthony Azzopardi, 1984]. In 1988, he produced his full-scale Native ballet *In the Land of Spirits*. His television and film scores include *As Long as the Rivers Flow*, *The Trial of Standing Bear*, and *Divided Loyalties: The Life and Times of Joseph Brant*. He was named an officer of the Order of Canada in 1991.

Bell, Leland—(Odawa) Folk/Trad

A successful visual artist, Bell also made some inroads into music. His music combined traditional elements with spoken word in Anishnabe and acoustic instrumentation to invoke a moody atmosphere that reflected his cultural identity. The song "Mishomis" was included on the collection entitled *The Gathering*, produced by Billy Bryans, which received the Juno Award for Best World Beat Recording in 1992.

DISCOGRAPHY:
"Mishomis" [independent 1990] cassingle

Appearances:
The Gathering [Attic World 1990] comp
I Am an Eagle: The Music from the Legends Project [First Nations 1994] comp
Legends: I Am an Eagle [First Nations 1994] comp

Belladonna, Joey—(Iroquois) Rock

Born Joseph Bellardini, October 30, 1960, Oswego, New York. After moving to New York City, Belladonna fronted several heavy metal cover bands before gaining fame as the lead singer for Anthrax from 1985 to 1992. During this period, the group sold more than 8 million albums worldwide, generating several Gold albums and three Grammy nominations before Belladonna pursued a solo career. Known for composing vocal-oriented material that emphasizes his melodic style, his identity was made apparent in his anthemic composition "Indians" and the 1995 song "Injun." He enhanced his stage presence by wearing an eagle feather headdress, which became his trademark. His first solo album included Daren Scott, guitars; Joe Andrews, bass; Scott Schroeter, drums.

DISCOGRAPHY:
Spells of Fear [D-Rock 1998]
Belladonna [Mausoleum/EMI/BMG 1995]
Anthrax (lead vocals):
Madhouse: The Very Best of Anthrax [Island 2001] best of
Return of the Killer A's: The Best [Island 1999] best of
Armed and Dangerous [Island 1998, Japan]
Live: The Island Years [Island 1994]
Attack of the Killer B's [Island 1989/1991] Gold
Persistence of Time [Island 1990] Gold
State of Euphoria (Clean) [Island 1988]
State of Euphoria [Island 1988] Gold
I'm the Man [Island 1987] EP, Gold
Among the Living [Island 1987]
Spreading the Disease [Island 1985]
Armed and Dangerous [Island 1985]

Film and Video:
Anthrax: The Return of the Killer B's Video Anthology [Island 1999]
Oidivnikufesin NFV [Island 1988] seventy-five-minute live concert
Pledge Night (AKA: Hazing in Hell) [Paul Ziller, 1988] as Young Sid

Bezhig—Rock

Lineup: Jeff Richards (Shuswap), guitar/vocals; Joe Keesickquayash (Anishnabe), percussion, Brent (Potawatomi), bass. Formed in 1997, Toronto, Ontario. Bezhig recorded two demo CDs in the late 1990s and released a full album in 2002.

DISCOGRAPHY:
Tonto Was Cool [independent 2002]

Billie, Chief Jim—(Seminole) Folk

From Cyprus Swamp, Florida. Singer-songwriter, entrepreneur, and former tribal council chief of the Florida Seminoles, Billy received NAMA's Living Legend Award in 1999.

DISCOGRAPHY:
Seminole Fire: Legends and Stories [SOAR 2000] spoken word *See*: Contemporary Spoken Word: Legends
Alligator Tales [SOAR 1998]
Big Alligator [Seminole Records 1996]
Old Ways [Seminole Records 1995]
Seminole Man [Seminole Records 1993]
Native Son [independent 1986]

Billy, Chuck—(Pomo) Hardcore Metal
See: Star Nayea

Born June 23, 1962. Based in Oakland, California. As the lead singer of the explosive metal band Testament, Billy also made guest appearances with other metal acts. Formed in 1982 as Legacy, Testament is a founder of the Bay Area thrash movement. Despite its enormous commercial success, the band consistently released solid thrash albums without straying from its roots. A solid fan base was punctuated by a number of top-ten chart appearances. Billy's influences began with his older brother, who played guitar. He remembered, at age five, hearing the music of Jimmy Hendrix, Cream, and others, and later being impacted by the band KISS.

Testament Lineup: Chuck Billy, vocals; Eric Peterson, rhythm/lead guitars/backup vocals; Greg Christian, bass; James Murphy, lead guitars; Louie Clemente, drums.

DISCOGRAPHY:
First Strike Still Deadly [Burnt Offerings/Spitfire 2001]
The Gathering [Spitfire 1999]
Demonic [Burnt Offerings 1997]
Live at the Fillmore [Burnt Offerings 1995, United Kingdom] w/ Star Nayea
Low [Atlantic 1994]
Return to the Apocalypse [Atlantic 1993] EP
Souls of Black [Atlantic 1990]
Practice What You Preach [Atlantic 1989]
The New Order [Atlantic 1988]
Live at Eindhoven [Megaforce 1987]
The Legacy [Megaforce/Atlantic 1987]

Appearances:
James Murphey:
Feeding the Machine [Shrapnel 1999]
Convergence [Shrapnel 1996]
Stuck Mojo:
Rising [Century Media 1998]

Bird, Barry—(Anishnabe) Folk/Gospel

Based in Saint Catharines, Ontario, Bird recorded music he loved the most. Playing fiddle, dobro, mandolin, rhythm guitar and singing vocals, he was accompanied by Charles Rogers on bass, Tom Longboat on banjo, and Marilyn Monague on backup vocals.

DISCOGRAPHY:
Barry Bird Sings Ojibway [independent 1996]

Bird, Gordon—(Mandan-Hidatsa-Arikira) Country/Rock *See*: Featherstone; Flute Music

The patriarch of the family band Featherstone, Bird also founded the label of the same name. The music is a unique mix of powwow, flute, country, and rock, with 49er-style lyrics (*See*: Powwow Music: Introduction).

DISCOGRAPHY:
Catch Your Dreams [Featherstone 1997]
Generation to Generation [Featherstone 1996] w/ Jackie Bird
Music of the Plains [Featherstone FR-400] flute
Move on Up [Featherstone 1994]
You're So Far Away/Indian Nation [Featherstone FT-2009]
Live at the Logo [Featherstone 2005]
Gordon Bird Sings Traditional/Contemporary American Indian Songs [Featherstone FT-1001]

Singles:
"Summertime Blues/Something Else" [Featherstone FT-2016] cassingle

Bird, Jackie—(Mandan-Hidatsa) Folk/Rock/Trad *See*: Featherstone; Robbie Robertson

A multitalented musician and female hoop dancer, Bird was also the drummer for the Bird family band Featherstone. She describes her music as Indian blues/rock that combines a variety of contemporary influences with traditional 49ers (*See*: Powwow Music: Introduction), exemplified in her recording of the song "Lovesick Blues." She also excels in powwow dance styles, including fancy shawl dancing.

DISCOGRAPHY:
With Love, Honor, and Respect [Featherstone 2001]
Lady [Featherstone 1996]

Singles:
"Honey Love Me/Wild Horse" [Featherstone FRS-2012] cassingle
"Just Because/I'm Crying Looking for You" [Featherstone 1990] cassingle
"Lovesick Blues/Whirlwind Rider" [Featherstone 1990] cassingle

Appearances:
Robbie Robertson:
Contact from the Underworld of Redboy [Capitol 1998]
Various:
Sacred Spirit II: More Chants and Dances of the Native Americans [Higher Octave Music/Virgin 2000] comp

Bird, Sherry—(Mandan-Hidatsa) Country *See*: Featherstone

Sherry Bird excels in music, traditional dance, and visual art and was the bass player for the family group Featherstone.

DISCOGRAPHY:
"I'm the One Who Loves You/Sad Movies" [Featherstone FRS-2010] cassingle

Bird, Suzanne—(Plains Cree) Country

Winnipeg-based singer with an impressive vocal quality, but hampered by stage fright; broke out of her shell only long enough to record one album.

DISCOGRAPHY:
Heart Full of Soul [Rayne 1989] cass

Appearances:
Aboriginal Showcase [Sunshine 2001] comp

Bird Family—(Dakota) Folk/Rock *See*: Featherstone

Bisi, Martin—(Chicano) Alternative Rock

Bordering on the experimental with songs sung in English and Spanish, Bisi recorded his first album with former King Crimson and Gentle Giant notables Fred Frith and Bill Laswell (*See*: Stevie Salas).

DISCOGRAPHY:

See Ya in Tiajuana [New Alliance 1995]
   w/ Las Cochinas
All Will Be Won [New Alliance 1991]
Creole Mass [New Alliance 1989]

Black, Jimmy Carl—(Comanche)
Rock

Born James Inkanish Black, February 1,
1938, El Paso, Texas. Raised in Anthony
on the Texas–New Mexico border, Black
studied trumpet in high school. His early
influences included Elvis Presley, Muddy
Waters, and Howlin' Wolf. His musical
origins are traced to the blues, Tex-Mex,
cowboy rock, and bump 'n' grind backup
music for strippers. He did a stint with the
U.S. Air Force but left it in 1958, at which
time he had a wife and three children.
Black started a short-lived country-and-
western trio (without a bass player) called
Three Guys. He recorded his first single
in 1962 with the Keys on a pressing of
one thousand copies. By 1964, he moved
to California and formed the Soul Giants
with Roy Estrada and Ray Collins, performing mostly R & B covers. The group's
singer and guitarist were drafted into military service and were replaced by Frank
Zappa. Zappa proposed that if they played
his music, they would become rich and
famous, wherein Black pointed out, "I
got famous, but I damn sure didn't get
rich!" A founding member of the Mothers
of Invention, Black became a creative
force. "I'm Jimmy Carl Black, and I'm the
Indian of the group" is the immortalized
self-introduction from their album *We're
Only in It for the Money*. Black was an
underpaid musician with five kids, and his
arguments and rants with Zappa were captured on tape and spliced into several early
albums, including the track "If We'd All
Been Living in California" from the album
Uncle Meat. His most notable performance
was the song "Lonesome Cowboy Burt"
from *200 Motels*. After Zappa disbanded

the Mothers of Invention, Black went on
to form Geronimo Black in 1971. Zappa
alumni Bunk Gardner, Don Preston, and
Black formed the Grandmothers in 1980
and pulled off a U.S. tour of sixty shows
in sixty-six days. The 1980 single "Trail of
Tears" exemplified Black's strengths as a
talented songwriter who expressed a direct
perspective on history.

   Throughout his career, Black played
with numerous acts, including the Lotus
Family, Jim Bowie, Captain Glasspack and
the Magic Mufflers, Big Sonny and the Lost
Boys, and Eugene Chadbourne (as the Jack
and Jim Show). In the 1990s, he finally
found enough work with Muffin Records
in Stuttgart, Germany, to live off his music.
He has become known as one of the best
interpreters of classic Zappa. His autobiography, published by the University of
Liverpool Press, was coauthored with Rod
Gillard of the Muffin Men.

DISCOGRAPHY:

When Do We Get Paid [Divine 1998]
Jimmy Carl Black and the Mannish Boys:
A Little Dab'l Do Ya [Amazing 1987]
Geronimo Black:
Welcome Back [Helios 1980]
Geronimo Black [UNI 1972]

Appearances (listed alphabetically):
Ant Bee:
Lunar Muzik [Divine 1998]
*Ant Bee with My Favorite Vegetables and
   Other Bizarre Muzik* [Divine 1994]
Austin Lounge Lizards:
Highway Cafe of the Damned [Watermelon
   1988; Sugar Hill 1999]
Big Sonny and the Lost Boys:
In Heat [Con Safo 1979]
Arthur Brown and Jimmy Carl Black:
Brown, Black, and Blue [Blue Wave 1991]
Captain Beefheart and the Magic Band:
Grow Fins: Rarities (1965–1982) [Revenant
   1999] best of
Eugene Chadbourne:
Communication Is Overrated [House of
   Chadula 2000]

Locked in a Dutch Coffee Shop [House of Chadula 1999]
Chadbourne Barber Shop [Airline 1996]
Uncle Jimmy's Master Plan [House of Chadula 1996]
Pachuco Cadaver [Fire Ant 1995]
Fundamental [House of Chadula 1993]
The Grandmothers:
The Eternal Question [Inkinish 2001]
Eating the Astoria [Obvious Music 1998]
Dreams on Long Play [Muffin USA 1995]
Who Could Imagine [Brain 1994; Network-Munich Records 1995]
A Mother of an Anthology [One Way 1993]
Looking Up Granny's Dress [Rhino 1982]
Official Grandmothers Fan Club Talk Album [Panda 1981]
An Anthology of Previously Unreleased Material [Rhino 1980] comp
The Keys:
"Stretch Pants/Just a Matter of Time" [Ultimate 1962] 45-rpm single
Frank Zappa and the Mothers of Invention:
200 Motels [Bizarre/Reprise 1971] sdtk
Weasels Ripped My Flesh [Bizarre/Reprise 1970]
Burnt Weeny Sandwich [Bizarre/Reprise 1969]
Uncle Meat [Bizarre/Reprise 1969]
Mothermania: The Best of the Mothers [MGM/Verve 1968] best of
Cruising with Reuben and the Jets [MGM/Verve 1968]
Lumpy Gravy [MGM/Verve 1968]
We're Only in It for the Money [MGM/Verve 1968]
Absolutely Free [MGM/Verve 1967]
Freak Out! [MGM/Verve 1966]

Film:
The True Story of 200 Motels [Roelof Kiers, 1989]
Uncle Meat [Frank Zappa, 1987]
Mondo Hollywood [Robert Carl Cohen, 1976]
200 Motels [Frank Zappa/Tony Palmer, 1971]
Ride for Your Life (AKA: Mourir Champion) [Robin Spry, 1967]

Blackfire—(Dineh) Heavy Metal

Lineup: Klee Benally, vocals/guitar; Jeneda Benally, bass/vocals; Clayson Benally, drums; with Jones Benally, traditional vocals (*See*: Traditional/Archival Solo), and Robert Tree Cody, flute (*See*: Flute Music).

Three siblings born in the heart of the land struggle at Big Mountain, Arizona, on the former Navajo/Hopi Joint Use Area, rose up to speak out with anger and insight. Traditional beliefs, punk/metal riffs, and lyrics focusing on unity and survival ignited Blackfire's explosive style that resonated with depth and energy. This unique character grabbed the attention of genre icons the Ramones. C. J. Ramone produced the *Blackfire* EP, and Joey Ramone worked as producer and vocalist for the *One Nation Under* album, his last project before he passed away. Heavy metal, rock, and punk serve as solid pillars for Blackfire's style and writing, but band members also cited a variety of other influences. Jeneda and Clayson said classical music was a favorite, and Klee, the serious but outgoing frontman, document frontline actions of the Native land struggle. Activists in the truest sense, they also perform traditional songs and dances with their uncle as the Jones Benally Family. They received a NAMA nomination for Best Independent Release in 1999, then embarked on a successful European tour in 2001. They later journeyed to North Africa and played at the Festival in the Desert in Essakne, Mali, alongside numerous local indigenous Tuareg musicians, notable African musicians such as Ali Farka Toure, and rock legend Robert Plant. Through a connection with Nora Guthrie, Blackfire became involved in a musically diverse project that set Woody Guthrie lyrics to new music. The trio emerged from the studio with a two-track EP, "Mean Things Happenin' in This World" and "Corn Song."

DISCOGRAPHY:
Woody Guthrie Singles [Tacoho Productions 2003] two-track EP

Blackfire: Clayson, Jeneda, and Klee Benally. Photo by John Running.

One Nation Under [Tacoho Productions 2001] w/ Joey Ramone, vocals

Blackfire [Tacoho Productions 1998] three-track CD w/ C. J. Ramone

Blackfire [Tacoho Productions 1994] five-track CD w/ Robert Tree Cody

Appearances:

Festival in the Desert [World Village Music 2003, Germany] comp

Peace and Dignity Journeys [Xicano Records and Film 2000] comp

Spirit of the Native American Indians [ARC Music 1999, United Kingdom, Germany] comp *See*: Traditional/Archival Compilations

Videos:

It Ain't Over [independent 2001]

Blackfoot—Rock *See*: NDN, Greg T. Walker

Original Lineup: Ricky Medlocke, lead, acoustic, slide guitar/lead vocals/dobro/mandolin; Charles Hargrett, lead guitar; Jackson Spires (Cherokee-Cheyenne), drums/vocals; Greg T. Walker (Creek-Choctaw), bass/keyboard/vocals; Shorty Medlocke, special harmonica appearances; former Uriah Heap keyboardist Ken Hensley, joined in 1983.

Formed in 1969, Jacksonville, Florida, with Medlocke, Walker, and Ron Sciabarasi as Fresh Garbage. After the usual fine-tuning, they became known as Blackfoot and enjoyed several Billboard Chart appearances: *Strikes* clocked in at number 42 in 1979; *Tomcattin'* made it to number 50; *Marauder* number 48 in 1981; *Siogo* number 82 in 1983, *Vertical Smiles* number 176 in 1984. The original lineup ended that year, with Bobby Berth replacing Hargrett. Spires left the band in 1986, when the Blackfoot corporation was finally dissolved. Medlocke continued using the Blackfoot name with a 1994 lineup that included former Wasp drummer Stet Howland and later Mark Woerpel on guitar, Bryce Barnes on bass, and John Howsley on lead/rhythm guitars. They released three albums in the late 1980s and early 1990s. Spires makes jewelry with a Web site for Internet sales and plays with the Southern Rock Allstars. The Allstars released a 1999 album, *Crazy Again*, with former members of Molly Hatchet and the Rossington Band: Charles Hart, Dave Hlubek, and Jay Johnson. Spires also teamed up with Walker and guitarist-songwriter Richard Luciano to work on the NDN project. Walker made earlier appearances on Cross Country's self-titled 1973 album released on the Atco label and on Lynyrd Skynyrd's *Street Survivors* [MCA 1977]. Hargrett continued making music while chronicling the band's history.

DISCOGRAPHY:

Hits You Remember—Live [Madacy 2001] best of
Live [EMI/Capitol 2000] best of
KBFH Blackfoot Live at the Palladium 1983 [King Biscuit's Sour Hour 1998]
Gimme Gimme Gimme [Bootleg 1996, Japan] four-CD box set of radio shows
Rattlesnake Rock n Roll: The Best of Blackfoot [Atco 1994] best of
The Best of Blackfoot [Rhino 1994] bootleg
Vertical Smiles [Atco 1984]
Siogo [Atco 1983]
Highway Song—Live [Atco 1982]
Marauder [Atco 1981]
Tomcattin' [Atco 1980]
Strikes [Atco 1979]
Flyin' High [Epic 1976]
No Reservations [Island 1975]

Singles:

"Morning Dew/Livin' in the City" [Atco 1985] twelve-inch vinyl
"Morning Dew/Livin' in the City" [Atco 1985] seven-inch vinyl
"Morning Dew/Livin' in the City" [Atco 1984] long and short promo seven-inch vinyl
"Teenage Idol/Run for Cover" [Atco 1983] seven-inch vinyl
"Teenage Idol/We're Goin' Down" [Atco 1983] twelve-inch vinyl
"Teenage Idol/We're Goin' Down" [Atco 1983] seven-inch vinyl
"Teenage Idol" [Atco 1983] long and short versions, seven-inch vinyl
"Send Me an Angel/Drivin' Fool" [Atco 1983]
"Highway Song (live)/Rollin' and Tumblin' (live)/Fly Away" [Atco 1982]
"Dry County/Too Hard to Handle/On the Run/Train Train" [Atco 1982]
"Interview/What It's About" [Atco 1982]
"Searchin'" [Atco 1981] stereo/mono promo seven-inch vinyl
"Searchin'/Payin' for It" [Atco 1981]
"Fly Away/Good Morning Searchin'" [Atco 1981]
"Fly Away" [Atco 1981] stereo/mono promo seven-inch vinyl
"Every Man Should Know Queenie/Highway Song" [Atco 1980]
"On the Run/Street Fighter" [Atco 1980]
"Spendin' Cabbage" [Atco 1980] stereo/mono promo seven-inch vinyl
"Gimme Gimme Gimme" [Atco 1980] stereo/mono promo seven-inch vinyl
"Gimme Gimme Gimme/In the Night" [Atco 1980] seven-inch vinyl
"Street Fighter/My Own Love" [Atco 1980]
"Train Train/Baby Blue" [Atco 1980]
"Train Train" [Atco 1979] long and short promo seven-inch vinyl
"Highway Song" [Atco 1979] long and short promo seven-inch vinyl
"Highway Song/Road Fever" [Atco 1979]
"Highway Song/Train Train" [Atco 1979]

Solo Work:

Ricky Medlocke:
After the Reign [Music for Nations 1994]
Sittin' on Top of the World [Music for Nations 1994]
Medicine Man [Music for Nations 1990]

Chilled to da Bone [Music for Nations 1990]

Guitar Slinger Song and Dance [Music for Nations 1990]

Ricky Medlocke and Blackfoot [Atlantic 1987]

Saturday Night [Atlantic 1987] twelve-inch vinyl

Closer to Heaven [Atlantic 1987] twelve-inch vinyl

Black Thunder, Brian; a.k.a. Brian Davey—(OJ-Cree) Folk/Rock *See*: Murray Porter

Born and raised in the Cree community of Moose Factory, Ontario. A capable performer, Davey created a minor hit with "Silver Dollar" in the early 1980s, when he shared the stage with Murray Porter, Lawrence Martin (Wapistan), and many other Native musicians throughout northern Ontario. His career hit an upswing in the mid-1990s with his first solo project; Buffy Sainte-Marie provided string arrangements on his 1995 album. Following a relatively active period with numerous cross-country concert appearances, his music career slipped into dormancy as he reentered the political world of social work in the Native community.

DISCOGRAPHY:
Spirit with a Mask [Bear Clan 1995]

Appearances:
Jammin' on the Bay [World Records WRC4-6404] comp

Music from the Powerhouse: In the Spirit of Sharing [World Records 1985] comp

Goose Wings [World Records 1981] comp

Blue Coyote—Jazz

Lineup: Devon Pena, guitars/charango/clay flute/piano/digital sampler/synthesizers/vocals; Larry Brannon, flute/clay flutes/digital sampler/synthesizers; Phil Rogers, alto saxophone/piano/eight-track engineering. Blue Coyote produced one album, which, although not widely distributed, was the result of a desire to play good music.

DISCOGRAPHY:
Blue Coyote: A Journey into Southwestern "Wilderness Jazz" [Music Coyotl 1998]

Blues Nation *See*: Tom Ware

Bobbish, Robert—(Cree) Rock

Born in Chisassibi, Quebec. An extensive roster of musicians appear with Bobbish on his first album, produced by Randall Presott, Jon Park-Wheeler, and Robert Bobbish, and engineered by Ken Freisen, Martin Russell, Jon Park-Wheeler, and Tracey Brown-Prescott. Career highlights include being an opening act for Blue Rodeo, Nazareth, and Susan Aglukark.

DISCOGRAPHY:
Lost Inside [Blue Thunder 1996]

Appearances:
James Bay Cree Youth Compilation Album [Cree Eeyou Productions 1996] comp

Bouvette, Reg—(Metis) Fiddle

Born April 23, 1923, Saint Vital, Manitoba. A legend of old-time and Metis fiddle music, Bouvette achieved national prominence throughout the 1960s, 1970s, and 1980s. Noted for his prominent style, he won numerous fiddle contests in both Canada and the United States. Most of his recordings were issued on the Sunshine Records label.

DISCOGRAPHY:
24 Greatest Hits [Sunshine 1999]

Barn Dance Favorites [Sunshine ssbct-475]

Waltz Favorites [Sunshine ssbct-474]

Reg Bouvette . . . A Fiddling Legend [Sunshine SSCT 474]

The King and the Princess [Sunshine ssbct-449] w/ Patti Kusturok

Special Anniversary Edition [Sunshine ssbct-444]

More Original Fiddling Gems [Sunshine SSCT 439]

Fiddling Gems [Sunshine ssbct-439]

Drops of Brandy [Sunshine ssbct-436]

Fiddling across the Border [Sunshine ssbct-425] w/ Jr. Daugherty

Lookin' Buck [Sunshine ssbct-412]

Red River Jig [Sunshine ssbct-402]

Homebrew [Sunshine ssbct-400]

Appearances:

Drops of Brandy and Other Traditional Metis Tunes [Gabriel Dumont Institute 2002] four-CD comp

20 Aboriginal Greatest Hits, Vol. 3 [Sunshine 2002] comp

Fiddle Legends [Sunshine 2000] comp

24 Golden Fiddle Greats [Sunshine 1998] comp

Boyd, Jim—(Colville Confederated Tribes) Folk/Rock *See*: Annie Humphrey, Winter Hawk, XIT

Born James Lee Boyd, January 1, 1956, Edwards Air Force Base, California; resides on the Lakes Band of the Colville Reservation, Washington.

In the early 1980s, Boyd played with the all-Native bands Winter Hawk and XIT. He returned to his home reservation and established Thunder Wolf Studios in Inchelium, Washington. Local celebrated author Sherman Alexie was a big fan of Boyd's work and initiated a collaboration of music and poetry. Their single "Small World" appeared on the Indigo Girl's project *Honor* (*See*: Contemporary Compilations). Boyd went on to create film scores and soundtracks with writer Alexie for director Chris Eyre's *Smoke Signals*, *Reservation Blues*, and *The Business*

Rez Bound: LaRae Wiley, Jerry Stensgar, Alfonso Kolb, Jim Boyd. Photo by Shelly Boyd; courtesy Thunder Wolf Productions.

of Fancy Dancing, with appearances in each release. His support work includes the CD project *Community Vision— Healthy Nations: Reducing Substance Abuse, Promoting Healthy Lifestyles, "A Way of Life Community."* The collaboration between Boyd and the Colville Tribes Healthy Nations Project dedicated the proceeds from the album sales to building stronger Native communities. Boyd wrote the music, and community members supplied the lyrics: Bessie Nugent, Laura Rivera, Justina Campbell, James Tonasket, Chris Shaffer-Louie, Mary Wahpat, Bob Louie, Shelly Boyd, Julie Phillips, Valerie Vargas-Thomas, and George Abrahamson.

Rez Bound Lineup (1999): Jim Boyd, guitar/vocals; Alfonso Kolb (San Luiseno), drums/percussion; Jerry Stensgar (Colville), bass; LaRae Wiley (Colville), keyboards/vocals.

Kyo-T Lineup (2003): Jim Boyd, guitar/vocals/harmonica/cedar flute; Alfonso Kolb, drums; Brad Green, keyboards; Marty Meisner, bass.

DISCOGRAPHY:

Going to the Stick Games [Thunder Wolf 2004]

Jim Boyd and Kyo-T Live [Thunderwolf 2003]
Live at the Met [Thunderwolf 2002]
w/ Alfonso Kolb
alterNATIVES [Thunderwolf 2001]
w/ Annie Humphrey
Community Vision—Healthy Nations [Thunderwolf 1999]
First Come Last Served [Thunderwolf 1997]
Reservation Blues [Thunderwolf 1996]
w/ Sherman Alexie
Jim Boyd [Thunderwolf 1996] CD EP
Spokane Language [Spokane Tribe of Indians 1996]
Unity [Thunderwolf 1993]
Reservation Bound [Thunderwolf 1986]

Singles:
"Rez Bound" [Thunderwolf 1999]
"Filtered Ways" [Thunderwolf 1995]

Appearances (listed alphabetically):
Annie Humphrey:
Edge of America [Makoche 2003] vocals/guitar
XIT:
Drums across the Atlantic [SOAR 1984] drums
Various:
The Business of Fancy Dancing [Falls Apart 2003] sdtk
Urban Skins, Vol. 1 [SOAR 1999] comp
Smoke Signals [Miramax 1998] sdtk
Indian Killer [Warner 1996] audio book, w/ Sherman Alexie *See*: Contemporary Spoken Word: Audio Books
Honor [Daemon 1996] comp, w/ Sherman Alexie
Talking Rain [Tim Kerr Records 1995] w/ Sherman Alexie

Videos:
XIT:
Without Reservation [SOAR 2002]

Boyer, Alfred "Hap"—(Metis) Fiddle

Born 1929, North Battleford, Saskatchewan. A legend in the field of traditional Metis fiddling, Boyer's unique playing style took him on international tours that earned him wide acclaim in his field of music.

DISCOGRAPHY:
Hap Boyer—Fiddling Metis Style [Turtle Island Music 1997]

Appearances:
Edmund Bull:
Indian Boy [Turtle Island Music 2000]
Various:
Drops of Brandy and Other Traditional Metis Tunes [Gabriel Dumont Institute 2002] four-CD comp
Gabriel's Crossing [Turtle Island Music 1997] comp

Boyer, Eugene—(Anishnabe) *See*: Carmen Jones, Wagon Burner Express

Born February 24, 1955, Sault Sainte Marie, Ontario. Boyer began playing music in the 1960s, first only by ear; then he studied at Humber College and then jazz at York University, Toronto, Ontario; guest instructors included guitarists Joe Pass and Lenny Breau (*See*: Jeari Czapla). After playing a gig in Winnipeg, Manitoba, with Wagon Burner Express, Boyer and the band received an invitation to be the opening act for keyboardist Chick Corea in Jacksonville, Florida. In 1994, Boyer began working full-time for GO Transit in Toronto, Ontario, and devoted less time to music.

DISCOGRAPHY:
The Jim Heineman/John T. Davis Quartet, Vol. 4 [independent 1991] guitars

Appearances:
Carmen Jones:
Stepping Out [independent 2003] producer-guitarist

Bravestone—Rock

Lineup: Ennis Jacob, vocals/keyboard; Lenny Jacob, guitar; Archie, guitar; Benji, bass; Norman Shewaybick, drums; Fred Jacob, producer.

Two brothers from Webequie, a small northern community of six hundred people located near Fort Hope in northwestern Ontario. Primarily self-taught musicians, they were raised around the old fiddle stylings of their uncles. They ventured south to the big city of Thunder Bay, Ontario, to record some tracks and released two albums on the Winnipeg-based Sunshine Records label.

DISCOGRAPHY:
Spirit of the North [Sunshine 1994]
Sittin' by the Window [Sunshine 1990]

Appearances:
24 Canadian Aboriginal Artists [Sunshine 1995] comp

Breach of Trust—Heavy Metal

Lineup: Marty Ballentyne, guitar/vocals; Colin Cheechoo, guitar/vocals; Zane Kryzanowsky, bass; William Aubut, drums.

Formed in 1994, based in Saskatoon, Saskatchewan. Following the success of their nationally televised video, the band signed with EMI Music in 2001 to release their first single, "Disease." While they developed a clean and heavy sound, their distinction as a premier rock act included subtleties of their Native identity. They recorded a cover of the Payola$ hit "Eyes of a Stranger" for the soundtrack for the film *Fubar* [Mike Dowse, 2002].

DISCOGRAPHY:
Songs for Dying Nations [EMI 2001]
Songs for Dying Nations [BOT 2000]
Dead Issue [Rockin' Rod 1995] EP

Singles:
"Disease" [EMI 2001]
"Complicated" [EMI 2001] album version/ radio edit

Appearances:
Fubar—The Album [Aquarius 2002] sdtk

Videos:
Disease [EMI 2001]
Who Am I? [independent 2000]

Bread, Philip "Yogie"— (Kiowa-Cherokee) Jazz/Blues

Born June 15, 1959. A traditional singer, dancer, and direct descendant of historical leaders Hunting Horse and Satanta, Bread took up their struggle using modern musical instruments. He worked in television and served as a cultural consultant for the film productions *Geronimo, An American Legend* [Walter Hill, 1992] and *Dances with Wolves* [Kevin Costner, 1990]. Bread later teamed up with bassist Dave Copenhaver to create *Thon-gya*, which received a NAMA nomination for Best Jazz Album, 1998. He also recorded with David Brown (Lakota-Muskogee-Creek), who has performed with many blues legends, including Albert King, Koko Taylor, and Stevie Ray Vaughn.

DISCOGRAPHY:
Brown, Bread, and Blues [independent 1999]
Thon-gya [Lunacy 1997]

Broken Walls—Gospel *See*: Jonathan Maracle

Lineup: Jonathan Maracle, lead vocals/ guitar; Linda Maracle, vocals/keyboards; Kris De Lorenzi, vocals/bass; Scott Offord, drums.

From Tyendinaga Mohawk Territory near Belleville, Ontario, Jonathan Maracle began recording his own brand of gospel after years of work with the community's gospel choir. His two brothers, Tom and David, also record their music in his twenty-four-track studio.

DISCOGRAPHY:
Rise Up Mighty Warrior [independent 2001]

Clearly His Voice [independent 2000]
Broken Walls [independent 1996]

Brule—(Lakota) New Age *See*: Red Nativity

Born Paul LaRoche June 23, 1955. Adopted at an early age, LaRoche found his way back to his Lakota roots. With the stage name Brule, he became the Hagood Hardy of Indian Country and headlined live piano performances, which made him one of the top-selling recording artists in contemporary Native music. He also composed the original score for Red Sky's 1998 theatrical stage production *Tribe*.

DISCOGRAPHY:
Star People [SOAR 2001]
One Nation [SOAR 1999]
Lakota Piano [Natural Visions/SOAR 1997]
Medicine River—Man and Nature [Natural Visions/SOAR 1997] w/ Tom Bee
We the People [Natural Visions/SOAR 1995]

Appearances:
Red Nativity:
One Holy Night [Red Sea 1997] w/ Robbie Bee
Various:
Tribal Legends [Earth Beat! 2002] comp
Awakening the Spirit [SOAR 2000] comp
Visions and Rhythms 2 [Natural Visions/SOAR 1998] comp

B. S. and the Truth—Heavy Rock

Lineup: Brian L. Stanger, guitar/vocals; Bruce Butler, bass; Kyle McDermott, drums; Jim Jackson, guitar.

DISCOGRAPHY:
Last of the Holdouts [Nervous Records 1998] five-track EP

Buckland, Charles; a.k.a. Charles Haddon—(Mohican) Rock

After releasing two albums in Japan with the group Phantom, Buckland did his first demo in 1995. He worked in theater, providing backup as a multidisciplinary musician. He studied music theory at the University of Miami and based himself in New York City with experience in Internet/digital broadcasting. His scores include the NAMA theme.

DISCOGRAPHY:
Land Is Life [independent 2000] w/ Soni Moreno *See*: Ulali
Spider Heart [independent 1999]

Built for Comfort—(Mohawk) Blues *See*: Corvairs

Lineup: Matt Tarbell, harmonica; Morris Tarbell, slide guitar; Paul LaRonde, bass; Larry Stringer, bass; Dave Sisson, drums; Mark Doyle, organ/percussion; Kim Lembo, backup vocals.

The Tarbell brothers founded the Corvairs and then the Built for Comfort blues band, which lasted into the late 1990s.

DISCOGRAPHY:
High Ballin' [Blue Wave 1996]
Keep Cool [Blue Wave 1993]

Bull, Edmund—(Cree) Country *See*: Powwow Music: Red Bull

An outstanding traditional singer, Bull was not as successful as a country music performer.
Lineup: Edmund Bull, vocals; Jay Ross, Jay Buettner, Neil Meckelborg, guitars; Shane Wooley, drums/percussion; Greg Edmund, Edgar Muenala, flutes; Greg Edmund, keyboards; Carl Krouger, bass; Hank Boss, steel guitar; Hap Boyer, fiddle.

DISCOGRAPHY:
End of the Trail [Turtle Island Music 2003]
   round dance
Indian Boy [Turtle Island 2000] country
I've Been Everywhere [Sweet Grass 1994]
   powwow

Appearances:
A Turtle Island Christmas [Turtle Island
   Music 2002] comp

Burch, Sharon—(Dineh) Country/
Folk *See*: A. Paul Ortega

Born December 8, 1959. Burch's first
recording appearance was with A. Paul
Ortega. The collaboration propelled her
career in the southwestern United States.
Her songs focus on family, land, and culture, with an alluring simplicity in her
songwriting. With the exception of her
1999 album, her material is performed
in Dineh as she accompanies herself on
acoustic guitar. *Touch the Sweet Earth*
received the NAIRD INDIE Award, Best
North American Native Music, 1995; a
NAMA nomination, 1998; *Colors of My
Heart* received a NAMA Record of the
Year, 2000.

DISCOGRAPHY:
Colors of My Heart [Canyon 1999]
Touch the Sweet Earth [Canyon 1995]
Yazzie Girl [Canyon 1989]
The Blessing Ways [Canyon 1984]
   w/ A. Paul Ortega

Appearances:
Jennifer Berezan:
Returning [Edge of Wonder 2001] vocals
Various:
Sacred Souls [Manteca 2001, United King-
   dom] comp
*World Music, the Rough Guide: Latin and
   North America, Caribbean, India, Asia,
   and Pacific*, Vol. 2 [World Music Net-
   work, Rough Guides NCOS, and the
   New Internationalist 2000] comp

Sharon Burch. Photo by John Running.

Songs of the Spirit, Vol. 2 [Triloka 2000]
   comp
Divine Divas [UNI/Rounder 1997] comp
Rainbow Sign [Rounder 1992] comp
*Music of New Mexico: Native American
   Traditions* [Smithsonian Folkways 1992]
   comp

Burning Sky—Folk/New Age *See*:
Sky Chasers, Aaron White

Lineup: Kelvin Bizahaloni (Dineh) cedar
flute; Aaron White (Dineh) guitar; Michael
Bannister, percussion (left the group in
2000).
   Based in Flagstaff, Arizona. Primarily
an instrumental band that crossed many
musical boundaries, Burning Sky transcended the simplicity of the New Age
genre by infusing folk and traditional elements. Their sound progressed with each

release but never went beyond the safety net of familiar style or lyrics. They played several notable performances, including U.S. president Bill Clinton's Inaugural Ball, January 1997; they enjoyed on-stage appearances with Bruce Cockburn, Buffy Sainte-Marie, and others. White recorded and released a solo project, *Full Moon Sessions,* in late 1999 under the auspices of Sky Chasers. White and Bizahaloni reunited with John Densmore (the Doors) to record *Spirits in the Wind,* which received a Grammy nomination for Best Native Music Album, a NAMA nomination for Best Instrumental Recording, and a NAMA award for Best Duo/Group of the Year, 2003. Singer Martha Redbone appeared on the title track of the album *A Simple Man.*

DISCOGRAPHY:
Spirits in the Wind [Canyon 2002] w/ John Densmore
Enter the Earth [Ryko 1998]
A Simple Man [Canyon 1996]
Creation [Canyon 1996]
Blood of the Land [Canyon 1996]
Burning Sky [Canyon 1994]

Appearances:
A Native American Odyssey [Putumayo 1998] comp
Tribal Waters [Earth Beat! 1998] comp
"Barbwire Mind" from *Acoustic Café* [NPR broadcast, January 13, 1997] vocal track
Voices across the Canyon, Vol. 2 [Canyon 1996] comp
Voices across the Canyon, Vol. 1 [Canyon 1996] comp

Burnt—Rock/World

Lineup: David Boulanger, vocals/acoustic guitar; Peter Baureiss, tabla/djembe; Marc Baureiss, electric guitar; Jake Bell, percussion; Chuck Copenace, trumpet; Steve Gauthier, bass; Atik Mason, saxophone; Neewa Mason, keyboard/vocals; Darrin Monkman, drums; Jason McLean, sitar; David Kramer, harmonica; Kristjanna

Oleson, viola/violin; Michelle Castle, didgeridoo; Rob Vaarmeyer, Tibetan bowl.

Formed in Winnipeg, Manitoba, 2000. The band received a Juno nomination for Aboriginal Recording of the Year, 2004.

DISCOGRAPHY:
Project 1: The Avenue [Sunshine 2003]

Singles:
"Deadmen" [Sunshine 2003]

Buster, Jessica—(Seminole) *See:* Paul Buster

The daughter of country singer Paul Buster, Jessica Buster recorded a four-track CD. After leaving for college in 2001, she found less time to record music.

DISCOGRAPHY:
Me and Grandpa [independent 1999] four-track CD

Buster, Paul; a.k.a. Cowbone—(Seminole) Country and Western

Born January 17, 1950, Big Cyprus Reservation, Florida. Based in Hollywood, Florida. Buster was influenced by the Grand Ole Opry, Hank Williams, and his own father, Junior Buster; his mother (Mary Annie Buster) bought him his first guitar. Throughout his life, he worked as a language teacher with preschool children and sang gospel with the Gulfstream Baptist Association. His dad gave him the name Cowbone, which came from the cattle era, when they chased down stray cattle and found nothing but bleached bones.

Cowbone Band Lineup: Paul Buster, vocals/guitar; Solomon Cypress, bass; Chunky, lead guitar; Ronnie Billie, drums; Paul Pettitt, sequencing/keyboards; J. Roberts, fiddle; Alan Kendle, steel guitar; Keith Ridenour, electric guitar; Miss Jessica, backup vocal.

DISCOGRAPHY:
Black Water Bayou [independent 2000]
Hi-Way 41 [independent 1998]

Campbell, David—(Arawak) Folk

A self-taught songwriter-singer, poet, painter, writer, and guitarist born in Guyana of an Arawak father and a Portuguese Guyanian mother, David Campbell currently resides in Vancouver, British Columbia. On the music scene for many years, Campbell was able to entertain audiences of all ages. His songs are filled with a simple charm and poetry, utilizing only voice and acoustic guitar. This musical minimalism attested to his craftsmanship as a diverse songwriter. His ability to write poignant material of political and historical subjects, coupled with a witty storytelling style, earned him notoriety on the Canadian folk music scene and in many Native communities as well. His first of fifteen or more albums was recorded and released through the Toronto-based Development in Education Centre. He moved to British Columbia in the late 1980s and continued to play the folk festivals and concerts throughout Canada.

Campbell made many radio and television appearances throughout his career, including CBC TV's childen's show *Mr. Dress Up*. He also performed at many children's festivals and at hundreds of elementary schools across Canada. His many career highlights include a concert at the Albert Hall in London, England. He composed music for the NFB film *Song of the Paddle* [Bill Mason, 1978] and was commissioned by the Vancouver School Board to record the album *People of the Salmon* in 1985. In August 2003, Campbell received a lifetime award from his country of origin, Guyana, for contributing to the arts and culture of that country. He has recorded twenty albums of original songs and toured extensively across Canada, England, Holland, Germany, the United States, Guatemala, and Guyana. He has written five books of poetry, including *Between Songs*, *Through Arawak Eyes*, and *Search*, all released independently. He has also appeared at various spoken-word events, including the Vancouver International Writer's Festival, the Free Press Festival, and the Young Writer's Conference in Vancouver. In February 2004, he received the World Poetry Life Time Award.

SELECTED DISCOGRAPHY:
Keepers of the Fire [independent 2001]
Let the People Dance [independent 1993]
West Coast [independent 1992]
Healing Circle, Vol. 1 [independent 1991]
Healing Circle, Vol. 2 [independent 1991]
Bound for the Sun [independent 1991]
My Kind of Song [independent 1991]
People of Turtle Island [independent 1990]
Hidden Tears [independent 1990]
The Earth and Us-Me [independent 1990]
Old What's His Name [independent 1989; originally *Through the Eyes of a Child*, 1981]
Twilight Rambler [independent 1986]
People of the Salmon [independent 1985]
Through the Eyes of a Child [Noona 1981]
Underneath the Blue Canadian Sky [Columbia 1979]
Song [Columbia 1978]
Pretty Brown [Columbia 1977]
Through Arawak Eyes [DEC 1974]
Sun Wheel [Decca 1972, United Kingdom]
Mr. Everywhere [Mercury Records 1970]
Young Blood [Transatlantic Records 1967]
David Campbell [Transatlantic Records 1966]

Singles:
"Dene Nation/We Are Not All Over" [Kevin Moynihan Audio-Visual Services 1976] seven-inch vinyl

Cardinal, Ron—(Metis) Fiddle

Lineup: Ron, Gary, and Lee Cardinal.

DISCOGRAPHY:
Big John-Fiddle Jam [Sunshine SSCT-477]

Castel, Sidney—(Cree)

From Mathias Colomb, Manitoba (formerly Pukatawagan). Castel began his professional music career playing the bars in Manitoba. His wife smashed his guitar each time she found him playing and made him promise never to perform again. After her death in the late 1980s, he began to revive his career. When he recorded the "Pukatawagan Song" in 2001, he received national attention. He passed away in 2003, in his midsixties.

DISCOGRAPHY:
Live at the Beaver Lodge [Sunshine 2003]
Live at the Beaver Lodge [Sunshine 2002] studio version

Appearances:
Pukatawagan 1st Annual Talent Search 2000 [Sunshine 2001] comp

Castillo, Randy—(Isleta Pueblo–Cherokee) Rock *See*: Red Thunder, Stevie Salas

1950–2002
Born December 18, 1950, Albuquerque, New Mexico. Castillo is known more for his ten-year collaboration with Ozzie Osbourne, but his musical journey began when he became a drummer in his high school marching band. He later worked with his father, a trumpet player, performing at weddings and parties. After several warmup stints in local bands, he headed for Los Angeles and played with the Wumblies in the 1970s. By 1981, he joined the New Wave band the Motels and then played with Lita Ford, former member of the Runaways. It was through Ford that he met Motley Crue. The band's drummer, Tommy Lee, introduced Castillo to former Black Sabbath vocalist Ozzy Osbourne. The 1985 meeting generated a ten-year stint of songwriting, recording, and touring. Through Sharon Osbourne, Castillo became the drummer for Motley Crue in

1999. In addition to his work with Ozzy and the Crue, Castillo also appeared on numerous tribute albums. Shortly after the release of *New Tattoo* in 2000, Castillo was diagnosed with squamous cell carcinoma, a form of cancer. After a hard fight with the disease, he passed away on March 26, 2002.

DISCOGRAPHY:

Appearances (listed alphabetically):
Black Sabbath:
Under Wheels of Confusion: 1970 . . . [Essential/Castle 1996]
Cage:
Cage [Nexus International 1997]
Lita Ford:
Dancin' on the Edge [Mercury/Vertigo 1984]
Bret Michaels:
Letter from Death Row [ULG 1998]
Motley Crue:
New Tattoo [EMI 2000]
Ozzy Osbourne:
Diary of a Madman/Bark at the Moon [Sony 1998]
Ozzman Cometh: Greatest Hits [Sony International 1997, United States]
Live and Loud [Epic 1993]
Mama I'm Coming Home [CBS/Sony 1992]
No More Tears [Epic 1991]
Just Say Ozzy [Epic 1990]
No Rest for the Wicked [Epic 1989]
Ultimate Sin [Epic/CBS 1986; Columbia/Sony 1990]
Stevie Salas:
Electric Powwow [Aquarius 1994]
Various:
Essential Metal Masters [Big Eye 2001] comp
Leppardmania: A Tribute to Def Leppard [Cleopatra 2000] comp
Humanary Stew? A Tribute to Alice [Cleopatra 1999] comp
Not the Same Old Song and Dance [Cleopatra 1999] comp
Rock: Train Kept a Rollin' [Sony 1999] comp

Buffy the Vampire Slayer (Original Sound-track) [CBS 1992] sdtk

Film:

Star Licks: The Master Sessions [Hal Leonard Corp. 2000] forty-five-minute instructional video

The Adventures of Ford Fairlane [Kenny Harlin, 1990] as Black Plague band member

Cavenaugh, Archie James—(Tlingit) Jazz *See*: Jim Pepper, Redbone

Born February 25, 1951, Wrangell, Alaska. A lifelong musician, Cavenaugh grew up in a musical household and formed rock bands in high school that were popular in the community. His work is heavily influenced by Bozz Scaggs, Stevie Wonder, and West Coast Chicano jazz/rock. He composed on guitar, and his wife, Melinda, wrote the lyrics. He first met Jim Pepper at a barroom gig in Alaska. Enthralled by what he heard, the singer jumped on stage and began improvising. Pepper later told him, "If anyone else had done that, I would've kicked their ass." Impressed with the singer's abilities, Pepper agreed to session on the recording that included members of Redbone. In 2000, Cavenaugh signed with Vivid Sound Corporation of Japan to record two new projects.

Cavenaugh's only album, *Black and White Raven*, features: Jim Pepper, saxophone/flute; Cavenaugh, guitar/vocals; former Redbone member Tony Bellamy, guitar/percussion/production; Redbone member Peter DePoe, drums/percussion; Redbone member Lolly Vegas, producer; Grant Reeves, alto saxophone; Mark Williams, trombone; Kenny Day, synthesizer/keyboards; Michael Spiro, percussion; Tag Henning, bass; Don Smith, trumpet; Charley Lee, drums; Dave Perry, percussion; Carrie Ernesti and Sammi Baker, backup vocals.

DISCOGRAPHY:
Black and White Raven [A&M 1980]

Chante; a.k.a. Chante Pierce— (Lakota) Folk/Trad

Chante recorded her first album with Earl Bullhead (*See*: Traditional/Archival Solo), Rick Ellis, Jack Lee, Duke Devine, Kevin Richard, and M. B. Gordy. That project was part of a larger healing and wellness initiative focused on recovery from alcohol and subsance abuse (*See*: Contemporary Spoken Word: Miscellaneous: *The Red Road to Sobriety*).

DISCOGRAPHY:
Nightbird [Great Spirit 1994]

Appearances:
Music from Turtle Island [Turtle Island Music 1999] comp

Chaput, Paul—(Metis) Folk/Blues

Born March 22, 1946, St. Boniface, Manitoba. A seasoned musician, poet, and actor, Chaput landed a role in the original 1969 production of Jerry Ragni, Jim Rado, and Galt MacDermot's musical *Hair*. He continued to perform in all mediums and worked as a television host, a film director, and a recording artist nominated for two Aboriginal Music Awards in 2002. His first solo release was a collection of original compositions performed on guitar. His second album displayed a greater lyrical sense, and he was accompanied by a full band. He maintained his professional course as an advanced structural consultant in addition to being a Registered in Human Relations health care practitioner; he also holds a degree in commercial arts and is a certified yoga instructor. In 2001, he hosted a bilingual (French-English) television series *Finding Our Talk* [Mushkeg/APTN] and directed the docudrama *Restoring the Circle*, which deals with restorative justice in northern Canadian Native communities.

DISCOGRAPHY:
Sweet Rain White Lights Red Blues [independent 2002]
Uncooked/Unplugged [independent 1999]

Charlie, Gerald—(Scowlitz) Blues

Born May 23, 1955. From British Columbia's Fraser Valley, Charlie found inspiration in the music of B. B. King and Muddy Waters. His musical career began in the 1980s when he formed the Black Owl Blues Band.
　Lineup: Gerald Charlie, guitar/vocals; Mike Wedge, bass; Graham Howell, sax; Chris Nordguist, drums; Terry Charlie drums.

DISCOGRAPHY:
Gerald Charlie and the Black Owl Blues [independent 1999]

Chartrand, Melanie—(Metis) Country/Folk

From Waterhen, Manitoba. Her single "No Way" from the album *Melanie* appeared at number 36 on the Canadian country charts. She performed for HRH Prince Albert Rainer and HRH Prince Charles in 1984. *Color Blind* received a Juno Award nomination for Aboriginal Recording of the Year, 1997.

DISCOGRAPHY:
Color Blind [Sunshine 1996]
Melanie Chartrand: Live at C-Weed's [independent 1995]
Melanie [independent 1993]

Appearances:
20 Aboriginal Greatest Hits, Vol. 2 [Sunshine 1998] comp

Cheechoo, Archie—(Cree) Country

Born February 20, 1948, James Bay, Ontario. The son of Sinclair Cheechoo, Archie Cheechoo had a life infused with music in northern Canada. Performing for more than twenty years, he recorded his first album in Philadelphia and Toronto with help from siblings Thelma and Vernon.

DISCOGRAPHY:
Child of the North [independent 1998]

Cheechoo, Clayton—(Cree) Rock

Born October 8, 1962. This bass player teamed up with twin sisters Lea Harper and Lyn Harper (a.k.a. Syren) and recorded a world music project of environmental consciousness, entitled *Wisdom of the Heart* [Magnum Opus 1993]. The album's single, "Let Them Live," was used to rally support for the land struggle being waged by Alberta's Lubicon Cree in the 1980s.

Cheechoo, Colin—(Cree) *See*: Breach of Trust

Cheechoo, James—(Cree) Fiddle

Born February 6, 1930. James Cheechoo is a member of the Moose Cree First Nation of James Bay. He learned the old fiddle tunes of his elders, who adopted the Irish and Scottish styles from trappers coming into the region. This form of playing had almost died out in the late twentieth century, when he decided to work on a project to record what he knew. "Shay Chee Man" is Cree for the three-masted ships that came to the Hudson Bay area during the fur-trading period.

DISCOGRAPHY:
Shay Chee Man [independent 1999]

Cheechoo, Lloyd—(Cree) Folk/
Country *See*: Morley Loon

Born September 14, 1956, East Main, Quebec. This guitarist, drummer, and man of many talents started to play professionally with Morley Loon in the mid-1970s. He later worked with many musicians, including Kenny Mianscum.

DISCOGRAPHY:

Appearances:
Kway [independent 2000] comp
Goose Wings [World Records 1981] comp

Cheechoo, Sinclair—(Cree) Fiddle

Born January 1, 1922, James Bay, Quebec. Growing up in East Main, Quebec, Sinclair Cheechoo eventually worked for the Hudson's Bay Company and settled in Moose Factory. His travels to various northern communities exposed his entire family to fiddle music and country styles that inspired years of performances and several recordings.

DISCOGRAPHY:
Sinclair Cheechoo Special [Sunshine 1994]
James Bay Cree Fiddler [Sunshine SSCT-448]

Appearances:
The Best Cree Fiddle Players of James Bay [Hughboy Records 1993] comp
Step Dance and Fiddle [Ojibway Cree Cultural Centre, NDA] comp

Cheechoo, Thelma—(Cree) Country
See: Archie Cheechoo

From the Moose Cree First Nation, James Bay, Ontario. Her musical roots took her around the James and Hudson Bay area in the mid-1980s, when she recorded her first song on an album entitled *The Cheechoo Family*. An opening performer at many folk music festivals and gatherings, she

also founded the Native Arts and Music Society in northern Ontario.

DISCOGRAPHY:
Pa Ma Sei Win [independent 1996]

Cheechoo, Vernon—(Cree) Country
and Western *See*: Archie Cheechoo,
Lawrence Martin

Born June 27, 1958. Vernon Cheechoo was raised on an island community on the Moose River several hundreds of miles from Moose Factory, Ontario, in the James Bay region. A self-taught musician raised in a musical family, he started playing in talent shows at the age of eight and recorded an album with his father, Sinclair, and sister Thelma. He also contributed two tracks to the *Goose Wings* album. His first album gained favorable reviews; his second release, *Touch the Earth and Sky*, received a Juno nomination for Best Music of Aboriginal Canada Recording, 2000. *The Right Combination* received a Juno nomination for Aboriginal Recording of the Year, 2003.

DISCOGRAPHY:
The Right Combination, Cheechoo and Martin [A Spirit Voice/EMI/Page 2002]
Touch the Earth and Sky [Darklight/Festival 1999]
Lonesome and Hurtin' [Dark Light/Denon 1993]

Appearances:
Dance Me Outside [Denon 1994] sdtk
Jammin' on the Bay [World Records WRC4-6404] comp
Goose Wings [World Records WRC1-2019 1981] comp

Videos:
Lonesome and Hurtin' [Bruce MacDonald, 1992]

Cheechoo Family—(Cree) Fiddle

DISCOGRAPHY:
Country and Fiddle [Sunshine SSCT-4137]

Cherokee Gospel Music—(Cherokee) Gospel

Lineup: Janis Ross Ballou, soprano; Nan Kingfisher Budder, alto; Chief Chad Smith; Deputy Chief Hastings Shade; the Cherokee National Children's Choir; Jamie Geneva and Janis Ross Ballou, choir conductors. All hymns were sung in the Cherokee language and recorded for the Cherokee national holiday; coproduced and recorded by the Cherokee Nations Cultural Resource Centre, Robbie Robinson, and Jeffrey Gray Parker (*See:* Coyote Zen).

DISCOGRAPHY:
Cherokee Gospel Music [Cherokee Nation 2000]

Cherokee National Children's Choir—(Cherokee) Gospel *See:* Rita Coolidge

Lineup: Holly Backwater, Rebecca Cook, Heather Crittenden, Alese Christie, Amanda Gibe, Devon Kirby, Kandra Liles, Ashley Proctor, Jon Ross, Kayla Sharp, Chris Smith, Samantha Spiker, Amy Watkins, Haley Noe, Holly Noe; w/ J. B. Dreadfulwater, choir leader. Also featuring: Rita Coolidge, vocals; Choogie Kingfisher, flute/vocals; Jeffrey Gray Parker, acoustic guitar; the Kenwood Emmanuel Baptist Church Choir.

A selection of gospel standards performed in the Cherokee language. Special guest Rita Coolidge performs "Amazing Grace." Additional material was written by Jamie McGee-Geneva, Jan Ballou, and Jeffrey Parker. The *Voices* album received a NAMA Award for Best Gospel/Christian Recording, 2002.

DISCOGRAPHY:
Voices of the Creator's Children [Cherokee Nation 2001] w/ Rita Coolidge

Cherokee National Youth Choir—(Cherokee) Gospel

Lineup: Holly Backwater, Heather Crittenden, Alese Christie, Rebecca Cook, Delilah Davis, Amanda Gibe, Paige Haines, Christina Hanvey, Vanessa John, Leslie Ketcher, Devon Kirby, Kandra Liles, Lora Miller, Haley Noe, Holly Noe, Tracy Pickup, Ashley Proctor, Megan Ross, Kinsey Shade, Kayla Sharp, Ryan Sierra, Christopher Smith, Amie Watkins, Caroline Buffalomeat, Walter Buffalomeat, Christina Catron, Pawnee Crabtree; w/ Jeffrey Gray Parker, composer. Narration provided by Jamie McGee-Geneva and Gil Silverbird. A collection of traditional gospel standards and original songs sung in the Cherokee language, with narration based on historical figure Redbird Smith from 1918.

DISCOGRAPHY:
Jesus Is Born Today [Cherokee Nation 2003]
Building One Fire [Cherokee Nation 2002] w/ Gil Silverbird

Cherokee Rose; a.k.a. Rose "Starfeather" Moore— (Cherokee) Country/Folk

Born January 28, 1966, Nashville, Tennessee. Moore began her music career in Minneapolis, Minnesota, "to satisfy a monumental itch to create." She took up the stage name Cherokee Rose and captured critical acclaim for her efforts. She conducted workshops on Native music and culture in education and toured internationally. The city of Albuquerque, New Mexico, proclaimed October 8, 1995, Cherokee Rose Day. Her remix of "Cradle Song" was included on *Pure Moods II:*

Sacred Spirits [Virgin 1994], with vocal appearances on *Sacred Spirits II* [Higher Octave Music/Virgin 2000]. In 2001, she worked on a spoken-word project with storyteller Eldrena Douma (Laguna Pueblo).

DISCOGRAPHY:
Chant [Clearlight Music 2001]
Love Medicine Music [Clearlight Music 1999]
To All the Wild Horses [Clearlight 1995]
Chant [Clearlight Music 1995]
Tracks South [Clearlight 1994]
Buckskin [Clearlight Music 1993] cass

Cherokee Rose and Silena—(Cherokee) Folk

This mother-daughter singing duo began performing in the 1980s.

DISCOGRAPHY:
Balanced by Tradition [Sunshine 2001]
Visions of History [Indian Country 1993] includes a song for Leonard Peltier
Walking against the Wind [Indian Country 1992]

Appearances:
20 Aboriginal Greatest Hits, Vol. 3 [Sunshine 2002] comp

Chief Jeff; a.k.a. Jeff Monague—(Anishnabe) Country/Folk

An elected chief of the Beausoliel First Nation, Christian Island, Ontario, Chief Jeff recorded original songs about barricades and bingo.
    Lineup: Chief Jeff, acoustic guitars/harmonica/lead vocals; Mitchell James, bass/rhythm/lead guitars/backup vocals; David Ashley, keyboards/backup vocals; Skip Newton, drums.

DISCOGRAPHY:
Rezervation Line [independent 1996]

Chief Rock—(Mohawk) Rap

Born Sino General, May 19, 1975, Six Nations Mohawk Territory of the Grand River, Ontario.
    A powwow (grass, hoop, fancy) dancer-singer and traditional Iroquois smoke dancer, Chief Rock also performs as a rapper and B-Boy with many Toronto-based artists. He recorded with the Stylelordz hip-hop network and appears in their video *Superlordz* (Loaded Films 2001). His debut album received a NAMA nomination for Best Rap/Hip-Hop, 2001. The album includes traditional singers Bill Crouse (*See*: Traditional/Archival Group) and Northern Cree Singers (*See*: Powwow Music), with Money G, Mayor Drama, and P Vincent; it successfully blended powwow styles with hip-hop.

DISCOGRAPHY:
The Relentless Warrior [independent 2001]

Appearances:
Stylelordz Hip Hop Network:
21 Artful Songs [stylelordz.com 2001]

Children of Earth—Poetry/Rock *See*: John Trudell

Lineup: Sage Ratt, Star Ratt, and Song Ratt. Three daughters of poet John Trudell recite their father's words with music provided by Mark Shark and Quiltman of the Graffiti Band. The recording is dedicated to the memories of Ricarda Star, Sunshine, and Eli Changing Sun.

DISCOGRAPHY:
A Child's Voice [Peace Company 1992]

Children of the Sun—Rock *See*: Derek Miller

Lineup: Derek Miller, vocals/guitar; Blaine Bomberry, vocals/guitar; Ohan Vandermeer, vocals/bass; Scott Berger, vocals/drums. From the Six Nations Territory of the Grand River, Ontario. This short-lived excursion into the world of rock allowed young musicians to cut their teeth in the studio. Derek Miller and others pursued solo careers.

DISCOGRAPHY:
Gentle Beginnings [independent 1993] cass

Chinle Galileans—(Dineh) Gospel

DISCOGRAPHY:
Chinle Galileans, Vol. 3 [Canyon 1980]
Chinle Galileans, Vol. 2 [Canyon 1975]
Chinle Galileans, Vol. 1 [Canyon 1975]

Church, Lorrie—(Cree-Metis) Country and Western

Born and raised in Meadowlake, Saskatche-wan, as Weei'Nakwa Mek'Wanak (Grey Feathers). She was one of sixteen children in her family. She has been an entertainer since childhood, her career encouraged by her parents. She went on to win Enter-tainer of the Year, Female Vocalist of the Year, Video of the Year, Single of the Year, and Most Promising Entertainer of the Year from the Saskatchewan Country Music Association in 1996, and then Enter-tainer of the Year in 1999 from the same association, when she was also nominated Wrangler Rising Star by the Canadian Country Music Association and for the National Aboriginal Achievement Award. Her video *Running Away*, which included an appearance by the Blackstone Sing-ers (*See*: Powwow Music), was nominated Best Music Video, American Indian Film Festival, San Francisco, 1999.

DISCOGRAPHY:
I Never Gave Up Hope [Eagle Hill 1999] enhanced

Videos:
I Never Gave Up Hope [independent 1998]
Running Away [independent 1998]

Clan/destine—Rock

Lineup: Chuck Harris (Hopi–Tohono O'odham), guitar; Frank Poocha (Dineh), keyboards/vocals; Dave Montour (Mohawk-Cayuga-Potowatomi), bass/flute; Juan Sanchez (Pueblo-Lakota), didgeridoo/per-cussion/vocals; Derrick Suwaima Davis, hoop dancer.

Based in Phoenix, Arizona. Sanchez also played with the group Rainbow Tribe, which released a six-song EP entitled *Mindsight*; Poocha previously played with Poetic Justice and Rasta Farmers; Mon-tour was Artist-in-Residence at the Heard Museum, Phoenix, Arizona; Harris devel-oped his guitar skills at the Hollywood Musician's Institute. *Deeply Rooted* re-ceived a NAMA Award for Best Pop-Rock Recording, 2000.

DISCOGRAPHY:
Amajacoustic [Rezdawgs 2000]
Deeply Rooted [Rezdawgs 1999]
Clan/destine [Canyon 1996]

Appearances:
Sacred Souls [Manteca 2001, United King-dom] comp
Voices across the Canyon, Vol. 3 [Canyon 1997] comp

Videos:
Clan/destine [Rezdawgs 2000]

Clearwater, Clarence—(Dineh) Folk

Lineup: Clarence Clearwater, vocals/gui-tar/percussion; Lance Tailfeathers, vocals/guitar/percussion (*See*: Keith Secola); Beulah Sunrise, vocals.

DISCOGRAPHY:
Ashkii bahi niya: Contemporary Music from Dinetah [Toledo 1992] six-track cass

Clearwater, Eddie—(Cherokee–African American) Blues *See*: Big Joe Williams

Born Eddie Harrington, January 10, 1935. Raised by his Cherokee grandmother in Mississippi, Harrington began playing guitar at age thirteen. He moved to Chicago in 1950, playing predominantly gospel and later developing his blues artistry after working with Magic Sam, Otis Rush, and others. In 1953, he emerged onto the blues scene as Guitar Eddy to record a number of 45-rpm singles. The name Clearwater later came about as wordplay on the name Muddy Waters. He became a great showman with a vast repertoire as he toured the blues clubs for more than twenty years. He gained wide acceptance in Europe after his first appearance there in the late 1980s. The left-handed guitarist played right-handed guitars, which he held upside down without altering the position of the strings. On the eve of the new millennium, he opened Reservation Blues, a restaurant/club at 1566 North Milwaukee Avenue in Chicago, Illinois.

DISCOGRAPHY:
Reservation Blues [Bullseye 2000]
Cool Blues Walk [Bullseye 1998]
Mean Case of the Blues [Bullseye 1997]
Boogie My Blues Away [Delmark 1996]
Help Yourself [Blind Pig 1992]
A Real Good Time—Live! [Rooster Blues 1990]
Blues Hangout [Evidence 1989]
Flimdoozie [Rooster 1986]
The Chief [Rooster 1980; reissued 1994]
Eddy Clearwater and Carey Bell [Wolf 1980, Austria]
2 X 9 [Charly 1979, United Kingdom; reissued on Fan Club 1991]
Live at the Kingston Mines [Fan Club 1978; reissued 1992]
I Don't Give a Damn If Whites Buy It [Red Lightnin' 1977, United Kingdom]
Black Night [MCM 1976, France]

Singles:
"True Love/Lonely Nights" [Cleartone 1975]
"Doin' the Model/I Don't Know Why" [Versa/Atomic H 1969]
"The Duckwalk/Honey Bee" [USA 1962]
"Cool Water/Baby Please" [LaSalle 1961]
"Hey Bernadine/A Real Good Time" [Federal 1961]
"Twist Like This/I Was Gone" [Federal 1961]
"All My Life/Chicago Jump" [Bandera 1960]
"Ain't That a Shame/Dancin' Time" [Redita 1960]
"A Minor Cha-Cha/I Don't Know Baby" [Atomic H 1959]
"Boogie Woogie Baby/Hill Billy Blues" [Atomic H 1958]

Appearances:
Highway Blues [Rounder 2000] comp
New Blues Hits [Bullseye 1997] comp
Essential Chicago Blues [House of Blues 1997] comp
Sweet Home Blue Chicago [Blue Chicago 1996] comp
Evidence Blues Sampler [Evidence 1992] comp
Chicago Blues Session, Vol. 23 [Wolf 1990, Austria] comp

Cochrane, Jesse—(Cree) Country

From Cochrane, Ontario, Jesse Cochrane moved throughout northern Ontario and Quebec, Canada. His one album was recorded in Nashville, Tennessee.

DISCOGRAPHY:
Indian Country [Sunshine SSCT-4225]

Conrad and Baton Rouge—(Cree) Country

Born February 9, 1968, Saskatchewan. Conrad's vocals are reminiscent of Billy Ray Cyrus (Cherokee) and Dwight Yoakam, a quality that helped win him the 1997 Big Country Talent Search. The single "Won't Be Back" was released internationally to radio and was included on the *Nashville North* sampler.

Baton Rouge Lineup: Conrad, acoustic guitar/vocals; Ken Burton, lead/rhythm guitar; Dave Chobot, keyboard/bass; Gary Dunitz, bass; Don Young, drums.

DISCOGRAPHY:
Hurry Up and Wait [Horizon Talent Agency 1998]

Constant, Leonard, and Cornelius—Gospel

DISCOGRAPHY:
Cree Hymns Alive [Sunshine 1995]

Coolidge, Priscilla—(Cherokee-Scottish) Pop/Rock *See*: Rita Coolidge, Jesse Ed Davis, Laura Satterfield, Walela

Born October 1, 1941, Nashville, Tennessee. Along with sister Rita, Priscilla was raised in a musical family with heavy gospel influences and a strong cultural foundation inspired by their Cherokee grandmother. As a backup singer, she performed not only with her sister, but also with many of the industry's most notable performers, including former husband Booker T. Jones. She helped form the group Walela with her daughter Laura Satterfield.

DISCOGRAPHY:
Flying [Capricorn 1979]
Gypsy Queen [A&M 4297]
Chronicles [A&M 1973]
Home Grown [A&M 1972]
Booker T. and Priscilla [A&M 1971] double vinyl

Appearances (listed alphabetically):
Marc Benno:
Marc Benno [A&M 1970]

Rita Coolidge:
Love Lessons [Critique 1992]
Satisfied [A&M 1979]
Fall into Spring [A&M 1974]
The Lady's Not for Sale [A&M 1972; MFP 1981]
Rita Coolidge [A&M 1971]
Bob Dylan:
Pat Garrett and Billy the Kid [Columbia 1973]
Little Wolf Band:
Wolf Moon [Triloka 1997]
Dream Song [Triloka 1995]
Bob Neuwirth:
Bob Neuwirth [Asylum 1974]
Robbie Robertson:
Contact from the Underworld of Redboy [Capitol 1998]
Music for the Native Americans [Capitol 1994]
Stephen Stills:
Stephen Stills [Atlantic 1970]
Walela:
Live in Concert [Sovereign Nation Preservation Project 2004]
Unbearable Love [Triloka 2000]
Walela [Triloka 1997]
Various:
Naturally Native [Silver Wave 2000] sdtk

Coolidge, Rita—(Cherokee-Scottish) Pop/Rock *See*: Cherokee National Children's Choir, Priscilla Coolidge, Jesse Ed Davis, Laura Satterfield, Walela; Flute Music: Andrew Vasquez

Born May 1, 1944, Nashville, Tennessee. Coolidge's Scottish and Cherokee roots along with gospel music were inspirational to her singing. She launched her career in the early 1960s doing commercial jingles in Memphis and recorded on the Pepper label. She later toured and sang backup for Marc Benno, Delaney, Bonnie and Friends, Stephen Stills, Eric Clapton, Glen Campbell, Joe Cocker, Jimmy Buffet, and others. Her relationship with Kris Kristofferson, as a duet and as a couple, marked a major turning point in her private life and her commercial success, which included Hollywood. She enjoyed numerous hit singles that scored on the Billboard Charts, including "Higher and Higher" from the film *Ghostbusters II* [Ivan Reitman, 1989] and "All Time High" from the film *Octopussy* [John Glen, 1983]. Coolidge is also a multiple Grammy Award winner, including the 1973 Country Duo/Group with Vocal for "From the Bottle to the Bottom" and the 1975 Country Duo/Group with Vocal for "Lover Please." A founding member of Walela, she appeared on Robbie Robertson's *Music for the Native Americans* and with the Cherokee National Children's Choir.

DISCOGRAPHY:

20th Century Masters Millennium Collection [A&M 2000] best of
Cherokee [Indelible 1998, United Kingdom]
Thinkin' about You [Innerworks 1998]
All Time High [A&M/Kaurussell LC-5064] best of
Rita Coolidge: Master Series [A&M/Polygram 1998] best of
Dancing with an Angel [A&M 1997, Canada]
Out of the Blues [Beacon 1996]
Behind the Memories [Polygram 1995, Japan]
The Collection [Polygram 1995] best of
Someday [K-Point Gold 1994, Czech Republic] released as *Fire Me Back*
For You [Polygram 1993, Japan]
Love Lessons [Critique 1992, United States]
Fire Me Back [Attic 1990]
Inside the Fire [A&M 1984]
Never Let You Go [A&M 1983]
Heartbreak Radio [A&M 1981] number 160 Billboard Pop Album Charts
Greatest Hits [A&M 1980] number 107 Billboard Pop Album Charts
Satisfied [A&M 1979] number 95 Billboard Pop Album Charts
Love Me Again [A&M 1978] number 32 Billboard Pop Album Charts

The Rita Coolidge Radio Special [A&M 1978] best of w/ interview segments
Anytime, Anywhere [A&M 1977] number 23 Billboard Country Album Charts; number 6 Billboard Pop Album Charts
It's Only Love [A&M 1975] number 85 Billboard Pop Album Charts
Fall Into Spring [A&M 1974] number 55 Billboard Pop Album Charts
Nice Feelin' [A&M 1973] number 135 Billboard Pop Album Charts
The Lady's Not for Sale [A&M 1972] number 46 Billboard Pop Album Charts
Rita Coolidge [A&M 1971] number 105 Billboard Pop Album Charts
Kris and Rita:
Natural Act [A&M/Polygram 1978] number 24 Billboard Country Charts; number 95 Billboard Pop Charts
Breakaway [Sony 1974/1991]
Full Moon [A&M 1973]
Jesus Was a Capricorn [CBS/Monument 1972]
Live at the Philharmonic [Sony 1972/1991]

Singles:

"All Time High" [A&M 1983] number 1 Adult Contemporary Billboard Charts; number 36 Billboard Pop Singles
"Only You" [A&M 1983] number 37 Adult Contemporary Billboard Charts
"Fool That I Am" [A&M 1981] number 46 Billboard Pop Singles; number 72 Billboard Country Singles
"Somethin' about You I Like" [Capitol 1980] w/ Glen Campbell
"I'd Rather Leave While I'm in Love" [A&M 1980] number 3 Adult Contemporary Billboard Charts; number 32 Billboard Country Singles; number 38 Billboard Pop Singles
"One Fine Day" [A&M 1979] number 66 Billboard Country Singles
"The Way You Do the Things You Do" [A&M 1978] number 20 Billboard Pop Singles
"The Jealous Kind" [A&M 1978] number 63 Billboard Country Singles

"Love Me Again" [A&M 1978] number 83 Billboard Country Singles

"You" [A&M 1978] number 3 Adult Contemporary Billboard Charts

"We're All Alone" [A&M 1977] number 1 Adult Contemporary Billboard Charts; number 7 Billboard Pop Singles; number 82 Billboard Country Singles

"Higher and Higher" [A&M 1977] number 2 Billboard Charts; number 5 Adult Contemporary Billboard Charts

"Mama Lou" [A&M 1973] number 94 Billboard Country Singles

"Loving Arms" [A&M 1973] number 98 Billboard Country Singles

"My Crew" [A&M 1972] number 99 Billboard Pop Singles

"Fever" [A&M 1972] number 76 Billboard Pop Singles

"Turn around and Love You" [Pepper 1969]

Appearances (listed alphabetically):

Marc Benno:
Minnows [A&M 1971]
Marc Benno [A&M 1970]
David Blue:
Stories [Asylum 1972]
Jimmy Buffett:
Hot Water [Island 1988]
Cherokee National Children's Choir:
Voices of the Creator's Children [Cherokee Nation 2001]
Eric Clapton:
Eric Clapton [RSO 1970]
Crosby, Stills, and Nash:
Crosby, Stills, and Nash [Atlantic 1969]
Bonnie Delaney and Friends:
Bonnie Delaney and Friends on Tour [A&M 1970]
Accept No Substitutes [A&M 1969]
Bob Dylan:
Pat Garrett and Billy the Kid [Columbia 1973] sdtk
Robbie Robertson:
Music for the Native Americans [Capitol 1994]
Stephen Stills:
Stephen Stills [Atlantic 1970]
Various:

Singing Our Stories [Full Regalia Productions 2000] comp

Film Soundtracks:
Grand Avenue [Daniel Sackheim, 1996] no recording available
Earthrise [1992]
Music for UNICEF Concert [NDA]
Splash [Ron Howard, 1984]
Octopussy [John Glen, 1983]
The Raccoons [Kevin Gillis, Polygram 1983] w/ Leo Sayer and Rupert Holmes
Coast to Coast [Joseph Sargent, 1980]
In Pursuit of DB Cooper [Robert Spottiswoode, RCA 1981]
A Star Is Born [Frank Pierson, 1976]
Pat Garrett and Billy the Kid [MCA 1973]

Film and Television Appearances:
The Muppet Show [Philip Casson/Pater Harris, 1978] as herself
A Star Is Born [Frank Pierson, 1976] as herself
Free to Be . . . You and Me [Bill Davis/Ian Steckier/Fred Wolf, 1974] as herself
Pat Garrett and Billy the Kid [Sam Peckinpah, 1973] as Maria
Mad Dogs and Englishmen [Robert Abel/Peter Adidge, 1971] as herself
Vanishing Point [Richard C. Sarafin, 1971] uncredited singer

Corvairs—(Mohawk) Blues *See*: Built for Comfort

Lineup: Matt Tarbell (Mohawk), vocals/harmonica; Morris Tarbell (Mohawk), guitar; Jerry Neely, keyboards; David Petrovich, drums; Boothe Johnson, bass; Wayne Daniels, guitar; Rod Zajac, saxophones.

Based in the Akwesasne Mohawk community, which is intersected by Ontario, Quebec, and New York State.

DISCOGRAPHY:
Fast Lane Livin' [independent 1990] cass

Coyote Zen—Folk/Rock *See*:
Cherokee National Children's Choir

Lineup: Jeffrey Gray Parker (Cherokee-Scottish), flute/guitars/percussion; Marci Von Broembsen, flute/percussion; Benny Gene Craig (Cherokee), harmonica/fiddle; Lisa LaRue, percussion.

Based in Tahlequah, Oklahoma. The name Coyote Zen is a metaphor for Father Sky and Mother Earth. The group's founder, Jeffrey Gray Parker (born June 3, 1956, Arkansas City, Kansas), created the project in order to record material relevant to the changing Cherokee culture. Parker worked as an audio engineer, producer, and studio artist. His recording and production credits include soundtracks for independent film and video; his performance credits include sessions with Buck Owens, Brewer and Shipley, Alice Cooper, Jefferson Starship, and others.

DISCOGRAPHY:
Medicine Dog [Dust Bowl 2000; PAW 2001]
Blood of Many Nations [Dust Bowl 1999]
Coyote Zen [Dust Bowl 1999]

Craig, Vince—(Dineh) Country

A humorist, singer, and motivational speaker, Craig created the comic strip, *Muttonman*, which appears in the *Navajo Times* newspaper. He plays guitar, traditional flute, and harmonica to accompany original songs rife with humor and biting social commentary. In concert, he opened for Dwight Yoakam, T. J. Shepard, Shenandoah, and many others. Craig also works with children on the Navajo Reservation to help develop self-esteem and wrote the theme song "Catch the Spirit" for the 1982 National Indian Youth Conference. His projects include a video on substance abuse for the Dineh Nation. With a degree in law, Craig has worked as a law clerk, a police academy director, tribal prosecutor, justice commissioner for the White Mountain Apache Tribe, and chief of probation and parole services with the supreme court of the Dineh Nation.

DISCOGRAPHY:
Song Weaver [VC-06]
Yer' Jus' Somehow [VC-05]
Cowboyz N' Stuff [VC-04]
Boarding School Fish Stories, Vol. 3 [VC-03]
Thank God for Polyester [VC-02]
Vincent Craig [Muttonwood Productions/ Canyon 1980]

Singles:
"The Navajo Code Talker Song/Goodbye Miss Rodeo" [Canyon 1981] 45 rpm

Videos:
I've Been Bingo-ed by My Baby [Nora Naranjo-Morse, 1996]

Cremo, Lee—(Mi'kmaq) Fiddle *See*:
Willie Dunn

1939–1999
From Eskasoni, Nova Scotia, Lee Cremo became a legend of East Coast fiddle music, earning worldwide acclaim. His first fiddle was a handmade instrument handed down from his great-grandfather, who had received it as a gift from a Scottish settler. Cremo could play a variety of instruments, including bass guitar, mandolin, and drums.

He won the Maritime Fiddling Championship six times; captured the Old Time Fiddling Contest in Dartmouth, Nova Scotia, three years consecutive from 1966 to 1968; won the Canadian title once and the Alberta Tar Sands Competition; was named World Champion Fiddler in the 1970s; and received the 1996 ECMA Aboriginal Recording of the Year for *The Champion Returns*. He shared the stage with many great performers, including Merle Haggard, Dolly Parton, and Johnny Cash, and he performed for Queen Elizabeth II. At the height of his career, Cremo almost faded into obscurity. When he signed on with Audat and released seven successful albums with tours throughout North America, he saw little or no financial return despite record sales. The company invoked an exclusive rights clause to his material and prohibited him from performing or releasing any recordings until the late 1980s. During those years, he worked different jobs on his home reserve as laborer, bus driver, and music teacher. He finally returned to the stage in 1991.

Two of his former music students, Ashley MacIsaac and Natalie MacMaster, invited their mentor to tour with them in 1994. Bad luck entered his life again when he broke his right arm, which he rebroke a short time later after slipping on a rain-drenched stage. Although he couldn't bend his bow arm more than ninety degrees, he continued to play. One of his last public appearances was the launch of the Aboriginal People's Television Network in 1998. Cremo became an international icon of fiddle music. His life was chronicled in the documentary films *Arm of Gold* and *Mi'kmaq Entertainers Cultural Showcase*. He passed away on October 10, 1999.

Eastern Variation Lineup: Gabriel Sylibay, bass; Wilfred Paul, lead guitar; Joseph MacMullen, piano; Peter Stevens, drums; James Poulette, rhythm guitar.

DISCOGRAPHY:

The Champion Returns [Cremo Productions 1995]
Cape Breton Fiddling [Audat 477-9088]
The Flying Fiddle of Lee Cremo [Audat 477-9077]
Lee Cremo [Audat 477-9050] produced by Bill Guest
The Cape Breton Fiddle of Lee Cremo and His Band [Audat 477-9032]
Lee Cremo and the Eastern Variation [Audat 477-9010]

Appearances:

Down Home Recordings, the Compact Collection: Fiddle Music and Song [Lismor 9027, United Kingdom] comp
Down Home, Vol. 1: An Historic Journey

Through Scotland to North America [Lismor 7012, United Kingdom] comp
Wood That Sings: Indian Fiddle Music of the Americas [Smithsonian Folkways 1997] comp *See*: Traditional/Archival Compilations
Creation's Journey [Smithsonian Folkways 1994] comp

Film:

Arm of Gold [Edwin Communications, 1986]

Croall, Barbara — (Odawa) Classical

Born November 8, 1966. Croall graduated from the University of Toronto in 1995, when she was selected to participate in a special music course in Orkney, Scotland, sponsored by the Scottish Chamber Orchestra and led by Sir Peter Maxwell Davies. Her composition *The Four Directions*, referring to Antonio Vivaldi's *Four Seasons*, premiered in 1997 with the Toronto Symphony Orchestra (TSO) and received the Glenn Gould Award for competition. Croall was the first woman composer to study music composition at Munich's 150-year-old Hochschule für Musik. She was recognized for possessing a distinct compositional voice and worked as composer-in-residence at the TSO in 1998. She also premiered her composition *When Push Came to Shove* with the TSO, conducted by Saraste. She combined various elements of Western and Native compositonal thinking and approach, simple melodies with major and minor chords and complex microtones. Her music is unusual in part because few Western composers use microntal structure (an interval smaller than a semitone) as notation becomes increasingly difficult with sixteenth tones and smaller. With the exception of electronic music, the microtone is not always available because most instruments cannot accommodate it, though a very few quarter-tone pianos were made. Mexican composer Julian Carrillo (1875–1965) was a major pioneer in microtonal music.

Cultee, Roger—(Quinalt) Rock

Cultee began playing music on his home territory on the West Coast and later moved to Albuquerque, New Mexico, to pursue an independent recording career.

DISCOGRAPHY:
Roger Cultee [Rez Tunes 1999] five-track EP
Native Sun [Rez Tunes 1996]

Culture of Rage; a.k.a. Heath St. John—(Apache-Lakota) Rap

Based in San Francisco, California. St. John's hard-core political message was heard at anniversary concerts for the 1969 Alcatraz takeover by Tribes of All Nations. He worked with the Youth Empowerment Program and the IITC and graduated from the Native American studies program at the University of California, Berkeley.
Lineup: Culture of Rage, songwriter/vocals; K. Nez (Dineh); M. Marin (Washo); Orlando Z. Jr. (El Salvadoran); Norma S. (Indonesian); V. Huff (African American); and M. Visovich.

DISCOGRAPHY:
Eyez Iz [independent 1996]
Urban Native Son [independent 1994] cass
Urban Indian [independent 1992] cass

Appearances:
Peace and Dignity Journeys [Xicano Records and Film 2000] comp

Curtis, Johnny—(White Mountain Apache) Gospel

Lineup: Johnny Curtis, lead guitar/vocals; David Seville, bass; Freddie Ringlaro, drums; David Forester, rhythm guitar.

DISCOGRAPHY:
The Christmas Album [independent 2000]
Mighty God [independent 1999]
Best of Curtis [Canyon 1994]
One for the Bearhats [independent no date]
Somebody Cares [independent no date]
Travelin' for Jesus, Vol. 8 [Canyon 1988]
Live in Concert [Canyon 1987]
In Loving Memories II [Canyon 1985]
Spirit of God [Canyon 1984]
In Loving Memories [Canyon 1981]
Johnny Curtis with Apache Gospel Sounds [Canyon 1980]
Leavin' This Reservation [Canyon 1978]
Apache Country Gospel [Canyon 1977]

C-Weed—Country See: Mitch Daigneault, Freebird Band, Errol Ranville, Jay Ross, Clyde Roulette; Powwow Music: Red Bull

Lineup: Errol Ranville, guitar/vocals; Randy Hiebert, electric guitars; Craig Fotheringham, electric/acoustic guitars/keyboards; Jim Flett, gut-string guitar; Dylan Evans, steel guitar; Clyde Roulette, slide guitar; Wally Ranville, bass/backup vocals; Don Ranville, drums; Clint Dutiaume, fiddle/backup vocals; Ed Birkett, percussion; Ronda Hart, backup vocals.
Millennium Lineup: Errol Ranville, Mike Bruyere, Elvis Ballantyne, Corny Michel, Mitch Daigneault.

Formed in Winnipeg, Manitoba, in the early 1970s by singer-songwriter Errol "C-Weed" Ranville and his brothers, Don and Wally. They landed their first gig as the house band at the Brunswick Hotel. Local venues were reluctant to hire them because they attracted rowdy audiences, so the band took to the road to find gigs outside the city. In 1981, they spent 297 days on the road traveling in a 1954 Western Flyer bus playing rodeos, dances, concerts, and powwows and appearing on syndicated television shows across Canada and the United States. Ranville was described by the music press as "the favorite Native son of the Canadian music industry." C-Weed's international tours included England, Scotland, and continental Europe; they shared the stage with Ricky Skaggs, the Judds, and many others. Their first single, a cover of Robbie Robertson's "Evangeline," rose to number four in Canada on the *RPM Weekly* Country Music Charts and stayed in the top five on many country music radio station charts. As a result, copies of the single were scarce because the pressing plant couldn't keep up with demand for the record. Their cover of "Hard Hearted Woman" enjoyed equal success. They received two MACA Awards in 1981 for Top Recording Artists and Song of the Year for "Evangeline." That same year the band received the CHMM-FM Radio Award, shared with the Harvey Henry Band; Ranville was also named Entertainer of the Year. Juno Award nominations included Country Group of the Year, 1985 and 1986, and Aboriginal Recording of the Year, 2001.

DISCOGRAPHY:
Run as One [c-weedband.com 2000]
  w/ Red Bull
The Older Songs of the 80s [c-weedband
  .com 2000] three-CD live best of
Goin' the Distance [RCA/Hawk 1983]
Flight of the Hawk, Vol. 2 [Sunshine SSCT-
  4079]
Flight of the Hawk, Vol. 1 [Sunshine SSCT-
  4078]
A Tribute to Southern Rock [Sunshine
  SSCT-4074]
High and Dry [Sunshine 1981]
The Finest You Can Buy [Sunshine 1980]

Singles:
"Magic in the Music/Draggin' the Bow"
  [RCA 1983]
"Magic in the Music" [RCA 1983]
"(Play Me) My Favourite Song" [RCA 1983]
"Clovis (New Mexico)/Draggin' the Bow"
  [RCA 50823]
"Hard Hearted Woman" [Sunshine 1981]

"Finest You Can Buy" [Sunshine 1980]
"Janine" [Sunshine 1980]
"Old Rodeo Cowboys" [Sunshine 1980]
"Evangeline" [Sunshine 1980]

Videos:
Old Rodeo Cowboys [Sunshine 1980]

Cyr, Richard—(Anishnabe) Folk

Cyr created political protest music with historical perspectives. The 1990 Oka crisis dominated much of his acoustic guitar-based material.

DISCOGRAPHY:
Drum [CYR-03 1993]
500 Years [CYR-02 1992]
Larceny by Trick [independent 1990]

Czapla, Jeari—(Plains Cree) Jazz

Born July 17, 1965, Peguis First Nation, Saint Boniface, Manitoba. Czapla took up guitar at the age of six. In 1986, he attended the University of Manitoba, learning classical guitar, and enrolled at the Lenny Breau School of Music under the direction of the founder's son, Chet Breau (Metis). He furthered his studies at the Toronto Conservatory of Music and moved to Edmonton, Alberta, to attend the Grant MacEwan College. After making the city his home, he formed his first band, the Uptown Shuffle, in 1995. Czapla has become a guitarist with the ability to play in any style or genre of music with impeccable results. His two-hands-on-the-fret style adopted from Lenny Breau (Cree-Metis; *See*: Ray St. Germain) included a ten-finger picking style similar to piano keyboard movements. Czapla wrote all the horn sections for his first self-produced album.

DISCOGRAPHY:
for ella [independent/Festival 2002]

Daigneault, Mitch—(Cree) Country
See: C-Weed

Born February 1972, Regina, Saskatchewan (Fishing Lake Band). Daigneault received his first guitar at age five and grew up listening to country radio. In 1989, he formed his first band in high school after moving to Beauval, Saskatchewan, and later enrolled at the Saskatchewan Indian Federated College in Saskatoon. He played numerous talent shows; received his recording engineer certificate in Chillicothe, Ohio; and by 1997 was playing gigs at C-Weed's Cabaret. He eventually joined C-Weed, then pursued a solo career while based in Battleford, Saskatchewan.

DISCOGRAPHY:
Keep On Believing [c-weedband.com 2002]

Appearances:
Run as One [c-weedband.com 2000]

Darkfeather—(Wampanoag) Rock

Original Lineup: Chris Waters, Mike Waters, Autumn Hawk. *Second Lineup*: Chris Waters and Ray Waters (Tispaquin).
   Formed in 1992, Massachusetts. Led by Chris Waters, the band went through several lineup changes until they re-recorded their only album.

DISCOGRAPHY:
Circle of Dawn [Waterfall RW002] cass

Davids, Brent Michael—
(Stockbridge-Munsee-Mohican)
Classical *See*: Keith Secola

Born June 4, 1959, Madison, Wisconsin. Specializing in the quartz crystal flute and guitar, Davids combined Native American song with Western compositional technique in his music. He received his bachelor's degree from Arizona State University in 1991 and his master's degree in composition from Northern Illinois University in 1981. Invited to Robert Redford's Sundance Institute in 1998 to create a score for Sherman Alexie's film *Indian Killer*, Davids was also awarded a residency as a McKnight Visiting Composer through the American Composers Forum. His commissioned works include the Joffrey Ballet: *Moon of the Falling Leaves*, 1991/1998; the Kronos Quartet, *The Native American National Anthem*, 1996, based on the AIM song (*See*: John Trudell: Quiltman and Tewahnee); and a fifteen-minute chamber piece for Apache violin (*See*: Traditional/Archival Solo: Chesley Goseyun Wilson). Davids's major work, *Pau Wau; A Gathering of Nations*, for MC and Orchestra: "A Day in the Life of a Powwow," premiered in 1999, with David Lockington conducting the New Mexico Symphony Orchestra, Sonny Tone-ke (Kiowa) serving as MC, and Raoul Trujillo doing the choreography. Other projects include *The Trial of Standing Bear: The Opera*, with the Omaha Opera Company, Omaha, Nebraska. His soundtrack project for *Dawn* features Joe Myers, guitar; Annie Humphrey, vocals (*See*: Contemporary Spoken Word: Legends [Miscellaneous]: *Whispering Tree*); Sule Greg Wilson, percussion; John Ebinger, acoustic bass.

DISCOGRAPHY:
Dawn [Blue Butterfly 2000] sdtk
Joe and the Blue Butterfly [Blue Butterfly 1998] w/ Joe Myers
Ni-Tcang [Blue Butterfly 1992]

Appearances (listed alphabetically):
Kronos Quartet:
Turtle People [Elektra/Nonesuch 1995]
Meukwekok Naxkomao: The Singing Woods [Elektra/Nonesuch 1994]
Mimi McBride:
You Are You [Eagle View Music 1995]
Keith Secola:
XV for Our Ancestors [Normal 1996, Germany]
Circle [AKINA 1992]

Brent Michael Davids creates modern classical music with a quartz flute. Photo by Carla Roberts; courtesy Brent Michael Davids.

Acoustic Aroma [AKINA 1991]
Time Flies Like an Arrow, Fruit Flies Like a Banana [AKINA 1990]
Various:
The Business of Fancy Dancing [Falls Apart 2003] sdtk

Davies, Harry, and the Quicksilver Express Band—(Cree) Country

Lineup: Harry Davies, rhythm guitar/vocals; Peter Sound, bass/backup vocals; Albert Auger, drums; Clint Dutiaume, lead guitar/fiddle/backup vocals (*See*: C-Weed). From Faust, Alberta (Lesser Slave Lake region).

DISCOGRAPHY:
The Bannock Song [Sunshine SSCT-4139]

Davis, Angelique—(Eastern Cherokee) Pop *See*: Litefoot

Davis, Jesse Edwin, III—(Kiowa-Comanche) Rock *See*: John Trudell

1944–1988
Born September 21, Norman, Oklahoma. Davis was raised in a musical family; his mother was a piano teacher and his father played drums in a Dixieland jazz band. After earning a degree in English from the University of Oklahoma in 1966, he started playing locally with school chums Leon Russell and Levon Helm, who lured him into the music world. He toured professionally with Conway Twitty and later moved to Los Angeles, where he sessioned with Gary Lewis and the Playboys, the

Monkees, the Tulsa Tops, Marvin Gaye, and, more notably, Taj Mahal. In addition to his guitar wizardry with the Fender Telecaster and Stratocaster, Davis also played piano on Taj Mahal's first three albums and learned slide guitar in 1968 while recording the song "Statesboro Blues." Known as Jesse "Ed" or "Indian Ed," Davis quickly became one of the most sought-after session guitarists of the 1970s. He also influenced legions of players, including Stevie Ray Vaughn, Duane Allman, and Dwight Yoakam's lead string Pete Anderson. Davis possessed a remarkable range that encompassed slide, R & B, blues, rhythm, country, and jazz. The crying solo on Jackson Browne's "Doctor My Eyes" and the liquid stylings Davis created for John Lennon's *Walls and Bridges* album remain some of his most memorable work. However, the rock 'n' roll lifestyle and the demands of long hours (sometimes playing three different sessions in one day) took their toll. As his success became cursed with drug and alcohol addictions, Davis finally entered the rehab program at the Eagle Lodge in California. He was working as a counselor at the Indian Free Clinic in Long Beach when he first heard the poetry of John Trudell on a cassette called *Tribal Voice.*

After hooking up with Trudell at one of the Graffiti Band shows, Davis offered to help produce and record new projects with Trudell. He became absorbed in the process of joining rock with poetry and traditional music. They received a 1987 Grammy nomination for Best Word and Best Rock Duo for the 1986 Peace Company release *AKA Graffiti Man*. Two 1987 shows at the Palomino Club and the Comedy Store in Hollywood turned into reunions for Davis. He and the Graffiti Band were joined onstage by Bob Dylan, John Fogerty, Taj Mahal, George Harrison, Nicky Hopkins, Buffy Sainte-Marie, actor Max Gail, and comedian Charlie Hill (*See*: Contemporary Spoken Word: Comedy). More recordings and tours swept Davis back into

aka Grafitti Man - JT/JED
Original Release 1986

John Trudell and Jesse Ed Davis merged music with poetry. Cover art courtesy Peace Company.

renewed creativity and old habits amid unfounded rumors of a stroke. A unique fusion of music and personalities suddenly ended. The result of a suspected drug overdose, Davis passed away on June 22, 1988, although Los Angeles police did not rule out homicide. His body was flown home to Oklahoma, where he received a traditional burial. Trudell reflected poetically on Davis's life with "The Needle" on his 1990 cassette release *Fables and Other Realities*; Billy Joe Shaver and Waylon Jennings paid tribute to Davis with the song "Oklahoma Wind" from the album *Tramp on Your Street* [BMG 1993], with Bill Miller, flute/chants. Few guitarists have achieved Davis's status as a session artist; his influence and talent are legendary. In 1998, he was finally recognized by the First Americans in the Arts with a Lifetime Musical Achievement Award and inducted into the Oklahoma State Hall of Fame, June 19, 2002.

DISCOGRAPHY:

Keep Me Comin' [Epic 1973, reissued Epic 1999, Japan] rare

This explosive and soulful blues and R & B album represents the pinnacle of Davis's solo career, with all original material cowritten with John Angelos. *Lineup*: John Angelos, harmonica/vocals; James Gordon, keyboards; Bob Glaub, bass; Jim Keltner, drums; Bobby Torres, congas (*See*: Gary Small); Felix Falcon, percussion; Bobby Bruce, fiddle; Bill Plummer, double bass; Jerry Jumonville, Howard Johnson, George Bohannon, Gary Barone, Clifford Scott, John Smith, Jacques Ellis, horns; Oma Drake, Julie Tillman, Carolyn Willis, Patti Daley, Chris O'Dell, Russell Saunkeah, John Angelos, Billy Davis, backup vocals.

Ululu [Atco 1972, reissued Epic 1999, Japan] rare

    Lineup: Mac Rebennack (a.k.a. Dr. John), Albhy Galuten, Leon Russell, Stan Szeleste, Larry Knechtel, keyboards; Donald Duck Dunn, Billy Rich, Arnold Rosenthal, bass; Jim Keltner, drums; the Charles Chalmers Singers, Merry Clayton, Vanetta Fields, Clydie King, Chuck Kirkpatrick, backup vocals.

¡Jesse Davis! [Atco 1971; reissued Sony 1990, Japan; Line 1990, Germany; Atlantic Records 1998] rare

    Lineup: Eric Clapton, Joel Scott Hill, guitars; Leon Russell, Larry Knechtel, Ben Sidran, Larry Pierce, John Simon, keyboards; Steve Thompson, Billy Rich, bass; Chuck Blackwell, Steve Mitchell, Bruce Rowland, Alan White, drums; Jerry Jumonville, James Gordon, Darrell Leonard, Frank Mayers, horns; Vanetta Fields, Merry Clayton, Clydie King, Gram Parsons, backup vocals. The cover painting was created by his father, Jesse Ed Davis II. Reissued in 1998 on the Atlantic Original Sound series for the label's fiftieth anniversary, with remastered sound and liner notes that mistakenly identify Davis as part of the group the Rising Suns.

"Santa Clause Is Gettin' Down" single from *Winter Warner Land* [Warner 1988] comp, double red vinyl

The Jesse Ed Davis Interview [Epic 1973] seven-inch vinyl w/ B. Michael Reed of KMET, Los Angeles, California *See*:

Contemporary Spoken Word: Interview Discs

My Captain/Sue Me Sue You Blues [Atco 1972, United Kingdom] seven-inch vinyl

Sessions (listed alphabetically):

Attitudes:

Attitudes [Darkhorse 1975]

Long John Baldry:

Welcome to Club Casablanca [Casablanca 1976]

Marc Benno:

Ambush [A&M 1972]

Minnows [A&M 1971; Polygram 2000] w/ Rita Coolidge

Wayne Berry:

Home at Last [RCA 0603]

David Blue:

Cupid's Arrow [Asylum 1976]

Brewer and Shipley:

Brewer and Shipley [Capitol 1974]

Jackson Browne:

The Next Voice You Hear: Best of Jackson Browne [Elektra/Asylum 1997] best of

Jackson Browne [Asylum 1972] a.k.a. *Saturate before Using*

Brian Cadd:

Yesterday Dream [Capitol 1978]

Captain Beefheart and the Magic Band:

The Dust Blows Forward: Anthology [Rhino 1999] best of

Blue Collar [MCA 1978; Edsel 1995] sdtk

David Cassidy:

When I'm a Rock 'n' Roll Star: The David Cassidy Collection [Razor and Tie 1996] best of

Home Is Where the Heart Is [RCA 1976]

The Higher They Climb the Harder They Fall [RCA 1975]

Eric Clapton:

Crossroads [Polydor 1988/1990] best of

No Reason to Cry [RSO 1976]

Happy, Happy Birthday Eric [Dandelion DLO17, 1976] rare bootleg

Gene Clark:

Flying High [A&M 1999] best of

American Dreamer [Raven 1997] best of

No Other [Asylum/Line 1974]

White Light [A&M 1972]

Gene Clark [Together 1969]

Leonard Cohen:

Death of a Lady's Man [Columbia 1977]
  Phil Spector, producer

Scott Colby:

Slide of Hand [SST 1987] comp D

Mac Davis:

Burning Thing [Columbia 1975]

Jackie DeShannon:

New Arrangement [Columbia 1975]

Neil Diamond:

*Classics: The Early Years/Jazz Singer/Beau-
  tiful Noise* [Sony 1997] best of three-CD
  box set

In My Lifetime [Columbia 1996, Sony 2001]
  best of

Beautiful Noise [Columbia 1976]

Dion:

To Be with You [Capitol 1975] Phil Spector,
  producer

Donovan:

Slow Down World [Epic 1976]

Dunn and Rubini:

Diggin' It [Prodigal 1976]

Bob Dylan:

Knocked Out Loaded [CBS 1986] special
  thanks

Fifth Dimension:

Earth Bound [ABC 1975]

Arlo Guthrie:

Together in Concert [Reprise 1975] w/ Pete
  Seeger

Last of the Brooklyn Cowboys [Reprise
  1973; Koch 1997]

Arlo Guthrie [Charterline 1972; Reprise
  1974; Koch 1997]

Emmy Lou Harris:

Portraits [Warner Archives 1996] best of

George Harrison:

Extra Texture [Apple 1975]

Concert for Bangladesh [Apple 1971]

Richie Havens:

Kent State: Original Sound Track [RCA
  1981] sdtk

John Lee Hooker:

Endless Boogie [MCA 1970; ABC 1971]

Live at Cafe Au Go Go [Blueway 1966;
  BGO 1967]

Lightnin' Hopkins:

It's a Sin to Be Rich [Gitanes 1972; Verve
  1993]

Tom Jans:

Eyes of an Only Child [Columbia/CBS
  1975]

Bert Jansch:

LA Turnaround [Charisma 1974]

Booker T. Jones and Priscilla:

Booker T. and Priscilla [A&M 1971]

Albert King:

Lovejoy [Stax 1971]

B. B. King:

LA Midnight [ABC 1972]

John Lennon:

Wonsaponatime [Capitol 1998] best of

Anthology [Capitol 1998] four-CD box set

Lennon Legend: The Very Best [Parlophone
  1998] best of

Lennon [EMI 1990] four-CD box set

Menlove Avenue [Capitol 1986/1990]

Walls and Bridges [Capitol 1975]

Rock N Roll [Capitol 1975]

Lennon and McCartney:

A Toot and a Snore in '74 [Mistral MM
  9225, 1992] rare bootleg

Taj Mahal:

*Legends of the Guitar: Rock of the 60s,
  Vol. 2* [Rhino/Guitar Player 1999]

Taj's Blues [Columbia Legacy 1992] best of

Taj [Polygram 1986]

Mariposa '76 [Mariposa 1977] comp

Music Keeps Me Together [CBS 1975]
  w/ the Intergalactic Soul Messenger
  Band

Happy to Be Just Like I Am [Columbia
  1971]

Live at Bill Graham's Fillmore West [Co-
  lumbia 1969] w/ Michael Bloomfield

Take a Giant Step [CBS 1969; Columbia
  Legacy 2000]

The Natch'l Blues [CBS 1969; Columbia
  Legacy 2000]

Taj Mahal [CBS 1968; Columbia Legacy
  2000]

Eric Mercury:

Eric Mercury [Mercury 1975]

Steve Miller:

Recall the Beginning: A Journey from Eden
  [Capitol 1973]

Keith Moon:
Two Sides of the Moon [MCA 1975; King Biscuit 1997]
Geoff Muldour:
Motion [Reprise 1976]
Tracy Nelson:
Time Is on My Side [One Way/MCA 1976]
Harry Nilsson:
Sandman [RCA 1978]
Duit on mon dei [RCA 1975]
Pussycats [RCA 1974] John Lennon, producer
Van Dyke Parks:
Clang of the Yankee Reaper [Warner 1976]
The Pointer Sisters:
That's a Plenty [Blue Thumb 1974]
Jim Pulte:
Out the Window [AU 1972]
Helen Reddy:
I Am Woman [Capitol 1972]
Alex Richman:
Salty [Capitol 11004]
The Rolling Stones:
Rock and Roll Circus [Abcko 1996] sdtk recorded 1968
Leon Russell:
Shelter People [Capitol 1971] w/ the Tulsa Tops
Buffy Sainte-Marie:
She Used to Wanna Be a Ballerina [Vanguard 1971]
Ben Sidran:
Little Kiss in the Night [Arista 1978]
Feel Your Groove [Capitol 1971/1976]
Ringo Starr:
Starr Struck: The Best of Ringo Starr [Rhino 1989] best of
Rotogravure [Atlantic 1976/1978/1992]
Duit on mon dei [RCA 1975]
Goodnight Vienna [Apple 1974; Alliance 1991/1996]
Rod Stewart:
A Night on the Town [Warner 1976]
Atlantic Crossing [Warner 1975/1988/2000]
Rod Taylor:
Rod Taylor [Asylum 1973]
Roger Tillison:
Roger Tillison's Album [Atco 1971]

John Trudell:
AKA Graffiti Man [Ryko 1992] best of
Heart Jump Bouquet [Peace Company 1987] cass
. . . But This Isn't El Salvador [Peace Company 1987] cass
AKA Graffiti Man [Peace Company 1986] cass
Valdy:
See How the Years Have Gone By [A&M 1975, United States] re-recording of the album *Valdy* [A&M 1975, Canada]
Various:
Blue Collar [MCA 1978; Edsel 1995] sdtk w/ Jack Nitzsche, Captain Beefheart, Ry Cooder, Lynyrd Skynyrd
Kent State: Original Sound Track [RCA 1981] sdtk w/ Grace Slick, Richie Havens, John Sebastian
The Legend of Jesse James [A&M 1980] w/ Levon Helm, Johnny Cash, Emmy Lou Harris, Charlie Daniels

Related Material:
Michael Rabon:
Michael Rabon and Choctaw [Abnack 1970] the song "Hollywood, California" gives reference to Davis

Day, Nick—(OJ–Cree) Trad/Rock *See*: Bearpaws

From Sandy Lake, Ontario. Day was the founder and former lead vocalist of Bear Paws; he later released a solo album performed in the Cree language.
Lineup: Nick Day, lead vocals/guitar; Danny Schur, keyboards/bass/drum/piano; James Creasy, lead/steel/acoustic guitar.

DISCOGRAPHY:
Kesakehen [Sunshine 1996]

December Wind—(Mohawk) Trad/
Folk/Rock *See*: Atsiaktonkie

Lineup: Atsiaktonkie, Terry and Darman
Terrence, Donald Sharrow, and Randy Fur-
nia. From Akwesasne Mohawk territory,
the band infused culture with contemporary music.

DISCOGRAPHY:
Sacred Voices [Canyon 1999]

Appearances:
Songs of the Spirit, Vol. 2 [Triloka 2000]
    comp
Voices across the Canyon, Vol. 4 [Canyon
    1999] comp

Deer, Louie; a.k.a. Os-ke-non-ton—
(Mohawk)

1890–1950
From Kahnewake, Quebec, Deer started
out a hunting guide in the Lake of Bay's
district. Leonora James Kennedy, a music
teacher from Toronto, Ontario, assisted
in bringing him into recording and commercial performance as a baritone. His
acclaimed appearances include in the CNE
in 1920 and in Coleridge-Taylor's *Hiawatha* at the Albert Hall, London. Deer's
work was released predominantly from
1920 to 1925, but four of his 78-rpm recordings appeared on Edward B. Moogk's *Roll
Back the Years*, released through the National Library of Canada. *The Happy Song*
was reissued in 1977 by CRIA and the National Library of Canada's celebration of a
century of recorded sound.

SELECTED DISCOGRAPHY:
The Happy Song [CRIA 1977] reissue

Dejarlis, Andy—(Metis) Fiddle

Regarded as an all-time fiddle great, Dejarlis recorded more than thirty-five projects.
He was the host of his own television show
on local cable in Montreal, Quebec, and

was host of a radio program after moving to
Winnipeg, Manitoba.

DISCOGRAPHY:
Latin America [Sunshine ssbct 495]
Waltz Favourites [Sunshine ssbct 476]
Red River Jig [Sunshine ssbct 460]
Back Again [Sunshine ssbct 434]

Appearances:
Fiddle Legends [Sunshine 2000] comp

Devlin, Peter—(Dene) Rock

Born April 13, 1973, Yellowknife, Northwest Territories. Devlin is a Toronto-based
guitarist who recorded with Canadian
bands Porno Beat and Blue Orange and
who appeared on the Blue Dog Pict album
Anxiety of Influence [Catwalk 1993].

**DJ Rolando; a.k.a. the Aztec
Mystic**—(Chicano) Techno

A member of the elusive Detroit-based
Underground Resistance crew. The vinyl
releases contain four remixes by Derrick
May.

DISCOGRAPHY:
Jaguar [UR/430 West 2000]
Aztlan [UR 49]
Knights of the Jaguar [UR 49]

Donavan, Mishi—
(Cree-Anishnabekwe) Country/Pop

Born July 21, 1964, Edmonton, Alberta.
Donovan's family roots can be traced
to Turtle Mountain, North Dakota, and
Sandy Beach, Alberta. Donovan developed
her talent in country and bluegrass to win
Sunshine Records Great Canadian Talent
Search. Critics were generous, and airplay was plentiful on Native radio stations
throughout North America. She made a
cameo appearance in the Canadian tele-

vision series *Lonesome Dove*. The album *The Spirit Within* received the Juno Award, Best Music of Aboriginal Canada Recording, 1998, and a nomination in the same category in 2001.

DISCOGRAPHY:
Journey Home [Arbor 2000]
The Spirit Within [Sunshine 1997]
Spirit in Flight [Sunshine 1996]

Appearances:
20 Aboriginal Greatest Hits, Vol. 3 [Sunshine 2002] comp
Native to Canada: Showcase of Aboriginal Musicians at WOMEX 2000 [Canada Council for the Arts 2001] comp
20 Aboriginal Greatest Hits, Vol. 2 [Sunshine 1998] comp
24 Canadian Aboriginal Artists [Sunshine 1995] comp

Videos:
Letting Go [Sunshine 1997]

Douglas, Ronnie—(Anishnabe) Blues

Born January 16, 1966, Orillia, Ontario. Douglas began playing professionally in 1991 and went on to win the 1999 Toronto Blues Society New Talent Search Contest. His performance at the Great Canadian Blues Festival in Toronto was recorded for national airplay by CBC Radio.

Lineup: Ronnie Douglas, guitar/vocals; Steve Thomas, harmonica; Steve Henry, bass; Dave Hewitt, drums.

DISCOGRAPHY:
Big Brother [RD 2001]
Ronnie Douglas Blues Band [RD 1999]

Appearances:
Skin Tight Blues [Sweet Grass/EMI 2002] comp
Mariposa Folk Festival 2001 [Mariposa Folk Foundation 2001] comp

Dreamspeak—Techno *See*: Russell Wallace; Contemporary Compilations: The Fire This Time

Russell Wallace combines techno beats with media soundbites to express perspectives of the Oka crisis of 1990, wherein an absent Canadian prime minister Brian Mulroney was derelict in his duties as the Canadian army was unleashed by the provincial government of Quebec to deal with a land dispute involving golf course expansion onto a traditional Mohawk burial ground.

DISCOGRAPHY:
Bloodlines [Spiral 1991] CD-EP
Indian Summer [Spiral 1991] cassingle

Dunn, Willie—(Mi'kmaq-Couashauck) Folk *See*: Chief Dan George, Kashtin, Shingoose

Born August 14, 1941, Montreal, Quebec. Dunn left the army at age twenty-three and embarked on a journey to become an underground folk music hero. He penned some of the most poignant songs of his time with material that focused on historical and social issues. He played with Jesse Winchester for the music used in the National Film Board documentary *Paper Boy* [Clay Borris, 1971]; additional soundtrack projects include *The Other Side of the Ledger* [Martin Defalco/Willie Dunn, 1972], *Cold Journey* [Martin Defalco, 1975] and *Incident at Restigouche* [Alanis Obomsawin, 1984]. He later created a film that focused on sixteen indigenous languages in North America entitled *Voice of the Land in Our People* [AFN 1998]. A pioneer, Dunn incorporated spoken-word elements of William Shakespeare and T. S. Elliot with the Akwesasne Drummers on his album *The Pacific*. The highly televised 1968 NFB ten-minute short based on his song "Crowfoot" used visuals and historical stills to create the forerunner of the music video. He achieved greater popularity in Europe than in North America, with special releases of his music licensed for European markets. His 1999 album *Metallic* is a best-of collection featuring traditional singer Jerry Saddleback and fiddler Lee Cremo. Selected tracks from the *Willie Dunn* album were used for the CBC radio program *Our Native Land*, hosted by Johnny Yesno. In 1999, Dunn received the Lee Cremo Award for Native Artists at the Tenth Annual Porcupine Awards. He was one of seven artists from Canada selected to showcase at the North American Folk and Dance Alliance in Cleveland, Ohio, in February 2000.

DISCOGRAPHY:
Son of the Sun [Trikont 2004, Germany]
Walking Eagle [Trikont 2004, Germany]
Metallic [Aural Traditions 1999] best of
Nova Scotia/Rattling along in a Freight Train [CBC Northern Service 1986] EP
The Vanity of Human Wishes [Trikont 1983, Germany]
The Pacific [CBC/Boot 1980, 1983] w/ Dario Domingues
Willie Dunn [Akwesasne Notes 1970; Kotai 1972]
Stories and Songs [CBC International 1971] EP
Willie Dunn [Summus 1969] mostly the same material from the 1967 release, with different cover art
Willie Dunn [Summus 1967] Johnny Yesno, producer

Appearances:
Native to Canada: Showcase of Aboriginal Musicians at WOMEX 2000 [Canada Council for the Arts 2001] comp
Festival to Go, Vol. 2 [Festival 1999] comp
Music from Turtle Island [Turtle Island Music 1999] comp
Silencing the Guns [Arthur Lamothe, 1997] sdtk
Here and Now: A Celebration of Canadian Music [Sony 1995] comp
Children of the World [Groupe Concept/ Musicor 1994] comp

Mariposa '76 [Mariposa 1977] comp
Ecstasy of Rita Joe [United Artists 1973] sdtk

Dutiaume Family—(Metis) Gospel

Lineup: Jimmy, Barb, Kenny, Bernice, Albert, Marlene, Marcel, Keith, Tom, Valerie, Frances, and Clint Dutiaume. The band's one album was recorded in Lorette, Manitoba.

DISCOGRAPHY:
A Metis Christmas [Turtle Island Music 1999]

Eagle, Bobby—(Lakota) Gospel

Eagle recorded several original songs that commemorated and honored Vietnam War veterans.

DISCOGRAPHY:
Heroes, Warriors, and Saints [SOAR 1991]

Eagle and Hawk—Alternative Rock

Original Lineup: Vince Fontaine (Anishnabe), guitars/vocals (founder-songwriter); Mike Bruyere (Anishnabe), percussion/ acoustic guitar/traditional vocals; Randy Booth, bass/vocals; Troy Westwood, lyrics/ vocals; Jason Bodner, lead vocals/guitar; Wayne Stranger, traditional vocals.

Formed in 1993 in Winnipeg, Manitoba. The band's eclectic rock and funk rhythms combined with Native sensibilites created a uniquely captivating sound with live shows that included pow-wow dancers. After more than a dozen international tours, Eagle and Hawk gained popularity throughout central Europe. Fontaine, Bruyere, and Booth played with Keith Secola from 1995 to 1997 and with Errol Ranville from 1997 to 1999, and they provided backup for Jerry Alfred and for Chester Knight and the Wind. Westwood wore number 7 as the kicker for the Canadian Football League's Winnipeg Blue Bombers. Booth, a veteran of the Canadian music scene, has played with Canadian mainstream artists Gerry Doucette, Idle Eyes, and Harlequin. Fontaine and Stranger were instrumental in organizing the Native music component at the 1999 Pan Am Games in Winnipeg.

DISCOGRAPHY:
Mother Earth [Arbor 2003]
On and On [Sunshine 2001]
Eagle and Hawk [TP Music/Rising Sun 2000]
Indian City [independent 1999]
Eagle and Hawk Live [independent 1998] EP
Medicine Wheel [independent 1997] w/ Jody Gaskin *See*: Flute Music
The Dream [independent 1997] w/ Troy Westwood, vocals

Appearances:
20 Aboriginal Greatest Hits, Vol. 3 [Sunshine 2002] comp

Selected Awards:
2004: Juno nomination, Aboriginal Recording of the Year, *Mother Earth*
2002: Juno Award, Aboriginal Recording of the Year, *On and On*
2001: Juno nomination, Best Music of Aboriginal Canada, *Indian City*
2001: NAMA nomination, Best Rock Album, *Indian City*
2000: Prairie Music Award nomination, Best Aborignal Recording, *Indian City*
1999: NAMA nomination, Best Group

Eagle Cloud, Leonard—New Age/Gospel

Born Leonard Howell, February 1953. Howell began recording in 1984 on a collaborative project called Okanagan Heat. He was later part of the Vancouver-based 1970s and 1980s band Pendragon. He utilized his indigenous musical experience and created several recordings based on a cultural theme.

DISCOGRAPHY:
Live in '99 [independent 2000]
An Eagle's Carol [independent 1997] Christmas album
Red Road [independent 1996]
Traveller [independent 1994]

Eagle Feather *See*: J. Hubert Francis and Eagle Feather

Earth Treaty—Rock/Trad

Lineup: Frank Steele, songwriter/lead vocals; Sherman Butler, drums/storytelling; Mark Rutherford, keyboards/vocals/productions; Becky Big Canoe, vocals; Joanne Powell, vocals; Gary Taylor, drums/vocals; Sandy Chochinov, bass; Peter Mueller, guitars; Eric Kidd, guitars.

DISCOGRAPHY:
Can't Cage a Spirit [FCS 1994] six-track cass

Echo Hawk, Roger—(Pawnee) Ambient

Echo Hawk utilized electronic music in a way similar to Tangerine Dream or Vangelis and so avoided New Age categorization. He completed a master's degree in Native American history at the University of Colorado, Boulder, and worked with his brother Walter on grave protection and repatriation. He revealed that "*Edges of the Earth* comes from a variety of roots influences of Pawnee heritage; however, this is not traditional Pawnee music."

DISCOGRAPHY:
Edges of the Earth: Aural Dream Meditations [WithOut Rez Productions 1996]

El Chicano—Rock

Original Lineup: Bobby Espinosa, organ; Andre Baeza, conga/percussion/vocals; Ersi Arvizu, vocal/percussion; Mickey Lespron, guitar; John De Luna, drums/percussion.

1974 Lineup: Bobby Espinosa, organ; Mickey Lespron, guitar; Andre Baeza, conga/percussion/vocals; Hector Regalado, drums/percussion; Brian Magness, bass; Jerry Salas, guitar; Eddie Rodriguez, drums/percussion.

DISCOGRAPHY:
Chicano Chant [MCA 1997] best of
Let Me Dance with You [Capitol/CBS 1984] twelve-inch dance single
This Is El Chicano [Shadybrook 1976]
Viva El Chicano! Their Very Best [MCA 1976]
The Best of Everything [MCA 1975]
Pyramid of Love and Friends [MCA 1975]
Cinco [MCA 1974]
El Chicano [MCA 1973]
Celebration [MCA 1972]
Revolucion [KAPP 1971]
Viva Tiredo [MCA 1970]

Appearances:
This Is . . . El Chicano [Varese 2000] best of
Latin Oldies, Vol. 4 [Thump Records 2000] comp
Latin Oldies, Vol. 3 [Thump Records 1999] comp
Latin Oldies, Vol. 2 [Thump Records 1998] comp
Latin Oldies, Vol. 1 [Thump Records 1998] comp
Chicano Power [Soul Jazz Records 1998] comp
Ay Califas: Raza Rock of the '70s and '80s [Rhino 1998] comp
Painting the Moment [Thump 1998] comp
Look of Love [Musicdisc 1997] comp
Chicano Chant [MCA Special 1997] comp

El Cochise—(Apache-Hopi) Country and Western

A Southwest favorite who performed in the classic country style.

DISCOGRAPHY:
Better Than Ever [Canyon 1980]
Chuck's Boogie [Canyon 1979]
Sad News [Canyon 1977]
Crazy Arms [Canyon 1971]

Emerson, Larry, and Skyward—(Dineh) Gospel

Lineup: Larry Emerson, lead vocals/lead rhythm guitar; Frances Emerson, Joanne Begay, Frankie Woodis, Emmett Fowler.

DISCOGRAPHY:
Now Is the Time [MER 1984]
Skyward Message [MER 0498]

Escovedo, Alejandro—(Chicano) Rock *See*: True Believers

Escovedo began his music career in the mid-1970s with the San Francisco–based punk band the Nuns; he later cofounded the moo-wave band Rank and File in 1979 and then played with the True Believers, with Buck McKane and Ry Cooder.

DISCOGRAPHY:
Bouronistis [Bloodshot 1999]
More Miles Than Money: Live 1994–1996 [Bloodshot 1998]
With These Hands [Ryko 1996] w/ Sheila E.
Thirteen Years [Watermelon 1994] best of
The End/Losing Your Touch [Watermelon 1994]
Gravity [Watermelon 1992]

Escovedo, Coke—(Chicano) Rock/ Jazz *See*: Azteca, Malo

Died July 13, 1986. This timbalist-percussionist was another cofounder of Azteca and formed the Escovedo Brothers Latin Jazz Sextet with siblings Pete and Phil. In addition to his solo albums, Escovedo sessioned with Herbie Hancock, Malo, Santana, Boz Scaggs, and others.

DISCOGRAPHY:
Disco Fantasy [Mercury 1977]
Comin' at Ya [Mercury 1976]
Coke [Mercury 1975]

Escovedo, Pete—(Chicano) Rock/Jazz
See: Azteca

Born July 13, 1935. This exceptional percussionist played with Malo, Santana, Con Funk Shun, and Billy Cobham, and he cofounded the 1970s group Azteca.

DISCOGRAPHY:
E Musica [Concord Jazz 2000]
E Street [Concord Jazz 1997]
Flying South [Concord 1995]
Mister E [Crossover 1987]
Yesterday's Memories: Tomorrow's Dreams [Crossover 1985]
Island [Es Go/Fantasy 1982]
Happy Together [Fantasy 1978]
Solo Two [Fantasy 1977]

Escovedo, Sheila; a.k.a. Sheila E.—(Chicana) Rock/Jazz *See*: Azteca

Born December 12, 1957, Oakland, California. The daughter of percussionist Pete Escovedo and formerly a percussionist for Prince, Sheila E. cut her teeth with the group Azteca and later played on two of her father's solo albums. She began her solo career in 1984 after being discovered by Prince and featured on his single "Let's Go Crazy/Erotic City" [Warner 1984]. Her second single, "The Belle of St. Mark," charted in both the U.K. and the U.S. top forty; her 1985 hit "A Love Bizarre" went to number 11, though her 1987 self-titled album failed to make a mark. She then

joined Prince's Sign o' the Times Tour in 1987. Throughout her career, Sheila E. has shared the stage and sessioned with many performers, including Babyface, Mariah Carey, Phil Collins, Con Funk Shun, the Crusaders, Celine Dion, Chante Moore, Billy Cobham, Ringo Starr, and others, and she appeared as the bandleader on Magic Johnson's *The Magic Hour*.

DISCOGRAPHY:
The Writes of Passage [Concord 2000] w/ the E Train Band
Sex Cymbal [Warner 1991]
Sheila E. [Paisley Park 1987]
Romance 1600 [Warner 1985]
The Glamorous Life [Warner 1984]

EPs/Singles:
"Sex Cymbal" [Warner 1991] w/ cassingle release
"The Glamorous Life" [Warner 1991]
"Cry Baby" [Warner 1991]
"Droppin' Like Flies" [Warner 1991]
"A Love Bizarre" [Paisley Park 1985]
"The Belle of St. Mark" [Warner 1984]
"Let's Go Crazy/Erotic City" [Warner 1984]

Videos:
Live Romance 1600 [Warner 1985]

Fairchuck, Len—(Metis) Fiddle

1932–2004
Born Leonard William Fairchuk, June 2, 1932, Winnipeg, Manitoba. During his professional career, Fairchuck was given the name "White Buffalo" by Chief George Pierre of the Acoma Nation of Washington State. In the 1950s, Fairchuck played the accordion in the Rhythm Ranch Boys, the backup band for Winnipeg entertainer and friend Ray St. Germain. Fairchuck was an accomplished artist, musician, and songwriter. He was best known as the host of *The Western Hour*, a CBC variety show filmed on lcation in countless communities throughout the province of Manitoba. The popular show ran Saturday afternoons

from 1977 to 1996 and showcased the fiddling, jigging, square dancing, and singing of the area residents. Fairchuck closed every program with, "God bless, and may the Great Spirit be with you." He died of heart failure on April 4, 2004.

DISCOGRAPHY:
Western Hour Fiddle Tunes [Sunshine 1995]
The Pioneers [Silver Spur SS-178 1967]

Fara—(Cree) Hip-Hop/R & B

Born Fara Jaylene Katcheech Palmer, November 16, 1972, North Battleford, Saskatchewan. Fara made her recording debut with Willie Dunn, Susan Aglukark, Don Ross, and Shingoose on the *Children of the World* project. She opened the 1997 North American Indigenous Games and made numerous television and radio appearances with extensive press coverage. Her single "Make It Up to You" placed eighth in the R & B category of the 1997 John Lennon Songwriting Contest, New York. She performed at the National Aboriginal Achievement Awards in Regina, Saskatchewan, in 1999 and received two Juno nominations for Aboriginal Recording of the Year, 1998 and 2000.

DISCOGRAPHY:
Pretty Brown [Black Moon 1999]
This Is My World [Black Moon 1997]

Appearances:
Vision Quest [independent 1997] comp
Here and Now: A Celebration of Canadian Music [Sony 1995] comp, w/ Willie Dunn
Children of the World [Groupe Concept/ Musicor 1994] comp

Videos:
Bring Back Yesterday [Black Moon 1999]
Pretty Brown [Black Moon 1999]

Featherstone—Trad/Rock *See:* Gordon Bird, Jackie Bird, Sherry Bird

Lineup: Jackie Bird, drums/vocals; Sherry Bird, bass/vocals; Lori Bird, percussion/ vocals; JoAnne Bird, synthesizer/vocals; Gordon Bird, guitars/vocals. Recorded several of their own independent projects and some powwow groups on the family label Featherstone. Based in Bookings, South Dakota.

DISCOGRAPHY:
Featherstone in Concert [Featherstone 1990] cass

Fernandez, Wade—(Menominee) Blues/Rock *See:* Mitch Walking Elk

Born November 9, 1968, Menominee Reservation, Wisconsin. This guitarist and singer-songwriter started his career in the 1980s as a session musician. *Black Wolf's Blues* received a NAMA nomiation for Best Rock Album, 2003.

DISCOGRAPHY:
Black Wolf's Blues [independent 2002]
Music for the 7th Generation [independent 2002]
Wiciwen Apis-Mahwaew [independent 2000]

Appearances:
Mitch Walking Elk:
Ain't No Simple Thing [Shaeila 1993]

Firecat of Discord—Jazz/Rock/ Country

Lineup: Maura Dhu, vocals; Josh Grinspoon, lead guitar; Bruce King, vocals/ rhythm guitar; Wes Studi, bass/vocals; Benito Concha, percussion (*See:* Red Thunder); Gary Storm, viola. Formed in 1995.

DISCOGRAPHY:
Firecat of Discord [independent 1998]

Fischer, Carl—(Cherokee) Classical

1912–1954

Born in California. Encouraged by his parents to pursue a career in classical music, Fischer began learning the violin at the age of seven, the accordion at ten, and the piano at twelve. In 1944, he met Frankie Laine and joined him as an accompanist for the remainder of his life. During international tours, Fischer complained of pains that grew steadily worse, but visits to the doctor revealed nothing. He died suddenly on March 27, 1954. His work *Reflections of an Indian Boy* represents a lifelong process. Much of the suite was never written down until its actual completion. In 1952, Victor Young offered to orchestrate the score and recorded the sessions, and Laine wrote lyrics for four sections. The tone poem, divided into nine parts, is a musical biography with original themes based on traditional music, rhythms, and thought. As a tribute to Fischer, the piece was first publicly performed on August 5, 1954, with Frankie Laine and the Cleveland Orchestra, with Victor Young, conductor.

DISCOGRAPHY:

Reflections of an Indian Boy: A Tone Poem [Columbia/CBS 1974 788-LP37576] w/ the Paul Weston Orchestra; reissued with black-and-white cover photo [Columbia Special Products ACL 788-LP37577]

Five and Country Senses—Trad/Folk

An unusual and rare collective of youths who recorded a 1971 album on Schreiber Island, Ontario, Canada. The project was produced by the Manitou Arts Foundation, with music conducted and arranged by Louis Ballard. Featured performers include artist Clayton Brascoupe, Michael Doxtator, Shirley Horse, and filmmaker Shirley Cheechoo. The album contained sendups of traditional songs from various regions across Canada.

Flawless—(Anishnabe) Rap *See*: Litefoot

A young MC from St. Paul, Minnesota, who hooked up with producer Litefoot to record one album.

DISCOGRAPHY:

Living Life Flawless [Red Vinyl 1999]

Appearances:

Red Ryders, Vol. 2 [Red Vinyl 1999] comp
Red Ryders, Vol. 1 [Red Vinyl 1999] comp

Flummies—Country/Folk

Lineup: Alton Best (born May 31, 1934; Labrador Metis), guitar/harmonica/vocals; Richard Dyson (born July 31, 1948; Labrador Metis), accordion/percussion; Leander Baikie (born December 20, 1961; Labrador Metis), rhythm and lead guitars/vocals; Eugene (Tunker) Campbell (born April 19, 1957; Labrador Inuit), acoustic lead guitar/vocals; Simeon Asivak (born March 2, 1961; Labrador Inuit), acoustic and electric guitars.

Original Lineup: Dyson, Best, Bob Lunnen, Winston White, and George Shiwak (1937–1998).

Formed in 1978, Goose Bay, Labrador. Singing original songs of the land and life of the region in a style typical of East Coast jigs, reels, and ballads. The band took its name from a traditional trappers' bread made from flour, salt, and baking powder. They were nominated in the ECMA category Best Aboriginal Music in 2001 and won that category in 2003; additional merits include the MIANL Award for Aboriginal Artist/Group of the Year in 2002 and an MIANL nomination in the same category in 2000.

DISCOGRAPHY:
Way Back Then [Kenamu Records 2002]
Labradorimiut [Kenamu Records 2000]
Songs of Labrador [Kenamu Records 1988]
 cass
Four Songs from Labrador [Kenamu Records 1986] vinyl EP

Related Projects:
"Tunker Campbell: My Sweet Lady" [Mukluk Studios 2003] single

Francis, J. Hubert, and Eagle Feather—(Mi'kmaq) Country/Rock
See: Ancestral Fire, Redbone

Lineup: J. Hubert Francis, lead vocals/guitar; Byron Simon, bass; J. F. Goguen, lead guitar; Scott Girvan, keyboards; J. J. Francis, drums.

The band broke nationally in 1990 when their first single, "Lady of the Evening," charted in Canada at number 35 and appeared in the Top 100 Country Singles in the United States. Hubert collaborated with author Melinda Camber-Porter on the book and film project *Badlands*. Their material is sung in English and Mi'kmaq. They received an ECMA nomination in 1995, Juno nominations for Aboriginal Recording of the Year in 1994 and 1998, and a NAMA nomination in 1999.

DISCOGRAPHY:
Message from a Drum [Bear Paw 1998]
No Boundaries [Bear Paw 1995]
Reverence [Sunshine 1993]

Appearances:
20 Aboriginal Greatest Hits, Vol. 3 [Sunshine 2002] comp
20 Aboriginal Greatest Hits, Vol. 2 [Sunshine 1998] comp
24 Canadian Aboriginal Artists [Sunshine 1995] comp

Free, Micki—(Cherokee-Comanche) Rock/Funk/R & B

Born in Texas. Free's stepfather was in the U.S. military service, and Free grew up in Germany. He moved to Los Angeles in the early 1980s to work as a session guitarist and singer-songwriter and was managed by Diana Ross. He worked with Wendy O. Williams of the Plasmatics and cowrote her song "Legends Never Die" with Gene Simmons of KISS. Free went on to play and collaborate with many performers, including Janet Jackson ("Come Give Me Your Love"), Prince, Babyface, Jon Brant (Cheap Trick), George Duke, Howard Hewitt, L. A. Reid, Trevor Rabin (Yes), Roger Taylor (Queen), and Tony Thompson (Chic). He has also worked with producer Jean Beavouir and KISS alumni Paul Stanley for the Crown of Thorns project.

Throughout Free's time with Shalamar, he shared four platinum records and four gold records, including the soundtrack for the film *Footloose* [Herbert Ross, 1984]. He received a Grammy Award for Best Album or Original Score Written for a Motion Picture in 1985 for *Beverly Hills Cop* [Martin Best, 1984] and had a platinum single in "Don't Get Stopped in Beverly Hills." He received a NAMA Award for Best Male Artist, 2002.

Free's passion for history and action is combined in his lifetime association with the California Desperados Mounted Shooting Club and the Single Action Shooting Society (SASS) which involves combinations of skilled rifle shooting and trick riding. As an actor, he has appeared in the television series *Tales of a Gun* [History Channel 2000].

SELECTED DISCOGRAPHY:
The Sun Chaser: Native American Flute Love Songs [independent 2003]
Electric Warrior/Gypsy Cowby [independent 2001]
Black Moon . . . Black Sun [independent 1993]

Appearances (listed alphabetically):
Crown of Thorns: *Hike It Up* [Now & Then 1994, United Kingdom] EP
Killer Thorns [Interscope 1994]
Crown of Thorns [Interscope 1993]
Janet Jackson: *Janet Jackson* [A&M 1982]
Shalamar: *Wake Up* [Solar Records 1990]
Circumstantial Evidence [Solar Records 1987]
Heart Break [Solar Records 1984]
Over and Over [Solar Records 1984]
Various: *Lambada* [Warner 1989] sdtk
Beverly Hills Cop [MCA 1985] sdtk
Footloose [Sony 1984] sdtk
DC Cab [A&M 1983] sdtk

Freebird Band—Country *See*: C-Weed, Hector Menow

Lineup: Fred Mitchell, vocals/guitar; Wally Ranville, vocals/bass; Dean Malcolm, vocals/guitar/fiddle; Don Ranville, drums; Craig Fotheringham, keyboards.

DISCOGRAPHY:
The Freebird Band—Recorded Live [P&L Promotions 1993]
The Freebird Band [independent 1992]

Full Ephekt—Rap

Lineup: Michelle Alvin, Amanda Janvier, Sonnie MacDonald, Frankie Bull, Alex Cantois, Spencer Auigbelle, Kelly Noskiye, Keith Ward.
Formed in 2000, Winnipeg, Manitoba. With members ranging in ages from nine to nineteen years old, the group strived to build awareness among Native youth about street life and drug abuse with a culture-positive perspective.

DISCOGRAPHY:
Full Ephekt [Sunshine 2001]

Appearances:
20 Aboriginal Greatest Hits, Vol. 3 [Sunshine 2002] comp

Funkdoobiest—Rap

Lineup: Tribal Funkster, Son Doobie, Tomahawk Funk (a.k.a. DJ Ralph Medrano), L. Muggerud, J. Vasquez, w/ Brett Bouldin. Formed in 1992.

DISCOGRAPHY:
The Troubleshooters [BuzzTone/RCA 1998]
Act on It [BMG 1997]
Brothas Doobie [Epic/Immortal/Sony 1995]
Which Doobie U B? [Epic/Immortal 1993]

Funky Aztecs—(Chicano) Rap

Lineup: A. Funky Aztec, lyrics; Peewee, 2PAC, Money B, Merciless, Indio, Loco-Motion, ALT (Another Latin Timebomb), vocals; Chino Josh Jones and John Santos, percussion; DJ Q-Bert and Jeremy Jackson, turntables; Lloyd Gregory, guitars. The Funky Aztecs' punchy grooves and tasty samples delivered messages of unity with barrio flavors. Later projects include *Day of the Dead*.

DISCOGRAPHY:
Chicano Blues [TNT 1992]

Gagnon, Marcel—(Carrier) Country/Folk

Born May 2, 1950, Ferndale, British Columbia; based in Prince George, British Columbia. Gagnon's early musical influences include Buddy Holly, Hank Williams, Pink Floyd, and Morley Loon. *Crazy Maker* received a Juno nomination for Aboriginal Recording of the Year, 2002.
Lineup: Marcel Gagnon, vocals/rhythm guitar; Don McLelland, bass; Trevor Bigam, drums/percussion; Jeremy Blattner, keyboard; Justin Frey, saxophone; Suzy Wigmore, flute; Arnold Faber, vibes; Dianna McNolty, vocals.

DISCOGRAPHY:
The Watchman—Tom Crow [VuFox 2002]
Crazy Maker [VuFox 2001]

Gamblin, Edward—(Cree) Country and Western

Born 1950, Norway House, Manitoba. Gamblin first began playing music at age sixteen and started his first band, the Cree Nation, in 1966. He formed much of his style after country artists such as Waylon Jennings and recorded more than sixty original songs, including his ballad for Wounded Knee entitled "Soldier Blue" (not to be confused with Buffy Sainte-Marie's song of the same name). With his group Northern Lobo (Dennis Dick, guitar; Danny Robertson, bass; Lloyd Arthurson, drums), Gamblin collaborated with Doug Sahm on the compilation *Flow Like a River*. Playing and recording for more than three decades, Gamblin has created an impressive legacy in Native country-and-western music that holds true to its roots.

DISCOGRAPHY:
Bright Blue Moon [Sunshine 2003]
Greatest Hits [Sunshine 2002]
Edward Gamblin [Sunshine SSCT-4106]
Soldier Blue [Sunshine SSCT-4094]
This Can't Go On [Sunshine SSCT-4058]
Don't Blame It on the Rain [Sunshine SSCT-4043]

Appearances:
20 Aboriginal Greatest Hits, Vol. 3 [Sunshine 2002] comp
Northern Legends [Sunshine 2000] comp
Flow Like a River [Rising Eagle Productions 1989] comp

Gardipy, Henry—(Metis) Fiddle

Born 1950, North Battleford, Saskatchewan.

DISCOGRAPHY:

Appearances:
Drops of Brandy and Other Traditional Metis Tunes [Gabriel Dumont Institute 2002] four-CD comp

Gaskin, Jody Thomas—(Anishnabe) Rock *See*: Eagle and Hawk; Flute Music

Born December 29, 1963, Saulte Sainte Marie, Michigan. A session player, Gaskin worked with the Winnipeg-based rock group Eagle and Hawk and recorded traditional cedar flute and contemporary albums.

DISCOGRAPHY:
Native American Flute Songs, Vol. 2 [Sunshine 1999]
. . . Part of Being Anishnabe [Sunshine 1995]
Native American Flute Songs, Vol. 1 [Sunshine 1995]

Appearances:
20 Aboriginal Greatest Hits, Vol. 3 [Sunshine 2002] comp
World's Best 49er Songs [Sunshine 2000] comp, w/ White Wolf Singers *See*: Powwow Music: Compilations
20 Greatest Aboriginal Hits, Vol. 2 [Sunshine 1998] comp
24 Canadian Aboriginal Artists [Sunshine 1995] comp

Geffre, Darren—(Blackfeet) Pop/Rock

Born in Browning, Montana. Geffre began his music career at age twelve and played in several bands by his midteens. His guitar work helped lay the groundwork for the original songs he recorded in collaboration with producers-songwriters Duncan Pain and Peter Amato. The single "If I Ever" received a NAMA nomination for Best Independent Recording, 2001.

DISCOGRAPHY:
Uncivilized [independent 2002]
Thunder Beings [independent 2000]

George, Chief Dan—(Shuswap)

1899–1981

Born Daniel Paul George (Geswanouth Slahoot–Teswahno), July 24, 1899, Burrard Indian Reserve Number 3, British Columbia. The renowned actor-author-statesman appeared on several recording projects and made important inroads for Native actors into the mainstream film industry. He served as chief of the Shuswap from 1961 to 1963. His famous 1967 Centennial Speech appears on the album *In Circle* with Vancouver-based folk/rock group Fireweed. He received an Oscar nomination for Best Supporting Actor for *Little Big Man* [Arthur Penn, 1970] and made numerous television appearances on *Bonanza* in 1959, *The Incredible Hulk* in 1978, and many other shows. His life story was the subject of two documentary films: *Today Is a Good Day* [Loretta Todd, 1998] and *Chief Dan George Speaks* [Jeff Howard, 1974]. He passed away September 12, 1981.

DISCOGRAPHY:

Proud Earth [Salt City 1975] w/ Arlene Nofchissey-Williams and Rick Brosseau
The Ecstasy of Rita Joe [United Artists 1973] w/ Willie Dunn, Paul Horn, Ann Mortifee, and George Ryga
In Circle [Can-Base 1972]
Little Big Man [Columbia 1967] sdtk w/ Dustin Hoffman and John Hammond

Selected Filmography:

Spirit of the Wind [Ralph Liddle, 1979] *See*: Buffy Sainte-Marie
The Outlaw Josey Wales [Clint Eastwood, 1976]
Harry and Tonto [Paul Mazursky, 1974]
Little Big Man [Arthur Penn, 1970]

Gilday, Leela—(Dene) Rock *See*: Arctic/Circumpolar Contemporary: Lucy Idlout

Born October 18, 1974, Yellowknife, Northwest Territories. With a formal degree in music after studying opera, Gilday began her singing career in the late 1980s. Her cool R & B, hip-hop-flavored style is progressive and lyrically conscious. A duet with Lucy Idlout performing Gilday's song "For This Land" was included on the live album *Truly Something*. Her album *spirit world, solid wood* received a Juno nomination for the 2003 Best Music of Aboriginal Canada. The album's first track, "Great Slave Shore," enjoyed national airplay on CBC Radio and on many Native radio stations; George Leach provided guitar work on the song "Anything at All."

DISCOGRAPHY:

spirit world, solid wood [Diva Sound 2002]
"Love Built" [Sunray Inc. 2000] single

Appearances:

True North Concerts—Truly Something [CBC North 2000] comp

Gladstone, Jack—(Blackfoot) Folk

Born April 8, 1958, Seattle, Washington. An outstanding athlete, Gladstone attended the University of Washington on a scholarship and earned a degree in speech communications along with a Rose Bowl ring. He returned to his roots in northwestern Montana, where he taught public speaking at Blackfeet Community College. This prolific singer-songwriter, whose vocal character bears a striking similarity to that of Gordon Lightfoot, turned his live shows into multimedia events by combining performance, sound, and image. He crafted his reverence for his culture and the land into witty and insightful lyrics. Tribute material includes Jim Thorpe, the Navajo Code Talkers, and the Hudson's Bay Company. Among many awards, he is the recipient of the Human Rights Award, Montana State University, Northern, 1997.

DISCOGRAPHY:

Buffalo Republic [Hawkstone 2000]
Legacy [Hawkstone 1998] best of

Buffalo Stew [Hawkstone 1998]
Buffalo Cafe [Hawkstone 1997]
Noble Heart [Hawkstone 1996]
Buckskin Poet Society [Hawkstone 1993]
In the Shadow of Mount Lassen [Hawkstone 1991]
Wolves on Sea and Plain [Hawkstone 1988]

Goertzen, Charlie—(Cree) Rock

Born April 22, 1980, Fort Vermilion, Alberta. Goertzen began recording at the age of eleven. Though he was not an Elvis Presley impersonator, his choice of cover material allowed him to put a little of the King's swank into his own vocal style.

DISCOGRAPHY:
Handful of Hope [Sunshine 1995]
Charlie Goertzen [Sunshine 1994]

Appearances:
24 Canadian Aboriginal Artists [Sunshine 1995] comp

Gon, David—(Dene) Country

Born 1953, Yellowknife, Northwest Territories. With a traditional upbringing, Gon recorded songs of the land and the people in a simple contemporary country music style.

DISCOGRAPHY:
Island Miles Away [CBC Northern Service 1987]

Gordon, Roxy—(Choctaw) Country/Folk

1945–2000
Born March 7, 1945, Ballinger, Texas. A renowned poet, singer, author, and activist, Gordon grew up in a musical family; his mom played piano in a Methodist church, and his grandfather played piano and French harp. Gordon attended the Uni-

Roxy Gordon's *Smaller Circles*. Courtesy Judy Gordon.

versity of Texas, Austin, and traveled to Montana and California in the late 1960s, where he worked with Rip Torn and Jim Morrison. He later moved to Albuquerque, New Mexico, to become editor of *Picking Up the Tempo*. After returning to Texas, he wrote for the *Coleman Chronicle* and the *Democrat Voice* newspapers in Dallas. His published works include *Some Things I Did* [Encino Press 1971] and *No Evidence* [Wowapi 1989] and two coauthored plays. As a performer, Gordon shared the stage and studio with Bob Dylan, Ernest Tubb, Leonard Cohen, Townes Van Zandt, and many others. His exploits with Van Zandt were notorious, and he sometimes used them as the subject of his poetry. In 1991, he was adopted by the Assiniboine Nation at Fort Belknap, Montana, and given the name First Coyote Boy. He passed away February 7, 2000, following a lengthy illness.

DISCOGRAPHY:
Townes Asked Did Hank Williams Ever Write Anything As Good As Nothing [Wowapi 2001] w/ Wes McGhee
Smaller Circles [Road Goes On Forever Records 1997, United Kingdom]
Roxy Gordon, Kerrville Live [Backporch Music 1996]

Crazy Horse Never Died [Sunstorm Records 1990, United Kingdom]

Appearances:
Jukebox Cowboy [Vinyl Junkie 1999] comp

Gospel Light Singers—(Dineh)
Gospel

Lineup: Alfred, Louis, Cynthia, and Stanley Jim; Sharon Yazzie; William Tso.

DISCOGRAPHY:
If That Isn't Love [Canyon 1986]
I'm Bound for That City [Canyon 1983]
Life's Railway to Heaven [Canyon 1982]
To My Mansion in the Sky [Canyon 1980]
Jesus Died for Me Long Ago [Canyon 1979]
Introducing the Gospel Light Singers [Canyon 1978]

GQ Smooth—(Cree-Saulteaux) Rap
See: TKO

Born April 14, 1972, Winnipeg, Manitoba. The brother of TKO attempted a short foray in recording.

DISCOGRAPHY:
"Prepare for What's to Come" [Knock 'em Dead Productions 1998] single
"Chief Rocker" [Knock 'em Dead Productions 1997] single

Green, Billy Joe—(Anishnabe) Blues

Born March 12, 1951, Shoal Lake, Ontario. A singer-songwriter for more than twenty years, Green recorded his first full-length album in 1996; some material was recorded by C-Weed. His ax style is raw blues that swings between ethereal rock and heavy metal. *My Ojibway Experience* features the Lake of the Woods Singers (*See*: Powwow Music) and earned a 2002 Juno nomination for Best Music of Aboriginal Canada Recording.

DISCOGRAPHY:
My Ojibway Experience: Strength and Hope, The Rockin' Blues of Billy Joe Green [independent 2000]
Roughin' It [Sunshine 1996]
Live at C-Weed's Cabaret, Vol. 2 [independent 1995]
Billy Joe Green [independent 1994] cass EP
Blues Man [Jamco 1994]

Appearances:
Skin Tight Blues [Sweet Grass/EMI 2002] comp
20 Greatest Aboriginal Hits, Vol. 2 [Sunshine 1998] comp

Haida—(Haida-Arapaho) Rap

Born 1977, Lander, Wyoming. Haida started recording in the mid-1990s and released an album that featured ALT (Another Latin Timebomb), Litefoot, Pura Fe, and Kid Frost.

DISCOGRAPHY:
The Haida Way [Red Vinyl 1998] w/ song for Leonard Peltier
Haida Way [Red Vinyl 1997] cass EP

Hamana, Butch—(Hopi) Country/Rock

DISCOGRAPHY:
Butch Hamana and the Big Bang Brothers Band [Canyon CR-7112]
Hamana [Canyon CR-7111]

Harjo, Joy—(Muscogee) Spoken Word/Jazz *See*: Contemporary Spoken Word: Audio Books: *Mankiller* and *The Woman Who Fell from the Sky*

Born 1952, Tulsa, Oklahoma. Noted author of numerous award-winning books of poetry and fiction, and editor of several anthologies, Harjo transgressed the boundaries of spoken-word performance with traditional, jazz, rock, and reggae music. A self-taught player, she cites Jim Pepper as a major influence; her compositions are lush tapestries of sound, image, and emotion. She's earned several honors for her written work and music, including the Lila Wallace-Reader's Digest Fund Writers' Award, the Oklahoma Book Award, the American Book Award, and a First Americans in the Arts Award. She toured internationally with her band Poetic Justice (a.k.a. Native Roots).

DISCOGRAPHY:
Letter from the End of the 20th Century [Red Horses 1996]
Furious Light [independent 1989] cass D

Appearances:
Cahokia: America's Lost City [TLC/BBC 1998] sdtk
Heartbeat 2: More Voices of First Nations Women [Smithsonian Folkways 1998] comp *See*: Traditional/Archival Compilations
Storytellers of the Pacific [1997] documentary, narration
Native American Currents [Silver Wave 1997] comp
Tribal Fires [Earth Beat! 1997] comp
Honor [Daemon 1996] comp
Before Columbus Foundation: Poets Read Their Contemporary Poetry [Folkways 1980] comp *See*: Contemporary Spoken Word: Poetry Compilations

Harvey Family Singers—Gospel

DISCOGRAPHY:
Let's Go Tell the World [Canyon 1982]

Hawk, Dennis—(Cherokee) Folk/New Age *See*: Flute Music

A guitarist with an admiration for the cedar flute, Hawk composed an eleven-track album dedicated to the sacred places of Turtle Island, with spoken-word pieces by Richard Awonohopay.

DISCOGRAPHY:
Many Trails [Hawk Sounds 1999]

Hawk Project—Jazz

Lineup: Dennis Yerry (Iroquois), flute/acoustic piano/percussion; Ken Littlehawk (Mi'kmaq), flute/vocals/percussion; Gus Mancini, bass clarinet/alto saxophone/synthesizer; Ken Lovelett, orthagonal lap drum/percussion/drums.

DISCOGRAPHY:
Let Us Put Our Minds Together [Yerry Music 1997]

Appearances:
The West [Sony Classical 1996] sdtk

Hawke, Thom E., and the Pineneedles *See*: Seventh Fire

Hawker, Ashton—(Dene) Country/Folk

Born in Fort McMurray and raised in Uranium City, Alberta. Ashton Hawker's album of original compositions includes Bill Cramer, guitar; Robert Wood, bass; Bill Workman, piano/keyboards; John Claverley, flute; Dane Cantera, drums/keyboards; Tanyss Nixi and Tina Hawker, background vocals.

DISCOGRAPHY:
Survivor [Sunshine 1995]

Henry, Len—(Metis) Country and Western

From Boggy Creek, Manitoba. Henry was raised in a musical family; his father played fiddle and harmonica, and his mother was a singer who bought him a mail-order guitar. He started playing country dances in the Roblin area and moved to Winnipeg in his late teens. In 1964, he joined the Mystics but later left the group to pursue a solo career. On March 29, 1981, Henry and his band, Good Company, won the fifth annual MACA Award for Most Popular Country Band (chosen by country music fans). Henry retired from the music business in Winnipeg, Manitoba.

Lineup: Al Gain, acoustic/steel guitar; Carman Moerike, acoustic/electric guitar; Graham Shaw, acoustic guitar; Jim Flett, acoustic guitar; Bill Merritt, Tim Kreiser, bass; Graham Shaw, Victor Davies, piano; Sonny Cape, Reg Kellin, drums; Lea Janes Singers; Victor Davies Singers; Winnipeg Local 190 strings and brass.

DISCOGRAPHY:
Don't Give a Damn Kind of Man [Downs Records DWNS-1000]

Henson, Lance—(Cheyenne) Rock/ Spoken Word

Known more for his literary talents, demonstrated in works such as *Another Song for America* [Point Riders Press, 1987/ 1991] and *In a Dark Mist* [Cross-Cultural Communications, 1992], Henson reads selected poems in collaboration with Not Moving, a collective of politically charged rockers popular in the Italian underground who adapted his poetry to song. The group released several albums dealing with struggle; many were dedicated to AIM.

DISCOGRAPHY:
Song of Myself [Wide 1989, Italy]

Hidden Mana—Gospel

Lineup: Murphy Platero, lead vocals/ rhythm guitar/acoustic guitar/keyboards; Jimson Ignacio, bass; McJohn Gordo, lead guitar; Jothem Harry, drums; Janice Platero, guitar/backup vocals.

From Canocito, New Mexico, Dineh musician Murphy Platero became active in the Christian music ministry in 1979 with his Morning Star Band and independently released *When Shall It Be?* in 1984. The group was nominated in the top ten of the Christian Music Talent Contest held by the Gospel Music Association.

DISCOGRAPHY:
Continue the Cause [CPR 2000]
Rain Mana Rain [CPR 1992]

Highway, Tomson—(Cree) *See*: George Leach, the Unceded Band; Contemporary Soundtracks: *Son of Ayash*

Born December 6, 1951, on a trapline near Lynn Lake, Manitoba. This renowned playwright, pianist, and composer scored many numbers for his award-winning plays, which include *Dry Lips Oughta Move to Kapuskasing*. The cabaret production of *The Rose* featured singers Star Nayea and Jani Lauzon. His first highly acclaimed book was *Kiss of the Fur Queen* [Doubleday 1998]. A cover of his composition "I'm Thinking of You" was recorded by the Unceded Band in 1997. He received three honorary degrees and was made a Member of the Order of Canada.

Hill, ElizaBeth—(Mohawk) Country

Born September 16, 1956, Six Nations Reserve, Grand River Territory, Ontario. Hill moved to Nashville, Tennessee, in 1986 to develop her craft as a songwriter. Ten years later she returned to Canada and performed in the Native music scene as a singer-storyteller. Her first album, steeped in country and folk roots, was recorded in both Nashville and Toronto. Her follow-up project, *Love That Strong*, received a Juno nomination for Best Music of Aboriginal Canada Recording, 2000; guest artists and cowriters include John Hiatt and Jamie O'Hara. She received two CAMA nominations for Best Female Artist and Best Producer, 2001.

DISCOGRAPHY:
Love That Strong [independent 1999]
When the Spirit Moves Me [independent 1993]

Appearances:
Kaha:wi [independent 2003] sdtk
Mariposa 2003 [Mariposa Folk Foundation 2003] comp
DownaBush [independent 1999] comp
Hearts of the Nations [Banff Centre for the Arts/Sweet Grass 1997] comp *See*: Traditional/Archival Compilations
I Am an Eagle: The Music from the Legends Project [First Nations 1994] comp

Hilliard, Dr. Quincy—(Lakota)
Classical

Dr. Quincy Hilliard worked as an assistant professor of theory and composition at the University of Southern Louisiana, Lafayette, Louisiana. After accepting a commission from Augustana College, Sioux Falls, South Dakota, Dr. Hilliard composed a symphonic piece entitled *Ghost Dance* to commemorate the 1890 Wounded Knee Massacre. The work was intended as a musical offering in recognition of South Dakota governor George Mickelson's 1990 declaration of a century of reconciliation. Presented in three movements, the work contains traditional instruments and historical monologue; it was also made available in manuscript form.

DISCOGRAPHY:
Moving within the Circle: Contemporary Native American Music and Dance [World Music Press 1993] Bryan Burton book/cass

Houle, Lawrence "Teddy Boy"—
(Anishnabe-Metis) Fiddle

Born October, 1938, Ebb and Flow Reserve, Manitoba, Canada. Based in Lockport, Manitoba. An energetic performer and accomplished player, Houle mixed several styles, including elements of Cape Breton, French Canadian, Scottish, Appalachian, and Native. His performances were accentuated with the percussive use of his feet for tempo, which also mimicked the footsteps of dancers.

DISCOGRAPHY:
Lawrence "Teddy Boy" Houle [Sunshine SSCT-442]

Appearances:
Wood That Sings: Indian Fiddle Music of the Americas [Smithsonian Folkways 1997] *See*: Traditional/Archival Compilations
Old Native and Metis Fiddling in Manitoba, Vol. 1 [Falcon Productions 1986] comp

Humphrey, Annie—(Anishnabikwe)
Folk *See*: Jim Boyd, Brent Michael Davids

Born and raised on the Leech Lake Reservation, Minnesota. Basically a self-taught musician since childhood, Humphrey went on to front various cover bands in her late teens. She released her first recording project in 1989 with Don Robinson in Minneapolis, Minnesota. After a four-year stint in the U.S. Marines, she left the service in 1994 and enrolled in the University of North Dakota. A year later she launched her recording career with her second independent release. After five years of playing venues throughout the United States, she signed with Makoche Records. She received NAMA nominations for Songwriter of the Year, Recording of the Year, Best Folk/Country Recording, Best Female Artist, 2001. For her album *Edge of*

America, Jim Boyd provided backup vocals and acoustic guitar work on the track "I'll Be There," and Keith Secola appeared on vocals for the song "Storm."

DISCOGRAPHY:
Edge of America [Makoche 2003]
The Heron Smiled [Makoche 2000] w/ John Trudell
Justice Smiled [independent 1995]
For the Children [independent 1989]

Appearances:
Jim Boyd:
alterNATIVES [Thunderwolf 2001]
Various:
Whispering Tree [Makoche 2000] comp, spoken word *See*: Contemporary Spoken Word: Legends (Miscellaneous)

Hunt, Bonnie Jo—(Lakota) Classical
See: Robbie Robertson

A lyric coloratura soprano, Hunt sang with the San Francisco Opera Company and the Bolshoi Opera Theatre. She also collaborated with Jean Richard and Tony Hymas on the 1990 double album *Oyate* and on Robbie Robertson's Native-themed projects. She founded Artists of Indian America in 1980 to help provide opportunities for Native youth. Hunt was honored in 1989 by the American Association of Retired Persons as one of twenty outstanding women as part of National Women's History Month.

DISCOGRAPHY:
A Time to Sing [independent 2003]
Spiritual Bouquet [independent 2002]
Wiyu'kcan (Contemplation) [independent 2000]
Inspiration, Vol. 2 [Artists of Indian America 1990] w/ Anna Husband, piano
Inspiration, Vol. 1 [Artists of Indian America 1989]

Appearances:
Robbie Robertson:

Contact from the Underworld of Redboy [Capitol 1998]
Music for the Native Americans [Capitol 1994]
Various:
Oyate [Nato/World 1990/1998, France] comp

Imperial, Linda—(Creek-Sicilian) NRG

Imperial's great-uncle was the renowned Native poet Alexander Posey. Possessing a richly textured voice, Imperial earned the title of NRG diva. She launched her music career in the 1970s, working with various disco, funk, and R & B acts such as Sylvester, the Weather Girls, the New York Jazz Explosion, and Gavin Christopher. She cofounded Loverde with Frank Loverde; their song "Die Hard Lover" hit the charts in 1983. She released solo projects on several dance labels and enjoyed chart appearances with numerous singles, including "Stranger", "Fire," and "Extra Credit," released on Columbia Records. Her coproduction of "Killing Me Softly" was nominated in the category Twelve-Inch Dance Record of the Year by the Hi-NRG Awards in 1992; "Get Here" hit number 2 on the DMA International Hi-NRG Charts.

DISCOGRAPHY:
Imagine [Inherit 1999]
All by Myself/Two Out of Three Ain't Bad [Interhit 1997]
Loverde:
Die Hard Lover/My World Is Empty [Moby Dick 1982] twelve-inch vinyl

Indian Chipmunks

Lineup: Dusty Miller, Louis Ballard, Paul Pahdocony, Chris White, and Millard Clarke (producer). Featuring Alvin Ahoyboy and His Chipmunk Singers.

DISCOGRAPHY:

The Indian Chipmunks, Vol. 2 [Indian Sounds 1984]

The Indian Chipmunks, Vol. 1 [Indian Sounds 1983]

Indigenous—(Dakota) Blues

Lineup: Mato Nanji, guitar/vocals; Wanbdi, drums/vocals; Pte, bass; Horse, percussion.

Composed of two brothers, a sister, and a cousin, Indigenous is a tightly knit group that borrowed heavily from Stevie Ray Vaughn and Jimi Hendrix. Schooled at home by their parents, Greg and Bev Zephier, the kids were immersed in traditional Native culture and musical training. In the 1960s and 1970s, their father played lead guitar in his own band, the Vanishing Americans. He was also a visual artist who created the logo for the IITC, an NGO (*See: Beyond Treaty* comp). He supported his children's band with expertise, encouragement, and insight from his own music experience, forbidding them to play in front of audiences until they practiced solidly for more than a year. After they cut their first album, however, a house fire took all of their possessions, including instruments, equipment, and the master tapes for their first two recordings. Always in full support of their love of music, their parents took out a loan for new equipment and instruments to help rebuild their musical lives. With the bank paid off after a year of gigs, the band hit the road and never looked back.

Their 1996 album, *Love in a Mist*, sold more than twenty-five thousand units in 1997. The band's first video release, *Things We Do*, won Best Music Video, American Indian Film Awards, San Francisco, California, 1998. After they opened for B. B. King on his 1999 summer tour, the blues great remarked, "Indigenous is someone America and the world should hear." The same year Indigenous was featured in the Jimi Hendrix tribute at Woodstock with television appearances on *Conan O'Brien* and *Austin City Limits*. In 1999, they hit the U.S. Radio and Records Rock Chart with three singles from the album *Things We Do*: "Now That You're Gone," number 9; "Things We Do" number 18; and "Got to Tell You," number 23. The album *Circle* reached number 12 on the Billboard Charts in late 2000 as the album's single "Rest of My Days" reached number 7 on Billboard's AAA Charts and number 9 on the Radio and Records AAA Chart. The second single, "Little Time," made number 18 on the Radio and Records Rock Chart and number 28 on the Radio and Records AAA Chart. *Live at Pachyderm Studio 1998* was named Best Blues Recording by NAMA, 2000.

DISCOGRAPHY:

Indigenous [Silvertone 2003]

Circle [Pachyderm 2000] w/ Jennifer Warnes

Live at Pachyderm Studio 1998 [Pachyderm 1999]

Things We Do [Pachyderm 1999] enhanced w/ new singles

Blues This Morning [Pachyderm 1998] EP

Things We Do [Pachyderm 1998]

Pachyderm Sessions [Pachyderm 1997]

Love in a Mist [independent 1996]

Live Blues from the Sky [independent 1995]

Awake [Kiva 1994]

Indigenous [independent 1992]

Singles:
"Little Time" [Pachyderm 2000]

Appearances:
Grant Hart:
Good News for Modern Man [Pachyderm 1999] w/ Mato Nanji
Various:
Honor [Daemon 1996] comp

Videos:
Indigenous Rocks, Live [Pachyderm 2001]

Live @ La Zona Rosa [Pachyderm 1999]

Things We Do [Pachyderm 1998]

Jackalope—Jazz *See*: Carlos Nakai Quartet, Larry Yanez

Lineup: R. Carlos Nakai, flute/trumpet/percussion; Larry M. Yanez, synthesizer/percussion; Darrell Flint, percussion; Richard Carbajal, guitar *(Weavings)*; Steve Cheseborough, guitar/percussion/E flat washboard; J. David Muniz, bass/classical guitar/synthesizer; Will Clipman, percussion *(Boat People)*.

This fusion style, described as synthacousticpunkarachiNavajazz, is played mainly by Nakai and Yanez, with different guest musicians on various albums.

DISCOGRAPHY:
Boat People [Canyon 1993]
Dances with Rabbits [Canyon 1993] Nakai/Yanez
Weavings [Canyon 1988]
Jackalope [Canyon 1986] Nakai/Yanez

Jackson, Tom—(Anishnabe) Country

Born 1949, One Arrow Reserve, Saskatchewan; raised in Winnipeg, Manitoba. Jackson has played the folk festival circuit extensively over the years. Adding acting to his performance credits, he starred in Tomson Highway's *Dry Lips Ought to Move to Kapuskasing*. His work in television and film include a guest appearance in *Star Trek: The Next Generation*, the film *Clear Cut* [Richard Bugajski, 1992], and *Shining Time Station* [PBS 1990]; he received a Gemini nomination for Best Actor in the CBC television series *North of Sixty* [Alliance 1994]. His album *No Regrets* received a 1995 Juno nomination for Aboriginal Recording of the Year. In 1998, *That Side of the Window* earned a Juno nomination, and the single "Before the Owl Calls My Name" won NAMA Song of the Year, San Francisco. Jackson's ongoing fund-raising efforts made a difference in the lives of the homeless with his annual television production of *The Huron Carole*. Other fund-raisers have included food drives as well as projects for the Manitoba flood victims of 1997 and survivors of September 11, 2001. He founded Tomali Records and Pictures in Calgary, Alberta. In 2002, he was named an officer of the Order of Canada for his music and humanitarian work.

DISCOGRAPHY:
On the Holiday Train [Tomali 2002]
The Huron Carole [Tomali 2001] interview disc
I Will Bring You Near [Tomali 2001]
The Best of the Huron Carole [Tomali 2000]
Home This Christmas [Tomali 1997]
That Side of the Window [independent 1997]
No Regrets [Peg 1994]
Sally Ann [Thunder 1990]
Love, Lust, and Longing [Sunshine 1990]
The Huron Carole [Thunder 1988/1995]
Tom Jackson [Rayne 1984] cass

Appearances:
True North Concerts—Truly Something [CBC North 2000] comp
North of 60 [Alliance Communications 1994] sdtk

Videos:
No Regrets [Peg 1994]

Film and Television:
Star Trek: The Next Generation [Corey Allen, 1994] episode 172, "Journey's End," as Lakanta
North of Sixty [Alliance Communications 1994]
Clearcut [Ralph Bugajski 1992]
Shining Time Station [PBS 1990]

Jana—(Lumbee) Pop/Dance

Born Jana Maria, 1976, Lumberton, North Carolina. In the mid-1990s, Grammy-nominated producer and songwriter Rodney Shelton was invited by a friend to hear a young Jana Marie, then lead singer for a local cover band called Peace'n Love. He was impressed by her talent, and their

Jana gave dance music a new twist. Photo by Andrew Eccles; courtesy T. E. Savage.

initial meeting led to Jana's first recording, Shelton's "What Am I to You," which went to the top forty on the Radio and Records Rhythmic Chart. The single exemplified her vocal range and ability and landed her a record deal with Curb Records' Los Angeles–based pop music division; they released four singles. In 1999, she was a featured performer for ESPRIT's fashion showcase tour and appeared on the premiere of *The Cindy Margolis Show* [CBS 2000]. The single "Ooh Baby, Baby" charted on Gavin, the Radio and Records Top 40 R & B Charts and appeared at number 40 and number 48 on the Radio and Records Charts; "More Than Life" made mid-April 2001 Hot Shot Debut at number 29 on the Billboard Hot Dance Music Maxi-Single Sales Chart and number 43 on the Billboard Dance Charts. She also cowrote "Kiss and Tell" for the Crystal

Lewis Grammy-nominated album *Fearless* [Interscope 2000].

DISCOGRAPHY (SINGLES):
"Stairway to Heaven" [Radikal/EMI 2001] CD single
"More Than Life" [Curb 2000] CD EP
"More Than Life" [Curb 2000] remixes
"Ooh Baby, Baby" [Curb 1999] Euro radio edit, dance remixes
"Ooh, Baby, Baby" [Curb 1999] remix single
"The Price" [Curb 1998] country singles
"Near Me" [Curb 1998] remix single
"What Am I to You" [Curb 1996] remix single

Appearances (listed alphabetically):
Gordon Grody:
Exclusively Yours [Sunbar 2180]
Shizou vs. Shizor:
Shizou vs. Shizor [Grand Royal/Digital Hard Corp 1997]

Jessup, Georgie—(Dakota) Rock/Pop

Lineup: Georgie Jessup, piano/vocals; Cochise Anderson, flute (*See*: Pura Fe).

In celebration of Native *berdache* culture ("two-spirited people," or gay), Jessup carries on the *winkte* tradition through contemporary music. S/he has opened for John Trudell, Deanna Bogart, NRBQ, and others. The liner notes describe a meeting with Lakota elder Frank Fools Crow (*See*: Contemporary Spoken Word: Testimonials and Memoirs:), who encouraged Jessup to continue on the two-spirited path.

DISCOGRAPHY:
American Holocaust [Winkte Music 1994]

Johnson, Eddie "King"—(Anishnabe) Folk

Traditional fiddle tunes and gospel songs recorded with Brian Johnson, Bismarck, North Dakota.

DISCOGRAPHY:
Together in God's Love, Vol. 2 [independent 1984]
My Kind of Gospel, Vol. 1 [indpendent 1984]
Chippewa Cajun, Vol. 2 [independent 1983]
Chippewa Cajun, Vol. 1 [independent 1981]
Chippewa Fiddle by Eddie "King" Johnson [independent 1980]

Johnson, Janice-Marie—(Stockbridge Munsee) Pop/R & B

Born 1956, Los Angeles, California. Johnson's father was a musician, and she grew up learning her chops singing in Los Angeles jazz clubs, where she opened for Miles Davis and others. She learned bass guitar when she was in college, and in 1971 she met other musicians to form the band A Taste of Honey: Percy Kibble, keyboards; Hazel Payne, guitar; and Donald Johnson, drums. They met Fonce Mizell and Larry Mizell, former Motwon producers, who helped sign the band to Capitol Records. They generated numerous multiplatinum hits, including "Boogie Oogie Oogie," "World Spin," and "Do It Good," as well as their version of Kyu Sakamoto's "Sukiyaki." This Grammy-winning group dissolved in the late 1980s. Johnson continued to tour and record and later moved to Wisconsin and created Native-roots projects with Robert Tree Cody (*See*: Flute Music).

DISCOGRAPHY:
"Until the Eagle Falls" [Tastebuds 2002] w/ Robert Tree Cody, single
Hiatus of the Heart [Tastebuds 2000]
One Taste of Honey [Capitol 1984] number 67 R & B charts
A Taste of Honey (selected discography):
Back to Back Hits [EMI/Capitol 2002]
Classic Masters [Capitol 2002]
Beauty and the Boogie [Capitol 1997]
A Taste of Honey [Capitol 1997]
Golden Honey [Capitol C2-916398]
Anthology [One Way 1994] best of

Twice As Sweet [Capitol 1981]
Another Taste [Capitol 1979]
Ladies of the Eighties [Capitol 12173]
Videos:
Until the Eagle Falls [Tastebuds 2001] w/ Robert Tree Cody

Johnson, Lee—(Cherokee) Classical

Johnson composed several pieces on the Trail of Tears Cherokee removal. Artists on the album *Trail of Tears* include J. B. Dreadfulwater, vocals; Tommy Wildcat, flute (*See*: Flute Music); Jack Gallup, guitar; the Cherokee Choir; and others. Some of the liner notes are written in Cherokee syllabics.

DISCOGRAPHY:
Trail of Tears [Platinum/Intersound 1998]

Johnson, Nancy—(Plains Cree–Irish) Folk *See*: Carmen Jones

Born September 16, 1955, Toronto, Ontario. Johnson grew up in a musical environment and recorded her first album in 2000.

DISCOGRAPHY:
Pretty Good Sign [Migizi Music 2001]

Jones, Carmen—(Anishnabekwe) Folk

Born March 21, 1958, Garden River, Ontario. In a lifetime of involvement in music and the music industry, Jones was inspired by a number of women artists. With bluegrass, folk, and jazz influences, her original material expresses personal experiences. She has been backed by prominent Toronto musicians, including Eugene Boyer (keyboards/guitar/producer), Jim Heinemen (saxophone/flute; *See*: Wagon Burner Express), and Nancy Johnson (percussion/backup vocals).

DISCOGRAPHY:
Stepping Out [independent 2003]

Jones, Charlie—(Choctaw) Gospel

Born in 1917. Recorded in Fayetteville, Arkansas, Jones sang his collection of Christian hymns in Choctaw; the album includes a songbook.

DISCOGRAPHY:
Choctaw Singing with Charlie Jones [VIP 1994]

Julian B—(Muskogee-Creek) Rap *See*: Shadowyze

Born in 1970. Formerly based in Oklahoma, Julian released his first recording on the SOAR label, gaining some airplay and attention. His millennium project includes Denver-based MC D-Town Brown and Shadowyze, who appear on the track "Free Leonard Peltier."

DISCOGRAPHY:
Upcoming Demo Tracks [Soul Food 2000]
Once upon a Genocide [Warrior/SOAR 1994]

Appearances:
Shadowyze:
World of Illusions [Backbone Records 2002]
Spirit Warrior [Warrior/SOAR 200]

Kalpulli—(Chicano) Rap *See*: Aztlan Underground

Lineup: Phoenix Voice, Urban Native Son, Maloc Cuixin, Long Wind, Yaotl and Bull Dog of Aztlan Underground, Tekolotl, Hue Hue Coyotli, and Shane Bright Path.

Rap from the front lines with words in Nahuatl, Lakota, English, and Spanish, reflecting the band members' diverse backgrounds and origins. Their music contains traditional Peruvian and North American indigenous beats and samples combined with conscious rhymes.

DISCOGRAPHY:
Mixkoatl [Xicano Records and Film 1999]

Kashtin—(Innu) Folk/Rock/Trad *See*: Claude McKenzie, Phillipe McKenzie, Morley Loon, Florent Vollant

Lineup: Claude McKenzie, electric guitar/vocals/harmonica; Florent Vollant, acoustic guitar/vocals/traditional drumming; Gaetan Essiambre, Normand Dube, guitars; Jean Francois Fabiano and Normand Bourdeau, drums/percussion; Daniel Bonin, bass; Rejean Bouchard, acoustic/electric guitars.

A lifelong relationship between Claude McKenzie and Florent Vollant led to the formation of the group that was initially started by Phillipe McKenzie. The duo hit the stage in 1984, performing in their Innu (Montagnais) home reserve of Maliotenam, Quebec, and later emerged as a household name in the world music scene in 1989. They achieved international acclaim almost immediately after opening for the Gipsy Kings in Montreal as their innocent but catchy melodies gained substantial airplay and produced healthy record sales. Kashtin's name was taken from the Innu word for "tornado" and aptly describes their ascent to fame. The first album sold more than 150,000 copies in six months, earning double-platinum status in Canada and gold in France within seven weeks of its release, topping the 500 Best-Selling Chart and the top-fifty charts in Europe. By the year's end, album sales totaled more than 225,000 units, which was an astounding achievement considering they recorded their music in a language spoken by fewer than ten thousand people. A year later the duo received four of Quebec music industry's Felix Awards, including Album of the Year, Best First Album, Best Country-Folk

Album, and Lighting Design and Sound for Live Performances. Despite all the attention and acclaim, their music was banned from airplay in Quebec during the Oka crisis of 1990. However, their second release, *Innu*, sold more than 80,000 units, giving it gold status in Canada. Additional projects and guest appearances include Robbie Robertson's *Music for the Native Americans*. Robertson also appeared on their third album, *Akua Tuta*, which received a 1995 Juno nomination for Aboriginal Recording of the Year and includes their first English single, "Son of the Sun," written by Willie Dunn. The duo continued to appear together amid rumours of a breakup, but by the late 1990s they were releasing solo projects. For a Native act to perform in an indigenous language and nevertheless gain international success was an impressive and unexpected achievement.

DISCOGRAPHY:

Akua Tuta [Groupe Concept/Musicor 1994]
Innu [Groupe Concept/Musicor 1991]
Kashtin [Groupe Concept/Musicor 1989]

Singles:

"Tshinuau vous autres/All of you" [Groupe Concept/Musicor 1991] w/ interview
"Ishkues fille/Girl" [Groupe Concept/Musicor 1991]
"Tshinanu/Tipatshimun/Harricana/E Uassiuian" [Groupe Concept/Musicor 1989]

Appearances:

Robbie Robertson:
Music for the Native Americans [Capitol 1994]
Various:
True North Concerts—Truly Something [CBC North 2000] comp
Putumayo Presents a Native American Odyssey [Putumayo 1998] comp
Silencing the Guns [Arthur Lamothe, 1997] sdtk

Songs of the Spirit [Worldly/Triloka 1996] comp
Due South: The Television Soundtrack [Nettwerk/EMI 1996] sdtk
Here and Now: A Celebration of Canadian Music [Sony 1995] comp
Children of the World [Groupe Concept/Musicor 1994] comp
Dance Me Outside [Denon 1994] sdtk

Videos:

Akua Tuta; Ashtam Nashue; Son of the Sun [Groupe Concept/Sony 1994]
Ishkuess; Harricana [Groupe Concept 1991]
Tshinanu; Euassiuian; Tipatshimun [Groupe Concept 1989]

Kearney, Christopher—
(Cheyenne-Araphao) Folk/Rock

Born December 6, 1951, Toronto, Ontario. Raised in San Francisco's Bay Area, Kearney later served in the Vietnam War from 1969 to 1970. He moved back to Toronto in the early 1970s, where Gordon Lightfoot helped him record the single "A Theme for Jody" on Lightfoot's Early Morning Productions. After signing with Capitol Records, Kearney became a musician of some renown. His material reflected cultural roots and the pitfalls of love, war, desire, and fame. Along with the Stampeders in 1972, he represented Canada at the Seventh Rio International Song Festival in Rio de Janeiro, Brazil. Kearney's last Canadian recording was "(Letter from) Sarajevo," written with Scott Lane and Neil Dobson. This benefit project enlisted the talents of Sylvia Tyson, Molly Johnson, Ian Tyson, Tom Cochrane, Rick Emmett, Murray McLaughlin, the Niagara Children's Choir, Bryan Adams, and others.

DISCOGRAPHY:

China [CBS/Epic 1981] w/ Danny McBride and Bill King
Sweet Water [Capitol/EMI 1974] w/ Jackson Hawk

Pemmican Stash [Capitol/EMI 1973]
Christopher Kearney [Capitol/EMI 1972]

Singles:
"Steady Ground/Runnin' Child" [Capitol 1975] seven-inch vinyl
"One Helluva Rock 'N' Roll Band/Young-bird" [Capitol 1973] seven-inch vinyl
"Loosen Up/Let It Be Gone" [Capitol 1971] seven-inch vinyl
"Country Lady/Rocking Chair Ride" [Capitol 1971] seven-inch vinyl
"A Theme for Jody" [Early Morning Productions/MCA 1970] seven-inch vinyl

Appearances:
Canadian Artists [Warner 1993] comp

Keenan, Irene, Jr. — (Hochunk) Blues/ Rock

Based in Wisconsin. Keenan's throaty vocals are reminiscent of Janis Joplin's, with a Michelle Shocked undertone. Her album is an impressive onslaught of strong vocals and well-directed musical energy.

DISCOGRAPHY:
Dreamer Has Awaken [independent 2001]

Keplin, Ryan; a.k.a "Fiddlin' Lefty" — (Anishnabe) Country

Born March 11, 1971, Belcourt, North Dakota. An exceptional left-handed fiddle player who is equally adept at playing guitar (acoustic and bass) and drums. He writes and performs his own material and teaches at Turtle Mountain Community Elementary School.

DISCOGRAPHY:
Keplin's Breakdown [Sunshine 2000]
Fiddlin' Lefty [Sunshine SSBCT 447]

Keshane, Mike, and Whitestone — Country Gospel

DISCOGRAPHY:
Rich Man [Sunshine SSCT 6014]

Kid Frost — (Chicano) Rap *See*: Haida, Latin Alliance, Litefoot

This East Los Angeles rapper first made waves with his solo project *Hispanic Causing Panic* and with collaborations with Latin Alliance. His collaboration with Litefoot in the mid-1990s resulted in some tribal-based, politically conscious projects that included the gangster attitude of the rap genre coupled with a lyrical and musical strength that established a large commercial presence for Kid Frost in the hip-hop scene. Later projects include *When Hell A. Freezes Over* with Slowpain, *Smile Now Die Later*, and *East Side Story*. Kid Frost was featured in the photo-essay book *Who Shot Ya?* [Harper Collins 2002] by photographer Ernie Paniccioli (Anishnabe), with text by Kevin Powell.

DISCOGRAPHY:
When Hell A. Freezes Over [independent 1998]
Hispanic Causing Panic [Virgin 1990]

Kinrawk — Rock

Lineup: Lance Tailfeathers, lead vocals/ guitars/synthesizer; Garrett Tailfeathers, drums/backup vocals (*See*: Keith Secola); Curt Tailfeathers, bass/backup vocals; Myron Fox, acoustic/electric guitars. From Lethbridge, Alberta, Canada.

DISCOGRAPHY:
Red, Raw, and Ready [SOAR 1991]

Kiowarini—(Wendat) Folk/Pop

This group recorded at Studio DBM in Montreal, Quebec, in the late 1960s or early 1970s. Its strange mix of folk and Native music gave its material something of a tourist flavor. Additional musicians included Michel Deguire, Robert Turmel, Pierre Sauve, Norman McLellan, Pierre Martin, Claude Vincent, Pierre Clement, Marc Lalonde, Ovila Blais, and Norman Bouchard (producer). The front cover of their one album features Kiowarini, with Micheline Kawina Gros Louis.

DISCOGRAPHY:
Chante le dernier soufflé de sa nation [PAX 6608/POO-63]

Knifewing—(Chiricahua Apache) Rock/Trad

Born January 2, 1957. Knifewing Segura, performer and artisan, is known predominantly for his jewelry and visual art. His music entails historical and cultural subjects in a contemporary style; along with his twelve-string guitar, he uses a variety of traditional instruments.

DISCOGRAPHY:
One Spirit Two Worlds [independent 1997]
First American Heroes—Instrumental [independent 1991]
First American Heroes [independent 1991]

Knight, Chester, and the Wind— (Cree) Rock *See*: Arctic/Circumpolar: Lucy Idlout

The Wind Lineup: Chester Knight (born April 18, 1956, Muskoday First Nation, Saskatchewan), guitar/vocals; Hal Shrank, drums/percussion; Brent Taylor, lead guitar/rhythm/bass; Vernon Knight, Thelma Knight, Don Froese, backup vocals.

Knight combined his unique style of singing and songwriting with cultural and historical references in a sharp lyrical framework. Knight's performances included major festivals across Canada and the Grammy Nominee Showcase in Hollywood, California, February 26, 2002. He received a CAMA for Best Group, 1999; Outstanding Aboriginal Recording at the Prairie Music Awards, 1999; three Juno nominations for Aboriginal Recording of the Year, 1997, 2000, and 2003. *Falling Down* was reissued in the United States as *Windfall*.

DISCOGRAPHY:
Standing Strong [Arbor/SOAR 2002]
Falling Down [Falcon's Dream 1999] reissued as *Windfall* [SOAR 2001]
Freedom [Falcon's Dream 1996]

Appearances:
The Juno 2000 Collection [CARAS 2000] two-CD comp
Urban Skins, Vol. 3 [SOAR 2000] comp
Urban Skins, Vol. 1 [SOAR 1999] comp
Festival to Go [Festival Records 1998] comp

Videos:
Pocohontas [Falcon's Dream 1999]

Koljademo—New Age/Folk/Rock

Lineup: Lennie Gomes (Pomo), bass/vocals; Cal Hopper (Pomo), vocals; Tom Hayashi (Japanese), synthesizer/piano; Randy Quan (Japanese), guitar; with Pomo elders Eleanor Stevenson Gonzales and Cornelius Jack Stevenson.

The project was named after Pomo elder Josephine Green Stevenson (1853–1936). The group's music is based on traditional Pomo teachings, culture, and history from precontact to colonialism. Their work features archival taped voices of Pomo elders Eleanor Stevenson Gonzales and Cornelius Jack Stevenson (1902–83).

DISCOGRAPHY:
Destined Love Traveller [Natural Visions/ SOAR 1998]

Appearances:
Alcatraz Is Not an Island [James Fortier, 2002] score

Koskanuba—(Blackfoot) Powwow Rock

Lineup: Cherrilene Cardinal, lead vocals; Helmer Twoyoungmen, vocals/guitar; Faron Twoyoungmen, lead guitar; Lance Twoyoungmen, Native drums; Fred Powderface, drums. From Morley, Alberta.

DISCOGRAPHY:
Koskanuba Kehew Wetchin [KMFN 1995]

Appearances:
Music from Turtle Island [Turtle Island Music 1999] comp

Kotay, Ralph—(Kiowa) Gospel

Kotay specialized in singing gospel hymns in the Kiowa language in the 1970s.

DISCOGRAPHY:
Traditional Kiowa Hymns, Vol. 4 [Indian Sounds IS-3503]
Traditional Kiowa Hymns, Vol. 3 [Indian Sounds IS-3502]
Traditional Kiowa Hymns, Vol. 2 [Indian Sounds IS-3501]
Traditional Kiowa Hymns, Vol. 1 [Indian Sounds IS-3500]

Appearances:
Comanche Church Hymns, Vol. 1 [Indian Sounds IS-3551] comp

Laderoute, Eugene—(Metis) Fiddle

An award-winning and respected fiddle player, Laderoute recorded mostly original material.

DISCOGRAPHY:
Fiddle Fire [Sunshine ssbct 422]
Rosin on the Bow [Sunshine ssbct 419]

Appearances:
Fiddle Legends [Sunshine 2000] comp

LaFarge, Peter—(Narragansett) Folk
See: Ancestral Fire, Tomas Obomsawin, Jim Pepper, Keith Secola

1931–1965
Born in Fountain, Colorado, though no official birth certificate exists. A folk music pioneer, LaFarge composed consciousness-raising songs that placed him front and center in the folk music scene of the early 1960s and that influenced many contemporary songwriters. Adopted by Oliver LaFarge, author and one-time Indian agent in the U.S. Southwest, Peter grew up with an understanding of Native culture and politics.

LaFarge hosted his own radio show at age fourteen, in Colorado Springs, Colorado. In his late teens, he indulged in his passions for rodeo riding and singing, and jammed with blues artists Josh White, Big Bill Broonzy, and Cisco Houston. He enlisted in the U.S. Navy in the late 1940s and served in Korea, where he was awarded five Battle Stars. After suffering injuries from rodeo riding and amateur boxing, he studied at the Goodman School of Theater in Chicago, then moved to New York City. He became a local favorite in Greenwich Village, where he was often joined onstage by contemporaries Bob Dylan, Dave Van Ronk, Ramblin' Jack Elliot, and Pete Seeger. He later met up with a blossoming Buffy Sainte-Marie; together, they worked on Native activism when he formed the Federation for American Indian Rights.

His songs, later covered by Johnny Cash on the album *Bitter Tears* [Columbia 1964], propelled LaFarge to greater notoriety. Cash raised the ire of narrow-minded critics who called for his resignation from the Country Music Association for recording such outspoken material.

Known for his strong vocal ability, crafty wordsmithing, and minimalistic guitar work, LaFarge opened the doors for future generations of Native performers. In expressing his views on the injustices against indigenous people in America, his music was prophetic to the coming era of Indian activism as songs such as "The Ballad of Ira Hayes" reached the top of the country charts. His activities spanned music, rodeo riding, athletics, stage acting, and theatrical writing. He was a regular contributor to *Sing Out! Folk Song Magazine* and a contributing editor for *Broadside* magazine. He married Danish singer Inger Neilsen, who appears on his *Peter Lafarge Sings Women's Blues* album; she recorded her own project, *Danish Folk Songs* [Folkways FW-8819]. LaFarge died suddenly on October 27, 1965, in New York City. The official cause of death was a stroke, though some suspected foul play.

DISCOGRAPHY:

Songs of the Cowboys/Iron Mountain and Other Songs [Bear Family 1992] CD
As Long as the Grass Shall Grow/On the Warpath [Bear Family 1992] CD
On the Warpath [Folkways 1965]
Peter LaFarge Sings Women's Blues [Folkways 1964; Verve 1965]
Songs of the Cowboys [Folkways 1964]
Peter LaFarge Sings Love Songs [Folkways CS-2534]
As Long as the Grass Will Grow [Folkways 1963, reissued 1968]
Iron Mountain and Other Songs [Folkways 1962]
Ira Hayes and Other Ballads [Columbia 1961] rare

Appearances:

Cowboy Songs from Folkways [Smithsonian Folkways 1991; Rounder 1992] comp
Newport Folk Festival [Vanguard 1991] live comp
An Anthology of North American Indian and Eskimo Music [Folkways 1973] comp

Covers of LaFarge's Songs (listed alphabetically):

Ancestral Fire:
"Drums" on *Honouring Who We Are* [Bear Paw Music 2002]
Johnny Cash:
"The Ballad of Ira Hayes" on *Bitter Tears* [Columbia 1964]
"The Ballad of Ira Hayes" appears on at least ten Cash albums.
Bob Dylan:
"Ballad of Ira Hayes" on *Bob Dylan* [Columbia 1973]
Kinky Friedman:
"Ballad of Ira Hayes" on *Lasso from El Paso* [Epic 1976; Varese 1999]
"Ballad of Ira Hayes" on *From One Good American to Another* [Fruit of the Tune 1995]
Tom Obomsawin:
"Indian Drums," "Ira Hayes," "The General" on *Abenakis* [Canyon 1990]
Jim Pepper:
"Senecas (As Long as the Grass Will Grow)" and "Drums" on *Pepper's Powwow* [Embryo 1971]
Pete Seeger:
"Ira Hayes" on *Little Boxes and Other Broadsides* [Smithsonian Folkways 1965]
"Coyote My Little Brother" on *God Bless the Grass* [Sony 1998]
Keith Secola:
"Crimson Parsons" on *Circle* [AKINA 1992]
Patrick Sky:
"Ballad of Ira Hayes" on *Patrick Sky* [Fontana 1965]
Townes Van Zandt:
"Ira Hayes" on *Road Songs* [Sugar Hill 1994]
"Ballad of Ira Hayes" on *Highway Kind* [Sugar Hill 1997]

Lamanite Generation—Gospel

Lineup: Arlene Nofchissey Williams, vocals (*See*: Chief Dan George); John Rainer, flute (*See*: Flute Music); Al Harrington, narration; Michael Campbell, vocals; Carnes Burson, words and music.

Andean ensemble: Edgar Zurita, flutes;
Julio Ortiz, vocals/guitar.

Hawaiian ensemble: Shawn Keliliiki,
Jody Wihongi, Manu Sekona, Hama Sadler,
vocals; Kenneth Makuakane, Randy
Ngum, words/music; Ron Saltmarsh, Ron
Simpson, instruments.

Formed at Brigham Young University as
a musical variety show, this group's work
encompasses North American, Andean,
and Hawaiian music.

DISCOGRAPHY:
Go My Son [Proud Earth/Canyon 1988;
   Tantara Records 1994]
From the Eagle's Bed [BYU 1989]
The Lamanite Generation [BYU 1985]

**Lambert, Burt, and the Northern
Express**—(Anishnabe) Country/Rock

Lineup: Burt Lambert, Ronald Garneau,
Lance Azure, Mike Hamley. From Belcourt, North Dakota.

DISCOGRAPHY:
Just Arriving [independent 1979]

LaRue, Lisa—(Cherokee) New Age/
Traditional *See*: Coyote Zen

LaRue's album was recorded with Joan Hill
(Chee-se-quah and Creek) and Greg Ellis,
percussion.

DISCOGRAPHY:
Beloved Tribal Women [Natural Visions/
   SOAR 1994]

Appearances:
Awakening the Spirit [SOAR 2000] comp

Latin Alliance—(Chicano) Rap

Lineup: Kid Frost, ALT, Markski, Mellow
Man Ace, and Ralph M (turntables); album
produced by Will Roc and Tony G.

DISCOGRAPHY:
Latin Alliance [Virgin 1991]

Laughing, Lawrence—(Mohawk)
New Age *See*: Joanne Shenandoah

Born 1961. Theatrical performer, storyteller, and traditional vocalist. Laughing's
Silver Wave albums offer a collection
of modern interpretations of traditional
songs, with acoustic backup from Tom
Wasinger and Mark McCoin. Laughing
appears with Rebecca Chartrand (Anishnabekwe), Happy Laughing, and Norm
Lussier on *Music from the XIII Pan-Am
Games*.

DISCOGRAPHY:
Now Our Minds Are One [Silver Wave
   2000]
On Ji Da [Sunshine 1999] w/ Rebecca Char-
   trand
Orenda [Silver Wave 1998] w/ Joanne
   Shenandoah

Appearances:
Tribal Legends [Earth Beat! 2002] comp
Bears [Silver Wave 2001] sdtk
Prayer for Peace [Silver Wave 2000] comp
Music from the XIII Pan-Am Games [Water
   Lily Records 1999] sdtk

Lauzon, Jani—(Metis) Folk/Rock/
Blues *See*: Tomson Highway

Born September 29, 1959, Kimberley,
British Columbia. Lauzon started singing
professionally at age seventeen in Vancouver's club scene. Finding her way to
Manitoulin Island, Ontario, she connected
deeply with Anishnabe roots and traditional teachings. Musician, puppeteer,
and actor, she was nominated in 1994 for
a Dora Mavor Moore Award for her role
in Tomson Highway's *Rez Sisters*. Her
album *Blue Voice New Voice* received a
Juno nomination, Best Music of Aboriginal
Canada Recording, 1995; *Thirst* received

the same nomination in 1999. While working with the Toronto-based Centre for Indigenous Theatre, she wrote and performed *The Scrubbing Project* with Michelle St. John (*See*: Contemporary Soundtracks: *The Business of Fancy Dancing*) and Monique Mojica. She made her directorial debut with the production *Waiora*, written by Hone Kouka (Maori), 2003.

DISCOGRAPHY:
Thirst [Ra 1998]
Blue Voice New Voice [Ra 1994]
The Panthers [independent 1993] cass
Double Take [independent 1986] cass
Jani, Jazz Live [independent 1985] cass
Jani and the Soda Jerks [independent 1984] cass
"Don't Tell Me" [independent 1982] cassingle
Eleven O'Clock Blues Band [independent 1982]

Appearances (listed alphabetically):
Susan Hookong:
Diamonds [DWS 1995]
Kanatan Aski:
Kanatan Aski [Dark Jaguar 1993]
Crystal Lynn Shawanda:
Will You Love Me Too? [independent 1994] backup vocals/flute
boo Watson:
Opening Moves [independent 1999] backup vocals/flute *See*: Unceded Band
Various:
Skin Tight Blues [Sweet Grass/EMI 2002] comp
Music from Turtle Island [Turtle Island Music 1999] comp
Songs for Chiapas "Off the Record" [Ra Records 1999] comp
Heartbeat 2: More Voices of First Nations Women [Folkways 1998] comp *See*: Traditional/Archival Compilations
Hearts of the Nations [Banff Centre for the Arts/Sweet Grass 1997] comp *See*: Traditional/Archival Compilations
Dreamcatchers [Polygram 1995] comp
Here and Now: A Celebration of Canadian Music [Sony 1995] comp

Stuck on a Cold Steel Pole [Duke Street 1995] comp
Summerfolk [GBFS 1995] comp
Toronto Blues Today [Toronto Blues Society 1995] comp
Duncan Campbell Scott [NFB 1994] sdtk
Jenny's Song [Laughing Dog Plays 1994] radio play
Heart and Soul [Velvet 1993] comp
Lupi, the Great White Wolf [Debahjumujig 1993] sdtk
The Making of Warriors [CBC 1993] sdtk
Sacajewea [CBC 1992] sdtk
Son of Ayash [Native Earth Performing Arts 1992] score

Lavallee, Wayne—(Cree-Metis) Rock

Born May 9, 1971, Vancouver, British Columbia. Lavallee studied guitar and music theory at the Douglas Academy of Music, Surrey, British Columbia. He combined experimental rock and folk with a vocal character reminiscent of Geddy Lee of Rush. Based in Vancouver, Lavallee performed throughout the region and recorded with Russell Wallace and Sandy Scofield.

Lineup: Wayne Lavallee, vocals/guitar; Barry Meldrum, drums; Pat Meldrum, bass/electric guitar/keyboards; Tracy Williams, harmonica; Jason Burnstick, mandolin/flamenco guitar; Barry Meldrum, drums; Russell Wallace, vocals/chants; traditional singers: Kaya George, Cedar George, Debbie Parker, Jesus Parker, Ruben George, Damian George, Justin George, Amy Marie George, and Chief Leonard George.

DISCOGRAPHY:
Green Dress [independent 2004]
Liv Again [independent 2000]

Appearances (listed alphabetically):
Sandy Scofield:
Riel's Road [Arpeggio 2002]
Russell Wallace:
Chinook Winds [Banff Centre 2000]

Lavi, Lara—Folk/Rock *See*: Song
Catchers

Raised in a serious musical family and classically trained, a very young Lavi studied
under Andre Previn and at the age of sixteen toured and sang backup for Buddy
Guy. The musical diversity of her background allowed her to branch out into
other areas. She formed her own band, Red
Dog Zen, before becoming cocreator of
Song Catchers and co-owner of the Seattle-
based label Very Juicy Records. She has
also served as the attorney for the Muckle-
shoopt and other Northwest nations.

DISCOGRAPHY:
Inside the Red Room [Very Juicy Records
     1998]

Lawrence, Eddy—(Mohawk) Folk/
Blues

Born in Kahnewake, Quebec, Lawrence
released more than eight very obscure
independent albums.

SELECTED DISCOGRAPHY:
Going to Water [Snowplow Records 2001]

Leach, George—(Stl'atl'imx) Blues/
Rock *See*: Leela Gilday

Born September 27, 1976. A visual artist
with a passion to play music, Leach decided to teach himself some chords on the
guitar. In 1996, he moved into acting, with
roles in television, film, and theater productions, including Tomson Highway's
Mortality, staged by the Toronto-based
Volcano Theatre Company in 2002. His
blistering blues slide style combines with
rock-steady stamina in both his up-tempo
tracks and his ballads. His debut album
received two CAMA Awards for Best Male
Artist and Best Rock Album, 2000. The
video single *Young Enough* earned Best
Video at San Francisco's American Indian

Film Festival, 2002, and national airplay
on both MUCH MUSIC and APTN. He
has opened for many well-known artists,
including Bo Diddley, Robbie Robertson,
Susan Aglukark, and Great Big Sea. As his
reputation grew, he collaborated with guitarist Domenic Troiano (the Guess Who).
His numerous television appearances include the series *Music Works* [CBC 2003].

DISCOGRAPHY:
Just Where I'm At [independent 2000]

Appearances (listed alphabetically):
Leela Gilday:
spirit world, solid wood [Diva Sound 2002]
Florent Vollant:
Katak [D7 Recordings 2003]
Various:
20 Aboriginal Greatest Hits, Vol. 3 [Sun-
     shine 2002] comp

Videos:
Young Enough [Big Soul Productions/
     APTN 2002]

Lederman, Anne—(Metis) Fiddle

Lederman was one of the first researchers of Metis music to compile and present
material on old Native and Metis fiddle
styles.

DISCOGRAPHY:
Fiddlesong [independent 2002]
Scatter the Ashes: Music of Old Ontario
     [independent 1999]

Appearances:
*Old Native and Metis Fiddling in Mani-
     toba*, Vol. 2 [Falcon Productions 1987]
     comp, producer
*Old Native and Metis Fiddling in Mani-
     toba*, Vol. 1 [Falcon Productions 1986]
     comp, producer

Lee, Jess—(Metis) Country

Former lead singer and bassist for the Juno-nominated Midnite Rodeo Band, which included in its lineup lead guitarist Lloyd Shingoose and guitarist Ed Molyski. This producer and songwriter pumped out four hit albums on RCA in the 1980s. Lee's credentials include the British Columbia Country Music Association's Song of the Year Award for "Honky Tonk Love Affair" and its Country Male Vocalist of the Year, as well as a Juno nomination for Best Music of Aboriginal Canada Recording, 1996.

Based in British Columbia, where the tragic events of the Gustafson Lake standoff in 1995 turned outrage into musical expression on Lee's 1995 album. Lee also recorded songs of the Metis experience and performed with champion fiddle player Calvin Volrath in 1995.

DISCOGRAPHY:
Sacred Ground [12th Street 1995]
Honky Tonk Love Affair [Music Line 1991; Spinner Music 1992]

Videos:
Sacred Ground and *Walking the White Line* [12th Street 1995]

Leupp Family Singers—(Dineh) Gospel

DISCOGRAPHY:
Leupp Family Singers, Vol. 1 [Canyon 1987]

Litefoot—(Eastern Cherokee) Hip-Hop *See*: Haida, Kid Frost, Mistic

Born Gary Paul Davis, circa 1970, Oakland, California. Though Davis likes a shroud of mystery about his origins, he was raised in Tulsa, Oklahoma, where he earned a football scholarship to attend the University of Tulsa. In 1988, his sister Angelique, who was singing professionally in Los Angeles, California, asked him to pen some rhymes for a rap she wanted to include on her recording. With his interest piqued, he entered and won the national Rap Search Contest.

He started his professional career in 1992 with his first release, *Money*. A major label executive snubbed Litefoot's approach to being the "first Native rapper" and told him, "all Indians ever buy is alcohol." The experience galvanized Litefoot's resolve to make it as an independent artist. He established Red Vinyl Records and turned to acting; his Hollywood earnings helped bolster a recording career. He later signed on several Native artists, including Haida, the Prophet, Flawless, flute players Tommy Wildcat and Funmaker (*See*: Flute Music), and collaborated with Kid Frost, Tony G, and others in the larger hip-hop scene. His starring role in *Indian in the Cupboard* earned him a Best Actor award from First Americans in the Arts and helped him break more fully into the mainstream. His roles in other films, including *The Song of Hiawatha* and *Mortal Kombat II*, brought his second Best Actor Award from First Americans in the Arts, and his work in *Kull the Conqueror* garnered his third Best Actor Award from First Americans in the Arts. He won the NAMA Best Rap Artist in 1998 and its Best Rap/Hip-Hop Recording for *Rez Affiliated* in 2000 and was featured in the photo-essay book *Who Shot Ya?* [Harper Collins 2002], photography by Ernie Paniccioli (Anishnabe) and text by Kevin Powell.

DISCOGRAPHY:
Native American Me [Red Vinyl 2003]
The Messenger [Red Vinyl 2003]
Tribal Boogie [Red Vinyl 2001]
Rez Affiliated [Red Vinyl 1999] w/ Warpaint and Coolio
The Clown Kutz [Red Vinyl 1999] bonus tracks
The Lite Years: The Very Best of Mr. Litefoot 1985–1999 [Red Vinyl 1999] w/ interview clips

The Life and Times [Red Vinyl 1998]
Good Day to Die [Red Vinyl 1996] w/ Kid
  Frost
The Messenger [Red Vinyl 1995]
"Cherokee Stomp Dance"/"For My People"
  [Red Vinyl 1995]
Seein' Red [Red Vinyl 1994]
"Native Tongue" [Red Vinyl 1993] cassingle
The Money [Red Vinyl 1992]

Appearances:

Eschikagou Powwow 2000 LIVE! [Gather-
  ing of Nations Records 2001] comp *See*:
  Powwow Compilations
*Litefoot Presents the Sounds of Indian
  Country* [Red Vinyl RVR-0970] comp
The Red Ryders, Vol. 2 [Red Vinyl 1999]
  comp
The Red Ryders, Vol. 1 [Red Vinyl 1999]
  comp

Film and Videos:

Picture of Priority [Red Vinyl 1999] live
  concert
Kull the Conqueror [John Nicolella, 1997]
The Song of Hiawatha [Jeffrey Shore, 1997]
Mortal Kombat II [Alan Rudolph, 1995]
Indian in the Cupboard [Frank Oz, 1995]

Little Elk, David—(Lakota) Rock

Born October 31, 1961, Mobridge, South
Dakota. A longtime session player and language and cultural instructor, Little Elk
built his own recording studio and created several projects that promoted the
traditional values of health and spirituality.

DISCOGRAPHY:

Wana Wahi [Rez Boy 2000]
Elk Dreamer [Rez Boy 2000]
David Little Elk [Rez Boy 1996] cass
Malakota Wana Wahi [Rez Boy 1994] cass

Little Wolf; a.k.a. Jim Wilson—
(Choctaw) *See*: Robbie Robertson,
Tulku, Walela

Born and raised in Texas, Little Wolf
worked with the Cheyenne Tribal Council in Lame Deer, Montana; he cofounded
Polygram's country/rock band Blue Northern with Billy Cowsill (of the Cowsills)
and earned a number 1 country single and
six top-ten pop and country singles. He is
also long-time collaborator with Grammy
Award winner Queen Ida.

  Lineup: Jim Wilson, instrumental-
ist/composer/producer (most notably of
Robbie Robertson's *Music for the Native
Americans*); Geoffery Gordon, drums/per-
cussion; Walela and Paula Nelson (Willie
Nelson's daughter), backup vocals; Robbie
Robertson, guest guitar appearance; Jim
Stalling, bass; John Bartlit, drums.

DISCOGRAPHY:

Wolf Moon [Triloka 1997] w/ Walela and
  Robbie Robertson
Entering the Circle [Worldly/Triloka 1997]
Dream Song [Worldly/Triloka 1995]

Lomayesva, Casper—(Hopi-Dineh)
Reggae

Born Calvin Arthur Lomayesva, September 28, 1967, Winslow, Arizona. When
Freddie McGregor first performed in
northeastern Arizona's Hopiland in 1985,
turntable DJ, singer, performer, and phi-
losopher Casper Lomayesva (pronounced
Lo-ma-da-wa) ventured to Jamaica to seek
out the roots of reggae. Thereafter, fronting
his band 6-0-2, he chose a musical form
that best conveyed the lyrics of culture
and politics while combining soul, R & B,
and rock grooves. His first album stirred
interest, prompting cross-country tours
and airplay that inspired a second release.
Citing his grandfather as a major influence, Lomayesva looked to his traditional
roots and created his own unique style of
reggae. Band members and session players

Casper Lomayesva's *Sounds of Reality* (2000) transformed reggae into Native expression. Courtesy Third Mesa Music.

Casper Lomayesva. Photo by Neal Ullstead.

who have worked with Lomayesva include William Banks, Danny Clarke, Jamie Cirrito, Isaac Lomayesva of the Bear Shield Singers, members of 6-0-2, and others. *Sounds of Reality* received a NAMA Award for Best World Music, 2001.

DISCOGRAPHY:
Sounds of Reality [Third Mesa Music 2000]
Original Landlord [Third Mesa Music 1997]

Singles:
"Brother Leonard" [Third Mesa Music 2003] w/ Quiltman *See*: John Trudell
"Honor the People" [Third Mesa Music 2003]

Appearances:
Urban Skins, Vol. 2 [Warrior/SOAR 1999] comp
Urban Skins, Vol. 1 [Warrior/SOAR 1999] comp
Dread in America, Vol. 3: *Thousand Years of Peace* [Natural Mystic 1997] comp
Dread in America, Vol. 2: *Babylon Burns* [Natural Mystic 1995] comp

Longacre, Ernest Clayton—(Tsalagi) Folk

Indian Head Penny Band Lineup: Ernest Clayton Longacre, lead vocals/acoustic guitars/drum; Duffy Williams (Paiute), bass/mandolin; Kevin Blackwood (Cherokee), drums; Bob Smith (Cherokee), lead/electric guitars; Ann Marie Ruijacich, violin; Elliot Rodriguez (Taino), bongos/background vocals; Julio Feliciano (Taino), congas/timbales/background vocals; Jair, maracas/tambourines/shakers; Heritage Boys Drum: Laurence Magee (Cere), John Blankenship (Cherokee), Laurence Walves (Assiniboine), Ian LaFontaine (Anishnabe); backup singers: Shiloh Marie Longacre (Tsalagi), Bryna Lawrence (Squamish), Pamela Johnston (Anishnabekwe), Nikolai Brown (Chikasaw), Susan Colfield (Cherokee), Paula Wilson (East Coast Tsalagi).

DISCOGRAPHY:
In the Spirit of Crazy Horse [Longacre
Music 1997] four-track EP

Longboat, Timothy John—
(Mohawk) Classical

Born August 7, 1959, Six Nations Reserve,
Grand River Territory, Ontario. Described
as a composer of new music, Longboat incorporates pop rock with compositions
that use Native instruments within a Western musical framework. His formal education includes enrollment at the University
of Miami, Coral Gables, Florida, where
he graduated with a bachelor's degree in
music composition (including jazz) and a
doctorate in music composition, media
writing, and production, as well as diplo-
mas in recording engineering and recorded
music production from Fanshawe College,
London, Ontario.

He composed orchestral pieces using
Native notalidies and jazz harmonies with
a chromatic palette. Among his smaller
chamber works, his composition "A Distant Bluebird" utilizes traditional instruments such as the eagle bone whistle, horn
shaker, hand drum, and dancers' bells,
with the narration of E. Pauline Johnson's
poem "The Birds' Lullabye" (See: Contemporary Spoken Word: Poetry Recordings).
Many of his works were influenced by
Stravinsky and Debussy, but they utilize
atonal jazz harmonies; his pop-rock creations favor a mature jazz sound similar
to that of Steely Dan or Jackson Browne.
His instruments of choice for composition
include acoustic and electric guitars and
piano.

Longbottom, Ted—(Metis) Folk

Longbottom has been recognized as an
emerging contemporary artist whose material focuses on historical events relating
to the Metis, fur traders, and soldiers. His
baritone voice commands attention within
an upbeat folk repertoire.

Lineup: Ted Longbottom, vocals/guitar;
Daniel Koulack, bass/mandolin/spoons/
bodhran; Murray Pulver, guitar; Bill Spor-
nitz, saxophone; Ben Mink, violin; Geoff
Butler, accordion/flute; Rob Lee, drums;
Ken Whitely, David Wall, Pat Patrick,
Cathy Fink, Marcey Marxer, Shannon
David, Chuck McCandles, background
vocals.

DISCOGRAPHY:
River Road [Festival 2001]
Longbottom [Longbottom 1997]

Appearances:
The Rough Guide to the Music of Canada
[World Music Network 2003, United
Kingdom] comp

Loon, Morley—(Cree) Folk/Trad *See*: Ancestral Fire, Marcel Gagnon, Kashtin

1948–1986
Born May 8, Mistassini, Quebec. A musical ambassador of the James Bay Cree,
Loon traveled throughout North America
delivering his musical message during
the political struggle of the 1970s. While
living in British Columbia, he cofounded
the band Red Cedar, which performed at
the 1980 Black Hills Survival Gathering
in South Dakota, sharing the stage with
Floyd Westerman, the Thunderbird Sisters,
Bonnie Raitt, and others. Singing predominantly in the Cree language, Loon developed a unique style that a wide audience
enjoyed, and he gained national airplay,
paving the way for similar artists. Kashtin cites Loon as a major influence who
inspired the group to write and perform
in their own language. He passed away on
July 14, 1986, following a lengthy illness,
but he left a legacy that continues to inspire performers in the northern region
where he originated.

DISCOGRAPHY:

North Country [independent 1984] cas-single

Cree Songs [CBC Northern Service QCS-1302] six-track EP w/ R. Daignault, flute; J. Kelly, percussion

Songs Sung in Cree Composed and Sung by Morley Loon [CBC Northern Service QC-1271] five-track vinyl EP

Northland My Land [CBC/Boot 1982]

Appearances:

Sweet Grass [CBC North 1982; Trikont 1993, Germany] comp

Los Mocosos—(Chicano) Rock/Hip-Hop

Lineup: Piero El Malo, vocals; Happy Sanchez, bass; Roberto Quintana, percussion; Sebastian Ponti, drums; Steve Carter, keyboards; Andy "El Guero" Stern, guitar; the Hitz Squad, horns/vocals: Gordon Ramos, tenor/alto sax/vocals; Victor Castro, trombone/vocals; Joe Kaline, baritone sax/vocals.

From San Francisco's Mission District, Los Mocosos, or the Inner City Latin Groove Rebels, hit the scene like a tidal wave only to witness the notoriety enjoyed by their contemporaries Ozomatli.

DISCOGRAPHY:

Shades of Brown [Six Degrees 2001]
Mocos Locos [Aztlan 1998]

Appearances:

New World Party [Putumayo 1999] comp

Loud Silence—(Dineh) Rock

Lineup: Ron Lopez, vocals/guitar; Chris Jones, bass; Ray Jones, drums.

DISCOGRAPHY:

Loud Silence [independent 1996]

Lunar Drive—Ambient Rez House

In an attempt to develop workable descriptions for some of the recent music hybrids, I came up with *ambient rez house* to identify categorically the work of Lunar Drive. The term is derived from their blend of ambient (a form of electronica) and house music (a later comination based on funk and disco), combined with elements of jazz, blues, techno, and powwow music.

Lineup on first recording: Sandy Hoover, Count Dubulah, Kevin Locke (*See*: Flute Music), Sam Minkler, Reuben Fast Horse, Henrik Takkenberg, John Benally, Tom Bedonie, Phil Lane Sr. *Lineup on second recording*: Sandy Hoover, Reuben Fast Horse, Ed Walksnice, Rey Cantil, Franklin Khan, Cindy Busher.

Formed in 1996, Flagstaff, Arizona. Combining traditional songs with soundbites, poetry, and techno music, their first release quickly climbed to number 5 on the European world music charts.

DISCOGRAPHY:

All Together Here [Beggars Banquet 1999]
Crying, Looking for You [Nation 1996, United Kingdom] five-song EP
Here at Black Mesa, Arizona [Nation 1996, United Kingdom]

Appearances:

Tribal Fires [Earth Beat! 1997] comp

Videos:

Here at Black Mesa, Arizona [Nation/Beggar's Banquet 1997]

MacIntyre, Brenda; a.k.a. Special Ice—(Metis)

Based in Toronto, Ontario, MacIntyre worked with keyboardist Steve Cogdell and singer Lisette Cogdell at Lionheart Studio (*See*: Contemporary Compilations: The Fire This Time) and recorded a handful of hip-hop/reggae singles. She later formed the hand-drum duo Spirit Wind in 2000 with singer Zainab Amadahy and the band

Midnight Rainbow with the Cogdells and drummer Ken Skinner.

DISCOGRAPHY:
Spirit Wind:
Soul Talkin [independent 2003]
Breathing the Wind [independent 2001]
Midnight Rainbow:
Never Too Late [independent 2002]
Special Ice:
"Bimishay" [independent 1996] cassingle
"Rock-A Talk" [independent 1994] cassingle

Appearances:
As Special Ice:
Impact Music—Sequence 1.0 [Impact 1995] comp
The Gathering: A Compilation of Toronto World Music [Attic World 1990] comp

MacKenzie, Mack—(Mi'kmaq) Rock
See: Three O'Clock Train

Born Malcom MacKenzie, Lincoln, Maine. Founding member of the influential 1980s group Three O'Clock Train, MacKenzie all but disappeared from the music scene after the band's demise. He returned in the mid-1990s to record a solo album and to produce the *Three O'Clock Train* anthology. Two of MacKenzie's compositions appeared in the NFB drama *Train of Dreams* [John N. Smith, 1987].

DISCOGRAPHY:
Mack MacKenzie [Justin' Time 1996]
Three O'Clock Train Anthology [Just a Memory 1996]
"It Takes a Lot to Laugh, It Takes a Train to Cry" B.D. [CBC/Justin' Time 1991]

Malo—(Chicano) Rock/R & B/Jazz

Original Lineup: Jorge Santana, guitar; Pablo Tellez, bass; Arcelio Garcia, lead vocals/percussion; Richard Kermode, piano/organ/percussion; Leo Rosales, tim-

bales/congas/percussion/backup vocals; Hadley Caliman, tenor/baritone saxophone/flute; Forrest Buchtel, trumpet; Luis Gasca, trumpet/flugelhorn.

1994 Lineup: Arcelio Garcia, lead/backup vocals; Martin Cantu, lead/backup vocals; Gabriel Manzo, lead guitar/backup vocals; Tony Menjavar, congas; Gibby Ross, timbales/congas; David George, drums; Victor Pantoja, percussion; Gary Fisher, keyboards; Ramiro Quezada Amador, bass; Steve Rocha, trombone; Carlton Smith, trumpet; Andy Najera, saxophone.

Formed in 1970, San Francisco, California. Referred to as the "poor man's Santana," the group released two albums in their first year out and hit the top-fifteen charts, with the single "Suavecito" at number 18 in 1972. Jorge enlisted Santana percussionists Coke Escovido and Victor Pontoja, as well as Richard Kermode and Luis Gasca, who played in Janis Joplin's Kozmic Blues Band. Gasca had also played with Count Basie, Woody Herman, and Mongo Santamaria. Into the 1990s, long after the original band split up, Garcia and Pontoja continued to play under the Malo name with new material. Several best-of albums and collections followed, with inclusion in compilations such as *Latin Legends Live* and *'70s Smash Hits*, Vol. 6 [Rhino 1993].

DISCOGRAPHY:
Unreleased Vintage Tracks [independent 1998]
Rockin' the Rockies [independent 1997] twenty-fifth anniversary album
Best of Malo [Crescendo 1996]
Senorita [Crescendo 1995]
Malo V [Traq Records 1977]
Ascension [Warner 1974]
Evolution [Warner 1973]
Dos [Warner 1972]
Malo [Warner 1972]

Appearances:
Ay Califas: Raza Rock of the '70s and '80s [Rhino 1998] comp

Chicano Power [Soul Jazz Records 1998]
comp

Man-i-tones—(Cree) Country and Western

Lineup: Roni Beardy, lead vocals/acoustic guitar; Lenny Keno, electric guitar; Eddie Munroe, bass guitar; Brian Beardy, drums/harmonica/vocals.

From Garden Hill, Manitoba. In the 1960s, the various group members attended school in the larger southern communities in the province. When they later traveled to the city of Winnipeg, they returned with many musical influences and recorded an album of rock and country standards.

DISCOGRAPHY:
The Manitones [Sunshine 2001]

Maracle, Jonathan, and Linda Maracle—(Mohawk) Gospel *See*: Broken Walls, Yodeca

Lineup: Jonathan Maracle, rhythm guitar/vocals; Linda Maracle, backup vocals; Andrew Martin, drums/backup vocals; Petri Leppikargis, lead guitar; Mark Shaw, bass.

Jonathan Maracle began recording the local Tyendinaga Mohawk Elders Choir in his recording studio on the Tyendinaga Reserve in southern Ontario. Maracle Studios have recorded projects by David Maracle and Tom Maracle (*See*: Flute Music) and the Peacemakers Drum (*See*: Powwow Music).

DISCOGRAPHY:
Broken Walls [independent 1996]

Appearances (listed alphabetically):
Gary Lalonde and Tundra:
Isumataq [Padger 1992]
Yodeca:
Unsigned 05 [NXNE 2003] comp
Earth Fusion [independent 2001]

Marchand, Donna—(Metis) Folk

Battling the adoption process to find her roots, Marchand studied law and made music a form of activism.

DISCOGRAPHY:
In from the Cold [independent 1998]

Martin, Don Patrick—(Mohawk) Rock/Trad *See*: Mighty Mohawks

Born February, 4, 1957, Kahnawake, Quebec. Martin was raised in a musical family, learning the rudiments from his uncles, Slim Martin and Wallace Martin, who formed the Mighty Mohawks in the 1960s. Providing a musical response to the Oka siege of 1990, Martin combined progressive rock and political statements, all wrapped in Mohawk cultural perspectives and music. With help from friends, supporters, and numerous session players in Europe, he recorded the album in Amsterdam, Holland. The project received substantial airplay and interest on both sides of the Atlantic Ocean. He also appeared in the film *Black Robe* [Bruce Beresford, 1991].

DISCOGRAPHY:
So—This Is America [independent 1991, Holland]

Appearances:
The Fire This Time:
Still Dancing on John Wayne's Head [Extreme 1998] comp
Basslines and Ballistics [Extreme 1991] comp

Martin, Lawrence; a.k.a. Wapistan—(Cree) Country/Trad *See*: Vernon Cheechoo

Born January 12, 1956, Moose Factory, Ontario. This former manager of Wawatay, northern Canada's all-Native communications network, and former mayor of the town of Sioux Lookout, Ontario, turned his attention to music. He was the first winner in the newly established Juno Awards category Best Music of Aboriginal Canada Recording in 1994 for his second album *Wapistan*. His follow-up album, *Message*, was nominated in the same Juno category in 1996. *The Right Combination* received a Juno nomination for Aboriginal Recording of the Year, 2003.

DISCOGRAPHY:
The Right Combination, Cheechoo and Martin [A Spirit Voice/EMI/Page 2002]
Message [First Nations 1995]
Wapistan Is Lawrence Martin [First Nations 1993]
Let's Play Cowboys and Indians [Wawatay 1993] cass

Appearances:
Here and Now: A Celebration of Canadian Music [Sony 1995] comp
I Am an Eagle: The Music from the Legends Project [First Nations 1994] comp
Legends: I Am an Eagle, Radio Special and Interview Clips [First Nations 1994] spoken word *See*: Contemporary Spoken Word: Interview Recordings
Music from the Powerhouse [World Records 1985] comp
Goose Wings [World Records 1981] comp

Videos:
Wache Ay [First Nations 1993]

Martinez, Yolanda—(Apache) Country/Pop

Based in Las Cruces, New Mexico. Martinez is one of eleven children. In addition to being an Arizona-based art gallery owner, Martinez also does Web-based sales and marketing. She lived and worked as a commercial fisher, picture framer, and gallery owner on Kodiak Island, Alaska, for eight years. In 1991, she began to pursue traditional influences in music and later incorporated into her music contemporary flavors that reflect her heritage.

DISCOGRAPHY:
Lonely Warrior [MART 1999]
Dreaming Woman [MART-04]
Prairie Mother [MART-03]
Native Heartbeat [MART-02]
Resounding Spirituality [MART 1992]

Marty Dredd—(Blackfoot) Reggae

Based in Maui, Marty Dredd maximized the language of reggae with a proliferation of albums. He was also included on the compilation album *Reggae Ambassadors Worldwide*, Vol. 1.

DISCOGRAPHY:
Reggae Suite [Five Corners Music 1999]
Versatile Roots [Five Corners Music 1998] w/ Kris Kristofferson
Live! [Five Corners Music 1997]
Reggae for Love [Five Corners Music 1996]

Appearances:
Dread in America, Vol. 2: *Babylon Burns* [Natural Mystic 1995] comp

Mason, Andy—(Mohawk-Cayuga) Folk/Rock

Born December 14, 1962, Toronto, Ontario. A grassroots activist, Mason worked in theater and music to express his perspectives on Native rights. In the mid-1980s, he released a cassette demo with his Crosby, Stills, Nash, and Young tribute band Four Way Street. While based in Ottawa, he played in several groups, including Seventh Fire, Chapter 23, and the Celtic-based Crooked Ham. After moving to Vancouver, British Columbia, in 1998, Mason recorded fifteen years of original material for his debut album. The material drew from Native, bluegrass, and R & B influences, with songs for Big Mountain and Leonard Peltier. The original recording of "Long Walk 49" was made in 1985 through the Ontario Institute of Studies in Education, Toronto.

DISCOGRAPHY:
Long Walk 49 [Raven Hymn 2001]
Four Way Street [independent 1987] cass

Maytwayashing, Cliff—(Cree) Fiddle

DISCOGRAPHY:
Flaming Arrow [Sunshine SSCT-479]
Native Fiddlin' Fever [Sunshine SSCT-443]

McArthur, Maurice—(Nakota) Country/Rock

From Pheasant Rump Nakota Band, Kisbey, Saskatchewan. The track "Tribute to J. J." is dedicated to the Winnipeg-based activist who was shot by police under questionable circumstances; "Take a Stand" was influenced by the 1990 Oka crisis; "Blind Justice" was written for Donald Marshall, a Mi'kmaq man falsely accused of a murder he didn't commit. Other songs are dedicated to McArthur's family and the sacred drum.

Lineup: Clint Dutiaume, fiddle/guitar (*See*: C-Weed); Danny Schur, keyboard/bass/drums; Chantal Kreziazuk, vocals.

DISCOGRAPHY:
Justice Now [Sunshine 1991]

Appearances:
20 Greatest Aboriginal Hits, Vol. 2 [Sunshine 1998] comp

McBride, Mimi—(Lakota) Pop *See*: Brent Michael Davids

Lineup: Mimi McBride, vocals; Joey Trujillo, acoustic/electric guitars; Tim Roth, lead guitar; Kenny Poe, keyboards; Mario Mendivil, bass; Mike Barton, drums; Keith Johnson, traditional drum; Brent Michael Davids, flute.

DISCOGRAPHY:
You Are You [Eagle View Music 1995]

McCabe, Glen—(Metis) Folk/Rock

Born in Winnipeg, Manitoba. McCabe has performed across Canada and internationally. His style is as varied as his human experience. He has also combined traditional healing with his Ph.D. in clinical psychology to help stem family violence.

DISCOGRAPHY:
3rd Degree [Harvelle Music 2002]
Strange Empires [Harvelle Music 1998]

McKenzie, Claude—(Innu) Rock *See*: Kashtin

Born 1967, Schefferville, Quebec. The rockin' half of Kashtin continues on, but a little older and a lot wiser. Material on his first solo recording was sung in Innu, English, and French, backed with hard-strumming acoustics. *Innu Town* received a Juno nomination for Best Music of Aboriginal Canada Recording, 1997; the video single won Best Video at the 1999 American Indian Film Festival, San Francisco, California. He appeared on the Canadian television special *Solstice Rouge* [Prime 2001].

DISCOGRAPHY:
Pishimuss [L-Abe 2004]
Innu Town [Groupe Concept/Musicor 1996]

Appearances:
Urban Skins, Vol. 3 [Warrior/SOAR 2000] comp

Videos:
Innu Town [Groupe Concept/Musicor 1996]

McKenzie, Phillipe—(Innu) Pop/Rock

Some pre-Kashtin work features musicians Phillipe McKenzie, Florent Vollant, James Kelly, and Marc St-Onge. *Mistashipu* is the original Kashtin roots album—the musical birthplace of a traditional and contemporary hybrid.

DISCOGRAPHY:
Indian Songs in Folk Rock Tradition [CBC Northern Service QCS-1422] minivinyl EP
Mistashipu—Great River [CBC/Boot 1982]

Means, Russell—(Lakota)

Born November 10, 1939, Pine Ridge, South Dakota. This Hollywood/AIM personality not only survived, but flourished amid much controversy, most of which was of his own making. After working as a dance instructor in Los Angeles in the 1960s, he propelled his public image through political notoriety as a prominent figure of Indian activism in the early 1970s. His autobiography, *Where White Men Fear to Tread* [St. Martin's Press 1995], was written with Marvin J. Wolf.

DISCOGRAPHY:
Where White Men Fear to Tread [St. Martin's Press 1996] audio book *See*: Contemporary Spoken Word: Audio Books
The Radical [Warrior/SOAR 1994]
Electric Warrior [Warrior/SOAR 1993]

Appearances:
Cash on Delivery: A Tribute to Johnny Cash [CMH 1999] comp
Natural Born Killers [Interscope 1994] sdtk

Selected Film and Television Appearances:
Song of Hiawatha [Jeffrey Shore, 1997]
Pocahontas [Disney Studios 1995]
Natural Born Killers [Oliver Stone, 1994]
Last of the Mohicans [Michael Mann, 1992]
Shining Time Station [PBS 1989]

Medicine Dream—Folk

Lineup: Paul Pike (Mi'kmaq), lead vocals/guitar/keyboard/bass/flute/traditional drumming; Buz Daney (Choctaw), lead tra-

ditional vocals/drumming; John Fields, keyboards/backup vocals; Cea Anderson Nicklie, backup vocals; George Newton (Aluet-Inupiak), lead guitar/vocals; Patrick Lind (Aluet), bass/vocals; Chuck Henman (Apache-Dineh), drums/vocals; Paulette Sierra-Moreno, spoken word.

Medicine Dream's music combines contemporary instrumentation with traditional influences and New Age music. A portion of the profits from *Mawio'mi* were earmarked for sobriety and recovery programs.

DISCOGRAPHY:
Tomegan Gospem [Canyon 2002]
Mawio'mi [Canyon 1999]

Appearances:
Tribal Legends [Earth Beat! 2002] comp

Medicine Men—Rock

Lineup: Paul Little Eagle Carlos, guitar/vocals; Frank Giroux, percussion/drums; Jaoe Cerrato, bass/backup vocals; Louis Gray Eagle, flute; Cochise Anderson, Phil Balzono, Soni Moreno, Pura Fe, backup vocals.

Based in New York City, the group made a measurable impact throughout the eastern United States and Canada in the wake of indigenous peoples' anti-Columbus activities.

DISCOGRAPHY:
Keepers of the Sacred Fire [Savage 1992]
Dig Out the Hatchet [Savage 1992]

Menard, Andrea—(Metis) Jazz/Blues

Born January 5, 1975, Flin Flon, Manitoba. Based in Saskatoon, Saskatchewan, Menard appeared in Tomson Highway's play *Rez Sisters*; in several independent films, including *Betrayed* [Anne Wheeler, 1999] and *Skipped Parts* [Tamra Davis 1998], and in numerous national tele-

Andrea Menard revived 1940s jazz sounds with original material. Photo courtesy Helen Tansey.

vison shows in Canada as well. A talented singer-songwriter, Menard delivered an impressive vocal performance of 1940s jazz style in her highly acclaimed one-act, one-woman play *The Velvet Devil*.

DISCOGRAPHY:
The Velvet Devil [Velvet and Hawk Productions 2002]

Appearances (listed alphabetically):
Edmund Bull:
Indian Boy [Turtle Island Music 2000] backup vocals
Curtis Cardinal:
No Lies [Turtle Island Music 2002] backup vocals
Winston Wuttunee:
The Best of Winston Wuttunee [Turtle Island Music 2001] backup vocals
Various:
A Turtle Island Christmas [Turtle Island Music 2002] comp

Menow, Hector—(Cree) Country/ Rock *See*: Freebird Band, Errol Ranville

From Norway House, Manitoba. Menow recorded his first album with help from the Freebird Band, featuring Wally Ranville, Don Ranville, and Dean Malcolm. The title song of his 1994 release is named for Helen Betty Osborne, a young Native woman from Winnipeg, Manitoba, who was murdered by a gang of non-Native youths. The youths were finally brought to justice after decades of silence from townspeople and law enforcement.

DISCOGRAPHY:
Her Spirit Cries [Sunshine 1994]

Appearances:
24 Canadian Aboriginal Artists [Sunshine 1995] comp

Meshers—(Metis) Folk

Lineup: Eldred Mesher, Selby Mesher, Ford Mesher, Wayne Mesher, and Flora Mesher-Riley. From Happy Valley–Goose Bay, Labrador.

DISCOGRAPHY:
Echoes from across the River [The Music Reel 2002]

Meshikamau—(Innu) Rock *See*: Tipatshimun

Lineup: Andrew Penashue, vocals/guitar; Melvin Penashue, vocal/keyboards; Kevin Nuna, electric guitar; Gerome Pone, bass; Kim Fontaine, drums/bass.
    From Happy Valley–Goose Bay, Labrador. A raw performance of three-chord rock laden with ballads focused primarily on culture and the land and sung in the Innu language. Influenced by Kashtin on their first album, Meshikamau developed a greater sense of exploration on their second release.

DISCOGRAPHY:
Nika [Innu Nation 2001]
Meshikamau [Eagle Studios 1996]

Midnight Mist—(Cree-Metis) Fiddle

Lineup: Bill Bryant, fiddle; Elmer Cote, fiddle; Dave Bryant, lead guitar; Kevin Strong Quill, rhythm guitar; Frank Cote, bass.

DISCOGRAPHY:
First Time Out [Sunshine SCCT-486]

Mighty Mohawks—(Mohawk) Country and Western *See*: Don Patrick Martin

Lineup: George Hill, Allen Stacey, Slim Martin (all from Kahnawake, Quebec); Wally Moon (Restigouche, Quebec); Princess Moonbeam (Clarenceville, Quebec); Boots Bernie (Richabucto, New Brunswick).

Formed in 1958 and billed as "Canada's Country Boys," the Mighty Mohawks performed covers of country hits and original material sung in Mohawk, French, and English while sporting feathered headdresses and Mohawk haircuts. Their most memorable gig was at Montreal's EXPO '67. Reissues include *Memories* and *Canada's Stars of Country*.

DISCOGRAPHY:
Great Country Music Stars [GPH-403 1991] cass
Capture Country [Arc 1965]

Appearances:
George Hill Sings Again with Friends [independent 1994] comp

Miller, Bill—(Mohican) Folk/Rock/ Blues *See*: Jesse Ed Davis, Robert Mirabal, Joanne Shenandoah

Born Fush-ya Heay Aka (Bird Song), January 23, 1955, Stockbridge-Munsee Reservation, Wisconsin. A talented singer-songwriter, Miller has held a delicate balance between ballads and protest songs, with a clever use of lyric and storytelling technique combined with a musical sensitivity. Miller's talent with the guitar, flute, and piano appear in the work of many other Nashville-based recording artists.

His love of music was apparent since childhood, when he enjoyed the usual stints with various bands and styles throughout his teenage years. He left the reservation to study art at the University of Wisconsin and later attended the Lake School of Art and Design in Milwaukee. In 1984, he moved to Nashville to pursue a career as a singer-songwriter. He later signed with Warner Western and developed a musical craft that is appealing to both country and Native audiences. After five years with Warner Records, Miller created his own label but also signed with other entities, including Vanguard and Paras Recordings. His material encompasses love songs, historical ballads, and social commentary, as featured on his breakout album *Reservation Road*, produced by Richard Bennett. "Ghost Dance" received a NAMA Award for Song of the Year, and was named Artist of the Year, 1999. He was featured in the book *Nashville: Pilgrims of Guitar Town* by Robert Hicks and Michel Arnaud [Stewart, Tabori, and Chong 2000].

DISCOGRAPHY:
Cedar Dream [Paras 2004]
Spirit Songs: Best of Bill Miller [Vanguard 2003]
A Sacred Gift [Paras 2002]
Spirit Rain [Sol 2002]
Hear Our Prayer [Paras 2000]
Healings Waters [Paras 1999, United Kingdom]
Ghost Dance [Sol 1998]
Raven in the Snow [Warner 1996]
Native Suite [Warner Western 1996]
  w/ Robert Mirabal
Red Road [Warner Western 1993]
  w/ Smokey Town *See*: Powwow Music

Reservation Road—Bill Miller Live [Rosebud/Vanguard 1992]
Loon, Mountain, and Moon [Rosebud 1991]
The Art of Survival [Rosebud 1990]
Old Dreams and New Hopes [Windspirit 1987]
Native Sons [Windspirit 1982]

Singles:
"Ghost Dance" [Sol 1998]
"River of Time" [Reprise 1995]

Appearances (listed alphabetically):
Bellamy Brothers:
Sons of Beaches [Intersound 1995] flute
Alison Brown:
Look Left [Vanguard 1994] flute
Marty Brown:
Wild Kentucky Skies [MCA 1993] flute/rainstick
Solomon Burke:
Proud Mary: The Bell Sessions [Sundazed 2000] photography
Kate Campbell:
Moonpie Dreams [Compass 1997] percussion/flute
Steve Green:
Letter [Sparrow 1996] flute
Hal Ketchum:
Sure Love [Curb 1992] flute
Robert Mirabal:
Mirabal [Warner 1997] vocals
Michael Martin Murphey:
Land of Enchantment [Warner 1989]
Billy Joe Shaver:
Tramp on Your Street [BMG 1993]
Joanne Shenandoah:
Eagle Cries [Red Feather 2001]
Beau Williams:
Higher [Light/A&M 1990]
Various:
This Land Is Your Land: Songs of Unity [Music for Little People 2002] comp
Naturally Native [Silver Wave 2000] sdtk
Women of Faith: Outrageous Joy [1999] comp
A Native American Odyssey [Putumayo 1998] comp
Narada World: Global Vision [Narada 1997] two-CD comp

Between Father Sky and Mother Earth [Narada 1995] comp
Big Country for One and All [Music for Little People 1995] comp
Sioux City (AKA: Ultimate Revenge) [Lou Diamond Phillips, 1994] sdtk
Legends: I Am an Eagle [First Nations 1994] comp
Wild West [Mogul Entertainment/Telepictures Productions 1993] sdtk

Miller, Derek—(Mohawk) Rock *See*: Keith Secola, Shingoose

Born October 29, 1976, Six Nations Reserve, Grand River Territory, Ontario. This angst-ridden, ax-wielding guitarist played in local bands Children of the Sun and Universal Light (Ken Hoover, bass; Mark Vanni, drums). Miller didn't have to try too hard to grab attention with his flashy guitar style. He developed his craft after Robbie Robertson and others, including Link Wray and his power-chord style. He also honed his talent through recording many of his songs as independent demo releases. Eventually he toured and recorded with Keith Secola's Wild Band of Indians and later collaborated with Moontie Sinquah. *Music Is the Medicine* received the Juno Award for Aboriginal Recording of the Year and the FAITA Award for Best Musical Achievement, 2003. Miller also appears on *Indian Time III* [Global/Bravo 2003].

DISCOGRAPHY:
Music Is the Medicine [Arbor/SOAR 2002]
Bootleg [independent 2000] w/ Moontie Sinquah and Universal Light
Sketches [independent 1999] EP
Derek Miller and Universal Light [independent 1995] cass
Derek Miller [independent 1994] cass

Appearances (listed alphabetically):
Children of the Sun:
Gentle Beginnings [independent 1993] cass
Lucie Idlout:

E5-770: My Mother's Name [Arbor 2003]
Chester Knight:
Standing Strong [Arbor/SOAR 2002]
Keith Secola:
Finger Monkey [AKINA 1999]
Tru Rez Crew:
"I'm a Lucky One" [independent 2002]
  single
Various:
Urban Skins, Vol. 3 [SOAR 2000] comp

Miller, Dusty *See*: Indian
Chipmunks, Tom Ware, XIT

Miller, Josh, and 3 Wheel Drive—
(Mohawk) Blues/R & B

Lineup: Josh Miller, guitar/vocals; Darrin
Jamieson, drums; Dane Ngahuka (Maori),
bass.
   From Six Nations Reserve, Grand River
Territory, Ontario. This band mixes original blues, funk, and jazz with covers,
including material by Stevie Wonder. In
2001, Miller created the Soul Kings, a new
group with Blaine Bomberry and Keith
Silver.

DISCOGRAPHY:
Josh Miller and 3 Wheel Drive [Fourth
  Wheel Productions 1997]

Miller, Rebecca—(Mohawk) Country/
Rock

Born 1977, Six Nations Reserve, Grand
River Territory, Ontario. Miller first won
the Ontario-based 1996 YTV Youth Vocal
Awards for artists nineteen years of age
and under. "Listen to the Radio" was produced by Randall Prescott. Miller toured
throughout the United States and Canada
and performed on the nationally televised
Aboriginal Achievement Awards in 1997.

DISCOGRAPHY:
Listen to the Radio [Warner 1998]

Singles:
"Listen to the Radio" [BMG 1994]

Mirabal, Robert—(Taos Pueblo) Rock
See: Bill Miller

Born 1967, Taos Pueblo, New Mexico.
Mirabal made an impact with his album
Land, an experimental recording of traditional flute and percussion released
internationally on Warner Western. The
project earned him the New York Dance
and Performance Bessi Award in 1992.
His second project for the label, *Mirabal*,
included producer Michael Wancic (John
Mellancamp), producer Mark Andes (Heart
and Firefall), guitarist Andy York, drummer Kenny Aronoff, and singer-songwriter
Eliza Gilkyson. Mirabal crossed over into
rock, where he displayed versatile abilities as a songwriter and received a NAMA
Award for Best Songwriter of the Year,
1998. *Taos Tales* won the same honor in
2000 while generating critical acclaim in
Gavin and *Billboard* magazines. He was
featured in the PBS specials *Spirit* and *One
World* in 1999 and *Music from a Painted
Cave* in 2001.

DISCOGRAPHY:
Indians Indians [Silver Wave 2003]
Music from a Painted Cave [Silver Wave
  2001]
Taos Tales [Silver Wave 1999]
Mirabal [Warner Western 1997]
Warrior Magician [Silver Wave 1996]
Native Suite [Warner Western 1996] w/ Bill
  Miller
Land [Warner Western 1995]
Song Carrier [MTI 1995]
Something in the Fog [independent 1988]
  cass
Sys-to-le: Flute Songs [independent 1987]
  cass

Selected Appearances (listed alphabetically):
Robby Bee and the Boyz:
Reservation of Education [SOAR/Warrior 1990] flute/backup vocals
Peter Kater:
Red Moon [Silver Wave 2003] vocals
Michael Martin Murphy:
Sagebrush Symphony [Warner 1995] flute/percussion
Various:
Prayer for Peace [Silver Wave 2000] comp
Urban Skins, Vol. 1 [Warrior/SOAR 1999] comp
Under the Green Corn Moon [Silver Wave 1998] comp
Native American Currents [Silver Wave 1997] comp
The Santa Fe Sampler [MTI 1995] comp

Mistic—(Dineh) Rap *See*: Litefoot

From Two Gray Hills, New Mexico. Mistic released his first album with Cherokee rapper Litefoot. His later material focuses more on street life, rescue from gangs, culture-positive survival, and struggle.

DISCOGRAPHY:
Tribal Scars [2TE-1001]
Rezurection [Red Vinyl Records 1996]

Mitchell, Esau—(Anishnabe) Gospel

Mitchell's album was recorded independently in Southampton, Ontario, with Bill Mankiss, keyboards; Lloyd Banks, dobro/steel guitar; Victor Pasowisty, vocals/acoustic guitar; Lynn Russwurm, bass; Philip Ritchie, acoustic guitar; Velma Soloman, Bernetta Thompson, Dorothy Jones, Sylvia John, backup vocals.

DISCOGRAPHY:
The Sounds of Ojibwe Gospel [independent NDA]

Mixashawn—(Maheekanew) Jazz

Almost eccentric, but definitely creative, Mixashawn is best known for his work with Bobby McFerrin. His experimental vocals and rhythms are based on traditional songs. From his release *Plastic Champions*, the track "Omni Pop" details the rhythmic influences traditional music made on rock 'n' roll, combining elements of Chuck Berry, Jim Pepper, and traditional 49ers.

DISCOGRAPHY:
Plastic Champions [independent 1992] cass
Native Songs and Stories [independent 1991] cass

Appearances:
Keith Secola:
Wild Band of Indians [AKINA 1997] soprano saxophone

Mnjikaning Ojibwe Singers—(Anishnabekwe) Gospel

Lineup: Lorraine McRae, Shirley Shilling, Irene Snache.

DISCOGRAPHY:
Native Gospel Songs: Chippewas of Rama First Nation [independent 1994] cass

Mohawk Blood—(Mohawk) Rock

Lineup: Aronhiakons Hemlock, guitar/vocals; Frank Zacharie, bass/backup vocals; Cam Giroux, drums; Kario, lyrics.

The song "Listen to the Eagle's Cry" was inspired by the Oka crisis of 1990, when the Canadian military and Quebec police invaded the three Mohawk territories of Kahnesetake, Kahnawake, and Akwesasne. The second track, "Have You Seen the Dawn," was originally recorded for the video/book project *Where Eagles Dare to Soar* [NDA], dealing with Kevin White, a young Cree man and his struggle with AIDS.

DISCOGRAPHY:
Mohawk Blood [independent 1991] cass EP

Monias, Ernest, and Sons—(Cree) Country/Rock/Gospel

From Cross Lake, Manitoba. Monias gained popularity in many Native communities throughout northern Manitoba and western Canada with his straight ahead down-home country style.

DISCOGRAPHY:
A Tribute to Hank Williams [Sunshine 2003]
The Gospel Side of Ernest Monias [Cherish/Sunshine 1997]
Innu Nikamu [Sunshine 1997]
Greatest Hits [Sunshine SSCD 4262]
Ernest Monias and Sons: Neechee [Sunshine SSCT 4111]
Ernest Monias and the Shadows: Best Regrets [Sunshine SSCT 4087]
Be a Woman to Me [Sunshine SSCT 4083]
Original Recordings [Sunshine SSCT 4082]
Ernest Monias and the Shadows [Sunshine SSCT 4063]
You're Still the One [Sunshine SSCT 4039]
Ernest Monias and the Shadows [Sunshine 1983]
The Gospel Side [CRCT 6008]
Rain Music [independent 1979] produced by Ray St. Germain

Appearances:
20 Aboriginal Greatest Hits, Vol. 3 [Sunshine 2002] comp
20 Greatest Aboriginal Hits, Vol. 2 [Sunshine 1998] comp
An Aboriginal Christmas, Vol. 1 [Sunshine 1997] comp
24 Canadian Aboriginal Artists [Sunshine 1995] comp
A Northern Christmas [Sunshine SSCD-4180]

Montana, Joe, and the Roadrunners—(Hualapai) Country and Western

Lineup: Joe Montana, lead guitar/vocals; Del Havatone, rhythm guitar; Neil Jackson, drums/lead guitar; Chum Shrum, bass. Montana played the southwestern United States for many years.

DISCOGRAPHY:
Joe Montana and the Roadrunners, Vol. 4 [independent 1981]
Joe Montana and the Roadrunners, Vol. 3 [independent 1979]
Joe Montana and the Roadrunners, Vol. 2 [independent 1978]
Joe Montana and the Roadrunners, Vol. 1 [Canyon 1974]

Montano, Frank; a.k.a. Anakwad—(Anishnabe) Folk *See*: Soulfood; Flute Music

Born March 25, 1941, Red Cliff, Wisconsin. Montano contructed his own cedar flutes to accompany his contemporary compositions. He was also active in the protection of Natives' intellectual property rights.

DISCOGRAPHY:
Reservation Reflections [independent 1988]

Appearances:
Soulfood:
Breathe [Candescence/Musik International 1997] two-CD set
Various:
An Aboriginal Christmas, Vol. 1 [Sunshine 1997] comp

Montour, Tara-Louise—(Mohawk) Classical

Considered Canada's foremost Native classical violinist, Montour was given the name Tara-Louise Perrault after her adoption at five weeks of age in 1972. She traced her roots to the Kahnawake Mohawk territory on the south shore of the St. Lawrence River. Raised in a musical family, she studied at the Conservatoire de Musique, Montreal; the Licentiate of Music, McGill University, Montreal; the Masters of Music, Northern Illinois University; and the Academia Musicale, Chigiana, Italy. She was a laureate of many competitions, including the Montreal Symphony's Shell Matinee Series; the 1998 XVI Commonwealth Games Arts Festival, Kuala Lampur, Malaysia; and the Mostly Music Series in Chicago. She was a guest artist in Cremona, Elba, and Siena, Italy, as well. In 1994, she appeared with Susan Aglukark to perform a composition written by John Kim Bell for the opening of the National Aboriginal Achievement Awards in Ottawa, Ontario; she also performed under the direction of conductor Boris Brott in Vancouver in 1997. Her original work *Farewell to the Warriors* blends traditional Native music with Bartok and Prokofiev. *Farewell to the Warriors* premiered February 2000 in Toronto, Ontario, with the I Virtuoso Chamber Orchestra.

Moody X 2—(Cree) Pop *See*: Powwow Music: Little Thunderbird Singers

Sisters Natashia (born 1986) and Alexandria (born 1987), best known for their involvement with the Little Thunderbird Singers, recorded some country songs for kids of all ages.

DISCOGRAPHY:
You and I [Sunshine 1998]
We Are Children of Today [Sunshine 1997]

Appearances:
20 Greatest Aboriginal Hits, Vol. 2 [Sunshine 1998] comp
An Aboriginal Christmas, Vol. 1 [Sunshine 1997] comp

Moon, Brian, and Rare Breed—(Mohawk) Country *See*: Mighty Mohawks

Based in Montreal, Quebec, a product of a musical family, Moon began performing at age five. In 1989, he was nominated in two Canadian Country Music Competition categories. Since then, he has worked with many country artists, including Mel Tillis, Leroy Van Dyke, and Jerry Reed.

DISCOGRAPHY:
Brian Moon and Rare Breed! [Sunshine SSCT-4226]
Temporarily Single [Sunshine SSCT-4073]
2 Old Flames [Sunshine SSCT-4064]

Moore, Rose—(Cherokee) Country/ Folk *See*: Cherokee Rose

Moore, Russell "Big Chief"—(Akimel O'odham) Jazz

1912–1983
Born August 13, 1912, Bapchule, Arizona. Moore grew up at Gila Crossing in District 6 (Gila River Indian Community) with his two brothers, Clark and Everett. He was eleven years old when his father passed away, at which time he was sent to Blue Island, Illinois, to live with his uncle William, a Chicago-based music teacher. Introduced to the piano, drums, and several brass instruments, Moore learned trombone at the Sherman Institute, a residential school. He went on to play in the big bands, and by 1935, after moving to Los Angeles, he joined Lionel Hampton and Eddie Barefield. Four years later he shifted his focus to Dixieland jazz in New Orleans and worked with Oscar Celestin, Kid Rena, A. J. Piron, and Paul Barbarin. After stints with Ernie Fields, Harlan Leonard, and Noble Sissle, Moore joined Louis Armstrong's Big Band and the Louis Armstrong Sextet (1944–47); the band members ap-

peared as themselves in the film *New Orleans* [Arthur Lubin, 1947]. In 1952, Moore went on to work with jazz greats Rudy Braff, Pee Wee Russell, Eddie Condon, Wild Bill Davison, Jimmy McPartland, Tony Parenti, and others. A year later he toured Europe with Mezz Mezzrow and recorded with Sidney Bechet, Buck Clayton, and Mezzrow. During this time, Moore recorded two titles on the Vogue label and one on Trutone Records.

In January 1957, he married Ida Powless from Oneida, Wisconsin; they later adopted two children, Randy and Amy. In 1959, he was sponsored by the NCAI to help build morale among Native youth, so he established a scholarship fund.

Moore joined Louis Armstrong's All Stars (1964–65), replacing Trummy Young as first trombone, and was featured prominently on the album *Hello Dolly* [Kapp 1964; MCA 1980]. He went on to front his own Dixieland jazz band and frequently played in Canada. He recorded with Quincy Jones and Cozy Cole in 1977; toured England in 1981 with Ken Smith; played the inaugural balls for Presidents Kennedy, Johnson, and Nixon, and the royal wedding of Prince Charles and Lady Diana. In addition to trombone, he also played bass guitar, saxophone, and sang baritone. The annual Russell Moore Music Fest was established in September 1998 on the Gila River Reservation near Phoenix, Arizona, where he often played at community events.

"Big Chief" Moore's Powwow Jazz Band lineup (1973–75): Russell Moore, trombone; Ed Oleer, cornet; Dick Wellstood, piano; Gene Ramey, bass; Jack Williams, drums.

DISCOGRAPHY:

Russell "Big Chief" Moore, Vol. 2 [Jazz Art 1975]

Russell "Big Chief" Moore's Powwow Jazz Band [Jazz Art 1973]

Appearances (listed alphabetically):

Louis Armstrong:

Very Best of Louis Armstrong [Universal International 2002]

C'est si bon: Rockin' Chair [Proper 2001]

Legendary Satchmo: 100 Years [Prestige Elite 2001]

Legendary Satchmo, Vol. 1 [Prestige Elite 2001]

Satchmo in the Forties [ASV/Living Era 2001]

Louis Armstrong: The Complete RCA Victor Recordings [RCA 1997/2001] four-CD best of

Blues for Yesterday [Avid 2000]

100th Birthday Celebration [RCA 2000]

New Orleans: The Soundtrack [Giants of Jazz/Jazz Crusade 1999]

Louis Armstrong 1946–1947 [Classics 1998]

American Icon [Hip-O 1998]

All-Time Greatest Hits [MCA 1994]

Louis Armstrong [Laserlight 1992; Universal Special Products 1995; Delta 1996]

Essential Louis Armstrong [Vanguard 1990/1993; Polygram 1992; Charly 1995]

Hello Dolly [Kapp 1964; MCA 1980; Drive Records 1993; Legacy 2000]

Jazz Collector Edition [Delta 1990]

Satchmo's Greatest Hits, Vol. 4: *1946* [RCA 731-051 Serie Black and White, Vol. 39, France]

Satchmo's Greatest Hits, Vol. 3: *1933–1946* [RCA 731-050 Serie Black and White, Vol. 38, France]

The Blues Are Brewin' [RCA 1946]

Sidney Bechet:

Jazz at Storyville [Pumpkin Records 1951]

Condon's Floor Show [TV Broadcast, New York, August 6, 1949]

Sidney Bechet Jam Session [Vogue Integrale 1949, Sweden; Phontastic NOST 7602] three-LP set

Jam Session [Blues Final, Pleyel, Paris, 1949] w/ Charlie Parker

Ernie Fields and His Orchestra:

Just Let Me Alone [W24961-A T-Town Blues/Vocalion 1939]

Blues at Midnight [Town Blues/Vocalion 1939]

High Jivin' [Town Blues/Vocalion 1939]

Bless Your Heart [Town Blues/Vocalion 1939]
Leonard Gaskin:
Leonard Gaskin at the Downtown Strutters' Ball 1962 [Swingville 1962]
Lionel Hampton:
Old Fashioned Swing [Jazz Hour 1995] best of
Lionel Hampton and the Cozy Cole All-Stars:
Tribute to Louis Armstrong [Jazz World 1999]
Quincy Jones:
Q: The Musical Biography of Quincy [Rhino 2001] best of
Charlie Parker:
Bird's Eyes, Vol. 12 [Philology 1949] best of
Swingville All-Stars:
Memphis Blues 1962 [Good Time Jazz 1997]
Various:
Jazz Cities: New Orleans, Chicago, New York, Kansas City [Radio France 2000] comp
New Orleans Original Soundtrack [Soundtrack Factory 2000] sdtk
Dr Jazz Sampler 1951–1952 [Storyville Records 1993] comp

Morning Star—(Mi'kmaq) Trad/Folk

Lineup: Alex and Richard Poulette (Mi'kmaq), lead vocals/chanting; George Paul (Mi'kmaq), lyrics; Four the Moment, backup vocals; Matt Minglewood, organ; Matt Foulds, drums; Ed Woodsworth, bass; Fred Lavery, acoustic guitars; Ralph Dillon, piano; Gordie Sampson, acoustic/electric guitars; J. P. Cormier, fiddle/acoustic guitars; Al Bennett, bass; Stewart MacNeil, accordion; Tom Roach, drums; Gordie Sampson, acoustic guitar; Joel Denny, Native flute; Bruce McPhee, bagpipes.

With upbeat music and great backup performers, the Poulette brothers created a unique blend of traditional fusion music. Their material reflects on Mi'kmaq teach-ings combined with the importance of cultural survival, resistance, and the experience of boarding schools, with lyrics sung in English and Mi'kmaq. The band received the ECMA Award for Aboriginal Recording of the Year in 2000.

DISCOGRAPHY:
A Little More Understanding [independent 1999]

Nadjiwan, Marc—(OJ-Cree) Rock

Born January 3, 1970, Lynn Lake, Manitoba. Originally billed as part of a trio, Nadjiwan entered the music scene by means of several folk festivals throughout the province of Ontario. The original lineup included Marc Nadjiwan, guitar/vocals; Robin Ranger, bass/vocals; Jeff Nelson, drums/percussion/hand drum (the latter two Anishnabe from Thunder Bay, Ontario). His self-titled debut release reflected similarities to Blue Oyster Cult, whereas his second album was more acoustic based; his third was a return to the rock guitar rudiments of the first. His music is described as a superlative blend

Marc Nadjiwan's cover for *Awake*, 2000.
Courtesy Heading North Music/Marc Nadjiwan.

of traditional and modern forms of music. He continues to develop as a songwriter and recording artist with producer Ron Skinner.

DISCOGRAPHY:
Awake [Heading North 2000]
Free [Heading North 1998]
Brother [Heading North 1994/2002]

Appearances:
Mariposa Folk Festival 2001 [Mariposa Folk Foundation 2001] comp
Urban Skins, vol. 3 [SOAR 2000] comp

Nakai Quartet, R. Carlos—Jazz *See*: Jackalope, Redhouse Family; Flute Music

Lineup: R. Carlos Nakai, flute; Amo Chip, keyboards/soprano, tenor, alto saxophone/vocals; Will Clipman, drums/percussion; J. David Muniz (Apache), bass/keyboards/guitar/vocals *(Kokopelli's Cafe)*; Mary Redhouse (Dineh), bass/vocals *(Big Medicine)*.

R. Carlos Nakai created numerous combinations centered on traditional flute music. The Nakai Quartet developed a Native-flavored jazz combined with African beats.

DISCOGRAPHY:
Ancient Future [Canyon 2000]
Big Medicine [Canyon 1998]
Kokopelli's Cafe [Canyon 1995]

Napoleon, Art—(Cree) Folk/Blues

Napoleon began performing in 1991, blending the music of two cultures. He entered the folk music circuit by opening for performers such as Valdy, Faith Nolan, and Kashtin. After returning home to work with Native youth, he was elected chief. Napoleon's music bears resemblences to that of Charlie Musselwhite and Steve Earle, while taking influences from his traditional roots.

Lineup: Art Napoleon, lead/backup vocals/acoustic guitar/harmonica/percussion; James Oldenburg, electric/slide guitar/backup vocals/drums/keyboards; Tim Leacock, backup vocals/acoustic guitar/dobro; Reddon Whiteman, moose scrapers/percussion; children of the Moberly Lake School; and others.

DISCOGRAPHY:
Outta the Woods [independent 1996]

Natay—(Dineh) Rap

Born May 31, 1973, Shiprock, New Mexico, Navajo Reservation. Based in Albuquerque, Natay brought the reality of street life and youth gangs to light with his first release.

DISCOGRAPHY:
TNT [independent 2001]
A Place Called Survival [SOAR 1998]

Natay, Dineh rapper. Photo courtesy Robby Bee.

Appearances:
Urban Skins, Vol. 3 [SOAR 2000] comp
Urban Skins, Vol. 2 [SOAR 1999] comp
Urban Skins, Vol. 1 [SOAR 1999] comp

Native Flamenco—Native Flamenco
See: Redhouse Family, Ruben Romero
and Lydia Torea

Lineup: Ruben Romero, flamenco guitar;
Robert Tree Cody, flute (*See*: Flute Music);
Tony Redhouse, percussion; John Murray,
bass.

The continuing pursuit of the most
outlandish hybrids provided the opportunity to hear Joaquin Rodrigo's "Aranjuez"
played on the traditional flute. *Native Flamenco* received a NAMA Award for Best
World Music Recording and Best Latin
Recording, 2000.

DISCOGRAPHY:
Native Flamenco [Canyon 1999]

Native Roots—Reggae *See*: Joy
Harjo, Red Earth

Lineup: John Williams (Dakota), flute/
sequencing/bass/drums; Skheme (Santa
Ana Pueblo), vocals/lyrics; Victor Vigil
(Jemez Pueblo), percussion; William Bluehouse Johnson (Isleta-Dineh), rhythm/
lead guitars; Carlos Johnson, second lead
guitar; Rolando Hall, bass; Susan Williams (Dakota), drums; Rachelle Williams
(Dakota), backup vocals.

With members of Joy Harjo's backup
band Poetic Justice, this Albuquerque-
based group dedicated their talents to the
sound and spirit of reggae with a conscious
Native philosophy. Shkeme performed
with the Rio Grande Singers (*See*: Powwow Music) and the Gathering of Nations
Dance Troupe. Williams has worked in
reggae and Caribbean bands since the early
1980s, with stints in Central America,
Asia, and Europe.

DISCOGRAPHY:
Rain Us Love [Warrior/SOAR 2001]
Place I Call Home [Irie Culture 1998;
SOAR 1999]

Appearances:
Urban Skins, Vol. 2 [SOAR 1999] comp
Urban Skins, Vol. 1 [SOAR 1999] comp

Navajo Sundowners—Country and
Western

From Farmington, New Mexico.

DISCOGRAPHY:
The Navajo Sundowners, Vol. 13 [Canyon
1976] w/ Cody Bearpaw
The Navajo Sundowners, Vol. 12 [Canyon
1976]
The Navajo Sundowners, Vol. 11 [Canyon
1975]
The Navajo Sundowners Dance, Vol. 10
[Canyon 1974]
The Navajo Sundowners, Vol. 9 [Canyon
1974]
The Navajo Sundowners Gold, Vol. 8
[Canyon 1974] best of
The Navajo Sundowners, Vol. 7 [Canyon
1974]
The Navajo Sundowners, Vol. 6 [Canyon
1974] w/ Harold Mariano
The Navajo Sundowners, Vol. 5 [Canyon
1973]
The Navajo Sundowners, Vol. 4 [Canyon
1973]
The Navajo Sundowners, Vol. 3 [Canyon
1973]
The Navajo Sundowners, Vol. 2 [Canyon
1973]
The Navajo Sundowners, Vol. 1 [Canyon
1973]

NDN—Rock *See*: Blackfoot, Greg T. Walker

Lineup: Greg T. Walker (Creek-Choctaw), bass/keyboards/vocals; Richard Luciano, guitars; Bob Hatter, rhythm/lead/slide guitars; William Ellis (Hochunk), drums; Mike Bush, backup vocals/percussion; Carol Bush, backup vocals; Doug Wallantyne, flute on the track "Home"; Dorian Sanchez, chants.

Founding member of the group Blackfoot, Walker pursued his dream of creating a culturally relevant band. The new musical incarnation combined the rock and acoustic guitar majesty of Rick Luciano with traditional flavors. Walker's other collaborations include work with Donald Johns and Co., Dee Dee Nichols, Headband, and the Southern Rock All-stars.

DISCOGRAPHY:
Warriors' Pride [Red Nations 1999]

Videos:
Times We've Had [Thunderous Nations Productions 1999]

Nelson, Tracy Lee—
(Kumayaay-Luiseno) Blues

Nelson was raised in the Los Angeles area. His past musical exploits include the formation of a punk band, Johnny and the Dingbats, and later of the Madd Vampires. He's shared the stage with John Trudell, Strawberry Alarm Clock, Charlie Hill (Oneida), and others, and has played with Redbone and the Song Catchers. Nelson identified blues as an appropriate choice of music for Natives because "we've been oppressed for 500 years; it's a natural outlet of expression." His Native Blues Band included Johnny Lord on drums and Don Durham on bass.

DISCOGRAPHY:
Commodity Blues [independent 2003]
500 Years of the Blues [independent 1999]

New Breed—Rap *See*: Red Power Squad

Lineup: Derek Mason (Mase the Project Poet); Misty Potts (Lady Poet); Victor Bird (So Nice); T. Brabec and D. Mason, music; additional personnel, Conway K. (Red Power) and Sauzi Delver.

DISCOGRAPHY:
Life's Journey [Black Eagle 1996]

Appearances:
Urban Skins, Vol. 2 [SOAR 1999] comp

Newton, Wayne—
(Powhatan-Cherokee) Lounge

Born April 3, 1942, Roanoke, Virginia. Said to be a direct descendant of Pocahontas, "Mr. Entertainment" has recorded more than one hundred albums and starred in numerous movies and Las Vegas shows.

Nighthawk, Jessie—(Cherokee) Folk/Rock

Based in Lancaster, Pennsylvania.
1998 Lineup: Jessie Nighthawk, vocals/acoustic guitar; Jim Beer, vocals/acoustic guitar; David White Buffalo (Lakota) chants/drum; Caroline Fisher, flute; Christine Crowl, backup vocals/harp/guitar; George Keynser, electric/acoustic guitar; John Elder, bass; Andrew Botham, keyboards/vocals/bass; Mike Christe, percussion.

DISCOGRAPHY:
Ghost Dance: The Last Hope [Sacred Fire 1998]
So Long My Noble Red Man [Sacred Fire 1997]

Nitatshun—(Innu) Rock

Lineup: Edmund Benuen, rhythm guitar/vocals; Etienne Riche, bass; Stanley Pokue, rhythm guitar/lead vocals. A guitar-heavy outfit backed with drum programming, Nitatshun performed all original material sung in the Innu language.

DISCOGRAPHY:
Numushum [Innu Nation 2002]

Nofchissey, Arlene; a.k.a. Arlene Nofchissey Williams— (Dineh) Folk
See: Chief Dan George, Lamanite Generation

Nofchissey was invited to China in the summer of 1999 for the July Fourth celebration at the U.S. embassy with the Spirit Eagle Dancers from Provost, Utah. When the Chinese government extended an invitation to her to perform in Mongolia for the national Nadaam Festival, a correspondent for a foreign entertainment magazine claimed she was there seeking her roots (that's those Bering Strait land-bridge theorists for you)!

DISCOGRAPHY:
Encircle [Proud Earth 1989] w/ John Rainer Jr. *See*: Flute Music
Go My Son [Proud Earth/Canyon 1988] w/ Lamanite Generation
Proud Earth [Salt Lake City 1975] w/ Chief Dan George

No Reservations—Folk/Rock

Lineup: Kevin Shaganash, guitar/vocals; Mark Seabrook, rhythm guitar; Shawn Corbiere, lead guitar/percussion/vocals; Jennifer Brunelle, percussion/vocals; Dan Amadio, drums/percussion, Dave Heneberry, bass.

Based in Sudbury, Ontario. *Necessary* received a Juno nomination for Best Music of Aboriginal Canada, 1998. The band blended elements of electric folk with acoustic rock music, and their material carries a heavy politicized character that makes for a challenging but easy sound.

DISCOGRAPHY:
Hollywood Indian [independent 1998]
Necessary [independent 1997]
No Reservations [independent 1996] cass
Demo Sessions [independent 1995] cass

Numkena, Wil—(Dineh) New Age/Country

DISCOGRAPHY:
Various Native American Artists: Solo Flights Two, Vol. 2 [SOAR 1994] comp

Obomsawin, Alanis—(Abenaki) *See*: Shannon Two Feathers; Traditional/Archival Solo

Born August 31, 1931, Lebanon, New Hampshire. Poet, singer, and filmmaker Obomsawin made several appearances in the folk music scene and released a few obscure recordings of spoken word and song. Her critical documentaries include *Incident at Restigouche* [NFB 1978] and *Kahnesetake* [NFB 1991], filmed during the crisis at Oka, Quebec, in 1990.

1991 Lineup: Francois Richard, flute; Mario Giroux, violin/cello; Marie-France Richard, oboe; Domenique Luc Tremblay, violin; Jean Vanasse, arranger; Alain de Grosbois, producer.

DISCOGRAPHY:
Bush Lady [Wawa 1991]
Bush Lady [CBC 1985]
Indian Songs [CBC Northern Service QC-1406] six-track vinyl EP
Indian Songs [CBC Northern Service QC-1406]

Appearances:
Your Silence Will Not Protect You [Maya Music 1988] comp
Mariposa [Mariposa 1977] comp

Obomsawin, Tomas—(Abenaki)
Blues

Obomsawin started playing music at the age of twelve and developed a deep interest in the blues. As a community activist, he worked on treaty rights in New England and Quebec. His experiences were the inspiration for his first album, which also includes protest songs by Peter LaFarge and Floyd Westerman. As Obomsawin began work on a second album, he faded from the music scene.

DISCOGRAPHY:
Abenakis [Canyon 1990]

Ojibwa Choir—(Anishnabe) Gospel

Lineup: Chief North Star (Dalton Jacobs), Adely Muskrat, Allen Taylor, Gladys Taylor, Aileen Irons, Inez Knott, Alex Knott, Austin McPue, John Jacobs, Victor Johnson, Amos Irons.

Billed as Chief North Star's Singers, the Ojibwa Indian Choir dressed in traditional garb and sang Christian hymns in the Anishnabe language. Their album, subtitled *A Unique Blending of Voices in the Indian Tongue*, was produced by William Montaigne.

DISCOGRAPHY:
Ojibwa Choir [Montaigne Limited Edition CT-31087]

Om—(Chicano) Techno

Though Om's one recording is primarily a techno-based album, acoustic guitars and some rock-based music appear on tracks that carry hints of traditional drumming.

DISCOGRAPHY:
namaste [Aztlan Records 1998]

One in the Chamber—(Chicano)
Heavy Metal

Lineup: Javier, Eymos, Cheyenne, Jose, Felipea. With a sound reminiscent of Rage Against the Machine, this band's message was culture, survival, and resistance.

DISCOGRAPHY:
One in the Chamber [Quetzal Music/Olin Records 1997]

One Star, Lloyd—(Lakota) composer/
singer

Born on the Rosebud Sioux Reservation, South Dakota. One Star was hired as the traditional music consultant for the feature film *A Man Called Horse* [Elliot Silverstein, 1970]. He later worked in a similar capacity on the television series *Star Trek: The Next Generation* [Paramount Pictures, 1987–94].

DISCOGRAPHY:
A Man Called Horse [Columbia OS 3530] sdtk

Ortega, A. Paul—(Mescalero Apache)
Trad/Folk *See*: Sharon Burch, Joanne Shenandoah

Born Anthony Paul Ortega, August 26, 1937, Riconda Valley, New Mexico. Ortega was raised in traditional surroundings in the southwestern United States. As a youth in the 1950s, he won several awards for war dancing and visual art in Albuquerque, New Mexico. After leaving the U.S. Army, Ortega studied at Chicago's Allied Institute of Technology and Design and "fooled with the blues," playing bass in various bands in the Old Town section. He developed new interpretations of traditional songs on acoustic guitar "to sensitize people about the music and the culture." His first album contained the song "What Is an Indian," written by Ralph Keene. On his second album, *Three Worlds*, he protested the U.S. government's relocation policy of the 1950s with the song "Chicago"; the melody is based on the country classic "Streets of Laredo" (originally composed by Raymond B. Evans and Jay Livingston; performed by Marty Robbins). Ortega made his first recording in a church in San Francisco in 1962; the one thousand pressings were sold out in the first week of release. Ortega later signed with Phoenix-based Canyon Records, who reissued his first album and recorded all of his subsequent releases.

Beginning in the 1970s, Ortega continued his recording career, worked in youth education, toured the world as a musician and a lecturer, and served his community as a traditional healer for the Bureau of Indian Affairs Indian Health Services in New Mexico until 1998. He introduced traditional healing lodges for patients who observed traditional healing with modern medicine. In 2004, he was continuing to work on new recording projects.

The *Three Worlds* album includes the following personnel: Joe Jojola (Isleta Pueblo); Tom Setopkewa (Hopi); Judy Skenandore (Oneida); Sandra Shieja (Santa Clara Pueblo); Virginia Shanta (Mescalero Apache); John Truitt, flute; Michael Booth, bass.

DISCOGRAPHY:
Loving Ways [Canyon 1991] w/ Joanne Shenandoah
Blessing Ways [Canyon 1984] w/ Sharon Burch
Three Worlds [Canyon 1974]
Two Worlds [Rose 1964; Canyon 1973]

Appearances:
Music of New Mexico: Native American Traditions [Smithsonian Folkways 1992] comp
Oyate [Nato/World 1990/1998, France] comp
Beyond Treaty: An Evening with Friends of the International Indian Treaty Council [independent 1986] comp

Osborne, William—(Cree) Country

From northern Manitoba, Osborne released one mini-album of original country songs.

DISCOGRAPHY:
It Ain't Been Easy [independent 1995] cass EP

Ozomatli—(Chicano) Rap *See*: Red Earth

Lineup: Tony Lujan, trumpet; David Hidalgo, accordion; David Ralicke, trombone/baritone saxohone; Paul Livingstone, guitar; Ulises Bella, clarinet/tenor saxophone/guitar; Cut Chemist, turntables; Asfru Sierra, trumpet; Wil-Dog Abers, bass; DJ Kid WIK, turntables; Tylana Enomoto, violin; Jose Espinoza, alto sax; William Marrufo, drums; Andy Mendoza, drums; Alfredo Ortiz, timbales; Raul Pacheco, guitar; Justin Poree, percussion; Chali 2na, rap; Jiro Yamaguchi, percussion/tabla.

DISCOGRAPHY:
Embrace the Chaos [Almo Sounds/Interscope 2001]
Ozomatli: Holland Bonus Tracks [Universal International 2000]
Cut Chemist Suite [Almo Sounds 1999] EP
Super Bowl Sundae [Almo Sounds 1999] EP single
Ya Llego [Almo Sounds 1999] EP
Ozomatli Sampler [Almo Sounds 1998] cass
Ozomatli [Almo Sounds 1998]

Appearances:
Never Been Kissed [Capitol 1999] sdtk
Ed TV [Ron Howard, 1998] sdtk
Very Bad Things [Interscope/Polygram 1998] sdtk, enhanced CD
Sociadad = Sociadad [BYO Records 1997] comp

Painted Pony—Blues

Lineup: Jony James, vocals/guitar; Oren Doxtator (Oneida) drums/backup vocals; Don Powless (Mohawk), bass; Joleen Williams (Seneca), vocals/keyboards; Al Gator, saxophones. Based in New York State.

DISCOGRAPHY:
Drove Me Crazy [independent 1994]

Pappy Johns Band—(Mohawk) Blues

Lineup: Faron Johns, vocals; Lorne Greene, lead guitar/backup vocals; Chris Johns, guitars/backup vocals; Don Powless, bass/vocals; Oren Doxtator, drums/percussion; Al Kroll, alto saxophone; Murray Porter, keyboards.

Based on the Six Nations Reserve near Brantford, Ontario. This collective of veteran musicians with a strong local following made several national television appearances in Canada and played the Chicago Blues Festival in 2003. Faron Johns appeared on the dance performance soundtrack album *Kaha:wi.*

DISCOGRAPHY:
Full Circle [independent 2003]
Blame It on Monday [independent 2001]

Appearances:
Skin Tight Blues [Sweet Grass/EMI 2002] comp
Kaha:wi [independent 2003] sdtk

Patterson, Rick—(Kyuquot) Rock

Lineup: Rick Patterson, vocals/drums/percussion/guitar; Clyde Roulette, Ed Molyski, guitars; Chief Fraser Andrew, vocals; the Arrows to Freedom Singers; Joel Sacks, Daryl Hok, Bob Walker, bass; Tom Carter, keyboard/percussion; Charlie Hase, steel guitar; Marcie Nokony, violin; Gil Herman, saxophone. Based in Vancouver, British Columbia.

DISCOGRAPHY:
Spirit of the Wolf [independent 1992]
The Message Is Clear [independent 1990] cassingle

PeaceMaker—Heavy Metal

Lineup: Mark Nabess, vocals/acoustic guitar; Jesse Green, lead/rhythm guitars; Greg Mentuck, lead/rhythm guitars; Donny Ducharme, bass/vocals; Shawn Parenteau, drums.

Formed in 1993. Nabess, the primary songwriter for this Winnipeg-based group, penned conscious lyrics dealing with social problems and cultural survival. Selected tracks appeared on a Winnipeg radio station compilation entitled *Homegrown*, vol. 3.

DISCOGRAPHY:
Reservation Dog [Sunshine 1996]
Peacemaker [Jamco 1994]
Sacred Ground [independent 1992]

Singles:
"21st Century Indian" [independent 2000]

Appearances:
Homegrown, Vol. 3 [CITI-FM 1997] comp

Videos:
Reservation Dog [independent 1996]
Sacred Ground [independent 1994]

Pekeshemoon—(Algonquin) Rock

Lineup: Moe Mitchell, vocals/acoustic guitar; Lucien Poucachiche, vocals/bass; Mario Thomas, vocal/electric guitar; Alex Cheezo, synthesized guitar; Edward P, drums. From the Abitibi region of northern Quebec. Formed in 1997.

DISCOGRAPHY:
Nadegam [SDC Mahigan 1997] four-track EP

Jane Peloquin turns activism to musical power.
Photo courtesy Brian Wright-McLeod.

Peloquin, Jane—(Metis) Folk

Born 1959. From northern Ontario, Canada, Peloquin became a favorite solo acoustic performer on the Native folk and coffee house scene in the 1980s in Toronto, Ontario. Her political and social activism inspired her songwriting.

DISCOGRAPHY:

Believe in Your Dreams [independent 1985] cass

Pepper, Jim—(Muscogee Creek–Kaw) Jazz *See*: Archie Cavenaugh, Joy Harjo, Peter LaFarge, Mixashawn, Pura Fe

1941–1992

Born in Portland, Oregon, 1941. A self-described urban Indian, Pepper was taught the traditional aspects of his culture after the family moved to Oklahoma. An eclectic entertainer since childhood, Pepper played clarinet, studied tap dancing and traditional hoop dancing, and in high school fronted his own band called the Spices.

After moving to New York City in the early 1960s, Pepper met guitarist Larry Coryell; in 1964, they formed the Free Spirits with Bob Moses on drums, Columbus Baker on rhythm guitar and vocals, and Chris Hills on bass. They released two rock/jazz albums that laid the foundations of a new free-form jazz style known as fusion. Pepper wielded an ability to switch from tenor, alto, and soprano saxophones with ease and could play the flute with equal skill. He possessed an incredible range and created textures that enabled him to blend and split notes, harmonies, and tones without electronically stacking his playing. Pepper combined traditional music with jazz and produced melodies that represented the splicing of cultures and music, most notably in his signature song "Witchi Tai To." Recorded in 1968, "Witchi Tai To" appeared at number 69 on the U.S. pop charts for five weeks. The song was based on a peyote chant made by his grandfather, Ralph Pepper, who was a road man with the NAC. Ralph had learned saxophone in residential school and taught Jim the art of improvisation. A cross section of artists have covered the song, including Harper's Bizarre on their album *Feelin' Groovy*, Jan Garbarek on *Witchi Tai To*, and Chuck Florence on the tribute album *Remembering Jim Pepper*.

After the Free Spirits disbanded in 1968, Pepper went on to record with Keith Jarrett and reunited with Hills to form Everything Is Everything. He also sessioned with dozens of artists and appeared on the Classics IV hits "Spooky" and "Stormy." His first solo album, *Pepper's Powwow*, features his father, Gilbert Pepper, spoken word/chants; Ravie Pepper, flute; Larry Coryell, guitar; Jim Jemmott, bass; Tom Grant, piano; Spider Rice, drums; and

Herbie Mann, producer. The disc blends country, jazz, and rock with covers of Peter LaFarge numbers and traditional chants, including "Witchi Tai To." In 1971, Pepper and his wife, Caren Knight, moved to Alaska for eleven years, where he continued to play and record. While working as a deep-sea fisherman, he witnessed the tragic loss of five friends at sea, and the Peppers returned to Oregon. Friend and contemporary, trumpet player Don Cherry helped Pepper with his definitive "comeback album," *Comin' and Goin'*. By the mid-1980s, Pepper was touring and recording in Europe with Stanton Davis, Mal Waldron, Marty Cook, John Betsch, Ed Schuller, and many others. Pepper's performance at the International Jazz Festival in Münster, Germany, on May 19, 1990, was released posthumously as *Remembrance* in 1994.

A respected member of the Native community, Pepper often visited the reservations when touring North America. After succumbing to lymphoma, he passed away in Portland, Oregon, on February 10, 1992. His life story was presented in the documentary *Pepper's Powwow* [Sandra Osawa, 1994].

DISCOGRAPHY:

Witchi Tai To: The Music of Jim Pepper [Tutu 2002] best of
Live at New Morning, Paris [Tutu 1999]
Remembrance [Tutu 1994]
Camargue [Pan 1989] w/ Claudine Francois
Art of the Duo [Tutu 1989] w/ Mal Waldron
West End Avenue [Nabel 1989]
The Path [Enja 1988]
Bear Tracks [Extraplatte 1988]
Dakota Song [Enja 1987]
Comin' and Goin' [Europa 1983; Island 1987; Polygram 1991]
Pepper's Powwow [Atlantic/Embryo 1971] w/ circular dye-cut gatefold cover; rare

Singles:

"Polar Bear Stomp" [Alaska Hit Singles AHS-001 1981/1984] composed 1974

Appearances (listed alphabetically):

Archie Cavenaugh (Tlingit):
Black and White Raven [A&M/Cavenaugh 1980]
Classics IV:
Spooky [Imperial 1967]
Marty Cook:
Red, White, Black, and Blue [Tutu 1988, 1995]
Nightwork [Enja 1986]
Larry Coryell:
Improvisations: Best of Vanguard [Vanguard 1999] box set
Basics [Vanguard 1968]
Everything Is Everything:
Hey Look What I Found! Vol. 9 [Mavis CD-4509] comp
Vanguard Collector's Edition [Vanguard 1997] comp, box set
Witchi Tai To [Vanguard/Apostle VRS-35082] number 69 Billboard Pop Charts for five weeks, 1969
Everything Is Everything [Vanguard/Apostle 1969]
The Free Spirits:
I Want to Be Free [ABC 1967; Paramount 1968]
"Tattoo Man/Girl of the Mountain" [ABC 1967] seven-inch single
Outta Sight Outta Sound [ABC 1966; Paramount 1967]
David Freisen, E. Moore, Jim Pepper, etc.:
Remembering the Moment [Soul Note 1994] reissue
The Fugs:
Belle of Avenue A. [Reprise 1969]
Tom Grant:
View from Here [Verve/Polygram 1993] reissue
Charlie Haden, Carla Bley, etc.:
Ballad of the Fallen [ECM 1983; Polygram 1990/1993; ECM 2000]
Keith Jarrett:
Foundations: The Keith Jarrett Anthology [Rhino 1994]
Foundations [Atlantic 1968]
Gordon Lee Quartet:
Land Whales in New York [Tutu 1982]
Essra Mohawk:

Sandy's Album Is Here at Last [Bizarre/
  Verve 1969; Edsel 1995]
Bob Moses:
When Elephants Dream of Music [Grama-
  vision 1982/1993]
Paul Motian:
Misterioso [Soul Note 1983/1987]
Jack of Clubs [Soul Note 1985]
The Story of Maryam [Soul Note 1983/
  1993]
Cam Newton:
*Welcome Aliens: Party Music for the First
  Authentic Landing* [Inner City 1979]
Cole Porter:
Porter for Sale [Jazzfest 1997] reissue
Ray and the Wolf Gang:
The Blues Can't Turn You Loose [Gray Cats
  Music Productions 1988]
Nana Simopoulos:
Wings and Air [Enja 1986]
Mal Waldron:
Devils and Hymns [High Tide 1989]
  w/ magazine *Musica Jazz* no. 10/97, Italy
Mal, Dance, and Soul [Tutu 1988]
More Git Goat [Tutu 1988]
Quadralogue at Utopia, Vol. 1 [Tutu 1987]
Art of the Duo [Enja 1986]
Peter Walker:
Second Poem to Karmela [Vanguard 1969]
World Music Orchestra:
East West Suite [Granit Records 1990]
Various:
Gramavision 10th Anniversary [Grama-
  vision 1991] comp
Oyate [Nato/World 1990/1998, France]
  comp
International Jazz Festival, Münster '88
  [Tutu 888-110] comp
ECM Spectrum, Vol. 1 [ECM 1987] comp

Covers (listed alphabetically):
Brewer and Shipley:
"Witchi Tai To" on *The Best of Brewer and
  Shipley* [Kama Sutra 1976]
Chuck Florence:
"Witchi Tai To" on *Remembering Jim
  Pepper* [Saxophile 1999] tribute album
Jan Garbarek:
"Witchi Tai To" on *Witchi Tai To* [ECM
  1973]

Harper's Bizarre:
"Witchi Tai To" on *Feelin' Groovy* [Warner
  1967]

Peters, Aaron—(Saulteaux) Rock

Born 1971, Long Plain First Nations, Manitoba. Peters combined his radio and television training with his music, which he
calls "bannock rock." His rockudrama/
music video about residential schools,
called *Perfect Crime*, garnered a gold
medal at Worldfest, Charleston, North
Carolina, for Best Music Video (New Artist) and a Blizzard Award nomination from
the Manitoba Motion Picture Industry for
Best Music Video. His second album, produced by Basil Karahalios and Don Marks,
was recorded in his hometown, Winnipeg,
Manitoba. The album's single, "Alone in
the Rain," was used in the CBC television
series *The Rez.*

DISCOGRAPHY:
Sasquatch [independent 2000]
Don't Say Reality [independent 1996]
Unafraid [independent 1994] cass

Appearances:
An Aboriginal Christmas [Sunshine 1997]
  comp

Videos:
The Day I Ran Away [Sasquatch 2000]
Perfect Crime [Native Multimedia Produc-
  tions 1996]
On the Other Hand [Native Multimedia
  Productions 1996]

Pettiford, Oscar—(Choctaw–Cherokee–African American) Jazz

1922–1960

Born September 30, 1922, midnight, Ok-
mulgee, Oklahoma. Raised in Mississippi, Pettiford began playing piano in
1933 and bass in 1935, performing with

his eleven siblings, his Choctaw mother, and his Cherokee African father, Harry "Doc" Pettiford. His father, a veterinarian, ordered his son to embark on a music career in the family band, known as Doc Pettiford and His Family Orchestra, which included older siblings Leontine, Harry, Cecile, Ira, Margie, and Alonzo, and the younger children Rosemay, Helen, Katherine, Alice, and Joseph. They spent enough time in Minneapolis to call it home but disbanded after Doc passed away in 1943.

That same year, Pettiford joined Charlie Barnet with bass player Chubby Jackson and developed a twin-bassed band. The following year, OP, as Pettiford was called, started the first be-bop band with Dizzy Gillespie. OP became one of the top bass players as well as a bop pioneer and the first major cello soloist in jazz. He formed the Oscar Pettiford Orchestra and the New Oscar Pettiford Sextet, later playing in Harlem with Gillespie; the Esquire All Stars with Mildred Bailey; Coleman Hawkins; Woody Herman; Duke Ellington (from 1945 to 1948); Louis Armstrong (See: Russell Moore); Eddie Bert's All Stars; the Birdlanders; Art Blakey; Clifford Brown; Kenny Burrell; Red Rodney; Earl Hines; Charles Mingus; and many others. He recorded several rare and original sides on Bethlehem Archives, Avenue Jazz, Paramount, Jazzland, Fantasy, Debut/OJC, Black Lion, and Affinity Records and recorded with Thelonius Monk, Stan Getz, and Bud Powell.

OP led an all-star band on a USO tour to Japan and Korea in 1951; he played New York City from 1952 to 1958, then England, and later performed with drummer Jimmy Pratt and Stan Getz in Scandanavia. His appearances as himself in the films *The Crimson Canary* [John Hoffman, 1945] and *Und noch frech dazu AKA: And Saucy at That* [Rolf Von Sydow, 1959] attest to his popularity. Recognized by his peers for his exceptional bass playing, he was awarded the *Metronome* magazine and Jazz All-Star awards in 1944 and 1945. His work was described as melodically innovative; he possessed great technical skill and breathtakingly accurate intonation, both issuing from a vast musical knowledge. While playing with Woody Herman, OP substituted his bass for a cello, more as a joke, but unwittingly developed a unique place for the instrument in the jazz idiom. He not only developed the cello as a solo instrument, but turned his attention to writing music while mending a broken arm. Memorable tracks include "Tricotism," "Minor Seventh Heaven," and "Chasin' the Bass." A legend in the world of jazz, OP died in the Fiedfredericksberg Hospital in Copenhagen, Denmark, September 18, 1960.

The New Oscar Pettiford Sextet Lineup: Oscar Pettiford, cello; Phil Urso, tenor; Charles Mingus, bass; Julius Watkins, French horn; Walter Bishop, piano; Percy Brice, drums.

SELECTED DISCOGRAPHY:
Bass Hits [Pearl 1998]
The New Oscar Pettiford Sextet [Fantasy/ Debut 1984]
Bohemia after Dark [Charly/Affinity 1984] reissue of *The Finest of Oscar Pettiford*
The Finest of Oscar Pettiford [Bethlehem 1976] recorded 1955
The Legendary Oscar Pettiford, Featuring Attila Zoller [Black Lion 1976] recorded 1959
Live at Jilly's [Atlantic 1965]
The Essen Jazz Festival All Stars [Fantasy 1964]
My Little Cello [Fantasy 1964]
Last Recordings by the Late, Great Bassist [Jazzland 1962]
Oscar Pettiford: Classics of Modern Jazz [Jazzland 1962]
Montmartre Blues [Black Lion 1959]
O.P.'s Jazz Men [Paramount 1957]
Oscar Pettiford and His Birdland Band [Spotlite 1957]
Deep Passion [Impulse 1956]
Orchestra in Hi Fi [ABC 1956]
Oscar Pettiford in Hi Fi [Paramount 1956]

Jazz Mainstream [Bethlehem 1955]
Another One [Bethlehem 1955]
Bass by Pettiford/Burke [Bethlehem 1954]
Oscar Pettiford Modern Quintet [Bethlehem 1954]
Basically Duke [Bethlehem 1954]
Oscar Pettiford Sextet [Vogue 1954]
The New Oscar Pettiford Trio [Debut 1953]
The New Oscar Pettiford Sextet [Debut/OJC 1953]
First Bass [IAJRC 1953]
Discoveries [Savoy 1952]

Pine Family Singers—(Anishnabe)
Gospel

Lineup: Donna, Gertrude, Dan Jr., Bev, Gail, Doreen, Edith, Betty, Lana, Geraldine, Willard, and Morley Pine.

From Garden River First Nation in Ontario, Canada, the Pines are descendants of Shingwaukonce (Little Pine). Hymns sung in Anishnabe reveal a long history of cultural preservation within conversion to Christianity. These songs of praise and thanksgiving handed down through generations were recorded in Sault Sainte Marie, Ontario.

DISCOGRAPHY:
The Pine Family Singers [independent 1999] cass

Porter, Murray—(Mohawk) Blues
See: Pappy Johns Band; Flute Music: Paul and Jason Hacker; Contemporary Spoken Word: Legends (Miscellaneous)

Born Murray Steven Porter, June 24, 1960, Six Nations Reserve, Grand River Territory, Ontario. Self-described as "a red man in a white man's world singing the black man's music," Porter started playing in the early 1970s and has toured internationally. He was a featured performer in the 1995 television special *Blues on Ice*, which blended figure skating and live blues

music; additional performers included Olympic skaters Elvis Stojko, Brian Orser, singer-songwriter Murray McLaughlin, and others. Porter joined the Pappy Johns Band in 2001. He was nominated Best Songwriter, Maple Blues Award, 2004.

DISCOGRAPHY:
1492: Who Found Who? [First Nations 1994]
1492: Who Found Who? [independent 1991] cass
Last Stand [independent 1989] cassingle

Appearances:
Pappy Johns Band:
Full Circle [indepedent 2003]
Various:
Skin Tight Blues [Sweet Grass/EMI 2002] comp
Backroads: Worlds [independent 2000] comp
Downa Bush: The Future of Aboriginal Music [independent 1999] comp
Blues on Ice [CBC 1995] television special
Toronto Blues Today [Toronto Blues Society 1995] comp
Lacrosse: The Creator's Game [Ken Murch, 1994] sdtk, documentary
I Am an Eagle: The Music from the Legends Project [First Nations 1994] comp
Legends: I Am an Eagle [First Nations 1994] comp

Videos:
TV Repairman [First Nations 1994]

Princess Pale Moon—(Cherokee)

Word Records certainly took its chances in releasing this strange little curio without the foresight of any possible future hauntings; it was recorded in Nashville, with arrangements by Bill Pursell and special thanks to Silver Hair and Morning Star Greenlee.

DISCOGRAPHY:
Walk in Beauty [Word Records 1977]

Psychotic Aztecs—(Chicano) Rock

Lineup: Tito Larriva, vocals/guitar; Steven Medina, guitar; John Auila, bass/vocals; Johnny "Vatos" Hernandez, drums/percussion. Aztecan expression from the raw materials of punk and metal.

DISCOGRAPHY:
Santa Sangre [Grita! 1998]

Pura Fe—(Oneiowa-Tuscarora) Vocalist *See*: Haida, Medicine Men, Jim Pepper, Raphael, Robbie Robertson, Tonemah, Ulali

Based in New York City, this Broadway alumnus studied with Martha Graham, danced with the American Ballet Theater, sang with the Mercer Ellington Orchestra, and sang backup on numerous projects, including commercial jingles.

A founding member of Ulali, she gained notoriety in the late 1980s as a featured performer at the 1989 WOMAD Music Festival in Toronto, Ontario. Pura Fe (Pure Faith) was billed as a singing group featuring M. Cochise Anderson, Soni Moreno Primeau, Louis Mofsie, Kenneth Littlehawk, Jim Roach, Matoaka Little Eagle, Franc Menusan, and the Young Blood Singers (*See*: Powwow Music). The second cassette recording includes the track "Condor Meets the Eagle," which commemorates the five hundred years since the Columbus invasion and gained popularity on Native and community radio. *Caution to the Wind* received international airplay as Pura Fe made several appearances on recordings with many other artists, including the Andean group Kanatan Aski's *Condor Meets the Eagle* [independent 1993], which received a Juno nomination for Best Global Recording, 1994. Her 1991 video *Follow Your Heart's Desire* won Best Music Video from the American Indian Film Festival, 1996.

DISCOGRAPHY:
Caution to the Wind [Shanachie 1995]

Ladies Choice [independent 1992] w/ Soni Romero
Pura Fe, Vol. 2 [independent 1989] cass
Pura Fe, Vol. 1 [independent 1988] cass

Singles:
"Museum Cases" [independent 1992]

Appearances (listed alphabetically):
Haida:
The Haida Way [Red Vinyl 1998]
Raphael:
Half-Breed Blues [independent 1997]
Tonemah:
The Ghosts of St. Augustine [Red Sky Productions 1997]
Various:
Songs for Chiapas "Off the Record" [Ra Records 1999] comp
The Fire This Time: *Dancing on John Wayne's Head* [Extreme 1995] comp

Videos:
Pepper's Powwow [Sandra Osawa, 1994]
Follow Your Heart's Desire [AICH 1991]

Quinto Sol—(Chicano) Reggae *See*: Aztlan Underground

Lineup: Mizraim R. Real, vocals/guitar; Tino Torres, vocals; Martin Perez, bass; Javier Villalobos, drums; Caesar Villalobos, guitar/keyboards; Bernie Bran, percussion; Sal Magalion, timbales; Mondo Ganzalez, congas; Steve Gomez, bongos; Ray Ray, keyboards.

Quinto Sol (the Fifth Sun) employed bilingual lyrics with outspoken perspectives on colonialism, resistance, social issues, police violence, the EZLN, and the uprising in Chiapas, Mexico, in 1994.

DISCOGRAPHY:
Kwikakali [Xicano Records and Film 1999] two-CD set

Appearances:
Peace and Dignity Journeys [Xicano Records and Film 2000] comp
Sociadad = Suciadad [BYO Records 1997] comp

Rage Against the Machine—Rock
See: Aztlan Underground

Lineup: Zach de la Rocha (Chicano), vocals; Tom Morello (Chicano), guitars; Brad Wilk, drums; Timmy C., bass; Eric B., turntables.

Rage is perhaps one of the most notorious bands to brandish a political view with an emphasis on human rights and liberation struggles. Although the group had three platinum albums, critics still felt that they took too many chances in bringing attention to the cases of political prisoners Leonard Peltier and Mumia Abu Jamal. Frontman de la Rocha has worked with barrio kids in East Los Angeles and assisted in community projects.

DISCOGRAPHY:
Renegades [Sony 2000]
Star Profile [Master Rights 2000]
Battle of Los Angeles [Epic 1999]
Evil Empire [Epic 1996]
Justify Those That Die [Kiss the Stone
    1993, Italy] recorded live in Amsterdam
Rage Against the Machine [Epic 1992]

Singles:
"Guerrilla Radio/Without a Face" [Epic
    1999]
"Fuck the Police" [Epic 1999]
"People of the Sun" [Epic 1996]
"Bulls on Parade" [Epic 1996]
"The Ghost of Tom Joad" [Epic 1996]
"No Shelter" [Epic 1992]
"Bombtrack" [Epic 1992] four-track EP
"Freedom/Take the Power Back" [Epic
    1992]

Videos:
Live in Concert [Epic 1997]
The Ghost of Tom Joad [Epic 1996]
Zapata's Blood [Epic 1996]
Freedom (for Leonard Peltier) [Epic 1992]

Rain Dance—Rock

Lineup: Mardy Lucier Porte, guitars/ vocals/harmonica/cedar flute; Nick Chiarore, drums/percussion/backup vocals;

Dove, bass/background vocals; Adam Songchow, lead vocals.

Porte and Songchow made some headway as soloists and session players despite the band's short life span.

DISCOGRAPHY:
Peyote [Sunshine 1995]

Ranville, Errol—(Cree) Country/Rock
See: C-Weed

Born August 1, 1953. Founder and mainstay of C-Weed, the country-and-western Native band, Ranville helped generate more than forty awards and eight albums with the group. He launched his solo career in the 1980s and operated the C-Weed Cabaret in Winnipeg, Manitoba. On his first album, he cowrote much of the music with Ra McGuire of the Canadian rock band Trooper. The album spawned two singles, "Still the One" and "Janine." Ranville later revived C-Weed and launched the cweed.com record label.

DISCOGRAPHY:
I Wanna Fly [C-Weed 2000]
The Cowboy Code [independent 1996]
I Want to Fly [Thunder 1990]

Videos:
Last of an Old Cowboy's Dream [independent 1986]

Raphael—Folk
DISCOGRAPHY:
Half-Breed Blues [independent 1997]
    w/ Pura Fe

Appearances:
Songs for Chiapas "Off the Record" [Ra
    Records 1999] comp

Raynor, Marg—(Metis) Folk

Based in Perkinsfield, Ontario. Raynor, a teacher and singer-songwriter, performed extensively throughout the central region of the province. She received the Georgian Bay Music Association Award for Folk Music in 1995.

DISCOGRAPHY:

Keeper of Stories [independent 1999]
Mist upon the Water [independent 1997]

R. Carlos Nakai Quartet *See*: R. Carlos Nakai

Red Blaze—Country

Lineup: Ray Villebrun, lead vocals/acoustic rhythm guitar; P. J. Jacobson, bass/harmony vocals; Rob Turner, drums/percussion/harmony vocals; Duane Lasas, lead guitar/harmony vocals; with Fred Nabess, lead guitar; Greg Edmunds, keyboards/saxophone; Denise Lanceley, backup/harmony vocals; Dean Bernier, fiddle; Peggy Vermette, backup/harmony vocals. Formed in 1994, Saskatchewan, Canada.

DISCOGRAPHY:

Sound of Thunder [independent 2001]
   w/ Ray Villebrun
Memories and Daydreams [Turtle Island
   Music 1998]

Appearances:

A Turtle Island Christmas [Turtle Island
   Music 2002] comp
Still the Eagle Flies [SICC 1995] comp,
   w/ Ray Villebrun

Redbone—Rock *See*: Archie Cavenaugh

Original Lineup: Lolly Vegas (Yaqui-Shoshone), vocals/guitar; Pat Vegas (Yaqui-Shoshone), vocals/electric bass; Tony Bel-lamy (Yaqui), vocals/guitar; Pete DePoe (Cheyenne), drums (replaced by Arturo Perez, 1971, and by Butch Rillera, 1973).

Formed in 1968, Los Angeles, California. Redbone's first album was a two-record set—unusual for an initial release. The name Redbone was derived from Cajun slang for "half-breed." Though California-based, the band specialized in Louisiana swamp rock mixed with funk and soul. Brothers Pat Vegas and Lolly Vegas, who founded the group, were born in Fresno, California, and grew up around the migrant farmworkers, who brought many musical influences, including Cajun and Louisiana roots music. The farm community of Jerico became the basis for the autobiographical song of the same name.

After moving to Los Angeles in the early 1960s, the Vegas brothers found work as songwriters and session artists. Their film scores included the 1964 James Landis spy-spoof *Nasty Rabbit AKA "Spies A Go-Go,"* Elvis Presley's *Kissin' Cousins* [Gene Nelson, 1964], and the 1967 surfploitation flick *It's a Bikini World* [Stephanie Rothman, 1967]. They teamed up with Leon Russell and Delaney Bramlett to form the houseband for ABC's teen music show *Shindig* (1964–66). In 1966, they released a live recording on Mercury Records entitled *Pat and Lolly Vegas Live at the Haunted House*, which was recorded at the Los Angeles hot spot and coproduced by Russell Garrett and Snuffy Garrett. Performing as the Avantis, the brothers released *Hotrodders Choice* on the Del-Fi label. Lolly was hired as the arranger for Jim Ford's *Harlan County* album, released on White Whale Records in 1969, and played lead guitar on a rare track, "The Deuce Coupes."

The brothers' session work included stints with Glen Campbell, Sonny and Cher, and many others. Their song "Niki Hokey," recorded by P. J. Probert, reached number 23 on the Billboard Charts in 1967 and set the stage for the birth of an all-Native group. The idea formed when the

Vegas brothers met guitarist Tony Bellamy during backup sessions for Odetta and John Lee Hooker (*See*: Jesse Ed Davis). Bellamy had started out playing Spanish guitar at his parents' restaurant in Los Angeles and then in bands on the local club circuit. Bobby Womack introduced the trio to drummer Pete DePoe (born Last Walking Bear, Neah Bay Reservation, Washington). DePoe had learned the drum at ceremonies and powwows, then later moved into contemporary percussion. David Garibaldi, drummer for the 1970s funk and R & B band Tower of Power, cited DePoe as a major influence and credited him for creating an influential style known as the King-Kong Beat, which contained the same cadence found in Puerto Rican dance music the *bomba* and the *cua*. The pattern that DePoe developed involved playing a ride beat on the bell of his cymbal, with the remainder of the drumming played underneath. That technique was exemplified in Redbone's song "Prehistoric Rhythm."

After forming Redbone, the Vegas brothers, Bellamy, and DePoe signed a five-album deal with Epic Records, and although they went through three drummers within a span of four years, they managed to produce a string of hits. In 1971, Elton John identified Redbone as his favorite band. Their Billboard Chart appearances included "Maggie," number 45 from December 1970 to February 1971; "Witch Queen of New Orleans," number 21 from November 1971 to February 1972; "Come and Get Your Love," number 5 in 1974. The 1974 album, *Turquoise Dreams Through Beaded Eyes*, features guest singers Bonnie Bramlett (*See*: Rita Coolidge), Merry Clayton, and Clydie King (*See*: Jesse Ed Davis). Their songs of struggle include "Alcatraz," "Chant: 13th Hour," and "Wovoka." Although Redbone enjoyed great commercial success, their albums never sold well, and by the late 1970s the band folded. Numerous best-of albums were released

throughout the 1990s as the Vegas brothers continued to perform as Redbone. They made a guest appearance at NAMA in 1998 and were inducted into the Rock 'n' Roll Hall of Fame in Cleveland, Ohio, in 2002.

DISCOGRAPHY:
The Essential Redbone [Sony 2003] best of
Take Two [Sony 2002]
To the Bone [Sony 1998] best of
Redbone Breaks [Ubiquity 1997]
Golden Classics [Sony/Collectibles 1996] best of
Live [Avenue/Rhino 1994] recorded 1977
Greatest Songs [Curb 1994] best of
The Best of Redbone [Dominion 1990] best of
Cycles [RCA 1977] rare
Come and Get Your Redbone [Epic 1975] best of
The Best of Redbone [Epic 1974; Dominion 1976; K-Tel 1991] best of
Turquoise Dreams Through Beaded Eyes [Epic 1974]
Wovoka [Epic 1974]
Already Here [Epic 1972]
Message from a Drum [Epic 1972]
Potlatch [Epic 1970]
Red Bone [Epic 1970] double vinyl

Pat Vegas and Lolly Vegas:
Pat and Lolly Vegas at the Haunted House [Mercury 1966 SR-61059]
performing as the Avantis:
Hotrodders Choice [Del-Fi 1966]
performing as the Sharks:
Robot Walk [Apogee 1964]
Big Surf [Sapien 1963]

Singles:
"Give Our Love Another Try/Funky Silk" [RCA 1977]
"Checkin' It Out" [RCA 1977]
"I've Got to Find the Right Woman" [Epic 1975]
"One More Time/Blood Sweat And Tears" [Epic 1974]
"Come and Get Your Love" [Epic 1974] number 5 Billboard Charts
"Only You/Rock and Roll" [Epic 1974]

"Suzi Girl" [Epic 1974]

"Suzi Girl/Interstate Highway" [Epic 1974]

"Wovoka/Clouds in My Sunshine" [Epic 1973]

"Come and Get Your Love/Day to Day" [Epic 1973]

"We Were All Wounded at Wounded Knee/ Speakeasy" [Epic 1973, Holland]

"We Were All Wounded at Wounded Knee" [Epic 1973]

"Message from a Drum/One Monkey" [Epic 1972]

"Fais Do/Already Here (Brujo)" [Epic 1972]

"Poison Ivy/Condition Your Condition" [Epic 1972]

"The Witch Queen of New Orleans/Chant: 13th Hour" [Epic 1971, France]

"Witch Queen of New Orleans" [Epic 1971] number 21 Billboard Charts 1971–72

"Light as a Feather/Who Can Say?" [Epic 1970]

"Crazy Cajun Cakewalk Band/Night Come Down" [Epic 1970]

"Maggie" [Epic 1970] number 40 Billboard Charts

Appearances (listed alphabetically):

Archie Cavenaugh:

Black and White Raven [A&M/Cavenaugh 1980] session backup

Brenda Patterson:

Keep On Keepin' On [Epic 1971] session backup

Various:

Latin Oldies, Vol. 4 [Thump Records 2000] comp

Latin Oldies, Vol. 3 [Thump Records 1999] comp

House of Blues: Essential Southern Rock [A&M 1997] comp

Back to the 70s [Dominion 1987; K-Tel 1990; Castle 1994; Madacy 1997] comp

Dance Me Outside [Denon 1994] sdtk

Rock of the '70s, Vol. 3 [Dunhill 1992; DC 1995] comp

Golden Years: 1974 [Dominion 1990; K-Tel 1993] comp

Super '70s, Vol. 1 [Dominion/K-Tel 1993] comp

Rock Artifacts, Vol. 2 [Sony 1991] comp

Rock Artifacts, Vol. 1 [Columbia/Legacy 1990] comp

Music People [Columbia 31280] comp

Different Strokes [Columbia 1971] comp

Covers (listed alphabetically):

Abstracts:

"Any Old Time" on Abstracts [Pompeii 1968]

Bus Stop:

"Come and Get Your Love" on Little Faster [Ripe and Ready 1995]

Dave Edmunds:

"Juju Man" on Anthology 1968–1990 [Rhino 1993]

"Juju Man" on Best of Dave Edmunds [Swan Song 1981]

"Juju Man" on Get It [Swan Song 1977]

J. Hubert Francis and Eagle Feather:

"Message from a Drum" on Message from a Drum [Bear Paw 1998]

"Alcatraz" on Reverence [Sunshine CD 4190]

Aretha Franklin:

"Niki Hokey" on Lady Soul [Atlantic 1968; Rhino 1995]

Joy Unlimited:

Groove with What You Got [Mercury 1970]

Minnesoda:

"Maggie" on Minnesoda [Capitol 11102]

The Premiers:

"I Won't Be Back Next Year" on Farmer John [WB 1964]

Real McCoy:

"Come and Get Your Love" on Another Night [Arista 1994]

Rock Buster:

title track on Crazy Cajun Cakewalk Band [CBS 48/49]

Swamp Mama Johnson:

"Niki Hokey" on Swamp Mama Johnson [BMS 1995/1998]

Film Soundtracks:

Dance Me Outside [Bruce MacDonald, 1994]

It's a Bikini World [Stephanie Rothman, 1967]

Nasty Rabbit AKA "Spies A Go-Go" [James Landis, 1964]
Kissin' Cousins [Gene Nelson, 1964]

Red Bow, Buddy—(Lakota) Country
See: Contemporary Spoken Word: Testimonials and Memoirs: *Frank Fools Crow*

1949–1993
Born Pine Ridge, South Dakota. Stories of Red Bow's birth are surrounded in poetic mystery. Abandoned as an infant, he was found on the steps of an elderly couple's home on the reservation and given the name he carried throughout his life. Red Bow learned the traditional ways and values he eloquently conveyed in country ballads. He enlisted in the U.S. Marine Corps in the late 1960s and later found his way back to the reservation to pursue a career in music. He recorded his first single in July 1976 on Mr. Dog Music, a small independent label based in Rapid City, South Dakota. This recording sparked his love of music and revealed a remarkable talent. Red Bow played and recorded predominantly with producer Dik Darnell. He passed away on March 28, 1993. A NAMA Award was dedicated to his memory in 1998 with a performance by Floyd Westerman and Joanne Shenandoah.

DISCOGRAPHY:
BRB [Native Spirit/Variena 1993] memorial reissue
Black Hills Dreamer [Tatanka 1991]
Journey to the Spirit World [Tatanka 1983]
BRB [First American 1980]

Appearances:
Music from Turtle Island [Turtle Island Music 1999] comp

Red Earth—Rock/Funk/Reggae

Lineup: Adrian Wall, bass/vocals; Ira Wilson, lead vocals/rhythm guitar/sax; Jeff

Drummerman, drums/percussion/vocals; Christian Orellana, percussion/pipes/flute/vocals; Carl Bluehouse Johnson, lead guitar/keyboard/vocals/bass; Monica X. Delgado, trumpet/vocals; Jason Botten, trumpet (replaced by John Simms); Itideki Imai, trombone (replaced by Kenneth Beaupre); guest vocalists include Skheme of Poetic Justice/Native Roots and Star Nayea (on *When Worlds Collide*).

Formed in 1995, Albuquerque, New Mexico. NAMA Award, Debut Artist/Group of the Year, 2000.

DISCOGRAPHY:
Zia Soul [Tribal Stew 2003]
Live! [Tribal Stew 2001] EP
When Worlds Collide [Third Mesa 1999]
Red Earth [Third Mesa 1998] EP

Appearances:
Ouch! Welcome to Albuquerque [Soeyermom Records 1999] comp

Redhead, Roy—(Cree) Country/Pop

Born October 21, 1957, York Factory, Manitoba. His one album contains lengthy compositions with uplifting messages; it was produced by Craig Fotheringham (*See*: C-Weed). Redhead was elected chief of his community in the 1990s.

DISCOGRAPHY:
Towards the Light [Saposka 1999]

Redhouse Family—(Dineh) Jazz *See*: Native Flamenco, R. Carlos Nakai Quartet; Flute Music

Lineup: Charlotte Redhouse, vocals; Mary Redhouse, bass/vocals; Vince Redhouse, tenor saxophone/guitar; Tony Redhouse, percussion; Lenny Redhouse, drums; Larry Redhouse, piano/keyboards; Rex Redhouse, traditional vocals.

Rex was born and raised in the Four Corners area of the Dineh Nation, served in

The Redhouse Family. Photo by John Running.

World War II, and later earned a degree in business from Santa Clara University; he created the Redhouse Dancers in 1969. Charlotte has worked in different visual art mediums, including traditional Dineh jewelry. Mary has worked in education, provided music for PBS documentaries, recorded with the R. Carlos Nakai Quartet, and appears on the William Eaton Ensemble album *Naked in Eureka*. Vince played in an acid-jazz band in northern California. Tony has worked in art, dance, and music while performing and recording with Robert Tree Cody (*See*: Flute Music) and Rob Wallace. Lenny played with several groups in Tucson, Arizona, and performed as a traditional dancer with the Redhouse Dancers. Larry has performed throughout the southwestern United States as a solo pianist and also dances with the Redhouse Dancers.

The Redhouse Family's *Urban Indian* (1997), combined culture with jazz. Courtesy Canyon Records.

DISCOGRAPHY:

Urban Indian [Canyon 1997]

Appearances:
Voices across the Canyon [Canyon 1997]
comp

Related Projects:
Vince Redhouse:
Faith in the House [SOAR 2002] Grammy
nomination, 2003

Red Nativity—Gospel

A collection of seasonal carols performed
and arranged by Robby Bee and Paul La
Roche (a.k.a. Brule).

DISCOGRAPHY:
One Holy Night [Red Sea 1997]

Red Power Squad—Hip-Hop *See*: New Breed

Lineup: Conway Kootenay (Mr. K), Howard
Horseman (MC-REDD-E), Vincent Rain,
Jordan James, and Leo James.
    Formed in 1998, Edmonton, Alberta.
The group started out promoting drug-
and alcohol-free lifestyles through their
rap combined with powwow dancers and
break dancers. Their 2003 album marked
a shift to a more commercial direction
with rhymes composed of sexually explicit
material. They have shared the stage with
Maestro Fresh Wes, 2Rude, and many other
mentors.

DISCOGRAPHY:
Triumph [Red Power Squad 2003]
Total Kaos [Red Power Squad 2002]
Bad Medicine [Octave 2000]

Red Road Ensemble *See*: Robbie Robertson

Red Thunder—Pop/Trad

Lineup: Robby Romero, vocals/acoustic
guitar/traditional percussion; Benito Concha, traditional drums/percussion/vocals
(*See*: Tonemah; *Beyond Treaty* comp);
Mazatl Galindo, traditional flutes/percus-
sion/vocals; Paul Martinez, acoustic bass/
bass clarinet/vocals; additional performers
include Mike Concha, Richard Moves
Camp, Curtis Milk, Stevie Salas, Randy
Castillo, Charles Gasper, Dakota Rene, and
Cam Jr.
    Formed in 1990, in Washington, D.C.
Romero provided the catalyst for the
project, which grew from an Earth Day
performance. Once he had developed a
formula and a platform, he launched his
cultural and environmental content in the
band's character. He produced a half-hour
"world alert" video special, *Sacred Earth*,
which aired on MTV and VH-1, placing
the band front and center in the media's
attention, with a guest spot on the PBS
children's television series *The Puzzle
Place* and MTV's *Free Your Mind Campaign* in 1997. While based in Los Angeles,
California, Red Thunder continued to
play throughout the United States, show-
casing an eclectic mix of dance beats,
reggae rhythms, and rock, mixed together
in a vortex of traditional Native icons.
After the group dissolved, Romero continued to perform as a solo act while still
using the name Red Thunder. He released
a number of short videos, including the
thirty-minute *Thunder Storm* [MTV 2002].

DISCOGRAPHY:
American's Last Frontier [ETR 1075]
Hidden Medicine [independent 2002]
Heartbeat [Eagle Thunder 2001] dance
    remix single
Makoce Wakan [Eagle Thunder/Koch 1995]
Red Thunder [Eagle Thunder 1994] EP

Appearances:
Hidden Medicine [Eagle Thunder 1999]
    sdtk
Urban Skins, Vol. 1 [SOAR 1999] comp

Red Thunder (Robby Romero, *left*) with Bonnie Raitt. Photo by Agnes Patak.

Robby Romero:
Tears and a Journey [Eagle Thunder 2002]

Singles:
"Paint the World" [Eagle Thunder 2001]
"The Night You Called It a Day" [Eagle Thunder 2001]

Videos:
Hidden Medicine [Eagle Thunder 1999]
Sacred Ground [Eagle Thunder 1995]
Heart Beat [Eagle Thunder 1995]
Is It Too Late [Julien Temple, 1991]

Red Thunder Native Dance Theatre
See: Powwow Music

Revolver—(Dineh) Rock

Lineup: Hondo Baldwin Louis, lead vocals/rhythm guitar; Aanor Baldwin Louis,

drums; Richard "Ric" Davis Jr., lead guitar; Aaron Francisco, bass. This all-Dineh rock band from Window Rock, Arizona, recorded their first album in Utah.

DISCOGRAPHY:
Resolve [Cool Runnings 2000]

Reynosa, Carlos—(Chicano) Acoustic
See: Keith Secola

This California-based fashion photographer enlisted a legion of players to set his softer side to moody compositions of love and happiness. He helped establish the Native youth program Life Love Earth with Joanne Shenandoah and others.

DISCOGRAPHY:
Wiseman [independent 2000]
Sunrise [independent 2000]
Carlos Reynosa [Sacred Circle 1996]

Appearances:

Keith Secola:

Homeland: An Original Soundtrack
 [AKINA 2000]

Various:

Naturally Native [Silver Wave 2000] sdtk

Rhyne, Ken—(Tuscarora) Blues

A musician who was an architect or an architect who plays music—either way Rhyne is an exceptional harmonica player, with talent likened to that of Charlie Musselwhite, James Cotton, and Paul Butterfield. A veteran player based in Georgia and North Carolina, Rhyne has performed with George Thorogood and the Destroyers, Elvin Bishop, Koko Taylor, Johnnie Shines, and Gregg Allman. His first release includes the talents of William Alvarez, Van Miller, James Calvin, T. K. Lively, Henry Parrilla, Ricky Fargo, Jimmy O'Neill, Michael Hoskin, and Butch Mudbone.

DISCOGRAPHY:

Caught You White Handed [Fat City
 Records 2001]

Appearances:

Skin Tight Blues [Sweet Grass/EMI 2002]
 comp

Riley, Billy Lee—(Cherokee) Rockabilly

Born in Pocohontas, Oklahoma. A talented session guitarist/harmonica player, Riley worked in Hollywood, California, where he began his professional music career in 1961. He worked with many notable stars, including Ricky Nelson, Sammy Davis Jr., Johnny Rivers, the Ronettes, and the Beach Boys.

SELECTED DISCOGRAPHY:

In Action [GNP/Crescendo 1964]

Rinker, Al—(Coeur d'Alene) Jazz *See*: Mildred Bailey

1907–1982

Born Alton Rinker, December 20, Tekoa, Washington. Brother of the great Mildred Bailey and member of the original Paul Whiteman Rhythm Boys vocal trio that included Bing Crosby and Harry Barris. Rinker started out in Spokane, Washington, managing the Musiclanders, and lured childhood friend Bing Crosby into the entertainment business. Crosby was studying law and decided that a career in entertainment was much more appealing. In 1925, Rinker and Crosby traveled to Los Angeles to visit Rinker's sister, Mildred, who found them work singing while she put them up in her house. They were billed as Two Boys and a Piano in the Morrisey Music Hall Revue. A year later orchestra leader Paul Whiteman hired the boys for a national tour. Whiteman created the Rhythm Boys with the introduction of Harry Barris. After Crosby's solo career took off, the trio broke up, and Rinker worked as a producer for CBS Radio. He composed several songs, including "Dreamsville," "Let's Choo Choo to Idaho," and "You Can't Do Wrong Doin' Right." The latter two compositions appeared in the film *Duchess of Idaho* [Robert Z. Leonard, 1950]. Rinker passed away June 11, 1982, in Burbank, California.

DISCOGRAPHY:

Paul Whiteman's Rhythm Boys:

"Sweet Li'l/Ain't She Sweet?/Mississippi
 Mud/I Left My Sugar Standing in the
 Rain" [Victor 20783]
"Miss Annabelle Lee/Up Chillun, Wake
 Up" [Victor 21104]
"Birmingham Bertha/Am I Blue?" [Vocalion
 1296]
"Dixie Lee/Delta Bound" [Vocalion 2620]
"I Need You/When It's Sleepy Time Down
 South" [Brunswick 6174]
"It's You/River, Stay 'Way from My Door"
 [Brunswick 6192]

"I'm Going Home/Then You're Drunk" [Bluebird 8649]

"Bump It/I Know That You Know" [Decca 1584]

"I'm Walkin' This Town/Call Me Darling" [Decca 1730]

"Keystone Blues/New Orleans Hop Scotch Blues" [Decca 18095]

"Sweet Georgia Brown/Way Down Yonder in New Orleans" [Decca 18439]

"He's a Different Type of Guy/The Blues Jumped a Rabbit" [Decca 18440]

Jimmy Noone:

Ace of Hearts [Brunswick BL-58006] ten-inch vinyl

Jazz at the Apex [Brunswick AH-84]

Jimmie Noone and Johnny Dodds:

Battle of Jazz, Vol. 8 [Brunswick BL-58046] ten-inch vinyl

Jimmie Noone and Earl Hines:

At the Apex Club [Decca DL-9235]

Tommy Ladnier:

Blues and Stomps [Riverside 1026] ten-inch vinyl

Rising Cree—(Cree) Rock

David Cree and Bernadette Cree, originally from the Paul Cree Indian Band near Edmonton, Alberta, offered a sound resembling that of Kashtin.

DISCOGRAPHY:
North American Breed [DMT/Suncor 1995]

Ritchie, Paul—(Anishnabe) Folk

Ritchie recorded one album in Toronto, then disappeared from the scene to work as an Ottawa bureaucrat.

DISCOGRAPHY:
October Stranger [Broken Treaty 1980]

Rivers, Jimmie—(Cherokee) Country Swing

Born Jimmie Fewell, 1926, Hockerville, Oklahoma. This talented but obscure singer-songwriter toiled nightly in bars opening for Bob Wills, Lefty Frizzell, and Ernest Tubb. He played six- and twelve-string guitars, double-neck guitar, and trumpet. His playing style went beyond the margins of country, with bebop runs and influences of swing. He was a regular at DeMarco's 23 Club in Brisbane, California, in the late 1950s and early 1960s, where many live recordings were made and gradually released as a collection in 1995. Rivers was also inducted into the Western Swing Hall of Fame.

The 1995 album includes Jimmie Rivers on guitar and trumpet, Gene Duncan on rhythm guitar, Vance Terry on steel guitar, and Rivers's group, the Cherokees.

DISCOGRAPHY:
Jimmie Rivers and the Cherokees featuring Vance Terry: Western Swing 1961–64: Brisbane Bop [Joaquin Records 1995]

Singles:
"Hot Rod Lincoln/Jimmy's Riff" [Veltone 1960]

"Home on rhe Rockin' Range/So Much Crying" [Check 1960]

"I Don't Love Nobody/Jazz Me Blues" [Cavalier 1957]

Robertson, Robbie—(Mohawk) Rock

See: C-Weed, Jesse Ed Davis, Kashtin, George Leach, Little Wolf, Derek Miller

Born Jaime Robbie Robertson, July 5, 1943, Toronto, Ontario. A founding member of the Band, Robertson grew up in Toronto and visited his Mohawk relatives each summer on the Six Nations Reserve near Brantford, Ontario, discovering another side of his ancestry and a love of music. Learning guitar from his uncles on the rez,

Robbie Robertson and Buffy Sainte-Marie at the 1992 Juno Awards. Photo by Barry Roden; courtesy EMI.

he warmed up to the stage with Ronnie Hawkins and the Hawks. Hawkins recorded Robertson's songs "Hey Boba Lu" and "Someone Like You" in 1960. Through playing with the Hawks, Robertson met Bob Dylan and embarked on another music venture. The Band was formed in 1967 and became one of the most successful groups of its day.

Robertson's brilliant soundtrack work and arranging, writing, and playing were structured toward success as his keen business sense guided the way. A good friend of director Martin Scorsese, Robertson broadened his creativity in numerous aspects of the film industry, including acting. After phenomenal achievement with the Band, he stepped back from the spotlight to examine his Native roots.

Robertson released a self-titled solo album that carried elements of the Native renaissance in a celebration of culture. Some tracks from this 1987 album were used in the film *Powwow Highway*. Robertson began focusing predominantly on Native musicians, including his soundtrack for the PBS miniseries *Music for the Native Americans*, produced by Jim Wilson, whose album *Wolf Moon* [Triloka 1997] featured Robertson on guitar.

Robertson's studio band the Red Road

Ensemble featured Walela; Doug Wallentyne; Kashtin; Pura Fe; Patrick Leonard; Bonnie Jo Hunt; Louis Mofsie and the Silver Cloud Singers (*See*: Powwow Music); Ulali; Alex Acuna and Sebastian Robertson, drums/percussion; Benito Concha (*See*: Firecat of Discord, Red Thunder, *Beyond Treaty* comp); Bill Dillon and Tony Green, bass.

Similar inspiration led to Robertson's next project, *Contact from the Underworld of Redboy* (Grammy nomination for Best Producer, 1999; Juno Award for Best Music of Aboriginal Canada Recording, 1999), which accompanied the PBS documentary *Making a Noise*. The album's single "Unbound" was also featured in the film *Grey Owl*.

The 1998 album *Contact* opens with an archival recording of Leah Hicks-Manning, John Trudell's late mother-in-law. Featured performers include Joanne Shenandoah; James Bilagody (*See*: Traditional/Archival Solo); Rita Coolidge; Cree Summer; Bonnie Jo Hunt; Anthony Begaye; Benito Concha; Maztl Galindo; Verdell Primeaux and Johnny Mike (*See*: Peyote Solo and Group); Six Nations Women Singers (*See*: Traditional/Archival Group); Howie B.; DJ Premier; Jackie Bird; Star Nayea; Caroline MacKendrick; Rupert Browne; Tim Gordine; Chief Jake Thomas and Leonard Peltier, guest voices.

Robertson's early production and session work includes Neil Diamond's *Beautiful Noise*. His life was the subject of the Bruce MacDonald film *Road Songs: A Portrait of Robbie Robertson*, released in 2001. Robertson performed with members of the Red Road Ensemble (Walela, Sadie Buck, and Jim Wilson) at the opening of the 2002 Winter Olympics in Salt Lake City, Utah.

SELECTED DISCOGRAPHY:
Classic Masters [Capitol 2002] best of
Contact from the Underworld of Redboy [Capitol 1998]
Music for the Native Americans [Capitol 1994]

Storyville [Geffen 1991]
Robbie Robertson [Geffen 1987]

Singles:
"Unbound" [Capitol 1998]
"Contact from the Underworld of RedBoy" [Pussy Foot 1998] three-song red vinyl EP w/ Howie B
"Vanishing Breed," from *Discover the Rhythms of Native Voices* [EMI 1996, Holland] comp
"Mahk Jchi" [Capitol 1994] vinyl EP dance remixes
"What about Now" [Geffen 1991]

The Band:
The Capitol Years: 1968–1977 [Toshiba 1990, Japan]
To Kingdom Come [Capitol 1989]
The Band Gift Set [Capitol 1989]
Il Rock 5 [EMI 1988]
The Band Story [Toshiba 1988, Japan]
Rock of Ages, Vol. 1 [Capitol 1982]
Stage Fright [Toshiba/EMI 1980, Japan]
Anthology [Capitol 1978]
The Last Waltz [Warner 1978]
Islands [Capitol 1977]
Best of the Band [Capitol 1976]
Masters of Rock [EMI 1975]
Northern Lights Southern Cross [Capitol 1975]
In Concert [Capitol 1973]
Moondog Matinee [Capitol 1973]
Cahoots [Capitol/EMI 1971]
Stage Fright [Capitol/EMI 1970]
The Band [Capitol/EMI 1969]
Music from Big Pink [Capitol/EMI 1968]

Appearances (listed alphabetically):
Neil Diamond:
Classics: The Early Years/Jazz Singer/Beautiful Noise [Sony 1997] three-CD box set
Beautiful Noise [Columbia 1976]
Little Wolf Band:
Wolf Moon [Triloka 1997] w/ Walela
Ringo Starr:
Starr Struck: The Best of Ringo Starr [Rhino 1989] best of

Goodnight Vienna [Apple 1974; Alliance 1991/1996]

Videos:
Unbound [Capitol 1998]
Showdown at Big Sky [Capitol 1987]

Film and Television:
Revisiting the Last Waltz [Stephen Altobello, 2002] as himself
Road Songs: A Portrait of Robbie Robertson [Bruce MacDonald, 2001] television documentary
Any Given Sunday [Oliver Stone, 1999] music
Grey Owl [Richard Attenborough, 1999] music
Wolves [David Douglas, 1999] IMAX documentary: narration
Making a Noise: A Native American Musical Journey with Robbie Robertson [PBS 1998] documentary
Cousin Bette [Des McAnuff, 1998] special thanks
Asteroids: Deadly Impact [Eitan Weinreich, 1997] television documentary: narration
Phenomenon [John Turteltaub, 1996] feature film: producer
Dakota Exile [Kristian Berg/Darren Renville, 1996] historical documentary: narration
The Crossing Guard [Sean Penn, 1995] as Roger
Concert for the Rock and Roll Hall of Fame [1995] television
Robbie Robertson: Going Home [Findlay Bunting, 1995] television
Jimmy Hollywood [Barry Levinson, 1994] music
U2: The Making of the Movie "Rattle and Hum" [Barry Devlin, 1988] television: narration
Powwow Highway [Jonathan Wacks, 1988] music
The Color of Money [Martin Scorsese, 1986] music
The King of Comedy [Martin Scorsese 1983] music
Visiting Hours AKA: The Fright AKA:

Get Well Soon, French Canadian title:
Terreur a l'hopital central [Jean-Claude
Lord, 1982] as Matthew
Carny [Robert Kaylor, 1980] feature film:
producer-writer, appeared as Patch
Raging Bull [Martin Scorsese, 1980] music
The Last Waltz [Martin Scorsese, 1978]
concert film: producer, appeared w/ the
Band
Eat the Document [Bob Dylan, 1972] docu-
mentary: as himself

Selected Awards:
2003: National Aboriginal Lifetime
Achievement Award
1999: Juno Award, Aboriginal Recording of
the Year, *Contact from the Underworld
of Redboy*
1995: Juno Award, Producer of the Year;
Juno Aboriginal Recording of the Year
nomination, *Music for the Native Americans*
1991: Grammy nominations, Best Rock
Vocal Performance (Solo), Best Engineer,
Storyville
1988: Juno Awards, *Robbie Robertson*;
CARAS Juno Hall of Fame Inductee, the
Band
1987: Grammy nomination, Best Rock/
Vocal Album, *Robbie Robertson*

Rogers, Will—(Cherokee) *See*:
Contemporary Spoken Word:
Testimonials and Memoirs

Romero, Joanelle Nadine—(Apache)
Blues

This sister of Robbie Romero also starred
in *Powwow Highway* [Jonathan Wacks,
1988] and composed a single for the PBS
special *American Holocaust*, 1999.

DISCOGRAPHY:
Indian Country Blues [independent 1995]
Joanelle Nadine Romero [independent
1995]

Rosita Stone—(Chicana) Folk/Rock

This Toronto-based singer-songwriter performed with a smooth voice and a sultry
demeanour. Her first recording includes
the talents of Greg Brozek, guitars; Bob
Sibony, drums/percussion; Etrik Lyons,
bass; and Mike Fonfaira, keyboards.

DISCOGRAPHY:
Heavy Sex Vibe [independent 1993] cass

Ross, Don—(Mi'kmaq-Scottish) Jazz/
Folk/Rock/Classical *See*:
Contemporary Spoken Word:
Miscellaneous: *Sugar Blues*

Born November 19, 1960, Montreal, Quebec. Ross began to work on his music
career after graduating from the music
department of York University, Toronto,
1983. He is the only person to win twice
the prestigious annual U.S. National
Fingerstyle Guitar Championship in
Winfield, Kansas, 1988 and 1996. A true
innovator of guitar composition and technique, he employs elements of jazz, folk,
rock, and classical in his style, which he
has labeled "Heavy Wood." *Guitar Player*
magazine described his work as "dazzling"
with signature jazzy chording, walking
bass lines, smooth runs of alternating fret-
ted and open strings, percussive knuckle
whacks, sweet timbres, and a groove.
Passion Session was recorded in Berlin's
Passionskirche (the Church of the Passion)
while Ross was on tour in Europe.

DISCOGRAPHY:
Robot Monster [Narada 2003]
Huron Street [Narada/Virgin 2001] best of
Passion Session [Narada 1999]
Loaded. Leather. Moonroof [Columbia/
Sony 1997]
Wintertide [Columbia/Sony 1996] Christ-
mas album
This Dragon Won't Sleep [Columbia/Sony
1995]
Three Hands [Duke Street 1992]

Don Ross [Duke Street 1990]
Bearing Strait [Duke Street 1989]

Appearances:
Narada Guitar [Narada 2000] two-CD
  comp
The Worlds of Narada [Narada 1999] comp
Masters of Acoustic Guitar [Narada 1999]
  comp
Guitar Finger Style [Narada 1998] comp
*Here and Now: A Celebration of Canadian
  Music* [Sony 1995] comp, w/ Willie Dunn
Children of the World [Groupe Concept/
  Musicor 1994] comp
Jenny's Song [Laughing Dog Plays 1993]
  radio play

Film and Videos:
*The Fingerstyle of Don Ross and His Gui-
  tar* [New Media Video Concepts 1995]

Ross, Jay—(Metis) Country/Gospel
See: Edmund Bull, C-Weed

Born December 18, 1972, La Ronge, Saskatchewan. Ross spent his early childhood
commuting between Winnipeg, Manitoba,
where he attended elementary school, and
Molansa, Saskatchewan, where he spent
summers with his extended family. He
began playing drums at age eight and guitar at age twelve. He started playing in
gospel bands in the 1980s and made the
easy transition to country music in the
1990s. In 2000, he met up with Errol Ranville and joined C-Weed, where he found
opportunities to write and record his own
music.

DISCOGRAPHY:
This Old Town [c-weedband.com 2003]

Roulette, Clyde—(Anishnabe) Blues
See: C-Weed

From Sandy Bay Reserve, Manitoba.
"Slidin' Clyde" started playing in the
1970s and earned a reputation through his
unique guitar style. He shared the stage
with Stevie Ray Vaughn, Matt "Guitar"
Murphy, Dickie Betts, and many others.

DISCOGRAPHY:

Appearances:
Rick Patterson:
Spirit of the Wolf [independent 1992]
C-Weed:
Goin' the Distance [RCA/Hawk 1983]
Flight of the Hawk, Vol. 2 [Sunshine SSCT-
  4079]
Flight of the Hawk, Vol. 1 [Sunshine SSCT-
  4078]
A Tribute to Southern Rock [Sunshine
  SSCT-4074]
High and Dry [Sunshine 1981]
The Finest You Can Buy [Sunshine 1980]

Sainte-Marie, Buffy—(Plains Cree)
Folk/Rock *See*: Brian Black Thunder,
Jesse Ed Davis, Peter LaFarge,
Shingoose, Floyd Westerman

Born February 20, 1941, Piapot Reserve,
Saskatchewan, Canada. Sainte-Marie once
described herself as "a full-blooded Cree
who is one-sixth folk singer." Adopted as
an infant by part Mi'kmaq parents, she
was raised in Maine. She was three years
old when she first started playing piano,
but then she switched to guitar at age
sixteen. As a teenager, she returned to
Saskatchewan. She collected the choke-
cherry branches on the Piapot Reserve for
the mouthbows that she used in performances.
    While attending the University of Mas-
sachusetts, she played the Saladin Coffee
House on weekends. After graduation in
the early 1960s, she decided to try her
luck at singing in New York City's Greenwich Village coffeehouse scene. Bob Dylan
liked her songs at Gerde's Folk City and
suggested she also try the Gaslight. A
couple of times she shared the bill with
folk music legend Peter LaFarge (Narra-
gansett). Her unique vocal style, timeless

lyrics, and compositions created immediate interest. Robert Shelton's review of her at this time in the *New York Times* described her as "one of the most promising new talents of the folk scene." The *Boston Herald* described her as "a phenomenal talent." Maynard Soloman of Vanguard Records then signed her to the label. In 1963, shortly before recording her first album, *It's My Way*, she had a long engagement at a coffeehouse in Florida. Although blessed with good health, she developed bronchitis. Her medical treatment led to an addiction to codeine, inspiring the song "Cod'ine" from her debut album.

The opening track on side one of *It's My Way* was the politically charged historical ballad "Now That the Buffalo's Gone," but the album's big single was "Universal Soldier." Banned from airplay and described by the press as the anthem of the anti–Vietnam War movement, the song was nevertheless covered by Donovan and Glen Campbell, placing Sainte-Marie front and center in both the music and the political scenes. She had originally signed away the publishing rights to the song for a dollar, but she managed to buy it back ten years later for twenty-five thousand dollars. Meanwhile, she enjoyed enormous popularity with an international schedule of capacity concerts and television appearances, including the the Tonight Show, Rowan & Martin's Laugh In, Merv Griffin, Dick Cavett, and the Andy Williams Show in 1966.

As an artist, she broke new ground in recording. Her 1969 release *Illuminations* was the first electronic quadraphonic vocal album; and pioneered the use of early synthesizers; and for *Performance* [Nicolas Roeg, 1969] she utilized multitracking on her mouthbow segments. Her 1992 album, *Coincidence and Likely Stories*, was created on a Macintosh computer.

Chart appearances include Elvis Presley's cover of "Until It's Time for You to Go," which reached number 40 on the Billboard Pop Charts and number 68 on the U.S. Billboard Country Charts in 1972, and soared to number 5 in the United Kingdom. Numerous covers of "Until It's Time for You to Go" include a version by Helen Reddy on her album *Long Hard Climb* [Capitol 1973]. Other artists who have covered her material include Chet Atkins, Janis Joplin, the Boston Pops Orchestra, the Indigo Girls, and many more. In 1972, she had three singles on the U.S. Billboard Pop Charts: "I'm Gonna Be a Country Girl Again," number 98 for three weeks; "Mr. Can't You See," number 38; "He's an Indian Cowboy in the Rodeo," number 98 and number 14 for nine weeks in Canada (one year after Canadian content regulations went into effect). At the same time in Europe and the United Kingdom, "Soldier Blue," the title track from the 1970 Ralph Nelson film, enjoyed immense popularity.

Sainte-Marie signed to MCA in 1974 and released *Buffy* and *Changing Woman*. She then moved on to ABC Records in 1976 and released *Sweet America*, which contained the original version of "Starwalker," written for AIM. The record label went under shortly after the album's release. In 1992, she included a digitized remake of "Starwalker" on *Coincidence and Likely Stories*, with sampled sounds of a powwow at the opening of the song and a six-second vocal of Ben Blackbear Sr. and the Ironwood Singers (*See*: Powwow Music) into the first line of the second verse.

In addition to scoring several films and television shows, she was a five-year cast member on the children's television program *Sesame Street* in 1976. She won the Academy Award for Best Song in 1983 for "Up Where We Belong" from the film *An Officer and a Gentleman*. The track, composed with former husband Jack Nitzsche, was performed by Joe Cocker and Jennifer Warnes.

In the 1980s, she spent most of her time at her island home in Hawaii raising her son, Dakota Wolfchild, and returned to performing in 1992 with the ground-breaking album *Coincidence and Likely Stories*. The CD contains the anthemic "Bury My Heart at Wounded Knee" and launched an international tour of her computer-generated digital paintings, one of which she used for the CD cover. Her subsequent 1996 best-of album, *Up Where We Belong*, received the Juno Award for Aboriginal Recording of the Year, 1997; guest artists on the album include Stoney Park and Edmund Bull with the Red Bull Singers (*See*: Powwow Music).

In 1988, she was presented with the Louis T. Delgado Award as Native American Philanthropist of the Year for raising self-esteem in all children while creating a cross-cultural exchange and a more accurate core curriculum. Since the late 1990s, she has focused her efforts on developing the educational Cradle Board Teaching Project, an interactive computer program subtitled *Science through Native Eyes*, which links Native with non-Native schools through the Internet. This type of work was nothing new for Sainte-Marie; she developed her first educational project, the Nihewan Foundation for American Indian Education, in 1968.

She received her Ph.D. in fine arts and was an honors graduate in Oriental philosophy and teaching from the University of Massachusetts, Amherst; she also received an honorary doctorate from the University of Regina, Saskatchewan, and an honorary doctor of letters from Lakehead University, Thunder Bay, Ontario. She has served as adjunct professor of fine art at Saskatchewan Indian Federated College, Regina, Saskatchewan; and York University, Toronto, Ontario; as an Evans Chair Scholar at Evergreen State College, Olympia, Washington; and visiting teacher of digital arts at the Institute for American Indian Arts, Santa Fe, New Mexico. She was named an officer of the Order of Canada and received the American Indian College Fund's Lifetime Achievement Award.

DISCOGRAPHY:

Best of the Vanguard Years [Vanguard 2003] best of

Up Where We Belong [Angel/EMI 1996]

Interview Disc [Capitol/EMI 1992]

Coincidence and Likely Stories [Chrysalis 1992]

The Best of Buffy Sainte-Marie [Vanguard 1986] two LPs

Live at Carnegie Hall [Vanguard 1985] bootleg

The Best of Buffy Sainte-Marie [Vanguard-Midline 1982]

The Best of Buffy Sainte-Marie, Vol. 2 [Vanguard 1981] two LPs

Spotlight on Buffy Sainte Marie [Vanguard 1981, United Kingdom] best of, two LPs

Spirit of the Wind [Attla 1979] sdtk w/ William Ackerman

Sweet America [ABC 1976]

A Golden Hour of Buffy Sainte Marie [Pye 1976, United Kingdom] best of

Changing Woman [MCA 1975]

Buffy [MCA 1974]

Quiet Places [Vanguard 1974]

Native North American Child: An Odyssey [Vanguard 1974] best of

Concert Canadien: Buffy Sainte Marie and Beverly Glenn Copeland [CSPS 847A] interview disc with songs from MCA and Vanguard recordings

Moonshot [Vanguard 1972] number 134 on the U.S. pop charts for eight weeks

She Used to Wanna Be a Ballerina [Vanguard 1971] number 182 U.S. pop charts six weeks; w/ Jesse Ed Davis, Neil Young and Crazy Horse, Jack Nitzsche, Ry Cooder, Merry Clayton, Russ Titleman, Gayle Levant, Bobby West; and others

Illuminations [Vanguard 1969]

I'm Gonna Be a Country Girl Again [Vanguard 1968] number 171 U.S. pop charts for seven weeks

Fire, Fleet, and Candlelight [Vanguard 1967] number 126 U.S. pop charts for six weeks

Little Wheel Spin and Spin [Vanguard 1966] number 97 U.S. pop charts for ten weeks

Many a Mile [Vanguard 1965]

It's My Way [Vanguard 1964]

Singles:

"Fallen Angel/Soldier Blue" [Chrysalis 1992] w/ reggae and dub versions

"The Big Ones Get Away/I'm Going Home/Contralosophy" [Chrysalis 1992, United Kingdom]

"Soldier Blue/I'm Gonna Be a Country Girl Again" [Flashback 1983]

"Look at the Facts/Where Poets Go" [ABC 1976]

"Sweet America/Starwalker" [ABC 1976]

"Starwalker: For the American Indian Movement/Free the Lady" [ABC 1976]

"Take My Hand for a While/Tall Trees in Georgia" [Vanguard 1976]

"I'm Gonna Be a Country Girl Again/Now That the Buffalo's Gone" [Vanguard 1975]

"Love's Got to Breathe and Flower/Nobody Will Ever Know It's Real But You" [MCA 1975]

"Soldier Blue" [Vanguard 1974]

"Generation/Sweet, Fast Hooker Blues" [MCA 1974]

"I Can't Take It No More/Native North American Child: An Odyssey" [MCA 1974]

"Waves/Sweet Little Vera" [MCA 1974]

"I Can't Believe the Feeling When You're Gone/Waves" [MCA 1974]

"Jeremiah/I Wanna Hold Your Hand" [Vanguard 1973]

"He's an Indian Cowboy in the Rodeo/Not the Lovin' Kind" [Vanguard 1972] number 98 U.S. Billboard Pop Charts; number 14 in Canada for nine weeks

"Moonshot/Mr. Can't You See" [Vanguard 1972] number 38 U.S. Billboard Pop Charts

"Until It's Time for You to Go/She Used to Wanna Be a Ballerina" [Vanguard 1971]

"Helpless/Now You've Been Gone a Long Time" [Vanguard 1971]

"She Used to Wanna Be a Ballerina/Moratorium" [Vanguard 1971]

"Soldier Blue/Moratorium" [Vanguard 1971]

"Soldier Blue/Until It's Time for You to Go" [Vanguard 1971]

"Better to Find Out for Yourself/The Circle Game" [Vanguard 1970]

"He's a Keeper of the Fire/Better to Find Out for Yourself" [Vanguard 1969]

"I'm Gonna Be a Country Girl Again/From the Bottom of My Heart" [Vanguard 1969]

"Better to Find Out for Yourself/Sometimes I Get to Thinkin'" [Vanguard 1968]

"I'm Gonna Be a Country Girl Again/The Piney Wood Hills" [Vanguard 1968] number 98 U.S. Billboard Pop Charts for three weeks

"The Piney Wood Hills/Soulful Shade" [Vanguard 1968]

"The Circle Game/Until It's Time for You to Go" [Vanguard 1967]

"Jusqu'au Jour Ou Tu Partiras/Until It's Time for You to Go" [Vanguard 1967]

"Timeless Love/Lady Margaret" [Vanguard 1966]

"Universal Soldier/Cripple Creek" [Vanguard 1965]

"Until It's Time for You to Go/The Flower and the Apple Tree" [Vanguard 1965]

Appearances (listed alphabetically):

Brian Black Thunder:

Spirit with a Mask [Bear Clan 1995] string arrangements

Donovan:

7 Tease [Epic 1974] percussion/backup vocals

Steve Gillette:

Steve Gillette [Vanguard 1967] percussion

Neville Brothers:

Brothers Keeper [A&M 1990] backup vocals

New Riders of the Purple Sage:

Adventures of Panama Red [Columbia 1973] backup vocals

Mark Nine:

This Island [Underworld Records 1994] backup vocals

Earl Scruggs:

Anniversary Special [CBS 1975] backup vocals

Floyd Westerman:

The Land Is Your Mother [Full Circle Productions 1984] piano

Various:

Our Voice Is Our Weapon and Our Bullets Are the Truth [Red Wire Magazine 2003] comp

Classic Love at the Movies [Decca/Universal 2000] comp

Vanguard Collectors Edition [Vanguard 1997] comp, four-CD box set

The 1997 Juno Awards [CARAS 1997] comp

Tapes for Timor [Hands Free Records 1996] comp

Mariposa '95: 35th Anniversary [Mariposa 1996] comp

Listen to the Music: '70s Female Singers [Rhino 1996] comp

The 1995 Juno Awards [CARAS 1995] comp

Heartbeat: Voices of First Nations Women [Smithsonian 1995] comp *See*: Traditional/Archival Compilations

Northern Exposure, Vol. 1 [NE 1992] comp

In the Spirit of Crazy Horse [Four Winds Trading 1992] comp

Troubadours of the Folk Era, Vol. 1 [Rhino 1992] comp

Greatest Folksingers of the 'Sixties [Vanguard 1986] comp, two-LP set

An Officer and a Gentleman [Island 1982] sdtk, composer

Bread and Roses: Festival of Acoustic Music [Fantasy 1979] live at the Greek Theater, University of California, Berkeley

Greatest Folk Singers of the '60s [Vanguard 1972]

The Strawberry Statement [MGM 1970] sdtk

Performance [Warner 1969] sdtk; rare tracks "Dyed Dead Red" and "Hashishin" w/ Ry Cooder

Revolution [United Artists 1968] sdtk; "Co'dine" performed by Quicksilver Messenger Service

Videos:

Up Where We Belong [David Storey, 1996] forty-seven minutes

The Big Ones Get Away [Chrysalis 1992]

Film and Television:

Indian Time III [Global/Bravo 2003] performer

Snow White and the Seven Dwarves [HBO 1995] animated: music and voice

The Broken Chain [Lamont Johnson, 1993] historical drama: as Seth's wife

Son of the Morning Star [Mike Robe, 1991] historical drama: as the voice of Kate Bighead

Where the Spirit Lives [CBC 1989] television drama: music; title track "I'm Going Home" released on *Coincidences and Likely Stories*

Indian Time [CTV 1989] performer

Uranium [NFB 1988] documentary: narration

Broken Rainbow [Earth Works 1986] documentary: translation voice

Stripper [Jerome Gary, 1985] documentary: music

Great Spirit in the Hole [Chris Spotted Eagle, 1983] documentary: music

An Officer and a Gentleman [Taylor Hackford, 1982] feature film: title music

Harold of Orange [independent 1982] drama: music

Spirit Bay [CBC 1981] television series: theme music

Spirit of the Wind [Ralph Liddle 1979] biographical drama: music

Sesame Street [CTVW 1976–81] television series: cast member

Soldier Blue [Ralph Nelson, 1970] feature film: title music

Festival [Murray Lerner, 1967] documentary: music

Selected Awards:

1998: Native American Music Association Best Pop Artist

1997: Juno Award, Aboriginal Recording of the Year, *Up Where We Belong*

1997: Gemini Award, Best Performance in a Television Special

1996: FAITA Lifetime Musical Achievement Award

1995: CARAS Juno Hall of Fame Inductee

1994: SRIA Lifetime Achievement Award

Salas, Stevie "No-Wonder"—
(Mescalero Apache) Rock/R & B/Soul/
Funk

Born November 17, 1965, San Diego, California. Salas's father served in the U.S. Marines and thereafter settled the family in San Diego. In high school, Salas began playing in a punk band that recorded two self-produced EPs. He quickly became an outstanding guitarist who unwittingly tailored his sound after Jimi Hendrix. Though he was also directly inspired by Bootsy Collins, his individuality is recognizable through the energy and style of his playing.

Salas moved to Los Angeles in 1985 to find work as a musician. Penniless, and unemployed he found solace at Baby-O, a popular Los Angeles recording studio, and crashed on the couch while soliciting artists for session work. When George Clinton was recording an album, he woke Salas at 3:00 A.M. and asked him to add a few guitar chords. Salas seized the moment and stunned Clinton with his blazing guitar licks. Through Clinton, Salas was introduced to Bootsy Collins. Three years later, Salas worked with Don Was on the Was (Not Was) project *What Up, Dog?* and appeared in the house band on the television series *Fame* [Christopher Gore, 1987].

It wasn't long before Salas found his way into film, where he supplied all of the guitar work and the guitar hands for George Carlin's character in *Bill and Ted's Excellent Adventure* [Stephen Herek, 1989]. Along with Randy Castillo and traditional percussionist Benito Concha, Salas joined Robby Romero's Red Thunder project. The short foray into Indian show biz inspired Salas to return to the mainstream music industry. The 1992 *Hardware* album, recorded with Bootsy Collins and drummer Buddy Miles, showcased poignant material dedicated to 1492 and the Leonard Peltier story. Salas went on to form Nicklebag in 1994, with Bernard Fowler and then toured with Rolling Stones guitarist Ron Wood. The momentum increased with *Electric Powwow*, recorded with Deep Purple guitarist Glenn Hughes, singer Sass Jordan, Norwood Fisher of Fishbone, Terrence Trent Darby, Cheap Trick guitarist Rick Neilson, drummers Randy Castillo and Matt Sorum, among many others. By 1998, he was performing with Rod Stewart—which prompted Mick Jagger to invite Salas to tour the release of his solo album, *Goddess in the Doorway* [Virgin 2001].

During his career, Salas has worked with Eddie Money, Bill Laswell, Carmine Apice, Michael Hutchence of INXS, and many more well-known artists. He has also produced for Glenn Hughes, the Jeff Healey Band, and numerous others. On July 30, 2003, Salas joined Sass Jordan onstage at the Rolling Stones Toronto benefit concert for health workers with an audience of five hundred thousand people. He is also featured in the book *50 Greatest Guitarists of All Time* [Guitar Player Magazine, 1996].

SELECTED DISCOGRAPHY:
The Soulblasters of the Universe [Yamaha 2004, Japan]
Shapeshifter [Surfdog/Sony 2003/Yamaha 2004, Japan]
Sol Power [Pony Canyon 1999, Germany]
Seoul Power [Pony Canyon 1998, Korea]
Sometimes Almost Never Was [Pony Canyon 1998]
Le Bootleg/Live in Paris [USG 1997, Germany]
Anthology of Stevie Salas Colorcode 1987—1994
[Polystar 1996, Japan]
Alter Native Gold [Indianee 1996, Germany]
Alter-Native [Pony Canyon 1995]
Back From the Living [Polygram/Pavement 1995]
Electric Powwow [Aquarius/Polygram 1994]
Stuff [Island 1991]
Colorcode [Island 1990]

Singles:
"Cover Me in Noise" [Pony Canyon 1997]
"Start Again" [Geronimo 1995–96, Japan]
"Tell Your Story Walkin'" [Polystar 1994, Japan]
"The Harder They Come" [Island IS459, United Kingdom] seven-inch vinyl
"The Harder They Come" [Island 12IS 459, United Kingdom]
"The Harder They Come/Blind/Indian Chief" [Island CID-459, United Kingdom] CD

Appearances (listed alphabetically):
George Clinton:
Some of My Best Jokes Are My Friends [Capitol 1985]
Bootsy Collins:
What's Bootsy Doin'? [Columbia 1988]
Glenn Hughes:
Different Stages [Shrapnel 1999] best of
Way It Is [Shrapnel 1999]
Hardware:
Third Eye Open [Ryko 1992] w/ Buddy Miles and Bootsy Collins
Sass Jordan:
Sass . . . Best of Sass Jordan [Aquarius 2003] best of
Rats [Aquarius 1994]
Racine [EMI 1992]
Eddie Money:
Essential Eddie Money [CMC 2003] best of
Nothing to Lose [Columbia 1988]
Mr. Fiddler:
With Respect [1990]
Nickel Bag:
Mas Feedback [Pony Canyon/WEA 1997]
Nickelbag: 12 Hits and a Bump [Pony Canyon/WEA 1995]
Red Thunder:
Makoche Wakan [Eagle Thunder 1995]
State of Mind:
State of Mind [Fog Area 1991]
Terence Trent Darby:
TTD's Vibrator [Sony 1995]
Was (Not Was):
What Up, Dog? [Chrysalis 1988]
Various:

Black Night: The Deepest Purple Deep Purple Tribute [Warner 1989] comp

Film:
Being Mick [Kevin Macdonald, 2001] documentary
Small Soldiers [Joe Dante, 1998]
Bill and Ted's Excellent Adventure [Stephen Herek, 1989]
Next of Kin [Atom Egoyan, 1984]
Action Jackson [Craig R. Baxley, 1988]
Big Shots [Robert Mandel, 1988]

Sand Creek—Rock *See*: Keith Secola

Lineup: Eugene Ridgely, Ben Ridgely, Gail Ridgely, Paul Moss, Bob Toahty, Julene Christian. Arapaho band from Wyoming.

DISCOGRAPHY:
Endless Flight [Canyon 1981] D

Santana, Carlos—(Chicano) Rock/Jazz *See*: Malo

Born July 20, 1947, Autlán, Mexico. Moved to San Francisco in 1961. He has produced a staggering number of recordings in his career, as a soloist and session guitarist, a feat acknowledged with a Grammy sweep in 1999. He founded the Milagro Foundation, an entity dedicated to providing medical, financial, and educational assistance to children. In addition to his popular music persona, Santana has also given aid to indigenous struggles in America and Mexico.

Santana, Jorge—(Chicano) Rock/Jazz *See*: Malo

Born June 13, 1954, Autlán, Mexico. Brother of Carlos and five other siblings, the younger Santana pursued a music career that helped establish the group Malo.

DISCOGRAPHY:
It's All about Love [Tomato 1979]
Jorge Santana [Tomato 1978]

Santoka—Country/Rock

Lineup: Tara and Eric Bravo.

DISCOGRAPHY:
Fire in Your Heart [Indian Sounds 9201]

Satterfield, Laura—(Cherokee) *See*: Robbie Robertson, Walela

Born March 25, 1964, Nashville, Tennessee. A founding member of the trio Walela and daughter of Priscilla Coolidge. Satterfield began as a session backup singer. She was the lead vocalist on the single "Unbound" from Robbie Robertson's *Contact from the Underworld of Redboy*, which made the charts and readied the ground for her debut album. She continues to perform with Walela while pursuing her own music projects in California.

DISCOGRAPHY:
Dirty Velvet Lie [Triloka 2000]

Appearances (listed alphabetically):
Rita Coolidge:
Love Lessons [Critique 1992]
Neil Diamond:
Christmas Album, Vol. 2 [Sony 1994; Columbia 1995]
Up on the Roof: Songs from the Brill Building [Columbia 1993]
Bruce Hornsby and the Range:
Harborlights [RCA 1993]
Robbie Robertson:
Contact from the Underworld of Redboy [Capitol 1998]
Music for the Native Americans [Capitol 1994]

Schreiber, Pam—(Anishnabekwe) Folk/Rock

Born February 3, 1958. Beginning her music career in her midteens and pursuing it for many years, Schreiber left the scene for more than a decade, but then returned with an independent album of original songs.

DISCOGRAPHY:
Language of the Heart [independent 2000]

Scofield, Sandy—(Cree-Saulteaux-Metis) Folk *See*: Wayne Lavallee

Born in Windsor, Ontario. This singer-songwriter continually gains acclaim from her first release. Her work has appeared on several compilation albums, including the benefit release for Greenpeace, *Save Howe Sound*. She fronted the polka-punk band the Crimpolines early in her Vancouver-based career. She has worked in film and theater while making several appearances at major folk festivals throughout Canada. Her television appearances include *Indian*

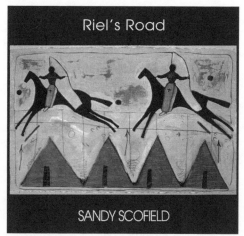

Sandy Scofield's second album *Riel's Road* (2000) won acclaim in Canada. Courtesy Sandy Scofield. Cover art: George Littlechild's "The Land Called Morning."

Time III [Global/Bravo 2003] (*See*: Shingoose).

DISCOGRAPHY:
Ketwam [Kokum Records 2002]
Riel's Road [Arpeggio 2000]
Dirty River [Arpeggio 1994]

Appearances (listed alphabetically):
Bourne and MacLeod:
Moonlight Dancers [Attic 1992] backup vocals
Dobb and Dumela:
One Drop [Festival 1992] backup vocals
Stephen Fearing:
The Assassin's Apprentice [Sony 1994] backup vocals
Various:
The Juno Collection [CARAS 2004] comp
Exposed Roots [Canada Council 2003] comp
Global Mystique [Tandem Music 2003] comp
Our Voice Is Our Weapon and Our Bullets Are the Truth [Red Wire Magazine 2003] comp
Skin Tight Blues [Sweet Grass/EMI 2002] comp
Western Canadian Music Awards Nominees [independent 2002] comp
Grrrls with Guitars [Aural Traditions 1999] comp
West Coast Sacred Music Festival [Festival 1999] comp
West Coast World Music Compilation [PMIA 1999] comp
Mariposa Folk Festival [Mariposa] comp
New Women's Voices [CBC/Variety 1993] comp
Aboriginal Women's Voices [ANDPVA 1992] comp *See*: Traditional/Archival Compilations
Routes West [Festival 1990] comp
Save Howe Sound [Fluid Records 1990] comp

Selected Awards:
2004: Juno nomination, Aboriginal Recording of the Year, *Ketwam*

2003: WCMA, Most Outstanding Aborignal Recording, *Ketwam*
2002: WCMA for Best Aboriginal Music, *Riel's Road*
2001: Juno nomination, Aboriginal Recording of the Year, *Riel's Road*
2000: AMA for Best Single, Best Alternative Recording, *Riel's Road*
1995: Juno nomination, Best Independent Song, *Dirty River*

Secola, Keith—(Anishnabe) Folk/ Rock *See*: Dennis Banks, Annie Humphrey

Born July, 28, 1957, Cook, Minnesota. Secola was raised in a musical family with champion fiddle players and powwow singers. While attending Mesabi Community College, he began to develop considerable guitar skills, with strong interests in traditional music. He wrote the love song "Zogipoon" as part of a language requirement for his Native American studies major at the University of Minnesota, Minneapolis, 1982. His signature hit, "Indian Car," was composed in 1985 and combines

Keith Secola's Wild Band of Indians discover Europe. Courtesy Keith Secola/AKINA.

the essence of traditional 49er songs with rock music. After moving to Tempe, Arizona, Secola established his own AKINA label and released several albums in Germany on the Normal label.

Touring internationally, he has shared the stage with numerous and notable performers, including Jackson Browne, Buffy Sainte-Marie, and Toots and the Maytalls. Much of his material is well crafted, entertaining, and compelling and is played by excellent musicians. *Finger Monkey* received a NAMA Award for Best Independent Recording, 2000; *Homeland* received a NAMA Award for Best Instrumental Recording, 2001.

Wild Band of Indians Lineup: Garret Tailfeathers, drums; Guy Ivester, bass; Brent Michael Davids, quartz crystal flute; Mixashawn, soprano saxophone; Delphine Tsinajinnie, backup vocals (*See*: Traditional/Archival Solo); and the Sand Creek Band.

Wild Band of Indians Millennium Lineup: Moontie Sinqua (Hopi-Tewa-Choctaw), traditional percussion/singing; Derek Miller, guitar/vocals/percussion; Matt Jones, drums/vocals; Jimmy Vickers, bass/vocals. *Kokopelli's Blues* features John Densmore of the Doors and Jim Creegan of the Barenaked Ladies.

DISCOGRAPHY:
Kokopelli's Blues/Sea of Cortez [AKINA 2001] three-track EP
Homeland: An Original Soundtrack [AKINA 2000] w/ the Indigo Girls and Carlos Reynosa
Finger Monkey [AKINA 1999]
XV for Our Ancestors [Normal 1996, Germany] limited edition live album
Wild Band of Indians [AKINA/Normal 1996, Germany] reissued domestically 1997
Encircle [AKINA/Normal 1994, Germany] European reissue of the 1992 album
Circle [AKINA 1992]
Acoustic Aroma [AKINA 1991]

Time Flies Like an Arrow Fruit Flies Like a Banana [AKINA 1990]
Indian Cars [AKINA 1985, 1989] cass

Appearances (listed alphabetically):
Dennis Banks:
United We Stand—Refusing to Fall [RCR 9770]
Annie Humphrey:
Edge of America [Makoche 2003] vocals
Various:
Alcatraz Is Not an Island [James Fortier, 2002] score
20 Aboriginal Greatest Hits, Vol. 3 [Sunshine 2002] comp
Skin Tight Blues [Sweet Grass/EMI 2002] comp
Urban Skins, Vol. 1 [SOAR 1999] comp
Tribal Fires [Earth Beat! 1997] comp
Honor [Daemon 1996] comp
Dance Me Outside [Rez Films/Denon 1994] sdtk
Ojibway Music from Minnesota: A Century of Song for Voice and Drum [MHS 1989/1997] comp

Videos:
Wild Band of Indians [AKINA 1997] w/ Star Nayea
Rockin' Warriors [Andy Bausch, 1999]

Related Projects:
Moonty Sinquah Appearances:
Joanne Shenandoah:
Warrior in Two Worlds: The Life of Ely Parker, Seneca Chief and Brigadier General [Red Feather 2000] sdtk
Tara Nevins:
"Troubles," single from *Mule to Ride* [Sugar Hill 1999]

Serrato, Greg—(Apache) Blues

Born May 7, 1957, Orange, California. A guitarist, Serrato was influenced by Freddie King, Jimi Hendrix, and Buddy Guy and worked with Robin Trower's drummer Bill Lordan. Memorable performances include the Grand Ole Opry in 1992 and the

2001 Blues Fest in Windsor, Ontario, with Double Trouble and Jeff Healey.

DISCOGRAPHY:
Blue Condition [Crying Sky Records 2003] recorded in 1995
Live at Modesto's State Theater [independent 2002]
Like a Tornado [J-Bird Records 2001]
Holy Smokes [J-Bird Records 1999]
Child of the Blues [J-Bird Records 1998]
On the Down Side [Crying Sky Records 1994] w/ 4th Street Blues Band

Appearances:
Shades of Blue [Bonaroo Records 1999] comp

Seventh Fire—Rock

Formed in 1985, Ottawa, Ontario, as Art and Soul, this band also performed as Thom E. Hawke and the Pineneedles in 1988 and became Seventh Fire in 1989.

Original Lineup: Allan Deleary, a.k.a. Thom E. Hawke (Anishnabe, born April 20, 1959, Detroit, Michigan), vocals/samples/percussion/keyboards; Cheryl Riley, vocals; John Macias, drums/percussion; Dave Deleary (Anishnabe, born November 6, 1957, Detroit, Michigan; *See*: Russell Wallace), bass/vocals/keyboards/acoustic guitar/vocals; Joe DiGangi; Greg Young-Ing, spoken word; Patrick Andrade, coproduction; Wayne Williams; Marty Jones; Simeon.

1991 Lineup: Allan Deleary; John Maracle (Mohawk), guitar/vocals/whales; Harold Sotomayor, keyboards; Peter DiGangi, guitars/bass/vocals/samples/harp; John Macias; Marty Jones, drum programming; Jarbiheey David Gidi, vocals/percussion; Rebecca Belmore, Florene Belmore, Greg Young Ing, Kateri Damm, spoken word.

1994 Lineup: Thom E. Hawke, lead vocals/tuba/lead xylophone; Dave Deleary; Miche Jette, rhythm guitars/vocals; Terry Whiteduck, lead guitars; Terry Owen, saxo-

phone; Eduardo Flores Suarez, drums/percussion, replaced by John Habel (Dakota).

Principal founder Allen Deleary fused powwow with Frank Zappa and Motown influences, rap, reggae, rock, and theatrical elements. He applied satirical lyrics with searing insight to historical and political realities. Seventh Fire's initial recordings turned heads, burned ears, and helped set them apart from their contemporaries. The term *diverse* may describe one aspect of their performances, but *eclectic* captures the nature of their collective musical attitude. They backed numerous spoken-word artists, including Toronto dub poet Lillian Allen, and appeared onstage with the German band Dissidenten. Four years after Seventh Fire disbanded around 1996, founder Allen Deleary labored to jump-start the band, but with little success. In 2002, guitarist Peter DiGangi revived some of their older tracks and created newer versions inspired by current events.

DISCOGRAPHY:
The Cheque Is in the Mail [independent 1993; First Nations Music 1994]
Well—What Does It Take? [Technawbe 1990] cass

Appearances:
Native American Music [Rough Guide 1998, United Kingdom] comp
The Fire This Time:
Till the Bars Break [Irresistible/Maya/Revolutionary IMR14 1991] comp

Videos:
The Cheque Is in the Mail [independent 1993]

Related Projects (listed alphabetically):
Art and Soul:
Your Silence Will Not Protect You [Maya 1988] comp
No Apparent Solutions [Wawatay 1987] video
Allan Deleary:
Native Legends and Storytelling [Glooscap Communications Group 1989] spoken

word *See*: Contemporary Spoken Word: Legends (Miscellaneous)

Dave Deleary:
Between Heaven and Earth [independent 2000] *See*: Flute Music: David Maracle
Don't Stay Out Late Tonight [independent 1992, 1997] cassingle

Pete DiGangi:
We Talk You Listen [independent 2002]

Thom E. Hawke and the Pine Needles:
Buffalo Cliff Collection [Technawbe 1988] o/p
Ho Wuh [Wawatay 1988] video

Severight, Grant—(Metis) Country/Folk/Rock

DISCOGRAPHY:
Life Is a Circle [Medicine Music 1996]

Appearances:
Music from Turtle Island [Turtle Island Music 1999] comp

Shadowyze—(Creek-Cherokee) Rap
See: Julian B

Born Shawn Enfinger April 20, 1972, San Antonio, Texas. A veteran performer of the rap genre, with beginnings somewhere in the early 1990s, steadily gained notoriety in the larger rap music scene. Shadowyze became more politicized after returning from Chiapas, Mexico, transferring his impressions on the experience into rhymes and beats with unforgiving fervor. A portion of album sales were slated for the indigenous people of Chiapas.

DISCOGRAPHY:
World of Illusions [Backbone/Red Earth 2002]
Spirit Warrior [SOAR 2000]
Ancestor Spirits [independent 2000]
Murder in Our Back Yard [independent 1999] CD, vinyl EP
Put Yer Dukes Up [Bulletproof 1994]
Keep It Rollin' [Bulletproof 1993]

Shawanda, Crystal Lynn—(Anishnabekwe) Country

Born 1981, Wikwemikong, Manitoulin Island, Ontario. This budding singer has performed in her home territory and as far away as Nashville, Tennessee, winning awards and attention along the way. She recorded her first release at the age of thirteen.

DISCOGRAPHY:
Raging Heart [independent 1998] w/ Jani Lauzon and Leland Bell
Will You Love Me Too? [independent 1994]

Shearman, Valerie—(Cree-Metis) Country/Rock

Originating from Calgary, Alberta, this seasoned vocalist with roots in folk, rock, and country music released her first independent recording in 1997. Shearman relaxed her efforts in the scene after becoming a first-time mother, but those who heard her rich vocal abilities dreamed of more to come.

DISCOGRAPHY:
Valerie Shearman [independent 1997]

Sheffer-Tate, Jerod—(Chickasaw) Classical

Born 1968, Norman, Oklahoma. Sheffer-Tate earned his bachelor's degree in piano performance and a master's in piano and composition from the Cleveland Institute of Music; his first composition, *Winter Moons*, a ballet score, was performed by the Colorado Symphony Orchestra and the Minnesota Orchestra in 1993, 1994, and 1996. His concerto *Apela Isskonosi* premiered in Ohio, New York, and Colorado. The operetta score for *Diva Ojibway* was commissioned by Native Earth Performing Arts in Toronto in 1994. He also worked as a composer for the series *First American*

Journal at Native American Television in Minneapolis, as staff accompanist and lecturer for the Academy of Colorado Ballet 1996 and 1998 Intensive Programs, and as keyboardist with the second national tour of *Miss Saigon* and the third national tour of *Les Miserables*.

Dream World Blesses Me was commissioned by the New Jersey Chamber Music Society and premiered at the Jersey City Museum, 1997. In that same year, he was commissioned by the Dale Warland Singers, Minneapolis, for his choral composition "Itti' Bo'li"; he was also selected as composer-in-residence for the Kennedy Center for the Performing Arts and National Symphony Orchestra American Residency program, Wyoming. *Iyaaknasha' for Double Bass and Orchestra* was commissioned by James VanDemark of the Eastman School of Music and premiered in 1993 with the Ohio Chamber Orchestra. Recorded in 1998, featuring James Van-Demark on double bass, the piece "Iyaak-nasha'" is based on a Chickasaw-Choctaw memorial song. The album also contains "Circle of Faith," composed by the late Alton Howe Clingan and performed with the Young Nation Singers and the Pro-Musica Chamber Orchestra of Columbus, Ohio, with the words of Chief Seattle narrated by John Belindo (Kiowa-Dineh) of the American Indian Radio on Satellite network; translations by Vi Hilbert (Upper Skagit); Timothy Russell, conductor. The text was from the January 12, 1854, speech by Suquamish leader Chief Seattle during a meeting with Isaac I. Stevens, first governor of Washington Territory—not to be confused with the 1970s movie script.

DISCOGRAPHY:
Circle of Faith: The Words of Chief Seattle and Iyaaknasha' [d'Note Classics 1998]

Shehan, Steve—(Cherokee) World Beat

Composer and percussionist Steve Shehan brings two cultures together in his work with Baly Othmani (Algerian Tuareg). Their collaborations began in 1985, leading to their first North American release. Baly's instrumental and vocal ensemble has toured the Middle East and Europe since 1979.

DISCOGRAPHY:
Assarouf [Worldly/Triloka 1997]

Appearances:
Made to Measure, Vol. 26 [Crammed Discs 1990] comp

Shenandoah, Joanne—(Oneida) Trad/Contemporary *See*: A. Paul Ortega, Carlos Reynosa, Robbie Robertson, Masie Shenandoah and Liz Robert, Floyd Westerman; Flute Music: Mary Youngblood

Born Joanne Lynn Shenandoah, June 23, 1957, Oneida Nation, New York State. The daughter of Onondaga chief Clifford Shenandoah and Clan Mother Masie Shenandoah, Joanne was given the name Tekalihwa khwa (She Sings). She grew up with music around her as her father played jazz guitar and her mother sang gospel songs and numerous other influential styles of music. Although Shenandoah excelled in music throughout her school years, she found work in a software company.

As a single mother, she began her music career with the release of a country album in 1988. She began to combine traditional Iroquois philosophy and music with contemporary sounds. She gained a reputation for combining Iroquois social songs and contemporary genres, including New Age, classical, techno, and rock. She has received more than three dozen music awards and done extensive world-

Joanne Shenandoah, one of the most prolific Native recording artists. Photo courtesy Silver Wave Records.

wide tours; her recording projects include soundtracks and guest vocals on many other releases. She contributed extensively to the CD-ROM version of *Indian in the Cupboard* [Frank Oz, 1995]; performed with Eastman Philharmonia Orchestra for the *Skywoman* project; opened Woodstock II, New York, 1994; played at William Clinton's Presidential Inaugural Ball with a private performance for First Lady Hillary Clinton and Mrs. Tipper Gore.

In addition to the 1999 Bose music industry sampler, her work also appears on the soundtrack for the PBS documentary *Warrior in Two Worlds: The Life of Ely Parker*. Other recordings include *A Path of Beauty* [Nature Company] and *Sun Child* [Open Mind Music, Spain]. In January 2002, Shenandoah was special guest artist at the Wegmans Pops Series concert with the Syracuse Symphony Orchestra for the world premier of her orchestral song set *Skywoman: Legends of the Iroquois*, Grant Cooper, conducting. *Peacemaker's Journey* was nominated for Best Native Music Recording Grammy Award, 2001. *Eagle Cries* received a Grammy nomination in the same category and features special

guests Bruce Cockburn, Neil Young, Bill Miller, and Mary Youngblood. Shenandoah became president of Round Dance Productions, a nonprofit foundation dedicated to the preservation of Iroquois culture. She was featured in two television specials, *Dancing on Mother Earth* [PBS 2003], a documentary, and *Sky Woman: Legends of the Iroquois* [PBS 2004], with Bill Miller and R. Carlos Nakai.

DISCOGRAPHY:
Covenant [Silver Wave 2003]
Peace and Power [Silver Wave 2002] best of
Eagle Cries [Red Feather 2001]
Warrior in Two Worlds: The Life of Ely Parker, Seneca Chief and Brigadier General [Red Feather 2000] sdtk
Peacemaker's Journey [Silver Wave 2000]
Orenda [Silver Wave 1998] w/ Lawrence Laughing
All Spirits Sing [Music for Little People 1997] children's album
Matriarch [Silver Wave 1996]
Lifeblood [Silver Wave 1995] w/ Peter Kater
Once in a Red Moon [Canyon 1994]
Loving Ways [Canyon 1991] w/ A. Paul Ortega
Joanne Shenandoah [Canyon 1988] country

Singles:
"Nature Dance" [Sun Child/Warner/WEA no date, Germany]

Appearances (listed alphabetically):
Elmer and Friends:
Freedom Rocks [Featherwind Productions 1997]
Robbie Robertson:
Contact from the Underworld of Redboy [Capitol 1998]
Masie Shenandoah and Liz Robert:
Sisters: Oneida Iroquois Hymns [Silver Wave 2003]
Various:
Tribal Legends [Earth Beat! 2002] comp
Sacred Souls [Manteca 2001, United Kingdom] comp
Oliver Shanti's Shaman 2 [Sattva 2000, Germany] comp

Prayer for Peace [Silver Wave 2000] comp
Naturally Native [Silver Wave 2000] sdtk
Wolves [Silver Wave 1999] sdtk
Prophecy [Hearts of Space 1999] comp
Under the Green Corn Moon [Silver Wave 1998] comp
Native American Currents [Silver Wave 1997] comp
When Eyes Meet [Shanachie 1997] comp
Tribal Fires [Earth Beat! 1997] comp
Songs of the Spirit [Triloka 1996] comp
Tribal Voices [Earth Beat! 1996] comp
A Winter Celebration [Silver Wave 1995] comp, w/ Peter Kater
I Am Walking: New Native Music [Narada 1995] comp
Heartbeat: Voices of First Nations Women [Smithsonian Folkways 1995] comp *See*: Traditional/Archival Compilations
How the West Was Lost, Vol. 2 [Silver Wave 1995] sdtk
More Music from Northern Exposure [MCA 1994] sdtk
Dance Me Outside [Rez Films/Denon 1994] sdtk
In the Spirit of Crazy Horse [Four Winds Trading 1992] comp
Oyate [Nato/World 1990/1998, France] comp

Selected Awards:

2002: Honorary Doctorate of Music, Syracuse University, Syracuse, New York
2000: NAMA Best Short and Long Form Music Video, *Warrior in Two Worlds*
1999: NAIRD INDIE Record of the Year nomination, *Orenda*
1998: NAMA Female Artist of the Year and Best Children's Album, *All Spirits Sing*
1997: NAIRD INDIE, Record of the Year, *Matriarch*
1996: Native American Woman's Recognition Award for Outstanding Musical Achievement
1994: FAITA Native American Musician of the Year; Pulitzer Prize nomination in music

Shenandoah, Masie, and Liz Robert—(Oneida) Trad/Gospel *See*: Joanne Shenandoah

Masie Shenandoah, vocals, a Wolf Clan Mother of the Oneida nation, married Elwood Falcon (Oneida), and they had five daughters and one son. She was always active in both traditional art forms and contemporary music, including acoustic guitar and singing. As a clanmother, she was responsible for the spiritual, social, and political welfare of the community. Elizabeth Robert, vocals, was Masie's identical twin, married to Raymond Robert Obomsawin (Abenaki), who had two daughters and two sons. With a degree in nursing, Liz served the residents of the Oneida Indian Territory. The hymns were selected and performed with Masie's daughter Joanne Shenandoah, with instrumentation by Tom Wasinger.

The history of the connection between the Oneida language and European religious song texts and hymns began in the 1700s. Through colonialism and war, the Iroquois people were decimated. Christianity influenced the development of the Handsome Lake Code and its prophet, Skan'lahawi, the Great Peacemaker. The traditional basis of the Code was derived from the original Great Law (Gayanerakowa) observed by the People of the Longhouse (Haudenosaunee).

DISCOGRAPHY:

Sisters: Oneida Iroquois Hymns [Silver Wave 2003] w/ Joanne Shenandoah

Shingoose; a.k.a. Curtis Jonnie—(Anishnabe) Folk/Rock *See*: Floyd Westerman; Contemporary Spoken Word: Poetry Recordings: Duke Redbird, Comedy: Charlie Hill

Born October 26, 1946, Rosseau River Reserve, Manitoba. Adopted at the age of four by a Mennonite missionary family in Steinbach, Manitoba, Shingoose grew

SHINGOOSE · BALLAD OF NORVAL

The song "The Ballad of Norval," written and performed by Shingoose, pays tribute to the painter Norval Morrisseau in the NFB film *The Paradox of Norval*. Photo courtesy Curtis Jonnie.

up singing in church choirs. After moving to the United States as a teenager, he joined the Boys Town Concert Choir of Nebraska. He reclaimed his family name Shingoose and chose a career in show business. "Goose" went on to work with Glen Campbell, the Roy Buchanan Blues Band, Bruce Cockburn, and many others in mainstream music. By the early 1970s, he was involved with Native theater groups and the folk festival circuit throughout North America and performed the song "The Ballad of Norval" in the documentary *The Paradox of Norval* [NFB 1974]. He formed Headband Records and released his first album in 1988; the song "Reservation Blues" became a concert favorite with comedian Charlie Hill (*See*: Contemporary Spoken Word: Comedy) and Floyd Westerman.

As a television producer, he created the *Indian Time* television special [CTV 1989] with Buffy Sainte-Marie, Charlie Hill, Max Gail, and Laura Vinson; *Indian Time II* [CTV 1995] included Joanne Shenandoah, Tom Jackson, dancer Margo Kane, and Kashtin; *Indian Time III* [Global/Bravo

2003] featured Derek Miller, Buffy Sainte-Marie, and Sandy Scofield. Along with Sainte-Marie, actor Don Francks, and talent agent Elaine Bomberry, Shingoose assisted in creating the Best Music of Aboriginal Canada category for the CARAS Juno Awards. Other projects include the original score for the documentary *They Call Me Chief* [Don Marks, 2001].

DISCOGRAPHY:
Natural Tan [Headband 1988, 2001]
The Ballad of Norval [CBC 1979]
Native Country [independent 1975] EP
  w/ Bruce Cockburn

Appearances:
Bruce Cockburn:
The Further Adventures of Bruce Cockburn [Island/True North 1978] backup vocals
Various:
Here and Now: A Celebration of Canadian Music [Sony 1995] comp, w/ Willie Dunn
Legends: I Am An Eagle, Radio Special and Interview Clips [First Nations Music 1994] narration *See*: Contemporary Spoken Word: Interview Recordings
Children of the World [Musicor/Groupe Concept 1994] comp

Shouting Mountain—Rock

Lineup: Ashley, vocals/flute; Eli Bitsoe, percussion/vocals; Marty Sims, bass; Larry Gaines, guitars/vocals; Leo Leta, drums.

DISCOGRAPHY:
Summit [Rock Power Records 1999]

Silver Canyon—(Mi'kmaq) Country

Lineup: Danny O'Donnell, Donnie Elliott, Trudy Elliott, Randy Currie, Cheryl Currie; album produced by Donnie Chapman and Silver Canyon. Based in New Brunswick, Canada.

DISCOGRAPHY:
Kindred Spirit [Silver Canyon 1994]

Simard, Billy—(Cree) Folk/Rock

Born June 27, 1948, Manigotogam, Manitoba. A veteran performer, Simard gained popularity in many Native communities throughout northern Manitoba and western Canada.

DISCOGRAPHY:
Seeing with My Heart [Sunshine SSCT-4327]
Don't Stop the Music [Sunshine SSCT-4026]

Appearances:
Northern Legends [Sunshine 2000] comp
20 Aboriginal Greatest Hits, Vol. 2 [Sunshine 1998] comp
24 Canadian Aboriginal Artists [Sunshine 1995] comp
A Northern Christmas [Sunshine SSCD-4180] comp

Simon, Conrad—(Mi'kmaq) Rock

From Big Cove, New Brunswick. A programmer, musician, composer, and progressive rock instrumentalist, Simon won a sponsorship from Yamaha Canada. Hired by the company to conduct guitar workshops in the Atlantic region, he increased his reputation as a brilliant programmer with blazing guitar techniques.

DISCOGRAPHY:
Instrumezzo [Dungeon Music 1995]

Sinclair, Esau—(Metis) Fiddle

From Grand Rapids, Manitoba. Sinclair is internationally renowned for his fiddle style, which combines traditional native and Metis elements with old Scottish styles.

DISCOGRAPHY:
Adeline's Waltz [Sunshine SSCT 487]
Grand Rapids Breakdown [Sunshine SSCT-471]
Big John McNeil [Sunshine SSCT-467]

Sky Chasers—Folk/Rock *See*: Burning Sky, Aaron White

Lineup: Aaron White, guitar/flute/vocals/percussion; Tommy Lee, flute; John Katz, guitar.

DISCOGRAPHY:
Full Moon Sessions [independent 2000]

Slowhand—(Cree) Rock

Lineup: Curtis Neoniak, rhythm guitar/vocals; Dale Delaronde, rhythm guitar/vocals; Alvin Chartrand, lead guitar; Calvin Nepinak, bass/slide guitars; Conrad McKay, drums; Mike Catheway, fiddle. From Pine Creek, Manitoba.

DISCOGRAPHY:
Stranded [Sunshine 2000]

Appearances:
20 Aboriginal Greatest Hits, Vol. 3 [Sunshine 2002] comp

Small, Gary—(Northern Cheyenne) Blues

Originally from Montana, but based in Portland, Oregon. A respected guitar player, Small mixed rock, reggae, and blues to tell stories of historical and cultural significance. While working at the local Indian healthcare organization, he offered his talents to create successful fund-raisers and benefit concerts. For these concerts, he assembled a formidable percussion section, including former Santana drummer Graham Lear and Joe Cocker percussionist Bobby Torres (*See*: Jesse Ed Davis); additional backup was given by the Fabulous Thunderbirds and other guest musicians.

DISCOGRAPHY:
Wild Indian [Medicine Tail Music 2001]
Cheyenne Blue Revisited [AKINA 2001]
Cheyenne Blue [Medicine Tail Music 1998]
    as Reverend Gary Small and the Deacons

Appearances:
Skin Tight Blues [Sweet Grass/EMI 2002]
comp

Smith, Keely—(Cherokee) Jazz

Born Dorothy Jacqueline Keely Smith, March 9, 1932, Norfolk, Virginia. In 1948, entertainer Louis Prima appeared in her hometown of Norfolk, Virginia, and hired Smith at an audition; she made their first recording in 1949. They were married on July 13, 1953, and had two daughters, Toni and Luanne. As a duet, they received the 1958 Grammy Award for Pop Duo/Group of the Year for their signature song "That Old Black Magic." When they signed with Capitol Records, Prima stipulated that Smith sign her own recording deal; they later left the label for Dot at the end of the 1950s. In 1961, Smith filed for divorce, citing extreme mental cruelty. In 1965, she married record producer Jimmy Bowen, but they were later divorced. Her rise to prominence came from her association with Prima, though his success can in part be attributed to her energetic showmanship and good-humored swing that accompanied his comedic trumpet act. They were a hit in Las Vegas and shared the stage with the biggest stars, including Frank Sinatra, who affectionately called her "my li'l Injun." Although Smith is associated mostly with Prima, she established herself as a singer of renown. Her debut album *I Wish You Love* went gold and received a Grammy nomination. She also starred in *Thunder Road* opposite Robert Mitchum.

Her millennium album *Swing, Swing, Swing* reached number 5 on Billboard's Top Jazz Album Charts, 2000; *Keely Sings Sinatra* received a Grammy nomination for Best Traditional Pop Vocal Album, 2001; *Keely Swings Basie Style—With Strings* was number 14 on the Billboard Charts in 2003.

SELECTED DISCOGRAPHY:
Keely Swings Basie Style—With Strings [Concord 2002] number 14 Billboard Top Jazz Album Charts
Keely Sings Sinatra [Concord Jazz 2001]
Swing Swing Swing [Concord Jazz 2000] number 5 Billboard Top Jazz Album Charts
I'm in Love Again [Fantasy 1985]
Doin' the Twist [Fantasy 1980]
Little Girl Blue [Reprise 1973]
Little Girl New [Reprise 1969]
Keely Smith Sings the Beatles [Reprise 1965]
Keely Smith Wishes You a Merry Christmas [Dot 1963]
Cherokeely Swings [Dot 1962; Jasmine 1994]
Dearly Beloved [Dot 1961]
What Kind of Fool Am I? [Dot 1961]
A Keely Christmas [Dot DLP-25345]
Swing You Lovers [Dot 1960]
Be My Love [Dot DLP-3387]
Twist with Keely Smith [Dot 1960]
Because You're Mine [Dot 1959]
Swingin' Pretty [Capitol 1959]
Politely! [Capitol 1958]
I Wish You Love [Capitol 1957]

Appearances:
Louis Prima:
Las Vegas Prima Style [Capitol T-1010]
Wildest! [Dot 1957]
Capitol Recordings [Capitol 1956]
Angelina [Capitol 1950]
Beepin' and Boppin' [Capitol 1949]

Film:
Louis Prima: The Wildest! [Don McGlynn, 1999] documentary
Hey Boy, Hey Girl [David Lowell Rich, 1959] as Dorothy Spencer
Senior Prom [David Lowell Rich, 1958] as herself
Thunder Road [Arthur Ripley, 1958] as Francie Wymore

Smith Family Gospel Singers—
(Dineh) Gospel

Lineup: Marsha Smith, lead vocals; Nona Lou Etsity, tenor; Vernita Halwood, alto; Dan Smith Jr., bass guitar/bass vocals; Roscoe Smith, acoustic guitar; Wilbert Tso, electric guitar; Deanne Bahe, bells.

DISCOGRAPHY:
Sweet Beulah Land [Canyon 1989]
A Navajo Christmas: Carols in Navajo and English [Canyon 1988]
Touching Jesus [Canyon 1987]
The Smith Family Gospels Singers with the Thunders [Canyon 1983]

Song Catchers—Trad/Jazz/Rock *See*: Lara Lavi; Powwow Music: American Indian Dance Theater

Lineup: Lara Lavi, lead vocals/spoken word; Charles Neville, soprano saxophone/spoken word; Arlie Neskahai, traditional vocals (*See*: Powwow Music); Mark Cardenas, keyboards; Maurice Jones Jr., bass; Ben Smith, drums; Morgan Fichter, violin; Danny Mangold, space guitar; William Wittman, electric guitar; Mark Smith, Robert Charles, Ryan Wilson, Ted Napoleon, Ron Tso, Joann Baptist, Bruce Baptist, traditional drumming and singing.

Formed in 1991. Their 1994 album won immediate acclaim for its mix of contemporary jazz, rock, traditional, and spoken-word elements. Relating traditional perspectives on historical and contemporary themes, it remains indelibly tasteful with talent and substance.

DISCOGRAPHY:
Dreaming in Color [A&M/Horizon 1994]

Sons of Membertou—(Mi'kmaq) Trad/Folk *See*: Traditional/Archival Group

Soulfood—Ambient

Lineup: DJ Free; Arapata; Frank Montano, a.k.a. Anakwad (*See*: Flute Music). Trance/ambient mixes combining Maori, Lakota, and Anishnabe elements with global instruments, all wrapped in studio technology to produce rhythmic and melodic tracks.

DISCOGRAPHY:
Breathe [Candescence/Musik International 1997] two CDs

Appearances:
Prophecy [Hearts of Space 1999] comp

Soul Kings—Blues

Formed in 1999, Six Nations Territory of the Grand River, Ontario. The individual players of this band are seasoned musicians who have played widely throughout North America. Their first recording together is a great mix of blues, rock, funk, and soul.

Lineup: Josh Miller, guitar/vocals; Keith Silver, bass/vocals; Blaine Bomberry, guitar/vocals; Frank Miller, drums.

DISCOGRAPHY:
Soul Kings [Joshmusic 2001]

Appearances:
Skin Tight Blues [Sweet Grass/EMI 2002] comp

Special Ice *See*: Brenda MacIntyre

Spirit Keepers—Folk/Blues/Trad

Lineup: Tom Goodman (Muscogee-Creek), didgeridoo/flutes/guitar/harmonica/percussion; Danny Bigay (Choctaw-Scots-Irish), flutes/percussion; Robert Bower, producer; guest appearances by Linda Holtz, vocals, and the Southern Nations Drum.

Former drummer for the Atlanta Rhythm Section, Bigay became a flute maker and creates his own line of jewelry and clothing. Goodman's father and grandfather played music with Sonny Terry, Brownie McGee, Robert Johnson, and many other players in the neighborhood where Bigay grew up. Bigay has created Native awareness projects in the education system, participated in community projects for children, and worked in wildlife preservation.

DISCOGRAPHY:
Sacred Ground [Intuitive Sound 1999]

Spirit Nation—Rock

Lineup: David Evans, Jimmy Waldo, Judy Crescenzo (Tucuhnut), and others. This band mixes nature sounds with world beats and traditional singing. Their 2001 release *Winter Moons* features Tamara Podemski (Anishnabekwe).

DISCOGRAPHY:
Winter Moons [Karuna/Razor and Tie 2001]
Spirit Nation [V2 Records 1998]

Star Nayea—Metal/Blues *See*: Chuck Billy, Red Earth, Robbie Robertson, Keith Secola

Born April 9, 1969. Based in New Mexico. Because Star Nayea was adopted in infancy, her lifelong search for her roots influenced her talent as a singer. Her powerhouse vocal performances in the 1999 musical *Tribe* earned her acclaim. She also appeared in Tomson Highway's *The Rose* and in concert with the heavy metal band Testament. *Somewhere in a Dream* received a NAMA nonination for Best Independent Recording, 2001.

DISCOGRAPHY:
Christmas Dream [independent 2001]

Somewhere in a Dream [independent 2000] five-track EP
Star Nayea [independent 1996] cass

Appearances (listed alphabetically):
Red Earth:
When Worlds Collide [Third Mesa 1999]
Robbie Robertson:
Contact from the Underworld of Redboy [Capitol 1998]
Testament:
Live at the Fillmore [Spitfire 1999]

Starr, Kay—(Iroquois-Irish) Jazz *See*: Mildred Bailey

Born Kathryn LaVerne Starks, Dougherty, Oklahoma, July 21, 1922. Her father, Harry Starks, was Iroquois, and her mother, Annie, was Irish. She began singing professionally in Dallas, Texas, when she was ten years old. After her aunt entered Kay into a talent contest at local radio station WWR Dallas, which she won. Kay stayed with the station, which eventually gave her a fifteen-minute show that aired three times a week and paid three dollars a night. She began her professional career in her early teens and became known as "the Kid." As her popularity grew along with a fan base that buried her in mail, the common misspelling of her name led to the use of Starr. The family moved to Memphis, Tennessee, where she landed a show at radio station WREC, called *Starr Time*, as she made regular appearances on the program *Saturday Night Jamboree*. In 1937, band leader and violinist Joe Venuti hired her under special contract that allowed her to stay in school while she worked as a performer. Two years later Starr went on to work with orchestra leader Bob Crosby and almost immediately thereafter with Glenn Miller, making her first recording with Miller on the Bluebird label. She finished high school in 1940 and moved to California to work again with Venuti. Starr joined Wingy Manone's New Orleans Jazz Band

and was hired by Charlie Barnet to replace
Lena Horne; she recorded with Barnet
on V-Discs and Decca in 1943. In 1945,
she recorded solo with Capitol Records on
their *Volumes of Jazz* series; made several
singles with the Lamplighter, Standard,
and Jewell labels; and finally signed with
Capitol in 1947. She become one of the
most consistent hit makers ever to sign
with the label. "I'm the Lonesomest Girl
in Town" made the top-30 charts. In the
spring of 1950, she had the number 2 song
with a cover of Perry Como's polka "Hoop
De Doo" and landed a major million seller
with "Bonaparte's Retreat"; her signature
song, "Wheel of Fortune," released in 1952,
stayed at number 1 for ten weeks. Although
her early recordings were steeped in jazz,
she later successfully blended pop sensibilities with rock in the 1955 hit "Rock
and Roll Waltz," which stayed at number 1
for six weeks, with equal popularity in the
United Kingdom. "Comes A-Long-A-Love"
also topped the charts in England. By 1960,
she was performing mainly in Las Vegas,
Nevada. Most of her work was with Capitol Records, but she also recorded on RCA
Victor, GNP, EMI, Stash, and Hindsight.

Her complete discography includes more
than 103 singles and B-sides, 14 EPs, more
than 33 box sets, and numerous guest appearances with other artists, including
Charlie Barnet, Nat King Cole, Tennessee Ernie Ford, Glen Miller, and Mildred
Bailey.

Kay Starr was Columbia Records' highest-paid
artist in the 1950s. Cover art courtesy Baldwin
Street Records.

SELECTED DISCOGRAPHY:
Kay Starr Country [GNP 2003]
Honeysuckle Rose [Stash 2003]
Encounter [MCA 2003]
Wheel of Fortune [ASV/Living Era 2003]
Jazz Singer [2002]
Kay Starr [Classic World 2002]
Kay Starr 1986 [Baldwin Street Music 2001]
The Essential RCA Singles Collection
   [Taragon 1999]
The Complete Lamplighter Recordings
   1945–1946 [Baldwin Street Music 1998]
The RCA Years [Collectors' Choice 1998]

Just Plain Country [Capitol 1970]
Back to the Roots [GNP 1969]
How about This [Paramount 1969]
When the Lights Go On Again [ABC 1968]
Tears and Heartaches/Old Records [Capi-
   tol 1966]
Fabulous Favorites [Capitol 1964]
I Cry by Night [Capitol 1962]
Kay Starr Sings, Vol. 2 [Coronet Records
   CX-179]
Kay Starr Sings [Coronet Records CX-106]
Movin' On Broadway [Capitol 1960]
One More Time [Capitol 1960]
Kay Starr: Jazz Singer [Capitol 1960]
Losers, Weepers [Capitol 1960]
Movin' [Capitol 1959]
I Hear the World [RCA Victor 1959]
Them There Eyes [Rondo-Lette 1958]
Rockin' with Kay [RCA Victor 1958]
Kay Starr [RCA Camden 1957] w/ Harold
   Mooney and His Orchestra
Blue Starr [RCA Victor 1957]
Songs by Kay Starr [Capitol 1956]
Swingin' with Kay Starr [Liberty 1956]
Singin' Kay Starr, Swingin' Erroll Garner
   [Modern 1956]
The One the Only Kay Starr [RCA Victor
   1955]
In a Blue Mood [Capitol 1955] ten-inch LP

The Hits of Kay Starr [Capitol 1954] ten-inch LP

Kay Starr Style [Capitol 1953] ten-inch LP

Songs by Kay Starr [Capitol 1950] ten-inch LP

Billboard Top 100:

"Four Walls" [October 27, 1962] number 92

"I'll Never Be Free" [June 19, 1961] number 94

"Foolin' Around" [March 20, 1961] number 49

"My Heart Reminds Me" [September 2, 1957] number 9

"Little Loneliness" [April 27, 1957] number 73

"Jamie Boy" [April 20, 1957] number 54

"Good Book" [September 8, 1956] number 89

"Things I Never Had" [September 8, 1956] number 89

"Love Ain't Right" [August 11, 1956] number 89

"Second Fiddle" [June 9, 1956] number 40

"I've Changed My Mind a Thousand Times" [February 4, 1956] number 73

"Rock and Roll Waltz" [January 17, 1956] number 1; gold record

"Good and Lonesome" [August 6, 1955] number 17

"If You Really Love Me" [April 25, 1954] number 4

"The Man Upstairs" [April 17, 1954] number 7

"Changing Partners" [December 5, 1953] number 7

"When My Dreamboat Comes Home" [October 17, 1953] number 18

"Allez-Vous-En" [June 20, 1953] number 11

"Half a Photograph" [June 6, 1953] number 7

"Side by Side" [January 31, 1953] number 3

"Comes A-Long-A-Love" [September 27, 1952] number 9

"Fool, Fool, Fool" [August 9, 1952] number 13; w/ the Lancers

"Kay's Lament" [July 26, 1952] number 18

"I Waited a Little Too Long" [May 31, 1952] number 20

"Wheel of Fortune" [February 16, 1952] number 1; gold

"Come On-A My House" [August 4, 1951] number 8

"Oceans of Tears" [June 30, 1951] number 15

"Oh, Babe!" [November 18, 1950] number 7

"I'll Never Be Free" [August 19, 1950] number 3; w/ Tennessee Ernie Ford

"Mississippi" [July 15, 1950] number 18

"Bonaparte's Retreat" [May 27, 1950] number 4

"Hoop De-Doo" [May 6, 1950] number 2

"You Were Only Foolin' (While I Was Falling in Love)" [December 4, 1948] number 16

"So Tired" [January 15, 1948] number 7

Film:

The Pied Piper of Hamelin [Bretaigne Windust, 1957] as John's mother

When You're Smiling [Joseph Santley, 1950] as herself

Make Believe Ballroom [Joseph Santley, 1949] as herself

Starr, Kinnie—(Mohawk-Irish) Funk/Hip-Hop/R & B

Based in Vancouver, British Columbia. This energetic and thoughtful singer-songwriter performs her trip-hop, funk, and soul with a sensual style that she prefers to call chunk-hop. This personality is the perfect vehicle to convey her message of consciousness, womanhood, and Native reality with a both subtle and outlandish artistic abandon.

She utilizes her passion for drums, guitar, and hip-hop in her first two albums, where she also rhymes in Spanish, English, and French. She won acclaim in Japan and Europe before making her mark in North America. Although she remained an underground diva for years in Vancouver, B.C., she quickly gained notoriety in an ever-widening musical circle. She was lead vocalist for the 2003 Cirque du Soleil adults-only production of *Zumanity* in Las Vegas, Nevada, and received a Juno nomination, New Artist of the Year, 2004.

DISCOGRAPHY:
Sun Again [Violet Inch 2003]
Tune Up [Violet Inch 2000]
Mending [Mercury 1997]
Tidy [Violet Inch 1996]
Learning 2 Cook [Violet Inch 1995] cass

Singles:
"Unbuttoned" [Violet Inch 1998] twelve-inch vinyl
"Woven/Rime Gone Rong" [Violet Inch 1996] seven-inch vinyl

Appearances:
Our Voice Is Our Weapon and Our Bullets Are the Truth [Red Wire Magazine 2003] comp

Videos:
Discovered [Universal 2000]

Starr, Lucille—(Metis-Anishnabekwe) Country *See*: Mighty Mohawks

Starr gained popularity in 1951 and wrote "The French Song," which became a hit in the 1960s and was covered by many artists, including the Mighty Mohawks.

St. Germain, Ray—(Metis) Rock/Pop/ Country *See*: Len Fairchuck; Ernest Monias

Born July 29, 1940, raised in St. Vital, Manitoba. St. Germain began his career in music in his early teens. By the age of sixteen, he began touring with a traveling radio show western band called the CKY Caravan from Bangor, Maine, to Winnipeg, Manitoba.

St. Germain began working in radio on CJOB and hosted *Country Cats and a Kitten*, with Wayne Funican, Roy Delarond, Albert Shorting, and Pat McMullin. He often toured with Hal Lone Pine (Harold Breau), Betty Cody, and their guitar-playing son, Lenny Breau (*See*: Jeari Czapla); his first 1958 recording, "She's a Square," features this legendary Metis jazz guitarist. In that same year, St. Germain won a CBC Talent Caravan Contest that started him off as a television host for *Music Hop Hootenanny*. He went on to host *My Kind of Country*, *Show of the Week*, *In Person*, *Time for Livin'* (written by Alan Thicke), and *Lorne Greene's Canada for the Fun of It*; he also made numerous guest appearances on other shows, including *The Tommy Hunter Show*. He wrote, produced, and hosted the award-winning series *Hits of Yesterday* for Global Television, syndicated nationally from 1978 to 1990.

Further work in Canadian television included *Ray St. Germain Country/Big Sky Country*, which featured country music stars such as Bobby Bare. St. Germain's work in television included the series *Rhythms of the Metis* and *The Road Show* for APTN; he was also the host of his own radio program, *The Metis Hour*, NCI-FM, Winnipeg, Manitoba.

DISCOGRAPHY:
My Many Moods [Arbor 2003]
Ray St. Germain, Greatest Hits, Vol. 1 [American Hall of Fame Recordings 1998] best of

Singles:
"She's A Square" [1958]
"If You Don't Mean It" [1958]

Supaman—(Crow) Rap

From Crow Agency, Montana. A rez-based rapper who displays skill with slick urban beats and rhymes, combining gospel with rap.

DISCOGRAPHY:
Supaman [independent 2002]

Tabor, Buddy—Country/Folk

Lineup: Buddy Tabor, guitar vocals; Bob Banghart, fiddle; Albert McDonnell, bass/vocals/percussion; Andy Ferguson, mandolin; Rachel Beck, backup vocals.

DISCOGRAPHY:
Meadowlark [independent 1998]

Tailfeathers, Olivia, and the Kainai Grassland Singers— (Blackfoot) Folk/Trad

Lineup: Olivia Tailfeathers, Sarah Black Plume, Bessie Black Rabbit, Jessie Black Water, Galena Brave Rock, Donovan Tailfeathers, Amber Weasel Head, Tanya White Man Left; Cheryl Davidsen, keyboards; Donovan Tailfeathers, cedar flute.

DISCOGRAPHY:
Niitsitapi [independent 2000]

Appearances:
Hearts of the Nations [Banff Centre for the Arts/Sweet Grass 1997] comp *See*: Traditional/Archival Compilations

Taylor, Billy—(Metis) Fiddle

DISCOGRAPHY:
Hometown Fiddle [Sunshine SSCT-494]

Thomas, Hubert—(Cree) Gospel

From Chinawawin Cree Nation. Thomas began playing guitar at age fourteen and learned Cree hymns from his family and his mentor Philip Sinclair.

DISCOGRAPHY:
Cree Hymns, Vol. 5 [Sunshine 2002]

Three O'Clock Train—Rock *See*: Mack MacKenzie

Lineup: Mack MacKenzie, lead vocals/guitar; Stuart MacKenzie, guitars; Pierre Perron, drums; Dave Hill, bass; Ivan Doroschuk, synthesizer; Stefan Doroschuk, guitar/fretless bass/synthesizer; Susan Joseph, piano.

Formed in 1984, Montreal, Quebec. They named their first recording after the Wig Wam Beach Music Fest in Kahnawake, Quebec. The group earned national acclaim before breaking up. The MacKenzies reformed the band with a new lineup in 1989. Mack MacKenzie's 1991 album is often cited as the group's third release.

DISCOGRAPHY:
Anthology: Wig Wam Beach/Muscle In [Just A Memory 1996]
Muscle In [Pipeline 1986]
Wig Wam Beach [Pipeline 1985] EP

Thunderbird Sisters—(Shinnecock-Montauk) Folk *See*: Morley Loon

Lineup: Becky Genia, vocals/guitar; Tina Tarrant, vocals/guitar; Holly Haile Davis, vocals/guitar; Ben Haile, bass/mandolin/backup vocals/producer. Chee Chee Thunderbird, Elizabeth Haile, Kim Makowski, and Randall Gregoire recorded the two-track EP *The Lord's Prayer*.

The grandchildren of Chief and Mrs. Thunderbird have been performing professionally since 1973. Notable performances include Carnegie Hall and backup vocals for Bonnie Raitt at the 1980 Black Hills Survival Gathering, South Dakota. The group provided the music for *Spirit of Turtle Island* [Alan Collins/Lenore Keeshig-Tobias, 1989]. They received the NAMA Award for Best Folk/Country Band, 2000.

DISCOGRAPHY:
Rise above My Enemy upon the Smoke [independent 2001]

Still Singin' [Thunderbird Sisters 1999]
w/ David Amram
The Lord's Prayer [Thunderbird Sisters 1999]
Live '85 [Thunderbird Sisters 1986]
Contemporary American Indian Songs [Smithsonian Folkways 37255]

Thunderchief; a.k.a. Francis Steindorf— (Winnebago-Hochungra) Folk

An educator and musician, Thunderchief performs concerts, lectures, and workshops for schools from kindergarten to university and works as an adjunct professor at Viterbo College, La Crosse, Wisconsin.

DISCOGRAPHY:
Good Medicine [independent 1999]
Native Realities [independent 1994]

Thunderkloud, Billy, and the Chieftones—(Tsimshian) Country

Born in northern British Columbia. With his brothers Jack, Barry and Richard, Billy Thunderkloud formed the Chieftones in 1964. They signed with 20th Century Records ten years later. 1976 Billboard Country Chart appearances include "Indian Nation," number 75 and "Try A Little Tenderness," number 50. The group later disbanded.

DISCOGRAPHY:
All Through the Night [Superior 1976]
Where Do I Begin to Tell the Story [Superior 1975]
What Time of Day [20th Century/GRT 1975]
Off the Reservation [20th Century/GRT 1973]

Singles:
"My Lady" [Polydor 1978]
"Oklahoma Wind" [Polydor 1977]
"Let Me Be Your Man" [Polydor 1977]

"Try a Little Tenderness" [Polydor 1976]
"Indian Nation" [Polydor 1976] number 75 Billboard Country Charts
"Pledging My Love" [Polydor 1976]
"Pledging My Love" [20th Century/GRT 1975]
"What Time of Day/When Love Is Right" [20th Century/GRT 1975]

Tiger Tiger—(Miccosukee) Rock

Lineup: Lee Tiger, bass/vocals/keyboards; Stephen Tiger, rhythm guitar/vocals; Gonzo Gutsens, Dennis Saunders, lead guitar; Ron Huff, drums/percussion.

A veteran band of the Miami club circuit, the Tiger brothers recorded original songs in the 1980s rock style.

DISCOGRAPHY:
Southern Exposure [Warrior/SOAR 2000]
Dream Scout [SOAR 1996]
Space Age Indian [SOAR 1995]

Appearances:
Urban Skins, Vol. 1 [SOAR 1999] comp

Videos:
Lay Your Burden Down [StingerHopanke/ Warrior/SOAR 2000]

Tipatshimun—(Innu) Rock *See*: Meshikamau

Lineup: David Penashue, rhythm guitar/ vocals; Kevin Nuna, lead guitar; Gregory Maxwell Penashue, keyboards; Brian Pone, bass.

From Happy Valley–Goose Bay, Labrador. Songs are sung in Innu with a primary focus on land, family, culture, and the struggle for justice. A talented David Penashue composed most of the material and performs lead guitar and vocals.

DISCOGRAPHY:
Pishum [Eagle Studios 2000]

Titla, Boe—(Apache) Country and Western

Born in Bylas, Arizona, Titla is a long-time favorite throughout the southwestern United States.

DISCOGRAPHY:
Boe Titla, Vol. 3 [BT 1998]
Boe Titla, Vol. 2 [BT 1995]
Memories of Point of Pines [BT 1990]

Tito and Tarantula—(Chicano) Rock

Lineup: Tito Larriva, vocals/guitars; Peter Atanasoff, guitars/vocals; Jennifer Condos, bass/vocals; Johnny "Vatos" Hernandez, drums/percussion/vocals; and an array of backup players.

Tito's music is a blend of classic riffs, with every groove on each disc packed with solid rock. His music is part of the score for *From Dusk Till Dawn* [Robert Rodriguez, 1996].

DISCOGRAPHY:
Hungry Sally and Other Killer Lullabies [Cockroach Records 1999]
Tarantism [Cockroach Records 1997]

TKO—(Cree-Saulteaux) Rap *See*: GQ Smooth

Born October 14, 1968, Winnipeg, Manitoba. Manager, rapper, and role model for Native youth, TKO (pronounced "taco") delivers rhymes to straighten the record on culture and history from a street-level perspective. *Welcome to the Playground* received a Juno nomination for Best Music of Aboriginal Canada Recording, 1999.

DISCOGRAPHY:
The Value of My Skin [Arbor 2001]
Welcome to the Playground [Sunshine 1997]

Appearances:
Arsenal [Knock 'em Dead Productions 2001] comp

20 Greatest Aboriginal Hits, Vol. 2 [Sunshine 1998] comp
Urban Skins, Vol. 2 [SOAR 1999] comp

Videos:
Shaman's Call See: Flute Music: R. Carlos Nakai

Tlen, Daniel—(Tutchone) Country/Rock

Based in the Yukon, Tlen began recording in Ottawa in 1987 for CBC Northern Service. He teamed up with Les McLaughlin, who produced Susan Aglukark's first album, and with Randall Prescott, a four-time Juno Award–winning country music producer. As a successful regional artist, Tlen and his band Fat Puppy were headliners for the CBC's annual True North concert series in Inuvik.

DISCOGRAPHY:

Appearances:
True North Concerts—Truly Something [CBC North 2000] comp
Skookum Jim's Gold [independent 1997] sdtk
The Yukon Collection [Caribou 1995] comp
Another Day in Paradise [CBC Northern Service 1987] comp

Tonemah—(Kiowa-Comanche-Tuscarora) Folk/Rock

Born Darryl Parker Tonemah, September 16, 1966. Based in Phoenix, Arizona, Tonemah combines durable vocals with radio-friendly music. While studying counseling psychology at the University of Nebraska, he was a featured vocalist in the 1998 stage production of *Tribe* and did some extra work for the film *The Last of the Mohicans* [Michael Mann, 1992].

His second album, *The Ghosts of St. Augustine*, includes traditional flute player Robert Tree Cody; percussionist Tony Redhouse (*See*: Redhouse Family); Pura Fe of

Tonemah with a custom-made Longbow guitar. Photo courtesy Tonemah.

the accapella trio Ulali; Benito Concha, percussion; Cary Morin of Atoll, guitar; Ray Hernandez, drums; and Tom Young, keyboards. The album earned him an Outstanding Musical Performance nomination by FAITA in 1997, and three NAMA nominations for Best Contemporary Album, Best Folk or Country Album, and Best Male Artist, 1998.

DISCOGRAPHY:
One in Every Crowd [Gladiola Records 2004]
A Time Like Now [Gladiola Records 2002]
Journal of My Misperceptions [Red Sky Productions 2000]
The Ghosts of St. Augustine [Red Sky Productions 1997]
Can You Hear Me? [Dakota Moon 1994]

Trezak, Dave "White Wolf"—
(Cherokee-Lakota) Blues/Country *See*: Flute Music

Born January 1, 1962, Ocala, Florida. With the Village of Many Tribes, Trezak released an anthemic album of political and social consciousness.

The Village of Many Tribes was the name of a group of talented session players that included Eddie Green from Steely Dan on drums; arranger Dale Herr of Los Angeles, Motown, and Nashville fame; and the Nashville String Machine. The project earned a NAMA nomination for Best Jazz Blues Roots Album. Trezak's country album is exemplary of the genre. Trezak also headed up the environmental initiative Save the Land Foundation Inc.

DISCOGRAPHY:
Native Country [Raven Moon 2000]
Medicine [Raven Moon 2000] flute music
Special Edition [independent 2000]
Save the Land [Raven Moon 1999]

Videos:
Save the Land [Raven Moon 1998]

Trials—Heavy Rock

Lineup: Ryan Quintana (Apache), guitars; Dean Green (Aztec), vocals; John Schrimsher, bass/vocals; Denny Pino (Choctaw), drums.

Based in New Mexico, Trials' only release has a commercial radio sound with lyrics that attempt to define the struggles of identity, alienation, and pride for Native people.

DISCOGRAPHY:
Thirteen [Black Cat Records 1998]

Trudell, John—(Santee) Poetry/Rock
See: Jesse Ed Davis, Annie Humphrey, Robbie Robertson

Born February 15, 1946, Omaha, Nebraska. Trudell served in the U.S. Navy from 1963 to 1967 during the Vietnam War. His involvement as spokesman for the Indians of All Tribes occupation of Alcatraz Island from 1969 to 1971 placed him on the FBI's "ten most wanted" list. He was the last active chairman of AIM before the position was dissolved; the FBI described him as "an eloquent speaker and an effective organizer." Arrested on contempt of court charges during the Leonard Peltier trials (1976), Trudell was brought before a retired judge and thrown in jail, during which time his life and his family's lives were threatened if he didn't end his activities. Months after being released, Trudell burned the American flag on the steps of the FBI building during a 1978 demonstration in Washington, D.C. His pregnant wife, Tina, his mother-in-law, Leah Hicks Manning (*See*: Robbie Robertson), and all four of the Trudell children perished in a house fire on Nevada's Duck Valley Reservation in 1979. The incident occurred twelve hours after Trudell's actions and under suspicious circumstances.

During his "survival time," Trudell began writing poetry as a form of therapy. His first cassette-only release, *Tribal Voice*, features work from his book of poetry. *Songs Called Poems* is backed with traditional singing by Quiltman Sahme and was produced by Jackson Browne. Although *Tribal Voice* was not the first time poetry was set to traditional music, it became the most successful and enduring album of its kind.

In 1985, guitar legend Jesse Ed Davis introduced himself to Trudell. Released on Trudell's Peace Company label, the collaborative *AKA: Graffiti Man*, produced by Davis, received a Grammy nomination in 1987 for Best Word and Best Rock Duo. Bob Dylan called it the "album of the year" and had it played over the PA system before each show during his world tour. *AKA Graffiti Man* sold more than twenty thousand copies in Europe alone. The follow-up project, . . . *But This Isn't El Salvador*, incorporated traditional music, rock, and spoken word.

Trudell's third demo release, *Heart Jump Bouquet*, is a blueprint for commercial-sounding material, with few tracks scoring points for lyrics. The cassette-only *Fables and Other Realities* contains "The Needle," an ode to Davis, with a special appearance by Kris Kristofferson. In 1992, Trudell signed with Ryko Records and re-released *AKA Graffiti Man* as a best-of album, but with some new material and remastered tracks that preserve some of Davis's last recordings. Davis had introduced Trudell to Mark Shark, a very competent player who eventually replaced Davis in the Graffiti Band. The second Ryko album, *Johnny Damas and Me*, shipped twenty-five thousand copies in the first three weeks of its February 1994 release and charted on the top-forty lists in Europe. On the *Oyate* project, Trudell recites the work of Barney Bush (*See*: Contemporary Spoken Word: Poetry) and his own poem "Crazy Horse," with Jeff Beck playing guitar; other ax men with whom Trudell has worked include Glenn Hughes of Deep Purple (*See*: Stevie Salas). Trudell's poem "Edge of America" was recorded by Annie Humphrey for the title song on her 2003 album of the same name.

In 1997, Trudell received the NAMA Living Legend Award, 1999; *Blue Indians* received NAMA Awards for Song of the Year, Producer of the Year, and Artist of the Year, 2000.

Bad Dog Lineup (formerly the Graffiti Band): Quiltman, traditional vocals; Mark Shark, guitar; Rick Eckstein, keyboards; Gary Ray, drums; Jackson Browne, executive producer.

DISCOGRAPHY:

The Collection 1983-1992 [Asitis/Effective Records 2003] six-CD box set
The Radio Interview [Asitis/Effective Records 2003] w/ ten songs
Bone Days [Asitis 2001]
Descendant Now Ancestor [Asitis 2000] speeches w/ poetry
Blue Indians [Dangerous Discs 1999]
Johnny Damas and Me [Ryko 1994]
AKA Graffiti Man [Ryko 1992] w/ Jesse Ed Davis
Fables and Other Realities [Peace Company 1990] w/ Kris Kristofferson
. . . But This Isn't El Salvador [Peace Company 1987] w/ Jesse Ed Davis
Heart Jump Bouquet [Peace Company 1987] w/ Jesse Ed Davis and Daryl Hannah
AKA Graffiti Man [Peace Company 1986] w/ Jesse Ed Davis
Tribal Voice [Peace Company 1983] w/ Quiltman, Madeline and Bark

Singles:

"A Face of God" [Asitis 2003]
"Broke the Light" [Asitis 2003]
"That Love" [Ryko 1994]
"Rant 'n' Roll" [Ryko 1994]

Appearances (listed alphabetically):

Bob Dylan:
Knocked Out Loaded [CBS 1986] special thanks

John Trudell. Photo by Agnes Patak.

Annie Humphrey:
Edge of Ameica [Makoche 2003]
The Heron Smiled [Makoche 2000]
Casper Lomayesva:
Sounds of Reality [Third Mesa 2000]
Various:
Whispering Tree [Makoche 2000] comp
Survival of the Sacred: A Spoken Word Event [Oh Yeah Productions 1998] cass; speeches by John Trudell and Corbin Harney recorded live in Santa Cruz, California
Basslines and Ballistics [Extreme 1995] comp EP *See*: The Fire This Time
Dancing On John Wayne's Head [Extreme 1995] comp *See*: The Fire This Time
Medium Rare: Ryko's 10th Anniversary [Ryko 1993] comp
Mountain Stage, Vol. 5 [Blue Plate 1993] comp
Neighbourhood Rhythms [Rhino 1984] two LP comp
No Nukes [Elektra/Asylum 1979] two LP

comp w/liner notes by Winona LaDuke (Anishnabekwe)

Oyate [Nato/World 1990/1998, France] two CD comp

Reggae on the River [Earth Beat! 1994] two CD comp

Still Dancing on John Wayne's Head [Extreme 1998] comp *See*: The Fire This Time

United States of Poetry [Mouth Almighty/Mercury/Polygram 1996] comp

Videos:

John Trudell Interview 4-22-03 [Effective Records 2003]

Rockin' the Rez [Ryko 1992]

Film:

Dreamkeepers [ABC/Hallmark 2003] as Coyote

A Thousand Guns [Russell Friedenberg 2002] as Wild Bill Charlie

Smoke Signals [Chris Eyre, 1998] as Randy Peone

Lewis and Clark: The Journey of the Corps of Discovery [Ken Burns, 1997] television: voice

Tushka [Ian Skorodin, 1996] docudrama: subject of

Extreme Measures [Michael Apted, 1996] as Tony

The Way West [Ric Burns, 1995] television: voice

On Deadly Ground [Steven Seagal, 1994] as Jonny Redfeather

Dark Blood [George Sluizer 1993] as Indian number 2

Thunderheart [Michael Apted, 1992] as Jimmy Looks Twice

Incident at Oglala [Michael Apted, 1992] documentary: as himself

Powwow Highway [Jonathan Wacks, 1988] as Louie Short Hair

Books:

Stick Man [Inanout Press 1994] o/p

Living in Reality—Songs Called Poems [Society of the People Struggling to Be Free, 1982] o/p

Living in Reality—A Story of Struggle [Society of the People Struggling to Be Free, 1981] o/p

Related Projects (listed alphabetically):

Children of Earth:

A Child's Voice [Peace Company 1992] cass; Trudell's daughters Song, Starr, and Sage Ratt perform their father's poetry; music by Mark Shark, Quiltman, and Rick Eckstein

Jim Page:

Whose World Is This [Liquid City 1996] Oregon-based singer and AIM supporter Jim Page reworked Trudell's poem "Tina Smiled," which appears on *Heart Jump Bouquet* and the Ryko release of *AKA Graffiti Man* in homage to Trudell's late wife

Quiltman (*See*: Traditional/Archival Solo):

Ravenous [Antonia Bird, 1999] sdtk

Quiltman and Tewahnee: Traditional Songs [independent 1996] cass; Quiltman Sahme and his son, Tewahnee, recorded the traditional songs from *Tribal Voice*

Mark Shark:

From the Heart [Peace Company 1997] Bad Dog guitarist Shark transformed Trudell's poetry into rock lyrics

True Believers—Rock

Lineup: Alejandro Escovedo, guitar/vocals; Javier Escovedo, guitar/vocals; Denny DeGorio, bass/harmonica/vocals; Kevin Foley, drums; Jon Dee Graham, guitar/lap steel/vocals.

DISCOGRAPHY:

Hard Road [Rykodisc 40287]

True Believers [EMI/Rounder 1986]

Tru Rez Crew—Rap

Lineup: Jon Garlow (Oneida), Harve Powless (Mohawk), Josh Harris (Seneca), Eric Martin (Tuscarora).

Formed in 1999, Six Nations of the Grand River Territory, Ontario, Canada.

The Tru Rez Crew's material draws from the members' experiences on the reservation as teenagers and is performed with raw energy, honest rhymes, and good music productions. They recorded their projects on the home computer and generated their succesful 2002 single "I'm a Lucky One," with Derek Miller, guitar; Lucie Idlout, backup vocals; and Inuit throat singers. *Ain't No Turning Back* received a CAMA Award, Best Rap Album, 2003.

DISCOGRAPHY:
Ain't No Turning Back [independent 2003]
It's Begun . . . [independent 2001]
Radio Singles [independent 2001] four-track EP
Native American Hip Hop [independent 2001] preview CD

Tuesday, Jason—(Anishnabe) Classical

Born in Big Grassy First Nation, 1975. Tuesday began playing at age sixteen. He studied at the Manitoba Conservatory of Music and Art in 1991 and thereafter at the University of Manitoba's School of Music. He captured the attention of classical guitar master Liona Boyd and appeared on the nationally televised *Aboriginal Achievement Awards* [CBC 1996].

Tulku—World Beat/New Age *See*: Little Wolf

Jim Wilson and Mitchell Markus employ samples, studio tracks, and live performances of music from around the world. Other musicians include Jai Uttal, Goeffrey Gordon of the Pagan Love Orchestra, and Vieux Diop from Senegal; there are also samples of the Tahitian Choir from the South Pacific and chants from India and North America. With rave reviews from New Age publications, the album

Transcendence reached number 9 on the jazz charts and on CMJ radio's New World Charts in 1997.

DISCOGRAPHY:
Transcendence [Triloka 1997]

Appearances:
Trance Planet [Triloka/Worldly 1996] comp

Turtle Mountain Boys—(Metis-Anishnabe) Country

Lineup: Wayne Poitra, bass; Todd Martell, lead guitar; Frank Martell, rhythm guitar; Derrick Dixon, drums/sax; Joe Swereda, fiddle; Wayne Link, steel guitar; Dick Schroeder, keys/vocals; Lee Thomas, guitar/vocals; Alvin Poitra, guitar/vocals.

DISCOGRAPHY:
Turtle Mountain Style "Originals" [Sunshine 1989]

2 Bears, Jackson—(Mohawk) Ambient Breaks

Born November 1, 1976, Brantford, Ontario. With a background in guitar, bass, drums, and classical piano, 2 Bears moved toward electronic music in 1997. His ambient techno beats layered with traditional singing and turntable sampling became a synthesis for the soundtrack for Kent Monkman's short film *Blood River* [Urban Nation 2000]. His Toronto club appearances help bring new dimensions to a growing movement in Native music as he continues to explore the possibilites of Native electronica.

Two Eagles, Vince—(Lakota) Folk/Rock

Born January 26, 1953, Wagner, South Dakota. Two Eagles works to develop a unique sound he calls *razz*, a combination of jazz and reservation-based music. With his band Otokahe (Beginnings), he incorporates flute, acoustic guitar, and rich vocals. A successful 1995 tour in Italy created international attention. He continues to perform throughout the United States.

DISCOGRAPHY:
In America [SOAR 1995]
People of the Earth [Max Records no date]
In the Night [Max Records no date]

Two Feathers, Shannon—
(Anishnabe) Country/Folk

An acoustic player from western Canada, Two Feathers released his recordings on IMI Records, based in Erickson, Manitoba.

SELECTED DISCOGRAPHY:
Dreams That Feed a Gypsy [IMI Records no date]
Separation Blue [IMI Records no date]

Singles:
"The Prisoner/Sweet Gypsy Hair" [RCA 1973]
"Separation Blue"/"The Prisoner" [IMI Records 1973]

Appearances:
Poundmaker's Lodge: A Healing Journey [Alanis Obomsawin, 1987] documentary: score

Ulali—Jazz/Trad *See*: Medicine Men, Pura Fe, Robbie Robertson, Spider Heart

Lineup: Pura Fe (Oneiowa-Tuscarora), Jennifer Kreisberg (Tuscarora), and Soni Moreno (Mayan-Apache).

Performing as a trio since 1991, Ulali toured extensively and made numerous recording appearances, including the Juno nominated *Hearts of the Nations* and the *Mission Impossible* soundtrack with U2. They were featured performers at Woodstock in 1994, at the Atlanta Olympic Games in 1996, and on *The Tonight Show*. They made important inroads into the mainstream with their fusion of traditional and gospel roots music, sweet harmonies, and jazzy a cappella. Their lyrics and poetry offer honest impressions of colonialism and cultural survival.

DISCOGRAPHY:
Mahk Jhi [Thrush 1996]
In the Spirit [independent 1993] cass
Ulali [independent 1992] cass
Corn Beans and Squash [independent 1991] cass

Appearances (listed alphabetically):
1 Giant Leap:
Braided Hair [Palm Pictures 2002] EP, backup vocals
1 Giant Leap [Palm Pictures 2001] backup vocals
Robbie Robertson and the Red Road Ensemble:
Music for the Native Americans [Capitol 1994]
Mahk Jhi [Capitol 1994] CD EP
Mahk Jhi [Capitol 1994] vinyl twelve-inch EP extended dance and ambient remixes
Speech:
Down South Productions [Vagabond 2002]
Dovie Thomason (*See*: Contemporary Spoken Word: Legends and Storytelling):
Lessons from the Animal People [Yellow Moon Press 1996]
Various:
Alcatraz Is Not an Island [James Fortier, 2002] score
Skin Tight Blues [Sweet Grass/EMI 2002] comp
Gathering of Nations Powwow 2001 [Gathering of Nations Records 2002] comp *See*: Powwow Compilations
Singing Our Stories [Full Regalia Productions 2000] comp
Songs for Chiapas "Off the Record" [Ra Records 1999] comp
Weaving the Strands: Music by Contemporary Native Women [Red Feather 1998] comp
Smoke Signals [Miramax 1998] sdtk

Honor [Daemon 1996] comp
Mission Impossible [Brian DePalma, 1996]
  sdtk
Global Divas [Rounder 1995] comp
Heartbeat: Voices of First Nations Women
  [Smithsonian 1995] comp *See*: Tradi-
  tional/Archival Compilations

Unceded Band—Blues/Rock *See*: Tomson Highway, Jani Lauzon

Lineup: Gloria Eshkibok (Anishnabewkwe),
vocals; boo Watson, keyboards; Sherry
Shute, lead guitar; Miche Hill (Mohawk),
bass.

This band's name originated from Eshkibok's home, the Unceded Territory of Wikwemikong. The group played extensively
throughout the 1990s, but generated very
few recordings before disbanding. Their
music was predominantly blues in flavor and rock in nature, with Native roots.
Shute is a superlative guitarist who sessioned with notable blues talents such as
Ellen McElwaine. Hill played and recorded
with the Vancouver-based Industrial Waste
Banned and recorded *Not Fit for Human
Consumption* [independent 1983] on cassette. Watson released her independent
project *Opening Moves* in 1999. Eshkibok
continued her acting career in film, television, and stage, with additional recording
appearances that include the score for
Blood River [Kent Monkman, 2003] (*See*:
Jackson 2 Bears). Their two-track release
includes Tomson Highway's "I'm Thinking
of You."

DISCOGRAPHY:
The Unceded Band [independent 1997] cass

Under the Northern Sky—Adult Contemporary

Lineup: Ron Kataquapit, J. Elliot, and
M. McGrath.

DISCOGRAPHY:
Facing Reality [independent 1991] cass

Valdez, Daniel—(Chicano) Folk

Primarily an acoustic player who offered
social commentary, Valdez penned songs
about Brown Pride, farmworkers, and indigenous roots to reflect a deep reverence
for the land. He starred with Edward James
Olmos in the 1981 film version of the Luis
Valdez play *Zoot Suit*, with original songs
by Valdez and Lalo Guerrero. Additional
acting and directing projects include *La
Bamba* [Luis Valdez, 1987], starring Lou
Diamond Phillips.

DISCOGRAPHY:
Mestizo [A&M 1974]

Appearances:
Ay Califas: Raza Rock of the '70s and '80s
  [Rhino 1998] comp
Zoot Suit [MCA 1981] sdtk

Villebrun, Ray *See*: Red Blaze

Vinson, Laura—(Cree-Metis) Country *See*: Shingoose; Contemporary Spoken Word: Interview Recordings

Born June 13, 1947, Jasper, Alberta. A veteran performer with numerous television
and radio appearances, predominantly in
western Canada, Vinson made her mark in
the Canadian country scene in the 1970s.

Vinson is the recipient of many awards,
including the CCMA Top Female Vocalist
1989, 1990, 1993; CCMA Album of the Year
and Best Roots/Traditional/Ethnic Artist
on Record, 1993; Performing Rights Organization of Canada's Songwriting Award;
Alberta Motion Picture Industry Award;
Alberta Achievement Award; PRO Canada
Award for Most Performed Song. She was
nominated for several Juno Awards for
Country Female Vocalist of the Year, 1979,
1981, 1983, 1985; and for Most Promising
Vocalist of the Year, 1980, 1981. Her television appearances include *Indian Time I*
[CTV 1989].

Free Spirit Lineup (1995): Laura Vinson, vocals/guitar; David Martineau, vocals/electric/acoustic/steel guitar/ dobro; Paul Martineau, backup vocals/percussion; Farley Scott, electric/acoustic bass; Maria Dunn, backup vocals/accordion/penny whistle; Christina Auger, Craig Auger, and John Keely, drummers/singers.

Redwyng Lineup (1977): Laura Vinson, vocals/guitar; Frank Walls, harp/steel/lead guitar; Wayne Saunders, vocals/bass/lead/rhythm guitar; Jim Hathaway, drums.

DISCOGRAPHY:
It Reminds Me [Me Ent 2001]
Point of the Arrow [Homestead 1999] re-recorded best of
Voices on the Wind [Homestead 1995]
Voices on the Wind: The Radio Special [Homestead 1995] w/ interview clips
Rise Like a Phoenix [Homestead 1991]
The Spirit Sings [Royalty 1989]
Adios Mexico [Royalty 1984]
High Fashion Queen [Royalty 1979]
First Flight [Royalty 1977] w/ Redwyng

Singles:
"Roots That Go Deep" [Homestead 1995]
"Let It Go" [Homestead 1995]
"Goodbye/Momma's Voice" [Royalty 1986]
"Sweet Mountain Music/Rollin' Slow" [Royalty 1980]
"High Fashion Queen/Rocky Mountain Skyline" [Royalty 1980]
"Mes Amis O Canada" [Royalty 1979]
"Northern Star/Sun Always Shines" [Royalty 1978]
"Empty Streets/First Flight" [Royalty 1978]
"Bluebird/Dirty Dan" [Royalty 1978]

Appearances:
20 Aboriginal Greatest Hits, Vol. 3 [Sunshine 2002] comp

Videos:
Daughters of the Dawn [Passion Music 1995]
Roots That Go Deep/Let It Go [Passion Music 1995]

Voice, Eric—(Anishnabe) Acoustic Rock

Born June 16, 1965, Kingston, Ontario. Voice was eight years old when he began playing music. His dominant musical influences were his family, but predominantly his grandfather, Lorne Sharbot, a violinist; contemporary influences were mainstream rock artists.

DISCOGRAPHY:
Inner Circle [Sunshine 2001]

Appearances:
20 Aboriginal Greatest Hits, Vol. 3 [Sunshine 2002] comp

Vollant, Florent—(Innu) Pop/Folk
See: Kashtin, Phillipe McKenzie

Born August 10, 1959, Maliotenam Reserve, Quebec. The musically mellow counterpart and traditional connection of Kashtin. One of Vollant's albums was recorded in the Innu language; the project features Richard Seguin, Ray Bonneville, Zachary Richard, Luce Default, Lucien Gabriel Jourdain, and Rejean Bouchard. Vollant also appeared in the Quebec television special *Uashtunamunam/Kaari:ho*, 2002. His album *Nipaiamianan* received a Juno Award for Aboriginal Recording of the Year, 2001.

DISCOGRAPHY:
Katak [D7 Recordings 2003]
Nipaiamianan [Avanti Stella/Musicor 1999]

Appearances:
The Rough Guide to the Music of Canada [World Music Network 2003]

Wagon Burner Express—Jazz *See*: Eugene Boyer, Carmen Jones

Lineup: Chris Martin, drums; Jim Heineman, tenor/soprano saxophone; Eugene Boyer, guitar; Victor Bateman, bass. A short-lived experiment between friends and collaborators, the heavy jazz fusion sound grabbed the attention of audiences wherever the band played. They were invited by keyboardist Chick Corea to open his show in Jacksonville, Florida, in 1989.

DISCOGRAPHY:
Wagon Burner Express [independent 1988] cass

Walela—Trad/Folk

Lineup: Rita Coolidge, Priscilla Coolidge, and Laura Satterfield.

Formed 1996. A family affair composed of Rita, sister Priscilla, and Priscilla's daughter, Laura. The group incorporates generations of music makers, with their grandmother's making an archival appearance on their first album. Debut Artist and Song of the Year for *Warrior*, NAMA, 1998.

DISCOGRAPHY:
Live in Concert [Sovereign Nation Preservation Project 2004] w/ DVD
Unbearable Love [Triloka 2000]
Walela [Triloka 1997]

Appearances:
Tribal Dreams [Earth Beat! 2001] comp
Naturally Native [Silver Wave 2000] sdtk
Singing Our Stories [Full Regalia Productions 2000] comp
Songs of the Spirit [Triloka 2000] comp
Wolves [Silver Wave 1999] sdtk
Saving Grace [Polygram 1998] comp
Tribal Fires [Earth Beat! 1997] comp
I Am Walking [Narada 1995] comp

Walker, Greg T.—(Creek-Choctaw) Rock See: Blackfoot, NDN

Born July 8, 1951, Jacksonville, Florida. Founding member and bass player for the 1980s band Blackfoot. Walker worked with many southern rock groups and appeared on Cross Country's self-titled album [Atco

1973] and on Lynyrd Skynyrd's *Street Survivors* [MCA 1977]. After Blackfoot, he explored other musical possibilities with the Native-themed project NDN.

Walker, Wendy—(Cree) Gospel/Folk

Born December 22, 1957, Winnipeg, Manitoba. While based in Calgary, Alberta, Walker appeared in several independent films, including *Borders* [Gil Cardinal, 1998] and recorded the Native version of "Oh Canada" for the CBC in 2000.

DISCOGRAPHY:
One Light [OTI Music 2003]
Shadow Dance [OTI Music 1996]

Walking Elk, Mitch—(Cheyenne) Folk/Rock

With conscious lyrics and a rich vocal quality emphasized by the high calibre of his guitar playing, Walking Elk's music encompasses blues, rock, and folk. Based in Wisconsin.

DISCOGRAPHY:
Peace and Dignity [Shaiela 2000]
Indians [Shaiela 1998]
Ain't No Simple Thing [Shaiela 1993]
Dreamer [Shaiela 1986]

Appearances:
In the Spirit of Crazy Horse: Songs for Leonard Peltier [Four Winds Trading 1992] comp

Wallace, Russell—(Stl'atl'imx) Techno/Trad/Experimental See: Dreamspeak; Traditional/Archival Group: Tzo'kam

Born January 24, 1965, Lillooet, British Columbia. An electronic musician, Wallace gained national airplay with "Indian Summer," his response to the 1990 Oka crisis.

In addition to work with other artists, he produced *Hearts of the Nations* (*See*: Traditional/Archival Compilations), scored several soundtracks for Native films and created the modern opera *Bones* in 2001 with Sadie Buck (*See*: Traditional/Archival Group: Six Nations Women Singers) and Seventh Fire's Dave Deleary.

DISCOGRAPHY:
Urban Coyote Project: Gathering [Red Planet Records 2002] EP, mixes
Tzo'Kam [Red Planet Records 2000] vocals
Chinook Winds: Aboriginal Dance 1996–97 [Banff Centre for the Arts 2000]
w/ Dreamspeak:
Bloodlines [Spiral 1991] CD EP
"Indian Summer" [Spiral 1991] cassingle

Appearances:
Wayne Lavallee:
Liv Again [independent 2000] backup vocals
Various:
The Fire This Time: *Basslines and Ballistics* [Extreme 1995] comp, keyboards

Ware, Tom—Blues

Lineup of Blues Nation: Tom Ware, guitar/vocals/drums; Dusty Miller, electric/slide guitar (*See*: Indian Chipmunks, XIT); Terry Sotigh, drums; Sonny Klinekole, bass; Aaron Connor, keyboards. Ware has been an underrated player on the Native music scene, with pioneering work recorded in the mid-1980s.

DISCOGRAPHY:
Tom Ware and Blues Nation [American Indian Music and Dance Show 1990]

Appearances:
Skin Tight Blues [Sweet Grass/EMI 2002] comp
Flow Like a River [Rising Eagle Productions 1989] comp

War Party—Rap

Lineup: Rex Smallboy, a.k.a. MC Noble; Karmen Omeosoo, a.k.a. Kool-ayd the Chubby Cree; Cynthia Smallboy, a.k.a. Girlie MC; Funky Red Brother; DJ Roach; Tom Crier, a.k.a. Big Stomp, coproducer.

Formed in 1995, Hobema, Alberta. Recipients of the 1995 Crystal Kids Youth Entertainment Award, War Party has also shared the stage with numerous performers, including Ice-T, Choclair, Ghetto Concept, MACK-10, Wu-Tang, and Litefoot.

The group enjoyed national media attention immediately following the release of their debut CD, which received high rotation on urban and reservation-based radio. In 2002, their video single "Feelin Reserved" was selected as a finalist at the Urban Music Association of Canada Awards and was screened at the First Peoples Film Festival in Montreal, Quebec. With sponsorship from the Tommy Hilfiger clothing company, they were invited to perform at the Telus World Ski and Snowboard Festival at Whistler, British Columbia. War Party's commercial success has enabled them to send their message of Native rights and reality to a much larger audience. Their second video release went into national rotation on MUCH MUSIC, Canada's equivalent to MTV. *The Reign* received the CAMA Award for Best Rap Album, 2001.

DISCOGRAPHY:
The Greatest Natives from the North [War Party 2003]
The Reign [Arbor 2000]

Appearances:
Our Voice Is Our Weapon and Our Bullets Are the Truth [Red Wire Magazine 2003] comp
Dig Your Roots [DYR 2002] comp

Videos:
Feelin Reserved II [War Party/Video Fact 2003]
Feelin Reserved [Arbor 2001]

Warpath—(Huichol–Tohono O'odam) Rap

Born Cesar Curiel Cordova, 1975. "Rap is the metamorphosis of oral storytelling traditions for the youth," declared the self-proclaimed mystic and visionary of the twenty-first century. He espouses theories on aliens, prophecies, visions, injustice, and cultural restoration. He also hosted his own television show on Buena Vision in southern California.

DISCOGRAPHY:
Y2K—Mission Critical [independent 1999]
Warpath [independent 1997]

Warriors Blood—(Mohawk) Rap

Lineup: Teyonienkwataseh, Thanaokate, and Tsionkweton, with Stacy Hill, backup vocals.

From Akwesasne Mohawk territory, Warriors Blood have based their material on the frontline struggles of Oka in 1990, the Zapatista uprising of 1994, and others. In their recordings, they pay tribute to the Great Law of the Iroquois Confederacy, the nation's women, and the Mohawk Warrior Society.

DISCOGRAPHY:
The Uprising [independent 2000] three-track EP

Appearances:
Blu 6 [Blu Magazine 2000] comp

Wayquay—(Anishnabekwe–Italian American) Hip-Hop

Born in Pennsylvania, based in New York City. Wayquay penned conscious lyrics/poems spliced with R & B, hip-hop, and rock; she also organized "Sunbow," a cross-country walk for the environment, and appeared in Robert Hein's 1997 film *Dreamland* and in the Canadian television special *Solstice Rouge* [Prime 2001].

DISCOGRAPHY:
Tribal Grind [Global Beat 1997]

Appearances:
Alcatraz Is Not an Island [James Fortier, 2002] documentary: poetry
Urban Skins, Vol. 2 [Warrior/SOAR 1999] comp

Westerman, Floyd—(Dakota) Country/Folk *See*: Dennis Banks, Morley Loon, Toman Obomsawin, Buddy Red Bow, Buffy Sainte-Marie, Joanne Shenandoah, Shingoose

Born August 17, 1935, Sisseton-Wahpeton Sioux Reservation, Veblen, South Dakota. At age two, Westerman was taken away from his parents and placed in a Catholic mission a few miles from the reservation. He saw his parents on weekends until age seven, when he was moved farther away to the government boarding school in Wahpeton, North Dakota. After the eighth grade, he was placed in Flandreau Indian School in Flandreau, South Dakota, where he learned to play the guitar. He went on to earn a degree in secondary education at Northern State Teacher's College in Aberdeen, South Dakota. During a break from college, he enlisted in the U.S. Marine Corps one-year reserve program.

Despite holding a degree in secondary education, he went into entertainment and played the bars in Denver, Colorado. He went back to school to study law, with intentions of helping his people. The era of 1960s political activism drew him in. He had already been traveling and playing venues when he met author Vine Deloria Jr. and lyricist Jimmy Curtiss. His law school years were curtailed when Deloria opened the way for Westerman to sign on with Perception Records in New York City. From there, he traveled the country as a featured performer. His first album became an important collection of Indian protest songs that have endured over time.

Floyd Westerman performs protest songs derived from experience. Photo by Agnes Patak.

He devoted his talents over the ensuing decades to playing benefit concerts for environmental and Native rights causes, including work with Sting and the Kaiapo people of Brazil. He has shared the stage with Buffy Sainte-Marie, John Trudell, Willie Nelson, Kris Kristofferson, Charlie Hill, Shingoose, and Max Gail. Westerman has appeared in several films, television series, and commercials, including *Dharma and Greg* [Chuck Lorre Productions, 1999], *The Broken Chain* [Lamont Johnson, 1993], *The X-Files* [Chris Carter, 1996], and *The Dakota Conflict* [PBS 1999].

DISCOGRAPHY:

Going Back: Yesterday, Today, and Tomorrow [West 101]

Custer Died for Your Sins/The Land Is Your Mother [Trikont 1993, Germany; Red Crow Creations 2001]

The Land Is Your Mother [Full Circle 1984] w/ Buffy Sainte-Marie, piano; Charlie Hill, 49er drum (*See*: Contemporary Spoken Word: Comedy); David Amram, flute; Jaime Quill Smith Band; Max Gail, piano; Merl Saunders, synthesizer; Christian Mostert, flute; Tana Larose Sanchez, Kelina Lobo, Sandy Blanco, vocals; Susan Lobo, Spanish interpretation; Jimmy Curtiss, lyrics; Vine Deloria, liner notes

Custer Died for Your Sins [Full Circle 1982] cass; re-recording of original release

Indian Country [Perception 1970] D, rare; recorded live at Town Hall, New York City, w/ Floyd Westerman, rhythm guitar/vocals; John Trivers, bass; Bob Abrahams, guitar; John Sadler, engineer

Custer Died for Your Sins [Perception 1969] first vinyl edition w/ gatefold cover; D, rare; w/ John Trivers, bass; Bob Abrahams, guitar; Jerry Shook, harp/dobro; Barry Lazarwitz, drums; Jimmy Curtiss, rhythm guitar; Pete Drake, steel guitar, Jimmy Curtiss, lyrics; Vine Deloria, liner notes

Appearances (listed alphabetically):
David Amram:
At Home around the World [Flying Fish 1980/1996]
Dennis Banks:
United We Stand—Refusing to Fall [RCR 9770]
Indian Nation:
Red Power [French Kiss 1991, France] Redcrow Euro interview
Lyrik & Jazz:
Wounded Knee [Wergo 1995, Germany] song lyrics translated into a German spoken-word and jazz project
Various:
Truth and Light: Music from the X-Files [Warner 1996] sdtk
Oyate [Nato/World 1990/1998, France] comp
Beyond Treaty [independent 1986] cass comp

Covers (listed alphabetically):
Edmund Bull:
"Chante Waste Wi" (retitled "Nichimos") on *Indian Boy* [Turtle Island Music 2000]
Christy Moore:
"Quiet Desperation" on *Christy Moore* [Atlantic 1988]
Tomas Obomsawin:
"Or Do You Care"; "Di Ni Shna Na"; "B.I.A. Blues"; "How Long Have You Been Blind"; "Joseph"; "To My Knees" on *Abenakis* [Canyon 1990]
Sally Rogers:
"La Tierra Estu Madre" on *Piggyback Planet* [Rounder 1989]
Joanne Shenandoah:
"Going Back" on *Joanne Shenandoah* [Canyon 1989]

Selected Films:
Grey Owl [Richard Attenborough, 1999] as powwow chief
Naturally Native [Valerie Redhorse, 1998] as Chairman Pico
The Brave [Johnny Depp, 1997] as Papa
Dusting Cliff 7 AKA: Last Assassins [William Molina, 1996] as Indian Bob

The Dakota: Native American Holocaust [PBS 1995] documentary: narration
Buffalo Girls [Rod Hardy, 1995] as No Ears
Lakota Woman [Frank Pierson, 1994] as Mary's grandfather
Clear Cut [Richard Bugajski, 1992] as Wilf
The Doors [Oliver Stone, 1991] as Shaman
Son of the Morning Star [Mike Robe, 1990] as Sitting Bull
Dances with Wolves [Kevin Costner, 1990] as Ten Bears
Renegades [Jack Sholder, 1989] as Red Crow
Powwow Highway [Jonathan Wacks, 1988] as the voice of White Cloud

White, Aaron—(Northern Ute–Dineh) Folk *See*: Burning Sky, Sky Chasers

Born September 6, 1962, Oakland, California. While on hiatus from the group Burning Sky, White formed an acoustic project called Sky Chasers, with flute player Tommy Lee, and created a heavy metal experiment called Super Chief. He scored soundtracks for independent film projects, including *Dough Boy* [Randy Red Road, 2000] and *Canyon De Chelley* [Bear Paw Productions 2000], provided music for National Public Radio's news program *All Things Considered*, and appeared on the compilation *Emerging Powers: Native American Rights Fund* [Red Feather 1999].

White Bear—Country/Folk

Lineup: Wil Dedam (Mi'kmaq) and Harvey Belliveau (Acadian); based in New Brunswick.

DISCOGRAPHY:
Last Stand [independent 1999]

White Eagle—(Lakota) Opera

1952–1995

From the Rosebud Sioux Reservation, South Dakota, White Eagle rose to prominence as an accomplished tenor opera singer with the Metropolitan Opera. He was a solo performer at a pre-presidential inaugural ball for George Bush Sr., which aired on CBS. He battled AIDS until the age of forty-three. The documentary of his life is called *White Eagle: How Sweet the Sound* [Brenda Farnsworth 1998].

Whiteface, Fredrick P.—(Lakota) Jazz

1922–2002

Born May 9, 1922, Pine Ridge, South Dakota. A self-taught musician who started out playing guitar in his first professional engagement at age eleven, Whiteface was allowed to travel and play only within a one-hundred-mile radius of his home. He graduated from St. Francis Mission High School in 1940 and enlisted into military service two years later. At age twenty, he attended the U.S. Navy Radio School at the University of Wisconsin. During World War II, he served in both the Atlantic and Pacific fleets aboard the *USS Big Her* and the *USS Cape Johnson*; he received an honourable discharge in 1945. While in service, he was selected as a saxophonist with the U.S. Navy Big Band Orchestra.

In civilian life after the war, Whiteface performed with numerous orchestras and fronted his own bands, the Club House Band and the New Flamingos, with his two daughters, his son, and a cousin in order to help defray their college expenses. Poor health kept him from playing for eleven years; then in 1981 he joined Rudy Hunter's Tones until 1989, when Hunter passed away.

For the next decade, Whiteface played with the Tommy Matthews Big Band and his own Freddy Whiteface Quartet. He was inducted into the Dakota Musicians Hall of Fame in 1995, the year that South Dakota governor William Janklow proclaimed April 20 Fredrick P. Whiteface Day.

At age seventy-four, he released his first album, *Mato Hota* (Grey Bear). The project was a mix of brassy sax with traditional songs that "encompassed Lakota music forms with the jazz idiom." The album's title song is a life story in music, with each passage and tempo relating to the different stages of Whiteface's life.

The lineup on *Mato Hota* includes: Chuck Childs, percussion; Billy Van Leuven, keyboards; Bob Shaw, keyboards; Lowell Sterling, bass; Stringbean Svenson, bass; traditional singers: David Braveheart; Elaine, Cody, Alzah and Dallas Eagle Boy; Paul, Randy, and Elaine Whiteface; Chuck Davis; Gemma Lockheart; Sandy Miller.

Whiteface received the NAMA Award for Best Blues/Jazz Artist and the Lifetime Achievement Award, 1998. He passed away Sunday, May 19, 2002, after a long battle with cancer.

DISCOGRAPHY:

Fred by Request [Fabulous 2000]
Mato Hota (Grey Bear) [SOAR 1997]

WigWam—(Anishnabe) Rock

Lineup: Norman Beaver, lead vocals/guitar; Cornelius Neshinapaise, vocals; David Wabasse, bass/acoustic guitar; Elias Wapasse, drums/percussion. From Summer Beaver, northwestern Ontario.

DISCOGRAPHY:

One Step at a Time [Sunshine 1996]
Adisokaan [Sunshine 1995]
Cry of the Wild [Sunshine 1993]

Appearances:

20 Aboriginal Greatest Hits, Vol. 3 [Sunshine 2002] comp
20 Aboriginal Greatest Hits, Vol. 2 [Sunshine 1998] comp

24 Canadian Aboriginal Artists [Sunshine 1995] comp

A Northern Christmas [Sunshine SSCD-4180] comp

Wiley, LaRae—(Colville Confederated Tribes) Rock *See*: Jim Boyd

Born in Washington State. A graduate of Eastern Washington University with degrees in history, music, and education, Wiley also studied voice and music at Whitworth College and Western Washington University. She made some of her first recording appearances as keyboardist and vocalist with Jim Boyd. Her smooth mix of blues, jazz, and rock focuses on culture and history.

DISCOGRAPHY:

Kelly Hill [Hummingtree Productions 2002]

Dissonant World [Hummingtree Productions 2002]

Wiley, Lee—(Cherokee) Jazz *See*: Mildred Bailey

1910–1975

Born October 9, Fort Gibson, Oklahoma. Known as the "Hot House Rose" after her signature song, Wiley was considered the musicians' singer. At age fifteen, she started singing on radio programs in New York City and developed the deep, sultry vocal style that captivated audiences for decades.

Wiley made her first professional debut in 1930 at the Paramount Show, grabbing the attention of orchestra leader Paul Whiteman. She later recorded with Johnny Green, the Casa Loma Orchestra, the Dorsey Brothers, Rodgers and Hart, George Gershwin and Ira Gershwin, Eddie Condon, and Cole Porter. Her major singles in the 1930s include "Got the South in My Soul," "Anytime, Anyday, Anywhere," and

Lee Wiley was known as the musicians' singer. Cover art courtesy Baldwin Street Records.

"Eerie Moan." She cut two superb sides in 1940, "Down to Steamboat Tennessee" and "Sugar." She married in 1943 and sang with her husband, Jess Stacy, until going back on the road as a solo performer, making numerous radio and television appearances.

Battling years of ill health, she went out in a blaze of glory at the 1972 Newport Jazz Festival. She succumbed to cancer three years later on December 11, 1975, in New York City. Like her contemporary, Mildred Bailey, Lee Wiley is remembered as a major influential contributor to the art of jazz singing.

SELECTED DISCOGRAPHY:

A Touch of the Blues [RCA 1957]

West of the Moon [RCA 1956]

Lee Wiley Sings Rogers and Hart [Storyville 1954]

Duologue [Black Lion 1954]

The Carnegie Hall Concert [Audiophile 1952]

Lee Wiley Sings Vincent Youmans [Columbia 1951]

Lee Wiley Sings Irving Berlin [Columbia 1951]

Music of Manhattan [Uptown 1950]

Night in Manhattan [Uptown 1950]

Reissues/Collections:

Legendary Song Stylist [Pulse 1999]

The Legendary Lee Wiley: Collector's Items 1931-1955 [Baldwin Street 1999]

Best of Jazz Singing, Vol. 1 [Baldwin Street Music 1998]

Back Home Again [Monmouth 1997]

Rarities: Thinking of You [Jazz Classics 1997]

Hot House Rose [Topaz 1996, United Kingdom/Germany]

Lee Wiley Sings George Gershwin and Cole Porter [MES 7034] originally released on 78 rpm by the Liberty Music Shop in 1939 and 1940, then reissued on the RIC label with different tracking

Lee Wiley 1931-1940 [L'art Vocal c. 1995]

Night in Manhattan [CSP 1995]

Are You Having Fun? A Celebration of Music [Audiophile 1994]

You Leave Me Breathless [Jass 1987]

The One and Only Lee Wiley [RIC Posterity Series 1981]

J. Stacy and Friends: Lee Wiley with Jess Stacy [Commodore/CBS 1980]

Lee Wiley "On the Air" [Totem 1977] radio work 1932–36

As Time Goes By [Bluebird c. 1956]

On the Air, Vol. 2 [Totem c. 1944]

Lee Wiley Sings Rogers and Hart and Harold Arlen [Monmouth-Evergreen MES 6807 c. 1940]

Lee Wiley Sings Ira and George Gershwin and Cole Porter [AUD 1994/Audiophile c. 1939]

I've Got You Under My Skin 1931–1937 [Vintage Jazz]

The Complete Lee Wiley 1931–1937 [Vintage Jazz]

Broadcasts and Rarities [JAS 1993 c. 1936]

Broadcasts and Rarities, Vol. 2 [JAS c. 1933]

I've Got You under My Skin [VJC 1933]

On the Air, Vol. 1 [Totem c. 1932]

Williams, "Big Joe"—
(Cherokee–African American) Blues

1903-1982

Born Joe Lee Williams, October, 16, 1903, near Crawford, Mississippi.

Williams played on a handmade guitar and enjoyed live music when performers came to town. He hit the road with the Rabbit Foot Minstrels, which included Ethel Waters as lead singer. He later played with the Birmingham Jug Band and recorded nine titles for Okeh Records in 1930. He recorded on several labels, including RCA, Arhoolie, Folkways, Milestone, Bluesville, and Testament Records beginning in 1935 and going on well into the 1960s; his most notable song is "Baby, Please Don't Go" [Bluebird 1935].

His nine-string Sovereign acoustic guitar was held together with adhesive tape and fitted with extra tuning pegs at the top of the stock and with a pickup under the strings to amplify the sound. He toured for decades as an ambassador of Mississippi Delta blues, performing and recording with Sonny Terry and Brownie McGhee, Lightnin' Hopkins, Memphis Slim, and Sonny Boy Williamson. As were many blues players from the South, Williams was born with Native lineage and raised on a reservation. (The book *Black Indians: A Hidden Heritage* by William Loren Katz [Simon Pulse, 1997] is very informative.)

Williams, Gary—(Anishnabe) Rock

Originating from Curve Lake Reserve, Ontario, Williams plied his craft with early 1990s rez rock bands Rockland County and Redline. With a message of culture and survival, he released his first recording in 1993.

DISCOGRAPHY:

Different Kind of Warrior [independent 1993] cass

Winter Hawk—Rock

Lineup: Niki Alexander, Frank J. Diaz de Leon, Alfonso Morris Kolb, Frankie Joe, Jim Boyd (1983).

Formed in the late 1970s, Winter Hawk was a lesser-known group that worked on the fringes of the West Coast music scene in the United States.

PARTIAL DISCOGRAPHY:
Red Rage [NDA] double album, features a song for Jim Thorpe
Dog Soldier [NDA]
Electric Warriors [NDA] produced by Tom Bee

WithOut Reservation—Rap

Original Lineup: Red Shadow; K-Wonda; J. Solo; and MC Hiddese (pronounced Hees), a.k.a. Chris Lamarr, who established WithOut Rez Records in 1996–97. This band was one of the first all-Native rap groups to emerge, but it was eventually overwhelmed by the larger rap and hip-hop scene.

DISCOGRAPHY:
WW II [WithOut Rez Productions 1999]
Are You Ready for WOR! [Canyon 1994]
Zero Tolerance [independent 1992] cass

Appearances:
Voices across the Canyon, Vol. 2 [Canyon 1996] comp

Wolf, Jimmy—(Mohawk) Blues

Born March 27, 1968. Playing professionally since 1990, Wolf has backed up players such as Jimmy Dawkins, Larry Davis, and Bill Doggett. He received a NAMA nomination for Best Blues Artist, 1999.

DISCOGRAPHY:
Jimmy Wolf [Red Reverend Records 2000]
Raw Blues [Red Reverend Records 1999]

Appearances:
Skin Tight Blues [Sweet Grass/EMI 2002] comp

Wolf River Band—(Menominee) Country and Western

Lineup: Daryl O'Katchicum, lead guitar/ fiddle/vocals; Dan Werner, pedal steel/ harmonica/vocals; Richard Awonohopay, bass/vocals; Richard Plass, drums/vocals. Based in northeastern Wisconsin.

DISCOGRAPHY:
The Journey Begins [independent 1997]

World Citizen—(Metis) Dance

Metis brothers Scott and Jeff Ward found inspiration for their music in their Native spirituality and the Baha'i writings. Based in Edmonton, Alberta.

DISCOGRAPHY:
World Citizen [independent 1997]

Wray, Link—(Shawnee-Cherokee) Rock 'n' Roll

Born Frederick Lincoln Wray Jr., May 2, 1929, Dunn, North Carolina. For many years, Wray recorded and toured throughout the world as the Granddaddy of Grunge, spawning generations of new guitar players. The Who guitarist Pete Townsend cited Wray as his primary influence.

Raised around gospel music, Link learned some stylings from local black blues and gospel players and started taking the instrument more seriously around 1947. After a stint in the army in 1949, he was discharged after contracting tuberculosis. With his brothers Doug and Vernon, he formed a country and rockabilly band and played the southern states with some radio appearances. After the return of tuberculosis in 1956, Link lost one of his lungs, severely limiting his vocal performances. A year later he formed Link Wray and the Ray Men (later the Wraymen), with brother Doug on drums. The names Ray Men/Wraymen both played on the guitarist's name and offered a futuristic feel to the band. The switchblade anthem "Rumble" was listed on the U.S. charts on April 28, 1958, lasting for fourteen weeks and reaching number 16.

Link's signature hit provided the electric guitar chord that rocked the foundations of the genre; the single "Rumble" sold more than a million copies. In pursuit of developing the right sound, Wray mail-ordered a Danelectro guitar because it had the right pickups, among other unusual features he needed. In additional experiments, he stacked four Premier amps, each with a fifteen-inch speaker and two six-inch tweeters, and turned them all up to ten. Still not satisfied, partially because he couldn't hear what he was playing (monitors didn't come into use until the early 1970s), Wray punched holes into the tweeters to get a fuzz distortion to generate the raw energy he was looking to create.

He founded Rumble Records in the late 1950s and continued live gigs throughout the East Coast, later signing on with Swan Records. Dismayed with the music industry and their impulse to mess with his creativity, Wray answered back in true roots style. Wray's Shack Three Track was just that, a chicken coop converted into a three-track recording studio. With no snare drum, Doug would use a can of nails for the percussive beats; the shack didn't have enough space to accommodate the amps, so they were miked through the window, with Telefunken microphones placed on top to allow the sound to leak through for the right overtones—instead of being tight to the amp for a sharp sound, which only produced amplifier noise. Link struck a deal with Polydor in 1970 to record more blues-based material.

Throughout the 1980s, European audi-ences wanted more of Link's music than audiences back home cared to support. He found a gal who dug his vibe, married her, and moved to Denmark, where he based his activities.

Although his discography contains an incredible number of titles, many albums are reissues and collections of previously recorded material. Some of his Indian-oriented instrumentals include "Shawnee," "Apache," "Comanche," "Genocide," and "Viva Zapata." In addition to live recordings, Link released two complete albums of all new material throughout the 1990s, *Indian Child* and *Shadow Man*, the latter being recorded on three tracks and in one take with drummer Rob Louwers and bassist Eric Greevers. Wray also produced the collection *Naughty Rhythms: The Best of Pub Rock*. The seventy-minute video *The Rumble Man* [JE 300N-NtSC/JE 300-Pal 1999, United Kingdom] was shot over two days in London and Manchester, England, during his 1996 European tour. The track "Rumble on the Docks" from the album *Shadowman* was used by Busch Breweries for their 2000 television advertising campaign.

Lucky Wray and the Palomino Ranch Hands Lineup: Link, guitar; Doug Wray, rhythm guitar; Shorty Horton, string bass; Dixie Neal, steel guitar; fronted by Vernon Wray.

DISCOGRAPHY:

Swan Singles Collection 1963–1967 [Sundazed 2004]
Rawhide [Collectibles 2003] best of
Guitar Legends: Link Wray [MI Plus 2003, Holland]
Live at the Paradiso (Griffin) [Magnum 2002]
Slinky: The Epic Sessions 1958–1961 [Sundazed/Sony 2002] two CDs
Law of the Jungle [Ace 2002]
Barbed Wire [Ace 2000]
The Rumble Man [1999, United Kingdom] seven-inch vinyl
Rock 'N' Rumble [Hallmark 309162]

The Sun Singles Collection [Rollercoaster 1997]

Walking Down the Street [Visionary 1997] live in London and Manchester

Shadowman [Ace 1997]

Rumble Man [Cleopatra 1997]

Missing Links, Vol. 4: *Streets of Chicago* [Norton 1997]

Missing Links, Vol. 3: *Some Kinda Nut* [Norton 1997]

Missing Links, Vol. 2: *Big City after Dark* [Norton 1997]

Missing Links, Vol. 1: *Hill Billy Wolf* [Norton 1997]

The Swan Singles Collection [Rollercoaster 1997]

Guitar Preacher: The Polydor Years [Polygram 1995] five-album collection o/p

Born to Be Wild: Live in the USA 1987 [Line 1995]

Link Wray and the Raymen: Mr. Guitar [Norton 1995]

Indian Child [Ball/Sony 1993] w/ rare vocal performances

Golden Classics [Sony Collectibles 1993] best of

Walkin' with Link [Sony 1992] reissue

Live in '85/Growlin' Guitar [Ace 1991; Big Beat 1995]

Apache/Wild Side of the City Lights [Ace 1990]

The Original Rumble [Ace 1989]

The Swan Demos '64 [Hangman 1989]

Live at the Paradiso [Line 1982]

Yesterday and Today [Ace 1982]

Good Rockin' Tonight [Ace 1982]

Too Fast to Live Too Young to Die [Private Stock 1982] w/ Robert Gordon

Bullshot [Passport/Visa 1979]

Early Recordings [Ace 1979]

Fresh Fish Special [Private Stock 1978] w/ Robert Gordon

Robert Gordon with Link Wray [Private Stock 1977]

Stuck in Gear [Virgin 1976]

Interstate 10 [Caroline 1975]

The Link Wray Rumble [Polydor 1974]

Tribute to Shorty Horton [Vermillion 1974] Swan outtakes

Rockin' and Handclappin' [Epic 1973]

Beans and Fatback [Virgin/Polydor 1973]

There's Good Rockin' Tonight [Union Pacific 1973]

Be What You Want To [Polydor 1973]

Rock 'n' Roll Rumble [Charly 1972]

Mordecai Jones [Polydor 1972] w/ Bobby Howard

Link Wray [Polydor 1970] U.S. pressing issued w/ die-cut gatefold cover

Yesterday and Today [Record Factory 1969]

On the Road [Guest Star 1449] Dave Dudley w/ Link Wray and the Raymen

Country Jubilee of Stars [Guest Star 1444] w/ Vernon Wray

Link Wray Sings and Plays Guitar [Vermillion 1964]

Jack the Ripper [Swan 1963; reissued P-Vine Records 1999]

Great Guitar Hits [Vermillion 1963]

Link Wray and the Wraymen [Epic 1959]

Singles:

"I Got to Ramble/She's That Kind of Woman" [Polydor 1974]

"Shine the Light/Lawdy Miss Clawdy" [Polydor 1971]

"Fallin' Rain/Juke Box Mama" [Polydor 1970]

"Fire and Brimstone/Juke Box Mama" [Polydor 1970]

"Rumble '69/Mind Blower" [Mr. G 1969]

"Rumble '68/Blow Your Mind" [Heavy 1968]

"Rumble Mambo/Hambone" [Okeh 1967] reissue

"Jack the Ripper/I'll Do Anything for You" [Swan 1967] reissue

"Let the Good Times Roll/Soul Train" [Swan 1966] w/ Kathy Lynn

"Ace of Spades (alt. version)/Hidden Charms" [Swan 1966]

"Batman Theme/Alone" [Swan 1966]

"Ace of Spades/The Fuzz" [Swan 1965]

"Girl from the North Country/You Hurt Me So" [Swan 1965]

"Please Please Me/Rumble '65" [Swan S-4211] unreleased

"Baby Watcha Gonna Do/Walkin' down the Street" [Diamond 1965]

"I'm Branded/Hang On" [Swan 1965]

"Good Rockin' Tonight/I'll Do Anything for You" [Swan 1965]

"Deuces Wild/Summer Dream" [Swan 1964] w/ the Raymen

"The Shadow Knows/My Alberta" [Swan 1964]

"Run Chicken Run/The Sweeper" [Swan 1963]

"Weekend/Turnpike USA" [Swan 1963]

"Hambone/Rumble Mama" [Okeh 1963] w/ Red Saunders and the Wraymen

"Jack the Ripper/The Black Widow" [Swan 1963]

"Dancing Party/There's a Hole in the Middle of the Moon" [Mala 1963]

"Poppin' Popeye/Big City Stomp" [Trans Atlas 1962] w/ the Raymen

"Jack the Ripper/The Stranger" [Rumble 1961] w/ the Raymen

Link Wray and the Wraymen Singles:
"El Toro/Tijuana" [Epic 1961]

"Ain't That Lovin' You Baby/Mary Anne" [Epic 1960]

"Trail of the Lonesome Pines/Golden String" [Epic 1960]

"Slinky/Rendezvous" [Epic 1959]

"Comanche/Lillian" [Epic 1959]

"Rawhide/Dixie Doodle" [Epic 1959] number 34 Hot 100 Charts

Link Wray and His Ray Men Singles:
"Rumble/The Swag" [Cadence 1958] number 16 Billboard Charts

"I Sez Baby/Johnny Bom Bonny" [Kay 1957] EP

"It's Music She Says/Sick and Tired" [Starday 1957]

"Got Another Baby/Watcha Say Honey?" [Starday 1957]

"Teenage Cutie/You're My Song" [Starday 1957]

Appearances (listed alphabetically):
Eggs Over Easy:
Good n Cheap [1972] producer
Robert Gordon:

Red Hot 1977–1981 [Bear Family 1995]

Robert Gordon Is Red Hot [Private Stock 1989]

Fresh Fish Special [Private Stock 1978]

Joe Welz:

Best of Joe Welz—Decades [1993]

Various:

Pulp Surfin' [Donna 1995] comp

Rockin' Rebels [independent 1992] comp

James Dean, Tribute to a Rebel [independent 1991] comp

Rock 'n' Roll Guitar Classics [K-Tel 1990] comp

History of Rock Instrumentals, Vol. 2 [1987] comp

Cadence Classics, Vol. 1 [Barnaby Records 1975] comp

Videos:
The Rumble Man [Cherry Red Films 2003, United Kingdom] DVD

Covers:
The Neville Brothers:
"Fallin Rain" on *Brother's Keeper* [A&M 1990]

Soundtracks:
Blow [Ted Demme, 2001]

Black Sheep [Penelope Spheeris, 1996]

Independence Day [Roland Emmerich, 1996]

Pulp Fiction [Quentin Tarantino, 1994] "Rumble" appears in the film only

This Boy's Life [Michael Caton-Jones, 1993]

Johnny Suede [Tom DiCillo, 1992]

Wuttunee, Winston—(Plains Cree) Trad/Folk

Born January 31, 1940, North Battleford, Saskatchewan. From the Red Pheasant Reserve. Wuttunee received most of his education in the province of Saskatchewan and completed high school in London, Ontario, and earned his degree in music from the University of Saskatchewan in Saskatoon.

Wuttunee enlisted in the Canadian army

in 1960, where he played clarinet in the Canadian Grenadier Guards Regimental Band. After eight years, he left the military and became music coordinator at the Saskatchewan Indian Cultural College (SICC) in 1973. Wuttunee helped develop a Cree language and cultural curriculum with music for the Indian Teachers Education Program. He left the SICC and began his career as an entertainer. After decades of performing, Wuttunee was voted Most Valuable Contributor to Aboriginal Art at the Blue Lantern Awards in 2001 and 2002; *The Best of Winston Wuttunee* received a CAMA Award for Best Aboriginal Recording, 2002; he also received the CAMA Lifetime Achievement Award, 2003.

DISCOGRAPHY:
When the Sun Sets over the World [Turtle Island Music 2003]
The Best of Winston Wuttunee [Turtle Island Music 2001] best of
Children's Songs Sung in Cree [Sunshine SSCT-4112]
Cree Christmas [Sunshine SSCT-4110]
Songs of the Northwest [Sunshine SSCT-4035]
Handsome Warrior [Sunshine SSCT-4033]
Reminiscing [Sunshine 1981]
Goosed by a Moose [Sunshine SSCT-4031] for children
Me and My Friends: Children's Songs [Sunshine SSCT 408] for children
See the Arrow [Sunshine SSLP-4004] w/ Duke Redbird *See*: Contemporary Spoken Word: Poetry Recordings

Appearances:
Sandy Scofield:
Ketwam [Kokum 2002] backup vocals
Various:
A Turtle Island Christmas [Turtle Island Music 2002] comp
20 Aboriginal Greatest Hits, Vol. 2 [Sunshine 1998] comp
An Aboriginal Christmas, Vol. 1 [Sunshine 1997] comp
24 Canadian Aboriginal Artists [Sunshine 1995] comp

A Northern Christmas [Sunshine SSCD-4180] comp
Mariposa '76 [Mariposa 1977] comp, w/ Duke Redbird

Wynne, Deborah—(Anishnabekwe) Folk

DISCOGRAPHY:
Whispering Wind [independent 1998]

XIT—Rock *See*: Tom Bee, Jim Boyd; Contemporary Spoken Word: Legends and Storytelling: Paul Goble

Original Lineup: A. Michael Martin, lead vocals/guitar; Leeja Herrera, drums/percussion; Jomac Suazo, bass; R. C. Gariss, lead guitar/piano; Tom Bee, lyrics.

1973 Lineup: Obie Sullivan, keyboards; Leeja Herrera, drums/percussion; Jomac Suazo, bass; R. C. Garris, lead guitar/piano; Chili Yazzie, percussion; Tom Bee, vocals; Tyrone King, percussion.

1977 Lineup: William Bluehouse Johnson, electric/acoustic guitar/backup vocals; Tom Bee, lead vocals/percussion; Maclovio Suazo, bass/backup vocals.

1981 Lineup: Jim Boyd, drums; P. J. West, guitar; Chuck Klingbiel, keyboards; Tom Bee, vocals.

XIT was formed in 1968; its name means "Crossing of the Tribes." XIT was one of a few all-Native bands in the 1970s delivering poignant statements with a unique blend of Native and rock music. Songwriter Bee sent out his material to various record companies in the hopes of selling some songs. His composition "We've Got Blue Skies" was purchased for the Jackson Five. Motown Records signed XIT in the early 1970s and recorded two concept albums, *Plight of the Redman* and *Silent Warrior*. The storyline of both projects traces the history of pre-European contact, the arrival of Columbus, and the ensuing upheaval into current times. With the political and

XIT, one of the most remembered bands of the 1970s. Photo by Alton Walpole; courtesy SOAR.

social revolution in America during the Vietnam War era of the 1960s and 1970s, combined with Native activism at Alcatraz Island and Fort Lawton, the group's message was met with mainstream resistance. Lyrically outspoken, their first album was banned from commercial radio airplay.

The band suffered its share of hardships and tragedy when Tyrone King (Dineh), XIT's percussionist and traditional dancer, was killed in a hit-and-run accident in 1981 while hitchhiking between Farmington and Shiprock, New Mexico. His brother, Jimmy King, the band's road manager from 1973 to 1978, passed away in the late 1980s following a lengthy illness; Chili Yazzie (Dineh) was shot by a hitchhiker in an attempted robbery, which resulted in the loss of his arm from lack of medical attention.

Remaining members Tom Ware and Jim Boyd—along with Dusty Miller (guitar), who played on and off with the band but didn't record with them—played a reunion show at the NAMA production in 1999 and a thirtieth-anniversary concert at Minnesota's Mystic Lake Casino, May 20, 2000. Hassled by rednecks over the years but loved by their fans throughout the world, XIT has remained one of the most remembered bands of its time.

DISCOGRAPHY:

Drums across the Atlantic [SOAR 1984/ 1995] recorded live in Switzerland, February 1981; the 1995 reissue contains five bonus tracks recorded in Anchorage, Alaska, 1984

Relocation [Canyon 1977; SOAR 1990] third official release

Back Trackin' [SOAR 1975] officially unreleased, though in circulation
Entrance [Canyon 1974; SOAR 1994/2000]
first recorded in 1968, released as the
band's third album
Silent Warrior [Rare Earth/Motown 1973;
SOAR 1989] produced by Tom Bee
w/ Mike Valvano
Plight of the Redman [Rare Earth/Mo-
town 1971; SOAR 1989/1999] originally
produced by Mike Valvano w/ Ralph
Terrana and Russ Terrana; gatefold cover
w/ inner sleeve band photo and lyrics

Appearances:
Urban Skins, Vol. 3 [SOAR 2000] comp
*Various Native American Artists: Solo
Flights Two*, Vol. 2 [SOAR 1994] comp
*Various Native American Artists: Solo
Flights*, Vol. 1 [SOAR 1991] comp

Videos:
Without Reservation [SOAR 2002] farewell
concert

Yanez, Larry—(Chicano) Jazz *See*:
Jackalope, R. Carlos Nakai Quartet

A founding member of the jazz group
Jackalope, Yanez, an accomplished key-
board player, released one solo album with
Kenny Eller on bass and percussion.

DISCOGRAPHY:
Suenos [Canyon 1989]

Yeagley, Dr. David—(Comanche)
Classical

Dr. Yeagley received his doctorate in musical science in piano performance from the
University of Arizona, along with degrees
from Oberlin, Emory, and Yale. In 1989,
he was the first American composer featured with an entire program at Beethoven
House Music Hall, Bonn, Germany (Beethoven's birthplace). His piano works have
aired on Connecticut Public Radio.

Yodeca *See*: Flute Music: David
Maracle

Lineup: David Maracle, flute/vocals/
percussion; Joe Lewis, guitars; Jacinthe
Trudeau, violin; Kevin Breit, mandolin/
guitars; Fergus Marsh, bass/Chapman
stick; Mark Rogars, drums; Dan Cutrona,
keyboards; Raju Singh, tablas; Amoy Levy,
backup vocals; Jonathon Maracle, backup
vocals (*See*: Broken Walls); Tyendinaga
Mohawk Elders Choir; Children's Choir;
Sherry Procunier, spoken word.

The album produced from this project,
initiated by David Maracle, was named
Best Alternative Album of the Year by
the Canadian Aboriginal Music Awards,
Toronto, Canada.

DISCOGRAPHY:
Earth Fusion [independent 2001]

Appearances:
*Unsigned 05: A Compilation of New Cana-
dian Music* [NXNE 2003] comp

Zuni Midniters—Country and
Western

From Zuni Pueblo, New Mexico, the Zuni
Midniters recorded mostly original material written by members Stanley Natewa
and Bill Crockett.

DISCOGRAPHY:
Our First Album [independent 04]
Our Sixth Album [independent 03]
Wanted [independent 02]
A Rainbow of Memories [independent 01]
Long Journey [Canyon 1985]
Land of Shalako [Canyon 1982]
My Land [Canyon 1982]

Section 3-B
Contemporary Compilation Recordings

An Aboriginal Christmas, Vol. 1
[Sunshine 1997]

Lineup: Jim Beer; Frank Montano; Lionel Desjarlais; Ernest Monias; Moody X2; Winston Wuttunee; Aaron Peters; Billy Simard.

America Fears the Drum
[Irresistible/Revolutionary 1992]

Nilak Butler performs the "Mourning Song." The album includes Daisy Zamora, former minister of culture in the Nicaraguan Sandanista government, whose poem "When We Return" is read by Puerto Rican poet Alfonso Texidor.

Arctic Refuge [Soundings of the Planet 1998]

A benefit album for the northern coastal plains to protect the calving grounds of the Porcupine caribou herd. The project was realized with the assistance of the Gwich'in Steering Committee and the Alaska Wilderness League and released through the Soundings of the Planet Records, based in Tucson, Arizona. Produced by Dean Evenson and Dudley Evenson. Main performers are Dean Evenson and Sarah Evenson, with additional tracks contributed by Dik Darnell (*See*: Buddy Red Bow); R. Carlos Nakai; Cornel Pewewardy; Tsa'ne Dos'e; Jerry Alfred; Sarah James. A portion of the album sales were donated to assist the Arctic National Wildlife Refuge.

Artists for Vision Quest
[independent 1997] *See*: Fara

Lineup: Fara Palmer; Amy Sky; Dan Hill; Raffi; Roch Voisine; Roy Henry Vickers, narration. A benefit album for Vancouver's Vision Quest Recovery Facility, initiated by master artist Roy Henry Vickers with the assistance of the Royal Canadian Mounted Police.

Louttit; David Sam; Peter Bosum; James Stewart.

Awakening the Spirit [SOAR 2000]

Lineup: Lisa LaRue; Samantha Rainbow; Cornel Pewewardy; Doug Spotted Eagle; Brule. A benefit recording with a portion of proceeds earmarked for the American Diabetes Association.

Ay Califas: Raza Rock of the '70s and '80s [Rhino 1998]

Lineup: Santana; Azteca; Malo; Cold Blood; Daniel Valdez; Sapo; Tower of Power; El Chicano; War; Los Lobos del Este de Los Angeles; Ruben and the Jets; Yaqui; Plugz; Cruzados; Los Illegals; Cheech and Chong; Con Safos; Tierra.

Backroads: Worlds [independent 2000]

Lineup: Doyle Bomberry, Dane Ngahuka, words/music/vocals/bass/drums (*See: Downa Bush* comp, Josh Miller); Murray Porter, vocals/keyboards; Mark Laforme, vocals/guitars/harmonica; Jason Martin, vocals/shaker; Jim Jacobs, Darren Martin, vocals; Troy Martin, electric guitar; Stan Szymkow, tenor/soprano saxophone; Chris Dahmer, organ/accordion/synthesizer; Steve Mancuso, percussion; Saidah Baba Talibah, backup vocals; Kahurangi Maori Dance Troupe of New Zealand, backup vocals. A collection of original blues songs from Six Nations Territory, Ontario.

The Best Cree Fiddle Players of James Bay [Hughboy Records 1993]

Lineup: Roger Weapenicappo; Matthew Mukash; Bobby Georgekish; Malcolm House; Sinclair Cheechoo; Clarence

Between Father Sky and Mother Earth: A Native American Collection [Narada 1995]

Lineup: R. Carlos Nakai; Bill Miller; Doug Wallantyne; Perry Silverbird; Tsa'ne Dos'e (*See*: Flute Music); Cornel Pewewardy; Chester Mahooty (*See*: Traditional/Archival Solo); Native Flute Ensemble; Primeaux, Mike, and Attson (*See*: Peyote Music Solo and Group); Charles Jefferson (Cherokee–African American) w/ Cynthia Jefferson and Mel Adams.

Beyond Treaty: An Evening with Friends of the International Indian Treaty Council [Mixtech Productions 1986]

Benefit concert for the International Indian Treaty Council (IITC, with NGO status), recorded in San Francisco. Featured performers include: Tlakaelel; Jeffrey Carpenter; Tony Gonzales; Bill Wahpepah; Floyd Westerman; Priscilla Vigil; Richard Archuleta; Benito Concha (*See*: Firecat of Discord, Red Thunder); David Amram; Maggie Banner; A. Paul Ortega; Chuck Banner; Jose Lucero.

Caribou Commons: Wildlands [Partners of Wildlands and Caribou Commons 1999]

Lineup: Matthew Lien, vocals/keyboards/producer; Hal Jordan, electric guitars; Danette Readman, guitar/vocals; Darcy Weavers, bass/vocals; Stephen Philip, flute/saxophone; Kevin Esposito, trombone; Gwich'in Nation speakers: Norma Kassi, Abraham John Jr., Gilbert James, Sarah James, Mary Tritt, Faith Gimmel (translation); Louis LaRose (Winnebago); Albert Whitehat Sr. (Lakota).

A collaboration between Native, northern artists and conservation groups that attempted to inspire people to help protect the calving grounds of the Porcupine caribou herd from oil development. The area spans 1,250 kilometers from Arctic Refuge, Alaska, to the Gwich'in village of Old Crow, Northwest Territories.

Chicano Power: Latin Rock in the USA 1968–1976 [Soul Jazz Records 1998]

Lineup: Sapo; Black Sugar; Chango; Harvey Averne Barrio Band; Tierra; Benitez; Malo; El Chicano; Mother Night; Sanatana; Toro; the Antiques. Brushed to the margins by musical and political purists, Chicanos trace their lineage to indigenous origins, romanticized as Raza Bronza. Those who embrace indigenous roots currently participate in a cultural revival and political consciousness. Groups that laid the musical foundation for these movements appear on this collection.

Children of the World: A Compilation of Some of Native Canada's Best Music [Groupe Concept 1994]

Lineup: Susan Aglukark; Willie Dunn; Kashtin; Fara Palmer; Don Ross; Shingoose. The EP contains new mixes with messages in First Nation languages accompanying previously released material.

Comanche Church Hymns, Vol. 1 [Indian Sounds IS-3551] gospel

Lineup: Pearl Pewo Ware; Velma Pewo Toosgah; Bill Ware; Marie Ware Criss; Marcella Delaware; Patricia Ware James; Sam and Jenny James; Ralph Kotay; Mildred

Kotay. Traditional hymns sung in the Comanche language.

Creation's Journey [Smithsonian Folkways 1994] *See*: Traditional/Archival Solo: D. J. Nez

Cree Christmas: Ahtahkakoop [Sweet Grass 1995]

Lineup: Marie Ahenakew; Eunice Little; Sheila Reimer; Chris Benjamin; Nina Dreaver; Ashton Masuskapoe; Marie Williams; Shelley Williams; Delores Greyeyes-Sand; Gordon Selkirk; and Terri-Ann Kendel. Christmas carols sung in Cree.

Cree Language Songs [Sunshine 2002]

Ruby Beardy and Victoria McCleod were born and raised in Norway House and Cross Lake, Manitoba. They worked as educators in their communities developing language and other curriculum for Native children. With Danny Schur, music.

Detras de nosotros estamos ustedes [Discos Armados 1999] *See*: *Rumours of War Jungle . . .* comp

Lineup: El Sub; Banda Bassotti; King Mafrundi; Fermin Muguruza; Dut; Hechos Contra el Decoro; Color Humano; Negu Gorriak; Quetzal; Aztlan Underground; Manu Chao; Joxe Ripiau; Wemean; P18; Todos Tus Muertos; Klaxon; Flor del Fango; RDE. Musicians from Aztlan, the Basque region of southern Spain, and Italy combine efforts to bring attention to the Zapatista struggle in Chiapas, Mexico. Neither sentimental nor opportunistic, the bulk of the material ranges from hard core to hip-hop to avante garde *folklorista*, with sampling and soundbites of Subcommandante Marcos, Ramona, and others.

Discover the Rhythm of Native Voices [EMI 1999, Holland]

Lineup: Features performers from around the world with previously released tracks by Robbie Robertson and Ulali from *Music for the Native Americans* and by Susan Aglukark from *This Child*.

Downa Bush: The Future of Aboriginal Music: A Compilation of Indigenous Artists [Studio Six Productions 1999]

Lineup: Dane Ngahuka, 1999 Juno and Grammy nomination for sound engineer on Robbie Robertson's *Contact from the Underworld of Redboy* (*See: Backroads* comp); Murray Porter; Mark LaForme; ElizaBeth Hill; Faron Jacobs; Jim Jacobs. Recorded at Studio Six, Six Nations Reservation, Brantford, Ontario.

Drops of Brandy and Other Traditional Metis Tunes [Gabriel Dumont Institute 2002] four CDs

Lineup: Mel Bedard; Reg Bouvette; Andy Dejarlis; Frederick Genthon; Emile Lavallee; Gary Lepine; John Arcand; Albert Boyer; Henry Gardipy; Gilbert Anderson; Richard Calihoo; Homer Poitras; Richard Lafferty; Edward Lafferty; and Trent Bruner. An accompanying book contains biographies, photographs, sheet music, and stories of Metis fiddle music.

Drum Songs and Painted Dreams, Vol. 8, no. 2 [Sunshine 1988]

Lineup: Kevin Locke; Winston Wuttunee; Skewk and Xaliki; Yupik Singers.

From the *Canadian Journal of Studies* in cooperation with Brandon University (Brandon, Manitoba) and Sunshine Records. The university's Native Music Symposium evening concert, March 1988.

Exiled in the Land of the Free [Columbia 1996]

Lineup: Bad Religion; Beastie Boys; Beaver Chief (*See*: Traditional/Archival Solo); Biohazard; Brother Sun (unreleased Native band); Corrosion of Conformity w/ Zack De la Rocha; Giant Sand; the Goats; J. G. Thirlwell; Rage Against the Machine; Sick of It All; Silica Gel; Superchunk; Mike Watt w/ Perry Farrell. A benefit album for the Leonard Peltier Defense Committee, compiled and coproduced by Reed Mullin (Corrosion of Conformity) and Van Riker.

Fiddle Legends [Sunshine 2000]

Lineup: Reg Bouvette; Andy Dejarlis; Eugene Laderoute; Marcel Meilleur.

The Fire This Time

The Fire This Time is a collective of artists who put out a series of recordings together. Tracks were taken from individual artist's recordings, and tracks from various recordings were sampled, so although The Fire This Time is technically a group, the recordings it released are more like compilations.

Lineup: Pat Andrade, production; Danny Thomas, bass; Russell Wallace, Augustus Pablo, Carl Ayton, keyboards; Santa Davis, drums; Scully, percussion; Errol Nazareth, samples; poets: Marcela A. Toro (Mapuche), Greg Young-Ing (Cree-Chinese), Oku Onura (Jamaican); voices: Chuck D., Harry Allen, John Trudell, Don Patrick Martin, Krystal Cook, Eagle Heart Singers. *Still Dancing on John Wayne's' Head* includes excerpts from Andrade's interview with Black Panther activist Assatta Shakur in Cuban exile. Although it contains remixes of many previously released tracks, personnel includes Michael Franti, Asian Dub Foundation, Carl Young, instruments; Don Patrick Martin (*See*: Contemporary Music), Kelly White (*See*: Traditional/Archival Compilations: *Heartbeat: Voices of First Nations Women*), Lionel Eustache (Shuswap), Amita Handa (Hindi) and Tanya Lena (Tamil), vocals; Pete DiGangi, bass/harmonica (*See*: Seventh Fire).

The 1995 release *Dancing on John Wayne's Head* includes South African poet Sandille Dikeni, Rupindeer Kaur, and the voices of Kerrie Charnley, Kelly White, Pura Fe, and Soni. *Till the Bars Break* received a Juno nomination, Best World Recording, 1992, and contains a legion of players, including Chuck D. samples; the Mad Professor; Henry Kaiser, guitar; James Henry, percussion/steel pan; George Cremaschi, acoustic bass; Jean Luc Mas, acoustic guitar; DJ Power, turntables; Henri Flood of the Beatnigs, Ron Nelson, former members of Violence and the Sacred; Don Paul; Seventh Fire; Florine Belmore and Rebecca Belmore; Delphine Armstrong, vocals; Chip Yarwood, flute/guitar/synthesizer; poetry by Jeannette Armstrong, Ahdri Zhini Mandiela, Benjamin Zephaniah, Greg Young-Ing; archival interview with Che Guevera, 1967.

DISCOGRAPHY:

Still Dancing on John Wayne's Head [Filter 1998, United Kingdom] remixes
Still Dancing on John Wayne's Head [Extreme 1998, Australia]
Dancing on John Wayne's Head [Extreme 1995] w/ Mikey Dread
Till the Bars Break [Cargo 1991] clear twelve-inch vinyl
Till the Bars Break [Irresistible/Maya/Revolutionary 1991]
Basslines and Ballistics [Extreme 1991]

Singles:

"I Love Tha Future" [Filter/Dorado 1998, United Kingdom] four-track twelve-inch vinyl
"Reluctant Warrior" [Filter/Dorado 1998] twelve-inch vinyl w/ Asian Dub Foundation and Michael Franti
"Basslines and Ballistics" [Extreme 1994–95] four-track EP
"At Least the American Indian Knows Exactly How They've Been Fucked Around" [Cargo 1991] four-track twelve-inch vinyl

Appearances:

Asian Dub Foundation:
Community Music [London Records 2000]
Various:
Mumia: Without Apology [Trade Roots 1999] comp
Killing Music [Filter/Dorado 1998, United Kingdom] comp
Elvis Never Meant Shit to Me [Filter/Dorado 1998] comp
Urban Renewal [Guidance Recordings 1997] comp

First Nation Gospel Jamboree
[Cherish Records 2002]

Lineup: William Bushey; Bill Hamelin, bass guitar; John McDonald (born on the Whitedog Reserve, Ontario); Art Shorting (born July 29, 1947, Winnipeg, Manitoba); Daniel Sinclair (born on the Little Saskatchewan First Nation); Al Fehr, steel guitar; Brian Bannab, harmonica; Hank Neafield, lead guitar.

Flow Like a River [Rising Eagle Productions 1989] cass

Lineup: Ed Gamblin and Northern Lobo (Norway House, Manitoba): Ed Gamblin, vocals; Dennis Dick, guitar; Danny Robertson, bass; Lloyd Arthurson, drums. Just the Boyz (Beauval, Saskatchewan): Bingo Kimbley, vocals; Fred Roy, bass; Mervin Morin, drums; Bill Roy, guitar. Tom Ware and

Bo Dock (Anadarko, Oklahoma): Batiste Jones, guitar; Melvin Scott, bass; Terry Tsotigh, drums; Smokey Hondolero, sax; James Haney, guitar; Tom Ware, vocals. Sir Doug Quintet: Doug Sahm, vocals/guitar; Augie Meyers, keyboards/accordion, Speedy Sparks, bass; Ernie Durawa, drums; Rocky Morales, sax. Recorded at the Fire Station in San Marcos, Texas; support also came from the Missinipi Broadcasting Corporation in La Ronge, Saskatchewan, Sipisishk Communications Inc., in Beauval, Saskatchewan, and the Norway House Indian Band, Norway House, Manitoba. The project was released as a fund-raiser to promote education and advancement in sport and performing arts for aboriginal people.

Gabriel's Crossing [Turtle Island Music 1997]

Lineup: Kelly Atcheynum; Hap Boyer; Henry Gardipy. The unique style of Metis fiddle music is performed by three of the most outstanding artists of their genre. The album is named in honor of Gabriel Dumont, who participated in the 1885 Metis Rebellion with Louis Riel. Gabriel's Crossing is the site of a ferry crossing on the South Saskatchewan River, north of the present city of Saskatoon, Saskatchewan.

The Gathering: A Compilation of Toronto World Music [Attic World 1990]

First Nations performers include Leland Bell and Special Ice. Billy Bryans, former drummer for Toronto-based bands the Parachute Club and Mama Quilla, created the project, which received the Juno Award for Best World Beat Recording, 1992.

Goose Wings: The Music of James Bay [World Records 1981 WRC1-2019]

Lineup: Lawrence Martin; Vern Cheechoo; Roger House; Brian Davey (*See*: Brian Black Thunder); Otterhead Drum; Lloyd Cheechoo; Norman Naveau. Additional musicians: Greg Spence, bass; Stan Louttit, drums; Brian Behie, guitar/bass/mandolin. The project brought together performers from northern Ontario and the James Bay region and was recorded at the Ojibway-Cree Cultural Centre, Timmins, Ontario.

Here and Now: A Celebration of Canadian Music [Sony 1995]

Lineup: Kashtin; Tudjaat; Stoney Park Singers; Lawrence Martin; Jerry Alfred and Medicine Beat; White Tail Singers (*See*: Powwow Music); Jani Lauzon; Johnny Landry; Willie Dunn w/ Susan Aglukark; Fara; Don Ross; Shingoose (*See: Children of the World* comp). CBC Radio Music, production; Canada Council for the Arts, executive production.

Honor [Daemon 1996]

Lineup Disk One: Ulali; Toad the Wet Sprocket; Bruce Cockburn; Exene Cervenka; Indigenous; Luka Bloom; Jane Siberry; Keith Secola and the Wild Band of Indians; Rusted Root; Reversing Hour. *Disc Two*: Bonnie Raitt and David Grisman; John Trudell; Victoria Williams; Latin Playboys; Soul Asylum; Sherman Alexie and Jim Boyd; Frank Hyde and Mike Jones; Indigo Girls; Matthew Sweet; Joy Harjo and Poetic Justice; Ulali. This benefit album for the Honor the Earth Campaign was the successful brainchild of the Indigo Girls. The double-disk release includes Native and non-Native performers, with rare tracks.

Huronia's A-Live, Vol. 1: *Lightning Rock* [independent 1993]

Lineup: Blue Barrie Jam Band; Distraction; Kevin Huggins; Humphrey Go-Cart; Rev; Michael Keith Group; King Size; Soldier; Larry Wilkes. Recorded in Barrie, Ontario.

I Am an Eagle: The Music from the Legends Project [First Nations 1994] *See*: Contemporary Spoken Word: Interview Recordings: *Legends*

Lineup: Leland Bell; Tammy Pierce w/ Murray Porter; ElizaBeth Hill; Lawrence Martin; the Legends Band (Jay Vern, keyboards; Milton Sledge, drums; Mike Chapman, bass; Danny Parks, guitars; Tom Roady, caribou drum/percussion; Jelly Roll, harp; Robert Bowlin, fiddle; Fred Satterfield, buffalo/caribou drums; Bruce Bouton, dobro; Joel Sonnier, accordions; Michael Black, Kim Morrison, Yvonne Hodges, background vocals).

I Am Walking: New Native American Music [Narada 1997]

Lineup: Andrew Vasquez; Gary Stroutos/ David Lanz; Little Wolf Band (R. Carlos Nakai, William Eaton, Will Clipman, Wind Travelin' Band, Oki Kano); Joseph Fire Crow; Joanne Shenandoah; Sacred Spirits; Walela.

In the Spirit of Crazy Horse: Songs for Leonard Peltier [Four Winds Trading 1992]

Lineup: Joanne Shenandoah; Mitch Walking Elk; Ellen Klaver; Carolyn Brittell; Larry Long; Alice Di Micele; Bruce Cockburn; Jim Page (*See*: John Trudell); Julie Robbins; City Folk; Buffy Sainte-Marie; Leonard Peltier.

James Bay Cree Youth Compilation Album [Cree Eeyou Productions 1996]

Lineup: David Cox Memorial Singers; Charles Hester; Miigwin; Blue Thunder; Thunder Nation; Francine Weislche; Chiislin; Joshua Iselhoff. Organized by the Cree Nation Youth Council of Eeyou Estchee, this recording represents nine Native communities in James Bay, northern Quebec.

Jammin' on the Bay [World Records WRC4-6404]

Lineup: The Harrapashires; Young Offenders; the Nakogee Band; Elmer Cheechoo Jr.; Vern Cheechoo; the Spence Band; John Rodrique. Recorded in collaboration with the Ojibway-Cree Cultural Centre in Timmins, Ontario, the Moosonee Friendship Centre, and Wawatay Communications.

Latin Oldies, Vol. 1 [Thump Records 1998]

Lineup: Thee Midniters; Santana; War; El Chicano; Lee Oskar; Rudy and the Cruisers; Aalon; Reney Rene; Rosie and the Original; Joe Bataan; Ralfi Pagan; McKinley Mitchell; Tierra.

Latin Oldies, Vol. 2 [Thump Records 1998]

Lineup: El Chicano; Patti Drew; James Brown; Joe Bataan; Brenton Wood; Stories; Johnny Chingas; Thee Midniters; Mary Wells; Ritchie Valens; War; Eric Burdon (featuring War); Sam the Sham and the Pharoahs; the Champs.

Latin Oldies, Vol. 3 [Thump Records 1999]

Lineup: The Delegations; Redbone; Thee Midniters; Willie Bobo; Frankie Karl; James Brown; Gene Chandler; War; El Chicano; Jorge Santana; Tierra; Breton Wood; Rene y Rene.

Latin Oldies, Vol. 4 [Thump Records 2000]

Lineup: Santana; Pete Wingfield; El Chicano; Teen Queens; Hugh Masakela; Thee Midniters; Tierra; Santa Esmerelda; Perez Prado; Randy Garibay; the Village Callers; Los Alacranes; Cannibal and the Head-hunters; Cal Tjader; Redbone.

Legends: I Am an Eagle [First Nations 1994] *See: I Am An Eagle* comp; Contemporary Spoken Word: Interview Recordings: *Legends*

Lineup: Pura Fe; Soni; Monique Mojica; Jenny, Betsy and Sadie Buck; Tammy Pierce (Cherokee); Murray Porter; Leland Bell; Bill Miller; ElizaBeth Hill; Bob Crawford (Algonquin); Murray Porter; Gloria Eshkibok; Jerry Sawanas (OJ-Cree); and the Legends Band (*See: I Am An Eagle* comp). A mix of contemporary and traditional Native music with legends told by Native story-tellers. An ambitious project that gathered together a large number of performers to bring Native legends to life, but that was much maligned by some Native people who thought it to be exploitive and opportunistic. Traditional legends were rewritten by the album's producer John James Stewart.

Lewis and Clark: Sounds of Discovery [Makoche 1999] *See*: Traditional/Archival Compilations

Litefoot Presents the Sounds of Indian Country [Red Vinyl 1999]

MacKenzie Music: Music of the MacKenzie Delta and South MacKenzie [CBC Northern Service Broadcast Recording 1991]

Lineup: Bob Mumford; Inuvik Drummers and Dancers; Charles Tizya; the Delta Good Time Band; Aklivik Delta Drummers and Dancers; Richard Provan; Mike Whiteside; Emmanuel Felix and William Nasogaluak; Annie Kasook; Claire Pemberton Pigott; Donald Kaglik; Drummers from Tuk; Pat Burke; Dave Sveinsen; the Gumboots; Wilf Bean.

Mariposa [Mariposa 1977]

Lineup: Akinsi Novalinga (Inuit); Lucie Amarualik and Alicie Tuauga (Inuit), throat singers; Samson Neacappo (Cree); Floyd Westerman; Alanis Obomsawin (Abenaki); Willie Dunn; Duke Redbird w/ Winston Wuttunee and the Ahbenoo-jeyug Singers (Anishnabe); Taj Mahal w/ Jesse Ed Davis. From the Mariposa Folk Festival, originally held on the Toronto Islands.

The Mexican Revolution [Arhooli 9041/4]

Four-record or CD set contains songs, anthems, and words from the 1911 revolution, featuring odes to Emiliano Zapata, Pancho Villa, Adalita, and others.

Mariposa Folk Festival, Toronto Island, 1975. *Left to right*: David Campbell, Shingoose, Duke Redbird, Paul Ritchie, Willie Dunn. Photo by Art Usherson.

Mighty Mohawks: Indian/Western Showband, George Hill Sings Again with His Friends [independent 1994] *See*: Mighty Mohawks

Lineup: George Hill; Donna Jacobs; Leo Diabo; Joe Running Deer; Sid Menard; Bobby T.; Ronnie Martin; Gary Rice; Bobby Donaldson; Ricky LeFevre; Guy Gagne; recorded in the Mohawk territory of Kahnawake.

Moving within the Circle: Contemporary Native American Music and Dance [World Music Press 1993]

The audio component that accompanied the Bryan Burton book of the same name. Although many of the traditional performers remain nameless, the nations represented include Yaqui, Dineh, Apache,

Haliwa-Saponi, Tigua Pueblo, Zuni, Nanticoke, Dakota, Seneca. Musicians credited for their appearance include Bryan Burton; Millard Clark (*See*: Indian Chipmunks); Tom Ware (*See*: XIT); Porcupine Singers (*See*: Powwow Music); Jackalope; Chester Mahooty (*See*: Traditional/Archival Solo); XIT; and Quincy Hilliard with excerpts from a symphonic work.

Music from the Powerhouse: In the Spirit of Sharing [World Records 1985]

From the Ojibway-Cree Cultural Centre in Timmins, Ontario, performers were recorded live at Manitoulin Island, Ontario. An admirable effort that contains tracking for song titles only, with no mention of the artists involved. Performers include Lawrence Martin, Brian Davey (a.k.a. Brian Black Thunder), and Murray Porter.

Music from Turtle Island: Contemporary Native American Music [Turtle Island 1999]

New material from veteran musicians and a taste of emerging talent. This twelve-track disc covers mostly country and folk territory with old and new songs from Willie Dunn; Buddy Red Bow; Chante Pierce; Chester Knight and the Wind; Peggy Vermette; Red Blaze; Cheryl Ogram; Denise Lanceley; Doug Moran; Jani Lauzon; Grant Severight; Koskanuba. Additional musicians include Zonnie Hawk, guitars/bass; Jason Ross, guitars/drums; Corny Michel, fiddle (See: C-Weed); Greg Edmunds, flute/keyboards; Ray Villebrun, bass; Ron Blankley, dobro/slide guitar; Kelly Parker, producer.

Music of New Mexico: Native American Traditions [Smithsonian Folkways 1992]

The companion recording to *Music of New Mexico: Hispanic Traditions*, includes Fernando Cellicion; John Rainer Jr. (See: Flute Music), Alton Nastacio, Florentine Johnson; Bernard Duran; Carl Tsosie; Ruben Romero, Ernest Martinez, Juan O. Lujan; the Garcia Brothers; Turtle Mountain Singers (See: Traditional/Archival Group); A. Paul Ortega w/ Sharon Burch; Geraldine Barney (See: Contemporary Music).

Native American Currents [Silver Wave 1997]

Lineup: R. Carlos Nakai, Peter Kater; Joanne Shenandoah; Robert Mirabal; Joy Harjo and Poetic Justice.

Native American Music: The Rough Guide [World Music Network 1998, United Kingdom]

Lineup: Walela; Sharon Burch; Judy Trejo; Joanne Shenandoah; Primeaux and Mike; Garcia Brothers; Blackstone Singers; Cornel Pewewardy; Blacklodge Singers; WithOut Reservation; The Fire This Time; R. Carlos Nakai; Robert Tree Cody; Burning Sky.

A Native American Odyssey [Putumayo 1998]

Lineup: Kashtin; Tudjaat; Andrew Vasquez; Bill Miller; Burning Sky; Jerry Alfred and the Medicine Beat; Jaramar (Huave); Binni Gula'za (Zapotec); Marlui Miranda (Amazon); Regional Vermelho E. Branco (Amazon); Los Incas (Andean); Bolivia Manta (Andean); Ezpresion (Andean).

Native to Canada: Showcase of Aboriginal Musicians at WOMEX 2000 [Canada Council for the Arts 2001]

Lineup: Wathahine (See: Traditional/Archival Solo); Coleman Beaver; Amos Keye Jr. (See: Traditional/Archival Group: Six Nations Singers); Harvey Dreaver; Lucie Idlout; Mishi Donovan; Calvin Vollrath; Willie Dunn.

A Northern Christmas [Sunshine SSCD-4180]

Lineup: Bear Paws; Lionel Desjarlais; Ernest Monias; Billy Simard; Wigwam; Winston Wuttunee.

Northern Legends [Sunshine 2000]

Lineup: Ernest Monias; Robbie Brass; Edward Gamblin; Billy Simard.

Old Native and Metis Fiddling in Manitoba, Vol. 1 [Falcon Productions 1986]

Lineup: Ebb and Flow; Bacon Ridge; Eddystone and Kinosta communities: Willie Mousseau; Walter Flett; Lawrence "Teddy Boy" Houle; Lawrence Flett; Albert Beaulieu; Emile Spence; Frank Desjarlais; Fred Lavasseur; Jack Ducharme; Angus McLeod; Jimmy Anderson; Eldon Campbell; Anne Lederman, producer (*See*: Contemporary Music).

Old Native and Metis Fiddling in Manitoba, Vol. 2 [Falcon Productions 1987]

Music from Camperville and Pine Creek, featuring Randy Fagnan, J. B. Ledoux, Stanley Sabiston, George DeMerais, Frank Catchaway, Roderick Ross, Little Joe Chartrand, Fred McKay, Hyacinth McKay, Rene Ferland; w/ Anne Lederman, producer (*See*: Contemporary Music).

Our Voice Is Our Weapon and Our Bullets Are the Truth [Red Wire Magazine 2003]

Produced by *Red Wire Magazine* in Vancouver, British Columbia, this album combines pre-released material from contemporary and traditional musicians, rappers, and poets. *Lineup*: Richard Ashley Joseph; Aztlan Undergound; Chrystos; Innersoulflow; Marc Longjohn; Nikki Maier; Manik w/ OS-12 and Chile; Vera Manuel; Namgis Singers; Larry Nicholson; Sandra Olsen; Skena Reece; Buffy Sainte-Marie; Sandy Scofield; Kinnie Starr; Richard Van Camp; Vera Wabegijig; War Party.

Oyate [Nato/World 1990/1998, France]

An obscure double album produced by Jeff Beck's former keyboard player Tony Hymas. He gathered several performers for an experimental project incorporating modern classical, jazz, and rock music with traditional and spoken-word elements. *Oyate* (a Lakota word for "nation" or "people") was inspired by and dedicated to the memories of historical leaders Crazy Horse, Manuelito, Satanta, Quanah Parker, Chief Joseph, Captain Jack, Black Kettle, Red Cloud, Geronimo, Lone Wolf, Cochise, and Sitting Bull. Hymas encouraged the artists to delve into musical styles completely different from what they are known for. Floyd Westerman delivers a traditional song with spoken word in Lakota on the track "Mahpiya Luta" and an aria entitled "Guipago"; Joanne Shenandoah sings heavy rock on "Naudah Cynthia"; John Trudell performs the poetry of Barney Bush ("Captain Jack") and is accompanied by Jeff Beck on Trudell's own poem "Crazy Horse." Recorded in January 1990, the album also contains Jim Pepper's last studio session with his composition "Lone Wolf." Traditional singing is performed by the Rock Creek Singers, Oley Little Eagle, George Archambault, and D. J. Nez; cedar flute players include Joseph Bellanger, Ed Wapp Wahpeconiah, R. Carlos Nakai, and Kevin Locke. Other rare tracks by Tom Bee, Bonnie Jo Hunt, Paul Ortega, and Hanay Geiogamah are exclusive to this album. In addition, a full orchestra of more than thirty classical musicians was conducted by Tony Hymas and Guy Le Querrec.

Peace and Dignity Journeys [Xicano Records and Film 2000]

Lineup: Aztlan Underground; Quinto Sol; Subsistencia; Victor E; La Paz; Virbatum; In Lak Ech; Culture of Rage; ITS; MSDC; Ground Keepers; Todos Vuelven; Blackfire;

Bulletproof; Blues Exp?; Sangre Pesada. A compilation/benefit album released in support of the Peace and Dignity Journeys, which seeks to unite nations from the Northern and Southern Hemispheres of Turtle Island. Two teams of runners set out to join in Mexico City, one began in Alaska and the other started from Tierra Del Fuego.

People of the Willows [Makoche 1999]

Lineup: Keith Bear, Gary Stroutsos, Nellie Youpee, and strings arranged by Jovino Santos Netos present a modern interpretation of traditional Mandan and Hidatsa songs.

Pine Ridge: An Open Letter to Allan Rock, Songs for Leonard Peltier [LPDC/Warner 1996]

Lineup: Sarah McLachlan; Jane Siberry; the Tragically Hip; Michael Ondaatje, spoken word; Tamara Williamson of Mrs. Torrence; Greg Keelor; Ashley MacIsaac (*See*: Lee Cremo); Bob Wiseman; Ursula; Anne Bourne; Jim Cuddy; the Skydiggers; Change of Heart; Molly Johnson; John Borra; Michelle McAdorey.

Several prominent Canadian music industry personalities contributed tracks in an effort to support Leonard Peltier, prompted by Greg Keelor and Jim Cuddy of Blue Rodeo. Sarah McLachlan's video *Unchained Melody* [Warner 1996] is connected to this project.

Plains Chippewa/Metis Music from Turtle Mountain [Smithsonian Folkways 1992]

Presented in four parts with archival and contemporary recordings. Pembina

Chippewa Drum Songs performed by the Pembina Chippewa Singers: Francis Cree (born 1920), Boy Joe Fayant (born 1910), Leo Wilkie (born 1935). French songs from elders to children performed by Della LaFloe (born 1904), Fred Parisien (born 1916), Gregory Davis (born 1908), and Alvina Davis (born 1907). Fiddle dance music performed by Fred Allery (born 1922), violin; Lawrence Keplin (born 1924), violin; Norbert Lenoir (born 1941), George Longie (born 1927), callers; Ray Houle (born 1938), harmonica. Contemporary fiddle, country, rock 'n' roll, and full-circle fiddle featuring: Mike Page (born 1939), violin; Dorothy Azure Page (born 1945), chorder; Thomas Belgarde (born 1958), rhythm/lead/guitar/vocals; Cary Poitra (born 1955), keyboards; Brian Johnson (born 1965), violin/vocals; Jim LaRocque (born 1953), lead guitar; Clayton Gourneau (born 1962), drums; Mac Bailey (born 1962), drums.

Prayer for Peace [Silver Wave 2000]

Lineup: Joanne Shenandoah; R. Carlos Nakai and Peter Kater; Robert Mirabal; Mary Youngblood; Alice Gomez; Lawrence Laughing; Michel Casson.

Prophecy: A Hearts of Space Native American Collection [Hearts of Space 1999]

Lineup: R. Carlos Nakai w/ Nawang Khechong; Primeaux and Mike; Joanne Shenandoah w/ Lawrence Laughing; Coyote Oldman and Soulfood (*See*: Contemporary Music).

Pukatawagan First Annual Talent Search 2000 [Sunshine 2001]

Lineup: Barbara Dumas; Demoley Nateweyes; Lorna Chadney; Sidney Castel;

Arnold Henderson; Michael Wiehe; Charlie Beardy. The Cree community of Pukatawagan, Manitoba, hosted a talent search; winners received recording opportunities and national radio airplay.

Red Ryders, Vol. 1 [Red Vinyl 1999]

Canada and U.S.–based rappers Flawless, Mistic, Daybi, Versatile, and Litefoot with ALT; coproduced by Funkdaddy and Tony G.

Red Ryders, Vol. 2 [Red Vinyl 1999]

Features rappers Flawless, Daybi, San Man, Mistic, and Litefoot.

Revolucion: The Chicano Spirit: A Selection of Chicano Grooves from the Early 70's [Follow Me 2001, France]

Lineup: El Chicano; Sapo; Coke Escovido; Cacers; Melom; Azteca; Tierra; Flash and the Dynamics; Massada.

The Rough Guide to the Music of Canada [World Music Network 2003]

Native musicians include Florent Vollant w/ Zachary Richard; Kanenhi:io; Longbottom; Tudjaat.

Rumours of War Jungle . . . Lacandona, Zapatista [Esan Ozenki 1998]

Lineup: Hubert Cesarion; Lumumba; DKP; P-18; GTI; Sree; 3thnicians; Pushy! and La Hundand Denise.

Sacred Souls [Manteca 2001, United Kingdom]

Lineup: Philip Cassadore; Clan/destine; R. Carlos Nakai; Robert Tree Cody; Wallace and Clipman; Joanne Shenandoah; Keith Mahone; Nakai, Eaton, and Clipman; Sharon Burch; Judy Trejo; Blacklodge; William Eaton Ensemble w/ Drepung Monks and Robert Tree Cody; Patsy Cassadore.

Sacred Spirit [Virgin/EMI 1994, United Kingdom]

This 1994 project features samples of traditonal music hijacked in the guise of cultural representation. Liner notes describe the archival source music as from the Menominee Tribe of Wisconsin, Kickapoo Indians of Texas, Massachusetts' Gay Head Wampanoag, Pascua Yaqui Tribe of Arizona, Louisiana's Tunica-Biloxi Tribe, Narrangansett Tribe of Rhode Island, and Poarch Creek Tribe of Alabama. Anonymous producers include "The Fearsome Brave," Jard Gorbohay, and New World Records; incidental music by Roger Tyler and Peter Kater (*See*: Flute Music: R. Carlos Nakai); single remixes were produced by Bravado, the Grid, Deep Recess, and Julian Mendelsohn.

DISCOGRAPHY:

Singles:
"Yeha-Noha" [Virgin 1994 DPRO-12750, United Kingdom]
"Yeha-Noha" [Virgin 1994 LC-3098, United Kingdom]

Appearances:
Escapes II [WEA/Warner 1997] comp

Sacred Spirit, Vol. 2: *Culture Clash* [Virgin/Rhythm and Blues Foundation 1997]

Arranged, mixed, and produced by the Brave with samples of John Lee Hooker; Dee Houndog Jeffs; Josef Spence and the Pinder Family; John Henry Barbee; Lightnin' Hopkins; Dick Gregory; and an unnamed cellist.

Sacred Spirit II: More Chants and Dances of the Native Americans [Higher Octave Music/Virgin 2000, United Kingdom]

A collection of ambient, New Age, and world music created by living contemporary Native performers and non-Native producers. Produced, mixed, and arranged by the Brave, w/ Eric Plummettaz and K. J. Jake; Native vocalists include Cherokee Rose, Nellie Two Bulls, Jackie Bird, Delany Apple, the White Wolfe Drummers, Jim White Wolfe, and Carlos Black.

Santa Fe Sampler [Musical Transformation Inc. 1995]

This Santa Fe–based CD includes three Native musicians: Robert Mirabal, Ruben Romero, and Daniel Jaramillo.

Singing Our Stories [Full Regalia Productions 2000]

Lineup: Rita Coolidge; Monk Sanders Family Singers; Namgis Traditional Singers; Ulali; Walela.

Skin Tight Blues: First Peoples Blues Compilation [Sweet Grass/EMI 2002]

Lineup: Blues Nation; Ronnie Douglas; Jani Lauzon; Butch Mudbone; Billy Joe Green; Pappy Johns Band; Murray Porter; Ken Rhyne; Sandy Scofield; Keith Secola; Gary Small Band; The Soul Kings; Ulali; Jimmy Wolf.

Sociadad = Suciadad [BYO Records 1997]

Lineup: Aztlan Underground; the Blues Experiment; Ollin; Ozomatli; Quinto Sol.

Solitudes: Raindance: Impressions of a Native Land [Solitudes 1995]

Juno Award–winning natural-sound recordist Dan Gibson w/ Howard Baer; Claude Desjardins; Ron Korb, flutes; Neil Donell, Beverly Glenn-Copeland, vocals; Cayuga words by Reginald Henry and Norm Jacobs (Cayuga).

Songs for Chiapas "Off the Record": Riding the Back of the Feathered Serpent [Ra Records 1999]

Lineup: Antonia Perez Vasquez; Bear Necessities; Alejadra Nunez; Raphael; Rolando Alvarez Giacoman; Ulali; Emailio Capistran; Michelle St. John; Jani Lauzon; Kanatan Aski w/ Pura Fe; Wayne St. John; Monique Mojica; Charlie Hill; Dane Ngahuka (*See: Downa Bush* and *Backroads* comps); Silver Cloud Singers (*See*: Powwow Music).

Songs of the Spirit [Worldly/Triloka 1997]

Lineup: Rita Coolidge; Coyote Oldman; 500 Nations; Kashtin; Little Wolf; R. Carlos Nakai w/ William Eaton; Native Flute Ensemble; Michael Stearns and Ron Sunsinger; Primeaux and Mike; Joanne Shenandoah; Doug Wallantyne w/ Brian Keane; featured alternate tracks of previously released material produced by Jim Wilson (*See*: Contemporary Music); Al Evers and Mitchel Markus.

Songs of the Spirit, Vol. 2 [Triloka 1999]

Lineup: Sharon Burch; Robert Tree Cody; December Wind; Lorain Fox; Robert Mirabal; Primeaux and Mike; Tony Redhouse; Joanne Shenandoah; Andrew Vasquez; Walela.

Step Dance and Fiddle [Ojibway Cree Cultural Centre no date]

Lineup: Sinclair Cheechoo; J. Keeash; Clarence Louttit; N. Naveau. No release date or information accompanies this cassette, released by the Ojibway Cree Cultural Centre, Timmins, Ontario, and produced by Dennis Austin, Stan Louttit, and Mel Stewart.

Still the Eagle Flies, Vols. 1 and 2 [Saskatchewan Indian Cultural Centre 1995] *See*: Powwow Compilations

Ray Villebrun and Cheryl Ogram.

Sweet Grass [CBC North 1982] *See*: Arctic/Circumpolar Compilations

Reissued in Germany on the Trikont label in 1993, this album contains live tracks of Morley Loon, Willie Thrasher, Willy Mitchell, and Roger House. Recorded in Val-d'Or, Quebec.

Tapes for Timor: 20 Years of Resistance to Genocide in East Timor [Hands Free Records 1996]

Lineup: Susan Aglukark; Ginger Baker Trio; Bonga; Peter Gabriel; U2; Mac-

Donald/Gang; Loreena McKennitt; Midnight Oil; Paul Morin; Buffy Sainte-Marie; Robert Wyatt; Xutos and Pontapes; Yothu Yindi.

The Third World Sings [Beaver Records 1974]

Lineup: The Conklin Minstrels w/ Deloris Tremblay; William Tremblay; Fred House w/ Ken Stoltz and the Nightlife Band. The Development Education Project and the Frontiers Foundation under the auspices of Operation Beaver produced an album of Native, Caribbean, Malaysian, and African songs.

Tribal Dreams [Earth Beat! 2001]

Lineup: Jerry Alfred; Joseph Fire Crow; Kevin Locke; R. Carlos Nakai and Peter Kater; Quiltman; Andrew Vasquez; Walela; Mary Youngblood.

Tribal Fires [Earth Beat! 1997]

Lineup: Jerry Alfred; Brule; Joy Harjo and Poetic Justice; Jani Lauzon; Lunar Drive; Robert Mirabal; Quiltman; Keith Secola; Song Catchers; Joanne Shenandoah; Ulali; Andrew Vasquez; Walela.

Tribal Gatherings [Music of the World MOW-154] *See*: Traditional/ Archival Compilations

Tribal Legends [Earth Beat! 2002]

Lineup: Brule; Joseph Fire Crow w/ Joseph Marshall; Lawrence Laughing; Kevin Locke; R. Carlos Nakai w/ William Eaton and the Blacklodge Singers; R. Carlos Nakai w/ Robert Tree Cody and Cliff

Sarde; Medicine Dream; Quiltman; Joanne Shenandoah; Andrew Vasquez.

Tribal Voices [Earth Beat! 1996]

Lineup: Jerry Alfred; Sharon Burch; Robert Tree Cody w/ Rob Wallace and Will Clipman; Joseph Fire Crow; Sissy Goodhouse; Kevin Locke; Primeaux and Mike; Quiltman; Joanne Shenandoah; Six Nations Women's Singers; Spirit of Song Singers; Ulali; Andrew Vasquez; Walela.

Tribal Waters [Earth Beat! 1998]

Lineup: Jerry Alfred; Keith Bear; Burning Sky; Joseph Fire Crow; Corbin Harney (Western Shoshone); Kevin Locke; Robert Mirabal; R. Carlos Nakai w/ Peter Kater; Primeaux and Mike; Quiltman; Andrew Vasquez; Mary Youngblood; Leib Ostrow w/ Agnes Patak and David Swenson, producers.

Tribal Winds: Music from Native American Flutes [Earth Beat! 1995/1996] *See*: Flute Compilations

True North Concerts—Truly Something [CBC North 2000]

Lineup: Peters Dury Trio; Kashtin; Leela Gilday with Lucy Idlout; Dave Haddock; Jerry Alfred; Cyrille Fontaine; Susan Aglukark; Matthew Lien; Top of the World Fiddlers; Charlie Panagoniak; Tudjaat; Daniel Tlen; Paul Andrew; Kim Barlow; Lee Manteville w/ Attagtaluk; Jason Akearjuk; Tom Jackson.

A Turtle Island Christmas [Turtle Island Music 2002]

Lineup: Amber Andrews; Edmund Bull; Curtis Cardinal; Brandy McKinnon; Andrea Menard; Connie Mike; Ray Villebrun; Winston Wuttunnee.

20 Aboriginal Greatest Hits, Vol. 2 [Sunshine 1998]

Lineup: Bearpaws; Jim Beer; Robbie Brass; Melanie Chartrand; Harry Davies; Mishi Donovan; Eagle Feather; Ray Fox; Edward Gamblin; Jody T. Gaskin; Billy Joe Green; Maurice McArthur; Ernest Monias; Moody X Two; Raindance; Billy Simard; TKO; Trapline; Wigwam; Winston Wuttunee.

20 Aboriginal Greatest Hits, Vol. 3 [Sunshine 2002]

Lineup: Jerry Alfred; Reg Bouvette; Cherokee Rose and Silena; Mishi Donovan; Eagle and Hawk; Eagle Feather; Full Ephekt; Edward Gamblin; Jody Gaskin; Arnold Henderson; Ingenuity; George Leach; Ernest Monias; On-ji-da; Keith Secola; Garry Settee; Slowhand; Laura Vinson; Eric Voice; Wigwam.

24 Aboriginal Artists/24 Greatest Hits, Vol. 1 [Sunshine 1995]

Bearpaws; Robbie Brass; Bravestone; Harry Davies; Mishi Donovan; Ray Fox; J. Hubert Francis and Eagle Feather; the Gardipys; Jody T. Gaskin; Charlie Goertzen; the Henry Brothers; Mike Henry; Richard McIvor; Ernest Monias; Hector Menow; Brian Moon; Rarebreed; Harve Settee; Billy Simard; Trapline; Weekend Warriors; Wigwam; Winston Wuttunee.

24 Golden Fiddle Greats [Sunshine 1998]

Lineup: Mel Bedard; Reg Bouvette; the Country Ramblers; Andy Dejarlis; Harvey Old Time Fiddlers; Eldon Jones; Yogi Klos; Eugen Laderoute; Clarence Levesque; Marcel Meilleur; Boris Nowosad; Brian Sklar.

Urban Skins, Vol. 1: *Tribal Pop Rock and More* [SOAR 1999]

Lineup: Robby Bee; Tom Bee; Jim Boyd; Chester Knight and the Wind; Casper Lomayesva; D. C. Lone Eagle; Robert Mirabal; Natay; Native Roots; Red Thunder; Keith Secola; Tiger Tiger; Vince Two Eagles.

Urban Skins, Vol. 2: *Tribal Rap and Reggae* [SOAR 1999]

Lineup: Boyz from the Rez; Casper Lomayesva; Natay; Native Roots; New Breed; TKO; Wayquay.

Urban Skins, Vol. 3: *Rock Collection* [SOAR 2000]

Lineup: Tom Bee; Chester Knight and the Wind; Claude McKenzie; Derek Miller; Nadjiwan; Natay; Tiger Tiger; XIT.

Various Native American Artists: Solo Flights, Vol. 1, SOAR Sampler Series [SOAR 1991]

Lineup: Cathedral Lake; Davis Mitchell; Billie Nez; Doug Wallantyne w/ James Bilagody and Tom Bee; XIT.

Various Native American Artists: Solo Flights, Vol. 2, SOAR Sampler Series [SOAR 1992]

Lineup: P. M. Begay; James Bilagody; Grayhorse Singers; Wil Numkena; Cornel Pewewardy; XIT.

Various Native American Artists: Solo Flights Two, Vol. 1, SOAR Sampler Series [SOAR 1993]

Lineup: Tom Bee; James Bilagody; Cathedral Lake Singers; Davis Mitchell; Billie Nez; Doug Wallantyne; XIT.

Various Native American Artists: Solo Flights Two, Vol. 2, SOAR Sampler Series [SOAR 1994]

Lineup: P. M. Begay; James Bilagody; Grayhorse Singers; Wil Numkena; Cornel Pewewardy; XIT.

Visions and Rhythms 1 [Natural Visions/SOAR-124]
Visions and Rhythms 2 [Natural Visions/SOAR 1998]

Lineup: Brule; Bob Conti; Red Nativity; Papa John and Daniel; Koljademo; Raven; Doug Wallantyne.

Voices across the Canyon, Vol. 1 [Canyon 1996]

Lineup: Sharon Burch; Burning Sky; Robert Tree Cody; William Eaton; R. Carlos Nakai; Northern Cree Singers; Primeaux and Mike; Red Tail Chasing Hawks; Joanne Shenandoah and A. Paul Ortega; Southern Scratch; Stephen Butler, series producer.

Voices across the Canyon, Vol. 2 [Canyon 1996]

Lineup: Blackstone Singers; Burning Sky; Robert Tree Cody and Rob Wallace; Jackalope; R. Carlos Nakai w/ William Eaton; Ed Lee Natay; Primeaux, Mike, and Attson; Ruben Romero and Lydia Torea; Joanne Shenandoah; WithOut Reservation.

Voices across the Canyon, Vol. 3 [Canyon 1997]

Lineup: Blacklodge Singers; Blacklodge Singers and the Canyon Symphony Orchestra; Clan/destine; William Eaton w/ Drepang Monks and Robert Tree Cody; R. Carlos Nakai w/ Paul Horn; R. Carlos Nakai Quartet; Primeaux and Mike; Redhouse Family; Red Tail Chasing Hawks; Judy Trejo.

Voices across the Canyon, Vol. 4 [Canyon 1999]

Lineup: Frank Afraid of His Horses and Ben Sitting Up; Robert Tree Cody w/ Wallace and Redhouse; December Wind; Hovia Edwards; Guy Jr. and Paul Guy Sr.; William Horncloud; R. Carlos Nakai and Paul Horn; Nakai Quartet; Nakai, Eaton, and Clipman; Northern Cree Singers; Primeaux and Mike; Wahancanka.

Voices across the Canyon, Vol. 5 [Canyon 2001]

Lineup: Blacklodge Singers; Sharon Burch; Jay Begaye; Robert Tree Cody w/ Ruben Romero and Tony Redhouse; Tree Cody w/ Xavier Quijas Yxayotl; William Eaton and Nawang Khechong; Medicine Dream; R. Carlos Nakai; Nakai w/ Will Clipman; Pima Express; Judy Trejo; Delphine Tsinajinne; Young Bird.

Weaving the Strands: Music by Contemporary Native Women [Red Feather 1998]

Lineup: Sharon Burch; Mishi Donovan; Alice Gomez; Joy Harjo; the Mankillers; Joanne Shenandoah; Mary Youngblood; Ulali; Walela; Paul Brotzman, producer.

Whispering Tree: Anishnabe Songs and Stories [Makoche 2000]

Spoken word and music by Annie Humphrey, Pato Hoffman, Larry Long, Anne Dunn and Friends, John Trudell.

Young Northern Voices [Bush League Records 1993]

Lineup: Features twenty-one songs developed and performed by school children in northern Saskatchewan, with Don Freed (Metis), the Northern Lights School Division, and the LaRonge First Nations. Additional musicians: Gary Walsh, dobro/banjo/tin whistle; Chris Lindgren, Celtic harp; Grant Lagimodiere, electric guitar/mandolin; Paddy Tutty, Merv Mahaffey, fiddle; Don Freed, guitar/jaw harp/harmonica; Glen Ens, snare drum; Dave Henrichs, octave mandolin; Del Ryan, rhythms/strings "and other things." Produced by Don Freed.

The Yukon Collection [Caribou 1995]

Lineup: Jerry Alfred and Medicine Beat; Dave Haddock; INCONNU; Manfred Janssen; Ladies Auxiliary; George McConkey and Bob Hamilton; Steve Slade; Daniel Tlen.

Section 3-C
Contemporary Soundtrack Recordings

Bears [Silver Wave 2001]

A National Wildlife Federation and Science North Presentation of a Primesco Film produced for IMAX theaters; original score by Violaine Corradi w/ Lyle Lovett, Claude Carmichael and Pat Wasner, Paul Reisler, Lawrence Laughing, Alice Gomez, Mary Youngblood (*See*: Flute Music).

The Business of Fancy Dancing [Falls Apart 2003]

Lineup: Jim Boyd w/ Alfonso Kolb; Brent Michael Davids; Jennifer Kreisberg (*See*: Contemporary Music: Ulali); Michelle St. John; Gene Tagaban (Tlingit), flute/drum; John Sires; Peter Himmelman; Swil Kanim; B. C. Smith; Neal Abrahamson.

Dance Me Outside [Rez Films/Denon 1994]

Lineup: Original score, Mychael Danna; Anishnabekwe Singers; Vern Cheechoo; Kashtin; Redbone; Keith Secola; Joanne Shenandoah; Dan Cecil Hill; R. Carlos Nakai (*See*: Flute Music); Headstones; Leslie Spit Trio; Ramones; Royal Scots Dragoon Guards.

Dead Man [12 Guage/Vapor Records 1996]

The album features the voices of Johnny Depp and Gary Farmer (Cayuga; *See*: Contemporary Spoken Word: Miscellaneous: *Jenny's Song*); with original music by Neil Young; John Hanlon, producer; Jim Jarmusch, director.

The Ecstasy of Rita Joe [United Artists 1973]

Written by George Ryga; the album's original compositions include "Sleepless Hours" and "Silver Train" by Willie Dunn (*See*: Contemporary Music). Other artists include Chief Dan George (*See*: Contemporary Music), John Avison, Peter Haworth; Paul Horn, flute (*See*: Flute Music: R. Carlos Nakai); Ann Mortifee, guitar; Doug Edwards, bass; Robbie King, electric piano; Kat Hendrikse, drums. Originally produced as a stage play by Vancouver's Playhouse Theatre Company in 1967 with Chief Dan George, this work was later commissioned by the Royal Winnipeg Ballet with the assistance of the Manitoba Indian Brotherhood, 1971.

500 Nations [CBS/Epic 1994]

Lineup: Peter Buffett, composer/producer; Chief Hawk Pope, vocals; Douglas Wallantyne, cedar flute; David Klagstad, guitar; Paul Gmeinder, cello; Dan Chase, percussion; Gordon Tootoosis, spoken word (*See*: Powwow Music).

Geronimo, An American Legend [Columbia 1993]

Lineup: Ry Cooder, guitar/I-beam/rudra veena; R. Carlos Nakai, flute; Jones Benally, vocals (*See*: Blackfire); Hoon Hoortoo Throat Singers of Tuva; Madjid Khaladj, tombak; David Lindley, bouzouki/mandolin; Michael Masley, water pipes/Lakota flute; Loren Marstellar, euphorium; Frank Morrocco, accordion; Suzy Katayama, accordion; Larry Corbett, cello; Van Dyke Parks, George S. Clinton, string and orchestra arrangements. Features several tracks scored by Nakai that appear on no other recording.

How the West Was Lost, Vol. 1 [Silver Wave SC-801]
How the West Was Lost, Vol. 2 [Silver Wave 1995]

Lineup: Music by Peter Kater w/ R. Carlos Nakai (*See*: Flute Music); the White Oak Singers; Joanne Shenandoah; Michael Moses Tirsch; Robert Jospe; Jonathan Edwards; Dave Palmer, percussion; Cecil Hooker, violin; Chris White, vocals; Marty Goodbear, vocals.

Kaha:wi [independent 2003]

Kaha:wi (She Cries) was a music and dance showcase written by choreographer Santee Smith (Mohawk); additional dancers included Carla Soto and Tamara Podemski (*See*: Spirit Nation). *Lineup*: Betsy Buck and Sadie Buck (*See*: Traditional/Archival Group: Iroquois Women's Singers); the Mohawk Hymn Singers of Six Nations (Sharell Martin, Karen Williams, Sandra Sault, Sheldon Johnson, Art Porter, Linda Hill, and Michelle Hill); ElizaBeth Hill; Faron Johns (*See*: Pappy Johns Band); Old Mush Singers (Alfred Key, Hubert Buck Sr., Amos Keye Jr. [*See*: Traditional/Archival Group: Six Nations Singers]); Tom Hill (Seneca); Gordon Buck (Seneca); Daniel Cecil Hill (*See*: Flute Music); Mavis Callihoo (Mohawk); Cheri Maracle (Mohawk); Randy Henry (Onondaga); Chris Warner (Onondaga); Rich Shadrach Lazar, percussions; Donald Quan, strings.

Légendes indiennes du Canada: Lespirit du Chef/Mandamin [Disques Ades 1982]
Légendes indiennes du Canada: Générique et musiques [Disques Ades 45t.11065]
Légendes indiennes du Canada: Pitchi le Rouge-Gorge [Disques Ades 45t. ALB-232]

Produced for CBC television by Daniel Bertolino with music by Vincent Davy and Osvaldo Montes.

Little Big Man [Columbia 1967]

The album features the voices of Chief Dan George (*See*: Contemporary Music), Dustin Hoffman, and cast; John Hammond, original music; Teo Macero, producer.

Louis Riel [Centrediscs 1985] three LPs

The Canadian Opera Company recorded live at the Kennedy Center, Washington, D.C. Harry Somers, music; Mavor Moore, libretto in collaboration with Jacques Languirand. Originally commissioned by the Floyd S. Chalmers Foundation to mark the centennial of Canada's confederation; first produced in 1967 by the Canadian Opera Company.

A Man Called Horse [Columbia OS 3530]

No release date on this little monster. Original score by Leonard Roseman, whose soundtrack albums for *East of Eden* and *Rebel* went gold; orchestration by Ralph Ferraro; Lloyd One Star (Lakota) from Rosebud, South Dakota, acted as Native music advisor and choral director; music credits for two tracks read: "Original Indian music performed by members of the Rose-

bud Sioux Tribe." The film was met with protest by Native people everywhere it played because of its inaccurate portrayal of the Lakota people of the 1700s.

More Music from Northern Exposure [MCA 1994]

Martin Breustle and Steve Turner, music supervisors; theme music by David Schwartz; Native performers who wrote original material for the soundtrack include Georgia Wettlin-Larsen and Joanne Shenandoah.

Naturally Native [Silver Wave 2000]

Murielle Hamilton; Arigon Starr; Bill Miller; Carlos Reynosa; Joanne Shenandoah; Walela (*See*: Contemporary Music); Mary Youngblood (*See*: Flute Music); the Mystic River Singers (*See*: Powwow Music); Donna Summer; Christafari; Juni Kae Randall.

North of Sixty [Alliance Communications 1994]

This CBC television series of the 1990s featured songs by Tom Jackson (*See*: Contemporary Music) and Bertha Norwegian (See: Arctic/Circumpolar Contemporary).

On Deadly Ground [Steven Segal, 1994] *See*: Arctic/Circumpolar Compilations and Soundtracks

The soundtrack features Inuit throat singers Middigak, Quanaq, and Timangiak Petaulassie.

Performance [Warner BS 2554] *See*: Buffy Sainte-Marie

Music by Jack Nitzsche from the Donald Cammell and Nicholas Roeg film, featuring performances by Mick Jagger, Randy Newman, the Last Poets, Merry Clayton (*See*: Jesse Ed Davis), and Ry Cooder with Buffy Sainte-Marie; Sainte-Marie's mouth bow solos composed exclusively for the soundtrack.

Powwow Highway [Handmade Films 1988] *See*: Robbie Robertson; Flute Music: Dan Cecil Hill

Although no official soundtrack was released, much of the music for the film was taken from the album *Robbie Robertson* [Geffen 1987]; traditional vocals during the film's opening credits are sung by Quiltman (*See*: John Trudell; Traditional/Archival Solo), and incidental flute music is played by Dan Cecil Hill.

Ravenous [20th Century Fox/Virgin 1999] *See*: John Trudell

Directed by Antonia Bird, with music/orchestra arrangements by Michael Nyman and Gary Carpenter; includes the vocal single "Weendigo Myth" performed by Quiltman (*See*: John Trudell; Traditional/Archival Solo).

Requiem for the Americas: Songs from the Lost World [Enigma 1989]

This recording and video project, a fund-raiser for the Save the Children Fund, was produced by Jonathan Elias. Performers include Ernie "Longwalker" Peters (Dakota), spoken word; Dan Cecil Hill (*See*: Flute Music); Xipe Totec Drummers and Dancers; Grace Jones; Martin Sheen and Charlie Sheen, spoken word; Jon Anderson;

Simon LeBon, vocals; Stewart Copeland; Ray Foote; Michael Bolton; and others; with archival poetry readings by Jim Morrison.

Riel [McCauley Music/GRT/CBC 1979]

Music composed and conducted by William McCauley; CBC/Green River teleplay written by Roy Moore; Raymond Cloutier as Louis Riel, Roger Blay as Gabriel Dumont, and Christopher Plummer as Prime Minister John A. MacDonald; George Bloomfield, director; released in English as *The Original Soundtrack Album* Riel (GRT 9230-1080) and in French as *Version sonore original du film* Riel (GRT 9230-1083).

Smoke Signals [Miramax 1998]

D. C. Smith, score; performers include Jim Boyd; Ulali; Eaglebear Singers; Dar Williams. The album received a NAMA Award for Best Compilation, 1999.

Son of Ayash [Native Earth Performing Arts 1992]

Tomson Highway's score for the Marsha Coffey production released as a fund-raiser for the Toronto-based Native Earth Performing Arts. Marsha Coffey, percussion/piano/synthesizer; Mica Barnes, vocals; Jani Lauzon, vocals; Michael Stewart, soprano/alto saxophones; Catherine Thompson, guitar/flute.

The Way West [American Experience/Shanachie 1995]

Music by Brian Keane. The album features Earl Bullhead (*See*: Traditional/Archival Solo); Bill Douglas, Doug Wallantyne; Dean Evenson; Will Galison; Whitefish Bay

Singers; Grayhorse Singers (*See*: Powwow Music); Ken Kosek; R. Carlos Nakai (*See*: Flute Music); Steve Roach; Barry Stramp; Brian Torff; Eric Weissberg; Metropolitan Opera Orchestra and others.

The West [Sony 1997]

The Ken Burns/Stephen Ives documentary series includes traditional music of the pioneers and Native Americans, such as the Kiowa Ruffle Dance, Lakota Flag Song, Cheyenne March Song, and the Joseph Honor Song. Music produced and arranged by Matthias Gohl.

Wolves [Silver Wave 1999]

Music for this IMAX production features Robbie Robertson with Primeaux and Mike (*See*: Peyote Solo and Group); Joanne Shenandoah with Lawrence Laughing (*See*: Contemporary Music); Mary Youngblood (*See*: Flute Music); Walela; Bruce Cockburn; Sacred Spirits; Paul Winter; Andy Quin; Michael Cusson.

Section 3-D
Contemporary Spoken-Word Recordings

Although music and spoken-word combinations are present in many cultures, they never had rock 'n' roll or powwow music for backup! In the 1980s, the poetry and spoken-word scene flourished, and it seemed that more women than men were releasing the majority of recordings. With a few exceptions, throughout the 1980s to early 1990s, much of the spoken-word material was released independently and backed with a variety of music styles, but predominantly a reggae and fusion style created expressly for spoken word, known as dub. Historically, one of the first contemporary poets to set her words to music was Pauline Johnson (*See*: Contemporary Music: Timothy Longboat), who in the late 1800s toured the world with a small chamber ensemble that accompanied her recitals. Other artists who used traditional Native music with poetry include Willie Dunn on his album *The Pacific*, where he recites William Shakespeare, with the Akwesasne Mohawk drummers providing the backbeat, and artists such as John Trudell and Joy Harjo (*See*: Contemporary Music).

Indian cowboy poets have enjoyed a long tradition, though not many recordings were ever made. Some recognition is required. Since the days of the horse culture to the modern rodeo, oral traditions have maintained an integral presence in the cowboy scene. From the Wild West shows of the 1880s to the advent of the motion picture industry, Indian cowboys have worked as stuntmen, actors, and wranglers; the most notable include Peter LaFarge, Will Rogers, and Yakima Canutt. Some of the late-twentieth-century Indian cowboy poets include Victor and Jack Runnels (Lakota), Elko, South Dakota; David Pratt (Dakota-Anishnabe), Gordon's Reserve, Saskatchewan; David Schildt (Blackfoot), Browning, Montana; Garry Gottfriedson (Secwepemc-Okanagan), Kamloops, British Columbia; Bob Annesley (Cherokee; *See*: Poetry Recordings); Henry Real Bird (Crow; *See*: Poetry Compilations: *United States of*

Poetry); and Roxy Gordon (Choctaw; *See*: Contemporary Music).

Subsection 3-D 1
Audio Books

American Indian Myths and Legends, Vol. 1 and 2 [Sunset Productions 1992]

Selected and edited by Alfonso Ortiz and Richard Erdoes, read by Jill Momaday (Kiowa).

Ancient Whispers [Blue Parrot 101 1997]

Read by Burt Reynolds (Cherokee).

Black Elk Speaks [Audio Literature 336]

From the book by John G. Neihardt, read by Fred Contreras (Tarahumara), w/ Chemo Candelaria (Ohlone), drumming and singing.

Bloody Knife: Custer's Favourite Scout [Makoche 11840]

Edited and narrated by Richard Collin.

Boots and Saddles: Life in Dakota with General Custer [Makoche 10749]

Written by Elizabeth Bacon Custer; read by Pay Guttensohn Ness.

The Boy Who Lived with Bears and Other Iroquois Stories [Harper Collins 1991]

Told by Joe Bruchac; Benjamin Franklin Award for Best Audio Recording, 1991.

Coyote and Rock and Other Lushoutseed Stories [Harper Collins 1992]

Told by Vi Hilbert (Upper Skagit) from the oral tradition of the first people of Puget Sound.

The Education of Little Tree [Audio Literature 351]

Written by Forrest Carter, read by Peter Coyote.

The First Dog and Other Chippewa-Cree Stories [Harper Collins 1992]

Told by Ron Evans (OJ-Cree-Assiniboine).

500 Nations [Random House 1994]

Written by Alvin M. Josephey Jr., read by Gregory Harrison, introduction by Kevin Costner.

The Flood and Other Lakota Stories [Harper Collins 1993]

Told by Kevin Locke (*See*: Flute Music).

Green Grass Running Water [Harper Collins/CBC 1994] *See*: Radio Plays: Thomas King (Cherokee-Greek).

How Rabbit Tricked Otter and Other Cherokee Animal Stories [Harper Collins 1991]

Told by Gayle Ross (Cherokee).

Indian Killer [Warner 1996] *See*: Poetry Recordings; Contemporary Music: Brent Michael Davids

Written and read by Sherman Alexie (Spokane).

Keepers of the Earth: Native American Stories [Fulcrum 1992]

Told by Joseph Bruchac from the book *Keepers of the Earth* by Michael J. Caduto and Joseph Bruchac, with additional music by Kevin Locke (*See*: Flute Music).

Mankiller [Audio Literature 389]

Autobiography of Wilma Mankiller, former chief of the Cherokee nation; read by Joy Harjo (Muscogee; *See*: Contemporary Music).

Message to the World [Sound Horizons 1992]

Words and music from the First World Conference of Indigenous Peoples, Kari Oka, Brazil, 1992.

Prison Writings: My Life Is a Sundance [St. Martin's Press/Mi Abuela 1999]

Excerpts from the book by Leonard Peltier (Dakota-Anishnabe) are read by editor Harvey Arden. *New Orleans Light Lineup*: Reverend Goat Carson, buffalo jawbone harp/backing vocals/harmonica; George Ingmire, drum/guitar; Harry Lenz, bass clarinet/saxophone; Michael Voelker, drums.

The Sacred Pipe [Audio Literature 1989]

John Neihardt's account of Black Elk's interpretations of Lakota ceremonial life read by Fred Contreras (Tarahumara), with drumming and singing by Chemo Candelaria (Ohlone).

Sacred Twins and Spider Woman and Other Navajo Creation Stories [Harper Collins 1992]

Told by Geri Keams (Dineh).

The Secret War Against the Black Panthers and the American Indian Movement [Maya Music 1988] cass, D

Read by Ward Churchill; Chip Yarwood, music.

Where Whitemen Fear to Tread [Audio Literature 1995]

Excerpts from the book read by author Russell Means (Lakota).

The Woman Who Fell from the Sky [W. W. Norton 1994]

Read by the author Joy Harjo (Muscogee; *See*: Contempoary Music).

Subsection 3-D 2
Children's Recordings

See: Contemporary Music: Vince Craig, Joanne Shenandoah, Winston Wuttunee

Begay, P. M. *See*: Traditonal/Archival Solo

Blacklodge *See*: Powwow Music

Children of Earth *See*: Contemporary Music: John Trudell

DISCOGRAPHY:
A Child's Voice [Peace Company 1992]

A Crow Named Joe and Circus Berzerkus [Pemmican 1996]

Peter Eyvindson.

The Indian Chipmunks, Vol. 1 [Indian Sounds 1983] *See*: Contemporary Music
The Indian Chipmunks, Vol. 2 [Indian Sounds 1984]

Featuring Alvin Ahoy-boy and His Chipmunk Singers. Produced by Millard Clark; with Louis Ballard, Dusty Miller, Paul Pahdocony, and Chris White.

Subsection 3-D 3
Comedy Recordings

Burnstick, Don—(Cree)

DISCOGRAPHY:
Redskin Radio [Sunshine 2003]
You Might Be a Redskin [Sunshine 1999]
Redskin Club [Sunshine 1998]

Craig, Vince *See*: Contemporary Music

Culture Clash—(Chicano)

This trio of comedic activists formed in 1984 on Cinqo de Mayo in San Francisco's Mission District. Other projects include *Radiomission* and a tribute to the Nuyorican (New York Puerto Rican) poetry and political movement of the 1970s.

DISCOGRAPHY:
Life, Death, and Revolutionary Comedy [Xicano Records and Film 2000] unreleased

Hill, Charlie—(Oneida)

A radio presentation of satirical monologues and skits on anthropology and society; Peggy Berryhill and Frank Blythe, producers.

DISCOGRAPHY:
Club Red [AIROS 2000]

Appearances:
Songs for Chiapas "Off the Record" [Ra Records 1999] comp *See*: Contemporary Compilations

Lacapa, Drew—
(Hopi-Apache-Tewa-Scots-Irish)

From Arizona, Lacapa offers perspectives on cultural quirks mixed with views of sexuality and politics.

DISCOGRAPHY:
4 Real [LM-70489] DVD
A One Night Stand in Paradise [DLMusic/ Knifewing Segura Records 2000]

Subsection 3-D 4
Interview Recordings

Buffy Sainte-Marie and Stewart Copeland [CSPS 847A] *See*: Contemporary Music

Interview clips from her first MCA release *Buffy* [1974].

Buffy Sainte-Marie: Interview Disc [Capitol/EMI/Chrysalis/Ensign 1992] *See*: Contemporary Music

Twenty-three answers with four song IDs, along with cues and times; to promote *Coincidence and Likely Stories*.

The Jesse Ed Davis Interview [Epic 1973] seven-inch vinyl *See*: Contemporary Music

Interviewer: B. Michael Reed of KMET, Los Angeles, California.

John Trudell: The Radio Interview [Asitis/Effective Records 2003] *See*: Contemporary Music

Ten songs from six albums released between 1983 and 1992, w/ eleven interview clips.

Kashtin: From the Album Innu [Musicor 1991 PPFLC-5021] *See*: Contemporary Music

Ten interview clips; contains the single "Tshinuau."

Laura Vinson: Voices on the Wind Radio Special [Homestead 1995] *See*: Contemporary Music

Host introduction with songs and interview clips.

Legends: I Am an Eagle, Radio Special and Interview Clips [First Nations Music 1994] *See*: Contemporary Compilations: *I Am an Eagle, Legends*

Narrated by Shingoose (*See*: Contemporary Music) w/ interview clips and selected tracks from the *Legends* project.

The Rita Coolidge Radio Special [A&M 1978] *See*: Contemporary Music

Tom Jackson: The Huron Carole [Tomali 2001] *See*: Contemporary Music

Legends and Storytelling

See: Audio Books

Billie, Chief Jim *See*: Contemporary Music

DISCOGRAPHY:
Seminole Fire [SOAR 2000]

Bruchac, Joseph—(Abenaki) *See*: Traditional/Archival Group: Dawnland Singers

DISCOGRAPHY:
Keepers of the Earth [Fulcrum 1992]
The Boy Who Lived with the Bears and Other Iroquois Stories [Harper Collins 1992]
Gluscabe Stories [Yellow Moon Press 1990]
Abenaki Stories [YMP-101]

Deloria, Vine, Jr.—(Lakota)

The stories are accompanied by Lakota songs.

DISCOGRAPHY:
Stories of the Lakota [Canyon 6151] D

Goble, Paul

DISCOGRAPHY:
Star Boy [Dakotah/SOAR 1994] music by XIT: "Birth" and "Awakening" *See*: Contemporary Music
Love Flute [Dakotah/SOAR 1993] w/ Bryan Akipa (*See*: Flute Music); Earl Bullhead (*See*: Traditional/Archival Solo); read by Tom Bee.

Hayes, Joe

DISCOGRAPHY:
And It Is Still That Way [Trails West 1988]
Coyote and Joe Hayes [Trails West 1983]

High Bear, Martin—(Lakota)

DISCOGRAPHY:
The White Buffalo Calf Woman [FC-3002]

Jumper, Betty Mae—(Seminole) *See*: Traditional/Archival Compilations: *Heartbeat: Voices of First Nations Women*

DISCOGRAPHY:
The Corn Lady [independent 1996]

Knockwood, Noel—(Mi'kmaq)

DISCOGRAPHY:
Mic Mac Language and Culture [independent 1999]

Locke, Kevin—(Lakota) *See*: Flute Music

DISCOGRAPHY:
The Flood and Other Lakota Stories [Harper Collins 1993]

Marshall, Joseph M., III—(Lakota)

"Native American wisdom on ethics and character." Excerpts from Marshall's book, with flute music by Keith Bear, Joseph Fire Crow, and Andrew Vasquez (*See*: Flute Music).

DISCOGRAPHY:
The Lakota Way [Makoche 2003]

McCormack, Tom

DISCOGRAPHY:
Tales from Western Tribes [independent 1995]

Mixashawn—(Maheekanew) *See:* Contemporary Music

DISCOGRAPHY:
Native Songs and Stories [independent 1991]

Peterson, Helen—(Makah)

DISCOGRAPHY:
Songs and Stories from Neah Bay [Canyon CR-6125]

Pratt, Vince E.

DISCOGRAPHY:
The Story of Iktomi [FC-3003]

Red Thunder Cloud

DISCOGRAPHY:
Songs and Legends of the Catawba, Vol. 2 [RTC-02]
Songs and Legends of the Catawba, Vol. 1 [RTC-01]

Ross, Gayle—(Cherokee)

DISCOGRAPHY:
How Rabbit Tricked Otter [Four Winds Trading]

Shenandoah, Joanne—(Oneida) *See:* Contemporary Music

DISCOGRAPHY:
All Spirits Sing [EB-72748]

Silverbird, J. Reuben— (Dineh-Apache) *See*: Flute Music

Narrated by J. Reuben with flute music by Perry Silverbird. The double album contains legends from various nations, including: Dineh, Zuni, Tohono O'odham, Akimel O'odham, Santo Domingo, Hopi, Apache, Tewa, Onondaga, Blackfoot, Anishnabe, Cheyenne, Pawnee, Paiute, Sioux, Choctaw, Cherokee, Seminole, Chickasaw, Creek, and Nez Perce. Additional musicians include Mark Linebury and Rob Russo, w/ traditional singers; recorded at Positron Studios, New York City, New York.

DISCOGRAPHY:
The World in Our Eyes: Native American Vision of Creation [Celestial Harmonies 1991]

Silverheels, Jay—(Mohawk) *See*: Radio Plays

1920–1980
Born Harry Smith, May 26, 1920, Brantford, Ontario, died March 5, 1980. The two-cassette and LP Caedmon releases were designed for the classroom with filmstrips, accompanying script, and teacher's guide by Dr. Jerry Blanche (Choctaw).

DISCOGRAPHY:
Indian Wisdom Stories [Caedmon CR532]
The Fire Plume [Caedmon 1973]

Appearances:
Here's Johnny: Magic Moments from the Tonight Show [Casablanca 1974] comp

Smith-Littlejohn, Cathy—(Cherokee)

DISCOGRAPHY:
Cherokee Legends, Vol. 2 [TCL10C770]
Cherokee Legends, Vol. 1 [TCL10C769]

Thomason, Dovie

DISCOGRAPHY:

Lessons from the Animal People [Yellow Moon Press 1996] w/ Ulali *See*: Contemporary Music

Wopila-A Giveaway [Yellow Moon Press-102] w/ Kevin Locke *See*: Flute Music

Tsonakwa—(Abenaki)

DISCOGRAPHY:

Echoes of the Night: Native American Legends of the Night Sky [TSP-7145] w/ Dean Evenson and R. Carlos Nakai *See*: Flute Music

Welcome the Caribou Man [T-1003]

Reflections [T-1001]

The Flood and Other Lakota Stories [T-1000]

Wilson, Chesley Goseyun *See*: Traditional/Archival Solo

Wilson, Elizabeth—(Nez Perce)

Songs and stories from ninety-one-year-old Elizabeth Wilson were originally recorded in October 1972.

DISCOGRAPHY:

Nez Perce Stories [Wild Sanctuary WSC-1601]

Legends (Miscellaneous)

American Indian Circles of Wisdom [independent 1995]

Read by Cheewa James. Featuring Mary Youngblood, flute; Frank Ryan, guitar; Awenede's Singers.

American Indian Myths and Legends

Read by Richard Erdoes and Alfonso Ortiz.

Drums across the Tundra [Wild Sanctuary 1992] *See*: Arctic/Circumpolar Compilations

The Elders Speak [Makoche 1999] enhanced CD-ROM

Mary Louis Defender Wilson (Dakota-Hidatsa) and Eagle Heart (Cree-Anishnabe). In 2000, this project received three NAMA Awards for Best Spoken Word Recording, Best Traditional Recording, and Best Historical Recording.

Enchanted Spring: An American Legend [Folkways 1966]

Told by Princess Nowedonah; incidental music by Dennis Starin.

Glooscap and His Magic: Legends of the Wabanaki [Caedmon 1979]

Read by Rita Moreno, produced by Kay Hill.

I Am an Eagle: The Music from the Legends Project [First Nations Music 1994]

Music and spoken-word interpretations of various legends; featuring ElizaBeth Hill, Bob Crawford, Murray Porter, Gloria Eshkibok, Lawrence Martin.

Inuit Legends [CBC 2002] two CDs

Jeannie Arreak-Kullualik and Annie Ford, translations; Jennifer Nalugnig, singing; Leah Shaw, producer.

My Relatives Say [Makoche 2001] enhanced

Traditional Dakota stories as told by Mary Louise Defender Wilson. Also known as Gourd Woman, Mary Louise was born into a family of traditional storytellers on the Standing Rock Reservation, South Dakota. For her work with language and her craft, she received a National Heritage Fellowship from the National Endowment for the Arts, a NAMA Award for Best Spoken Word Recording, the National Education Association's H. Council Trenholm Memorial Award for Human and Civil Rights, and a Notable Document Award from the Government Documents Round Table of the American Library Association.

Native American Legends [Castle/ Pulse 1998] bootleg

The album utilizes tracks lifted from archival recordings (public domain) from various nations, including Dineh, Sioux, Apache, Zuni, Flathead, San Ildefonso, Plains, and Canadian Plains.

Native Legends and Storytelling [Glooscap Communications Group 1989]

Walter Bonaise and Wilfred Peltier, story advisors; read by Allan Deleary (See: Contemporary Music: Seventh Fire).

Navajo Bird Tales [Caedmon 1970]

Told by Hosteen Clah Chee, recounted by Arthur Junaluska.

The Pueblo Indians in Story, Song, and Dance [Caedmon 1955]

Sung and told by Swift Eagle.

Sacred Twins and Spider Woman and Other Navajo Creation Stories [Harper-Collins 1992]

Traditional stories retold by Geri Keams (Dineh).

Voices from the Past Still with Us, Vol. 1 [Akwesasne Radio-CKON]
Voices from the Past Still with Us, Vol. 2 [Akwesasne Radio-CKON]

The series features quotes from historical leaders read in English and Mohawk, w/ synthesizer accompaniment.

Whispering Tree: Anishnabe Stories and Songs [Makoche 2000]
See: Contemporary Compilations

Featured performers include Annie Humphrey, John Trudell, Pato Hoffman, Larry Long, Anne Dunn and Friends.

Subsection 3-D 7
Poetry Recordings

Akiwenzie-Damm, Kateri— (Anishnabekwe)

Born February 3, 1965, Scarborough, Ontario. In addition to her appearance on Maya Music Group projects, Akiwenzie-Damm endured the long process of assembling a large complement of artists for her first independent recording project, including Maori hip-hop artists Tekupu (a.k.a. Dean Hapeta), DJ Rys B and DJ Koru; South American flute players Gucho Abanto and Marcos Arcentales of Kanatan Aski (*See*: Contemporary Music: Pura Fe); Algonquin-Mohawk musician Raven Polson-Lahache, Muscogee singer Johnny Thorpe, and poet Joy Harjo.

DISCOGRAPHY:
The Nishin Spoken Word Project [independent 2001]

Appearances:
Free Yourself Free Us All [Maya Music Group 1988] comp *See*: Poetry Compilations

Alexie, Sherman—(Spokane) *See*: Jim Boyd

Born October 7, 1966, Wellpinit, Washington. This celebrated author has made important contributions to contemporary Native literature; his collection of stories *The Lone Ranger and Tonto Fistfight in Heaven* [Atlantic Monthly Press 1993] was the basis for the film *Smoke Signals* [Chris Eyre, 1998].

DISCOGRAPHY:
Indian Killer [Warner 1996] audio book
Spokane Language [Spokane Tribes of Indians 1996]

Appearances:
Jim Boyd:

Reservation Blues [Thunder Wolf 1996]
Various:
Honor [Daemon 1996] comp *See*: Contemporary Compilations
Talking Rain [Tim Kerr Records 1995] comp

Annesley, Bob—(Cherokee)

Born February 11, 1943. Recognized for his work with awards for the 1986 Master Artist of the Five Civilized Tribes and membership in the American Indian and Cowboy Artists of America. Annesley's collection of poetry is accompanied by Fernando Cellicion and Doc Tate Nevaquaya, flute (*See*: Flute Music); Millard Clark, percussion.

DISCOGRAPHY:
Touch the Fire [Indian Sounds 1991]

Armstrong, Jeanette—(Okanagan)

Born 1948, Penticton Indian Reserve, British Columbia. Armstrong is an educator and lecturer on Native rights and author; her books include the acclaimed novel *Slash* [Theytus Books 1985].

DISCOGRAPHY:

Appearances:
Word Up [Virgin 1995] comp *See*: Poetry Compilations
Till the Bars Break [Maya/Revolutionary] comp *See*: Contemporary Compilations: The Fire This Time

Bush, Barney—(Shawnee) *See*: Contemporary Music: John Trudell

Born 1945. His work has been translated into French, Frisian, Macedonian, Serbian, Spanish, and Yugoslavian. An extension of the *Oyate* project featuring Tony Hymas, piano, and Tony Coe, clarinet; his two-

CD set of poetry and prose is mixed with modern classical, techno, and traditional music.

DISCOGRAPHY:
Remake of the American Dream, Vol. 1 [Nato 1990, France] w/ Shawnee Remnant Band Drum
Remake of the American Dream, Vol. 2 [Nato 1990, France] w/ Ed Tate Nevaquaya, flute
"Kintpuash" single from *Oyate* [Nato/ World 1990/1998, France] comp, read by John Trudell *See*: Contemporary Compilations

Connor, Celeste—(Chiricahua Apache)

Connor's work was recorded in San Francisco, with musicians Jeff Tomhave and Bruce Manning.

DISCOGRAPHY:
Cathexis [Komotion 1990]
A Vanity Project [Komotion 1990]

DeBassige, Mary Lou C.—(Anishnabekwe)

Born 1944, Whitefish River Reserve, Ontario, and grew up in West Bay on Manitoulin Island. DeBassige's seventeen-minute poem "West Bay Reservation" is included in a collection of short fiction by six women writers.

DISCOGRAPHY:

Appearances:
Some Imagining Women [Women's Press/ Verse to Vinyl 1989] comp

Gordon, Roxy—(Choctaw) *See*: Contemporary Music

Harjo, Joy—(Muscogee) *See*: Contemporary Music: Harjo, Kateri Akiwenzie-Damm; Audio Books

Henson, Lance—(Cheyenne)

Raised by his grandparents in Calumet, Oklahoma, Henson, a former marine, is a member of the Black Belt Association, the Cheyenne Dog Warrior Society, and the NAC (*See*: Peyote Music Solo and Group). He earned his bachelor's degree in English and a master's degree in creative writing. His album consists of short readings, and other work by Henson is set to music by the Italian heavy metal band Not Moving.

DISCOGRAPHY:
Song of Myself [Wide 1989, Italy]
In a Dark Mist [Cross Cultural Communications Press 1982] cass; translated from Cheyenne to English

Johnson, E. Pauline; a.k.a. Tekahionwake—(Mohawk)

1861–1913
Born March 10, 1861, Chiefswood Estate, Brantford, Ontario. This celebrated author and poet toured worldwide in times of massive upheaval for Native people. Educated and raised in a privileged class of both Mohawk and Canadian society, she enabled herself to speak out on behalf of Native rights through her performances. She passed away in Vancouver, British Columbia, March 7, 1913. Her most famous work, "The Song My Paddle Sings," was recorded by Hannah Polowy and Mitch Sago around 1967 and again in 2003 on a compilation by Six Nations writers.

DISCOGRAPHY:
The World of Pauline Johnson [Arc ACM-5004 Citation Series]

Appearances:
Onkwawennahson'a "Our Voices" [independent 2003] comp

Redbird, Duke—(Metis) *See*: Contemporary Music: Winston Wuttunee

Born March 18, 1939, Saugeen First Nations, Ontario. Troubadour, activist, journalist, filmmaker, entrepreneur, poet, and one-time member of the Company of Young Canadians. With Shingoose (*See*: Contemporary Music), he cowrote music for Glen Campbell and made several appearances at folk festivals during the 1970s. He released his first full album in 1999. As a visual artist, filmmaker, and restaurant owner, he also hosted a Native entertainment segment for City-TV, Toronto, Canada.

DISCOGRAPHY:
In Other Words [Staring in the Sun Music 1999]
Duke Redbird the Poet [Staring in the Sun 1994]

Appearances:
Winston Wuttunee:
See the Arrow [Sunshine SSLP-4004]
Various:
Mariposa [Mariposa 1977] comp *See*: Contemporary Compilations

Trudell, John—(Santee) *See*: Contemporary Music

Poetry Compilations

Aboriginal Hitch-Hike Rap [Maya Music Group 1988]

Words by Pat Andrade, music by J. Rock and the Conspiracy Crew w/ Sri.

America Fears the Drum [Irresistible/Revolutionary 1992]

Poetry and music project by San Francisco–based producer Don Paul, fashioned after the Maya Music projects; contains "Mourning Song" by Nilak Butler.

Before Columbus Foundation [Folkways 1980] *See*: Contemporary Music: Joy Harjo

Collection of poets from across America, featuring some of Harjo's first recorded performances.

The Death of John Wayne [Maya Music Group 1989] cass

A collection of poetry set to electronic, traditional, and reggae music; with Lee Maracle (Metis), Brian Wright-McLeod (Dakota-Anishnabe), Thom E. Hawke and the Pineneedles (*See*: Contemporary Music: Seventh Fire), HMS Dub, and Chip Yarwood.

The Fire This Time: *Till the Bars Break* [Revolutionary/Maya 1991] *See*: Contemporary Compilations

Lineup: Jeannette Armstrong, Henry Kaiser, Seventh Fire (*See*: Contemporary Music), Florene and Rebecca Belmore. Received a Juno nomination, 1992.

Free Yourself Free Us All [Maya Music Group 1988] cass

Lineup: Taylor Jane Green; Kateri Damm; Krin Thomas; Sonia Sanchez; Mary Carrielle; Victoria Freeman; J. Rock and the Conspiracy Crew.

Native American Meditations [New World Music 1999, United Kingdom]

Produced by Brooke and Steve Schiavi, this collection of songs, natural sounds with words, and quotations comes with the promise to connect the listener to Mother Earth and all the listener's relatives. Well, maybe not, but it is a well-produced selection with appearances by friends and family. Proceeds from album sales are earmarked for Pathways to Spirit, a nonprofit organization established to respond to emergencies on the Standing Rock, Cheyenne River, and Pine Ridge Reservations. Recorded on location in the Black Hills, South Dakota; narrators include P. J. Coyote Caller Birosik (Tungus-Chumash); Joe Chasing Horse (Lakota); June Dogskin (Lakota); Marvin and Nyla Helper (Lakota); Bernard Ice (Lakota); Timothy Kills-In Water (Lakota); Rosalie Little Thunder (Lakota); Everett Poor Bear (Lakota); Brooke and Steve Schiavi (Cherokee); Fred Sinkevich (Cherokee); David Swallow Jr. (Lakota); Cordell Tulley (Dineh). Musicians and singers include: Nyla Helper (Lakota); Eli Battese (Lakota); Ervin Buffalo Boy Pete (Dineh); Marvin Helper (Lakota); Christopher and Gabriel Lee (Dineh); Everett Poor Thunder (Lakota); Richard Valentine (Oneida); Justes Wilson (Lakota).

Oyate [Nato/World 1990/1998] *See*: Contemporary Compilations

Not strictly a spoken-word collection, this album does contain some rare tracks. Tom Bee performs "Dreamer of Visions," a poem about Sitting Bull, accompanied by modern classical and rock music. Barney Bush wrote "Kintpuash," a poem about Captain Jack, read by John Trudell, who also performs his own work, "Crazy Horse," with Jeff Beck on guitar. Paul Ortega recites "Cochise" with ambient music.

Poetry Is Not a Luxury [Maya Music Group 1987] cass

Poetry and music with Greg Young-Ing (Chinese-Cree), Ahdri Zhini Mandiela, Lee Maracle, Pineshi Gustin, Lenore Keeshig-Tobias (Anishnabekwe), Daniel David Moses (Lene Lenape), Afua Cooper, HMS Dub.

The Theft of Paradise [Maya Music Group 1988] cass

A collection of music and words by Macka B, No Means No, N. P. Rapper, Jeanette Armstrong, the Rhythm Pigs, and Rhythm Activism.

United States of Poetry [Mercury 1996]

A massive collection of poets, including Indian cowboy poet Henry Real Bird (Crow), who recites "That Driftwood Feeling," and John Trudell, who reads "Spirit Hunters." The companion video includes writer Jim Northrup (Anishnabe).

Your Silence Will Not Protect You [Maya Music Group MMG-8]

Ninety minutes of innovative work by black and Native poets and performers: the Beatnigs, Benjamin Zephania, Jeanette Armstrong, Lee Maracle, Chuck D., Kateri Damm, Celeste Connor, Macka B., Greg Young-Ing, Chris Martin (*See*: Contemporary Music: Wagon Burner Express), Afua Cooper, Neo Mafia, Art and Soul, Yared Tesfaye, Ahdri Zhini Mandiela, Pete Digangi (*See*: Contemporary Music: Seventh Fire).

Subsection 3-D 9
Radio Plays

See: Contemporary Spoken Word: Testimonials and Memoirs; Miscellaneous

Dead Dog Cafe, Vol. 1 [CBC Radio 1998]
Dead Dog Cafe, Vol. 2 [CBC Radio 1999]
Dead Dog Cafe, Vol. 3 [CBC Radio 2000]
Dead Dog Cafe, Vol. 4 [CBC Radio 2001]

Created by author Thomas King (Greek-Cherokee), the series ran from 1997 to 2000 on CBC Radio.

The Lone Ranger [Coca Cola/Mark 56 Records 1972]
The Lone Ranger [Nostalgia Lane 1977]

This radio series debuted in 1933 and ended in 1955, featuring the voices of Jack Deeds as the Lone Ranger, later replaced by George Seaton, and John Todd as Tonto. The television series featured Clayton Moore as the Lone Ranger and Jay Silverheels (a.k.a. Harry Smith) as Tonto, the only Native to fill the role (*See*: Legends and Storytelling); album produced by George Garabedian.

Straight Arrow [Nabisco/Mark 56 Records 1974]

From the original radio series that aired in the early 1930s. The Straight Arrow character was a full-blood Comanche also known as Steve Adams in the storyline. This was perhaps the first and only radio drama to feature a Native hero; album produced by George Garabedian. No credits

accompany the album, but further research into this era of radio is found in *The Great Radio Heroes* and *Jim Harmon's Nostalgia Catalogue* by Jim Harmon [McFarland 2001].

Subsection 3-D 10
Testimonials and Memoirs

Buffalo Bird Woman [Makoche 11147]

The narrative describes the Hidatsa, who lived near the Missouri River in western North Dakota during the late 1800s; read by Buffalo Bird Woman's great-great-granddaughter, Bonnie Goodbird Wells.

Caribou Commons: Wildlands [Partners of Wildlands and Caribou Commons 1999] *See*: Arctic/Circumpolar Compilations

Lineup: Gwich'in Nation speakers: Norma Kassi, Abraham John Jr., Gilbert James, Sarah James, Mary Tritt; Faith Gimmel, translation. Guest speakers: Louis LaRose (Winnebago); Albert Whitehat Sr. (Lakota).

Dr. Marius C. Barbeau: My Life in Recording Canadian Indian Folklore [Folkways Records and Service 1957] *See*: Traditional/Archival Solo

An Eskimo Woman Talks of Her Life [OISE 1973] *See*: Arctic/Circumpolar Traditional/Archival and Spoken Word

Frank Fools Crow: Holy Man [Native Spirit 1993] produced by Dik Darnell
Fools Crow [Tatanka 1977]

Produced by Dik Darnell and Buddy Red Bow (*See*: Contemporary Music). This 1997 vinyl recording has Chief Fools Crow speaking in Lakota on side one and interpreter Matthew King with the English translation on side two.

Indians and the Earth: Traditional Native Perspectives [NDA] cass

Traditional concepts and contemporary concerns including environment, law, and cosmology, presented by Natives.

Jim Thorpe: Olympic Gold Medalist 1912: The World's Greatest Athlete [Mark 56 Records 1983] two-record set

Produced by George Garabedian, created and edited by Robert W. Wheeler. Features excerpts from speeches and interviews with Jim Thorpe (1887–1953), Jack Dempsey, Dwight D. Eisenhower, George Halas, Tom Harmon, Burt Lancaster, Al Schacht, Leo V. Lyons, and others. Thorpe's 1912 Stockholm Olympic pentathlon and decathlon medals were finally returned five years before he was named Athlete of the Century in January 2000 by *Sports Illustrated* magazine. Thorpe signed on with the New York Giants, the Boston Braves, and the Cincinnati Reds, with a .320 batting average. He was also voted Greatest Football Player of the Half Century by the Associated Press in 1950 and voted Greatest American Football Player in History in a national poll in *Sport* magazine. His talents continue to be recognized and unmatched. In addition to a Pennsylvania town that bears his name, the Jim Thorpe Pro Sports Award was created in 1992, a thirty-two-cent U.S. postage stamp was unveiled in 1999, and May 26 is rec-

ognized as Jim Thorpe Honor Day. (*See*: Contemporary Music: Jack Gladstone.)

Maawanji'iding Gathering Together: Ojibway People, Lake Superior, Wisconsin [Brain Box 1999] CD-ROM

Survival of the Sacred [Oh Yeah Productions 1998]

Speeches recorded December 11, 1998, Santa Cruz, California: John Trudell (*See*: Contemporary Music) and Corbin Harney (*See*: Contemporary Compilations: *Tribal Waters*).

Will Rogers America's Legendary Humorist [Legacy International CD-449]
Will Rogers Original Radio Broadcasts [Mark 56 Records 1975]
Will Rogers' USA [Columbia Masterworks SG30546]

These recordings include highlights from the life of Cherokee humorist, actor, newspaper publisher, Indian cowboy, and California congressman Will Rogers (1879–1935). They are preserved recordings from live shows, interviews, and radio broadcasts. Rogers appeared on-stage nightly with Ziegfeld's Midnight Frolic Show beginning in 1915. Years later, as a syndicated columnist, he was ready to return to the new Ziegeld Follies with new material. He said, "Instead of paying some writer, or myself, to write funny things onstage, I turned to the Congressional Record. Congress has been writing my material for years!" The one-man stage production *Will Rogers' USA* featured James Whitmore in the title role; adaptation directed by Paul Shyre, produced by George Spota, with project consultant Will Rogers Jr.;

recorded live at the Mark Taper Forum Music Center, Los Angeles, California.

Subsection 3-D 11
Miscellaneous

Elders . . . New Voice [CKON FM/ Akwesasne Notes]

Thirteen-part series, circa 1980.

1. *The Opening Address*, Francis Boots
2. *The Creation Story*, Georgia Thomas
3. *The Great Law*, Ernest Benedict
4. *The Cycle of Ceremonies*, Tom Porter (*See*: Spoken Word: Miscellaneous: *Living Voices*)
5. *Plants and Medicines*, Edgar Jock and Tony Barnes
6. *Iroquois Government Models*, Ron LaFrance Sr.
7. *Plants and Their Spiritual Relationship*, Cecilia Mitchell
8. *The Coming of the Peacemaker*, Daniel Thompson
9. *Indian Education*, Ernest Benedict
10. *Diplomacy and the Use of the Wampum*, Francis Boots
11. *The Woman's Role in Iroquois Society*, Ann Jock
12. *Oral Traditions of Our People*, Christina Jock
13. *Conservation and the Environment*, Julius Cook

Honor the Grandmothers [Kitchen Table Productions 1992]

Featured speakers include Celene Not Help Him, Iola Columbus, Cecilia Montgomery, Alice New Holy, Stella Pretty Sounding Flute. Producers, Sarah Penman, Monika Bauerlein, Juanita Esponosa; music by Kevin Locke (*See*: Flute Music), Paula

Horne (*See*: Traditional/Archival Solo), Karen Artichoke, Katherine Grey Day, Donna Haukass (*See*: Powwow Music), Patty Wells.

Jenny's Song [Laughing Dog Plays 1991]

An audio documentary on AIDS w/ actors Eric Schweig, Jani Lauzon, Tina Bomberry, Carol Grey Eyes, Ron Cook, Jack Burning, Tonia Hill, Gary Farmer; title music by Don Ross and Jani Lauzon (*See*: Contemporary Music).

Living Voices/Voces vivas [Smithsonian/National Museum of the American Indian 2001] three CDs

A series of short audio profiles produced for unlimited radio broadcast and representing many ages, traditions, and perspectives. The forty different profiles, three to five minutes in length, are self-contained modules intended for cultural programs or station breaks or as a stand-alone series. *Voces vivas* was a single CD produced in Spanish. Voices include Rebecca Adamson (Cherokee-Swedish); Manuel Hernandez Aguilar (Tzeltal Maya); Mary Ann Andreas (Morongo); Haunani Apoliona (Hawaii); Mitchell Bush (Onondaga); Kapeka Chandler (Hawaii); Katsi Cook (Mohawk); J. R. Cook (Oklahoma Cherokee); Carrie Dann (Western Shoshone); Rosenda de la Cruz Vasquez (Tzotzil Maya); Frank Dukepoo (Hopi); L. Frank (Tongva-Acjachemen); Gksisedtanmoogk (Wampanoag); Diego Mendez Guzman (Tzeltal Maya); Raymundo Hernandez (Coalhuiltec); Linda Hogan (Chickasaw); Bob Haozous (Warm Springs Apache); Oscar Kawagley (Yupiaq); Carolyn Kualii (Hawaii); Iguaniginape Kungiler (Kuna); Chris LaMarr (Paiute-Pitt River; *See*: Contemporary Music: WithOut Reservation); Herbert Locklear (Lumbee); Dorothy

Lorentino (Comanche); Shayai Lucero (Laguna Pueblo); William A. Mehoja Sr. (Kaw); June Alaska Twitchell McAtee (Yup'ik); Richard Milanovich (Agua Caliente Cahuilla Apache); Robert Mirabal (Taos Pueblo; *See*: Contemporary Music); Autumn Morningstar (Choctaw-Blackfoot); Maria de Jesus Patricio (Nahuatl); Linda Poolaw (Delaware); Tom Porter (Mohawk); Puhipau (Hawaii); Lorene Sisquoc (Cahuilla Apache); Dolly Spencer (Inupiak); Marilyn St. Germaine (Blackfoot); Calvin J. Standing Bear (Lakota); Barbara Sutteer (Oklahoma Cherokee); Charlene Teters (Spokane); Josephine Wapp (Comanche).

The Red Road to Sobriety [Hazelden 1991; Kifaru Productions 1997]

This audio documentary on recovery from alcohol and substance abuse was produced by Peggy Berryhill and Dick Brooks.

Sugar Blues: Too Many Diabetic Indians [Laughing Dog Productions 1993]

This audio documentary on diabetes features an all-Native cast, including Margaret Cozry, Annie General, Ande Fuller, Eric Schweig, Vince Manitowabi, Pam Matthews. Music by Don Ross (*See*: Contemporary Music); Kelly McGowan, backup vocals; David Woodhead, fretless bass; Al Cross, drums; Matthew Fleming, percussion.

Three Messages from Ray Fadden [Akwesasne Notes 1980]

Recorded at the museum near Akwesasne, New York, this project offers the Iroquois perspective of history and of scientific, political, and societal structures.

SECTION 4
Flute Music

The flute has held a special place as an instrument of storytelling, courtship, healing, and entertainment in Native cultures throughout the continent from South America to the Tundra. The flute at one time was an instrument traditionally used by men to help bring them back into balance with themselves and to impart oral history within the community. Flutes vary in size and can be constructed from a variety of materials, including wood, cane, clay, antler, and bone. Some of the smaller ones are constructed of willow and are about the size of a penny whistle, with an open hole that contains a piece of wood that directs the air into one side of the tube. The largest flutes measure approximately four feet in length, and some have two air chambers. The smallest flute is the eagle bone (taken from the bird's ulna). Various lengths and sizes of the eagle bone are used only for certain melodies. The eagle bone whistle continues to be used in Sundance ceremonies but is also a part of the regalia of certain societies. At one time, it was also used as a hunting caller, and there was a complete philosophy on its history and use.

The most popularized type of flute is what's known as the Southern Plains Kiowa/Comanche end-blown block flute. A similar instrument also originated in the northeastern region of North America around Nova Scotia and Maine and was in wide use throughout the Woodlands region up until the mid-1700s. In the making of an end-blown block flute, two pieces of wood are hollowed out, leaving a small block of wood under the tone hole to force the air through the carved depression called the roost; usually, a carved bird is placed over the air hole, which is known as the nest; the bird can be adjusted to alter the tone. There are usually three to six finger holes; the wind hole at the other end is sometimes carved into a bird's head or any animal form, then decorated with any traditional symbol and perhaps dyed with colors.

For many decades after colonization, the art of flute playing was all but silent—kept alive by only a handful of artists in the twentieth century, including Doc Tate Nevaquaya, Tom Mauchahty-Ware, John Rainer, and Stan Snake. The late Hawk Littlejohn (1941–2000), a Cherokee flute maker from the Smoky Mountains, is an-other key figure credited with keeping the tradition alive.

The resurgence of the powwow in the mid-1970s was instrumental in reviving flute music by providing artists such as R. Carlos Nakai the opportunity to meet and learn about the flute and its history from the traditional people. Sadly, this revival would also open the door to years of commercial exploitation and misinterpretation resulting from a proliferation of recordings by non-Native and New Age opportunists. The tradition nevertheless endures and is even flourishing at a pace that has made this section necessary. Although biographical information is not provided for all the artists listed here, it is important to note the number of recordings that have been made in a relatively brief period of time in relation to the tradition itself.

Section 4-A
Flute Music Recordings

Akipa, Bryan—(Sisseton Wahpeton–Dakota)

DISCOGRAPHY:
Eagle Dreams [Makoche 2001]
Thunder Flute [SOAR 1998]
Mystic Moments [SOAR 1994]
The Flute Player [Makoche 1993]

Appearances (listed alphabetically):
Paul Goble (*See*: Contemporary Spoken Word: Legends and Storytelling):
Love Flute [Dakotah/SOAR 1993]
Takini (*See*: Traditional/Archival Group):
Musique et chants des Lakota Sioux [Le Chant du Monde 1994, France]
Various:
Alcatraz Is Not an Island [James Fortier, 2002] score
Across Indian Lands [SOAR 1999] comp *See*: Powwow Compilations
Soaring Hearts Tribal Peoples, Vol. 1 [SOAR 1996] comp *See*: Traditional/ Archival Compilations
Tribal Winds: Music from Native American Flutes [Earth Beat! 1996] comp

Anakwad; a.k.a. Frank Montano— (Anishnabe) *See*: Contemporary Music: Soulfood

Born March 25, 1941, Red Cliff Chippewa Reservation, Wisconsin. Anakwad began playing music in his midteens and continues today with several projects involving community elders, flute, drumming, and acoustic guitar.

DISCOGRAPHY:
Sky Spirits [Soul Food 2001]
Closing the Circle [independent 1994]
Spirit Visions [Northword Press 1994]
Lake Superior Visions [Northword Press 1994]
The Spirit Sings [Northword Press 1992]
Woodland Winds: The Woodland Consort [Chequamegon Music 1990]
Eternal Journey [independent 1989]
Reservation Reflections [independent 1988]

Barney, Geraldine—(Dineh) *See*: Contemporary Music; Traditional/ Archival Solo

DISCOGRAPHY:

Appearances:
Heartbeat: Voices of First Nations Women [Smithsonian Folkways 1995] comp *See*: Traditional/Archival Compilations
Music of New Mexico: Native American Traditions [Smithsonian Folkways 1992] comp *See*: Contemporary Compilations

Bear, Keith—(Mandan-Hidatsa) *See*: Contemporary Spoken Word: Legends and Storytelling: Joseph M. Marshall III

Bear began researching Mandan flute songs from historical archives. His *Earthlodge* album was recorded in a replica of the Mandan dwelling.

DISCOGRAPHY:
Earthlodge [Makoche 2000] enhanced
Echoes of the Upper Missouri [Makoche 1994]

Appearances:
Joseph M. Marshall III:
The Lakota Way [Makoche 2003]
Various:
People of the Willows [Makoche 1999] comp *See*: Contemporary Compilations
Lewis and Clark: Sounds of Discovery [Makoche 1998] comp *See*: Traditional/ Archival Compilations

Bellanger, Joe—(Anishnabe) *See*: Contemporary Compilations: *Oyate*

Bird, Gordon— (Mandan-Hidatsa-Arikira) *See*: Contemporary Music: Featherstone

DISCOGRAPHY:
Music of the Plains [Featherstone FS-4007]

Cedar Wind

Christine Ibach (Cree), traditional flute, with Al Jewer, classical flute. The project combines European and Native flute music.

DISCOGRAPHY:
Kindred Spirits
Feather on the Wind

Cellicion, Fernando—(Zuni Pueblo)

DISCOGRAPHY:
Kokopelli Dreams [Indian Sounds 1993]
Buffalo Spirit [Indian Sounds 1991] produced by Millard Clark
Traditional and Contemporary Indian Flute [Indian Sounds IS-5061]
Traditional Indian Flute [Indian Sounds 1988] produced by Millard Clark

Appearances:
Bob Annesley:
Touch the Fire [Indian Sounds 1991] *See*: Contemporary Spoken Word: Poetry
Various:
Tribal Winds: Music from Native American Flutes [Earth Beat! 1996] comp
Music of New Mexico: Native American Traditions [Smithsonian Folkways 1992] comp *See*: Contemporary Compilations

Chase, Brent—(Dineh) *See*: Contemporary Music: Ancient Brotherhood; Powwow Music: Four Mountain Nation Singers

Cody, Robert Tree— (Dakota-Maricopa) *See*: R. Carlos Nakai; Contemporary Music: Blackfire, Native Flamenco, Redhouse Family, Tonemah

The son of Iron-Eyes Cody, a prominent actor and cultural icon of the 1960s and 1970s, Robert found his path in music. An artist-in-residence for the Arizona Commission on the Arts, Cody also worked as a youth counselor and educator; he also traveled the powwow circuit as a traditional dancer and toured internationally as a traditional flute player. He successfully blended traditional music with various contemporary and cross-cultural themes and instruments, including flamenco. *Maze* received the NAMA Award for Best New Age Album, 1999, with Rob Wallace, keyboards; Tony Redhouse (*See*: Contemporary Music: Redhouse Family), percussion; Marlene Cody; Jim Lucero; Jones Benally (*See*: Contemporary Music: Blackfire), vocals.

DISCOGRAPHY:
Reflections [Canyon 2003] w/ Hovia Edwards
Native Brotherhood [New Earth 2001]
Crossroads [Canyon 2000]
Maze [Canyon 1998]
White Buffalo [Canyon 1996]
Dreams from the Grandfather [Canyon 1993]
Young Eagle's Flight [Canyon 1991]
Lullabies and Traditional Songs [Canyon 1990]
Traditional Flute Music North America [Canyon 1988]

Appearances (listed alphabetically):
Blackfire:
Blackfire [Tacoho 1994]
Todi Neesh Zhee Singers:
For All Eternity [Canyon 2001] *See*: Traditional/Archival Group
Tonemah:
The Ghosts of St. Augustine [Red Sky Productions 1997]
Various:
Tribal Legends [Earth Beat! 2002] comp *See*: Contemporary Compilations
Sacred Souls [Manteca 2001, United Kingdom] comp *See*: Contemporary Compilations
Voices across the Canyon, Vol. 4 [Canyon 1999] comp *See*: Contemporary Compilations

Robert Tree Cody. Photo by John Running.

Voices Across the Canyon, Vol. 1 [Canyon 1996] comp *See*: Contemporary Compilations

Councilor, Kyle—(Anishnabe) *See*: Powwow Music

From Northwest Bay, Ontario, Councilor also performed with the Spirit Mountain Singers.

DISCOGRAPHY:
Livin' the Good Life [Arbor 1999]

Appearances:
Spirit Mountain Singers:
Much Respect [Arbor 2000]
Spirit Mountain Singers [Sunshine SSCT 4294]
Thunder Drums, Vol. 1: *The Best of Arbor Records* [Arbor 2001] comp *See*: Powwow Compilations

Crane, Daniel—(Tsuu T'ina)

From the Tsuu T'ina Nation near Calgary, Alberta, Crane has created original songs, including "Bingo Warrior Blues" for the Red Thunder Native Dance Theatre (*See*: Powwow Compilations: *Bismarck Powwow*).

DISCOGRAPHY:
Spirit Dreams [independent 1997]

De Rocha, Troy—(Blackfoot)

From Heart Butte, Montana, De Rocha was raised by his grandparents. He first learned to play fiddle and mandolin before finding the traditional flute.

DISCOGRAPHY:
Shaman's Bone Whistle [independent 1986; reissued on Canyon Records 1996]
Listen My People [independent no date]

Edwards, Herman—(Okanagan)

DISCOGRAPHY:
Flute Music of the Okanagan [Canyon 1986]

Edwards, Hovia— (Shoshone-Dineh-Okanagan)

Edwards was fourteen years old and attending Blackfoot High School in Blackfoot, Idaho, when she recorded her first album. She has toured extensively with her father, Herman Edwards, a flute maker who taught her how to play. She has also performed as a soloist at the Center for the Arts, Scottsdale, Arizona, toured internationally, appeared on the PBS network, and performed at the opening ceremonies for the Winter Olympics, Salt Lake City, Utah, 2002.

DISCOGRAPHY:
Reflections [Canyon 2003] w/ Robert Tree Cody
Morning Star [Canyon 1998]

Appearances:
Voices across the Canyon, Vol. 4 [Canyon 1999] comp *See*: Contemporary Compilations

Estes, George—(Lakota) *See*: Contemporary Music: Dennis Banks

Lakota George created his first album of songs about love and war with electric music, poetry, and flute.

DISCOGRAPHY:
Flute Man [LGE 1998]
Voices of the Flute [LGE 1992]
Songs of a Different Flute: The Last Battle Cry [LGE 1990]

Appearances:
Dennis Banks:
United We Stand—Refusing to Fall [RCR 9770]

Fire Crow, Joseph—(Northern Cheyenne) *See*: Contemporary Spoken Word: Legends and Storytelling: Joseph M. Marshall III

Born in Montana and raised on the Northern Cheyenne Reservation, Fire Crow studied trumpet in primary school and flute from his college instructor, John Rainer. *Cheyenne Nation* received a Grammy nomination for Best Native American Music Album, 2001.

DISCOGRAPHY:
Legend of the Warrior [Makoche 2003]
Cheyenne Nation [Makoche 2000]
Fire Crow [Makoche 1995]
Rising Bird [JFC 1994]
The Mist [JFC 1992]

Joseph Fire Crow. Photo courtesy Makoche Records.

Appearances:
Joseph M. Marshall III:
The Lakota Way [Makoche 2003]
Various:
Tribal Legends [Earth Beat! 2002] comp
  See: Contemporary Compilations
Tribal Dreams [Earth Beat! 2001] comp
  See: Contemporary Compilations
Tribal Winds: Music from Native American Flutes [Earth Beat! 1996] comp

Funmaker—(Dakota) *See*: Contemporary Music: Litefoot

DISCOGRAPHY:
Flute Dreams [Red Vinyl 1997] w/ Tom Ware, guitars

Appearances:
Litefoot Presents the Sounds of Indian Country [Red Vinyl 1999] comp *See*: Contemporary Compilations

Gaskin, Jody Thomas—(Anishnabe) *See*: Contemporary Music: Eagle and Hawk; Powwow Music: Walking Wolf Singers

DISCOGRAPHY:
Native American Flute Songs, Vol. 2 [Sunshine 1999]

Native American Flute Songs, Vol. 1 [Sunshine 1995]
. . . *Part of Being Anishnabe* [Sunshine 1995]

Gomez, Alice—(Mestiza)

DISCOGRAPHY:
While the Eagle Sleeps [Talking Taco Records TTCD-130]

Appearances:
Bears [Silver Wave 2001] sdtk
Prayer for Peace [Silver Wave 2000] comp

Gutierrez, William—(Southern Ute–Dineh)

A veteran performer, Gutierrez has also scored soundtracks for Discovery Channel and PBS documentaries.

DISCOGRAPHY:
Keeper of the Songs [independent 1999]
Raven's Song [Indian Sounds 1997]
Eagle Canyon [Indian Sounds 1995]
Calling the Eagle [Indian Sounds IS-5076]

Appearances:
Tribal Winds: Music from Native American Flutes [Earth Beat! 1996] comp

Hacker, Jason—(Choctaw) *See*: Paul Hacker; Contemporary Music: Murray Porter

DISCOGRAPHY:
For Those Who Have Gone before Us [independent no date]
Horses Still Cry [independent no date]

Appearances:
Lacrosse: The Creator's Game [Ken Murch, 1994] documentary sdtk

Hacker, Paul—(Choctaw) *See*: Jason Hacker; Contemporary Music: Murray Porter

DISCOGRAPHY:
Winds of the Past, Vols. 1 and 2 [Hacker 1993]

Appearances:
Lacrosse: The Creator's Game [Ken Murch, 1994] documentary sdtk

Hawk, Dennis—(Cherokee)

Lineup: Dennis Hawk, guitar/percussion/flute; Richard Awonohopay, spoken word; coproduced by John Gibson.

DISCOGRAPHY:
Many Trails [Hawk Sounds 1999]

Henries, Hawk—(Nipmuc-Algonquin)
DISCOGRAPHY:
Tribal Winds: Music from Native American Flutes [Earth Beat! 1996] comp

Herring, Papa John
DISCOGRAPHY:
Tribility [Natural Visions 111] w/ Daniel Waldis
Earth Medicine [Natural Visions 1995]
Inner Windows [Natural Visions 1994] w/ Daniel Waldis, keyboards

Appearances:
Visions and Rhythms, Vol. 1 [SOAR 1998] comp *See*: Contemporary Compilations

High Eagle, J. C.—(Osage-Cherokee)

An influential flute player from Oklahoma, High Eagle has composed dozens of songs, performed with the Milwaukee Symphony Orchestra and the National Sym-phony Orchestra—including twenty shows in the Broadway production of *Makin' Whoopee!*—and scored for the television series *Walker, Texas Ranger*.

Hill, Dan Cecil—(Cayuga-Tuscarora)

Born October 13, 1949, Cattaraugus, New York. Hill's style is more experimental, combining sounds of nature with a variety of natural percussion instruments and flutes he has made from a variety of woods, ceramic, bone, and antler. He is also a silversmith.

DISCOGRAPHY:
Walk Through Creation [independent 1992] cass
Waterlands of Turtle Island [independent 1989] cass
Winter Night Song [independent 1987] cass

Appearances:
Joanne Shenandoah:
Warrior in Two Worlds [Red Feather 2002]
Various:
Kaha:wi [independent 2003] sdtk
Ice Storm [Ang Lee, 1997] sdtk
Dance Me Outside [Rez Films/Denon 1994] sdtk
Requiem for the Americas: Songs from the Lost World [Enigma 1989] comp/sdtk *See*: Contemporary Soundtracks
Powwow Highway [Handmade Films 1988] *See*: Contemporary Soundtracks

Karsten, Ralph
DISCOGRAPHY:
Bow and Arrow [Atma Sphere Music Systems 1994]
Grandfather's Gift [Atma Sphere Music Systems 1992]

Ketcheshawno—(Creek)

DISCOGRAPHY:

Riding the Wind [SOAR 1992] w/ Larry
   Gordon Dubois (Sac-Fox)

Kingfisher, Choogie—(Cherokee)
See: Contemporary Music: Cherokee
National Children's Choir

Appears on *Voices of the Creator's Children* [Cherokee Nation 2001] with Rita
Coolidge, the Cherokee National Children's Choir, and Jeffrey Parker.

Little Leaf, Charles—(Blackfoot)

Born and raised in Warm Springs, Oregon.
Little Leaf received his first flute from
R. Carlos Nakai in the late 1980s. He began
recording a few years later and established
Redwood Productions, specializing in
music and jewelry.

DISCOGRAPHY:

Heart of the Wolf [Redwood Productions
   2000] w/ Karen Therese
Ancient Reflections [Redwood Productions
   1999]
Whispers of Earth Medicine [Redwood
   Productions 1996] cass

Locke, Kevin—(Hunkpapa Lakota)
See: Contemporary Music: Lunar
Drive; Traditional/Archival Solo:
Evelyn "Sissy" Goodhouse

Born 1952, given the traditional name
Tokeya Inajin (The First to Arise). Since
the early 1970s, Locke has sought out traditional elders to learn about the flute,
including his uncle Abraham and the late
Richard Fool Bull, a one-hundred-year-old
elder and flute maker. Ed Wahpeconiah
(*See*: Contemporary Compilations: *Oyate*)
also helped Locke begin his journey. A
hoop dancer who performs with twenty-
eight hoops, Locke has performed in more
than seventy-one countries and remains
true to the traditional forms of the instrument. He provided flute music on Dovie
Thomason's *Wopila-A Giveaway* (*See*:
Contemporary Spoken Word: Legends and
Storytelling) and the score for *Dances with
Wolves* [Kevin Costner, 1990]. For *The First
Flute*, Locke received NAMA Awards for
Best Traditional Recording and Flutist of
the Year, 2000.

DISCOGRAPHY:

The First Flute [Makoche 1999] (interpre-
   tations of songs recorded 1911–14 by
   Frances Densmore)
Locke Box: Limited Edition Box Set
   [MC0122C] 4 cass
Open Circle [Makoche 1996] INDIE Award
   nominee
Keepers of the Dream, Vol. 2 of *Dream
   Catchers Series* [Earth Beat! 1994]
The Flash in the Mirror [Meyer 1993]
Dream Catcher [Earth Beat! 1992]
The Seventh Direction [Makoche 1990;
   Meyer 1994]
. . . Make Me a Hollow Reed . . . [indepen-
   dent 1990]
Lakota Love Songs and Stories [indepen-
   dent 1990] w/ spoken word
Love Songs of the Lakota [Indian House
   1983]
Lakota Wiikijo Olowan, Vol. 2 [Feather-
   stone FS-4004]
Lakota Wiikijo Olowan, Vol. 1 [Feather-
   stone FS-4001]

Appearances (listed alphabetically):
Evelyn "Sissy" Goodhouse:
Tiwahe [Makoche 1997]
Lunar Drive:
Here at Black Mesa, Arizona [Nation 1996,
   United Kingdom]
Various:
Tribal Legends [Earth Beat! 2002] comp
   See: Contemporary Compilations
Tribal Dreams [Earth Beat! 2001] comp
   See: Contemporary Compilations
Proud Heritage [Indian House 1996] comp
   See: Traditional/Archival Compilations

Tribal Winds: Music from Native American Flutes [Earth Beat! 1996] comp
Honor the Grandmothers [Kitchen Table Productions 1992] *See*: Contemporary: Spoken Word: Miscellaneous
Keepers of the Earth: Native American Stories [Fulcrum 1992] *See*: Contemporary Spoken Word: Audio Books
The Flood and Other Lakota Stories [T-1000] *See*: Contemporary Spoken Word: Audio Books
Drum Songs and Painted Dreams [Sunshine 1988] comp *See*: Contemporary Compilations
Our Sacred Land [Chris Spotted Eagle Productions 1984] sdtk

Lopez, Mac—(Shoshone)

DISCOGRAPHY:
Footprints of Our Ancestors [Whirlwind Studios 1999] w/ Tom Thompson
Wind Messengers [Whirlwind Studios 1996] w/ Lee Johnson

Maracle, David R.—(Mohawk)

Born February 15, 1962, Tyendinaga, Mohawk Territory, near Belleville, Ontario. A carver, visual artist, and self-taught musician, Maracle helped develop several creative projects with contemporary musicians, including Yodeca, with guitarist Dave Deleary of Seventh Fire (*See*: Contemporary Music).

DISCOGRAPHY:
Between Heaven and Earth [independent 2000]
Speaking Winds [independent 1999]
Caught Between Two Worlds [independent 1995]

Appearances:
Yodeca:
Unsigned—05 [NXNE/Indie Pool 2002] comp
Earth Fusion [independent 2001]

Maracle, Thomas B.—(Mohawk)

Born December 20, 1949, Tyendinaga Mohawk Territory, near Belleville, Ontario. Gallery owner and carver, Thomas Maracle began playing the flute through the inspiration of his land and family. Additional musicians in his recordings include Tammy Green Johnston, vocals; David Finkle, bass; Buzz Morrow, mandolin.

DISCOGRAPHY:
Different Vibes [independent 2001]
Spirit Land Band [independent 1998/2001]
Catch the Dream of the Flute [independent 1996]

Mauchahty-Ware, Tom— (Kiowa-Comanche) *See*: Powwow Music

Acclaimed flutist from Anadarko, Oklahoma, considered to be one of the best players of the genre.

DISCOGRAPHY:
Morning Star [Indian Sounds IS-5052]
Sunrise [Indian Sounds IS-5051]
The Traditional and Contemporary Indian Flute [Indian Sounds IS-5050]
Flute Songs of the Kiowa and Comanche [Indian House 1978]

Appearances:
Tribal Winds: Music from Native American Flutes [Earth Beat! 1996] comp

McDonald, Jerry—(Mohawk)

Lineup: Jerry McDonald, lead vocals/drums/rattles/flutes; Kris Delorenzi, bass violin/double bass; Jonathan Maracle (*See*: Contemporary Music) guitar/backup vocals/drums/keyboards; Rob Chapman, keyboards/bass; the Peacemakers Drum, drummers and singers.

DISCOGRAPHY:
Mohawk Transitions [independent 1998]

Mirabal, Robert—(Taos Pueblo) *See*: Contemporary Music

Nakai, R. Carlos—(Ute-Dineh) *See*: Contemporary Music: Jackalope, Nakai Quartet, Joanne Shenandoah

Born Raymond Carlos Nakai, April 16, 1946. Nakai is perhaps one of the most prolific and innovative artists of the genre. He enlisted in the military, where he took advantage of the music-training programs. After leaving the service, he studied traditional flute in 1972 and began recording in 1981. As with any flute player, Nakai was mostly self-taught and turned to traditional methods to study the history and mythology surrounding the instrument.

His 1989 album *Canyon Trilogy* went gold in 1997, selling more than five hundred thousand copies in the United States and was the first album of its genre to achieve such popularity. By 2002, Nakai had more than twenty-seven albums in commercial distribution, with more than 2 million album sales worldwide. The 1995 album *Feather, Stone, and Light*, recorded with William Eaton, made the Billboard Critic's Choice and topped the New Age album charts for thirteen weeks.

Nakai's music has been employed in many commercial venues, including Grand Canyon tours and Muzak on some southwestern U.S. regional airlines. Musical explorations and further collaborations include projects with Tibetan monk Nawang Khechong. Nakai coauthored one book, *The Art of the Native American Flute* [Canyon 1996], with ethnomusicologist David P. McAllester. *Sanctuary* received a Grammy nomination for Best Native American Music Album, 2004.

DISCOGRAPHY:
In Beauty, We Return [Canyon 2004] best of
Sanctuary [Canyon 2003]
Songs for Humanity [Silver Wave 2002] best of w/ Peter Kater

R. Carlos Nakai. Photo by John Running.

Fourth World [Canyon 2002]
In a Distant Place [Canyon 2000] w/ William Eaton, Will Clipman, and Nawang Khechong
Ancient Future [Canyon 2000] w/ the R. Carlos Nakai Quartet
Inner Voices [Canyon 1999] classical, w/ the Canyon Symphony Strings
Inside Monument Valley [Canyon 1999] w/ Paul Horn
Big Medicine [Canyon 1998] jazz, w/ the R. Carlos Nakai Quartet
Red Wind [Canyon 1998] w/ William Eaton and Will Clipman
Mythic Dreamer [Canyon 1998]
Winds of Devotion [Earth Sea 1998] w/ Nawang Khechong
Inside Canyon de Chelley [Canyon 1997] w/ Paul Horn

Two World Concerto [Canyon 1997] classical, w/ James DeMars, Blacklodge, and the Canyon Orchestra

Kokopelli's Cafe [Canyon 1996] jazz, w/ the R. Carlos Nakai Quartet

Improvisations in Concert [Silver Wave 1996] w/ Peter Kater

Feather, Stone, and Light [Canyon 1995] w/ William Eaton and Will Clipman

Island of Bows [Canyon 1994]

Native Tapestry [Canyon 1993] w/ James DeMars

Emergence [Canyon 1992]

Migration [Silver Wave 1992] w/ Peter Kater

Spirit Horses: Concerto for Native American Flute [Canyon 1991] w/ James DeMars

Ancestral Voices [Canyon CR-7010] w/ William Eaton and Blacklodge

Honorable Sky [Silver Wave SC-807]

Natives [Silver Wave 1990] w/ Peter Kater

Desert Dance [Celestial Harmonies 13-033]

Canyon Trilogy [Canyon 1989]

Sundance Season [Celestial Harmonies 1988]

Winter Dreams [Canyon CR-7007] w/ William Eaton

Carry the Gift [Canyon 1988] w/ William Eaton

Earth Spirit [Canyon 1987]

Journeys [Canyon 1986]

Cycles [Canyon 1985]

Changes [Canyon 1982]

Appearances:

Tsonakwa:

Echoes of the Night: Native American Legends of the Night Sky [TSP-7145] *See*: Contemporary Spoken Word: Legends and Storytelling

Various:

Tribal Legends [Earth Beat! 2002] comp, w/ William Eaton and Blacklodge *See*: Contemporary Compilations

Sacred Souls [Manteca 2001, United Kingdom] comp, w/ Clipman and Eaton *See*: Contemporary Compilations

Tribal Dreams [Earth Beat! 2001] comp, w/ Peter Kater *See*: Contemporary Compilations

Prayer for Peace [Silver Wave 2000] comp, w/ Peter Kater *See*: Contemporary Compilations

Voices across the Canyon, Vol. 4 [Canyon 1999] comp *See*: Contemporary Compilations

Prophecy: A Hearts of Space Native American Collection [Hearts of Space 1999] comp *See*: Contemporary Compilations

Voices across the Canyon, Vol. 3 [Canyon 1997] comp *See*: Contemporary Compilations

Native American Currents [Silver Wave 1997] comp *See*: Contemporary Compilations

World Flutes, Vol. 1 [Earth Sea Records 1997] comp

Narada World: Global Vision [Narada 1997] two-CD comp

Arctic Refuge [Soundings of the Planet 1996] comp *See*: Arctic/Circumpolar Compilations

Songs of the Spirit [Triloka 1996] comp *See*: Contemporary Compilations

Tribal Winds: Music from Native American Flutes [Earth Beat! 1996] comp, w/ William Eaton

Voices across the Canyon, Vol. 2 [Canyon 1996] comp *See*: Contemporary Compilations

Voices across the Canyon, Vol. 1 [Canyon 1996] comp *See*: Contemporary Compilations

The Best of Silver Wave, Vol. 3: *The Stars* [Silver Wave 1995] comp

Between Father Sky and Mother Earth [Narada 1995] comp

I Am Walking [Narada 1995] comp *See*: Contemporary Compilations

The Way West [Shanachie 1995] sdtk *See*: Contemporary Soundtracks

How the West Was Lost, Vol. 2 [Silver Wave 1995] sdtk *See*: Contemporary Soundtracks

How the West Was Lost, Vol. 1 [Silver Wave SC-801] sdtk *See*: Contemporary Soundtracks

Dance Me Outside [Rez Films/Denon 1994] sdtk *See*: Contemporary Soundtracks

Geronimo, An American Legend [Columbia 1993] sdtk *See*: Contemporary Soundtracks

Peyote [Dance Pool/Sony 1991, Germany] EP w/ Dag Lerner, Jam El-Mar

Oyate [Nato 1990, France] comp *See*: Contemporary Compilations

Selected Awards:

2003: NAMA Best Instrumental Recording, *Fourth World*

2001: NAMA nominations for Record of the Year, Duo/Group of the Year, and Best Instrumental Recording; Grammy nomination, Best New Age Album, *In a Distant Place*

2000: NAMA Best Instrumental Recording, *Inner Voices*

1999: NAMA Best Instrumental Recording, *Red Wind*; Grammy nominations for Best New Age Album, *Inner Voices* and *Inside Monument Valley*

1998: NAMA Best Instrumental Recording, *Two World Concerto*; Grammy nomination for Best New Age Album, *Inside Canyon de Chelley*

1994: Grammy nomination, Best Traditional Folk Album, *Ancestral Voices*; FAITA Outstanding Musical Achievement (Body of Work)

1992: Honorary Doctorate, the University of Arizona, Tucson; Arizona Governor's Art Award

Nevaquaya, Doc Tate—(Comanche)

1932–1996

Born July 3, 1932. Joyce Lee "Doc" Tate Nevaquaya, named after the family physician, Dr. C. W. Joyce, and nicknamed Doc. An accomplished visual artist and flute player, Nevaquaya had a reputation for playing hard-core traditional Comanche flute music, a style that was the result of researching and learning the old songs once thought to be lost. He incorporated the influences of the modern world in songs such as "Pizza Pie." Respected as a master of the instrument, he performed in the most distinguished concert halls and inspired a flute renaissance. In 1986, he received the National Endowment Award for keeping this art form alive. A year later the Comanche Nation of Oklahoma proclaimed the second Friday of October as Doc Tate Nevaquaya Day. He won international acclaim for his unique visual art style depicting traditional Comanche culture and history. He died on March 5, 1996. The 1999 *Legend and Legacy* release contains tracks from Doc Tate and his four sons, Edmond, Timothy, Calvert, and Sonny.

DISCOGRAPHY:

Legend and Legacy [Twin Bulls 1999]

The Master [Semihoye-Shawnee 1992] retitled: *Legends Are Forever*

Comanche Flute [Ethnic Folkways FE-4328 1979]

Appearances:

Bob Annesley:

Touch the Fire [Indian Sounds 1991] *See*: Contemporary Spoken Word: Poetry

Nevaquaya, Ed Tate—(Comanche)

See: Contemporary Spoken Word: Poetry: Barney Bush

Nevaquaya, Lean "Sonny"—(Comanche)

The son of Doc Tate presents his own variations of the instrument with songs for Vietnam War veterans.

DISCOGRAPHY:

Viva Kokopelli! [independent 1997]

Spirit of the Flute [Ancient Sun Music 1993]

Northrup, Ernie—(Hopi)

DISCOGRAPHY:

Hopi Mentor Grandfather [independent E717 1994] recorded at Desert Trax, Tucson, Arizona

Pewewardy, Cornel—(Kiowa-Comanche)

Born 1952, Lawton, Oklahoma. Pewewardy gained traditional knowledge from his uncle. He possesses a great interest in education and preserving traditional culture. He earned a Ph.D. in education and worked as assistant professor of teaching and leadership at the University of Kansas and as the principal of Mounds Park All Nations Magnet School, St. Paul, Minnesota; he received the Minnesota Administrators' Academy Transformational Award. In an effort to preserve the culture, he recorded "Comanche Hymns from the Prairie" with a group of Comanche elders and appeared on the Robbie Robertson project *Contact from the Underworld of Redboy*.

DISCOGRAPHY:

Warrior's Edge [Shortwave Records 1999]
Dancing Buffalo [Music of the World 1994] w/ Alliance West Singers
Spirit Journey [SOAR 1992]
Flute and Player Songs [TMI-02 1987]

Appearances (listed alphabetically):
Nicole LaRoche:
Passion Spirit [Natural Visions 2001]
Robbie Robertson (*See*: Contemporary Music):
Contact from the Underworld of Redboy [Capitol 1998]
Various:
Across Indian Lands [SOAR 1999] comp *See*: Powwow Compilations
Arctic Refuge [Soundings of the Planet 1996] *See*: Contemporary Compilations
Soaring Hearts Tribal Peoples, Vol. 1 [SOAR 1996] comp *See*: Traditional/ Archival Compilations

Between Father Sky and Mother Earth: A Native American Collection [Narada 1995] comp
Various Native American Artists: Solo Flights Two, Vol. 2 [SOAR 1994] comp *See*: Contemporary Compilations

Rainer, John, Jr.—(Taos Pueblo– Creek) *See*: Joseph Fire Crow; Contemporary Music: Lamanite Generation, Arlene Nofchissey; Traditional/Archival Solo

Rainer's work precedes much of what has become popular on the contemporary flute scene. He taught music of the Southwest at Brigham Young University in Provo, Utah.

DISCOGRAPHY:

Songs of the Indian Flute, Vol. 2 [independent 1986]
Songs of the Indian Flute, Vol. 1 [independent 1986]

Appearances:
Lamanite Generation:
Go My Son [Proud Earth/Canyon 1988; Tantara Records 1994]
Various:
Music of New Mexico: Native American Traditions [Smithsonian Folkways 1992] comp *See*: Contemporary Compilations

Rainer, Lillian—(Taos Pueblo–San Carlos Apache)

The daughter of John Rainer Jr., Lillian Rainer plays a small six-hole woman's flute made of cane from the San Carlos area in Arizona, where she was taught the songs by her father and grandmother. She attended Brigham Young University, Salt Lake City, Utah, to obtain a master's degree in social work.

DISCOGRAPHY:

Heartbeat: Voices of First Nations Women [Smithsonian Folkways 1995] comp *See*: Traditional/Archival Compilations

Red Tail Chasing Hawks

Lineup: Calvin Standing Bear (Oglala–Sicangu Lakota), flute; James Torres (Chiricahua Apache), keyboards.

DISCOGRAPHY:
Brother Hawk [Canyon 1996]
Eagle Dances in the Wind [Canyon 1995]

Appearances:
Voices across the Canyon, Vol. 3 [Canyon 1997] comp *See*: Contemporary Compilations
Voices across the Canyon, Vol. 1 [Canyon 1996] comp *See*: Contemporary Compilations

Rico, D. M.; a.k.a. Rainmaker—(Comanche)

In addition to plying his craft as a flute maker, David M. Rico has worked as a doctor in the U.S. Indian Health Services.

DISCOGRAPHY:
Distant Thunder [independent 1989]

Roybal, Ronald—(Tewa) *See*: Robert Tree Cody

Based in Santa Fe, New Mexico. A four-time NAMA nominee, Roybal specializes in traditional flute and classical guitar.

DISCOGRAPHY:
Eagle's Journey into Dawn [Native Heart Music 1999]
Visions of the Fourth World [Native Heart Music 1997]
Suite Santa Fe [Native Heart Music 1996] w/ classical/flamenco guitar

Appearances:
Robert Tree Cody:
Native Brotherhood [New Earth 2001]

Sekakuku, Alph—(Hopi)

DISCOGRAPHY:
Songs from the Fourth World [Four Winds Trading 1996] w/ John Huling

Shakra

Lineup: M. Saylors, cedar flutes; S. Powers, keyboards, guitars.

DISCOGRAPHY:
Double Rainbow [independent 1998]

Silverbird, J. Reuben—(Dineh-Apache)

Narrated by J. Reuben Silverbird with flute music by Perry Silverbird, the double album listed here contains legends from various nations, including Dineh, Zuni, Tohono O'odham, Akimel O'odham, Santo Domingo, Hopi, Apache, Tewa, Onondaga, Blackfoot, Anishnabe, Cheyenne, Pawnee, Paiute, Sioux, Choctaw, Cherokee, Seminole, Chickasaw, Creek, and Nez Perce. Additional musicians include Mark Linebury, Rob Russo, and traditional singers.

DISCOGRAPHY:
The World in Our Eyes: Native American Vision of Creation [Celestial Harmonies 1991] *See*: Contemporary Spoken Word: Legends and Storytelling

Silverbird, Perry—(Dineh-Apache)

The son of J. Reuben Silverbird, Perry Silverbird transcended his formal flute training to play what he describes as "free-spirit music." Additional appearances include the German-based project Big City Indians' (Native Indian Power Groove) album *Uncle Peyote*, a fund-raiser for radio station KILI-FM, Pine Ridge Reservation, South Dakota.

DISCOGRAPHY:
Spirit of the Fire [Celestial Harmonies 1993, Germany]
The Blessing Way [Celestial Harmonies 1992]

Appearances:
Between Father Sky and Mother Earth: A Native American Collection [Narada 1995] comp

Snake, Stan—(Ponca)

Regarded as a "granddaddy" of the traditional flute, Stan Snake remains an inspiration among many players in the genre. His only solo recording was produced by the Lamanite Generation Department of Music, Brigham Young University, Provo, Utah. He combines electric and traditional music, spoken word, and nature sounds.

DISCOGRAPHY:
Dawn of Love [independent 1984]

Sobylae, Emil

DISCOGRAPHY:
Where Earth Touches Sky [Astro 1996]

Tailfeathers, Donovan—(Blackfoot)
See: Contemporary Music: Olivia Tailfeathers and Kainai

DISCOGRAPHY:
Niitsitapi [independent 2000]

Talltree, Robert—(Anishnabe)

DISCOGRAPHY:
Sacred Journey [independent 1998]
Echoes of the Earth [Just Lucky 1997]

Tootoosis, Aaron—(Cree) *See*: Powwow Music: Wildhorse Singers

Tree Cody, Robert *See*: Cody, Robert Tree

Trezak, Dave "White Wolf"—(Cherokee-Lakota) *See*: Contemporary Music

DISCOGRAPHY:
Medicine [independent 2000]

Tsa'ne Dos'e; a.k.a. Arnold Richardson—(Sapone-Tuscarora)

From North Carolina. A carver and musician, Tsa'ne Dos'e (Last of the Wolves) has worked mostly in wood to construct his own flutes and sculptures.

DISCOGRAPHY:
Spirits in the Wind [SOAR 1996]
Moon Spirits [SOAR 1993]

Appearances:
Arctic Refuge [Soundings of the Planet 1996] *See*: Contemporary Compilations
Soaring Hearts Tribal Peoples [SOAR 1996] comp *See*: Traditional/Archival Compilations
Between Father Sky and Mother Earth: A Native American Collection [Narada 1995] comp

Two Hawks, Robert—(Cherokee)

DISCOGRAPHY:
Voices of the Earth [Featherstone FS-4008]

Andrew Vasquez. Photo courtesy Makoche Records.

Vasquez, Andrew—(Kiowa-Apache) *See*: Contemporary Spoken Word: Legends and Storytelling: Joseph M. Marshall III; Powwow Music: American Indian Dance Theater

Originally from Oklahoma, Vasquez started his career with the American Indian Dance Theater, where he learned to play flute. His first album enlists the help of Rita Coolidge, percussionist Epaminondas Trimis, bass player Miguel Garrido, keyboardist Jovino Santos Neto, and, in a special appearance, actor Rodney Grant. NAMA Best Male Artist of the Year, 2000.

DISCOGRAPHY:
V3: An American Indian [Makoche 1999]
Wind River [Makoche 1997] INDIE Award
    nominee
Vasquez [Makoche 1996]

Appearances (listed alphabetically):
American Indian Dance Theater:
American Indian Dance Theater [Broadway
    Limited Records 1984]

Joseph M. Marshall III:
The Lakota Way [Makoche 2003]
Various:
Tribal Legends [Earth Beat! 2002] comp
    See: Contemporary Compilations
Tribal Dreams [Earth Beat! 2001] comp
    See: Contemporary Compilations
Tribal Winds: Music from Native American Flutes [Earth Beat! 1996] comp

Wahpeconiah, Edd Wapp— (Sac-Fox-Comanche) *See*: Contemporary Compilations: *Oyate*

Walksnice, Ed—(Choctaw-Miwok) *See*: Contemporary Music: Lunar Drive

DISCOGRAPHY:
Cherished Memories [Sky Productions 1992]

Webster, Louis—
(Oneida-Menominee-Anishnabe)

DISCOGRAPHY:
Woodland Rhapsody [Sphere Music 1993]

Wettlin-Larsen, Georgia—
(Assiniboine-Nakota)

DISCOGRAPHY:

Appearances:
Heartbeat: Voices of First Nations Women
[Smithsonian Folkways 1995] comp *See*:
Traditional/Archival Compilations
More Music from Northern Exposure [MCA
1994] sdtk *See*: Contemporary Sound-
tracks

Whitewind—(Southern Ute) *See*:
Contemporary Music: Tom Bee

Whitewind cowrote "Voice of the Mountain" with Tom Bee for the film *Windtalkers* [John Woo, 2002].

DISCOGRAPHY:
Wind Dancer [SOAR 1996]

Appearances:
Across Indian Lands [SOAR 1999] comp
See: Contemporary Compilations

Widrick, Terry—(Mohawk)

Originally from upstate New York, Widrick later moved to Selkirk, Manitoba. This
craftsman, artist, and motivational speaker
bases his material on spirituality and culture; most songs are original compositions,
with the exception of the "Zuni Sunrise
Song" and "Amazing Grace."

DISCOGRAPHY:
By Sacred Waters [Sunshine 1995]

Wildcat, Tommy—(Cherokee) *See*:
Contemporary Music: Lee Johnson

Born in Park Hill, Oklahoma. Wildcat
began playing in 1994, utilizing different types of wood to produce a variety of
keys: the river cane flute (bamboo gathered
along the Illinois River) produces a high
G sharp; the poplar and wormy chestnut
produces an F minor; and cedar produces
a G sharp. Television appearances include
How the West Was Lost [PBS 1993].

DISCOGRAPHY:
The Fire People [Warrior Spirit Productions
1999]
Flames of Fire [Warrior Spirit 1998]
Trail of Tears [Platinum/Intersound 1998]
w/ Lee Johnson
Cherokee Flute Songs and Voices [indepen-
dent 1996]
Cherokee Voices [independent 1994]
Stomp Dances [Red Vinyl 1994]
Cherokee Dancers of Fire [Red Vinyl 1994]

Woerpel, Mark

DISCOGRAPHY:
Flute Songs of Mo-wa-Sah [NFIC 1998]

Youngblood, Mary—(Aluet-
Seminole) *See*: Contemporary Spoken
Word: Legends (Miscellaneous)

Born June 24, 1958. One of a growing number of female flute players, Youngblood is
regarded as the female Carlos Nakai. She
was classically trained for thirty years, beginning with piano and violin at age six,
flute and guitar at age ten. She approached
Native music with a great deal of respect
as a place where she could reaffirm her
roots. Youngblood has more than thirty
handmade flutes that are constructed from
diverse materials, including redwood,
cedar, bamboo, cane, pine, alder, red oak,
and PVC pipe. She received NAMA Best

Female Artist of the Year, Flutist of the Year, and Best New Age Recording for *Heart of the World*, 2000; *Beneath the Raven Moon* received the Grammy Award for Best Native Music Album of the Year, 2002.

DISCOGRAPHY:

Feed the Fire [Silver Wave 2004]
Beneath the Raven Moon [Silver Wave 2002]
Heart of the World [Silver Wave 1999]
The Offering [Silver Wave 1998]

Appearances:

Joanne Shenandoah:
Eagle Cries [Red Feather 2001]
All Spirits Sing [Music For Little People 1997]
Various:

Tribal Legends [Earth Beat! 2002] comp
   See: Contemporary Compilations
Bears [Silver Wave 2001] sdtk *See*: Contemporary Soundtracks
The Prophecy of the Eagle and the Condor [Silver Wave 2001] w/ Tito La Rosa
Tribal Dreams [Earth Beat! 2001] comp
   See: Contemporary Compilations
Prayer for Peace [Silver Wave 2000] comp
   See: Contemporary Compilations
Naturally Native [Silver Wave 2000] sdtk
   See: Contemporary Soundtracks
Heartbeat 2: More Voices of First Nations Women [Smithsonian Folkways 1998] comp *See*: Traditional/Archival Compilations
American Indian Circles of Wisdom [independent 1995] *See*: Contemporary Spoken Word: Legends (Miscellaneous)

Between Father Sky and Mother Earth: A Native American Collection [Narada 1995]

Lineup: R. Carlos Nakai; the Native Flute Ensemble; Cornel Pewewardy; Perry Silverbird; Tsa'ne Dos'e; Douglas Wallentyne; Primeaux, Mike, and Attson (*See*: Peyote Music); Chester Mahooty (*See*: Traditional/Archival Solo); Bill Miller; Charles Jefferson (*See*: Contemporary Music).

A Cry from the Earth: Music of the North American Indians [Folkways 1979] *See*: Traditional/Archival Compilations

Lakota, Anishnabe, Yuchi, Tohono O'odham. Recorded in 1927 by John Bierhorst.

The Indian Flute: Spiritual Songs of the American Indian [Red Rock Records 1992]

Taos Pueblo, Lakota, Crow, Northern Plains; no credits were provided on the recording.

Spiritual Songs of the American Indian: Flute Songs of the American Indian: The Gold Collection/Classic Performances [Deja Vu/Retro R2CD-4031]

Tribal Winds: Music from Native American Flutes [Earth Beat! 1996]

Lineup: Bryan Akipa; Keith Bear; Fernando Cellicion; Joseph Fire Crow; William Gutierrez; Hawk Henries; Kevin Locke; Tom Mauchahty-Ware; R. Carlos Nakai and William Eaton; Andrew Vasquez.

SECTION 5
Peyote Ritual Music

The recording of ceremonies is often regarded as inappropriate—a violation of a sacred observance—and is openly discouraged. However, Native American Church (NAC) members are permitted to record songs performed during ceremonies to help share and preserve the songs for personal use. On a commercial level, second to powwow, recorded peyote music is perhaps the only other widely diffused Native music on the market. First commercially released on the American Indian Sound Chiefs label between 1940 and 1950, the 78 rpm albums were initially intended for NAC members only. However, owing to its commercial appeal, peyote music has gained recognition within Native music categories of industry award shows, even surfacing in television commercials. Many of the singers, especially on older recordings, nonetheless still prefer anonymity, which is why there are few biographies in this section.

BRIEF HISTORY

The peyote medicine was used in the Southwest region of the United States and northern Mexico long before the arrival of Europeans; the establishment of formal entities such as the NAC are recent developments. The peyote ritual first came from Mexico (specifically from the Huichol and Tarahumara) to the White Mountain Apache in the 1870s, then to the Jicarilla and the Tonkawa, all of whom developed the basic ceremonial patterns used in the various styles of peyote meetings. By the late 1880s, the Comanche and Kiowa embraced the rituals and developed the basis for many of the songs and words. From there, the ceremony spread quickly throughout the Southwest as a highly organized religious movement. The northern migration of the practice included the Native peoples of Idaho, Montana, and the Dakotas until the influence was felt throughout most of North America. Oklahoma was predominantly the center of diffusion because of the gathering of many tribes through forced relocation there.

The three prominent figures engaged in the process of dissemination of the Peyote Way were John Wilson (Caddo-Delaware-French), Quanah Parker (Comanche), and Smithsonian archaeologist James Mooney (who helped establish the federally recognized NAC in 1918; 1937 in Canada). Whereas the ghost dance movement of the late 1800s was halted by U.S. military action, the peyote religion flourished despite resentment from both Native and white authorities.

The Christian elements found in the peyote ceremonies were incorporated both out of necessity and influence. The origin of the cast-iron kettle drum, for example, derives from the use of pots provided through trade as traditional drums were confiscated and destroyed under Indian policies of the day. The basic tenets observe a communal responsibility of goodness with no proselytization. The persistence of New Age cultural piracy and political agendas have placed great legal pressure on the use of the peyote sacrament.

Ceremonies or "meetings" are organized for many reasons, including birthdays, baptismals, graduations, weddings, wakes, observance of seasons, and other important occurrences. The key people within

the ceremony are the road man (priest or peyote chief), water woman, cedar man, drummer and singer, the door man, the fire man, the sponsor (the person who asked for the meeting), the patient (if it is a healing ceremony), friends, and supporters. The ceremony takes place either in a tipi or a house and lasts throughout the night until dawn, ending with a feast; the socializing lasts well beyond midday. On some occasions, meetings can take place over a period of days.

The ceremony involves prayer, meditation, song, and healing (both physical and spiritual); there is no dancing, as everyone sits in a circle around the sacred fire, with the ceremonial leaders (the drummer, the road man, the cedar man) sitting at the head of the altar directly across the tipi entrance located at the east (the door man and the fire man); all medicines and instruments are passed clockwise, as each singer takes his or her turn by holding the staff, sage, and feather in one hand while shaking the gourd in the other. Each singer sings a set of four songs accompanied by a pot (kettle) drum and gourd rattle. These meetings resemble other ceremonies in their natural symbolism, imagery, cosmology, and use of the elements fire, water, earth, and sky, including the crescent moon, waterbird, deer, corn, and other effigies. The intertribal elements of the ceremony, such as Winnebago and Apache influences on the structural basis combined with many words and prayers originating from the Comanche language, are prevalent. Teachings, prayers, and healing ceremonies take place throughout the night.

Although protocol varies from nation to nation, standard observances are recognized. In traditional Kiowa ways, women do not sing with the gourd, but provide backup or harmonize with the men; in other nations, the women sit together with each other and apart from the men, but in the Lakota ceremony women sit with their partners and sing with the gourd.

INSTRUMENTS

Four main musical instruments are used in the peyote ceremony: the cast-iron kettle water drum; the eagle bone whistle, which is used twice during the meeting by the road man when calling for midnight and morning water; the gourd rattle; and the human voice. The main herbs include sage, cedar, tobacco, and peyote.

The instruments and songs are simple, but very distinct. Stretched rawhide (deer or elk) is tied onto the cast-iron kettle water drum (derived from Tarahumara and Yaqui origins) with a thirty-foot cord that is held together with an arrangement of seven stones (usually turquoise approximately the size of an average marble) and placed along the drum's upper outer edge under the hide. The cord is wrapped around the stone held in position under the hide, then around the drum, then under and across the bottom of the drum to form an eight-pointed star pattern. The cord is tightened with a deer antler. Exotic hardwood is used for ornately carved drumsticks.

The squash gourd rattle is filled with stones, seeds, or beads and fitted with a straight thin handle usually made from exotic wood and approximately fourteen inches in length, sometimes with one and one-half inches protruding from the top of the gourd and finished with a brush of cropped horsehair attached to the very tip, which is surrounded in stripes of brightly colored feathers of a small bird, usually hummingbird feathers. The handle is usually highly polished and decorated with geometric patterns in rainbow-colored peyote-stitch beadwork (a technique that allows beads to form-fit any object). All manner of fans are decorated in the same way, often with macaw tail feathers of blue, red, yellow, and green. Eagle, hawk, and other raptor feathers are used, sometimes in conjunction with a wide variety of other birds, including those of the roadrunner, water hen, or pheas-

ant. The feathers are usually cut in very distinct ways to reflect the geometry of peyote spirituality. The roadman's staff— constructed of a wide selection of wood or man-made materials, decorated in the same manner as the gourd—creates a set of central implements integral to conducting the ceremony.

SONG STRUCTURE

There are four basic groups of peyote songs: harmonized songs, healing songs (usually sung without the drum or gourd), intertribal songs, and traditional songs. Many of the words for the songs are Comanche in origin. The songs are unique in form and performance; no other type of traditional singing is similar.

The music is simple, though of varied tempo, and has a set formula for opening and closing each song. The music consists of paired phrases typical of gospel hymns, with an initial arc in the melodic line. Most peyote songs have a definite rhythmic pattern with simple count divisions in two-four time and a metronome speed of 130 to 150.

This type of singing has developed its own very specific, unique, and immediately identifiable vocable style. Most verses and songs end in the same vocable refrain, "heya nay-no-way," on the tones or bass note of the melody. The singer signals the end of his song by vigorously shaking the rattle; the drummer hits the drum with five distinct separate beats at the end of one song, then quickly tips the drum to wet the drum head while creating a drop in the sound as the drum is tipped; the drumming resumes and follows a similar pattern throughout. There is a delicate and intricate interplay between drummer and singer, especially when the drummer and singer know each other. The drummer's thumb pressed on the drum head holds the tone at a constant pitch until the drummer slides it, which then drops the tone a fifth or more when the pressure is relaxed between songs. This technique can be used during the song to alter the pitch in order to accent the singer's performance. Between sets of songs, the drummer will blow into the drum at the upper rim where the hide folds over; the additional air gives the water-soaked drum skin a deeper sound to revitalize the tone.

Harmonized songs were first recorded in *Yankton Sioux Peyote Songs*, Vol. 2 [Indian House 1977]. The gospel or hymnlike attribute of the harmonized peyote song is a clear indication of the Christian influence on the music of the Peyote Way and on some elements of the ceremony itself. Peyote road man Joseph Shields Sr. (Yankton) describes the history of harmonized singing, which began on his reservation: "Right here is where I first heard this—it had to be in the 1930s. This group of men from the Crow-Creek Sioux belonged to a Presbyterian or Episcopal church over there. I was told that they even had a quartet. They never had medicine until they came over here to Greenwood, South Dakota. We never had first tenor, second tenor, bass, or anything. Then, they started to catch some songs and started singing with their wives and began harmonizing in the way they learned to arrange singers in harmony."

Intertribal songs are straight vocables of simple to complex patterns; all styles of songs are composed as either individual songs or sets of four. In all cases, the typical vocable refrain structure is used; in the case of morning songs, the Comanche word *yori* (meaning "the sun is coming up") is often used. Intertribals comprise a common melody and varying vocables that carry similar but continuously intricate patterns of melody and vocable text; they can be sung throughout the meeting and performed by anyone who knows them.

Traditional songs are specific to actions and functions within the ceremony itself and are sung in the traditional language (e.g., Sioux, Ponca, Dineh, and so on). Traditional songs include the opening (or starting song), midnight water song, early-morning water song, closing song, and healing songs (usually sung without gourd or drum), and they are sung at a specified time during the ceremony.

Armstrong, Alfred—
(Cheyenne-Caddo)

Lineup: Alicia Armstrong (Ute) and Francis Little Crow (Otoe).

DISCOGRAPHY:
Indian Lord's Prayer Songs [Canyon CR-8025]

Armstrong and Turtle

Lineup: Alfred Armstrong (Cheyenne-Caddo), Ralph Turtle (Southern Cheyenne), Wilbur Jack (Paiute-Wasco).

DISCOGRAPHY:
Chants of the Native American Church of North America, Vol. 3 [Canyon CR-6074]
Chants of the Native American Church of North America, Vol. 2 [Canyon CR-6068]
Chants of the Native American Church of North America, Vol. 1 [Canyon CR-6063]

Ashley and Aronilth Jr.—(Dineh)

DISCOGRAPHY:
Navajo Peyote Ceremonial Songs, Vol. 4 [Indian House IH-1544]
Navajo Peyote Ceremonial Songs, Vol. 3 [Indian House IH-1543]
Navajo Peyote Ceremonial Songs, Vol. 2 [Indian House IH-1542]
Navajo Peyote Ceremonial Songs, Vol. 1 [Indian House IH-1541]

Aunguoe, James—(Kiowa)

The peyote compilation albums listed here were originally recorded in Carnegie, Oklahoma, 1956, and reissued on Indian House 1996.

DISCOGRAPHY:

Appearances:
Kiowa Peyote Ritual Songs [American Indian Sound Chiefs 580] comp

Kiowa Peyote Ritual Songs [American Indian Sound Chiefs 549] comp

Bahe, Hosteen, and Bahe—(Dineh)

Lineup: Randy Bahe, Elroy Bahe, and Jefferson Hosteen.

DISCOGRAPHY:
Navajo Peyote Songs [Cool Runnings 1998]

Bahe, Irwin—(Dineh)

DISCOGRAPHY:
Azee'Beenahagaaji Tsodizin Sin, Vol. 2 [Cool Runnings 2000]
Azee'Beenahagaaji Tsodizin Sin, Vol. 1 [Cool Runnings 1997]

Bahe and Barton—(Dineh)

Lineup: Tony Bahe and A. Barton.

DISCOGRAPHY:
Morning, Healing, and Prayer Songs [DP-6066]

Bahe and Johnson—Dineh)

Lineup: Irwin Bahe and David Johnson from Chinle, Arizona.

DISCOGRAPHY:
Dineh Prayer Songs, Vol. 2 [Cool Runnings 2000]
Dineh prayer Songs, Vol. 1 [Cool Runnings 1998]
Navajo Peyote Prayer Songs [AIS01]

Barker and Butler *See*: Van Horn, Barker, and Clark

Lineup: Everett Barker (Sac-Fox) and Larry Butler (Dineh).

DISCOGRAPHY:
Peyote Songs, Vol. 2 [Canyon 1982]
Peyote Songs, Vol. 1 [Canyon 1981]

Begay, Anderson—(Dineh)

DISCOGRAPHY:
32 Peyote Prayer Songs [Gray Deer Arts 1992]

Begay, Calvin—(Dineh)

From Burnt Corn, Arizona.

DISCOGRAPHY:
Healing Vision [Cool Runnings 1998]

Bia, Andrew, Jr.

DISCOGRAPHY:
Running toward the Dawn [Kiva 1997]

Big Bow, Nelson—(Kiowa)

The American Indian Sound Chiefs recording was originally made at the Crow Agency, Montana, August 24, 1966, and reissued on Indian House in 1993; later recordings were made with Kenneth Cozad on March 22, 1997, and with Howard Cozad on June 3, 1998.

DISCOGRAPHY:
Kiowa Spiritual Peyote Songs, Vol. 3 [Indian House 1998]
Kiowa Spiritual Peyote Songs, Vol. 2 [Indian House 1997]
Kiowa Spiritual Peyote Songs, Vol. 1 [Indian House 1997]
Kiowa and Comanche Peyote Songs [American Indian Sound Chiefs 591; reissued Indian House 1993]

Black Bear, Eugene, Sr.—(Southern Cheyenne)

DISCOGRAPHY:
Peyote Songs [Canyon 8012] w/ Leo Yazzie
32 Southern Cheyenne Songs [Indian Records IR-792]
32 Southern Cheyenne Songs [Indian Records IR-791]

Blackfox *See*: Thomas Duran Jr.

DISCOGRAPHY:
Peyote Healing [Soar 1996]

Blackhorse—(Dineh)

Lineup: Richard Blackhorse and Delbar Blackhorse from Crow Springs, Utah.

DISCOGRAPHY:
Blackhorse [Cool Runnings 2000]
Prayer Songs for the New Millennium [Cool Runnings 1999]
Dineh Prayer Songs [Cool Runnings 1998]

Chenoah—(Lummi)

Chenoah Engawa, member of the Red Cedar Chapter, NAC, Lummi, Washington.

DISCOGRAPHY:
Sacred Fire [SOAR 1997]

Connahvichnah, Garrett— (Cheyenne)

DISCOGRAPHY:
32 Comanche and Southern Cheyenne Songs, Vol. 2 [Indian Records 7942]
32 Comanche and Southern Cheyenne Songs, Vol. 1 [Indian Records 7941]

Crowdog—(Lakota) *See*: Traditional/ Archival Group

Lineup: Henry, Leonard, and Mary Crow Dog, with Al Running.

DISCOGRAPHY:
Sing Out! The Folk Song Magazine, Vol. 24, no. 5 [1975] w/ soundsheet
Crowdog's Paradise: Songs of the Sioux [Elektra 1971]

Daukei, Horace, and Chester

DISCOGRAPHY:
Peyote Early Morning Chants [Canyon CR-6158]

Denny, Bill, Jr.—(OJ-Cree)

From Rocky Boy, Montana. *Lineup*: Bill Denny Jr., lead; Clinton Denny, drummer; Roberta Denny and Jerry Saddleback, harmonies (*See*: Contemporary Music: Willie Dunn).

DISCOGRAPHY:
Intertribal Peyote Chants, Vol. 6 [Canyon 1992]
Intertribal Peyote Chants, Vol. 5 [Canyon 1988]
Intertribal Peyote Chants, Vol. 4 [Canyon 1987]
Intertribal Peyote Chants, Vol. 3 [Canyon 1986]
Intertribal Peyote Chants, Vol. 2 [Canyon 1984]
Intertribal Peyote Chants, Vol. 1 [Canyon 1983]

Dupoint, Joe "Fish," and Tofpi— (Kiowa)

DISCOGRAPHY:

Appearances:
Faith, Hope, and Charity, Vols. 1 and 2 [1998] comps
Kiowa Peyote Songs [Canyon 1996] comp

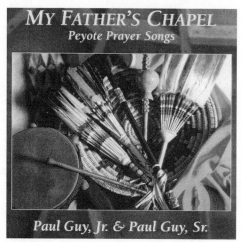

Guy and Guy's *My Father's Chapel* (1998), expressed culture and religious freedom. Courtesy Canyon Records.

Appearances:

Alcatraz Is Not an Island [James Fortier, 2002] score

Across Indian Lands [SOAR 1999] comp

Guy and Guy—(Dineh)

Lineup: Paul Guy Sr. and Paul Guy Jr.

DISCOGRAPHY:

My Father's Chapel [Canyon 1998]

Hoffman, Archie—(Shoshone)

DISCOGRAPHY:

32 Intertribal Songs, Vol. 4 [Indian Records 326]

32 Intertribal Songs, Vol. 3 [Indian Records 325]

32 Intertribal Songs, Vol. 2 [Indian Records 324]

32 Intertribal Songs Vol. 1 [Indian Records 323]

32 Intertribal Songs [Indian Records 329A]

32 Intertribal Songs [Indian Records 328A]

Appearances:

Intertribal Peyote Morning Songs, Vol. 2 [Indian Sounds IS-8061 1992] comp, w/ Dean Washa

Intertribal Peyote Morning Songs, Vol. 1 [Indian Sounds IS-8061 1992] comp, w/ Dean Washa

Duran, Thomas, Jr.—(Northern Arapaho)

DISCOGRAPHY:

Life Giver [Canyon 2002]

Connection to Mother Earth [Canyon 2001] w/ Delbert "Black Fox" Pomani

Flying High Woman—(Lakota)

Ethel Rachel Red Bear, born February 21, 1943, Norris, South Dakota; descendant of American Horse.

DISCOGRAPHY:

Flying High Woman [Cool Runnings 2000]

Guy and Allen—(Dineh)

Lineup: Paul Guy Jr. and Teddy Allen.

DISCOGRAPHY:

Peyote Strength [SOAR 1994]

Peyote Brothers [SOAR 1993]

Peyote Medicine [SOAR 1992]

Peyote Canyon [SOAR 1991]

Hoof, Leroy Magpie

DISCOGRAPHY:

Healing Songs [DP-4044]

Howlingwolf, Wesley—(Cheyenne)

DISCOGRAPHY:

32 Southern Cheyenne Songs, Vol. 2 [Indian Records 7911]

32 Southern Cheyenne Songs, Vol. 1 [Indian Records 7912]

Humming Bird, Edward—(Kiowa)

Recorded at Crow Agency, Montana, August 24, 1966.

DISCOGRAPHY:
Kiowa Peyote Ritual Songs [American Indian Sound Chiefs 590; reissued Indian House 1993]

Iron Shell, Ordell

DISCOGRAPHY:
Peyote Songs [Indian Sounds IS-5055]

James and Nez—(Dineh)

Lineup: Davidson James and Billie Nez.

DISCOGRAPHY:
Peyote Blessing [SOAR 1993]

James and Spencer—(Dineh)

Lineup: Davidson Kee James and Derald Spencer.

DISCOGRAPHY:
Dine Peyote Songs, Vol. 2 [Indian Sounds IS-1012]
Dine Peyote Songs, Vol. 1 [Indian Sounds IS-1022]

Johnson, David—(Dineh)

DISCOGRAPHY:
Sacred Prayer [Cool Runnings 1998]

Knight, Jimmy—(Dineh)

DISCOGRAPHY:
Navajo Healing Song [Canyon CR-6308]

Lewis, Kevin—(Dineh)

DISCOGRAPHY:
Navajo Peyote Songs, Vol. 2 [Indian Sounds IS-8002]
Navajo Peyote Songs, Vol. 1 [Indian Sounds IS-8001]

Littlecook and Botone

Lineup: Oliver, Steven, and O. J. Littlecook (Ponca-Otoe), along with Perry Botone (Otoe-Kiowa).

DISCOGRAPHY:
Songs of the Native American Church, Vol. 2 [Cool Runnings 2000]
Songs of the Native American Church, Vol. 1 [Cool Runnings 1999]

McClellan, Billy, Sr.—(Iowa-Otoe-Sac-Fox)

Recordings produced by Millard Clark (*See*: Contemporary Music: Indian Chipmunks).

DISCOGRAPHY:
Songs of the Native American Church, Vol. 2 [Indian Sounds IS-8052]
Songs of the Native American Church, Vol. 1 [Indian Sounds IS-8051]

Nakai and Primeaux

DISCOGRAPHY:
Peyote Songs by Nakai and Primeaux, Vol. 1 [Indian Sounds 1993]

Nez, Billie—(Dineh)

DISCOGRAPHY:
Peyote Songs from Navajoland [SOAR 1990]
32 Navajo and Intertribal Songs [Indian Records 776A]
32 Navajo and Intertribal Songs [Indian Records 775A]

Appearances:
Various Native American Artists: Solo Flights, Vol. 1 [SOAR 1991] comp *See:* Contemporary Compilations

Nez and Yazzie—(Dineh)

DISCOGRAPHY:
Peyote Voices [SOAR 1991]

Parker Singers

Lineup: Joe Standing Rock, Doug Standing Rock, Videl Standing Rock, George Stump, William Denny Jr., Clinton Denny. OJ-Cree singers from Rocky Boy, Montana.

DISCOGRAPHY:
Peyote Songs from Rocky Boy, Vol. 3 [Canyon CR-8024]
Peyote Songs from Rocky Boy, Vol. 2 [Canyon CR-8023]
Peyote Songs from Rocky Boy, Vol. 1 [Canyon CR-8022]

Primeaux and Dion

Lineup: Gerald Primeaux and Neulan Dion Jr.

DISCOGRAPHY:
In Loving Memory: Yankton Sioux Peyote Songs [Cool Runnings 1999]

Primeaux Family

DISCOGRAPHY:
32 Yankton Sioux Harmonizing Songs, Vol. 6 [Indian Records 1171F]
32 Yankton Sioux Harmonizing Songs, Vol. 5 [Indian Records 1171E]
32 Yankton Sioux Harmonizing Songs, Vol. 4 [Indian Records 1171D]
32 Yankton Sioux Harmonizing Songs, Vol. 3 [Indian Records 1171C]

32 Yankton Sioux Harmonizing Songs, Vol. 2 [Indian Records 1171B]
32 Yankton Sioux Harmonizing Songs, Vol. 1 [Indian Records 1171A]

Primeaux, Gerald, Sr.—(Yankton)

DISCOGRAPHY:
Yankton Sioux Peyote Songs [Cool Runnings 1999]

Primeaux and Mike *See:* Contemporary Music: Robbie Robertson

Lineup: Verdell Primeaux (Yankton Sioux) and Johnny Mike (Dineh). *Hours Before Dawn* received a Grammy Award, Best Native American Music Album, 2002.

DISCOGRAPHY:
Hours Before Dawn: Harmonized Peyote Songs of the Native American Church [Canyon 2002]
Bless the People [Canyon 2001]
Evolution: Generation to Generation [Canyon 2000]
Live in Harmony [Canyon 1999]
Gathering of Voices [Canyon 1998]
Peyote Songs of the Native American Church [Canyon 1998]
Sacred Path [Canyon 1997]
Peyote Songs in Sioux and Navajo [Canyon 1997]
Walk in Beauty: Healing Chants [Canyon 1996]
Peyote Songs in Sioux and Navajo [Canyon 1994] w/ Robert Attson
Healing and Peyote Songs in Navajo and Sioux [Canyon 1994] w/ Robert Attson
Peyote Songs in Sioux and Navajo [Canyon 1993]

Appearances:
Robbie Robertson:
Contact from the Underworld of Redboy [Capitol 1998]

Music for the Native Americans [Capitol 1994]

Various:

Enter Tribal [Canyon 2001] comp, w/ Cliff Sarde

Voices across the Canyon, Vol. 4 [Canyon 1999] comp *See*: Contemporary Compilations

Voices across the Canyon, Vol. 3 [Canyon 1997] comp *See*: Contemporary Compilations

Voices across the Canyon, Vol. 2 [Canyon 1996] comp *See*: Contemporary Compilations

Voices across the Canyon, Vol. 1 [Canyon 1996] comp *See*: Contemporary Compilations

Native Wisdom [Narada 1996] comp

Between Father Sky and Mother Earth [Narada 1995] comp, w/ Robert Attson *See*: Contemporary Compilations

Red Cloud—(Teton Lakota)

Lineup: Evert Redbear; Bernard, Myron, Avery, Jack, and Silas Red Cloud.

DISCOGRAPHY:

Circle of Belief: Voices of the 6th Generation [Cool Runnings 1998]

Secody, Eli—(Dineh)

DISCOGRAPHY:

The Following Generation: Navajo Prayer Songs [Canyon 2002]

Shields, Rev. Joseph, Sr.—(Lakota)

Rev. Joseph Shields Sr., with Duane L. Shields Sr.; recorded at Lake Andes, South Dakota, June 29, 1979.

DISCOGRAPHY:

Songs of the Native American Church [Indian House 1983]

Shields Singers—(Lakota)

Lineup: Joseph Shields III; Shane Shields; Lorenzo Shields Jr.

DISCOGRAPHY:

Songs of the Peyote Road, Vol. 2 [Canyon 1998]

Songs of the Peyote Road, Vol. 1 [Canyon 1997]

Siwash, Claude—(Shoshone-Paiute)

DISCOGRAPHY:

32 Shoshone Paiute Songs [Indian Records 1161A]

32 Shoshone Paiute Songs [Indian Records 1161B]

Turtle, Grover—(Southern Cheyenne)

DISCOGRAPHY:

32 Southern Cheyenne Songs, Vol. 3 [Indian Records 7932]

32 Southern Cheyenne Songs, Vol. 2 [Indian Records 7931]

24 Southern Cheyenne Songs [Indian Records 321]

Turtle, Ralph—(Southern Cheyenne)

DISCOGRAPHY:

Peyote Healing Songs of the Native American Church [Canyon CR-6094]

Bright Morning Star Songs [Canyon CR-6075] w/ Daniel Magpie (Southern Cheyenne)

Van Horn, Barker, and Clark

Lineup: Warren Van Horn (Cheyenne), Everett Barker (Sac-Fox), Albert C. Clark (Dineh).

DISCOGRAPHY:
Peyote Prayer Songs, Vol. 2 [Canyon CR-8019]
Peyote Prayer Songs, Vol. 1 [Canyon CR-8018]

Whiteyes, Alfred—(Omaha)

DISCOGRAPHY:
32 Omaha and Intertribal Songs [Indian Records 828A]

Woodty, Albert B.—(Dineh)

DISCOGRAPHY:
Navajo Tribal Peyote Songs [Cool Runnings 1998]

Yazzie, Alfred, and Family—(Dineh)

DISCOGRAPHY:
Peyote Songs, Vol. 2 [Indian Sounds IS-1013]
Peyote Songs, Vol. 1 [Indian Sounds 1993]

Peyote Music Compilation Recordings

Cheyenne Peyote Songs, Vol. 1
[Indian House 1975]
Cheyenne Peyote Songs, Vol. 2
[Indian House 1975]

Lineup: Allen Bushyhead; Lee R. Chouteau; Arthur Madbull; Toby Starr.

Comanche Peyote Songs, Vol. 1
[Indian House 1969]
Comanche Peyote Songs, Vol. 2
[Indian House 1969]

Lineup: Roy Simmons; Joe Niedo; Roy Wockmetooah; Roe Poafpybitty; Jessie Poahway; Ida Wockmetooah.

Delaware, Cherokee, Choctaw, Creek [Library of Congress L37] *See*: Traditional/Archival Compilations

Delaware peyote songs on a larger collection of traditional music.

Faith, Hope, and Charity, Vol. 1
[1998]
Faith, Hope, and Charity, Vol. 2
[1998]

Lineup Vol. 1: Daniel Cozad Sr., Kenneth Cozad, Howard Cozad, and Joe Fish Dupoint. Healing recordings for Charity Jane Cozad (born, October 19, 1995; died June 12, 1998); recorded at Medicine Park, Oklahoma, June 4, 1998.

Great Basin: Paiute, Washo, Ute, Bannock, Shoshone [Library of Congress L38] *See*: Traditional/ Archival Compilations

The album contains Ute peyote songs within a larger collection of traditional music.

Intertribal Peyote Morning Songs, Vol. 1 [Indian Sounds IS-8061 1992]
Intertribal Peyote Morning Songs, Vol. 2 [Indian Sounds IS-8062 1992]

Kiowa [Library of Congress L35]

Lineup: George Hunt and Matthew Whitehorse; recorded in 1941 and 1951.

Kiowa and Kiowa-Apache Peyote Ritual Songs [American Indian Sound Chiefs 548]

Lineup: Ernest Williams; Nathan Doyebi; Edgar Gouladdie; and Nelson Big Bow. Recorded at Carnegie, Oklahoma, 1964; reissued on Indian House 1996.

Kiowa-Comanche Peyote Songs [American Indian Sound Chiefs 507]

Lineup: Nelson Big Bow; Edgar Gouladdie; Harding Big Bow; and Walter Ahhaity. Recorded at Carnegie, Oklahoma, 1964; reissued on Indian House 1996.

Kiowa NAC Prayer Songs [Indian House IH-2542]

Kiowa Peyote Meeting [Ethnic Folkways 1965, 4601] three LPs

Various artists recorded in Anadarko, Oklahoma, by Harry E. Smith.

Kiowa Peyote Ritual Songs [American Indian Sound Chiefs 580]

Lineup: James Aunguoe; Ernest Redbird; Oscar Tahlo; Allan Tsontokoy; and Francis Tsontokoy. Recorded at Carnegie, Okla-

homa, 1956; reissued on Indian House in 1993.

Kiowa Peyote Songs, Vol. 1 [Indian House 2002]

Lineup: Kenneth Cozad; Howard Cozad; Herbert Redbird; Lonnie Emhoolah; Joe Fish Dupoint. Recorded at Hog Creek, Oklahoma, October 2000.

Kiowa Peyote Songs, Vol. 2 [Indian House 2002]

Lineup: Kenneth Cozad; Howard Cozad; Herbert Redbird; Lonnie Emhoolah; Joe Fish Dupoint. Recorded at Hog Creek, Oklahoma, October 2000.

Kiowa Peyote Songs [Canyon 1975] *See*: Traditional/Archival Compilations

Lineup: Bill Kaulaity, with Daniel Cozad and James Cozad. Recorded at Carnegie, Oklahoma.

Kiowa Prayer Songs, Vol. 1 [Indian House IH-2541]

Midnight and Morning Songs [Indian Sounds IS-3333]

Navajo [Library of Congress L41] *See*: Traditional/Archival Compilations

Peyote songs recorded in the late 1940s.

Navajo Peyote Ceremonial Songs, Vol. 1 [Indian House 1976]
Navajo Peyote Ceremonial Songs, Vol. 2 [Indian House 1977]
Navajo Peyote Ceremonial Songs, Vol. 3 [Indian House 1978]
Navajo Peyote Ceremonial Songs, Vol. 4 [Indian House 1979]

Lineup: Wilson Aronilith Jr. and Hanson Ashley. Recorded at Wheatfield, Arizona.

Navajo Wildcat Peak, Vol. 1: *Morning Peyote Songs* [Canyon 1977]
Navajo Wildcat Peak, Vol. 2: *Peyote Songs* [Canyon 1978]
Navajo Wildcat Peak, Vol. 3: *Morning Peyote Songs* [Canyon 1979]
Navajo Wildcat Peak, Vol. 4: *Morning Peyote Songs* [Canyon 1980]
Navajo Wildcat Peak, Vol. 5: *Peyote Songs* [Canyon 1987]

Navajo Wildcat Peak Youth [Canyon 1981]

Peyote, a Collection: Old Peyote Songs [Canyon CR-6054]

Lineup: David Apekaun (Kiowa); Morris Medicine (Cheyenne); Chief White Eagle (Cherokee); Chief Spotted Back Hamilton (Omaha); Johnny Buffalo (Bannock); Wilbur Jack (Paiute/Washo).

Peyote Early Morning Chants [Canyon CR-6158]

Lineup: Horace Dukei and Lee Chester; Kiowa and Comanche songs.

Peyote Healing Chants of the Native American Church [Canyon CR-6094]

Lineup: Ralph Turtle (Southern Cheyenne); album jacket by Kiowa artist Al Momaday.

Peyote Healing Songs [Sunshine 2001]

Lineup: Linus Woods; Eric Daniels.

Peyote Rite Chants [Canyon 1972]

Peyote Songs from Rocky Boy, Montana [Indian House] volume series

Ponca Peyote Songs, Vol. 1 [Indian House 1971]
Ponca Peyote Songs, Vol. 2 [Indian House 1972]

Ponca Peyote Songs, Vol. 1 (1971), one of many important recordings that helped preserve traditional values. Courtesy Indian House Records.

Ponca Peyote Songs, Vol. 3 [Indian House 1973]

Lineup: Harry Buffalohead; James Clark; Joe H. Rush; Franklin Smith; and Sylvester Warrior. Recorded at Ponca City, Oklahoma, April 6, 1971.

Washo Peyote Songs [Smithsonian Folkways 1965]

Peyote songs from the eastern slopes of the Sierra mountains of California and Nevada. Recorded by Dr. Warren d'Azevedo, Woodsfords, California.

Yankton Sioux Harmonizing Songs: 32 Intertribal Songs [Indian Records 1175A]

Yankton Sioux Peyote Songs, Vol. 1 [Indian House 1976]
Yankton Sioux Peyote Songs, Vol. 2 [Indian House 1977]
Yankton Sioux Peyote Songs, Vol. 3 [Indian House 1977]
Yankton Sioux Peyote Songs, Vol. 4 [Indian House 1978]
Yankton Sioux Peyote Songs, Vol. 5 [Indian House 1980]
Yankton Sioux Peyote Songs, Vol. 6 [Indian House 1980]

Yankton Sioux Peyote Songs, Vol. 2 (1977), first album of Native harmonized songs. Courtesy Indian House Records.

Yankton Sioux Peyote Songs, Vol. 7 [Indian House 1980]
Yankton Sioux Peyote Songs, Vol. 8 [Indian House IH-4378 1981]

Lineup Volumes 1–4: Joe Abdo Sr.; Quentin Bruguier; Lorenzo Dion; Asa Primeaux Sr.; Francis Primeaux; Duane Shields; and Joseph Shields Sr. Recorded July 6, 1976.

    Lineup Volumes 5–8: Rev. Joseph Shields Sr.; Joseph Shields Jr.; Joe Abdo Sr.; Duane L. Shields Sr.; Lorenzo Dion; and Philomene Dion. Recorded June 29, 1979, Lake Andes, South Dakota.

SECTION 6
Powwow Music

This introduction is not intended to provide all information related to powwows, but to offer some background in order to understand the song, album, and dance titles.

BRIEF HISTORY

A powwow is a gathering, a celebration, and an expression of appreciation for life through song and dance. It has always included a number of smaller ceremonies, rituals, and displays of hospitality and unity. The powwow is also a ceremony where songs and dances have developed over time. Moreover, it is a cultural evolutionary process that is in constant motion, changing each time the people dance.

The various origin stories of the powwow begin with the word itself. The term *powwow* is a derivative from an Algonquin term for "medicine man" or "priest" or "he who dreams" and relates to the family circle of sharing life. A Lakota story mentions a council of nations that was held in order to seek peace during the mid-1800s, which culminated in games, dances, and songs. The Anishnabe legend tells of the Original Man, who was lowered to Earth and walked carefully through creation, which is emulated in the dancers' steps.

During the late nineteenth century and well into the twentieth century, all Native cul-

"The drum is the heartbeat . . ." Photo courtesy Brian Wright-McLeod.

Powwow dancer. Photo by Agnes Patak.

Traditional dancer's eagle feather bustle. Photo courtesy Brian Wright-McLeod.

tural activities were banned by law in the United States and Canada, but they nevertheless survived underground. The evolution of the powwow has thus transpired within a relatively short period of time. In earlier days, the origin of a dancer could be identified by observing his or her dance style or beadwork. Contemporary powwow dancers incorporate anything that will attract the judges' attention, including bright materials, sequins, ribbons, patterns, designs, and beadwork that appeal to the dancer. Dance styles are also continually reinvented.

Contemporary influences have given rise to the distinction between traditional and contemporary song categories and to additional events connected to the powwow, including country music dances, rodeos, baseball games, fairs, concerts, and trade shows. The small traditional powwows, sponsored by families or single communities, culminate in a feast and giveaway. There is no prize money, and usually nothing is sold. Social powwows hosted by an array of groups such as Native student organizations and friendship centers promote cultural awareness and education. In stark contrast, the large commercial or competition powwows (for example, the Schemitzun World Championship of Song and Dance in Connecticut or the Gathering of Nations in Albuquerque, New Mexico) attract thousands of participants and offer large money prizes for dancers and singers. The geographical reach of the powwow is indeed international, including Hawaii and even Europe.

A certain etiquette needs to be observed when someone is attending powwows—formalities of respect followed at any cultural gathering. Rules about no drugs or alcohol and no pets near the arbor or dance area are enforced, and respect is to be shown to elders and veterans. There should be no casual dress, no revealing clothing, and no inappropriate recordings or photographs.

In the last years of the twentieth cen-

tury, powwow music surged in popularity to create a new industry. However, the continuing copyright issues persist as artists begin to understand their rights as songwriters and performers.

DANCERS AND DANCES

Blanket Dance
Traditionally, singers receive gifts of tobacco, food, or trade items. Dancers carry an unfolded blanket held at the corners and move clockwise around the outer edge of the dance area so spectators can toss donations into the center.

Buckskin *See*: Women's Traditional

Chicken Dance (Prairie Chicken Dance)
The dance imitates the mating rituals of the prairie birds. Originally, the Sioux carried their bustles into battle as sacred objects. An 1872 skirmish between the Sioux and the Crow resulted in the capture of one of the bustles. A second Crow war party was sent into the same area and was wiped out, except for one survivor. He was visited by spirits and was taught the songs and how to conduct the dance. The manner in which the drum is to be played symbolizes thunder, as thunder is understood to represent the voice of the Great Spirit.

Crow Hop
The single-beat version (slide song or slide step, a newer style) of the double-beat songs uses a trotting step. It is sometimes referred to as a single-beat Crow hop as opposed to the double-beat hop, where the dancer imitates the movements of the sage grouse.

The double-beat hop is also similar to the push dance, which was created by fusing the elements of the fox trot with the owl dance. The new name for the double-beat songs and the dance itself have gained wide acceptance in the powwow world.

49ers
The 49 songs or dances use a drum beat in three-four time while the singing is in

four-four time, similar to the round dance and rabbit dance songs. Typical 49 songs are known for their use of English lyrics that focus on love and heartbreak.

The Kiowa 49 was originally a war preparation ceremony. A war chief would go through camp singing war expedition songs, and those who enlisted would join in the singing, finally returning to the leader's tipi and singing throughout the night. In the late 1800s, war expedition songs transformed into social dances. By the early 1900s, the 49ers or war expedition songs had grown in popularity and were held after midnight, lasting sometimes until sunrise; the gatherings became known as the Comanche dances. Participants form a close circle around the singers and, with arms interlocked, move clockwise around the drum. As more people join in, a second, third, or fourth circle

forms around the first. A large dance can have as many as eight concentric circles of dancers.

One 49 origin story tells of how, in the early 1920s in Oklahoma, a traveling caravan featured *The Days of '49 Wild West Show*, in reference to the California gold rush days of 1849. The barker yelled all day long for a week, "Come on in, see the dancing girls of '49!" Later, one night when the dancing was in full swing, someone imitated the carnival barker and yelled, "Look at the dancing girls of '49!" However, the 49 dances became notorious because of the carousing that went on during them, and it took years before they were accepted openly in Native communities.

Another 49 origin story tells of fifty men from a reservation who enlisted to fight in World War II; all but one returned, and each of the remaining forty-nine men made a song for his fallen brother. Other versions tell the story so that forty-nine men are lost, and the remaining one soldier makes the songs.

Some of the original OJ-Cree doorway songs were converted into 49ers. The singers would make the rounds throughout a camp and were given gifts of food, tobacco, and other items collected in a blanket to be divided later among the singers.

Grass Dance or Omaha Dance
The grass dance was known as the Omaha society dance or the grass bustle dance in the mid-1800s by the Lakota, who received some of the rituals for the dance from the Omaha. In powwow circles, it's known as the traditional grass dance or the fancy feather dance. Around the 1870s, the Hidatsa introduced the grass dance to the Crow as the hot dance—or the double bustle. This is perhaps the forerunner of all traditional dances in the men's category. The original regalia of the Lakota grass dancer utilized braids and locks of grass tucked into the belt. The grass represented scalps taken in battle; the warriors were always the first to go ahead of the people to ensure safe passage, so they were

Jonathan Windy Boy, grass dancer, Alcatraz Thirtieth Anniversary Gathering, 1999. Photo by Agnes Patak.

the first dancers to prepare the dance area. The associated songs and dances became known as the grass dance. In the 1950s, the dancers were referred to as northern fancy dancers. Contemporary outfits use long, brightly colored yarn fringe to represent the original regalia; no bustle is worn. The steps are intricate and physically demanding as the dancers move in any direction and often pivot in reverse. Each step represents part of a story relating to the origin of the dance as the movements emulate the flattening of the tall grasses with the feet.

HOOP DANCE

The hoop dance was originally a healing ceremony, and the hoops were used only once. This athletic style also carries deep elements of myth and spirituality. The dancer utilizes a series of willow hoops (though contemporary materials are common), as many as thirty, depending on the dancer's experience, to create patterns that relate creation stories, animals, birds, or the earth. The hoop dances take place as an exhibition or competition within their own category.

Jingle Dress

The *jingle dress, straight jingle*, or *side step/slide* are terms related to the jingle dress category. The side step requires that the dancer's feet are held together and never leave the ground; the dancer must slide her feet to the rhythm of a syncopated double beat. The dresses are decorated with rows of tiny cone-shaped bells which were originally made from trade tin or copper.

The jingle dress came from an Anishnabe healing ceremony around 1875 when the daughter of an Anishnabe man became very ill. He was shown the vision of a dress that would heal his daughter; her health improved each time she danced. While origin stories vary, informants cite 1918 when the Jingle Dress Society began to emerge in northeast Ontario.

Men's Fancy Dance

The men's fancy dance originated in Oklahoma in the 1920s as the "crazy chicken." The fancy bustle dance or fancy dance requires total body movement with intricate footwork and physical agility. The style has transformed over time, becoming more athletic as the dancer spins, dips, kicks, splits, flips, and drops to the knee while keeping time with the drum. As the name indicates, the regalia is perhaps the most colorful and utilizes any bright colors, such as baby blue, bright orange, or pink with an upper and lower bustle of feather circular arrangements tipped with brightly colored fluffs. The dancer usually wears a headband or roach, ribbon shirt, breach clout or apron, shorts, fur leggings with sleigh bells fastened at the top near mid-calf of each leg, and moccasins. The dancer sometimes uses matching dance sticks (wands or quirts) to twirl in time with the performance.

Men's Traditional Dances

Men's traditional categories contain various styles from each nation and region, which defines each dance in its own terms, including the use of old buckskin (buckskin outfits and eagle-bonnet headdresses) and round bustle.

Old Style Prairie Chicken Dance (Siksika/ Picunni). One of the oldest dances and imitates the mating rituals of the prairie chicken.
Omaha Dance. Sometimes referred to as a grass dance that grew from the Ponca Heluska or He-thus-ka society dance.
Owl Dance. A social dance for couples and sung with the hand drum; women choose the partner.

Rabbit Dance

The rabbit dance is a very old style and the only Sioux dance for couples. The couples face forward with their hands joined and arms crossed in front of each other. As each dancer moves clockwise around the drum, the left foot takes the forward step almost as a low hop, and the right foot slides up close, but variations on the basic steps have been developed. The beat is a one-two loping rhythm, with the second beat of the drum louder than the first; the lyrics are often of an amorous nature and can contain English words similar to the 49er songs. The origin story of the rabbit dance song relates the travels of a young boy who became lost in a blizzard and heard music. He followed the sound, which led him to a group of jackrabbits, among whom one was singing with a small hand drum while the others danced two by two with a hopping step.

Round Dance *See*: 49ers
There are a variety of round dance songs and round dances, depending on who you talk to. They can be sung with the hand drum (Kahomani songs) or the big drum. Round dance is also a healing circle that has maintained a long existence throughout North America. With a heavy syncopated beat, it is usually sung without words; people form a circle and dance clockwise while stepping to the left and dragging the right foot into place; the name for this dance can also be translated from Lakota as the "dragging feet dance." The round dance or two-step that originated on the Plains is a couples' dance that allows spectators to join in and dance around the drum. The typical round dance song form contains a lead, a second (a repeat of the lead that overlaps the lead), the chorus or main verse with words, first ending (vocables), and final ending.

In western Canada, round dances typically occur during the long winter months, but they can also be performed throughout the year as social gatherings that offer courting opportunities. The round dance is also part of a larger series of drum dances that take place from October to midwinter (e.g.: Christmas Day, New Year's Day), Treaty Day, and early spring. Round dances are also conducted to stimulate community solidarity and reunion. They incorporate elements from other dances, such as the rabbit dance (singer and hand

drummers are stationary as the dancers move to a double meter, clockwise single file, never touching), the Cree dance (similar to rabbit but in triple meter), and the tea dance, where singer and hand drummers begin the song, then lay drums on the ground, holding hands, facing each other to form a half-circle, which is completed as a circle when the dancers join in (*See*: Traditional/Archival Compilations: *1962 Dogrib Tea Dance*). In the early days, they used buckets of very strong tea (sometimes local herbs mixed with tobacco), which later were replaced by regular tea.

The hand drum is held in one hand with the index and middle finger firmly placed on the underside of the drum head; each time the drummer strikes the drum with a drum stick held in the other hand, he drags his fingers along the back underside of the drumhead to create a resonance (almost a buzzing sound) with every second beat. Large gatherings take place where hundreds of drummers assemble to share songs. Competition powwows have categories for hand drumming and round dance singing.

Side-Step *See*: Jingle Dress
In the side-step dance, the women form a circle in the dance area, and the syncopated beat keeps the dancers moving in quick time while facing inward, moving up and down, keeping their feet tight together at the ankles and sliding and moving them to the left in a clockwise motion around the drum. They stop and raise their fans or feathers during the honor beats.

Slide-Step *See*: Crow Hop

Smoke Dance
The smoke dance originally grew from the Mohawk warrior society and was part of the thunder dance, which expresses appreciation for the natural elements. In the 1930s, the dance developed the fast footwork that demands agility and stamina. By the late 1990s, it became a popular dance category in many eastern powwows.

Snake Dance

The snake dance is a follow-the-leader social dance for all participants and spectators.

Sneak-up Dance

The sneak-up dance is a warrior's dance where the dancer depicts the sneaking up on an enemy either to scout or to attack or to retrieve a fallen comrade. It stems from a greater body of war songs and drum dances. Songs and dances are divided into two parts: the dancers move as if they are scouting for enemies; the drum rolls; then the dancer rises up and steps in time with the evenly quickened tempo.

Straight Fancy Dance

Straight fancy dance is a warm-up for fancy dance competitions. The dancers stand very straight—hence, the name of the song.

Women's Fancy Dance

Women's fancy dance began in the 1940s in Oklahoma and was brought north by young women attending boarding schools in the 1950s. During World War II, when many of the men left the reservations to enlist into military service, the women took up key roles in the workplace and in certain ceremonies to keep the culture alive. Some of these responsibilities ovelapped into social functions, including powwow drumming and dancing. The young women were attracted to the more physically demanding features of fancy-dancing and initially adopted the men's dance regalia complete with roaches and bustles. The overall transformation of the women's outfit was a gradual process. With respect to traditional philosophies, the woman is viewed as the bringer of life; the elders considered the new style to be scandalous in part because the women's feet were never supposed to leave the ground. Regardless, a highly competitive category for women dancers emerged.

Women's Fancy Shawl

Women's fancy shawl dancing evolved in the North during the 1960s. The women wear brightly colored cloth dresses accented with ribbonwork and beaded accessories; they may wear a single upright eagle plume or a beaded crown. The basic movements involve fast forward and backward foot shuffles, with the shawl draped over the dancer's back and arms to evoke a floating or flying motion. Some of the dance steps are akin to Scottish Highland dancing, with an upright stance and swinging foot motions and legwork that includes hops, turns, dips, and spins. There are more arm movements in fancy shawl dancing than in the women's fancy dance, where there are more head movements and faster footwork. Dancers with experience in both styles describe the fancy shawl dance as being "more feminine," whereas women's fancy dance allows for more creativity in movement. Nevertheless, both styles demand physical endurance.

Women's Traditional

Women's traditional (buckskin, cloth buckskin, or southern buckskin) dancers wear traditional buckskin regalia with traditional designs of beadwork, quillwork, cowry shells, hairpipe bone jewelry, dintalium shell, and elk teeth; more lenient dances allow cloth dresses. The dancers can wear fully decorated yokes, hide dresses, leggings, moccasins, conch belts, necklaces, shawls, fans, and feathers fastened to their hair, and they may carry eagle feather fans or a single feather. The dance requires the women to stand in one place and gently move up onto the balls of the feet and back down onto the heels and turn from one side to the other in unison with the drum, stopping at the last drum beat.

THE DRUM

The drum is sacred and represents the earth or the circle of life. The singer's high-

Diane Montoya, traditional dancer, Alcatraz Thirtieth Anniversary Gathering, 1999. Photo by Agnes Patak.

All singers in the group who sit at the drum have round-headed drum sticks and follow the lead and second lead singers. The small hand drum has only one membrane stretched over an octagonal or round frame that ranges from ten inches to eighteen inches in diameter and is about four inches deep. Alternating names for the performers who sing at the drum include *drummers-singers, singers, drum,* or *drum group.*

ELEMENTS OF THE POWWOW

Giveaway is a ceremony for which a family or individual will prepare for a year in advance. It is an honoring ceremony or a memorial for a family member. The person being honored distributes gifts among the people; generosity is regarded as a spiritual virtue that acknowledges balance in spirit and physical worlds.

"Grand Entry" is the first song of the powwow, which officially opens each day of the gathering. All of the dancers in full regalia enter the circle from the east near the drums and the announcer's podium. Various origin stories about "Grand Entry" also cite the influence of the Wild West shows of the 1800s, in which everyone entered the arena at the same time; other references name the Sundance, where dancers enter the arbor at the east.

The color guard, composed of Native veterans, carry the eagle staff and the Canadian and U.S. flags and lead the procession. The flag song is sung, followed by the veteran's song. The sneak-up song (a warrior's song) follows the veteran's song. The colors are retired at the closing of each day.

The powwow princess, who represents the virtues of the people, leads the veterans and elders. The head male dancer is followed by the male traditional dancers, who are followed by the head woman dancer, who leads the women dancers; behind them are the male fancy dancers, then the female shawl dancers and the children (or

pitched falsetto, found in northern-style singing, represents the first cry of a newborn child. Several styles of drums vary in size and construction, including the big drums, hand drums, water drums, and log drums.

The large drums are constructed of hide membranes stretched across a circular wooden frame usually three feet across and a foot deep, and they are placed on a blanket on the ground or suspended by a custom-made stand. Many groups beginning in the 1960s and through the 1980s used bass drums from contemporary kits.

Tiny Tots). Depending on the nature and location of the powwow, sometimes all head dancers enter together.

Judging utilizes a point system. Dancers are arranged in categories of styles and age groups, and contestants are judged on their outfits and regalia, performance, and style. A good dancer is one who dances to the song rather than to the beat of the drum. Drums are judged on their singing ability, range, knowledge, cohesion, and performance of any song at a moment's notice when called upon by the MC.

Powwow singing is strophic, with interior repetition such as hymns; each strophe is referred to as a *push-up* by the drummers-singers or as a *round* by dancers. The voice is used at a higher pitch at the beginning of each strophe; an incomplete repetition divides the strophe into two parts. Four push-ups are described as eight repetitions in Western music theory, which identifies four complete and four incomplete. An entire song can be a push-up; if an MC asks a drum group for four push-ups, the group will sing the song four times through.

As with most Native singing, the pentatonic scales are used in powwow music; songs often have four verses or *starts*. The music consists of vocables sung in melodic contours descending from high to low. The lead singers of the northern style often use a falsetto to introduce the beginning of the song and verse. The women stand outside the ring of drummers seated around the instrument and sing one octave higher than the men; they do not sing lead, but come in during the second half of the song.

Powwow songs include traditional songs that are generally word songs; straight songs are composed of vocables only, with all melody. Songs with vocables for the lead, second, and first part, and with words

for the second part of the song are known as *intertribals*. Traditional songs originate from old ceremonial or society songs that have evolved to become known as flag songs, memorial songs, honor songs, veterans' songs, victory songs, and grass dance. Traditional songs use a regular beat with a melodic structure and either words or vocables.

The songs are typically composed of two halves, as the second part echoes the first. The song begins with the lead singer, who starts out with a high falsetto, indicating to the group which song they are to sing and echo, then moves to a lower register as the opening phrasing continues. At the end of the first half, there is a slight pause, then the second half begins. Honor beats (loud single beats, usually four) are placed at intervals, indicating to the drummers and dancers that the song will continue or end. After the song has been sung once through, the lead singer will repeat the lead solo line, indicating that the song will be sung again. The lead singer adds a "tail," which picks up the song at the beginning of the second half. Songs are usually sung four times through.

Song styles include northern style and southern style. The region including the Northern Great Plains and the Great Lakes, generally the northern U.S. states, and all of Canada are referred to as "northern." The songs originating from these locations are northern style. Southern style is commonly identified as coming from the territory south of the Oklahoma/Kansas region. The southern-style singing utilizes the lower register, without the high falsetto common in northern-style singing. The differences include more than just songs or dance styles, but also involve origins, regalia, and history.

Section 6-A
Powwow Music Recordings

Alliance West Singers—(Kiowa) Southern Style *See*: Traditional/ Archival Group

Lineup: Vincent and Joe Toya, Chuck Gibbon, Kurt Adakai, Kevin Adakai, Tommy Spotted Bird, and Cornel Pewewardy (*See*: Flute Music).

DISCOGRAPHY:

Appearances:
Spirit of the Native American Indians [ARC Music 1999, United Kingdom/ Germany] comp
Dancing Buffalo [Music of the World 1994] w/ Cornel Pewewardy

All Nation Singers—(Intertribal) Northern Style

Lineup: Larry Walker, Clint Green Crow, John Morris, Keith Smith, Asay Thin Elk, Cliff Robertson, Wesley Hansen, Janice Walker, Karen Natewa. Recorded live on the Flandreau Indian School Campus, March 1983.

DISCOGRAPHY:
Flandreau Indian School [Featherstone FT-4002-C]

Appearances:
A Celebration of First Nations [Craggle Rock 1993] comp

American Indian Dance Theater— (Intertribal)

Lineup: Wade Baker; Saunders Bearstail Jr.; Hanay Geiogamah (*See*: Contemporary Compilations: *Oyate*); Chester Mahooty (*See*: Traditional/Archival Solo); Arlie Neskahi (*See*: Contemporary Music: Song Catchers); Andrew Vasquez (*See*: Flute Music); Norwyn Wesley, stage direction; Barbara Schwei, producer. The 1984 album received a Grammy nomination for Best Traditional Folk Album, 1989.

DISCOGRAPHY:
American Indian Dance Theater [Broadway Records 1984]

Appearances:
Pulse, a STOMP Odyssey [Six Degrees Records 2003] sdtk

Arawak Mountain—(Intertribal) Northern Style

Lineup: Al Boldeagle (Taino-Arawak), Louie Tureyguari (Taino-Arawak), Ray Elk Silva (Laguna Pueblo), Tree Ceibo Rivas (Taino-Arawak), Cliff Standing Deer Mathias (Taino–Carib–Eastern Cherokee), Lizzy Sarobey (Taino-Arawak), Joan Henry (Jicarilla Apache).

Based in New York State. The group's cultural diversity represents the reunion of the indigenous people from the North and South, symbolized by the eagle and the condor, respectively.

DISCOGRAPHY:
Honoring the Ancient Ones [SOAR 1996]
Feel the Thunder [SOAR 1995]

Ashland Singers—(Cheyenne) Northern Style

Lineup: Daniel Foote, LaForce Lonebear, Henry Sioux, Corlett Teeth, Harvey Whiteman, Oran Wolfback, Wesley Black Wolf. Recorded at Lame Deer Montana, May 12, 1974.

DISCOGRAPHY:
Northern Cheyenne War Dance [Indian House 1974]

Assiniboine Jrs.—(Assiniboine-Sioux) Northern Style

Lineup: Curtis Assiniboine, Glen Tait, Darryl Kingbird, Curtis Meeches, Shane Red Star, Kenny Pratt, Darren Cameron,

Hank Hotain, Feralin and Cyril Assiniboine. From Long Plain, Manitoba.

DISCOGRAPHY:
Tribute to Feralin [Wacipi Records 2001]
Powwow Songs, Vol. 5 [Canyon 1993]
Live at O'odham Tash, Vol. 4 [Canyon 1992]
Powwow Songs, Vol. 3 [Canyon 1992]

Appearances:
Gathering of Champions: The Winners' Circle [SOAR 1995] comp
Gathering of Nations Pow-Wow 1994 [SOAR 1995] comp

Assiniboine Singers—(Assiniboine-Sioux) Northern Style

DISCOGRAPHY:
Live at Dakota Tipi [Featherstone FT-1014]

Appearances:
Gathering of Champions: The Winners' Circle [SOAR 1995] comp

Atsa Butte—(Dineh) Northern Style

Lineup: Junior, Cleavon, Ivan, and Janell Succo; Tanya and Myron Brown; Adrian and Alvin Yazzie; Jeremy Kenneth; C. Bengi Pioche; Mirand King. Recorded live at Lake Valley, New Mexico.

DISCOGRAPHY:
N 2 Tha Millennium [Cool Runnings 2001]

Bad Canyon Wellpinit—(Spokane) Northern Style

Lineup: Ben, Evelyn, Rachel, Rose, Mary, Paul, Mavis, Albert, and Chico Corral. Recorded at the 1980 Omak Powwow. From Washington State.

DISCOGRAPHY:
Powwow Songs [Canyon CR-6174]

Appearances:
Omak Powwow 1980 [Canyon CR-6175]
  comp

Badger Singers—Northern Style

DISCOGRAPHY:
Songs of Ed King Eagle [Canyon 1996]

Badlands Singers—(Assiniboine-Sioux) Northern Traditional

Original Lineup: Lyle Denny, Rusty Denny, Gary Drum, Ben Gray Hawk, Gerald Lambert, Gary Red Eagle, Adrian Spotted Bird Sr., Leland Spotted Bird, Matthew Big Fork, and Roy Azure III.
  1994 Lineup: Bill Runsabove, Delray Smith, Chuck Spotted Bird, Merle Tendoy, and Harry Three Stars Jr.
  Founded by Seymour Eagle Speaker, Fort Peck, Montana, 1972.

DISCOGRAPHY:
Live at Santa Fe [Indian House 1994]
Live at United Tribes, Vol. 2 [Indian House 1980]
Live at United Tribes, Vol. 1 [Indian House 1980]
Kahomini Songs [Indian House 1978]
Badlands Singers at Home [Indian House 1978]
Live at Bismarck [Indian House 1977]
Sounds of the Badlands Singers [Indian House 1976]
Assiniboine Sioux Grass Dance [Indian House 1974]

Appearances:
Proud Heritage [Indian House 1996] comp
  See: Traditional/Archival Compilations

Bad Medicine—(Kiowa) Southern Style

Lineup: DeWayne Tofpi (Kiowa-Ute), Suni Deer (Kiowa-Creek), Gene Ray Ahboah

(Kiowa), Glen Ahhaitty (Kiowa-Comanche), Joe "Fish" Dupoint (*See*: Peyote Music), Walter Ahhaitty (Kiowa-Comanche).
  From Carnegie, Oklahoma, Bad Medicine was named World Champions of Southern Style Singing, Schemitzun, 1996.

DISCOGRAPHY:
Blast from the Past [Sweet Grass 2002]
Dance Your Style, Vol. 2 [Canyon 1996]
Southern Style Powwow Songs [Canyon 1996]

Appearances:
Mitataht askiy: Sweet Grass Records 10 Years [Sweet Grass 2003] comp
Gathering of Nations Powwow 2001 [Gathering of Nations Records 2001] comp
Schemitzun World Championship 2000: Southern Style [Turtle Island Music 2001] comp
Best of the Best Schemitzun '93–99 [Sweet Grass 1999] comp

Bad Nation; a.k.a. Oyate Sica—(Lakota-Dakota) Northern Style

Lineup: Kevin Wright; Richard Hudson; Glenn Shields; Whitney Recontre; Mike Spears; Emil Flute; Gerald, Clark, and Darrell Zephier; Doug Grey Owl; Chris and Ron Estes. From the Crow Creek and Lower Brule Reservations in South Dakota.

DISCOGRAPHY:
Live at the Black Hills Powwow [Medicine Wheel 2000]
Straight from tha Rez [Medicine Wheel 1999]

Appearances:
Black Hills: 16th Annual Powwow [Arbor 2003] comp
Sacred Spirit II [Higher Octave Music/Virgin 2000] comp *See*: Contemporary Compilations

Bad River—Northern Style

Lineup: Joe Dan Rose, Dan Powless, Ed Mayotte, Matt O'Claire, Francis Stone, Robert Leoso. Based in Bad River, Wisconsin.

DISCOGRAPHY:

Appearances:
Honor the Earth Powwow Songs of the Great Lakes [Ryko 1990] comp

Battle River—(Anishnabe) Northern Style

Lineup: Kevon, Don, and Gerald Kingbird; Mike Roy; Jon Prentice; Bob Barrett; Phibs Baker; Elliot Cloud; Terry Sengoles; Justin Smith; Frank Graves; Greg Thomas; Monica Prentice; Cecil Nepoose; Willy Strong. From Red Lake, Minnesota, Battle River was named Northern Style World Singing Champions, Schemitzun, 1998.

DISCOGRAPHY:
Live from the Rez [Turtle Island Music 2000]
Couple for the Road [Arbor 1999]

Appearances:
Champion Hand Drum Songs [Arbor 2003] comp
Women's Fancy Dance Songs [Arbor/ Native American Heritage Series 2003] comp
Thunder Drums, Vol. 2: *The Best Powwow Songs from the World's Best Drums* [Arbor 2002] comp
Schemitzun 2000: Hand Drum Songs [Sweet Grass 2001] comp
Schemitzun World Championship 2000: Northern Style [Turtle Island Music 2001] comp
Schemitzun World Championship 2000: Round Dance Singing [Turtle Island Music 2001] comp
Thunder Drums, Vol. 1: *The Best of Arbor Records* [Arbor 2001] comp
Schemitzun World Championship Round Dance Singing [Turtle Island Music 2000] comp
Bear Spirit [Turtle Island Music 1999] comp
Best of the Best Schemitzun '93–99 [Sweet Grass 1999] comp
Hinckley Powwow Northern Style [Arbor 1999] comp
Spirit of the Wolf [Turtle Island Music 1998] comp
Red Lake Nation [Turtle Island Music 1996] comp
United Tribes International Powwow [Makoche 1995] two-CD comp
Hinckley Grand Celebrations Powwow 1995 Northern Style [Sunshine SSCT-4283] comp
C.I.S. 20th Annual Powwow [Sunshine SSCT-4172] comp
White Earth Powwow [Sunshine SSCT-4173] comp

Bear Claw—Northern Style

Lineup: Ron, Rodney, and Steve Mallory; William Hendsley; Stuart Decorah. Based in Hertel, Wisconsin.

DISCOGRAPHY:

Appearances:
Honor the Earth Powwow Songs of the Great Lakes [Ryko 1990] comp

Bear Creek—(Anishnabe) Northern Style

Lineup: Hokie Clairmont; Rob Essex; Tom Hare; Nick Heavson; Nitanis Landry; Lenny and Trevor LeBlanc; Luke McCoy; Andrew Nahwegahbow; Chris Neveau; Justin Perreault; Joe, John, Kevin Syrette; Mike Tegosh; Darrell Thunderchild; Mike Willis. Based in Sault Sainte Marie, Ontario.

DISCOGRAPHY:
The Show Must Go On [Arbor 2003]
Live [Arbor 2001]

Appearances:
Women's Fancy Dance Songs [Arbor/
 Native American Heritage Series 2003]
 comp
*Thunder Drums, Vol. 2: The Best Pow-
 wow Songs from the World's Best Drums*
 [Arbor 2002] comp
Eschikagou Powwow 2000 LIVE! [Gather-
 ing of Nations Records 2001] comp
Gathering of Nations Powwow 2001
 [Gathering of Nations Records 2001]
 comp
Relentless Warrior [Gathering of Nations
 Records 2001] comp
*Thunder Drums, Vol. 1: The Best of Arbor
 Records* [Arbor 2001] comp
*Gathering of Nations Pow-Wow: Mil-
 lennium Celebration, Vol. 1: Various
 Northern Drums* [SOAR 2000] comp
Voices from Thunderchild Powwow Songs
 [Turtle Island Music 2000] comp

Big Bear—(Cree) Northern Style

Originally formed in 1973 with Willy
Okanee, Leslie Jack, George Weeseekase.
 1997 Lineup: Gerald, Luke, Willard,
Gary Sr., and Everette Okanee; Cornell
Tootoosis; Bill Runsabove; Jason Butler;
Cornelius Arkinson; Anthony Standing
Rock. From Thunderchild, Saskatchewan.

DISCOGRAPHY:
Live at Fort Hall [Indian House 2002]
Spirit Dancer [Sweet Grass 2000]

Appearances:
*37th Annual Milk River Indian Days Pow-
 wow Live at Fort Belknap, Montana*
 [Sweet Grass 2003] comp
Voices from Thunderchild Powwow Songs
 [Turtle Island Music 2000] comp

Big Soldier Creek—(Potawatomi)
Northern Style

Lineup: Dawn One Feather; Trilby, Bad-
ger, Karen, Adrian, and Greg Wah-was-uck.

They chose their name after the Big Soldier
family from the Prairie Band of Potawatomi, Mayette, Kansas.

DISCOGRAPHY:
*Beautiful Way of Life: Potawatomi Songs
 for the Northern Drum* [WithOut Rez
 Productions 1999]

Black Eagle—(Jemez Pueblo)
Traditional Hand Drum

Lineup: Malcolm, Emmett, Elston, Lloyd,
David Yepa Sr.; Glendon and Delvin Toyo;
Terrence and Kendrick Casiquito; Fidel
Fragua; Keven Gachupin.
 Formed in 1989. Their album *Life Goes
On: Hand Drum and Round Dance Songs*
received a Grammy nomination for Best
Native American Music Album, 2002; *Fly-
ing Free* received the Grammy Award for
Best Native American Music Album, 2004.

DISCOGRAPHY:
Flying Free [SOAR 2003]
*Life Goes On: Hand Drum and Round
 Dance Songs* [SOAR 2000]
Soaring High [SOAR 1999]

Appearances:
The Best of the Northern Boys [SOAR 1999]
 comp

Blackfeet Singers; a.k.a. Pat
Kennedy and the Blackfoot
Singers—(Blackfoot) Northern Style
See: Scalp Lock, Green, Kennedy
Singers

Lineup: Pat Kennedy, Thomas NorRunner,
Edwin Calfrobe, Victor Surechief.

DISCOGRAPHY:
Powwow Songs [Canyon CR-6132]
Old Blackfeet Powwow Songs [Canyon
 CR-6119]
Blackfeet Pow-Wow Songs [Canyon 1974]
From the Land of the Blackfeet [Canyon
 CR-6095]

Blackfoot A-1 Club Singers—
(Blackfoot) Northern Style

Lineup: Andy Axe, Dennis Black Rider, Nick Breaker, Ralph Crow Chief, Raymond Crow Chief, Philip Little Chief, Gerald Sitting Eagle, Marcel Weasel Head. Recorded at Gleichen, Alberta, July 26, 1972.

DISCOGRAPHY:
Powwow Songs, Vol. 2 [Indian House 1973]
Blackfoot A-1 Singers, Vol. 1 [Indian House 1973]

Blackfoot Crossing—(Siksika) Northern Style *See*: Traditional/Archival Group

Lineup: Fred Breaker, Radford Blackrider, Rod Scout, Joe and Eldon Weaselchild, Herman Yellow Old Woman, Dennis Blackrider, Julius Delaney, Irvin and Fredrick Johnson, Larry Whyte. From Siksika First Nation, Alberta; recorded August 12, 1989, Gleichen, Alberta.

DISCOGRAPHY:
Blackfoot Crossing [Indian House 1989]

Appearances:
Bismarck Powwow [Sunshine 1993] comp
Onion Lake Powwow 1992 [Sunshine SSCT-4149] comp

Blackfoot Oldtimers—(Blackfoot) Northern Style

Lineup: Alex Scalp Lock, Leo Pretty Young Man, Marcel Weasel Head, Henry Sun Walk, Peter Calf, Frank Turning Robe Sr.

DISCOGRAPHY:
Songs from the Past [Canyon CR-9004]

Blacklodge—(Blackfoot) Northern Style *See*: Arlie Neskahi/White Eagle Singers; Flute Music: R. Carlos Nakai

Lineup: Ken, Louise, Elgin, Erwin, Mike, John, Thomas, Shawn Scabby Robe, and Thomas Shawn.

Based in White Swan, Washington, Blacklodge is one of the most popular and probably the most recorded drum group. With more than twenty albums on the Canyon label alone, Blacklodge has maintained the integrity of powwow singing and explored successful hybrids with other music forms, including a collaboration with classical music orchestras. Blacklodge was named Contemporary World Champions, Schemitzun, 1999, and Drum Group of the Year, NAMA 2000; and they received Grammy nominations for Best Native American Music Album, 2001, 2002, and 2004.

DISCOGRAPHY:
Veterans' Honor Songs [Canyon 2003]
It's Been a Long Time Comin' Round Dance Songs [Canyon 2001]
Weasel Tail's Dream: The Tradition Continues [Canyon 2001]
Tribute to the Elders [Canyon 1999]
World Hand Drum Champions '98 [Sweet Grass 1998]
The People Dance: Recorded Live at Wellpinit [Canyon 1998]
Round Dance Tonight! Recorded at Wildhorse [Canyon 1997]
Enter the Circle: Recorded Live at Coeur D' Alene [Canyon 1997]
Powwow Songs for Kids [Canyon 1996]
Powwow Songs Recorded Live at White Swan [Canyon 1996]
Intertribal Powwow Songs Recorded Live in Arizona [Canyon 1996]
Powwow Songs, Vol. 11 [Canyon 1995]
Round Dance Songs [Canyon 1994]
Powwow People [SOAR 1994]
Live at Schemitzun 1994 [Sweet Grass 1994]
Powwow Songs, Vol. 9 [Canyon 1993]

Veteran's Honor Songs [Canyon 1993]
Live at Red Lake, Vol. 1 [Sunshine 1993]
Powwow Wow [SOAR/Spalax 1992, France]
Live at Red Lake, Vol. 2 [Sunshine SSCT-4176]
Live Recording [Sunshine SSCT-4150]
Powwow Songs, Vol. 7 [Canyon CR-16213]
Live at Fort Duschesne [Canyon 1991]
Intertribal Powwow Songs [Canyon 1991]
Intertribal Powwow Songs, Vol. 4 [Canyon 1990]
Powwow Highway Songs [SOAR 1990]
Powwow Songs Recorded Live [Canyon 1990]
Powwow Songs Recorded Live [Canyon 1989]
Powwow Songs, Vol. 1 [Canyon 1987]

Appearances:
Mitataht askiy: Sweet Grass Records 10 Years [Sweet Grass 2003] comp
Champion Hand Drum Songs [Arbor 2003] comp
Drum Beats: 18 Powwow Groups [Sunshine 2002] comp
Tribal Legends [Earth Beat! 2002] comp; w/ R. Carlos Nakai and William Eaton *See*: Contemporary Compilations
World's Best Memorial Songs [Sunshine 2002] comp
Schemitzun 2000: Hand Drum Songs [Sweet Grass 2001] comp
Schemitzun World Championship 2000: Round Dance Singing [Turtle Island Music 2001] comp
Sacred Souls [Manteca 2001, United Kingdom] comp *See*: Contemporary Compilations
World's Best Fancy Dance Songs, Vol. 2 [Sunshine 2001] comp
World's Best Intertribal Songs [Sunshine 2001] comp
World's Best Round Dance Songs, Vol. 2 [Sunshine 2001] comp
World's Best Veteran Songs, Vol. 1 [Sunshine 2001] comp
World's Best Fancy Dance Songs, Vol. 1 [Sunshine 2000] comp
Powwow 2000 [Sunshine 2000] comp

Schemitzun World Championship Round Dance Singing [Turtle Island Music 2000] comp
World's Best Powwow Drum Groups [Sunshine 2000] comp
Across Indian Lands [SOAR 1999] comp *See*: Traditional/Archival Compilations
The Best of the Northern Boys [SOAR 1999] comp
Best of the Best Schemitzun '93–99 [Sweet Grass 1999] comp
World's Best Grass Dance [Sunshine 1998] comp
World's Best Jingle Dress Songs [Sunshine 1998] comp
American Warriors: Songs for Indian Veterans [Ryko 1997] comp *See*: Traditional/Archival Compilations
Voices across the Canyon, Vol. 3 [Canyon 1997] comp *See*: Contemporary Compilations
World's Best Round Dance Songs [Sunshine 1997] comp
Gathering of Nations Pow-Wow 1994 [SOAR 1995] comp
Gathering of Nations Pow-Wow 1993 [SOAR 1994] comp
A Celebration of First Nations [Craggle Rock 1993] comp
Gathering of Nations Pow-Wow 1992 [SOAR 1993] comp
Gathering of Nations Pow-Wow, Vol. 1 [SOAR 1992] comp
Onion Lake Powwow 1992 [Sunshine SSCT-4149] comp

Blackstone Singers—(Cree)
Northern Style *See*: Contemporary Music: Lorrie Church

Lineup: Randy, Darrell, and Laurence Paskimin; Clint Frank. Formed in 1987, Sweetgrass, Saskatchewan. One of the top award-winning powwow groups, their titles included World Champions, Schemitzun, 1996 and 1999.

DISCOGRAPHY:

Round Dance Singin' [Canyon 2003]
  w/ Logan Alexis Singers
*On the Oregon Trail: Pow-Wow Songs
  Recorded Live at Simnasho* [Canyon
  2003]
Pictures of You: Round Dance Songs [Canyon 2002]
Around the Horn: Pow-Wow Songs Recorded Live at Couer D'Alene [Canyon 2002]
September Rain [Turtle Island Music 2002]
Wagon Trail [Blackstone Music 2000]
Buffalo Cloud [Noon Records 1998]
Powwow Songs [Canyon 1994]
Pow-wow Recorded Live! [Canyon 1993]
Powwow Songs, Vol. 3 [Canyon 1993]
Powwow Songs Live at Fort Duschesne [Canyon 1992]
Contest Songs Live! [Canyon 1991]

Appearances:

*Mitataht askiy: Sweet Grass Records 10
  Years* [Sweet Grass 2003] comp
*Northern Cree and Friends: Round Dance
  Songs Recorded "Live,"* Vol. 1 [Canyon 2002] comp
Gathering of Nations Powwow 2001
  [Gathering of Nations Records 2001]
  comp
Gathering of Nations Pow-Wow: Millennium Celebration, Vol. 1: *Various
  Northern Drums* [SOAR 2000] comp
Best of the Best Schemitzun '93–99 [Sweet
  Grass 1999] comp
Thunderchild '98 [Turtle Island Music
  1999] comp
Native American Music [Rough Guide
  1998, United Kingdom] comp
Indian Graffiti: Noon Records Greatest
  [Noon Records 1998] comp
Gathering of Nations Pow-Wow 1995
  [SOAR 1996] comp
Voices across the Canyon, Vol. 2 [Canyon 1996] comp *See*: Contemporary
  Compilations
A Celebration of First Nations [Craggle
  Rock 1993] comp

The Boyz—(Intertribal) Northern
Style *See*: Eyabay, Young Bird

Lineup: Everette Moore; Marlin Dickenson; Lakota, Bonnie, and April Clairmont;
Reuben Crowfeather; Opie Day-Bedeau;
Jeremy Dearly; Charles Lasley; Darian
Wakefield; James Day; Phillip St. John; Pat
De Cora.

Based in Minneapolis, Minnesota. The
Boyz was one of the first powwow recording groups to use hip-hop song titles to
reflect the influence of their urban surroundings.

DISCOGRAPHY:

Life and Timez of TBZ [Arbor 2000]
World Wide [Noon Records 1999]
Boyz 'n the Hood [Noon Records 1998]
*The Boyz: Recorded Live at Haskell Indian
  Nations University* [Turtle Island Music
  1996]

Appearances:

*Mitataht askiy: Sweet Grass Records 10
  Years* [Sweet Grass 2003] comp
Champion Hand Drum Songs [Arbor 2003]
  comp
*The Best of Hinckley Powwow Northern
  and Southern Style* [Arbor 2003] comp
Thunder Drums, Vol. 2: *The Best Powwow Songs from the World's Best Drums*
  [Arbor 2002] comp
Hinckley Powwow Northern Style [Arbor
  2001] comp
Schemitzun 2000: Hand Drum Songs
  [Sweet Grass 2001] comp
*Schemitzun World Championship 2000:
  Round Dance Singing* [Turtle Island
  Music 2001] comp
Thunder Drums, Vol. 1: *The Best of Arbor
  Records* [Arbor 2001] comp
*Schemitzun World Championship Round
  Dance Singing* [Turtle Island Music
  2000] comp
Bear Spirit [Turtle Island Music 1999]
  comp
*Ermineskin Cree Nation Pow-wow: Live at
  Bear Park* [Sweet Grass 1999] comp

Indian Graffiti: Noon Records Greatest [Noon Records 1998] comp

Spirit of the Wolf [Turtle Island Music 1998] comp

Gathering of Nations Pow-Wow 1996 [SOAR 1997] comp

United Tribes International Powwow [Makoche 1995] two-CD comp

Hinckley Grand Celebrations Powwow 1995 Northern Style [Sunshine SSCT-4283] comp

Hinckley Powwow, Vol. 2 [Sunshine 1995] comp

Minnesota Powwow Songs [Sunshine SSCT-4174] comp

Brave Scout Singers—(Intertribal) Northern Style

Lineup: Sid Brave Scout-Moore, Ted and Dot Moore, Pete Moore Sr., Ock Newrider, Cricket and Tee Tee Shields, Edward and Sydnna Yellowfish, Conrad Gayly, Rick Tosee, Dynomite Mitholo, Gwendy Williams. The singers represent Otoe, Missourian, and Pawnee Nations.

DISCOGRAPHY:
Brave Scout Singers—Northern Style [Canyon 1980]

Broken Wing—(Cree) Northern Style

Lineup includes lead singer Clement Mitsuing. Recorded live at Prince Albert Penitentiary; the album is the first powwow recording made within the walls of a penal institution.

DISCOGRAPHY:
Broken Wing Singers [Sweet Grass 1994]

Brown Eagle—(Intertribal) Northern Style

Lineup: Jamie, Barrie, Joey, Mark, and Chris Mandamin; Howard and Mark Carpenter; Andrew Letander; Brandon Bunting; Vincent Quewezance; David, Jeremiah, Ricky, and Jeremy McDonald.

DISCOGRAPHY:
Brown Eagle, Vol. 4 [Sunshine 1996]
Brown Eagle, Vol. 3 [Sunshine SSCT-4197]
Brown Eagle, Vol. 2 [Sunshine SSCT-4175]
Brown Eagle, Vol. I [Sunshine SSCT-4147]

Appearances:
Drum Beats: 18 Powwow Groups [Sunshine 2002] comp
World's Best Fancy Dance Songs, Vol. 2 [Sunshine 2001] comp

Brown, Tanya

DISCOGRAPHY:
Tonto's Fury [Cool Runnings 1998]

Buckaroos—(Anishnabe) Northern Style

Lineup: Leroy, Strong, and Johnny Smith.

DISCOGRAPHY:
The Buckaroos [Featherstone FT-1008]

Bucks—(Ho-Chunk) Northern Style

Lineup: Kelly and John Herman (Ho-Chunk); Herman Logan (Winnebago); O. C. Earth (Winnebago); Nate and Danny Ante (Bad River Chippewa); Ron Preston (San Carlos Apache); Wayne Moore (Kiowa); Hardon Dovel (Oklahoma Cherokee); R. J. Smith (LCO Chippewa); Kenny Addey; Ray Ackley; Charles Belisle; Darrell Hill; Sid White; Tom Johnson (Oneida).

DISCOGRAPHY:
Comin' Alive [Rez Cue Records 2000]

Appearances:
Thunder on the Lake [Arbor 2003] comp
Relentless Warrior [Gathering of Nations Records 2001] comp

Gathering of Nations Powwow 2001
[Gathering of Nations Records 2001]
comp

Buffalo Lake Singers—(Dakota) Northern Style

Lineup: Fred Holy Bull, Baby Gary Holy Bull, Gary Holy Bull Sr., Sam Hapa, Hank Hotain, Carl Essie, Harold Blacksmith, Donald Buffalo, Gary Taylor, Irene Yuzicapi, Rita Holy Bull. From Sioux Valley, Manitoba.

DISCOGRAPHY:
Schemitzun World Championship of Song and Dance [Sweet Grass 2001]
Buffalo Lake Singers [Sunshine SSCT-4184]

Appearances:
Mitataht askiy: Sweet Grass Records 10 Years [Sweet Grass 2003] comp

Buffalo River Dene Drummers— (Dene) Traditional Hand Drum

Lineup: Marius Catarat, Gilbert Benjamin, Phillip Sylvestre, Darren Billette, James Sylvestre. From northern Saskatchewan, Canada.

DISCOGRAPHY:
The Saskatchewan Indian Cultural Centre Presents [SICC 1993]

Appearances:
Still the Eagle Flies, Vols. 1 and 2 [SICC 1995] comp

Bull, Edmund—(Cree) Northern Style
See: Red Bull; Contemporary Music: Edmund Bull

From Little Pine First Nation, Cutknife, Saskatchewan.

DISCOGRAPHY:
End of the Trail [Turtle Island Music 2003]
round dance

Indian Boy [Turtle Island Music 2000]
country songs
I've Been Everywhere [Sweet Grass 1994]

Appearances:
Mitataht askiy: Sweet Grass Records 10 Years [Sweet Grass 2003] comp
World's Leading Round Dance Songs [Sweet Grass 1996] comp

Burntside Lake—(Anishnabe-Cree) Northern Style

Lineup: James, Joe, Ron, Gene, and Jim Beshey; Delwyn Wilson; Pat Pierre; Tony Northrup; Rick Myers; Terry Goodsky; Eric Kingbird; Elroy Lightfeather; Jordan Cloud; Bobby Adams; Darrel Deep; Jones Dallas; and Jerry Stillday.

DISCOGRAPHY:
Str8up [Arbor 2000]

Appearances:
Thunder Drums, Vol. 1: *The Best of Arbor Records* [Arbor 2001] comp

Cache Lake; a.k.a. Saddle Lake Singers—(Cree) Northern Style

Lineup: Willy Roy, Lloyd, Norris, and Edward Cardinal; William Delver; Sam and Louis McGilvery; Leo Brighteyes.

Formed in 1993, Saddle Lake First Nations, Alberta. The group began with four singers and grew to fifteen members under the direction of their teachers and mentors Leo, Lyman, and Hector McGilvery, who formed the group known as the Saddle Lake Singers in the 1950s. Cache Lake dedicated their first release to these singers, who kept the music alive when traditional values and customs were outlawed by the Canadian government, which enforced harsh penalties.

DISCOGRAPHY:
Keeping the Tradition [Sweet Grass 1996]

Calf Robe Singers—(Blackfoot) Northern Style

Lineup: Stephanie, Stephen, Bonnie, Marvin, Teena, and Sunshine Calf Robe; Kyle Crow; Lisa Starlight; Linda Rabbit; Kerry Day Chief; Darryl Black Plume.

DISCOGRAPHY:
Powwow Songs [Canyon 1995]
The Next Generation [Canyon 1993]
Family Powwow [SOAR 1992]

Calgary Drummers—(Blackfoot) Northern Style

Lineup: Frank Sr., Frank Jr., and Randy Turning Robe; Roy Big Head; Fred Breaker; Al Keeper; Radford Good Eagle.

DISCOGRAPHY:
Calgary Drummers [Canyon CR-9002]

Carlson Singers—(Blackfeet) Northern Style

Lineup: Pat Merlin, Ervin Quentin Carlson, Jim Black Wolf, Edwin Little Plume, Jim Crawford, Lloyd Reevis, Gerald Whiteman.

DISCOGRAPHY:
Powwow Songs [Canyon CR-6179]

Cathedral Lake Singers—(Intertribal) Northern Style *See*: Jay Begaye, Arlie Neskahi; White Eagle

Original Lineup: Jay and Tinesha Begaye (Dineh); Art Cleveland; John, Laurie, Wendy, Harriet, Kathy, Janet, and Jeanine Terbasket. Based in Keremeos, British Columbia. They acknowledge Arlie Neskahi for his teachings and the White Eagle Singers.

DISCOGRAPHY:
Live at Window Rock [Canyon 1999]
American Powwow [SOAR 1993]
Powwow Songs, Vol. 3 [SOAR 1992]
Powwow Songs, Vol. 2 [SOAR 1991]
Powwow Songs, Vol. 1 [SOAR 1990]

Appearances:
Gathering of Nations Pow-Wow, Vol. 1 [SOAR 1992] comp
Various Native American Artists: Solo Flights, Vol. 1 [SOAR 1991] comp *See*: Contemporary Compilations

Cedar Dale—(Kiowa) Southern Style

Lineup: Louis Maynahonah Jr.; Michael Topaum; John Hamilton; Ewan Kaulaity Jr.; George Red Bird; Gerald McIntosh; Roscoe Conklin Jr.; Ron Anquoe; Sally Kerchee-Maynahonah. Recorded in Oklahoma City, Oklahoma.

DISCOGRAPHY:
Cedar Dale Singers [Arbor 1999]

Cedar Tree—(Intertribal) Southern Style

Lineup: Jason Porter, Jody Cummings, Jeff Bailey, Dan Addis, Austin Sebastian, Bob Tenequer, Michael and John Mark Rose. From Geary, Oklahoma, the group took its name from elder Harold Cedar Tree (Cheyenne-Arapaho).

DISCOGRAPHY:
Schemitzun World Championship of Song and Dance [Sweet Grass 1997]

Appearances:
Gathering of Nations Pow-Wow: Millennium Celebration, Vol. 2: *Various Southern Drums* [SOAR 2000] comp

Chemewa Singers—(Intertribal) Northern Style *See*: White Eagle

Lineup: Arlie Neskahi (Dineh), Nathan Williams (Yakima), Annie Evans (Blackfeet), Gina Big Beaver (Kootenai), Michelle Crowe (Yakima). From the Chemewa Indian School, Salem, Oregon. Performance highlights include the World's Fair EXPO '74, Spokane, Washington.

DISCOGRAPHY:

Intertribal Powwow Songs [Canyon 1987]
Chemewa Indian School Singers [Canyon 1985]

Chief Cliff Singers—(Blackfeet) Northern Style

Lineup: Mike Kenmille, Clifford and Clayton Burke, Arleen Adams, Gina Big Beaver, Kenny Lozeau, Francis Auld. These Montana-based singers worked closely with Don Pullen and his band to create a successful hybrid of jazz and powwow compositions.

DISCOGRAPHY:

Appearances:
Don Pullen:
Common Sacred Ground [Blue Note 1995]

Chief Jimmy Bruneau School Drummers—(Dene) Traditional Hand Drum

Lineup: Angus Beaulieu, Peter Eyakfwo, Jeffery Football, Ricky Drybones, Michel Rabesca, David and Joe Tlokka. From Rae Edzo, Northwest Territories.

DISCOGRAPHY:

Drum Dance Music of the Dogrib [Canyon CR-16260; Vintage Recordings Series no. 19]

Chi-Geezis—(Anishnabe) Northern Style

Lineup: Bill and Carmen Antoine, Dean Roy, Chris Endanawas, Greg Dayfox.

DISCOGRAPHY:

Jingle Dress Songs, Vol. 6 [Sunshine Records 1999]
Sta-Ta-Hah [Sunshine SSCD-4365]
Ambae Neemdah—Let's Dance [Sunshine SSCD-4312]
Esgkiamdek [Sunshine SSCD-4311]
Kee Sam Owin [Sunshine SSCD-4277]
Songs of the Ojibway/Odawa [Sunshine SSCD-4276]

Appearances:

Drum Beats: 18 Powwow Groups [Sunshine 2002] comp
World's Best Crow Hop Songs [Sunshine 2001] comp
World's Best Intertribal Songs [Sunshine 2001] comp
World's Best Round Dance Songs, Vol. 2 [Sunshine 2001] comp
World's Best Veteran Songs, Vol. 1 [Sunshine 2001] comp
Powwow 2000 [Sunshine 2000] comp
World's Best Fancy Dance Songs, Vol. 1 [Sunshine 2000] comp
World's Best Powwow Drum Groups [Sunshine 2000] comp
World's Best Tiny Tot Songs [Sunshine 2000] comp
World's Best Jingle Dress Songs [Sunshine 1998] comp
The Best of Ontario Powwow Groups [Sunshine 1997] comp
World's Best Round Dance Songs [Sunshine 1997] comp

Chiniki Lake—(Nakota) Northern Style

Lineup: Clifford Powderface; Charles, Frank, and Paul Daniels; Arron, Cameron, Orville, and Kevin Keywake; Cliff Jr., Johnny, and Curt Jim. Formed in Morley,

Alberta, in 1977 by Rod Hunter and Clifford Powderface.

DISCOGRAPHY:
Nakota [Sweet Grass 1996]
Recorded Live at Carry the Kettle [Sweet Grass 1996]
Chiniki Lake Singers, Vol. 4 [Sunshine 1993]
Stoney Powwow Songs [Canyon CR-9003 1980]
Chiniki Lake Singers, Vol. 3 [Sunshine 1979]
Chiniki Lake Singers, Vol. 2 [Sunshine 1978]
Chiniki Lake Singers, Vol. 1 [Sunshine 1977]

Appearances:
World's Best Crow Hop Songs [Sunshine 2001] comp
World's Best Intertribal Songs [Sunshine 2001] comp
Best of Alberta [Sunshine 1997] comp
United Tribes International Powwow [Makoche 1995] two-CD comp
Shake the Feathers: Live at Peguis Powwow '93 [Sunshine SSCT-4204] comp
SIFC Annual Powwow [Sunshine SSCT-4168] comp

Chi Nodin—(Anishnabe) Northern Style

Lineup: Brian Moore; Darryl Ostamis; Mike Tegosh; Joe, John, Joel and Kevin Syrette; Sunny Roach-Syrette; Nick Hewson; Harvey Goodsky Jr.; Rob Essex; Tom Peters; Chris Neveau; James Roach; Heidi Goodwin; Theresa Hindsley. Recorded live at Batchewana First Nation, Ontario. From Rankin First Nation, Ontario.

DISCOGRAPHY:
At Batchewana Pow Wow [Sunshine SSCT-9696]
Sault Ste Marie [Sunshine SSCT-4293]
Chi Nodin [Sweet Grass 1996]

Appearances:
Powwow 2000 [Sunshine 2000] comp
Toronto Powwow [Sunshine 1998] comp
The Best of Ontario Powwow Groups [Sunshine 1997] comp
White Earth Powwow [Sunshine SSCT-4338] comp

Common Man Singers—(Lakota) Northern Style *See*: Traditional/Archival Solo: Earl Bullhead

Lineup: Earl and Tim Bullhead, Ken Billingsley, Jody Luger, Cedric and Evelyn (Sissy) Goodhouse (*See*: Traditional/Archival Solo), Gabe Kampeska, J. D. Buckley, Duane Steele.

DISCOGRAPHY:
Songs for the Common Man [SOAR 157]
Spirit of Song [Makoche 1995]
Signals from the Heart [SOAR 1992]

Copper Creek—(Cree) Northern Style

Lineup: Jeff, Steve, Arnold, Tanya, Alex, and Quincy Moosomin; Steven Wahobin; Earl McLeod; Jason Stone; Chopper Chekosis; Walter Oxebin; Orville Stone; Scott and Quinton Bull. Formed in 2002 with members from the Mosquito, Bear's Head, and Cree Man Band, Saskatchewan.

DISCOGRAPHY:
Descendants [Sweet Grass 2003]

Couchiching—(Anishnabe) Northern Style

DISCOGRAPHY:
Lake of Many Winds [Maracle Studios SC4-5141]

Cozad—(Kiowa) Southern Style *See*: Traditional/Archival Group

Lineup: Kim, Charlene, Mabel, Freddie, Leonard, Vernon, Barbara, Velma, Leonard Sr., Rusty Sr., Marie, Naomi, Kimberly T., James, Daniel, Joe, Andrew, Kenneth, Patrick Jr., and Larry Cozad.

The originators of this group, Larry Cozad and Leonard Cozad Sr., began recording traditional songs in the 1960s. The group was the Schemitzun Southern Style World Champions in 1999.

DISCOGRAPHY:
Live at Red Earth [Sweet Grass 1996]
Schemitzun Live Championship Singing 1995 [Sweet Grass 1995]

Appearances:
Mitataht askiy: Sweet Grass Records 10 Years [Sweet Grass 2003] comp
Gathering of Nations Powwow 2001 [Gathering of Nations Records 2001] comp
Hinckley Powwow Southern Style [Arbor 2001] comp
Thunder Drums, Vol. 1: *The Best of Arbor Records* [Arbor 2001] comp
Gathering of Nations Pow-Wow: Millennium Celebration, Vol. 2: *Various Southern Drums* [SOAR 2000] comp
Best of the Best Schemitzun '93–99 [Sweet Grass 1999] comp
Hinckley Powwow Southern Style [Arbor 1999] comp
Gathering of Nations Pow-Wow 1996 [SOAR 1997] comp
Gathering of Nations Pow-Wow 1995 [SOAR 1996] comp
Gathering of Nations Pow-Wow 1993 [SOAR 1994] comp

Crazy Horse Singers—(Lakota) Northern Style

Lineup: Terry Spoonhunter, Delbert New Holy, Grant Weston, Joe Pecotte, Brian Thunder Hawk, Sam Long Black Dog, Emmanuel Black Bear, Charlie Eagle Hawk, Reuben Looks Twice, Bruce Bad Milk. From Fort Yates, North Dakota.

DISCOGRAPHY:
Oglala Style [Wakinyan Records 2003]

Cree Spirit—(Cree) Northern Style

Lineup: Craig, Ross, Terrance, Linus, Morley, Derek, Blair, Jarvis, Lonnie, Perry, and Jason Littletent; Stacey Poorman; Gary and Howard Dustyhorn.

DISCOGRAPHY:
Cree Spirit, Vol. 4 [Sunshine 1995]
Cree Spirit, Vol. 3 [Sunshine SSCT-4208]
Cree Spirit, Vol. 2 [Sunshine SSCT-4159]
Cree Spirit [Sunshine SSCT-4142]

Appearances:
Powwow 2000 [Sunshine 2000] comp
The Best of Saskatchewan [Sunshine 1997] comp
SIFC Annual Powwow [Sunshine SSCT-4168] comp

Cree White Tail—(Cree) Northern Style

Lineup: Gitchie Cheechoo Jr.; P. J. Davey; Honey Boy Danyluk; Dave Hookimaw; Mike Wabano; Craig Trudeau; Lester, Kirby, and Deano Minaskum.

DISCOGRAPHY:
Live at Skydome [Sweet Grass 1998]

Crooked Lake Agency—(Cree) Northern Style

Lineup: Albert Isaac Jr.; Bob Natewa; Calvin Isaac Jr.; Trevor Ewack; Charles Buffalo Calf Jr.; Rook and Jason Spavier; Eric Redwood; J. R. McArthur; Shan Buffalo Calf; Terry and Bernard Bob. From Cowessess First Nation, Saskatchewan.

DISCOGRAPHY:
The Good Ol' Days [Sweet Grass 1997]

Appearances:
Mitataht askiy: Sweet Grass Records 10 Years [Sweet Grass 2003] comp
Ermineskin Cree Nation Pow-wow: Live at Bear Park [Sweet Grass 1999] comp
Thunderchild '98 [Turtle Island Music 1999] comp
Spirit of the People [Sweet Grass/EMI 1996] comp

Crowe Singers—(Cree) Northern Style

Lineup: David Whip Cote; Ricki Kitchemonia; Harvey Solly Cote; Terry Doo-Zim Lynx; Evan Nick Lavallee; Dion and George Keewatin; Arron Kakaraway; Derrick Crowe; Nathen Pelly; Brent Asapace; Alvin and Kelly Quewezance. From Keeseekoose First Nations, Saskatchewan.

DISCOGRAPHY:
Crowe Singers [Arbor 2001]

Appearances:
Thunder Drums, Vol. 2: *The Best Pow-wow Songs from the World's Best Drums* [Arbor 2002] comp

Crowfoot Drummers—(Blackfoot) Northern Style

Lineup: Robert, Henry, Leo, Gary, and Aldon Sun Walk; Don Scalp Lock; Bruce and Norman Calf Robe; Willy Mills.

DISCOGRAPHY:
Blackfoot Powwow Songs [Canyon CR-9009]

Crying Woman—(Cree) Northern Style *See*: Traditional/Archival comp

Lineup: Celina Bird Jones and Marcella Bird Wuttunee. Based in Fort Belknap,

Montana, originally from the Thunderchild Reserve in Saskatchewan.

DISCOGRAPHY:
Dancing Spirits [Sweet Grass 1994]

Appearances:
Heartbeat: Voices of First Nations Women [Smithsonian/Folkways 1995] comp *See*: Traditional/Archival Compilations
Heartbeat 2: More Voices of First Nations Women [Smithsonian Folkways 1995] comp *See*: Traditional/Archival Compilations

Da Bad Boyz—(Intertribal) Northern Style

Lineup: Farley Cardinal, Pater Favel, Chris Sleigh, Brian Blackkettle, Kevin Sandy, Galen Bullbear, Norvin Eaglespeaker. Formed in 1995, based in Alberta.

DISCOGRAPHY:
Y.2.D.B.B. [Stoney Records 1999]

Dakota Hotain—(Dakota) Northern Style

Lineup: Henry, Edward, and Michael Hotain; Ronald Hill; Brian Pratt; Karl Essie; Kenny Pratt. From Dakota Tipi, Manitoba.

DISCOGRAPHY:
Songs of the Dakota, Vol. 2 [Sunshine SSCT-4069]
Dakota Hotain [Sunshine SSCT-4059]

Dakota Travels—(Dakota) Northern Style

Lineup: Frank, Terence, Tyrone, Wilson, and Thomas Brown; Sam Hapa; Steve Eyahapi; Patrick McArthur; Lori Pratt; Audrey Wambdisha. Former members of the Sioux Assiniboine and the Dakota Travelers created a new group.

DISCOGRAPHY:
Live @ Prairie Island [Arbor 2002]

Appearances:
Round Dance Songs, Vol. 2 [Arbor/Native American Heritage Series 2003] comp

Dead Horse Creek—(Anishnabe) Northern Style

Lineup: Wayne Creighton; Ryan, Clement, Charles, and Owen Gustafson; Shawn Gullingham; Norma Barratt; Charlie O'Keese. From Thunder Bay, Ontario.

DISCOGRAPHY:
Dead Horse Creek, Vol. 2: *Live* [Sunshine SSCT-4323]
Dead Horse Creek, Vol. 1 [Sunshine SSCT-4322]
Dead Horse Creek, Vol. 1 [Sunshine 1997]

Appearances:
World's Best Intertribal Songs [Sunshine 2001] comp
World's Best Round Dance Songs, Vol. 2 [Sunshine 2001] comp
World's Best Fancy Dance Songs, Vol. 1 [Sunshine 2000] comp
The Best of Ontario Powwow Groups [Sunshine 1997] comp

Delia and the Waskewitch Boys— (Cree) Northern Style *See*: Spirit Whistle

Lineup: Delia, Irving, and Brian Waskewitch.

DISCOGRAPHY:
Under the Same Sky [Sweet Grass 2004]
Round Dance [Sweet Grass 2002]

Appearances:
Mitataht askiy: Sweet Grass Records 10 Years [Sweet Grass 2003] comp

Denver Dakota Singers—(Sioux) Northern Style

Lineup: Ken Little, Sherman and George Ironshield, Frank Trujillo, Conrad and George Little, Thomas Teegarden.

DISCOGRAPHY:
Powwow Songs [Canyon 1980]

Denver Indian Singers—(Intertribal) Northern Style

Lineup: Don Malnourie, Keith Fox, Ken and Conrad Little, John Black Bear.

DISCOGRAPHY:
The Denver Indian Singers [Canyon 1973]

Dineh Nation Jrz—(Dineh) Northern Style

Lineup: Randall Beaver, Farrell Nez, Jamie Bedonie, Anthony Betoney, and Orlando Dugi. Formed in 1994, Dineh Nation, Arizona.

DISCOGRAPHY:
Live at Southern Oregon University [SWR 6969]
STR8 TRPN [Cool Runnings 1998]

Dreaver, Mervin—(Cree) Northern Style

Lineup: Mervin and Marshall Dreaver, Ken Pooyak, Archie Moccassin, Marc Long John, John and Shorty Thomas, and Brad Crane. From Big River Cree First Nation, Saskatchewan.

DISCOGRAPHY:
Gone but Not Forgotten [Sweet Grass 1998]

Appearances:
Whitefish Jrs.:
Round Dance Songs [Sweet Grass 1995]
Various:

World's Leading Round Dance Songs
[Sweet Grass 1996] comp

Drum Circle—(Intertribal) Southern Style

Lineup: Lonnie Harrington (Seminole-Cherokee-Choctaw), Red Thunder Walking (Maya-Aztec-Cherokee), Lone Wolf (Taino-Arawak), Donna Spirit Wind (Aluet-Cherokee), Mahir El Eagle Sunwalker (Cherokee), Ricca Windhorse (Cherokee-Choctaw), Jerry Greyhawk (Jicarilla Apache–Taino). Formed in 1992 as the Drum Circle for the Northeastern Native American Association, Queens, New York.

DISCOGRAPHY:
Drum Circle Singers [Sunshine 1998]

Appearances:
SECC Earth Band [Sunshine 1998] comp

Drumming Hill—(Intertribal) Northern Style

Lineup: Ken and Don Pooyak; Vince Albert; Ken Snakeskin; and Wesley Weenie.

DISCOGRAPHY:
Drumming Hill [Sweet Grass 1997]

Eaglebear Singers—Northern Style
See: Contemporary Soundtracks: *Smoke Signals*

Eagle Claw—Northern Style Youth Drum

Lineup: Waylon, Terrence, Bradley, and Preston Littletent; Bradley Nehnepowisk; Jason Gavin; Roy Ryan; and Ira McNabb. The first album of original songs was performed by singers ranging in ages from five to fifteen years old. Recorded in Regina, Saskatchewan.

DISCOGRAPHY:
Round Dance Songs [Sunshine 1996]
  w/ Kirby Littletent
Eagle Claw [Sunshine SSCT-4207]

Appearances:
37th Annual Milk River Indian Days Pow-wow Live at Fort Belknap, Montana [Sweet Grass 2003] comp
Schemitzun 2000: Hand Drum Songs [Sweet Grass 2001] comp
World's Best Crow Hop Songs [Sunshine 2001] comp
World's Best Fancy Dance Songs, Vol. 2 [Sunshine 2001] comp
World's Best Tiny Tot Songs [Sunshine 2000] comp
The Best of Saskatchewan [Sunshine 1997] comp
Hinckley Powwow, Vol. 1 [Sunshine 1995] comp

Eagle Creek—(Dineh)

Formed in 1988, Dinnehotso, Arizona.

DISCOGRAPHY:
After Midnight [Rez Cue Records 1999]
Dine Powwow Songs—Recorded Live [Cool Runnings 1998]

Eagle Heart—(Intertribal) Northern Style *See*: Contemporary Music: Clayton Cheechoo

Lineup: Jimmy and Oliver Dick (James Bay Cree), Malcolm Norris (Mohawk-Anishnabe), Brian Marion (Cree), Marie Gaudet (Anishnabekwe), and Loretta Tait (Gitskan).
  Based in Toronto, Ontario. The group made many mainstream crossovers, including work with producer Jack Lenz in 1985 for *Pedahbun* (New Dawn), the Fire This Time's *Still Dancing on John Wayne's Head*, and a nationally televised commercial in 1995.

DISCOGRAPHY:
Songs from Mother Earth [Holborne Distributing AAPCD 004]
Eagle Heart Singers/Drummers [NWS002 1990]

Appearances:
The Fire This Time:
Still Dancing on John Wayne's Head [Extreme/Filter 1998] comp *See*: Contemporary Compilations
Dancing on John Wayne's Head [Extreme 1995] comp *See*: Contemporary Compilations
Syren:
Let Them Live: A Tribute to the Lubicon Cree [Kennisis Music 1990]

Eagle Hill—(Dakota-Anishnabe) Northern Style *See*: Windy Rock Singers

Lineup: Roy Coyote; Keith, Don Jr., Pearl, Garnet Jr., Mark, and Marlene Henry; Corey Littlejohn; Arnold Smith; Lydell Alexander; Felix, Jan, Barry, and Karen Antoine; Rodney Patrick; Murray Starr; Billy Jo Atkinson; and Rodney Patrick.

DISCOGRAPHY:
Eagle Hill [Sunshine SSCT-4144]

Appearances:
Ermineskin Cree Nation Pow-wow: Live at Bear Park [Sweet Grass 1999] comp
The Best of Saskatchewan [Sunshine 1997] comp

Eagle Mountain—(Lakota) Northern Style *See*: Traditional/Archival Compilations Recordings: Amérique du Nord

From Kyle, South Dakota. In 1999, the group won the Della Lovejoy Singing Contest, which allowed them to compete in the World Championship of Song and Dance at Schemitzun.

DISCOGRAPHY:

Appearances:
Best of the Best Schemitzun '93–99 [Sweet Grass 1999] comp
Songs of the Oglala Nation: Native American Powwow [Turtle Island Music 1998] comp
Wisconsin Intertribal [Sunshine SSCT-4216] comp

Eagle Society—(Blackfoot) Northern Style

Lineup: Robert, Henry, Trent, Wesley, and Gary Sun Walk; Donald Scalp Lock; Clarence Wolfleg; Ed Calf Robe Jr. Recorded at Clueny, Alberta, September 21, 1989.

DISCOGRAPHY:
Blackfoot Grass Dance Songs: Siksika Nation [Indian House 1990]

Eagle Spirit Singers—(Cherokee) Northern Style

Lineup: Henry Sultner, Frank Horn, Jeremy Ross, Philip Dersch, Kyle Shaffer, Mitch Sterner, Matt Barron, Chris Lapes, Andy Deardorff. Formed in 1995. Their first album was recorded live at the 1998 Cherokee Festive Memorial Day Weekend hosted by the Southeastern Cherokee Confederacy of Pennsylvania Earth Band's Fifth Annual Powwow, Ambler, Pennsylvania.

DISCOGRAPHY:
Eagle Spirit Singers [Sunshine 1998]

Eagle Tail—(Dakota) Northern Style

Lineup: Andy, Dave, Marlin, Charles, M. J., Marshall Sr., and Sage Demarce; Donovan Redroad; Wes Big Track; Kid Little Sky; Duane and Lee Jackson. Based in North Dakota.

DISCOGRAPHY:

Jammin' on the Rez [Arbor 2002]
Singing for the People [Sweet Grass 1999]
Powwow Songs Recorded Live [Canyon CR-16245]
Eagle Tail, Vol. 2 [Sunshine SSCT-4177]
Eagle Tail [Sunshine SSCT-4140]

Appearances:

Round Dance Songs, Vol. 2 [Arbor/Native American Heritage Series 2003] comp
World's Best Memorial Songs [Sunshine 2002] comp
World's Best Women's Traditional Songs [Sunshine 2002] comp
World's Best Veteran Songs, Vol. 1 [Sunshine 2001] comp
World's Best Jingle Dress Songs [Sunshine 1998] comp
United Tribes International Powwow [Makoche 1995] two CDs
Bismarck Powwow [Sunshine 1993] comp

Eagle Whistles—(Lakota-Dakota)
Northern Traditional *See*: New Town Singers

1973 Lineup: Alex Gwin, Saunders Bears Tail Jr., Murphy Sitting Crow, Dean Fox, Ronnie Smith, Michael Driver, Francis Driver Jr., Wade Baker.

1999 Lineup: Bill and Floyd Runsabove, Dean Fox, Charles Eaglespeaker, Merle Tendoy, Mike LaFromboise, Wade Baker, Rick Stewart, Ross Wise Spirit.

From Mandaree, North Dakota; 1984–85 International Singing Champions.

DISCOGRAPHY:

Live at Crow Fair [Indian House 2000]
Eagle Whistles 1986–87, Vol. 2 [High Star 1987]
Eagle Whistles 1986–87, Vol. 1 [High Star 1987]
Live at Bismarck, North Dakota [Featherstone FT-1013]
Live at Mandaree [Featherstone FT-1007]

Eastern Eagle Singers—(Mi'kmaq)
Northern Style *See*: Contemporary Music: J. Hubert Francis and Eagle Feather

Lineup: Brian, Gary, and Ivan Knockwood; Greg Marn; Jonothan Marshall; Billy and David Meuse; Mark, Colin, and Jason McDonald; Simon Nevin; Mike and Nathan Sack; Darren Myo; and Scott Taylor. Recorded in Halifax, Nova Scotia. From Indian Brook, Nova Scotia.

DISCOGRAPHY:

Sacred Flight [Arbor 2002]
East Side Connection [Sunshine 1998]
Traditionally Yours [SOAR 178]
Maq Attaq [SOAR 1995]

Appearances (listed alphabetically):

J. Hubert Francis and Eagle Feather/Ancestral Fire:
Honouring Who We Are [Bear Paw Music 2002]
Nicole LaRoche:
Passion Spirit [Natural Vision 2001] contemporary
Various:
Women's Fancy Dance Songs [Arbor/ Native American Heritage Series 2003] comp
Alcatraz Is Not an Island [James Fortier, 2002] score
Thunder Drums, Vol. 2: *The Best Powwow Songs from the World's Best Drums* [Arbor 2002] comp
World's Best Women's Traditional Songs [Sunshine 2002] comp
Powwow 2000 [Sunshine 2000] comp
World's Best Jingle Dress Songs [Sunshine 1998] comp

Eden Valley Pow-wow Club—
(Blackfoot) Northern Style

Lineup: Don Rider; Jack and Dora Crawler; Jacqueline, Didrienne, and Lorinda Rider; Bruce Beaver. Recorded in Calgary, Alberta.

DISCOGRAPHY:
Stony Pow-wow Songs [Canyon 1975]

Elk Nation Singers—(Olglala) Northern Style

Lineup: William Good Voice Elk III, Stanley and Charles Good Voice Elk, John Stewart. From Pine Ridge, South Dakota.

DISCOGRAPHY:
Spirit Drum [NS-51014]

Elk's Whistle—(Lakota) Northern Style

Lineup: Kim Worme; Angelo, Gordon, Riel, Jason, and Jeremy Wasteste; Robert Schuyler; Mike Esquash; Sage Worme; Robert Standing; Wislon Brown; Terry Grey; Anthony, Mark, and Joseph Favel; Curtis and Larry McKay. From Sioux Valley, based in Saskatchewan, Canada.

DISCOGRAPHY:
Still with Us—Wambdi Hokshida [Turtle Island Music 2003]
Indian Style [WREH 031]
Just Jammin' [WREH 011]
Ten Years Later [WREH 003]
Live at Schemitzun World Championship of Singing and Dance 1994 [Sweet Grass 1995]
Elk's Whistle, Vol. 3 [SICC 1994]

Appearances:
Mitataht askiy: Sweet Grass Records 10 Years [Sweet Grass 2003] comp
Black Hills: 16th Annual Powwow [Arbor 2003] comp
Just Jamming [Wacipi Records 2000] comp
Songs of the Spirit: The Best of Sweet Grass [Sweet Grass/EMI 1995] comp
Still the Eagle Flies, Vols. 1 and 2 [SICC 1995] comp
Hinckley Grand Celebrations Powwow 1995 Northern Style [Sunshine SSCT-4283] comp

Shake the Feathers: Live at Peguis Powwow '93 [Sunshine SSCT-4204] comp
Gathering of Nations Pow-Wow 1992 [SOAR 1993] comp

Eyabay—(Anishnabe) Northern Style
See: The Boyz

Lineup: Lee Lussier Jr., Terry St. John, John Morris Sr., Darren Defoe, Clint Greencrow, Darren Cook, Poie Day Bedeau, Roger White Jr., Philip St. John Jr., Ron Lussier, Jason Kingbird, David Henrywood.

Eyabay Jrs. are John Morris Jr., Anthony Greencrow, Verny Morris, Darren Defoe Jr., Chon Gaila, and Chauncey Morris.

From Red Lake, Minnesota, Eyabay was named Contemporary Champions, Schemitzun, in 1995, 1997, and 1998.

DISCOGRAPHY:
Miracle [Arbor 2002]
Ain't Nuthin' but a "E" thang [Sunshine 2000]
Live 2000 (E2K) [Arbor 1999]
The Best of Eyabay [Sunshine 1999]
No Limit [Arbor 1999]
4-Life, Vol. 4 [Sunshine 1998]
Thugs N Harmony, Vol. 3 [Sunshine SSCT-4332]
Keep Their Heads Ringing [Turtle Island Music 1996]
Eyabay, Vol. 2 [Sunshine SSCT-4270]
Eyabay, Vol. 1 [Sunshine SSCT-4233]

Appearances:
Mitataht askiy: Sweet Grass Records 10 Years [Sweet Grass 2003] comp
Round Dance Songs, Vol. 2 [Arbor/Native American Heritage Series 2003] comp
Women's Fancy Dance Songs [Arbor/Native American Heritage Series 2003] comp
Drum Beats: 18 Powwow Groups [Sunshine 2002] comp
Thunder Drums, Vol. 2: *The Best Powwow Songs from the World's Best Drums* [Arbor 2002] comp

World's Best Women's Traditional Songs [Sunshine 2002] comp

Schemitzun 2000: Hand Drum Songs [Sweet Grass 2001] comp

Schemitzun World Championship 2000: Round Dance Singing [Turtle Island Music 2001] comp

Thunder Drums, Vol. 1: *The Best of Arbor Records* [Arbor 2001] comp

World's Best Crow Hop Songs [Sunshine 2001] comp

World's Best Intertribal Songs [Sunshine 2001] comp

World's Best Fancy Dance Songs, Vol. 1 [Sunshine 2000] comp

Powwow 2000 [Sunshine 2000] comp

Schemitzun World Championship Round Dance Singing [Turtle Island Music 2000] comp

World's Best Powwow Drum Groups [Sunshine 2000] comp

World's Best Tiny Tot Songs [Sunshine 2000] comp

Bear Spirit [Turtle Island Music 1999] comp

Best of the Best Schemitzun '93–99 [Sweet Grass 1999] comp

Champion Round Dance Songs, Vol. 1 [Arbor 1999] comp

Hinckley Powwow Northern Style [Arbor 1999] comp

Spirit of the Wolf [Turtle Island Music 1998] comp

World's Best Round Dance Songs [Sunshine 1997] comp

Red Lake Nation [Turtle Island Music 1996] comp

Hinckley Grand Celebrations Powwow 1995 Northern Style [Sunshine SSCT-4283] comp

Hinckley Powwow, Vol. 2 [Sunshine 1995] comp

Hinckley Powwow, Vol. 1 [Sunshine 1995] comp

SIFC Powwow Live '95 [SICC 1995] comp

Still the Eagle Flies, Vols. 1 and 2 [SICC 1995] comp

United Tribes International Powwow [Makoche 1995] two CDs

White Earth Powwow [Sunshine SSCT-4338] comp

Eya-Hey Nakoda—(Nakota) Northern Style

From Stoney-Wesley Reserve, Alberta.

DISCOGRAPHY:

Live at Chilliwack [Turtle Island Music 1997]

Sacred Mountains [Turtle Island Music 1996]

Appearances:

Northern Cree and Friends: Round Dance Songs Recorded "Live," Vol. 1 [Canyon 2002] comp

Schemitzun 2000: Hand Drum Songs [Sweet Grass 2001] comp

Schemitzun World Championship 2000: Northern Style [Turtle Island Music 2001] comp

Bear Spirit [Turtle Island Music 1999] comp

Spirit of the Wolf [Turtle Island Music 1998] comp

First Nations Singers—Northern Style

DISCOGRAPHY:

First Nations Singers [Sunshine SSCT-4183]

Appearances:

Thunder Bear Powwow [Sunshine SSCT-4188] comp

Fly-In Eagle—(Cree) Northern Style

Lineup: Clyde, Dion, and Carl Kennedy; Jonas and Quinton Tootoosis (Cree); Devere Tsatoke (Kiowa-Comanche); Arnold Pete; Allan Bonaise; Quinton Checkosis (Cree).

DISCOGRAPHY:

Dream Time [Turtle Island Music 2004]

Bro Style [Cool Runnings 2000]

Tearin' It Up [Turtle Island Music 1999]
Thunder Shaker [Turtle Island Music 1998]
Fly-In-Eagle Singers [Sunshine 1998]
Red and Blue Powwow Songs [Canyon 1997]
Thunder Shaker [Turtle Island Music 1997]
The Second Wave: Straight Powwow Songs, Vol. 3 [Canyon 1996]
The Straighter the Better [Canyon 1995]
Powwow Songs [Canyon 1994]

Appearances:
Northern Cree and Friends: Round Dance Songs Recorded "Live," Vol. 1 [Canyon 2002] comp
Voices from Thunderchild Powwow Songs [Turtle Island Music 2000] comp
Bear Spirit [Turtle Island Music 1999] comp
Standing Our Ground [Turtle Island Music 1999] comp
Thunderchild '98 [Turtle Island Music 1999] comp
Cree Nation [Turtle Island Music 1998] comp
Spirit of the Wolf [Turtle Island Music 1998] comp
The Best of Saskatchewan [Sunshine 1997] comp
Spirit of the People [Sweet Grass/EMI 1996] comp
Still the Eagle Flies, Vols. 1 and 2 [SICC 1995] comp
A New Beginning, 1894–1994: St. Michael's College [Sweet Grass 1994] comp
The Sound of Champions [Sweet Grass 1994] comp
SIFC Annual Powwow [Sunshine SSCT-4168] comp

Fort Kipp Singers—(Sioux) Northern Style *See*: Maddog Singers; Traditional/Archival Group

Lineup: Jim Black Dog; Clarence, Buddy, and Pat Adams; Archie Bear Cub Sr.; Clifford Young Bear; Buzzy Red Eagle; Jim and Brad Buffalo Calf; Eunice Alfrey; Lillian

Ogle; Diane Chase; Loretta Bear Cub; Jerry, Kipp, and Clarice White Cloud.

DISCOGRAPHY:
Fort Kipp Celebration [Canyon 1983]
'77 Live [Canyon 1978]
Fort Kipp Celebration [Canyon 1976/1977]
Montana Grass Dance Songs [Canyon 1974]
At Fort Qu'Appelle [Canyon 1971]

Fort Oakland Ramblers—(Ponca) Southern Style

Lineup: Perry Lee Batone Jr., Jim Grant, James Kemble, Garland Kent Jr., Gregory Lieb, Oliver and Stephen Little Cook, Don and Henry Patterson, Jade Roubedeaux, Sophia Buffalohead, Tesa Good-Eagle, Roberta McIntosh, Dobbin Monoessy. Recorded at White Eagle, Oklahoma, March 21, 1992.

DISCOGRAPHY:
When He Paints His Face [Canyon CR-6281]
Oklahoma Intertribal and Contest Songs [Indian House 1993]

Fort Yates Singers—(Sioux) Northern Style

DISCOGRAPHY:
Live! Fort Yates Celebration [Featherstone FT-1010]

Four Little Feathers—Northern Style

Lineup: Adrien and Jason Kejick, Kelly Okanee, Derek Kelly, Bruce Landon, Steven Fisher, Patrick and Stanley Skead.

DISCOGRAPHY:
Four Little Feathers [Sunshine SSCT-4141]

Appearances:
World's Best Fancy Dance Songs, Vol. 2 [Sunshine 2001] comp

The Best of Saskatchewan [Sunshine 1997] comp

Four Mountain Nation Singers—
(Dineh) Northern Style

Lineup: Rudy, Henry, Ernie, Emerson, Emery, Vertina, and Percy Thompson; Darrell Harrison; Shawn Wero; Ronald and Deanna Todacheenie. Recorded in Leupp, Arizona, with A. Brent Chase (*See*: Contemporary Music: Ancient Brotherhood) on flute.

DISCOGRAPHY:
Navajo Chants, Vol. 1: *Powwow Songs* [Astro Music 1996]

Free Spirit—(Mi'kmaq) Northern Style

Lineup: Garry Knockwood, Michael and Vaughen Doucette, Roy Henry, Greg Marr, Mike Sack, Vincent Marshall, Anthony and Darrel Morris. Their 1990 album was recorded at Indian Brook Reservation, Nova Scotia.

DISCOGRAPHY:
Mic Mac (Mi'kmaq) Songs [Sunshine 1990]

Appearances:
World's Best Round Dance Songs, Vol. 2 [Sunshine 2001] comp
World's Best Round Dance Songs [Sunshine 1997] comp

Grassy Narrows Singers—
(Anishnabe) Northern Style

DISCOGRAPHY:
Grassy Narrows Singers [Sunshine SSCT-4296]

Appearances:
World's Best Memorial Songs [Sunshine 2002] comp

World's Best Women's Traditional Songs [Sunshine 2002] comp
World's Best Veteran Songs, Vol. 1 [Sunshine 2001] comp
Powwow 2000 [Sunshine 2000] comp
Best of Manitoba [Sunshine 1997] comp

Grayhorse—(Kiowa) Southern Style

Lineup: Jack, Redcloud, Jim, Rick, Warren, and Jimmy Anquoe; Louis Sheridan; Jason Goodblanket; Jimmy Reeder; Laverne Littlecalf. From Oklahoma, Grayhorse recorded traditional Kiowa gourd dances and powwow songs.

DISCOGRAPHY:
Spirits Who Dance [SOAR 1996]
Shake It Up [SOAR 1995]
Gourd Talkers [SOAR 1993]

Appearances:
Doug Wallentyne:
Human Rites [Natural Visions/SOAR 1993]
Various:
The Way West [American Experience/ Shanachie 1995] sdtk *See*: Contemporary Soundtracks
Gathering of Nations Powwow 1993 [SOAR 1994] comp
Various Native American Artists: Solo Flights Two, Vol. 2 [SOAR 1994] comp

Grey Eagle—(Cree) Northern Style

Lineup: Brian Paul, Percy and Lori Moosapayo; Jeffrey Moyah; Blair Mountain; Randy Frenchman; Eugene, Clayton, Elton and Wesley Cardinal. From Long Lake, Alberta.

DISCOGRAPHY:
Stars in Your Eyes [Sweet Grass 1993]

Appearances:
World's Leading Round Dance Songs [Sweet Grass 1996] comp

Grey Fox Singers—(Dakota)
Northern Style

Lineup: Philip, Joseph, Philmore, Burton, and Victor Jackson; Matthew Little; Mike Creeley; Milton Miller; Wambi Gill; Paul Little Sr.; Sam Crawford; Tom Flute.

DISCOGRAPHY:
Grey Fox Singers [Arbor 1999]

Appearances:
Thunder Drums, Vol. 1: *The Best of Arbor Records*, Vol. 1 [Arbor 2001] comp

Hanisha—(Anishnabe) Northern Style

Lineup: Tommy White; Murphy, Thomas Sr., Thomas Jr., and Marvin Paypompee; Stewart Nash; David Kabestra; Howard, Teddy and Leslie Copenace; Billy Girard; Johnny Namaypoke; Ogeekitas Kiueg; Peter, Joyce, Isavel, and Allan White. From Naotkamegwanning First Nation (Whitefish Bay), Ontario.

DISCOGRAPHY:
Hanisha, Vol. 3 [Sunshine 1997]
Hanisha, Vol. 2 [Sunshine 1996]
Hanisha, Vol. 1 [Sunshine 1995]

Appearances:
World's Best Memorial Songs [Sunshine 2002] comp
The Best of Ontario Powwow Groups [Sunshine 1997] comp

Hawk River—Northern Style

Lineup: Percy, Sydney, Daisy, Richard, Shane, and Misty Potts; Aaron Bird; Adrian Bull; Keith Rain; Tracy, Stephanie, Tony, and Lance Alexis. Based in Gleneuis, Alberta.

DISCOGRAPHY:
Nikoodi Rhythm [Sunshine 1999]
Hawk River [SICC HR011693]

Appearances:
Best of Alberta [Sunshine 1997] comp

Hays Singers—(Gros Ventre)
Northern Style

Lineup: Bobby and Carol Talks Different, Edith and Gordon Lodge. Based in Fort Belknap, Montana.

DISCOGRAPHY:
Gros Ventre Songs [Canyon CR-8003]

Haystack—(Cree) Northern Style *See*: Haystack Ramblers

Lineup: Jonathan and Arthur Windy Boy, Sherwin Obey, Bob Natewa, A. Taite Honadick, R. G. Harris, Junior MacArthur, John Murie, Delvin Keeswood, Lloyd Irvine, Adrian Main. Recorded at Piapot, Saskatchewan, August 16–18, 1996. Originally formed in the mid-1980s at Rocky Boy, Montana, with Jonathan, Alvin, and John Windy Boy Sr.; Eric Sampson; and Murray Blacksmith.

DISCOGRAPHY:
Live at Piapot [Indian House 1997]

Appearances:
Gathering of Nations Pow-Wow 1996 [SOAR 1997] comp
Hinckley Powwow, Vol. 2 [Sunshine 1995] comp
Hinckley Powwow, Vol. 1 [Sunshine 1995] comp
Shake the Feathers: Live at Peguis Powwow '93 [Sunshine SSCT-4204] comp
Bismarck Powwow [Sunshine 1993] comp

Haystack Ramblers—Northern Style
See: Rocky Boys

DISCOGRAPHY:
Songs from Rocky Boy Powwow [Canyon 1973]

Heart Butte Singers—(Blackfoot) Northern Style

Lineup: Fred and Beatrice Marceau, Tom Bear Grant, Gordon Clarence, Gary, Franklin and Ernest Comes At Night, Clifford and Jolene Eagle Speaker, Chuck Dusty Bull.

DISCOGRAPHY:
Powwow Songs, Vol. 2 [Canyon 1986]
Powwow Songs, Vol. 1 [Canyon 1981]

Heartland Singers—Northern Style

Lineup: Morley, Wes, and Blaine Cooke; Edmond and Ralph Poochay; Chris Oudie; Billy Torrance; Russell and Bryce Buffalocalf.

DISCOGRAPHY:
Heart and Soul [Sunshine 2000]

Hi Bull—Northern Style

Lineup: Raymond, Gary, Derek, Sonny, Wayne, Linus, and Priscilla Hotomani; Peter and Jaimie Parisian; Dustin Johnson; Terry Delmore; Cal Hunt; Todd and Sterling Crowe.

DISCOGRAPHY:
Hi Bull [Sunshine SSCT-4162]

Appearances:
Best of Manitoba [Sunshine 1997] comp

High Bull—Northern Style

DISCOGRAPHY:
Sioux Songs [Indian Records IR-1193]

High Noon—(Cree) Northern Style

Lineup: Ted Noon, Tim Whiteyes, Ron Noon, Bob Taylor, Louis Doctor, Jack Littlechild, Devere Tsatoke, Dale Roberts, Calvin King, Faron Lujan, Bill Runsabove, Willard and Luke Okanee, Sean Sherman, Alvin Lightening, Jim Todome. Formed in 1974, Thunderchild Reserve, Saskatchewan. Among numerous awards, High Noon was named Original Style Champions, Schemitzun in 1995, 1996, and 1998.

DISCOGRAPHY:
Have Drum Will Travel: Pow-wow Songs Recorded Live at Siksika [Canyon 2003]
Original Style Champions [Wacipi Records 1999]
Live at Taos [Indian House 1998]
On the Trail Again [Noon Records 1998]
High Noon [Sweet Grass 1997]
Original Style World Champions '95 [Sweet Grass 1996]
High Noon World Champs [Sweet Grass 1995]
High Noon [Sweet Grass 1995]

Appearances:
Mitataht askiy: Sweet Grass Records 10 Years [Sweet Grass 2003] comp
Hinckley Powwow Northern Style [Arbor 2001] comp
Schemitzun 2000: Hand Drum Songs [Sweet Grass 2001] comp
Schemitzun World Championship 2000: Northern Style [Turtle Island Music 2001] comp
Schemitzun World Championship 2000: Round Dance Singing [Turtle Island Music 2001] comp
Schemitzun World Championship Round Dance Singing [Turtle Island Music 2000] comp
Best of the Best Schemitzun '93–99 [Sweet Grass 1999] comp
Ermineskin Cree Nation Pow-wow: Live at Bear Park [Sweet Grass 1999] comp
Hinckley Powwow Northern Style [Arbor 1999] comp
Thunderchild '98 [Turtle Island Music 1999] comp
Indian Graffiti:Noon Records Greatest [Noon Records 1998] comp
Songs of the Spirit: The Best of Sweet Grass [Sweet Grass/EMI 1995] comp

The Sound of Champions [Sweet Grass
1994] comp

Ho hwo sju Lakota Singers—
(Lakota) Northern Style

Lineup: Franklin Bear Running, Romanus
Bear Stops, Berdell Blue Arm, Steve Charg-
ing Eagle, Kenneth Young Bear, Zona Bear
Stops, Lorraine Charging Eagle, Darlene
Young Bear. Recorded at Red Scaffold,
South Dakota, May 16, 1974.

DISCOGRAPHY:
Traditional Songs of the Sioux [Indian
House 1975]

Hope Lake Singers—(Anishnabe)
Northern Style

DISCOGRAPHY:
North West Bay, Ontario [Sunshine 1996]
Hope Lake Singers [Sunshine SSCT-4292]

Appearances:
World's Best Jingle Dress Songs [Sunshine
1998] comp

Hopi Sunshield Singers—(Hopi)
Northern Style

Lineup: Rickey Coochwytewa, Stan-
for Lomakema, Clifton Seweiumptewa,
Stewart and Pat Tewawaina, Delbridge
Honanie, Alonzo Dewakuku, Vinton Lonnie, Timmie Mowa, Jake Poleviyouma.

DISCOGRAPHY:
Northern Style Powwow Songs [Canyon
1982]

Indian Creek Singers—(Dineh)
Northern Style

Lineup: Drew, Nate, Art, Franco, and Tim
Warren; Cali and Earl Lameman; Herm,
Melvin, and Damon Begaie; Ray Dez;

Shawn Eskie; Phlanty Poyer and Sheldon
Shebala.

DISCOGRAPHY:
Powwow Jammin' [SOAR 1994]
Powwow Season [SOAR 1993]

Appearances:
Gathering of Nations Pow-Wow 1993
[SOAR 1994] comp

Indian Nation—(Intertribal) Northern
Style *See*: Rocky Boy

Lineup: Joseph, Frank, Irma, John, Sugar
Ray, Rodney, and Wilson Totus; Gary
Smith; Frank Eaglespeaker; Merle Tendoy.
Recorded at the Second Annual Wildhorse
Powwow, Umatilla, Oregon, July 4–6, 1996.
Members represented Yakima, Umatilla,
Blood, and OJ-Cree nations. Formed in
1981, White Swan, Washington, by Sammy
Colwash.

DISCOGRAPHY:
Indian Nation [Indian House 1997]

Ironwood Singers—(Lakota)
Northern Style

Lineup: Founded by Ben Black Bear Sr.,
w/ Kenny Haukass, Harvey Larvie, Ernie
Running, David White, Erwin Yellow
Robe. A long-time favorite of Sioux-style
powwow singing, Ironwood also specialized in traditional songs and duties within
their community.

DISCOGRAPHY:
Live at Schemitzun [Sweet Grass 1998]
Live at the 106th Rosebud Fair [Indian
House 1983/1987]
*Traditional Songs of the Sioux: Live at
Rosebud Fair—1978* [Indian House 1980/
1995]
Sioux Songs from Rosebud [Canyon 1978]

Appearances:
Proud Heritage [Indian House 1996] comp
See: Traditional/Archival Compilations

Hinckley Powwow, Vol. 2 [Sunshine 1995] comp

Hinckley Powwow, Vol. 1 [Sunshine 1995] comp

Kau-ta-noh Jrs.—(Intertribal) Northern Style

Lineup: John Oxendine II (Tuscarora); David, Oniyas, Timothy, Miranda, Tracy, and Tere Locklear (Tuscarora); Brian Graham (Tuscarora); John Chavis (Lumbee); Quinn Lowry (Lumbee); Sam Pedro (Tuscarora); Billy Joe Brooks; Donovan and Yolinda Joe (Dineh); Eric Freeman (Lumbee); Darice Sheppard (Lumbee); April Whittmore (Lumbee-Cheraw-Tuscarora); Vanessa Locklear (Lumbee); Chris Ammons (Coharie); Kay Oxendine (Haliwa-Saponi). Formed in 1998, Robeson County, North Carolina.

DISCOGRAPHY:
Kau-ta-noh Jrs. [Sunshine 2002]

Kennedy, Pat, and the Blackfoot Singers *See*: Blackfeet Singers

Kicking Woman—(Blackfeet) Northern Style

Lineup: Maynard Kicking Woman (Blackfeet), K. J. Bear Medicine (Blackfeet), Casey Eagle Speaker (Blood), Paul Old Chief Sr. (Blackfeet), Iris Heavy Runner (Blackfeet), Stan Pretty Paint (Crow), Lloyd Little Plume (Blackfeet), Tonia Gurdipee (Assiniboine-Sioux). Based in Montana.

DISCOGRAPHY:
Pikuni Style [Canyon 2000]
Our Way of Life [Canyon 1999]
A Tribute to Merlin Kicking Woman [Sweet Grass 1997]
Powwow Songs, Vol. 8 [Canyon CR-16253]
Intertribal Powwow Songs [Canyon CR-16224]

Powwow Songs, Vol. 6 [Canyon CR-16223]
The New Kicking Woman Singers: Intertribal Powwow Songs Recorded Live! [Canyon 1989]
The New Kicking Woman Singers [Canyon CR-6200]
Contest and Intertribal Songs [Canyon CR-6183]
Powwow Songs [Canyon CR-6181]
Intertribal Powwow Songs, Vol. 1 [Canyon 1981]

Kingbird Singers—(Anishnabe) Northern Style

Lineup: McKinley, Vernon, Royce, and Mark Kingbird; Michael and Gerald Hawk; Roger White; Vincent Belcourt. From Red Lake, Minnesota.

DISCOGRAPHY:
The Kingbird Singers [Canyon CR-6170]
Chippewa Grass Dance Songs [Canyon CR-6106]

Appearances:
Hinckley Powwow Northern Style [Arbor 2001] comp
Wisconsin Intertribal [Sunshine SSCT-4216] comp
C.I.S. 20th Annual Powwow [Sunshine SSCT-4172] comp
White Earth Powwow [Sunshine SSCT-4338] comp
White Earth Powwow [Canyon CR-6171] comp
Ojibway Music from Minnesota: A Century of Songs for Voice and Drum [MHS Press 1989/1997] comp *See*: Traditional/Archival Compilations

Ksai-Spai—(Blackfoot) Northern Style

Lineup: Wayne and Dean Plume, George White Man, Dominic Cross Child, Joe and Wayne Beebe, Theresa Plume, Georgina White Man, Diana Bull Shield.

DISCOGRAPHY:
Songs from the Blood Reserve [Canyon CR-6133]

Lake of the Woods Singers—
(Anishnabe) Northern Style *See*: Contemporary Music: Billy Joe Green

Lineup: Patrick, Stanley, and Waylon Skead; Ed, Roger, Dexter, and Herb Green; Lorne Redsky; Brennan Wapioke; Mike and Steven Fisher. From Shoal Lake, Ontario.

DISCOGRAPHY:
Songs of Thunder [Arbor 2002]
Honouring Our Elders [Arbor 2000]

Appearances:
Billy Joe Green:
My Ojibway Experience: Strength and Hope [independent 2000]
Various:
Thunder Drums, Vol. 2: *The Best Pow-wow Songs from the World's Best Drums* [Arbor 2002] comp
Thunder Drums, Vol. 1: *The Best of Arbor Records* [Arbor 2001] comp

Lake Region Singers—(Sioux) Northern Style

Lineup: Paul Little, Kenny Merrick Sr., Elmer White Sr., Carl, and Sam Merrick; Buddy Ross; Nathan Jones; Vic Jackson; Stacy Feather; Elmer White Jr.

DISCOGRAPHY:
Grass Dance Songs from Devils Lake [Canyon CR-8004]

Lake Vermillion Singers—
(Anishnabe) Northern Style

Lineup: Jeff Boshen Jr.; Joel Boshen; Terry Lightfeather Sr.; Terrence, Dan, and Harold Lightfeather; Arthur Dupree; Jerome Johnson Sr.; Derreck DeFoe; Dan Houle; Terry

Goodsky; Jeremy Wilson Sr.; Billy Wilson; Billy Morrison; Chad Morrin; Charlene Lightfeather; Heidi and Leah Goodwin; Tania Goodsky.

DISCOGRAPHY:
Onamani Zaaga-Igan [Arbor 1999]

Appearances:
Women's Fancy Dance Songs [Arbor/ Native American Heritage Series 2003] comp
Champion Round Dance Songs, Vol. 1 [Arbor 1999] comp

Little Axe—(Siksika) Northern Style
See: Traditional/Archival Group

Lineup: Stacey Axe; Trini and Trevor Back Fat; Radford Black Rider; Delford and Henry Three Suns; Kirk Yellow Fly; Harry Bull. From Siksika First Nation, Alberta.

DISCOGRAPHY:
Live at Beardy's [Sweet Grass 1999]
Chicken Dance Songs [Indian House 1998]

Appearances:
Mitataht askiy: Sweet Grass Records 10 Years [Sweet Grass 2003] comp

Little Boy Singers—(Blackfoot) Northern Style

Lineup: Daphne, Arnold, and Eugene Alexis; Darren, Donald, and Douglas Rain; Kimberly, Jennifer, Darcy, Dwight, and Sharon Paul; Lyndon and Leon Aginas; Jeff Moosomin. Based in Alberta, Canada.

DISCOGRAPHY:
Round Dance Songs [Canyon 1993]
Intertribal Powwow Songs [Canyon 1993]
Round Dances [Canyon 1992]
Intertribal Powwow Songs [Canyon 1991]
Powwow Songs for the Blood Reserve [Canyon 1990]

Little Corner Singers—(Blackfoot) Northern Style

Lineup: Clyde Heavy Runner; Woodrow and Keith Kicking Woman; Mike LaFramboise; Myron and Gayle Heavy Runner; K. J. Bear Medicine; Stan Whiteman.

DISCOGRAPHY:
Powwow Songs [Canyon 1986]

Little Earth—(Sioux) Northern Style

Recorded in Minneapolis–St. Paul, Minnesota.

DISCOGRAPHY:
Live! in the Twin Cities [Featherstone FT-1009]

Little Island Cree—(Cree) Northern Hand Drum

Lineup: Joey, Dale, Alvin, Clayton, and Jonathan Chief; Gerald Waterhen; Jeffrey Crookedneck; Clifford Ochuschayoo. From Island Lake Cree First Nation, Saskatchewan. Awards include World Hand Drum Champions, Schemitzun, and a Juno nomination for Best Music of Aboriginal Canada Recording, 1998.

DISCOGRAPHY:
Round Dance Blues [Turtle Island Music 2004]
Shadow of the Island [Turtle Island Music 2001]
Indian Country [Sweet Grass 2000]
For Old Times Sake [Sweet Grass 1998]
Little Island Cree [Sunshine 1997]
World Hand Drum Champions [Sweet Grass 1997]
Little Island Cree [Sweet Grass 1996]
Warrior [Sweet Grass 1996]
Little Island Cree [Sunshine SSCT-4181]

Appearances:
37th Annual Milk River Indian Days Powwow Live at Fort Belknap, Montana [Sweet Grass 2003] comp

Northern Cree and Friends: Round Dance Songs Recorded "Live," Vol. 1 [Canyon 2002] comp
World's Best Round Dance Songs, Vol. 2 [Sunshine 2001] comp
World's Best Fancy Dance Songs, Vol. 2 [Sunshine 2001] comp
World's Best Fancy Dance Songs, Vol. 1 [Sunshine 2000] comp
Best of the Best Schemitzun '93–99 [Sweet Grass 1999] comp
Thunderchild '98 [Turtle Island Music 1999] comp
World's Best Grass Dance [Sunshine 1998] comp
The Best of Saskatchewan [Sunshine 1997] comp
Gathering of Nations Pow-Wow 1996 [SOAR 1997] comp

Little Otter Singers—(Anishnabe) Northern Style

Lineup: Pete and Erik Gahbow, George Gauthier, Darrell Kingbird, Robert Sam, Larry Smallwood, Auddie Conner, Gerald Kingbird, Corey Joseph, Ron Brandt. Formed in 1979.

DISCOGRAPHY:
The Return [Arbor 2002]
Way Up North with Little Otter [Noc Bay 1998]
Come Dance to Our Music [Sunshine 1998]
Little Otter [Sunshine 1997]
Around the World for a Song [Ryko/World 1991] comp

Appearances:
Thunder on the Lake [Arbor 2003] comp
The Best of Hinckley Powwow Northern and Southern Style [Arbor 2003] comp
Jingle Dress Side Step Songs [Arbor 2001] comp
Hinckley Powwow Northern Style [Arbor 2001] comp
World's Best Crow Hop Songs [Sunshine 2001] comp

World's Best Intertribal Songs [Sunshine 2001] comp
Powwow 2000 [Sunshine 2000] comp
World's Best Powwow Drum Groups [Sunshine 2000] comp
World's Best Jingle Dress Songs [Sunshine 1998] comp
World's Best Round Dance Songs [Sunshine 1997] comp
Hinckley Grand Celebrations Powwow 1995 Northern Style [Sunshine SSCT-4283] comp
Honor the Earth Powwow Songs of the Great Lakes [Ryko 1990] comp
Minnesota Powwow Songs [Sunshine SSCT-4174] comp
White Earth Powwow [Sunshine SSCT-4338] comp
Wisconsin Intertribal [Sunshine SSCT-4216] comp
White Earth Powwow [Sunshine SSCT-4173] comp

Little Pine Singers—(Cree) Northern Style *See*: Red Bull

Lineup: Walter, Edmund, Albert and Lally Bull.

DISCOGRAPHY:
Cree Powwow Songs [Canyon 1977]

Little Shell Singers—(Hidatsa) Northern Style

Lineup: Alfred Driver Sr., Byron Brady, Delvin Driver Sr., Malcolm Wolf, Glen Fox Jr.

DISCOGRAPHY:
Hidatsa Songs [Canyon 1974]

Little Spirit—Northern-Style Youth Drum

Lineup: Priscilla, Sheena, and Marsha Hototmani; Jamie and Angie Parisian; Allison

and Tana Daniels; Vanesa McKay; Angie and Michelle Champagne.

DISCOGRAPHY:
Little Spirit Singers [Sunshine 1996]

Appearances:
Best of Manitoba [Sunshine 1997] comp

Little Thunderbird Singers— Northern-Style Youth Drum *See*: Contemporary Music: Moody X Two

Lineup: Tiffany, Rene, and Danielle Yetman; Natashia and Alexandria Moodie; Deidre Primrose; Jenna Walker; Candice Linklater.

DISCOGRAPHY:
The Little Thunderbird Singers [Sunshine 1997]

Appearances:
World's Best Tiny Tot Songs [Sunshine 2000] comp

Lodge Creek—(Anishnabe) Northern Style

Lineup: Chase Sayer, Joey Waterhen, Eric Chief, and others.

DISCOGRAPHY:
Round Dance Songs [Sunshine 2002]

Logan Alexis—(Nakota) Northern Style *See*: Blackstone Singers

Lineup: Logan, Eugene, Arnold, Robbie, and Daphne Alexis; Craig Lewis; Frank Hart; John Scabbyrobe; Leon Aginas. From Alexis, Alberta.

DISCOGRAPHY:
Christmas Time Has Come [Arbor 2003] enhanced
Logan Alexis, Vol. 2 [Sweet Grass 1997]
Round Dances [Sunshine SSCT-4130]

Appearances:

Blackstone Singers:

Round Dance Singin' [Canyon 2004]

Various:

Mitataht askiy: Sweet Grass Records 10 Years [Sweet Grass 2003] comp

Drum Beats: 18 Powwow Groups [Sunshine 2002] comp

Northern Cree and Friends: Round Dance Songs Recorded "Live," Vol. 1 [Canyon 2002] comp

World's Best Round Dance Songs, Vol. 2 [Sunshine 2001] comp

Powwow 2000 [Sunshine 2000] comp

World Renowned Hand Drum Lead Singers, Vol. 2 [Sunshine 2000] comp

World Renowned Hand Drum Lead Singers, Vol. 1 [Sunshine 2000] comp

World's Best Powwow Drum Groups [Sunshine 2000] comp

Best of Alberta [Sunshine 1997] comp

World's Best Round Dance Songs [Sunshine 1997] comp

Lone Buffalo Singers—(Lakota) Northern Style

Lineup: Ephraim Hill Sr., Zach Thompson, Louis Garcia, Norman Adams.

DISCOGRAPHY:

Sioux Songs from Devils Lake [Canyon CR-8005]

Lone Eagle Creek Singers— Northern Style

Lineup: Ambrose, Darren, Bernard, and Jason Tapaquon; Quentin O'Watch; Perry McNabb; Craig Lavallee; Darwin Asapace; Mike Pratt; Wendell Benjoe; Kevin, Robert, and Jeff Cappo.

DISCOGRAPHY:

Lone Eagle Creek Singers [Sunshine SSCT-4198]

Maddog Singers—(Crow) Northern Style

Lineup: Seymour Eagle Speaker; Dale, Henry Sr., and Robert Old Horn; Stanley Pretty Paint; Bill Runsabove; Merle Tendoy; Barbara Bearskin; Rachel Three Irons. Double-beat songs of the Crow Nation were preserved and handed down from Alphonso Child in the Mouth. In the late 1950s, some of these songs, performed by Jim Black Dog (*See*: Fort Kipp Singers) with Finnegan Baker (*See*: Mandaree), include songs called "Crow hop," a nickname for the double-beat songs. The dancers emulate prairie birds during their mating season, moving in any direction, even backward.

DISCOGRAPHY:

Double Beat Songs of the Crow [Indian House 2000]

Mandaree—(Mandan-Hidatsa-Arikira) Northern Style *See*: New Town Singers

Original Lineup: Sidrick, Bill, Norman, and Clement Baker; Bert Yellow Wolf. *Millennium Lineup:* Norman, Clement, Sidrick, Scott, and Wade Baker; Mike Short Bull; Fred Morsette; Angus and Rex Fox. From Fort Berthold, North Dakota.

DISCOGRAPHY:

Live at Ft. Belknap [Sweet Grass 2003]

Live at Crow Fair 2000 [Indian House 2001]

For the People [Arbor 2000]

Live at Stanford [Sweet Grass 1996]

Schemitzun Live: Championship of Song and Dance [Sweet Grass 1995]

A Tribute to Billy Baker [Sweet Grass 1995]

Live at Bismarck [Featherstone FT-1012]

Live! New Town, North Dakota [Featherstone FT-1004]

Powwow Songs [Canyon 1977]

Mandan Hidatsa Songs [Canyon 1974/1995]

Appearances:

Mitataht askiy: Sweet Grass Records 10 Years [Sweet Grass 2003] comp

37th Annual Milk River Indian Days Powwow Live at Fort Belknap, Montana [Sweet Grass 2003] comp

Thunder Drums, Vol. 2: The Best Powwow Songs from the World's Best Drums [Arbor 2002] comp

Thunder Drums, Vol. 1: The Best of Arbor Records [Arbor 2001] comp

Gathering of Nations Pow-Wow: Millennium Celebration, Vol. 1: Various Northern Drums [SOAR 2000] comp

Standing Our Ground [Turtle Island Music 1999] comp

Hinckley Powwow, Vol. 2 [Sunshine 1995] comp

Hinckley Powwow, Vol. 1 [Sunshine 1995] comp

Songs of the Spirit: The Best of Sweet Grass [Sweet Grass/EMI 1995] comp

United Tribes International Powwow [Makoche 1995] two-CD comp

Mankillers—(Intertribal) Northern-Style Women's Drum

Lineup: Genevieve Markussen, Maggie Eskobedo-Steele, Carolyn Dunn-Anderson, Irma Amaro-Davis, Tina Toledo-Rizzo, Rain Archambeau-Marshall, Geneva Shaw, Michon Eben, Kristy Orona-Ramirez, Sawar Young.

DISCOGRAPHY:

Comin' to Get'cha [SOAR 1999]

All Woman Northern Drum Group [With-Out Rez Productions 1997]

Mauchahty-Ware, Tom, and Millard Clark *See*: Flute Music (Mauchahty-Ware); Contemporary Music: Indian Chipmunks; Contemporary Spoken Word: Poetry: Bob Annesley

DISCOGRAPHY:

Powwow Specialty Dance Songs from Oklahoma [Indian Sounds IS-6001]

The Contest Is On: Trick Dance Songs, Vol. 2 [Indian Sounds IS-2011]

The Contest Is On: Trick Dance Songs, Vol. 1 [Indian Sounds IS-2020]

Powwow Songs from Oklahoma, Vol. 2 [Indian Sounds 2002]

Powwow Songs from Oklahoma, Vol. 1 [Indian Sounds 2001]

Round Dance Songs from Oklahoma, Vol. 4 [Indian Sounds IS-1004]

Round Dance Songs from Oklahoma, Vol. 3 [Indian Sounds IS-1003]

Round Dance Songs from Oklahoma, Vol. 2 [Indian Sounds IS-1002]

Round Dance Songs from Oklahoma, Vol. 1 [Indian Sounds IS-1001]

Maza Duta—(Nakota) Northern Style

Lineup: Daniel, Ira, Matthew, Leslie, Joel, Patrick, Little Eagle, and Crystal McArthur; Tracy Delorme; Stephen Eashappie; Terrence and Tina Brown; Marietta Akachuk. Formed in 1997, Pheasant Rump, Saskatchewan.

DISCOGRAPHY:

Maza Duta [Sunshine 2001]

Appearances:

Drum Beats: 18 Powwow Groups [Sunshine 2002] comp

McGilvery and Green—(Cree) Northern Style

Gordon McGilvery (born April 30, 1942) and Francis Green, from Saddle Lake and Bear Hills–Muskwachees, Alberta, respectively. These singers are keepers of generations-old round dance songs handed down by Gordon's father, Peter McGilvery.

Lineup for *All in the Family*: Gordon, David, Ferlin, and Aaron McGilvery; Ben Cardinal.

DISCOGRAPHY:
All in the Family: Old Time Cree Round Dance Songs [Canyon 2003] Gordon McGilvery
Shining Elbow [Sweet Grass 1998]
For the First Time: Round Dance Songs [Sweet Grass 1995]

Appearances:
Northern Cree and Friends: Round Dance Songs Recorded "Live," Vol. 2 [Canyon 2003] comp
Northern Cree and Friends: Round Dance Songs Recorded "Live," Vol. 1 [Canyon 2002] comp
Stick Game Songs, Vol. 1 [Arbor 2002] comp *See*: Traditional/Archival Compilations
World's Leading Round Dance Songs [Sweet Grass 1996] comp
Songs from the Battleford Powwow [Canyon 1975] comp

Medicine Drum — (Anishnabe) Northern Style

Lineup: Darrell, Arian, and Myron Medicine; Dave Medicine Jr.; John, Fred, Shannon, and Sandra Copenace; Marshall Morriseau. From Big Island First Nation, Ontario.

DISCOGRAPHY:
Medicine Drum [Sunshine SSCT-4324]

Appearances:
The Best of Ontario Powwow Groups [Sunshine 1997] comp

Meskwaki Nation — (Mesquakie) Northern Style

Lineup: Lydell and Jarvis Bear; Gee St. John; Jaro Jackson; Cody and Jeremy King; Willis Davenport; Chago and Gubba Hale; Brenton, Quinton, and Martel Pushetonequa. Formed in 1994, Tama, Iowa.

DISCOGRAPHY:
2002 Live @ Iowa City, Haskell University [independent 2003]
Live at Hinckley [WRMN 007]

Appearances:
The Best of Hinckley Powwow Northern and Southern Style: 11th Annual Powwow Grand Celebration [Arbor 2003] comp
Gathering of Nations Powwow 2001 [Gathering of Nations Records 2001] comp
Gathering of Nations Pow-Wow 1998: Various Drum Groups [SOAR 1999] comp
Red Lake Nation [Turtle Island Music 1996] comp

Metcalf, Leonard — (Lakota) Northern Style

DISCOGRAPHY:
Sioux Songs [Indian Records 1194]

Midnite Express — (Intertribal) Northern Style *See*: The Boyz, Eyabay, Mystic River, Meskwaki Nation

The lead singers of four drum groups created a new group to explore the boundless possiblities of powwow singing.

DISCOGRAPHY:
2002 — Live from Minnesota [independent RCR-9661 2003]
From Dusk to Dawn [independent RCR 2002]

Appearances:
The Best of the Hinckley Pow Wow Northern and Southern Style [Arbor 2003] comp

Moose Mountain Nakota Singers—
(Nakota) Northern Style

Lineup: Charlie Maxie; Lynelle and Charlie Big Eagle; Tracy Delorme; Joe Bunn; Josh Kakakaway; Willie Kennedy; Peter Bigstone; Eric Akachuk; Annette, Yvonne, and Gilbert Lonechild; Angoe, Joan, Sara, Wan, T. J., and Wallace McArthur; Sandy and Elmer Lonethunder.

Group members from various Nakota communities, including Whitebear First Nation, Manitoba, and Pheasant Rump and Ocean Man, Saskatchewan.

DISCOGRAPHY:
Kahomani Songs [Sunshine 2002]
Kahomani Songs, Vol. 2 [Sunshine 1999]
Kahomani Songs [Sunshine 1999]

Appearances:
Drum Beats: 18 Powwow Groups [Sunshine 2002] comp
Powwow 2000 [Sunshine 2000] comp
World's Best Powwow Drum Groups [Sunshine 2000] comp

Moosomin, Art—(Cree) *See*: Mosquito

DISCOGRAPHY:

Appearances:
Straight from the Heart: Tribute Album [Turtle Island Music 1999] comp

Mosquito—(Cree) Northern Style

Lineup: Art Moosomin; Quinn, Jeff, Susanne, Joanne, Diane, and Roseann Moosomin; Clayton Chief; Marshall Dreaver; Randy Harris; Shorty and Lorraine Thomas. From Mosquito First Nation, Saskatchewan.

DISCOGRAPHY:
You Belong to Me [Sweet Grass 1998]
Keep Me in Your Heart [Sweet Grass 1995]
For the Young at Heart [Sweet Grass 1994]

Appearances:
Mitataht askiy: Sweet Grass Records 10 Years [Sweet Grass 2003] comp
World's Leading Round Dance Songs [Sweet Grass 1996] comp

Mountain Soul—(Cree) Northern Style *See*: Smallboy Singers

Lineup: Elmer and Calvin Rattlesnake; Clay, Craig, Avery, J. K., Tyrone, Fred, Reinhart, Ira, Ian, and Daniel Roan; Stuart Morin; Jayson and Dale Zorthian.

From Hobema–Cree Camp, Alberta. In 1969, founding members of Mountain Soul approached various elders such as Windyboy, Wolfchild, Sam Windyboy, and Harry Shade and his singers, in Cardston, Alberta, and received traditional teachings relating to the original powwow ceremonies.

DISCOGRAPHY:
Live at Ft. Belknap [Sweet Grass 2003]
Mountain Soul in the Valley of the Sun, Vol. 2 [Indian House 2001]
Mountain Soul in the Valley of the Sun, Vol. 1 [Indian House 2001]
Soul Lives On [Sweet Grass 2000]

Appearances:
Mitataht askiy: Sweet Grass Records 10 Years [Sweet Grass 2003] comp
37th Annual Milk River Indian Days Powwow Live at Fort Belknap, Montana [Sweet Grass 2003] comp
Northern Cree and Friends: Round Dance Songs Recorded "Live," Vol. 2 [Canyon 2003] comp
Ermineskin Cree Nation Pow-wow: Live at Bear Park [Sweet Grass 1999] comp
Thunderchild '98 [Turtle Island Music 1999] comp

Mystic River—(Intertribal) Northern Style

Lineup: Seymor Eaglespeaker, Jim Genia, Bill Runsabove, Tyson Merrick, Mike Thomas, Kenny Merrick Jr., Sheldon Sundown, Jack Bull, Brian Kelly, Chris Newell, David Morsett. Based in Connecticut.

DISCOGRAPHY:
Live on the Trail [Wacipi Records 2000]
Schemitzun World Championship of Song and Dance [Sweet Grass 1997]
Live at the Crow Fair [Sweet Grass 1996]

Appearances:
Mitataht askiy: Sweet Grass Records 10 Years [Sweet Grass 2003] comp
Jingle Dress Side Step Songs [Arbor 2001] comp
World's Best Round Dance Songs, Vol. 2 [Sunshine 2001] comp
Gathering of Nations Pow-Wow: Millennium Celebration, Vol. 1: *Various Northern Drums* [SOAR 2000] comp
Naturally Native [Silver Wave 2000] sdtk *See*: Contemporary Soundtracks
Gathering of Nations Pow-Wow 1998 [SOAR 1999] comp
Standing Our Ground [Turtle Island Music 1999] comp
Toronto Powwow [Sunshine 1998] comp

Nakoda Lodge—(Nakota) Contemporary Northern Style

Lineup: Everett Hunter, Cory Smith, Randy Hunter, Kaylen and Trent Hunter, Lane Bearspaw.

From Morley, Alberta, this group of young singers redefined powwow music to much criticism and acclaim when they infused modern technological enhancements to create a new sound. *Dark Realm* received a Juno nomination for Best Music of Aboriginal Canada, 2002. Everett Hunter's techno album *Psycho Dancing* received an ECMA nomination for Best Aboriginal Album, 2004.

DISCOGRAPHY:
World's Best Chicken Dance Songs [Sunshine 2002]
Dark Realm [Stoney Records/Sunshine 2001]
Chico's Trail [Stoney Records/Sunshine 2001]

Appearances:
Drum Beats: 18 Powwow Groups [Sunshine 2002] comp

Related Projects:
Everett Hunter:
Psycho Dancing [independent 2003] contemporary music release

Neskahi, Arlie—(Dineh) *See*: White Eagle; Contemporary Music: Song Catchers.

An award-winning singer who released six albums on Canyon Records with the White Eagle Singers; toured with the American Indian Dance Theater; worked with the Song Catchers in the early 1990s; recorded with Paul Winter's *Prayer for the Wild Things*, 1995 Grammy Award; scored for theater, film, and video; was musical director for *Home Again*, Oregon Trail Project, 1998; and created his own Internet business in 1995, entitled Rainbow Walker. He appears on vocals and flute on the track "Eagle's Jump" from the *Sounds of Portland* compilation CD released in 1999, with Leroy Critcher, guitar/percussion/soundscapes.

Nettiyewpwat—Northern Style

DISCOGRAPHY:
Nettiyewpwat [Sunshine SSCT-4193]

New Town Singers—(Intertribal) Northern Traditional

Members of Mandaree, the Eagle Whistles, and the Old Scout Singers.

DISCOGRAPHY:
Live at Dakota Dance Clan Celebration [Featherstone FT-1003]

Nighthawk—(Crow) Northern Style

Lineup: Cedric Walks Over Ice; Billy Norman; Clement Baker (Mandaree, North Dakota); Matthew and Jim Black Dog (Fort Kipp, Montana). The group originated in the 1960s as the Night Time Hot Dance Society Singers. All members belong to the traditional Crow singing society based in Montana.

DISCOGRAPHY:
War Dance Songs [Arbor 2003]
Night Hawk Singers [Sweet Grass 1996]

Nikamok—(Cree-Metis)

Joe Naytowhow (Woodland Cree) from Sturgeon First Nation, Saskatchewan, and Cheryl L'Hirondelle-Waynohtew (Metis) from Lac la Biche, Alberta. Their songs stem from traditional northern-style hand drumming, which the duo infused with new interpretations that reflected contemporary influences, such as gospel and blues. The duo has performed at music festivals and traditional gatherings throughout Canada.

DISCOGRAPHY:
Nikamok [Miyohtakwan 2000]

Appearances:
Ookpic:
Pond Dynamics [Ookpic Pie 1992]

Noon Express—Northern Style

DISCOGRAPHY:
Round Dance and Other Songs [Noon Records 1998]
Powwow Songs [Noon Records 1997]

North Buffalo Cree Singers (Cree)—Northern style

Lineup: Jamie Cook, Daniel, Eli, and Ferley Constant; Mike Head; Quinton Cowley; Garry Munro Jr.; Nolan Moore.

DISCOGRAPHY:
North Buffalo Cree Singers [Sunshine 1994]

Appearances:
Best of Manitoba [Sunshine 1997] comp

Northern Cree Singers—(Cree) Northern Style *See:* Randy Wood, Young Bird; Contemporary Music: Chief Rock

Lineup: Steve and Randy Wood; Warren Shirt; Ferlin and Aaron McGilvery; Shane Dion; Verlon Gould.

From Saddle Lake, Alberta. They received a NAMA nomination for Duo/Group of the Year, 2003; *Rockin' the Rez* received a Grammy nomination for Best Native American Music Album, 2002; *Still Rezin'* received a Grammy nomination for Best Native American Music Album, 2004.

DISCOGRAPHY:
Rezonate: Powwow Songs Recorded Live at Saddle Lake [Canyon 2004]
Round Dance Jam [Canyon 2003]
Youngbird and Northern Cree: Double Platinum—Powwow Songs Recorded Live at Hobbema [Canyon 2003]
Still Rezin': Pow-wow Songs Recorded Live at Saddle Lake [Canyon 2002]
Rockin' the Rez: Powwow Songs Recorded Live at Saddle Lake [Canyon 2000]
Second Song . . . Dancers' Choice [Canyon 2000]

Showtime: Round Dance Songs [Canyon 2000]

Here to Stay [Canyon 1999]

In Our Drum We Trust [Canyon 1999]

Honor the Eagle Feather [Canyon 1998]

It's Time to Round Dance! [Canyon 1998]

Come and Dance! Powwow Songs Live at Whiteriver [Canyon 1996]

Live at Lummi [Canyon 1996]

Powwow Recorded Live! [Canyon 1994]

Powwow Songs Recorded Live [Canyon 1993]

Northern Cree Singers, Vol. 4: *"No Word Songs Please"* [Canyon 1993]

Live at Fort Duschene [Canyon 1992]

Powwow Songs [Canyon 1992]

Powwow Songs [Canyon 1991]

Appearances:

Chief Rock:

The Relentless Warrior [independent 2001]

Various:

Northern Cree and Friends: Round Dance Songs Recorded "Live," Vol. 2 [Canyon 2003] comp

Northern Cree and Friends: Round Dance Songs Recorded "Live," Vol. 1 [Canyon 2002] comp

Schemitzun 2000: Hand Drum Songs [Sweet Grass 2001] comp

Schemitzun World Championship 2000: Round Dance Singing [Turtle Island Music 2001] comp

Schemitzun World Championship Round Dance Singing [Turtle Island Music 2000] comp

Voices across the Canyon, Vol. 4 [Canyon 1999] comp *See:* Contemporary Compilations

World's Best Round Dance Songs [Sunshine 1997] comp

Voices across the Canyon, Vol. 1 [Canyon 1996] comp *See:* Contemporary Compilations

Hinckley Grand Celebrations Powwow 1995 Northern Style [Sunshine 1996] comp

Hinckley Powwow, Vol. 2 [Sunshine 1995] comp

Hinckley Powwow, Vol. 1 [Sunshine 1995] comp

Northern Plains Society Singers—
(Intertribal) Northern Style

Lineup: Sonny Mosquito (Blood-Creek), Glen Eagle Speaker (Blackfoot-Blood), Frank Mosquito (Cree), Dwynne Eagle Speaker (Blackfoot-Blood), Darrell Norman (Blackfoot), Steve Gunnyon (Anishnabe).

DISCOGRAPHY:

The Northern Plains Society Singers [Canyon 1980]

Northern Spirit—(Cree) Northern Style

Lineup: Clement and Oliver Mitsuing, Fred Campiou, Vince and Dave Kytwayhat, Greg and Brian Ernest, Lorne Crookedneck, Dave Larocque, Ed Seegerts, Alvin Paskimin, Ray Anderson. Formed within the Native Brotherhood at the Regional Psychiatric Centre, Saskatoon, Saskatchewan.

DISCOGRAPHY:

Northern Spirit Singers [Sweet Grass 1995]

Northern Wind—(Anishnabe) Northern Style

Lineup: Gabe and Farrell Desrosiers, Harvey Goodsky, Eddie Greene, Justin Handorgan, Dean Jouradain, Bruce and Rod Crow, Mike Fisher, Pat Skead.

DISCOGRAPHY:

Whispering Winds [Arbor 2004]

Campfire [Arbor 2002] enhanced

Dance with Us [Arbor 2001]

Blazing Trails [Turtle Island Music 2000]

Ikwe-Nagamonan Jingle Dress Songs [Arbor 2000]

21st Century [Arbor 1999]

Northern Wind, Vol. 11 [Sunshine SSCT-4320]

Northern Wind, Vol. 10 [Sunshine SSCT-4319]

Northern Wind, Vol. 9 [Sunshine 1997]

Northern Wind, Vol. 8 [Sunshine 1996]

Northern Wind, Vol. 7 [Sunshine SSCT-4239]

Northern Wind, Vol. 6 [Sunshine SSCT-4205]

Northern Wind, Vol. 5 [Sunshine SSCT-4195]

Northern Wind, Vol. 4 [Sunshine SSCT-4170]

Northern Wind, Vol. 3 [Sunshine SSCT-4154]

Northern Wind, Vol. 2 [Sunshine SSCT-4128]

Northern Wind, Vol. 1 [Sunshine SSCT-4108]

Appearances:

Round Dance Songs, Vol. 2 [Arbor/Native American Heritage Series 2003] comp

Women's Fancy Dance Songs [Arbor/Native American Heritage Series 2003] comp

Drum Beats: 18 Powwow Groups [Sunshine 2002] comp

Thunder Drums, Vol. 2: *The Best Powwow Songs from the World's Best Drums* [Arbor 2002] comp

World's Best Memorial Songs [Sunshine 2002] comp

World's Best Women's Traditional Songs [Sunshine 2002] comp

Jingle Dress Side Step Songs [Arbor 2001] comp

Eschikagou Powwow 2000 LIVE! [Gathering of Nations Records 2001] comp

Hinckley Powwow Northern Style [Arbor 2001] comp

Thunder Drums, Vol. 1: *The Best of Arbor Records* [Arbor 2001] comp

World's Best Crow Hop Songs [Sunshine 2001] comp

World's Best Fancy Dance Songs, Vol. 2 [Sunshine 2001] comp

World's Best Intertribal Songs [Sunshine 2001] comp

World's Best Round Dance Songs, Vol. 2 [Sunshine 2001] comp

World's Best Veteran Songs, Vol. 1 [Sunshine 2001] comp

World's Best Fancy Dance Songs, Vol. 1 [Sunshine 2000] comp

Powwow 2000 [Sunshine 2000] comp

World's Best Powwow Drum Groups [Sunshine 2000] comp

World's Best Grass Dance [Sunshine 1998] comp

World's Best Jingle Dress Songs [Sunshine 1998] comp

The Best of Ontario Powwow Groups [Sunshine 1997] comp

World's Best Round Dance Songs [Sunshine 1997] comp

Gathering of Nations Pow-Wow, Vol. 1 [SOAR 1992] comp

Thunder Bear Powwow [Sunshine SSCT-4188] comp

Minnesota Powwow Songs [Sunshine SSCT-4174] comp

Oakdale—(Blackfeet) Northern Style

Formed in Fort Berthold, North Dakota, in the 1950s by Joe Black Bear, Warren Wolf, George Wolf, and Eugene Smith. The tradition of singing has lived on through Eugene Smith's grandchildren Kenny, Ron, Tracy, Mike, Lyle, Arthur, and Eugene Smith; and through Warren Wolf's great grandsons Charles Fox and Cody Seaboy.

DISCOGRAPHY:

Recorded Live at Carry the Kettle [Sweet Grass 1996]

Oakdale Singers [Sweet Grass 1996]

Old Agency Singers of the Blood Reserve—(Blackfoot) Northern Style

Lineup: Jim Chief Calf, John Chief Calf, Dominic Cross Child, Rick and Jarvie Day Chief, Dean Plume, Dan Weasel Moccasin Sr., Daniel Weasel Moccasin Jr., Stewart

Old Agency Singers of the Blood Reserve (1972), a vintage recording of old-style songs. Courtesy Indian House Records.

Weasel Moccasin. Recorded at Stand Off, Alberta, July 27, 1972.

DISCOGRAPHY:
Old Agency Singers of the Blood Reserve, Vol. 2 [Indian House 1972]
Old Agency Singers of the Blood Reserve, Vol. 1 [Indian House 1971]

Old Scout Singers—(Arikira) Northern Style *See:* New Town Singers

DISCOGRAPHY:
Live at White Shield, North Dakota [Featherstone FT-1005]

Omaha White Tail—Northern Style

Lineup: Tim Grant; Kelly, Tim, and A. J. Grant; J. R. Thomas; Brad Saunsoci; Kennard Parker; Blackbird and Jerome Sheridan. Formed in Omaha, Nebraska, 1989.

DISCOGRAPHY:
Kickin' It Up [Red Rock Productions 1999]
Schemitzun [Sweet Grass 1999]
To the Mothers [Sweet Grass 1998]

Live at Red Earth [Sweet Grass 1997]
Live at Carry the Kettle [Sweet Grass 1996}
Omaha Tribe of Nebraska [Sweet Grass 1996]

Appearances:
Mitataht askiy: Sweet Grass Records 10 Years [Sweet Grass 2003] comp

Otter Trail—(Intertribal) Southern Style

Lineup: Jose Roldan (Kogi-Arawak); Matt and Mandy Harmon (Nanticoke Delaware); Ron Gibson (Iowa-Shawnee); Al Bold Eagle (Arawak-Aztec); Mark Hicks (Eastern Cherokee); Urie Ridgeway (Nanticoke Delaware); David Buffalohead (Ponca-Kiowa-Comanche); Will Mosley (Nanticoke Delaware); Sean Keahna (Sac-Fox); Misty Nace (Anishnabe); Judy Gibson (Pawnee); Cherie Siebert (Eastern Cherokee).

Formed in 1992. *Family Song Southern Style* received a NAMA nomination for Best Powwow Album, 1998.

DISCOGRAPHY:
The Next Chapter [independent 2001]
Live at Marksville [independent 2000]
Family Song Southern Style [SOAR 1997]
Live from Hunter Mountain [independent 1992]

Appearances:
Gathering of Nations Pow-Wow 1998 [SOAR 1999] comp

Painted Horse—(Blackfoot) Northern Style

Lineup: Winston Wadsworth; Leo Wells; Craig First Rider; Tonka Howard; David, Michael, and Vince Meguinis; Billy, Blaine, Myron, and Morley Redwood; Bruce Starlight Jr.; Derrick Laboucan; Wesley Windyboy; Jason Belcourt.

Group members represent Blackfoot, Blood, Cree, Peigan, and Tsuu T'ina Nations, Alberta. Painted Horse placed in the top ten of the Contemporary Powwow category, Schemitzun, 1995.

DISCOGRAPHY:
Panee Xpress [Arbor 2003]
Live at Anapi [Sweet Grass 1998]
Good Ol' Days [Sweet Grass 1997]
Just Horsin' Around [Sweet Grass 1997]
Painted Horse [Sweet Grass 1996]

Appearances:
Mitataht askiy: Sweet Grass Records 10 Years [Sweet Grass 2003] comp
SIFC Powwow Live '95 [SICC 1995] comp
United Tribes International Powwow [Makoche 1995] two CDs

Parker Singers—
(OJ-Cree–Assiniboine)

Lineup: Videl, Kenny, Doug, and Russell Standing Rock; Irvin Denny; Ken Writing Bird. From Rocky Boy, Montana.

DISCOGRAPHY:
Cree Powwow Songs, Vol. 2 [Canyon CR-8031]
Cree Powwow Songs, Vol. 1 [Canyon CR-6091]

Pass Creek Singers—(Lakota)
Northern Style

Lineup: Adam Sparrow; Steve, Eternity, Thomas, Bobby, and Bloka DuBray; Waylon Gaddie; Mahpia Not Afraid; Dean Rouillard; Robert Rendon; Samuel Long; Chaske Johns; Santee Luke Witt. From Allen, South Dakota.

DISCOGRAPHY:
Generations [Turtle Island Music 1998]
Powwow Songs [Canyon 1993]

Appearances:
Songs of the Oglala Nation: Native American Powwow [Turtle Island Music 1998] comp
Gathering of Nations Pow-Wow 1993 [SOAR 1994] comp

Pawnee Yellowhorse—(Pawnee)
Southern Style

Lineup: Vance Horsechief Jr.; Phil Minthorn; Gary Leadingfox; Bryan Hodshire; Bunky and Debbie Echo Hawk; Jason Lightfoot; Jennifer Folsom-Minthorn; Colleen Gorman; Kay Hodshire; Vance Horsechief III, Greg Leadingfox; O. D. Moore; Marcie Muth; Carrie Howell.

DISCOGRAPHY:
Spirit of the Plains [WithOut Rez Productions 1996]

Appearances:
Schemitzun World Championship 2000: Southern Style [Turtle Island Music 2001] comp

Peacemakers Drum—(Mohawk) *See*: Flute Music: Jerry McDonald

Also known as the Tyendinaga Mohawk Singing Society, Deseronto, Ontario.

Pigeon Lake Singers—(Cree)
Northern Style

Lineup: Craig Lewis, Lester Brown, Leroy Whitestone, Blair Mountain, Lyle Chief, Isaac Thomas, Shawn Swampy, Clint Whitestone, Brad Pahtayken, Tahlee Redbird (Kiowa).

DISCOGRAPHY:
Cree Powwow Songs, Vol. 3 [Canyon 1995]
Powwow Songs [Canyon 1980]
Cree Tribal Songs [Canyon 1977]
Pigeon Lake Singers [Sunshine SSCT 4148]

Appearances:
World's Best Veteran Songs, Vol. 1 [Sunshine 2001] comp
World's Best Jingle Dress Songs [Sunshine 1998] comp
Best of Alberta [Sunshine 1997] comp
Onion Lake Powwow 1992 [Sunshine SSCT-4149] comp

Pipestone—(Anishnabe) Northern Style

Lineup: Ahsinees Larson, George Morrow III, Wendall Powless, John Anderson, Thomas Cain, Mikey DeMain, Jason Pettibone, Jerome Powless, Neal Quagon, Melvin White Jr., Mike Sullivan, John Morrow, Reggie Cadotte. From Lac Courte Oreilles Ojibwe Reservation, northern Wisconsin.

DISCOGRAPHY:
Pipestone [Arbor 2002]

Appearances:
Round Dance Songs, Vol. 2 [Arbor/Native American Heritage Series 2003] comp
The Best of Hinckley Powwow Northern and Southern Style [Arbor 2003] comp
Hinckley Powwow Northern Style [Arbor 2001] comp

Pipestone Creek—(Cree) Northern Style

Lineup: Vernon Chocan, Greg Whitestone, Isaac Thomas, Duane Chocan, Brad Pahtahken, Gary Waskahat, Grant Whitestone Sr., Darwin Jimmy, Blair Mountain. From Onion Lake, Saskatchewan.

DISCOGRAPHY:
Pipestone Creek and Friends: The Round Dance Way [Turtle Island Music 2004]
The Contest Is On [Turtle Island Music 2001]
We're Back to Stay [Turtle Island Music 2000]
Believing in Our Drum [Turtle Island Music 1998]
Respect Mother Earth [Sweet Grass 1994]
Pipestone Creek [Sweet Grass 1993]

Appearances:
Mitataht askiy: Sweet Grass Records 10 Years [Sweet Grass 2003] comp
Bear Spirit [Turtle Island Music 1999] comp
Cree Nation [Turtle Island Music 1998] comp

Spirit of the Wolf [Turtle Island Music 1998] comp
SIFC Powwow Live '95 [SICC 1995] comp

Plains Indian Singers—Northern Style

DISCOGRAPHY:
Powwow Songs [Canyon 16255]

Ponemah Chippewa Singers—(Anishnabe) Northern Style *See*: Kingbird Singers

Lineup: Greg Johnson, Johnson Kingbird, Joseph and George Dick. From Red Lake, Minnesota.

DISCOGRAPHY:
Chippewa [Canyon CR-6082]

Poor Boys—(Intertribal) Southern Style

Lineup: Geoff White, Quinton Anquoe, Michael Deer, Mike Gawhega, Mike Kihega, Amos Littlecrow, Knokkovlee Locust, Charles Logan, Rueben Tehaund, Marla White, Jo Jo Walker, Kaylene Deer, Shashauna Tehauno, Rachel Heap of Birds, Cekewe Locust.
Formed at Sequoyah Indian School, Oklahoma. The group members represent Kiowa, Comanche, Otoe, Iowa, Sac-Fox, Kickapoo, Ponca, and Shawnee Nations.

DISCOGRAPHY:
Oklahoma [Arbor 2003]
49er Songs, Vol. 1 [Arbor 2002]

Poplar Jrs.—(Lakota)
DISCOGRAPHY:
Sioux [Indian Records IR-1190]

Porcupine Singers—(Lakota)
Northern Style

1977 Lineup: James Clairmont, Severt Young Bear Sr., Ronnie Theisz, Francis Menard, Henry Green Crow, Philip Wright, Calvin Jumping Bull, David Clairmont.

1997 Lineup: Cedric and Melvin Young Bear, Severt Young Bear Jr., Clyde Squirrel Coat, Brian and Tom Thunderhawk, J. D. Goodhouse, Calvin Jumping Bull, Scott and Red Boy Means, Irving Tail, Kristian and Ronnie Theisz.

The roots of the Porcupine Singers began in the 1860s with the Young Bear family, Pine Ridge District, Pine Ridge Reservation, Porcupine, South Dakota. The generations of singers have passed on the group's name, and the group gained wide popularity in the 1970s and 1980s. They maintained a large repertoire of contemporary intertribal and old traditional Lakota songs and were one of the first drums to travel the powwow trail throughout North America. Active in traditional life, the singers often participated in many ceremonies and honored their drum with the name Oyate Ho Nah'um (the People Hear Its Voice). After long deliberations about recording traditional songs, the group felt it was necessary to preserve them in order to show how they should be sung and to provide a better understanding of the culture. By the late 1980s, they ceased traveling but continued singing locally; additional work includes the score for *Dances With Wolves* [Kevin Costner, 1990]. By the early 1990s, many of the Porcupine Singers had passed on, including Severt Young Bear Sr.; the remaining singers invited the Brotherhood Singers to record with them and eventually to carry on the Porcupine name. Their 1997 album *Songs from Porcupine: Honoring Irving Tail* includes songs made by former members in the early 1960s as well as traditional and current compositions.

DISCOGRAPHY:
New Years at Porcupine [Turtle Island Music 1997]
Songs from Porcupine: Honoring Irving Tail [Turtle Island Music 1997]
Traditional Lakota Songs: Canyon Vintage Series, Vol. 16 [Canyon 1997]
Keep the Traditions [Canyon 1995] w/Brotherhood Singers
Remembering the Singer [Canyon 1995] w/Brotherhood Singers
Rabbit Dance Songs, Part 2 [Canyon 1988]
Rabbit Dance Songs, Part 1 [Canyon 1987]
Live at the University of South Dakota [Canyon 1979]
Concert in Vermillion [Canyon 1979]
Traditional Songs of the Sioux [Canyon 1978]
At Ring Thunder [Canyon 1977]

Appearances:
Bear Spirit [Turtle Island Music 1999] comp
Songs of the Oglala Nation: Native American Powwow [Turtle Island Music 1998] comp
Spirit of the Wolf [Turtle Island Music 1998] comp
United Tribes International Powwow [Makoche 1995] two-CD comp

Red Bull—(Cree) Northern Style *See:* Little Pine Singers; Contemporary Music: Edmund Bull, C-Weed, Buffy Sainte-Marie.

Lineup: Irvin Waskewitch; Arnold Pete; Edmund, Earl, and Ross Bull; Art, Brian, Arnold, and Jeff Moosomin; Maurice Nicotine; Arnold Wuttunee; Joe Pahtaykan.

Formed in 1987, Little Pine Creek, Saskatchewan. Red Bull also opened for the 1994 Goodwill Games in Russia, Poland, Finland, and Sweden; performed on the track "Darlin' Don't Cry," cowritten by Edmund Bull and Buffy Sainte-Marie; and appeared on the television variety show *Rita McNeil and Friends* [CBC 1995]. They were named the World Hand Drum Champions, Schemitzun, in 1995, 1997, 1998, and 1999; *Dancing around the World* received a Juno nomination for Best Music of Aboriginal Canada Recording, 1996; *World Hand Drum Champs '98* received a Juno nomination for Best Music of Aboriginal Canada Recording, 2000.

DISCOGRAPHY:
Traditional [Turtle Island Music 2002]
Prairie Storm [Turtle Island Music 2001]
Millennium [Sweet Grass 2000]
Powwow 2000 [Sunshine 2000] comp
Best Of Red Bull [Sweet Grass 1999]
Red Bull, Vol. 2 [Sweet Grass 1999]
World Hand Drum Champs '98 [Sweet Grass 1998]
Having Fun Dancing [Sweet Grass 1998]
Gather the People: Live in Seattle [Canyon 1997]
"Have a Good Time" [Canyon CR-16265]
Mother Earth [Sweet Grass 1996]
Dancing around the World [Sweet Grass 1995]
Dance to Red Bull [SICC 1992]
Red Bull [SICC 1989]
Red Bull Singers [Sunshine SSCT 4092]

Appearances:
Mitataht askiy: Sweet Grass Records 10 Years [Sweet Grass 2003] comp
Drum Beats: 18 Powwow Groups [Sunshine 2002] comp
World's Best Memorial Songs [Sunshine 2002] comp
World's Best Women's Traditional Songs [Sunshine 2002] comp
World's Best Crow Hop Songs [Sunshine 2001] comp
Schemitzun 2000: Hand Drum Songs [Sweet Grass 2001] comp
Schemitzun World Championship 2000: Northern Style [Turtle Island Music 2001] comp
Schemitzun World Championship 2000: Round Dance Singing [Turtle Island Music 2001] comp
World's Best Round Dance Songs, Vol. 2 [Sunshine 2001] comp

Schemitzun World Championship Round Dance Singing [Turtle Island Music 2000] comp
Gathering of Nations Pow-Wow: Millennium Celebration, Vol. 1: *Various Northern Drums* [SOAR 2000] comp
Voices from Thunderchild Powwow Songs [Turtle Island Music 2000] comp
World's Best Powwow Drum Groups [Sunshine 2000] comp
World's Best Tiny Tot Songs [Sunshine 2000] comp
Best of the Best Schemitzun '93–99 [Sweet Grass 1999] comp
Thunderchild '98 [Turtle Island Music 1999] comp
The Best of Saskatchewan [Sunshine 1997] comp
World's Best Round Dance Songs [Sunshine 1997] comp
World's Leading Round Dance Songs [Sweet Grass 1996] comp
Songs of the Spirit: The Best of Sweet Grass [Sweet Grass/EMI 1995] comp
Still the Eagle Flies, Vols. 1 and 2 [SICC 1995]
United Tribes International Powwow [Makoche 1995] two CDs
The Sound of Champions [Sweet Grass 1994] comp
Bismarck Powwow [Sunshine 1993] comp
White Earth Powwow [Sunshine SSCT-4338] comp

Red Cloud Singers—(Lakota)
Northern Style

DISCOGRAPHY:
Sioux Songs, Vol. 2 [Indian Records IR-1198]
Sioux Songs, Vol. 1 [Indian Records IR-1199]

Red Creek Singers—Northern Style
DISCOGRAPHY:
Live at Fort Yates, North Dakota [Featherstone FT-1011]

Red Dog—(Cree) Northern Style

Lineup: Wavell and Wendell Starr; Sheldon, Shawn, and Ryan Poitras; Erroll, Gil Keewatin; Kelsey, Fred, and Dallas Starblanket; Gerald Moosemay; Charlie and Cassidy Goforth; Delvin Stanley; Jason Bellegarde; Tyler Favel. From Star Blanket Cree Nation, White Calf Reserve and Regina, Saskatchewan.

DISCOGRAPHY:
Plain and Simple [Sweet Grass 2001]

Appearances:
Mitataht askiy: Sweet Grass Records 10 Years [Sweet Grass 2003] comp

Red Earth Singers—(Mesquakie) Northern Style

Lineup: Homer Bear Jr., Edward Bear Heart Jr., Keith Davenport, Gerald McMaster, Adrian Pushetonequa, Wayne Pushetonequa, Richard Rice, Dean Whitebreast.

DISCOGRAPHY:
Red Earth of Tama, Iowa—"Live" [Indian House 1991]
Red Earth Singers [Indian House 1979]
Live at Bismarck [Indian House 1976]

Red Elk—(Taos Pueblo)

Formed in 1996 in New Mexico; formerly known as Elk's Trail.

DISCOGRAPHY:
On the Trail Again [SOAR 1998]

Appearances:
The Best of the Northern Boys [SOAR 1999]

Red Hawk Singers—Northern Style
See: Contemporary Music: Jim Beer

Lineup: Quentin Narcoosee Fuller III, Quentin Bear Fuller Jr., Bob Red Hawk, Jim Springfield, Marty Willits, Jeff Brings Plenty.

Red Hawk Singers, Vol. 2, was recorded live at the Third Annual Cherokee Indian Festival, Temple University, Ambler, Pennsylvania.

DISCOGRAPHY:
Red Hawk Singers [Sunshine 1998]
Red Hawk Singers, Vol. 2 [Sunshine 1996]
Red Hawk Singers, Vol. 1 [Sunshine 1995]

Appearances:
Drum Beats: 18 Powwow Groups [Sunshine 2002] comp
World's Best Memorial Songs [Sunshine 2002] comp
World's Best Fancy Dance Songs, Vol. 2 [Sunshine 2001] comp
World's Best Intertribal Songs [Sunshine 2001] comp
Powwow 2000 [Sunshine 2000] comp
World's Best Powwow Drum Groups [Sunshine 2000] comp
World's Best Tiny Tot Songs [Sunshine 2000] comp
World's Best Grass Dance [Sunshine 1998] comp
The Best of Ontario Powwow Groups [Sunshine 1997] comp
SECC Earth Band [Sunshine 1998] comp

Red House—(Intertribal) Northern Style

Lineup: Craig Stone (Metis-Cree), Ernest Big Medicine (Cheyenne–Oglala Lakota), Norman Williams (Dineh), Johnny Thorpe (Muscogee Creek), Ryan Ramos (Mississinewa Miami), Matt Moreno (Tarahumara), Les Peters (Yakima-Dineh), Anna Nazarian-Peters (Armenian), Delban Leslie (Hopi-Athabascan), Kenny Paul Hood Jr. (Shawnee), Adrian Tsosie (Hochunk-Dineh), Robert Schuyler (Dineh).

DISCOGRAPHY:
Between Two Worlds [Arbor 2003]
Round Dancin' Back to Cali [Arbor 2002]

Appearances:
Thunder Drums, Vol. 2: *The Best Pow-wow Songs from the World's Best Drums* [Arbor 2002] comp

Red Iron Singers—(Nakota) Northern Style

Lineup: Daniel, Patrick, Ira, Matt, Joel, and Crystal McArthur; Trey Delorme; Francher Kennedy; Charlie Big Eagle; Terrence Brown; Jackson Littlechief; Stephen Eashappie. From Pheasant Rump, Saskatchewan.

DISCOGRAPHY:
Dakota [Sunshine 2002]

Appearances:
Drum Beats: 18 Powwow Groups [Sunshine 2002] comp
World's Best Women's Traditional Songs [Sunshine 2002] comp

Red Leaf Singers—(Lakota) Northern Style

Lineup: Percy Roy; Willy, Alphonso, Pat and Howard Bad Hand; Burgess Yellow Cloud; Leo Chasing In Timber.

DISCOGRAPHY:
Songs of the Warrior [High Star 1985]

Red Leaf Takoja—(Lakota) Northern Style

Lineup: Howard, Terrie, Pat, Dale, and Al Bad Hand; Tom Teegarden; Richard Archuleta; Donna and Michelle Concha; Alice Martinez; Margaret Tyon. From the Red Leaf and Black Pipe communities of the Rosebud Reservation, South Dakota.

DISCOGRAPHY:
Echoes of the Universe [High Star 1988]
Live at Blue Lake [High Star 1985]

Red Nation Singers—(Lakota) Northern Style

DISCOGRAPHY:
Live at Fort Totten Days [Featherstone FT-1016]
Volume 1: Live at United Tribes 1987 [independent RNS-001] D
Dakota Tipi '84 Live [Featherstone 1985] comp

Red Scaffold—(Lakota) Northern Style

Lineup: Romanus Bear Stops, Steve Charging Eagle, Vernell Sitting Crow, Amos Cook, Loyd Bald Eagle, Roy Circle Bear, Ted Knife, Delvin Bowker, Burdell Blue Arm, Gloria Sitting Crow, Geraldine Bear Stops, Phyillis Bald Eagle.

Based on the Cheyenne River Reservation, South Dakota. Red Scaffold took the name for their group from their place of origin on the reservation. The group has recorded traditional powwow songs, including give-away and appreciation songs.

DISCOGRAPHY:
Red Scaffold [Sunshine SSCT-4212]

Appearances:
World's Best Fancy Dance Songs, Vol. 2 [Sunshine 2001] comp
H. V. Johnson Lakota Cultural Centre 1994 Spring Wacipi, Vol. 1 [Sunshine 1995] comp

Red Sons Singers—(Anishnabe) Northern Style

Lineup: Melvin Starr; Morley Redwood Jr.; Jeremy Hall; Sean, Chuck, George, and Willie Spence.

DISCOGRAPHY:
Red Sons Singers [Sunshine SSCT-4295]

Appearances:
World's Best Women's Traditional Songs [Sunshine 2002] comp

World's Best Fancy Dance Songs, Vol. 1
[Sunshine 2000] comp

Red Tail—Northern Style

Lineup: Luke Penney, George Meninick Jr., Shonto Pete, Raleigh Ellenwood, Dewey Miller, K. J. Redtail, Tony Smith, Juan Florez, Casey Wallahhee, Ted David, Joe Folts, Jay Dusty Bull, Sonny Qionto, D. J. and J. J. Meninick. From Lapwai, Idaho.

DISCOGRAPHY:
Red Tail, Vol. 2 [Arbor 2002]
Red Tail, Vol. 1 [Arbor 2000]

Appearances:
Round Dance Songs, Vol. 2 [Arbor/Native American Heritage Series 2003] comp
Women's Fancy Dance Songs [Arbor/ Native American Heritage Series 2003] comp
Hinckley Powwow Northern Style [Arbor 2001] comp
Thunder Drums, Vol. 1: *The Best of Arbor Records* [Arbor 2001] comp

Red Thunder Native Dance Theatre

Lineup: Farley Cardinal, Leo Wells, Chris Sleigh, Niso Bradford, Morley Redwood, Bonnie Lawrence, and John Green; Lee Crowchild, Denny Bellerose, Daniel Crane, flute; Peter D'Amico, guitar; Willy Joosen, keyboards. Formed in Calgary, Alberta, in 1987 by Lee and Aroha Crowchild.

DISCOGRAPHY:
Our Grandfathers' Journey [Black Bear Records 1997]

Appearances:
Bismarck Powwow [Sunshine 1993] comp

Red Wing Singers—(Intertribal) Northern Style

Lineup: Neil Hall; Chris Esquash; Brendan, Patrick, and Thomas Hall; Jeremy Thomas Jr.; Dan Thomas; Ernest Daniels; Anthony Moar; Colin Mousseau; Chris Robson.

DISCOGRAPHY:
Red Wing Singers [Sunshine SSCT-4334]

Rio Grande Singers—(Pueblo) Southern Style

Lineup: Tony, Faron, Floyd, Lloyd, and Myron Tortalita; Darrell Felipe; Mike and Emmet Garcia; Irvin Pino; J. E. Lujan Jr.; Isaac Lujan; C. Trujillo. From Taos Pueblo, New Mexico.

DISCOGRAPHY:
Turquoise Eyes [SOAR 1995]

Appearances:
Gathering of Nations Powwow 2001 [Gathering of Nations Records 2001] comp
Gathering of Nations Pow-Wow: Millennium Celebration, Vol. 2: *Various Southern Drums* [SOAR 2000] comp
Gathering of Nations Pow-Wow 1998 [SOAR 1999] comp

River Cree—(Cree) Northern Style

Lineup: Romeo Waskahat; Terence Plante; Gordon Ward; James Sharphead; Burton Plante; Darren and Francis Arcand; Jessie, Wayne, Bradley, and Lyle Morin.

DISCOGRAPHY:
Livin' in the Rez [Arbor 2002]

Appearances:
Women's Fancy Dance Songs [Arbor/ Native American Heritage Series 2003] comp
Thunder Drums, Vol. 2: *The Best Pow-*

wow Songs from the World's Best Drums [Arbor 2002] comp
Gathering of Nations Pow-Wow 1995 [SOAR 1996] comp

Rock Creek Singers—(Hunkpapa) Northern Style

Lineup: Fenton Takes the Hat, Oley Little Eagle, George Archambault, Lew Foote, Norman Shoe String, Dale Brave Crow, Tom Steele.

DISCOGRAPHY:
Powwow Songs [Canyon CR-8032]
Live! Fort Yates, North Dakota [Featherstone FT-1011]

Appearances:
Oyate [Nato/World 1990, France] *See*: Contemporary Compilations

Rockin' Horse Singers—(Intertribal) Southern Style

Lineup: Ricky and Shannon LeRoy, with group members from Otoe, Ponca, Omaha, Cherokee, and Tonkawa Nations.

DISCOGRAPHY:
Groundbreaker [Red Vinyl 1999]

Rocky Boy Chippewa-Cree Singers—(OJ-Cree) Northern Style

Lineup: Charles Gopher, John Meyers, Duncan Standing Rock, Lloyd Top Sky, Henry Wolfchild. Recorded at Rocky Boy, Montana, May 29, 1980.

DISCOGRAPHY:
Rocky Boy Chippewa-Cree Grass Dance Songs [Indian House IH-4401]

Rocky Boys—(Anishnabe-Cree) Northern Style *See*: Haystack Ramblers

Lineup: Rocky Stump, Alvin and John Windy Boy, Charles Gopher, John Meyers, Robert Flavel. From Rocky Boy Reservation, Montana.

DISCOGRAPHY:
Montana Homeland [SOAR 166]
Powwow Songs from Rocky Boy, Vol. 2 [Canyon CR-6154]
Powwow Songs from Rocky Boy, Vol. 1 [Canyon CR-6104]

Rocky Boy Singers—(Cree) Northern Style

Lineup: Lloyd Top Sky, Vern Gardipee Sr., Merle Tendoy, Kenny Standing Rock Sr., Recorded at Crow Agency, Montana, August 19, 2000.

DISCOGRAPHY:
Rocky Boy Chippewa-Cree Doorway Songs [Indian House 2001]

Appearances:
Champion Hand Drum Songs [Arbor 2003] comp
The Best of the Northern Boys [SOAR 1999] comp

Rocky Boy Singers—(Cree) Northern Style

Lineup: Charles, Kenneth, and Jonathan Gopher; Robert Taylor; Lloyd Topsky and Merle Tendoy Sr. Recorded at Rocky Boy, Montana, September 3, 1992.

DISCOGRAPHY:
Grass and Jingle Dress Songs, Vol. 2 [Indian House IH-4403 1993]
Grass and Jingle Dress Songs, Vol. 1 [Indian House IH-4402 1993]

Rocky Boy Singers—(Cree) Northern Style

Lineup: Wydel and James Stump; Louie Denn; Kenneth, Joe, and Russell Standing Rock. Recorded at Rocky Boy, Montana, January 29, 1972.

DISCOGRAPHY:
17 Chippewa-Cree (Rocky Boy) Songs [Indian Records 1972]

Rocky Boy Singers—(Cree) Northern Style *See*: Traditional/Archival Group

Lineup: Paul Eagleman, Charles Gopher, Bill Baker, John Gilbert Meyers, and Windy Boy. Recorded at Crow Agency, Montana, August 22, 1966

DISCOGRAPHY:
Chippewa-Cree Circle Dance [Indian House 1967; reissued American Indian Sounds Chiefs 2001]

Rocky Park—(Dineh)

Lineup: Alan Tsaipi; Sil Nelson; Mike Walker; Keno and Bryan Kelly; Ron Franklin; Erin Dickson; Carlos and Del Paddock; Ernie Tsosie; Jay Long; Bo Morgan; Tim Kellt; Arron Smith; Lorenzo McCabe; Marvin Foster; Darrell Jensen. From Leupp, Arizona, Navajo Reservation.

DISCOGRAPHY:
Rocky Park [Cool Runnings 1998]

Rose Hill—(Sac-Fox-Otoe-Kiowa) Southern Style

Lineup: Lloyd Gwin; Richard Williamson; Phil Dupoint; Harold Lynn Neconie; Roland Dean Barker; Amos Little Crow; Alan Tsoodle; Glen Ahhaitty; Gary Whitecloud Jr.; Moses and Michael Whitecloud. Formed in 1990.

DISCOGRAPHY:
Movin' On [Turtle Island Music 1997]
Live at Hinckley [Sweet Grass 1997]

Appearances:
Hinckley Powwow Southern Style [Arbor 2001] comp
Gathering of Nations Pow-Wow: Millennium Celebration, Vol. 2: *Various Southern Drums* [SOAR 2000] comp
Bear Spirit [Turtle Island Music 1999] comp
Hinckley Powwow Southern Style [Arbor 1999] comp
Spirit of the Wolf [Turtle Island Music 1998] comp
Gathering of Nations Pow-Wow 1995 [SOAR 1996] comp
Red Lake Nation [Turtle Island Music 1996] comp
Hinckley Grand Celebrations Powwow 1995 Southern Style [Sweet Grass 1995] comp
Gathering of Nations Pow-Wow 1993 [SOAR 1994] comp

Running Child—(Intertribal) Northern Style

Lineup: Bob Ironmaker Sr., Bob Ironmaker Jr., Ronny Doney Jr., Ron Doney, Mike Talksdifferent, Greg Rider, Todd Redbear, Dean Stiffarm. The members are Gros Ventre, Assiniboine, and OJ-Cree from Fort Belknap, Montana.

DISCOGRAPHY:
Strut Your Stuff [SOAR 1995]

Saddle Lake—(Cree) *See*: Cache Lake

Sage Point Singers—(Shoshone-Bannock) Northern Style

Lineup: Little Beaver, Gary, and Raphael Watson; Beuford Nipwater; Eric Whatomy;

Grayland Osborne; Lennis Jim; Dennis Moore; Alex Graves; Conrad and Ezra Benally (Dineh). Based in Fort Hall, Idaho. The original group was started by the patriarch, Gary Watson, in the 1960s.

DISCOGRAPHY:
Rockin' the Trail [independent 2003]
Indigenous: Live at EC Davis [independent 2002]
Live at Pyramid Lake [independent 2000]
Kickin' It [independent 1999]
Back to the Old School [independent 1998]
Powwow Cookin' [SOAR 119]

Appearances:
Gathering of Nations Pow-Wow: Millennium Celebration, Vol. 1: *Various Northern Drums* [SOAR 2000] comp

Saint Michael's Singers—(Lakota) Northern Style

Lineup: Ephraim Hill, Eugene Red Day, Ignatius and Philip Jackson.

DISCOGRAPHY:
Sioux Grass Songs and Round Dances [Canyon CR-6086]

Sarcee Broken Knife—(Tsuu T'ina) Northern Style *See*: Sarcee Bull Head Youth Club Singers

Lineup: Mike Meguinis; Charley Wood Jr.; Louise, Norma, and Michael Meguinis.

DISCOGRAPHY:
Powwow Songs, Vol. 2 [Canyon CR-9011]
Powwow Songs, Vol. 1 [Canyon CR-6135]

Sarcee Bull Head Youth Club Singers—(Tsuu T'ina) Northern Style

Lineup: Mike Meguinis; Charley Wood Jr.; Louise, Norma, and Michael Meguinis.

DISCOGRAPHY:
Songs of the Sarcee [Canyon 1975]

Sarcee Oldtimers—(Tsuu T'ina) Northern Style

Lineup: George Runner, Jim Dodging Horse, Frank One Spot, Willy Little Bear, Stanley Big Plume, Russell Big Crow.

DISCOGRAPHY:
Round Dance Songs [Canyon CR-9012]

Saskatchewan Northern Drum—(Cree) Northern Hand Drum

Lineup: Cedric and Frankie Moostoos, Clifford Ochuschayooo, Trevor Kahpeepatow, Lyle Chief, Paul Partridge, Gary Wahpistikwan. Formed in 1988, Joseph Bighead First Nation, Saskatchewan.

DISCOGRAPHY:
SaskNorthern Drum Round Dances [Sunshine SSCT-4117]

Appearances:
Toronto Powwow [Sunshine 1998] comp

Saulteaux First Nations Singers—(Saulteaux) Northern Style

Lineup: Archie, Dennis, David, Durwin, Leonard, Dolphus, Clayton, and Stanley Moccassin; Gary Awasis; Stewart Thomas; Fred Katcheech; Percy Stoney.

DISCOGRAPHY:
Round Dance Singers [Sweet Grass 1998]
Let's Go Round Dancin' [Sweet Grass 1995]

Scalp Lock, Green, Kennedy Singers—(Blackfoot) Northern Style

Lineup: Alex Scalp Lock, Francis Green, Pat Kennedy.

DISCOGRAPHY:

Songs from the Battleford Powwow [Canyon 1975]

Scalp Lock Singers—(Blackfoot) Northern Style

Lineup: Alex, Arthur, Irving, Aaron, Sheldon, and Junior Scalp Lock; Clarence Wolf Leg; Philip Little Chief. From the Siksika Reserve, Alberta.

DISCOGRAPHY:

Scalp Lock Singers [Canyon CR-9013]
The Canadian Blackfoot Indians [Lyrichord 1982] *See*: Traditional/Archival Compilations

Seekaskootch—(Cree) Northern Style

Lineup: Elroy Naistus, Lyle Chief, Peter and Tommy Lightning, Conroy Naistus. From Onion Lake and Samson Cree First Nation, Saskatchewan.

DISCOGRAPHY:

Guardian of the People [Sweet Grass 1997]
Live at Saulteaux 1995 [Sweet Grass 1995]
Live at Saskatoon Powwow [Sweet Grass 1994]
Seekaskootch [Sunshine SSCT 4182]

Appearances:

Mitataht askiy: Sweet Grass Records 10 Years [Sweet Grass 2003] comp
World's Best Women's Traditional Songs [Sunshine 2002] comp
World's Best Fancy Dance Songs, Vol. 2 [Sunshine 2001] comp
World's Best Round Dance Songs, Vol. 2 [Sunshine 2001] comp
Ermineskin Cree Nation Pow-wow: Live at Bear Park [Sweet Grass 1999] comp
Gathering of Nations Pow-Wow 1998 [SOAR 1999] comp
World's Best Grass Dance [Sunshine 1998] comp

The Best of Saskatchewan [Sunshine 1997] comp
World's Best Round Dance Songs [Sunshine 1997] comp
Songs of the Spirit The Best of Sweet Grass [Sweet Grass/EMI 1995] comp

Shadow Prey—(Dineh) Northern Style

Lineup: Larry Dashne Jr.; Tom, Harris, Nelson, Emerson, Luther, and Jason Yazzie; Chris Nelson; Daniel, Quincy, and Jefferson Begay; Billie Badonie Jr.; Ricky Clinton; Harold Archie. From Jeddito, Arizona.

DISCOGRAPHY:

Shadow Prey [Sweet Grass 1996]
Cool Runnings Powwow, Window Rock, Arizona [Sweet Grass 1995]

Siksika Ramblers—(Siksika) Northern Style

Lineup: Ken Healy, Norvin Eaglespeaker, Grant Many Heads, Herman Yellow Old Woman, Kent Ayoungman, Shane Breaker, Skip Wolfleg, Henry Red Crow, Paul McEvers.

DISCOGRAPHY:

Straight from the Rez [Canyon 2000]
Just for Old Time's Sake: Traditional Siksika Powwow Songs [Canyon 1998]

Silver Cloud Singers—(Intertribal) Northern Style *See*: Contemporary Music: Robbie Robertson

Lineup: Kevin Tarrant (Hopi–Ho-Chunk); Louis Mofsie (Hopi–Ho-Chunk); Dan Addi (Eastern Cherokee); Randy Whitehead (Flathead-Blackfeet); Lance Richmond (Mohawk); Ben Haile (Shinnecock); Alan Walsh (Cree).

Formed in 1991 and based in New York

City, Silver Cloud has played throughout the eastern United States and appeared in several contemporary music projects, including Robbie Robertson's *Music for the Native Americans*. Their first recording was dedicated to the memory of original founding member Michael Tarrant. Louis Mofsie cofounded the Thunderbird American Indian Dancers in 1963 and has worked with the American Indian Dance Theatre in New York City (*See*: Contemporary Music: Pura Fe).

DISCOGRAPHY:
Songs from the Clouds [AICH Productions 1997]
Silver Cloud [Sunshine 1996]

Appearances (listed alphabetically):
Jill McManus:
Symbols of Hopi [Concord Jazz 1984]
Robbie Robertson:
Music for Native Americans [Capitol 1994]
Various:
World's Best Women's Traditional Songs [Sunshine 2002] comp
Schemitzun World Championship 2000: Southern Style [Turtle Island Music 2001] comp
Powwow 2000 [Sunshine 2000] comp
Songs for Chiapas "Off the Record" [Ra Records 1999] comp *See*: Contemporary Compilations
World's Best Round Dance Songs [Sunshine 1997] comp

Sinte Ska—(Dakota) Northern Style

Lineup: Robert Sr., Steve, and Archie Fool Bear; Paul Roddegg III; William Manywounds; Casey Wise Spirit; George Red Eagle; Jim Picotte; Webb Three Legs; Monte Lebeau.

DISCOGRAPHY:
Sounds of the Pow-Wow [Sunshine SSCT-4185]

Appearances:
Bismarck Powwow [Sunshine 1993] comp

Sioux Assiniboine—
(Sioux-Assiniboine) Northern Style

Lineup: Frank and Terrence Brown; Jim Todome; Lenny Lonechild; Clyde Lonethunder; Herb May; Joe Mursette; Phibbs Baker; Sam Hapa; T. J., Armand, Amos, and Les McArthur; Audrey and Lori Pratt. From Pipestone, Manitoba.

DISCOGRAPHY:
Sioux Assiniboine Live Recording [Sunshine SSCT-4187]
Sioux Assiniboine, Vol. 3 [Sunshine SSCT-4152]
Sioux Assiniboine, Vol. 2 [Sunshine SSCT-4136]
Kahomini Songs [Sunshine SSCT-4115]

Appearances:
World's Best Intertribal Songs [Sunshine 2001] comp
World's Best Fancy Dance Songs, Vol. 1 [Sunshine 2000] comp
World's Best Jingle Dress Songs [Sunshine 1998] comp
Best of Manitoba [Sunshine 1997] comp
World's Best Round Dance Songs [Sunshine 1997] comp
United Tribes International Powwow [Makoche 1995] two-CD comp
Gathering of Nations Pow-Wow 1992 [SOAR 1993] comp
Shake the Feathers: Live at Peguis Powwow '93 [Sunshine SSCT-4204] comp
Minnesota Powwow Songs [Sunshine SSCT-4174] comp
Gathering of Nations Pow-Wow, Vol. 1 [SOAR 1992] comp

Sioux Travelers—(Sioux) Northern Style *See*: Traditional/Archival Group

DISCOGRAPHY:
12 Sioux Songs [Indian Records IR-1193]

Sioux Valley Juniors—(Sioux) Northern Style

DISCOGRAPHY:
Pezhin Wachipi: Grass Dance Songs [Canyon CR-6097]

Sioux Valley Singers—(Sioux) Northern Style *See*: Traditional/Archival Group

DISCOGRAPHY:

Appearances:
American Warriors: Songs for Indian Veterans [Ryko 1997] *See*: Traditional/Archival Compilations
H. V. Johnson Lakota Cultural Centre 1994 Spring Wacipi, Vol. 1 [Sunshine 1995] comp

Sizzortail—(Pawnee) Southern Style

Lineup: Arlen Goodfox, Steve Honeyestewa, Mark Wilson, Adrian Horsechief, Marty Thurman, Les Painter, Steve Byington.
    Formed in 1995. Sizzortail was named Southern Style World Champions, Gathering of Nations Powwow, 1998 and 1999.

DISCOGRAPHY:
Enuff Said [Arbor 1999]

Appearances:
Round Dance Songs, Vol. 2 [Arbor/Native American Heritage Series 2003] comp
Thunder Drums, Vol. 2: *The Best Powwow Songs from the World's Best Drums* [Arbor 2002] comp
Thunder Drums, Vol. 1: *The Best of Arbor Records* [Arbor 2001] comp
Gathering of Nations Pow-Wow: Millennium Celebration, Vol. 2: *Various Southern Drums* [SOAR 2000] comp
Hinckley Powwow Southern Style [Arbor 1999] comp

Smallboy Singers—(Cree) Northern Style *See*: Mountain Soul

Lineup: Charles Alexis; Charlie Favel; Stuart Morin; Calvin and Elmer Rattlesnake; Avery, Clayton, Craig, Fred, Ian, Reinhart, and Tyrone Roan. From Smallboy's Camp, Alberta.

DISCOGRAPHY:
Smallboy Singers [Indian House 1997]

Smokey Town—(Menominee) Northern Style *See*: Contemporary Music: Bill Miller

Lineup: Myron Pyawasit; Joey Awanohpay; Steven and Dana Waupoose; Gary Besaw; Cheyenne Pyawasit; Bedahbin Webkamigad. Formed in 1973, Menominee, Wisconsin.

DISCOGRAPHY:
The Next Generation [Noc Bay 1998]
Remembering [Noc Bay 1997]
Songs for the People [Sunshine 1997]
Smokey Town Singers [Sunshine 1997]
Live at LCO [independent RCR-9730]
Land of the Menominee [Sunshine SSCT-4221]

Appearances:
Bill Miller:
Red Road [Warner Western 1993]
Various:
Thunder on the Lake [Arbor 2003] comp
Hinckley Powwow Northern Style [Arbor 2001] comp
World's Best Intertribal Songs [Sunshine 2001] comp
World's Best Round Dance Songs, Vol. 2 [Sunshine 2001] comp
Powwow 2000 [Sunshine 2000] comp
World's Best Powwow Drum Groups [Sunshine 2000] comp
World's Best Tiny Tot Songs [Sunshine 2000] comp
World's Best Grass Dance [Sunshine 1998] comp

American Warriors:Songs for Indian Veterans [Ryko 1997] comp *See*: Traditional/Archival Compilations

World's Best Round Dance Songs [Sunshine 1997] comp

Honor the Earth Powwow Songs of the Great Lakes [Ryko 1990] comp

Smokey Valley—(Intertribal) West Coast Northern Style

Lineup: Francis James, Bobby Mercier, Keith Terbasket, Oscar James, Lidia Gabriel, Roxanne Terry, Rose Marie Sam, Gina West, Charlene Napoleon. Formed in 1994; group members are from the Sto:lo and Chehalis Nations of southwestern British Columbia.

DISCOGRAPHY:
West Coast Footslide [Arbor 2003]
Smokey Valley Singers [Sunshine 1997]

Appearances:
World's Best Memorial Songs [Sunshine 2002] comp
World's Best Fancy Dance Songs, Vol. 2 [Sunshine 2001] comp
World's Best Intertribal Songs [Sunshine 2001] comp
World's Best Fancy Dance Songs, Vol. 1 [Sunshine 2000] comp
World's Best Tiny Tot Songs [Sunshine 2000] comp

Snake Island Singers—(Intertribal) Northern Style

DISCOGRAPHY:
Out of the Blue [Red Rock 2000]

Songs of Bear Hills—(Cree) Northern Style

Lineup: Jack Bull, Arnold Pete, Francis Green, Melvin Stone, Ken Saddleback, Fredrick Raine, Melvin Abraham, Pete

Lightning, Garrison Deschamps, Florence Napoose, Margaret Green, Alexandra Moonias, Dee Dee Deschamps.

DISCOGRAPHY:
Round Dance Songs [Sweet Grass 1994]

Appearances:
World's Leading Round Dance Songs [Sweet Grass 1996] comp

Sons of the Oglalas—(Lakota) Northern Style

DISCOGRAPHY:
Sioux Songs [Indian Records IR-1195]

Southern Boys—(Intertribal) Southern Style

Lineup: Victor, Barbara, and Bobbie Tahchawwickah; Cheevers, Hyde, and Janaye Toppah; Timothy, Anthony, Ronald, Larry, and Althea Monoessy; Kelly Cable; Marvin Chasenah; Matt Little Creek; Darrell Cable Sr.

DISCOGRAPHY:
Live at St. Croix [Arbor 2003] enhanced
Todome [Arbor 2002]
Brothers for Life [Arbor 2002]
Deep Down South [Arbor 2001]
The Next Generation [Arbor 1999]

Appearances:
Round Dance Songs, Vol. 2 [Arbor/Native American Heritage Series 2003] comp
Champion Hand Drum Songs [Arbor 2003] comp
The Best of Hinckley Powwow Northern and Southern Style [Arbor 2003] comp
Thunder Drums, Vol. 2: *The Best Powwow Songs from the World's Best Drums* [Arbor 2002] comp
Relentless Warrior [Gathering of Nations Records 2001] comp
Schemitzun World Championship 2000: Southern Style [Turtle Island Music 2001] comp

Thunder Drums, Vol. 1: *The Best of Arbor Records* [Arbor 2001] comp
Hinckley Powwow Southern Style [Arbor 1999] comp

Southern Cree—(Cree) Northern Style

Lineup: Harlan and Keith Gopher; Ken Gopher Sr.; Clem Baker; Rod Sutherland Jr.; Glen Lewis; Jason Stone; Julio DeCora; Curtis Laliberte; Clinton Small (Cree); Tony Begay (Dineh-Hopi); Herb Augustine Jr. (Dineh-Arapaho); Ben Wise Spirit (Lakota); Clifton Goodwill (Lakota); Quanah LaRose (Ute); Ryan Burson (Ute).

Based in Montana; Southern Cree received a NAMA nomination for Best Powwow Recording, 2003.

DISCOGRAPHY:
Drum for Life: Cree Pow-Wow Songs [Canyon 2002]
Thunder and Lightning [Canyon 2001]
Keepin' It Real, Vol. 3 [Canyon 1999]
Southern Cree, Vol. 2: *Recorded Live at University of Arizona* [Canyon 1996]
Southern Cree, Vol. 1: *Get Up and Dance* [Canyon 1995]
Southern Cree Singers [SICC 1994]
Southern Cree at Beardy's [Sweet Grass 1994]
Southern Cree [SICC 1993]

Appearances:
Mitataht askiy: Sweet Grass Records 10 Years [Sweet Grass 2003] comp
The Best of Hinckley Powwow Northern and Southern Style [Arbor 2003] comp
Gathering of Nations Pow-Wow 1998 [SOAR 1999] comp
Gathering of Nations Pow-Wow 1996 [SOAR 1997] comp
Still the Eagle Flies, Vols. 1 and 2 [SICC 1995] comp

Southern Sun Singers—(Intertribal)

Lineup: Joe Liles, Derek Lowry, Mark Wagoner, Clyde Ellis, Linwood Watson, Jody and Jason Cummings, Chris Connor, Brian Simmons, Billy Hunt, Houston Locklear.

DISCOGRAPHY:
At Last [independent 2001]

Southern Thunder—(Pawnee) Southern Style

Lineup: Frank and Herb Adson, Kenny Bighorse Jr., Scott and Van Bighorse, Scott George, Oliver Little Cook, George Valliere, Chris White, Larry and Charlene Cozad, Mary George, Tesa Goodeagle, Andrea Kemble, Linda LaZelle, Georgia Tiger.

DISCOGRAPHY:
From the Heart, Vol. 2 [Indian House 1995]
From the Heart, Vol. 1 [Indian House 1995]
Reachin' Out [Indian House 1993]
Intertribal Songs of Oklahoma [Indian House 1992]

Appearances:
Proud Heritage [Indian House 1996] comp
See: Traditional/Archival Compilations

Southern Ute Singers *See*: Yellowjacket

Spirit Mountain Singers—(Anishnabe) Northern Style

Lineup: Kyle Councilor (*See*: Flute Music), Orville Councilor, Harold Lightfeather, Jeremy Davis, Mike Sullivan, Terry Goodsky, Joe Dick, Jason and Jaimie Petite.

DISCOGRAPHY:
Much Respect [Arbor 2000]
Spirit Mountain Singers [Sunshine SSCT-4294]

Appearances:
Thunder Drums, Vol. 1: *The Best of Arbor Records* [Arbor 2001] comp

Spirit Sand Singers—(Intertribal) Northern Style

Lineup: Michael, Kevin, Gerald, and Dempsey Esquash; Errol Cameron; Denny Hobson; Stewart Gordon; Ira Lavallee; Kevin Hart; Richard Blackbird; John and Ronald Martin; Melissa Nepinak; Jerilyn and Linda Esquash.

Formed in 1997 with singers ages seven to twenty-six years old. The members are from Swan Lake, Manitoba, and from Waterhen Lake and Piapot, Saskatchewan. Their music is used in the CBS television movie, *A Marriage of Convenience* [James Keach, 1998], with Jane Seymour.

DISCOGRAPHY:
Sacred Grounds [Arbor 1999]

Appearances:
Round Dance Songs, Vol. 2 [Arbor/Native American Heritage Series 2003] comp
Women's Fancy Dance Songs [Arbor/ Native American Heritage Series 2003] comp
Thunder Drums, Vol. 1: *The Best of Arbor Records* [Arbor 2001] comp
Champion Round Dance Songs, Vol. 1 [Arbor 1999] comp

Spirit Whistle—(Cree) Northern Style

Lineup: Irvine Sr., Irvine Jr., Debia, and Brian Waskewitch; Wendy Singer; Lee and Troy Tootoosis; Warren and Joe Wolf; Richard Moxin; Melvin Stone; Richard Moccasin; Freeman Trottier.

DISCOGRAPHY:
Round Dance [Sweet Grass 2001]

Appearances:
Mitataht askiy: Sweet Grass Records 10 Years [Sweet Grass 2003] comp

Spirit Wind Singers—(Intertribal) Northern Style

Lineup: Jim Mishquart; Patrick and Thomas Meshake; Johnny Pierre; Eddie Narcisse; Doug and Jeffrey Gagnon; Andy Atlookan; Derrick Megan; Tony Towedo; Ray Nobis; Dave Simard; George Ishabid; Lionel Atlookan; Steve Wesley.

DISCOGRAPHY:
Spirit Wind Singers [Sunshine 1995]

Appearances:
The Best of Ontario Powwow Groups [Sunshine 1997] comp
Hinckley Grand Celebrations Powwow 1995 Northern Style [Sunshine SSCT-4283] comp

Spotted Eagle Singers—(Blackfeet) Northern Style

Lineup: Troy Bull Bear; Irvin, Clarence, Kenny and Ed Spotted Eagle; Joe and Sam Scabby Robe; Marvin Weatherwax; Victor Sure Chief.

DISCOGRAPHY:
Intertribal Powwow Songs [Canyon 1986]

Appearances:
Eschikagou Powwow 2000 LIVE! [Gathering of Nations Records 2001] comp
Thunderchild '98 [Turtle Island Music 1999] comp

Spotted Lake Intertribal Singers—(Intertribal) Northern Style

Lineup: Ajia Kills Enemy (Lakota), Larry and Rick Kenoras (Okanagan), Voyne and Arnie Pierre (Okanagan), Robert Thomas (Coast Salish), Florence Thomas (Interior Salish), Duane Goulet (Cree).

DISCOGRAPHY:
Fraser Valley [Canyon CR-9006]

Spring Creek—(Cherokee) Northern Style

DISCOGRAPHY:
Spring Creek [Sunshine 1998]

Appearances:
SECC Earth Band [Sunshine 1998] comp

Standing Arrow Singers—(Iroquois) Northern Style/Traditional Iroquois

Lineup: Gesso, John, and Paul Thomas; Louie Thompson; Mitch Chubb (Mohawk); Alfred, Joey, and John White Crow (Seneca-Cayuga).

DISCOGRAPHY:
Powwow and Social Dance Songs, Vol. 3 [Akwesasne 1987]
Standing Arrow Singers, Vol. 2 [World Music Institute 1985]
Iroquois Social Songs [Akwesasne 1984]

Appearances:
Haitian and Native American Music [World Music Institute 1988] comp

Star Blanket Jrs.—Northern Style Youth Drum

Lineup: Gerald Moosemay; Victor and Aaron Starr; Maurice Desnomie; Sheldon, Ryan, and Albert Shawn Poitras; Derek, Dallas, and Kelsey Starblanket (Cree); Buffalo Campbell (Sioux-Anishnabe); Wavell Starr (Cree-Dakota).

DISCOGRAPHY:
Renegade and Rhythm [Wacipi 2000]
Kickin' It Live! [Turtle Island Music 1997]
Get Up and Dance [Canyon 1996]
"Make Your Feathers Shake" [Canyon CR-6268]
Live at Treaty Four [SICC 1994]
Star Blanket Jrs. [SICC SBJ91794]

Appearances:
Schemitzun World Championship 2000:
Northern Style [Turtle Island Music 2001] comp
Bear Spirit [Turtle Island Music 1999] comp
Gathering of Nations Pow-Wow 1998 [SOAR 1999] comp
Cree Nation [Turtle Island Music 1998] comp
Spirit of the Wolf [Turtle Island Music 1998] comp
Still the Eagle Flies, Vols. 1 and 2 [SICC 1995] comp
United Tribes International Powwow [Makoche 1995] two CDs
SIFC Annual Powwow [Sunshine SSCT-4168] comp

Videos:
Star Blanket Jrs. Recorded Live at the Treaty Four Gathering [SICC 1994]

Star Society—(Blackfoot) Northern Style

Lineup: Stan Whiteman, Stuart Bear Shield, Lois Gopher, Sheila Armstrong.

DISCOGRAPHY:
Blackfoot Forever [SOAR 1996]

Appearances:
The Best of the Northern Boys [SOAR 1999] comp
Gathering of Nations Pow-Wow 1993 [SOAR 1994] comp

Stoney Eagle—(Cree) Northern Style

Lineup: Kirby Jarvis; Craig, Derrick, Randy, Waylon, and Terrence Littletent; Joseph Kingfisher; Bradley Ititakoose; Bradley Nahnepowisk.

DISCOGRAPHY:
Round Dance Songs, Vol. 3 [Sunshine SSCT-4161]
Round Dances [Sunshine SSCT-4146]
Stoney Eagle [Sunshine SSCT-4143]

Appearances:

World's Best Round Dance Songs, Vol. 2 [Sunshine 2001] comp

World's Best Veteran Songs, Vol. 1 [Sunshine 2001] comp

World's Best Tiny Tot Songs [Sunshine 2000] comp

The Best of Saskatchewan [Sunshine 1997] comp

World's Best Round Dance Songs [Sunshine 1997] comp

Thunder Bear Powwow [Sunshine SSCT-4188] comp

SIFC Annual Powwow [Sunshine SSCT-4168] comp

Stoney Park's *Posse* (1996) represents a turning point in powwow recordings. Cover art by Ray McCallum; courtesy Sweet Grass Records.

Stoney Park—(Nakota) Northern Style *See*: Contemporary Music: Buffy Sainte-Marie

Lineup: Coleman Beaver; Coleman Beaver Jr.; Lenny, Greeves, and Harlan Beaver; John Blackbear; Kydd Littlesky; Jaycee Killspotted; Tahlee Redbird.

From Morley, Alberta. An acclaimed powwow group, Stoney Park crossed over into the mainstream with appearances on Buffy Sainte-Marie's album *Up Where We Belong*, on her televised induction into the Juno Hall of Fame in 1995, and on the track "Spider in My Room" from the Barenaked Ladies' album *Born on a Pirate Ship*. They won the World Champion, Schemitzun, 1993, and World Hand Drum Champions, Schemitzun, 1994; and they received a Juno nomination for Best Music of Aboriginal Canada Recording, 1994. Additional recording appearances include samples used in the score for *Blood River* [Kent Monkman, 2003].

DISCOGRAPHY:

Wolf Pack [Sweet Grass 2000]

Schemitzun World Championship of Song and Dance [Sweet Grass 1998]

Schemitzun Live [Sweet Grass 1997]

Posse [Sweet Grass 1996]

Looking for a Round Dance [Sweet Grass 1996]

Powwow Songs [Canyon 1995]

Don't Look Back [Sweet Grass 1995]

Schemitzun Live 1995 [Sweet Grass 1995]

Live at Hartford [Sweet Grass 1994]

Aude's Journey [Sweet Grass 1994]

World Champions Back to Back [Sweet Grass 1994]

Sweetgrass Presents . . . Stoney Park [Sweet Grass 1993]

Appearances (listed alphabetically):

Barenaked Ladies:

Born on a Pirate Ship [Sire/Reprise 1996]

Buffy Sainte-Marie:

Up Where We Belong [EMI 1996]

Various:

Blood River [Urban Nation 2003] sdtk

World's Best Tiny Tot Songs [Sunshine 2000] comp

Best of the Best Schemitzun '93–99 [Sweet Grass 1999] comp

Gathering of Nations Pow-Wow 1998 [SOAR 1999] comp

Best of Alberta [Sunshine 1997] comp

World's Best Round Dance Songs [Sunshine 1997] comp

Gathering of Nations Pow-Wow 1994
[SOAR 1995] comp
*Here and Now: A Celebration of Canadian
Music* [Sony 1995] comp *See*: Contemporary Compilations
Songs of the Spirit: The Best of Sweet Grass
[Sweet Grass/EMI 1995] comp
*A New Beginning, 1894–1994: St. Michael's
College* [Sweet Grass 1994] comp
Gathering of Nations Powwow 1993 [SOAR
1994] comp
Minnesota Powwow Songs [Sunshine 1994]
comp
The Sound of Champions [Sweet Grass
1994] comp

Sun Eagle Singers—(Dineh)
Northern Style

DISCOGRAPHY:
Sun Eagle Singers: Live [Cool Runnings
1998]
Sun Eagle Singers 1986 [High Star 1987]

Sweet Grass—(Cree) Northern Style

Lineup: Bruce, Gordon, Ross, Janet, and
Alvin Paskimin; Wesley Weenie; Gary Arcand; Garry Naytowhow; Jason Starchief;
Phillip and Trevor Cheekinew; Vincent
Fiddler; Raymond Albert; Darrell Moosomin. From Sweetgrass First Nation, Saskatchewan.

DISCOGRAPHY:
Round Dance Songs from Home [Turtle
Island Music 2004]
Indian Reservation [Noon Records 1998]
Family Tradition [Sweet Grass 1996]
Healing the Spirit [Sweet Grass 1995]
Sweet Grass Presents . . . Sweetgrass [Sweet
Grass 1994]

Appearances:
*Mitataht askiy: Sweet Grass Records 10
Years* [Sweet Grass 2003] comp
Voices from Thunderchild: Powwow Songs
[Turtle Island Music 2000] comp

*Ermineskin Cree Nation Pow-wow: Live at
Bear Park* [Sweet Grass 1999] comp
Indian Graffiti: Noon Records Greatest
[Noon Records 1998] comp
Songs of the Spirit: The Best of Sweet Grass
[Sweet Grass/EMI 1995] comp

Tail Wind—(Dakota) Northern Style

Lineup: Marcel, Christian, and Shawn
Bananish; Melvin and Rodney Greystick;
Fredrick and Terry Ottertail; Gary Whitefish; Angus and Ryan Oshawee; Harvey
Jorbon; Edward Atatise. From Lac La Croix
First Nations, Ontario.

DISCOGRAPHY:
Tail Wind [Sunshine SSCT-4151]

Appearances:
Best of Alberta [Sunshine 1997] comp

Ta-Otha Spirit—(Nakota) Northern
Style

Lineup: Jack, Robert, Shane, Keon, Floyd,
and Fergus Crawler; Oliver Hunter; Barry,
Dion, and Charles Wesley; Glen and Fred
Waskewitch; Harris Yazzie (Dineh).
    Formed in 1995 on the Kiska Waptan
Reserve, Alberta. Most of the members are
Nakota and Cree from Bighorn Nakota Reserve, Alberta; the group was named after
the legendary chief Ta-Otha.

DISCOGRAPHY:
Millennium 2000: New Beginnings [Turtle
Island Music 2000]
A Dream Takes Flight [Sweet Grass 1998]

Appearances:
*Ermineskin Cree Nation Pow-wow: Live at
Bear Park* [Sweet Grass 1999] comp

Teton Ramblers Jrs. —
(Cheyenne-Dakota) Northern Style

Lineup: Gordon High Bull, Cleveland High Bull Jr., Richard Lone Bear, Daniel Darrell, Mervin Smurf Small, William Buffalo Meat, Josh and Jazz Umtuch, Henry Big Fire, Rudy King III, Eugene Shoulder Blade, Judas Three Fingers. From Montana, the group carries on the generational teachings with their mentor Cleveland Holy Elk Boy.

DISCOGRAPHY:
Teton Ramblers Jrs. [Sweet Grass 1996]

Tha Tribe — (Intertribal) Northern Style *See*: Randy Wood

Lineup: Wayne Silas Jr. (Menominee-Oneida), Rocco Clark (Yakima), Wanbli Williams (Sioux-Anishnabe-Cheyenne), Shannon Ross (Cherokee), Jimmy Peters (Lakota), Ruben Littlehead (Northern Cheyenne), Jeremy Shield (Lakota-Crow), Donovan Likes Eagle (Mandan-Hidatsa), Gabe Cleveland (Ho-Chunk), Eddie Padilla (Sac-Fox), Kenny Coriz (Santo Domingo-Dineh), Adrian Harjo (Kickapoo-Seminole), Rusty Diamond (Pawnee-Otoe), Jancita Warrington (Menominee).

Formed in Lawrence, Kansas. Original songs are sung in Lakota, Ho-Chunk, Crow, and Menominee. The group received a NAMA nomination for Best Powwow Recording, 2003.

DISCOGRAPHY:
Best of Both Worlds: World One [Canyon 2004] w/ Randy Wood
Mad Hops and Crazy Stops: Pow-wow Songs Recorded Live in Chi-Town [Canyon 2003]
Winter Storm: Pow-wow Songs Recorded Live at M.S.U. [Canyon 2002]
N Action! Pow-wow Songs Recorded Live in San Carlos [Canyon 2001]
Live from Tornado Alley: Pow-wow Songs Recorded Live in Lawrence [Canyon 2000]
T2K [Canyon 2000]

Appearances:
Champion Hand Drum Songs [Arbor 2003] comp
Eschikagou Powwow 2000 LIVE! [Gathering of Nations Records 2001] comp
Gathering of Nations Pow-Wow: Millennium Celebration, Vol. 1: *Various Northern Drums* [SOAR 2000] comp
Gathering of Nations Pow-Wow 1998 [SOAR 1999] comp

Thunderchild, Vic — (Cree) Northern Style

Lineup: Vic, Ed, Harrison, and Raymond Thunderchild.

DISCOGRAPHY:
Vic Thunderchild and the Thunderchild Singers [Sunshine SSLP-4012]

Thunderhorse — Northern Style

Lineup: Robert and Kyle Lincoln, Cletis Mark, Andy Allen, Jeremy Bear, Paul Shipman, Pete Coter, Earnest Big Medicine, Dana Moyer, Kayaesbah Nave-Mark.

DISCOGRAPHY:
Native America [Arbor 2002]
Riding the Storm [Arbor 2001]

Appearances:
Round Dance Songs, Vol. 2 [Arbor/Native American Heritage Series 2003] comp
Thunder Drums, Vol. 2: *The Best Pow-wow Songs from the World's Best Drums* [Arbor 2002] comp
Gathering of Nations Powwow 2001 [Gathering of Nations Records 2001] comp
Gathering of Nations Pow-Wow: Millennium Celebration, Vol. 1: *Various Northern Drums* [SOAR 2000] comp

Thunder Mountain Singers—
(Anishnabe) Northern Style

Lineup: Clement, Owen, Ryan, and Grant Gustafson; Tony Towedo; Marcel Bananish; Chris Legarde; Norman Jordan; Peter Shebagabow; Warren Mainville; Derek Megan, Dave Menard, Dale Jack.

DISCOGRAPHY:
Thunder Mountain Singers, Vol. 2 [Sunshine 1994]
Thunder Mountain Singers [Sunshine 1993]
Recorded Live at White Swan, Washington [Canyon 1992]

Appearances:
World's Best Veteran Songs, Vol. 1 [Sunshine 2001] comp
Minnesota Powwow Songs [Sunshine SSCT-4174] comp

Tootoosis Family—(Cree) Northern Style

Lineup: John Tootoosis and his sons, Wilford, Austin, Gordon, Eric, Arsene, and Leonard.

DISCOGRAPHY:
The Drums of Poundmaker, Vol. 2 [Canyon 1977]
The Drums of Poundmaker [Canyon 1976; Vintage Series 1998]

Treaty of 1855—(Yakima-Wasco) Northern Style

Lineup: Leander, Delores, Anna, Coleen, Arlene, and Gary George. From Toppenish, Washington.

DISCOGRAPHY:
Intertribal Powwow Songs Recorded Live! [Canyon 1980]

Appearances:
Omak Powwow 1980 [Canyon CR-6175] comp

Treaty Six Ermin Skin Band—(Cree) Northern Style

Lineup: Alec Scalp Lock, Francis Green, Alfred Saddleback, Maurice Wolf, Eddie Bad Eagle, Ether Cut Arm, Frank Turning Robe, Marlene Mornin, Annette Stone Child, Carmen, Kelly, Elvin and Charlene Wolfe.

DISCOGRAPHY:
Powwow Songs [Canyon 1975]

Two Feathers—(Anishnabe) Northern Style

Lineup: Chuck and William Spence; Karis Robson; Brendan and Jeremy Hall; Chris Esquash; Ernest Daniels; Patrick, Richard, Freddy, Lindsy, and Darrin Roulette.

DISCOGRAPHY:
Two Feathers, Vol. 2 [Sunshine 1999]
Two Feathers, Vol. 1 [Sunshine 1997]

Appearances:
World's Best Memorial Songs [Sunshine 2002] comp
World's Best Fancy Dance Songs, Vol. 1 [Sunshine 2000] comp
Best of Manitoba [Sunshine 1997] comp

Two Medicine Lake Singers—
(Blackfoot) Northern Style

Lineup: Floyd Rider Sr., Cecile Rider, Al Potts, Raymond and Justine Croff.

DISCOGRAPHY:
Grass Dance Songs [Canyon 1984]
Powwow Songs [Canyon 1981]

Two Nation Singers—
(Cree-Assiniboine) Northern Style

Lineup: Frank and Clarence Moosomin, Percy Kiskotagen, Gerald and Vernon Baptiste, Pat Bugler.

DISCOGRAPHY:
Cree Round Dance Songs [Canyon 1981]

Umatilla Intertribal Singers—
(Intertribal)

Lineup: Richard Sam Sr., Randy "Tweety" Sam, Richard Sam Jr., Morris Sam, Ted Umtuch, Darren Black, Dana Sam.

The group was formed in 1966, and many of the originators have passed on: Dave Gone, Ed Morning Owl, Curtis Thompson, Francis McFarland, Lester Lewis, and Sam Jackson. The group members were from the Yakima, Nez Perce, Cree, Okanagan, Colville and Umatilla Nations, and represented three generations of singers.

DISCOGRAPHY:
For the People: Songs of the Northwest [WithOut Rez Productions 1996]

UMOn HAn Lodge Singers—
Northern Style

Lineup: Corwin, Evan, Bradley, Andre, and Lance Saunsoci; Dustin Griffin; Brian Morris Jr.; Brennan Lasley; Darrel Blackbird Jr. With the Tony Tuttle Canaries: Charlene Lasley, Adriana Saunsoci, Karina Drum, Rainelle Wright.

DISCOGRAPHY:
The Dream [Arbor 1999]

Wahpe Kute—(Dakota) Northern Style *See*: Traditional/Archival Music

The group was named World Hand Drum Champions, Schemitzun, 1993.

DISCOGRAPHY:
Best of the Best [Sweet Grass 1999] comp
Dakota Songs by Wahpe Kute [Featherstone FT-1002]

Appearances:
Wisconsin Intertribal [Sunshine SSCT-4216] comp

Walkin Bull—(Anishnabe) Northern Style

Lineup: Dino Smallwood, Daniel Buffalo, Jerritte and Garritte Caldwell, Nate King, Marvel Larose, Comanche Fairbanks, Hepi Crowfeather, Randy White, McAllen Garvin, Kevin Patterson, Siga Hindsley, Butter Luv. From northern Minnesota, Walkin Bull blends traditional and contemporary powwow styles.

DISCOGRAPHY:
Live at Oneida [independent 2002]
Walkin Bull [Arbor 1999]

Appearances:
Women's Fancy Dance Songs [Arbor/ Native American Heritage Series 2003] comp
Eschikagou Powwow 2000 LIVE! [Gathering of Nations Records 2001] comp
Hinckley Powwow Northern Style [Arbor 2001] comp
Schemitzun 2000: Hand Drum Songs [Sweet Grass 2001] comp
Thunder Drums, Vol. 1: *The Best of Arbor Records* [Arbor 2001] comp
Champion Round Dance Songs, Vol. 1 [Arbor 1999] comp

Walking Buffalo—(Cree) Northern Style

Lineup: Ralph Morin; Orville, Arnold, Lawrence, Rodney, and Rocky Morin; Sheldon Rainey; Clayton Keenatch; Marc Long John; Lyle Whitefish; Calvin Chocan; Jason Harris; Nathaniel Ottertail. Formed in 1994, Big River Cree, Saskatchewan.

DISCOGRAPHY:
Walking Buffalo [Sweet Grass 1998]
The Chase [Sweet Grass 1997]

Distant Voices [Sweet Grass 1996]
Walking Buffalo [Sweet Grass 1994]

Appearances:
Jingle Dress Side Step Songs [Arbor 2001]
comp
Gathering of Nations Pow-Wow: Millennium Celebration, Vol. 1: *Various Northern Drums* [SOAR 2000] comp
Ermineskin Cree Nation Pow-wow: Live at Bear Park [Sweet Grass 1999] comp
Thunderchild '98 [Turtle Island Music 1999] comp
Cree Nation [Turtle Island Music 1998] comp

Walking Wolf Singers—(Anishnabe) Northern Style

Lineup: Ray Stevenson, Murray Olson, Jody T. Gaskin (*See*: Flute Music; Contemporary Music), Trevor Sinclair, Danny Neapetung, Dean Smith, Lorne Redsky.

DISCOGRAPHY:
Walking Wolf Singers, Vol. 2 [Sunshine 2001]
Walking Wolf Singers, Vol. 1 [Sunshine 2000]

Appearances:
Drum Beats: 18 Powwow Groups [Sunshine 2002] comp
World's Best Memorial Songs [Sunshine 2002] comp
World's Best Women's Traditional Songs [Sunshine 2002] comp
World's Best Crow Hop Songs [Sunshine 2001] comp
World's Best Round Dance Songs, Vol. 2 [Sunshine 2001] comp
Powwow 2000 [Sunshine 2000] comp
World's Best Powwow Drum Groups [Sunshine 2000] comp
World's Best 49er Songs [Sunshine 2000] comp

Wandering Sound Singers—(Anishnabe) Northern Style

Lineup: Melvin Star, Morley Redwood Jr., Bruce Fontaine, Raymond Jack Jr., Ken Guiboche. Based in Manitoba, Canada.

DISCOGRAPHY:
Wandering Sound Singers [Sunshine SSCT-4201]

Appearances:
World's Best Women's Traditional Songs [Sunshine 2002] comp
World's Best Intertribal Songs [Sunshine 2001] comp
Best of Manitoba [Sunshine 1997] comp

Wandering Spirit—(Cree) Northern Style

From Frog Lake, Alberta, the group formed in the early 1980s.

DISCOGRAPHY:
First Tracks [Turtle Island Music 1999]

Wanesa—(Cree) Northern Style Women's Drum

Lineup: Amanda and Autumn Desjarlis; Pearl and Diana Henry. Formed, 1993, Dominion City, Manitoba. They used both big drum and hand drums to sing songs given to them by Sam Joseph from North Battleford, Saskatchewan.

DISCOGRAPHY:
Northern Lights Round Dance Songs [Sunshine 1998]

White Eagle—Northern Style

Original Lineup: Alroy, Albert, Arthur, Andrew, Arlie, and Aaron Neskahi; Allan Carl Neskahi III; and Allan Neskahi Jr. Formed in 1974, the group was host drum at Schemitzun Powwow, 1999.

DISCOGRAPHY:

White Eagle [Sunshine SSCT-4186]

Fifth Generation [Canyon 1993]

Intertribal Powwow Songs, Vol. 5 [Canyon 1988]

Love Songs, Vol. 4 [Canyon 1988]

Intertribal Powwow Songs, Vol. 3 [Canyon 1987]

Intertribal Powwow Songs, Vol. 2 [Canyon 1986]

Intertribal Powwow Songs, Vol. 1 [Canyon 1985]

Appearances:

World's Best Memorial Songs [Sunshine 2002] comp

World's Best Crow Hop Songs [Sunshine 2001] comp

World's Best Veteran Songs, Vol. 1 [Sunshine 2001] comp

Gathering of Nations Pow-Wow 1998 [SOAR 1999]

World's Best Grass Dance [Sunshine 1998] comp

Thunder Bear Powwow [Sunshine SSCT-4188] comp

Whitefish Bay—(Anishnabe) Northern Style *See*: Traditional/ Archival Group

Lineup: Andy, A. J., Tommy, Ryan, Ricky, Ramsay, Clarence, and Peter White; Tommy White Jr.; Charlie and Clarence Kelly; Hank and Darren Henry; Dale Jack. From Whitefish Bay First Nations, Ontario.

DISCOGRAPHY:

Anishnaabe Meenigoziwin, Vol. 10 [Sunshine 2002]

Powwow 2K [Arbor 2000]

Ndoo Te Mag [Arbor 1999]

Whitefish Bay Singers, Vol. 9 [Sunshine 1997]

Whitefish Bay Singers, Vol. 8 [Sunshine SSCT-4307]

Whitefish Bay Singers, Vol. 7 [Sunshine SSCT-4224]

Whitefish Bay Singers, Vol. 6 [Sunshine SSCT-4191]

Whitefish Bay Singers, Vol. 5 [Sunshine SSCT-4153]

Whitefish Bay Singers, Vol. 4 [Sunshine SSCT-4134]

Whitefish Bay Singers, Vol. 3 [Sunshine SSCT-4116]

Whitefish Bay Singers, Vol. 2 [Sunshine SSCT-4102]

Whitefish Bay Singers, Vol. 1 [Sunshine SSCT-4097]

Appearances:

Black Hills: 16th Annual Powwow [Arbor 2003] comp

Women's Fancy Dance Songs [Arbor/ Native American Heritage Series 2003] comp

Drum Beats: 18 Powwow Groups [Sunshine 2002] comp

Thunder Drums, Vol. 2: *The Best Powwow Songs from the World's Best Drums* [Arbor 2002] comp

World's Best Memorial Songs [Sunshine 2002] comp

Jingle Dress Side Step Songs [Arbor 2001] comp

World's Best Crow Hop Songs [Sunshine 2001] comp

World's Best Fancy Dance Songs, Vol. 2 [Sunshine 2001] comp

World's Best Intertribal Songs [Sunshine 2001] comp

World's Best Round Dance Songs, Vol. 2 [Sunshine 2001] comp

World's Best Veteran Songs, Vol. 1 [Sunshine 2001] comp

Powwow 2000 [Sunshine 2000] comp

World's Best Powwow Drum Groups [Sunshine 2000] comp

Champion Round Dance Songs, Vol. 1 [Arbor 1999] comp

World's Best Grass Dance [Sunshine 1998] comp

World's Best Jingle Dress Songs [Sunshine 1998] comp

The Best of Ontario Powwow Groups [Sunshine 1997] comp

World's Best Round Dance Songs [Sunshine 1997] comp

Hinckley Grand Celebrations Powwow 1995 Northern Style [Sunshine SSCT-4283] comp

Gathering of Champions: The Winners' Circle [SOAR 171 1995] comp

Gathering of Nations Pow-Wow 1994 [SOAR 1995] comp

Hinckley Powwow, Vol. 2 [Sunshine 1995] comp

The Way West [American Experience/ Shanachie 1995] sdtk *See*: Contemporary Soundtracks

Gathering of Nations Pow-Wow 1993 [SOAR 1994] comp

A Celebration of First Nations [Craggle Rock 1993] comp

Gathering of Nations Pow-Wow 1992 [SOAR 1993] comp

Shake the Feathers: Live at Peguis Powwow '93 [Sunshine SSCT-4204] comp

Gathering of Nations Pow-Wow, Vol. 1 [SOAR 1992] comp

C.I.S. 20th Annual Powwow [Sunshine SSCT-4172] comp

Ojibway Music from Minnesota: A Century of Song for Voice and Drum [MHS Press 1989/1997] comp

Whitefish Jrs. —(Cree) Northern Style

Lineup: Gordon Dreaver Jr.; Harvey, Brian, Percy, Archie, and Jerry Dreaver; Ronnie and Jeremy LaChance; Arnold Morin.

From Big River Cree Nation, Saskatchewan. Their various awards include World Hand Drum Champions, Schemitzun, 1997; Juno nomination, Aboriginal Recording of the Year, 2004.

DISCOGRAPHY:

In Honour of Percy Dreaver: Round Dance Songs [Sweet Grass 2003]

Live at Schemitzun [Sweet Grass 2003]

Cree Man [Sweet Grass 2000]

A Way of Life [Sweet Grass 1999]

Whitefish Jrs. [Sweet Grass 1997]

Life Giver [Sweet Grass 1996]

Forever Dancing [Sweet Grass 1995]

Live at Schemitzun [Sweet Grass 1994]

Hartford '94 [Sweet Grass 1994]

Traditions [Sweet Grass 1994]

In Honour of the Late Chief John Keenatch and Wife [Sweet Grass 1993]

Whitefish Jrs. [Sweet Grass 1993]

Aasomwaaypinace: A Tribute to Gabe White [Sunshine SSCT-4206]

Appearances:

Mitataht askiy: Sweet Grass Records 10 Years [Sweet Grass 2003] comp

Drum Beats: 18 Powwow Groups [Sunshine 2002] comp

Gathering of Nations Powwow 2001 [Gathering of Nations Records 2001] comp

World's Best Crow Hop Songs [Sunshine 2001] comp

Powwow 2000 [Sunshine 2000] comp

Voices from Thunderchild Powwow Songs [Turtle Island Music 2000] comp

Best of the Best Schemitzun '93–99 [Sweet Grass 1999] comp

World's Best Jingle Dress Songs [Sunshine 1998] comp

The Best of Ontario Powwow Groups [Sunshine 1997] comp

World's Leading Round Dance Songs [Sweet Grass 1996] comp, w/ Mervin Dreaver

Spirit of the People [Sweet Grass/EMI 1996] comp

Gathering of Champions: The Winners' Circle [SOAR 171 1995] comp

Gathering of Nations Pow-Wow 1994 [SOAR 1995] comp

Hinckley Powwow, Vol. 2 [Sunshine 1995] comp

Hinckley Powwow, Vol. 1 [Sunshine 1995] comp

Songs of the Spirit: The Best of Sweet Grass [Sweet Grass/EMI 1995] comp

Still the Eagle Flies, Vols. 1 and 2 [SICC 1995] comp

Gathering of Nations Pow-Wow 1993 [SOAR 1994] comp

Hinckley Grand Celebrations Powwow 1995 Northern Style [Sunshine SSCT 4283] comp
Gathering of Nations Pow-Wow 1992 [SOAR 1993] comp
Thunder Bear Powwow [Sunshine SSCT-4188] comp
Minnesota Powwow Songs [Sunshine SSCT-4174] comp

White Hawk—(Ponca) Southern Style

Lineup: Sterling Big Bear III; Sterling Big Bear Jr.; Lakota, Pat, Sarah, and Christine Big Bear; Gaylord, Evon, and Danny Boyer; Terry and RuthAnn Chives; Edwin Rodriguez; David Spenser; Jimmy and Dee Dee Wesaw; Carla Linder; Arthur and Mon'ee Zapata.

DISCOGRAPHY:
White Hawk [Arbor 2002]

White Lodge Singers—(Dakota) Northern Style

Millennium Lineup: Randy, Tony, and Jude Phelan; Jess Lussier; Junior Bear; Ambrose Phelan; Don Hunts Along; Jasper Young Bear; Leo Standish; Julian and Clair Fox; Dean Jourdain.

Original Lineup: Alonzo Young Bear Phelan; Ivan Young Bear; Vincent Hunts Along Sr.; George Wolf; Lee Old Mouse; Oliver and Leo Standish.

Formed in the 1950s, Mandaree, North Dakota.

DISCOGRAPHY:
White Lodge [Arbor 2001]
White Lodge Singers [Sweet Grass 1997]

Appearances:
Women's Fancy Dance Songs [Arbor/ Native American Heritage Series 2003] comp
Thunder Drums, Vol. 2: *The Best Powwow Songs from the World's Best Drums* [Arbor 2002] comp

Thunder Drums, Vol. 1: *The Best of Arbor Records* [Arbor 2001] comp

White Oak Singers *See*: Contemporary Soundtracks: *How the West Was Lost*

White Ridge—(Dineh) Northern Style

Lineup: Delbert Blackhorse; Paul, Darren, and Donovan Etsitty; Jonathan Yazzie; Nathan Largo; Ahley James; Louie Allen; Conrad Yanito; Sharlene Redhorse; Johnny and Conrad Begay. From Whiterock Point, Arizona.

DISCOGRAPHY:
The Spirit of Our Great Grandmother [Sweet Grass 1996]

Appearances:
Powwow 2000 [Sunshine 2000] comp

White Shield Singers—(Arikira) Northern Style

Lineup: Vincent Malnourie, David Little Swallow, Fred Morsette, John Fox, Terry Howling Wolf. Recorded in New Town, South Dakota, 1973.

DISCOGRAPHY:
Arikira Grass Songs [Canyon 1974]

White Swan Singers; a.k.a. Blacklodge—Northern Style

Lineup: Harry and Clayton Buck; William Whitegrass; Shawn Old Mouse; Alan, John, Shawn, Matthew, Erwin, Emerson, and Myron Scabby Robe.

DISCOGRAPHY:
Indian Summer [Turtle Island Music 1997]

Appearances:
Bear Spirit [Turtle Island Music 1999] comp

Spirit of the Wolf [Turtle Island Music 1998] comp

Whitetail—(Intertribal) Southern Style

Lineup: Kelly, Tim, A. J., Matthew Jr., Gregg, and Mike Grant; Dennis Thomas Jr.; Erwin Morris; John Morris Sr.; Mitchell Parker; Bridget Whipple; Jerome, Marq, and Blackbird Sheridan; Brad, Andre, and Louis Saunsoci. From Nebraska. Whitetail won the Southern Style Singing Competition, Hinckley Powwow, 2001.

DISCOGRAPHY:
For Our Elders [Arbor 2002]
Live at Hinckley [Arbor 2001]

Appearances:
Thunder Drums, Vol. 2: *The Best Powwow Songs from the World's Best Drums* [Arbor 2002] comp
Hinckley Powwow Southern Style [Arbor 2001] comp

White Tail Cree—(Cree) Northern Style

Lineup: David Okimaw (Cree); Marc Keekis (OJ-Cree); Doug Redbreast (OJ-Cree); Rodney Stanger (Algonquin); Brad Picody (OJ-Cree); Earl Danyluk (Cree); Gilbert Cheechoo (Cree); Adrian Sutherland (Cree); Craig Trudeau (Odawa); Chad McKenzie (Algonquin); Robin Deontie (Algonquin). An offshoot of the original White Tail Singers.

DISCOGRAPHY:
Live '00, Northern Style Powwow Songs [Red Rock Productions 2001]

Appearances:
Standing Our Ground [Turtle Island Music 1999] comp
Toronto Powwow [Sunshine 1998] comp

White Tail Singers—(OJ-Cree) Northern Style

Lineup: Lester Mianskum (Cree); Chris Couchie (Anishnabe); George Diamond-Oakes (OJ-Cree); Larry Hookimaw (Cree); Brian Wynne (Cree); Dean, Jonathan, and Kirby Mianskum (Cree); Chad McKenzie (Algonquin); Mark Meekis (OJ-Cree); David Ben Okimaw (Cree); Craig Trudeau (Odawa); Mike Wabano (Cree).

Formed in 1992, North Bay, Ontario. Some of the group's founding members, including Chris Couchie, began drumming at the North Bay Indian Friendship Centre in the late 1970s.

DISCOGRAPHY:
From the Heart [First Nations Music 1994]
Forever Dancing [First Nations Music 1993]

Appearances:
Here and Now: A Celebration of Canadian Music [Sony 1995] comp *See*: Contemporary Compilations
A Celebration of First Nations [Craggle Rock 1993] comp

White Whale Jrs.—(Nakota) Northern Style

Lineup: William and Wesley James; Darcy Paul; Vern Hunter; Michael, Cecil, Joel, Blair, and Jarrette Rain; Dale Desjarlais; Joe Bird. Formed in the 1970s in northern Alberta by the late Lazarous Rain.

DISCOGRAPHY:
White Whale Jrs. [Sweet Grass 1994]

Wildhorse Singers—(Cree) Northern Style

Lineup: Henry Gardipy Jr., Peter Lightning, Isaac Thomas, Devere Tsatoke, Colin Stonechild, Brad Crain, Pernelle Semaganis, Sean Waskahat, Jason Starchief, Donnie Spiedel, Jeff Moosomin, Quinton and Aaron Tootoosis.

DISCOGRAPHY:
Making Music [Turtle Island Music 2003]
Let It Ride [Sweet Grass 2000] w/ Aaron
   Tootoosis, flute
Wildhorse [Sweet Grass 1999]
Breaking Loose [Turtle Island Music 1998]
Wild Horse [Noon Records 1997]

Appearances:
*Mitataht askiy: Sweet Grass Records 10
   Years* [Sweet Grass 2003] comp
*Gathering of Nations Pow-Wow: Mil-
   lennium Celebration*, Vol. 1: *Various
   Northern Drums* [SOAR 2000] comp
*Ermineskin Cree Nation Pow-wow: Live at
   Bear Park* [Sweet Grass 1999] comp
Thunderchild '98 [Turtle Island Music
   1999] comp
Cree Nation [Turtle Island Music 1998]
   comp
Indian Graffiti: Noon Records Greatest
   [Noon Records 1998] comp

Willow Creek—(Lakota) Northern
Style

Lineup: Chris, Tyrone, and Carlos Mexi-
can; Eugene Condon; Martin, Marvin,
Justin, and Collin Holy; Harry Little Thun-
der; Andrew Little Moon; Arron Widow;
Brionne Blue Arm; Alex High Elk; Richard
Red Eagle. From Cheyenne River, South
Dakota.

DISCOGRAPHY:
Veteran Songs [Sunshine SSCT-4211]

Appearances:
World's Best Veteran Songs, Vol. 1 [Sun-
   shine 2001] comp
*H. V. Johnson Lakota Cultural Centre 1994
   Spring Wacipi*, Vol. 1 [Sunshine 1995]
   comp

Windy Rock Singers—
(Dakota-Anishnabe) Northern Style

Lineup: David Henry Jr.; Donald Henry Jr.;
Mark, Keith, and Jason Henry; Roy, Adrian,

and Jan Antoine; Lydell Alexander; Corey
Littlejohn. From Rosseau River Reserve,
Manitoba, this group was originally known
as Eagle Hill.

DISCOGRAPHY:
Windy Rock Singers [Sunshine SSCT-4166]

Appearances:
World's Best Crow Hop Songs [Sunshine
   2001] comp
World's Best Round Dance Songs, Vol. 2
   [Sunshine 2001] comp

Wisconsin Dells—(Hocak) Northern
Style

Lineup: Nelson, Dixon, and Kenny Funmaker. Formed in 1983, based in Wisconsin.

DISCOGRAPHY:
Schemitzun 1995 Live Championship
   [Sweet Grass 1995]

Appearances:
Thunder on the Lake [Arbor 2003] comp
World's Best Grass Dance [Sunshine 1998]
   comp
Wisconsin Intertribal [Sunshine SSCT-
   4216] comp

Wood, Randy—(Cree) Northern Style
See: Northern Cree Singers, Tha Tribe

A founding member of Northern Cree
Singers from Saddle Lake, Alberta. Wood
recorded a highly successful solo album of
round dance 49ers. The recording showcased his unique vocal majesty. *Round
Dance the Night Away* received a Juno
nomination for the Best Music of Aboriginal Canada and a Grammy nomination for
Native American Music Album, 2003.

DISCOGRAPHY:
Round Dance Blues [Canyon 2003]
Round Dance the Night Away [Canyon
   2001]

Appearances:
Tha Tribe:
Best of Both Worlds: World One [Canyon 2004]

Ya-iyo-waza—(Lakota) Northern Style

Lineup: Tim Black Bear; Simon Frazier; Kevin Red Buffalo; Eugene and William Condon. From Eagle Butte, South Dakota.

DISCOGRAPHY:
Ya-iyo-waza [Sunshine 1995]

Appearances:
World's Best Fancy Dance Songs, Vol. 2 [Sunshine 2001] comp
H. V. Johnson Lakota Cultural Centre 1994 Spring Wacipi, Vol. 1 [Sunshine 1995] comp

Yamparika Singers—(Ute) Northern Style

Lineup: Darren Cush, Baldwin Duncan, Ben Watts, Bradford Longhair, Leander Tapoof, Anson Manning. From Fort Duchesne, Utah.

DISCOGRAPHY:
Starting Young [SOAR 1994]

Appearances:
Across Indian Lands [SOAR 1999] comp

Yellowbird—(Intertribal) Northern Style *See*: Blackstone Singers, Fly-In Eagle, Northern Cree Singers, Seekaskootch, Wildhorse Singers, Young Spirit

Lineup: Norman, Merle, Dion, Conan, Tyson, Larson, and Marilyn Yellowbird; Walter, Peter, and Chum Lightning; Marlon Deschamps; Wayne Johnson; Nate and Kevin Littlechild; Dallas Waskahut; Clyde Tootoosis; Jacob Faithful; Rocky Morin.
Members of various powwow groups from Alberta and Saskatchewan formed to celebrate the round dance songs of Maskwacis Cree elder Norman Yellowbird.

DISCOGRAPHY:
Elite [Arbor 2003]

Yellowhammer—(Ponca) Southern Style

Lineup: Perry Lee Botone Jr., Mike Gawhega, Jim Grant, Wesley J. Hudson, James Kemble, Garland Kent Jr., Greg and Kinsel Lieb, John McIntosh.
Formed in 1990 as the Fort Oakland Ramblers, with members of the Ponca and Otoe-Missouria Nations. Southern Champions at Schemitzun in 1995, 1997, and 1998.

DISCOGRAPHY:
World Champions [Indian House 2001]
Yellowhammer [Turtle Island Music 1996]
Red Rock, Oklahoma [Indian House 1996]
Live at Hollywood, Florida [Indian House 1995]

Appearances:
Relentless Warrior [Gathering of Nations Records 2001] comp
Bear Spirit [Turtle Island Music 1999] comp
Best of the Best Schemitzun '93–99 [Sweet Grass 1999] comp
Spirit of the Wolf [Turtle Island Music 1998] comp
Gathering of Nations Pow-Wow 1995 [SOAR 1996] comp
Hinckley Grand Celebrations Powwow 1995 Southern Style [Sweet Grass 1995] comp
Hinckley Powwow, Vol. 2 [Sunshine 1995] comp
Hinckley Powwow, Vol. 1 [Sunshine 1995] comp
Gathering of Nations Pow-Wow 1993 [SOAR 1994] comp

Yellowjacket—(Intertribal) Southern Style

Lineup: Johnson B. Taylor; Jake, Tim, and Sheila Ryder; Billy Jack Baker; Jimmy Newton; Conrad Thompson; Frank Carson; Dwayne Manus; Dustin Teague; Michelle Chavez; Dan Jefferson; Terrille Medicine Bird; O. T. Sanky; Jeremy White Buffalo; Mike Pawnee Jr.; Young Bear; Ian Thompson; Raelynn, Patricia, and Johnita Taylor.

Formed by Johnson B. Taylor and Johnson K. Taylor as the Southern Ute Singers. Group members represent Pawnee, Southern Ute, Ponca, Otoe, Cheyenne and Dineh. Gathering of Nations Southern Drum Champions, 1996.

DISCOGRAPHY:
Tribute [WithOut Rez Productions 1999]
Yellowjacket [WithOut Rez Productions 1997]

Appearances:
Gathering of Nations Powwow 2001 [Gathering of Nations Records 2001] comp
Gathering of Nations Pow-Wow 1998 [SOAR 1999] comp
Standing Our Ground [Turtle Island Music 1999] comp
Gathering of Nations Pow-Wow 1996 [SOAR 1997] comp

Young Bird—(Intertribal) Southern Style *See*: The Boyz, Northern Cree Singers

Lineup: Curtis, Don, Juaquin, Jennifer, Rebecca, and June Hamilton–Young Bird (Cheyenne-Sauk-Fox); Poncho Brady (Hidatsa-Mandan); Jason Smith (Pawnee-Kiowa-Sauk-Fox); Ruben Watan (Cheyenne-Arapaho); Glen Ahhaitty (Kiowa-Comanche); G. C. Tsouhlarakis (Creek-Dineh); Jeff Miller (Omaha); Jancita Warrington (Menominee); Andrea Kemble (Osage-Ponca); Rusty Diamond (Pawnee-Otoe).

Their album *Change of Life* received a 2002 Best Native American Music Album Grammy nomination.

DISCOGRAPHY:
YB Style [Canyon 2003]
Youngbird and Northern Cree: Double Platinum—Powwow Songs Recorded Live at Hobbema [Canyon 2003]
Change of Life Oklahoma Pow-wow Songs [Canyon 2001]
Youngbird and The Boyz: Down 4 Life [Canyon 2001]
Live at Shakapee [Canyon 2000]
Deja Vu: Powwow Songs from Oklahoma [Canyon 1998]

Appearances:
Hinckley Powwow Southern Style [Arbor 2001] comp
Gathering of Nations Pow-Wow: Millennium Celebration, Vol. 2: Various Southern Drums [SOAR 2000] comp

Young Blood Singers—(Cherokee) Northern-Style Eastern Drum *See*: Contemporary Music: Pura Fe

Lineup: Christopher and Jeff Pegram, Wayne Duncan (Cherokee); Arthur Crippery, Micah Hunter, Andrew Coffee, Weyhan and Honovi Smith (Shinnecock).

DISCOGRAPHY:
Young Blood Singers, Vol. 3 [Sunshine 1998]
Young Blood Singers, Vol. 2 [Sunshine 1996]
Young Blood Singers, Vol. 1 [Sunshine 1995]

Appearances:
World's Best Memorial Songs [Sunshine 2002] comp
World's Best Women's Traditional Songs [Sunshine 2002] comp
SECC Earth Band [Sunshine 1998] comp
World's Best Crow Hop Songs [Sunshine 2001] comp

Young Eagle Cree—(Cree) Northern
Style

DISCOGRAPHY:
Young Eagle Cree [SICC YEC-122984]

Appearances:
Thunderchild '98 [Turtle Island Music
    1999] comp
SIFC Powwow Live '95 [SICC 1995] comp
White Earth Powwow [Sunshine SSCT-
    4173] comp

Young Grey Horse—(Blackfoot-
Assiniboine-Cree) Northern
Style

Lineup: Arlen Sharp, Joe Kicking Woman,
Corey and Chazz Eagle Speaker, Arlan
Edwards, Anjoe Scabby Robe, Durand Bear
Medicine, Pat Armstrong, Galen Sharp,
Jon Powder Face, Everett Armstrong, Duey
Bear Medicine, Kenneth Gopher, James
Big Beaver, Arlen Sharp, Kevin Calf Robe,
Linus Fish.

DISCOGRAPHY:
Tha Vibez [Arbor 2002]
TP Creepin' [Arbor 2000]
It's Just a Tribe Thang [Canyon 1999]
Generations [Canyon 1998]

Appearances:
Women's Fancy Dance Songs [Arbor/
    Native American Heritage Series 2003]
    comp
Thunder Drums, Vol. 2: *The Best Pow-
    wow Songs from the World's Best Drums*
    [Arbor 2002] comp
Thunder Drums, Vol. 1: *The Best of Arbor
    Records* [Arbor 2001] comp

Young Grey Horse Society—
(Blackfoot) Northern Traditional

Lineup: Wayne, Thelma, Denise, Durand,
Kevin, Armand, Neola, Wanda, Milana,
Michele, and Leland Bear Medicine; Joe

and Emily Scabby Robe; Don Parsons; Nels
Costel.

DISCOGRAPHY:
Powwow Songs [Canyon CR-6193]
Powwow Songs [Canyon CR-6184]
Songs of the Blackfeet [Canyon 1977/1999]

Young Kingbird—(Anishnabe)
Northern Style *See*: Kingbird Singers,
Ponemah Chippewa Singers

Lineup: Mark, Dallas, Nayghaj, Verlin,
Jim, Randy, Lance, and Matthew Kingbird;
Chad Goodrider; Frankie Graves; Darren
Defoe; Sheldon Hawk; Jarret and Garret
Caldwell. From Red Lake, Minnesota.

DISCOGRAPHY:
A Warrior's Cry [Arbor 2003] enhanced

Appearances:
Champion Hand Drum Songs [Arbor 2003]
    comp
*White Earth 134th Annual Powwow Cele-
    bration* [Arbor 2003] comp

Young Scouts—(Cree) Northern Style

Lineup: Percy, Michael, and Jerry Dreaver;
Lori Wahobin; Tiff, Leo, and Terry Paske-
min; Marc Longjohn; Devere Tsatoke;
Delia Waskewitch; Wavell Starr; Bradley
Crane; Allen Bonaise; Dale and Rocky
Morin; Colin Chief; Oscar; Bob and Shel-
don Rainy; Micah Daniels; Troy Tootoosis;
Earl McLeod; Ja-Carny; Big J; Cliffton Cha-
kita; Michelle Sanderson; Wendy Singer;
Jeffry Crookedneck.
    Originally known as the Amigos, this
Saskatchewan-based group of lead sing-
ers grew from the strong tradition of hand
drumming.

DISCOGRAPHY:
Plan 2 Round Dance [Sweet Grass 2004]
    two-CD set
Meet Ya at the Round Dance [Sweet Grass
    2003]

Appearances:

Mitataht askiy: Sweet Grass Records 10 Years [Sweet Grass 2003] comp

Young Spirit—(Cree) Northern Style

Lineup: Jacob, Fred, and George Faithful; Clyde Tootoosis; Peter Quinney; Glen Lewis; Vincent Rain; Skyler Redstar; Bryce Morin; Kenny Paul Hood Jr.; Adrian Tsosie; Joanne Chamakese; Candace Gadwa.

DISCOGRAPHY:

Neechmus: Cree Round Dance Songs [Arbor 2002]

Appearances:

Round Dance Songs, Vol. 2 [Arbor/Native American Heritage Series 2003] comp

Thunder Drums, Vol. 2: *The Best Powwow Songs from the World's Best Drums* [Arbor 2002] comp

Zotigh—(Kiowa) Southern Style

Lineup: Ralph, Bill, Dennis, and Sharon Zotigh; Ephraim Atencio; Christian Boos; J. J. Brunner; Shawn Harjo; Duane Harris; Bob Murray Jr.; Ben and Robert Nakai; Edward Pacheco; Stephan Swimmer; Woody Vanderhoop; Jennifer Bitsie; Colleen Gorman; Nicky Kay Michael; Le Andra Peters; Sunny Rose Yellowmule.

Originally from Hobart, Oklahoma, this group is based in Albuquerque, New Mexico. (Zotigh: pronounced "zoe-tie"; translation: "Wood Drifting on the Water.") This award-winning group's songs were composed to accommodate both northern and southern styles of powwow dancing.

DISCOGRAPHY:

Millennium [Indian House 2000]

Schemitzun World Championship of Song and Dance [Sweet Grass 1999]

Zotigh [Sweet Grass 1998]

Powwow Songs from the South West [Indian House 1997]

Appearances:

Mitataht askiy: Sweet Grass Records 10 Years [Sweet Grass 2003] comp

Gathering of Nations Powwow 2001 [Gathering of Nations Records 2001] comp

Gathering of Nations Pow-Wow: Millennium Celebration, Vol. 2: *Various Southern Drums* [SOAR 2000] comp

Gathering of Nations Pow-Wow 1998 [SOAR 1999] comp

Gathering of Nations Pow-Wow 1996 [SOAR 1997] comp

Across Indian Lands [SOAR 1999]

Lineup: Bryan Akipa (*See*: Flute Music),
Teddy Allen, Jack Anquoe, Jaye Begaye
(*See*: Rio Grande Singers), Blacklodge,
Earl Bullhead (*See*: Common Man Singers; Traditional/Archival Solo), Eastern
Canada, Paul Guy (*See*: Peyote Music), Wil
Numkena, Cornel Pewewardy (*See*: Flute
Music), Alexander Santos, Whitewind (*See*:
Flute Music), Yamparika.

Section 6-B
Powwow Compilation Recordings

Bear Spirit [Turtle Island Music 1999]

Lineup: Battle River, The Boyz, Eyabay,
Eya-Hey Nakoda, Fly-In Eagle, Pipestone
Creek, Porcupine, Rose Hill, Star Blanket
Jrs., White Swan, Yellowhammer.

Best of Alberta [Sunshine 1997]

Lineup: Chiniki Lake, Hawk River, Logan
Alexis, Pigeon Lake, Stoney Park, Tail
Wind.

Best of the Best Schemitzun '93–99 [Sweet Grass 1999]

Lineup: Bad Medicine, Battle River, Blacklodge, Blackstone, Cozad, Eagle Mountain,
Eyabay, High Noon, Little Island Cree, Red
Bull, Stoney Park, Whitefish Jrs., Yellow
Hammer.

The Best of Hinckley Powwow Northern and Southern Style: 11th Annual Powwow Grand Celebration [Arbor 2003]

Lineup: The Boyz, Cumberland, Little
Otter, Mahnomen Creek, Meskwaki Nation, Midnite Express, Pipestone, Southern
Boys, Southern Cree, Young Bird, Yellowfeather, Young Kingbird.

Best of Manitoba [Sunshine 1997]

Lineup: Circle Strong, Grassy Narrows, Hi Bull, Little Spirit, North Buffalo, Plains Ojibway, Red Suns, Red Wind, Sioux Assiniboine, Two Feathers, Wandering Sound.

The Best of the Northern Boys [SOAR 1999]

Lineup: Black Eagle, Blacklodge, Moccasin Flats, Red Elk, Rocky Boy, Star Society.

The Best of Ontario Powwow Groups [Sunshine 1997]

Lineup: Chi Geeziz, Chi Nodin, Dead Horse Creek, Hanisha, Medicine Drum, Northern Wind, Red Hawk, Red Shadow (*See*: Traditional/Archival Group), Spirit Wind, Whitefish Bay, Whitefish Jrs.

The Best of Saskatchewan [Sunshine 1997]

Lineup: Cree Spirit, Eagle Claw, Eagle Hill, Eagle Singing, Fly-In Eagle, Four Little Feathers, Grey Buffalo, Little Island Cree, Red Bull, Seekaskootch, Stony Eagle.

Best of Saskatchewan Cultural Centre [SICC 093]

Bismarck Powwow [Sunshine 1993]

Lineup: Blackfoot Crossing, Black Whistle, Cannon Ball, Eagle Creek, Eagle Tail, Haystack, Red Bull, Red Thunder, Sinte Ska, Wood Creek.

Black Hills: 16th Annual Powwow [Arbor 2003]

Lineup: Bad Horse, Bad Nation, Black Bull Jrs., Cheyenne Creek, Crazy Horse, Elk's Whistle, Prairie Island, Lakota Tribe, Red Voice, Whitefish Bay.

A Celebration of First Nations: The 1992 Toronto International Powwow [Craggle Rock 1993]

Lineup: All Nation w/ Otonabee, Blacklodge, Blackstone, Northern Lake, Red Dawn, Summer Cloud, Wikwmikong, Whitefish Bay, White Tail, Young Nation.

Champion Hand Drum Songs [Arbor 2003]

Lineup: Battle River, Blacklodge, The Boyz, Red Lake, Rocky Boy, Southern Boys, Three Amigos, Tha Tribe, Young Kingbird, Woodlands.

Champion Round Dance Songs, Vol. 1 [Arbor 1999]

Lineup: Eyabay, Lake Vermillion, Spirit Sands, Walkin Bull, Whitefish Bay.

Chicken Dance Songs [Arbor/Native American Heritage Series 2003]

The CD contains fifteen tracks but no credits.

Chippewa-Cree Grass Dance Songs from Rocky Boy [Indian House 1980]

Lineup: Bear Paw Singers w/ Charles Gopher, John G. Meyers, Rocky Boy, Duncan Standing Rock, Lloyd Top Sky, Henry Wolfchild.

C.I.S. 20th Annual Powwow
[Sunshine SSCT-4172]

Lineup: Anishnabe, Battle River, Kingbird, Whitefish Bay. Recorded at Bemidji State University, Bemidji, Minnesota.

Cree Nation [Turtle Island Music 1998]

Lineup: Fly-In Eagle, Pipestone Creek, Star Blanket Jrs., Walking Buffalo, Wildhorse. Recorded live at the Saskatchewan Indian Federated College Powwow, 1997.

Crow Celebration [Canyon 1971]

Lineup: Arapaho, Assiniboine, Blood, Cheyenne, Cree, Crow, Kiowa, Mandaree, Mesquakie, and Yakima Nations.

Dakota Tipi '84 Live [Featherstone 1985]

Lineup: Assiniboine Singers (Portage La Prairie, Manitoba); Minneapolis Buckaroos (Minneapolis, Minnesota); Red Nation Singers (Tokio, North Dakota). Recorded at the Chief Gall Oyate Powwow, Dakota Tipi Reserve, Portage La Prairie, Manitoba.

Drum Beats: 18 Powwow Groups
[Sunshine 2002]

Lineup: Blacklodge, Brown Eagle, Chi-Geezis, Chi-key-wis Sons, Eyabay, Logan Alexis, Maza Duta, Moose Mountain, Nakoda Lodge, Northern Wind, Ojibway Travelers, Red Bull, Red Hawk, Red Iron, Red Shadow, Walking Wolf, Whitefish Bay, Whitefish Jrs.

Ermineskin Cree Nation Pow-wow: Live at Bear Park [Sweet Grass 1999]

Lineup: The Boyz, Crooked Lake, Eagle Hill, High Noon, Mountain Soul, R-Boyz, Seekaskootch, Sweet Grass, Ta-Otha Spirit, Walking Buffalo, Wildhorse.

Eschikagou Powwow 2000 LIVE!
[Gathering of Nations Records 2001]

Lineup: Bear Clan, Bear Creek, Cricket Hill, Iroquois Smoke Dance, Litefoot (*See*: Contemporary Music), Northern Wind, Shki Bmaadzi, Spotted Eagle, Tha Tribe, Walkin Bull.

Gathering of Champions: The Winners Circle: Best of 1992–1994 Gathering [SOAR 171 1995]

Lineup: Assiniboine, Assiniboine Jr., Whitefish Bay, Whitefish Jrs. A collection of champion drum groups from Canada.

Gathering of Nations Powwow
[Gathering of Nations Records 2001]

Enhanced, w/ contemporary songs written by Eddie Madden.

Gathering of Nations Pow-Wow, Vol. 1 [SOAR 1992]

Lineup: Blacklodge, Cathedral Lake, Northern Wind, Sioux Assiniboine, Whitefish Bay. Video: *12th Annual Gathering of Nations Pow-Wow* [GON Video 101] sixty minutes.

Gathering of Nations Pow-Wow: Millennium Celebration, Vol. 1: *Various Northern Drums* [SOAR 2000]

Lineup: Bear Creek, Blackstone, Kautenoh Jrs., Mandaree, Mystic River, Red Bull, Sage Point, Tha Tribe, Thunder Creek, Thunderhorse, Walking Buffalo, Wildhorse. Grammy nomination, Best Native American Music Album, 2002.

Gathering of Nations Pow-Wow: Millennium Celebration, Vol. 2: *Various Southern Drums* [SOAR 2000]

Lineup: Cedar Tree, Cozad, Eagle Claw, Rio Grande, Rose Hill, Sizzortail, Young Bird, Zotigh.

Gathering of Nations Pow-Wow 1992: Various Drum Groups [SOAR 1993]

Lineup: Blackstone, Elk Whistle, Sioux Assiniboine, Whitefish Bay, Whitefish Jrs. w/Wynton Marsalis, trumpet.

Gathering of Nations Pow-Wow 1993: Various Drum Groups [SOAR 1994]

Lineup: Cozad, Grayhorse, Indian Creek, Little Eagle, Noshame, Pass Creek, Red Sands, Rose Hill, Star Society, Stoney Park, Whitefish Bay, Whitefish Jrs., Yellowhammer.

Gathering of Nations Pow-Wow 1994: Various Drum Groups [SOAR 1995]

Lineup: Assiniboine Jrs., Black Lodge, Stoney Park, Whitefish Bay, Whitefish Jrs.

Gathering of Nations Pow-Wow 1995 [SOAR 1996]

Lineup: Blackstone, Cozad, Rio Grande, Rose Hill, Six Nations Women Singers (*See*: Traditional/Archival Group), Yellowhammer.

Gathering of Nations Pow-Wow 1996 [SOAR 1997]

Lineup: The Boyz, Cozad, Haystack, Little Island Cree, Redstone, Southern Cree, Yellowjacket, Zotigh.

Gathering of Nations Pow-Wow 1997 [SOAR 197 1998]

Gathering of Nations Pow-Wow 1998: Various Drum Groups [SOAR 1999]

Lineup: Atsa Butte, Horse Tail, Meskwaki Nation, Mountain Song, Mystic River, Otter Trail, Red Stone, Rio Grande, Seekaskootch, Star Blanket Jrs., Stoney Park, Southern Cree, Tha Tribe, White Eagle, Yellowjacket, Zotigh. Grammy Award, Best Native American Music, 2001; NAMA Award, Best Powwow Recording, 2000.

Gathering of Nations Pow-Wow 1999 [SOAR 2000]

Lineup: Bear Springs, Fly-In Eagle, High Noon, Masquakie Nation, MGM, Northern Cree, Painted Horse, Sage Point, Seekaskootch, Southern Cree, Stoney Park, Tha Tribe, Trail Mix, White Clay, Wild Horse.

Gathering of Nations Pow-Wow: Northern Gathering [SOAR 1999]

Gathering of Nations Pow-Wow: Southern Gathering [SOAR 1999]

Gathering of Nations Powwow 2000—Y2K! [Gathering of Nations Records 2001]

Lineup: Bear Creek, Blackstone, Gray Horse, Mandaree, Northern Wind, Red Bull, Red Horse, Rose Hill, Walking Buffalo, Wildhorse, Young Bird.

Gathering of Nations Powwow 2001 [Gathering of Nations Records 2001]

Lineup: Bad Medicine, Bear Creek, Jay Begay and the Rio Grande Singers, Blackstone, the Bucks, Cozad, Meskwaki Nation, Omaha Lodge, Thunderhorse, Ulali (*See*: Contemporary Music), Whitefish Jrs., Wild Boys, Yellowjacket, Zotigh.

Great Plains Singers [Canyon CR-6052]

Arikira, Kiowa, Northern Arapaho, Northern Cheyenne, Phoenix Plains, Ponca, Shawnee, Sioux, Southern Cheyenne.

Hinckley Grand Celebrations Powwow 1995 Northern Style [Sunshine SSCT-4283]

Lineup: Battle River, The Boyz, Dakota Nation, Eyabay, Elk's Whistle, Little Otter, Northern Cree, Spirit Wind, Whitefish Bay, Whitefish Jrs.

Hinckley Grand Celebrations Powwow 1995 Southern Style [Sunshine SSCT-4284]

Hinckley Grand Celebrations Powwow 1995 Southern Style [Sweet Grass 1995]

Lineup: No Shame, Rose Hill, Southern Slam, Yellowhammer.

Hinckley Powwow, Vol. 1 [Sunshine 1995]

Lineup: Dakota Nation, Eagle Claw, Eyabay, Haystack, Ironwood, Mandaree, Northern Cree, Red Spirit, Whitefish Bay, Whitefish Jrs., Yellowhammer. Recorded at the Third Annual Grand Celebrations Powwow, Hinckley, Minnesota, July 29–31, 1994.

Hinckley Powwow, Vol. 2 [Sunshine 1995]

Lineup: Dakota Nation, Eagle Claw, Eyabay, Haystack, Ironwood, Lakeshore, Mandaree, Northern Cree, Sioux Assiniboine, Whitefish Jrs., Yellowhammer. Recorded at the Third Annual Grand Celebrations Powwow, Hinckley, Minnesota, July 29–31, 1994.

Hinckley Powwow Northern Style [Arbor 1999]

Lineup: Battle River, Eyabay, High Noon, Meskwaki Nation.

Hinckley Powwow Northern Style [Arbor 2001]

Lineup: The Boyz, High Noon, Kingbird, Leech Lake, Lightning Boy, Little Otter, Northern Wind, Pipestone, Red Tail, Smokeytown, Walkin Bull.

Hinckley Powwow Southern Style
[Arbor 1999]

Lineup: Cozad, Rose Hill, Sizzortail, Southern Boys.

Hinckley Powwow Southern Style
[Arbor 2001]

Lineup: Cozad, Ham-lush-ka, Rose Hill, Whitetail, Young Bird.

Honor the Earth Powwow Songs of the Great Lakes [Ryko 1990]

Lineup: Bad River, Bear Claw, LCO Soldiers' Drum, Little Otter, Smokey Town, Three Fires Society Drum, Winnebago Sons. Recorded at Lac Court Oreilles; produced by Mickey Hart.

H. V. Johnson Lakota Cultural Centre 1994 Spring Wacipi, Vol. 1
[Sunshine 1995]

Lineup: Buffalo Lake, Cherry Creek, Red Scaffold, Sioux Valley, Tatanka, Willow Creek, Ya-iyo-waza. Recorded at Eagle Butte, South Dakota.

Indian Graffiti: Noon Records Greatest [Noon Records 1998]

Lineup: Blackstone, The Boyz, High Noon, Noon Express, Sweet Grass, Wildhorse.

Jingle Dress Side Step Songs [Arbor 2001]

Lineup: Little Otter, Mystic River, Northern Wind, Walking Buffalo, Whitefish Bay.

Just Jamming [Wacipi Records 2000]

Lineup: Elk Whistle and Horse Tail.

Manitoba First Nation, Vol. 1
[Sunshine SSCT-4286]
Manitoba First Nation, Vol. 2
[Sunshine SSCT-4287]

Manitoba Powwow Groups
[Sunshine 1997]

Lineup: Circle Strong, First Nations, Grassy Narrows, Hi Bull, North Buffalo Cree, Plains Ojibway, Red Sons, Red Wind, Sioux Assiniboine, Two Feathers, Wandering Sound.

Medicine Drum: Ontario Powwow Groups [Mariposa MPCD-3003, Germany]

Minnesota Powwow Songs
[Sunshine SSCT-4174]

Lineup: The Boyz, Heart of the Earth, Little Otter, Northern Wind, Stoney Park, Sioux Assiniboine, Thunder Mountain, Whitefish Jrs. Recorded live at Hinckley, Minnesota, May 1993.

Mitataht askiy: Sweet Grass Records 10 Years [Sweet Grass 2003]

Lineup: Bad Medicine, Blacklodge, Blackstone, The Boyz, Buffalo Lake, Edmund Bull, Cozad, Crooked Lake, Delia and the Waskewitch Boys, Elk's Whistle, Eyabay, High Noon, Little Axe, Logan Alexis, Mandaree, Mosquito, Mountain Soul, Mystic River, Omaha Whitetail, Painted Horse, Pipestone Creek, Red Bull, Red Dog, Seekaskootch, Southern Cree, Spirit

Whistle, Sweetgrass, Whitefish Jrs., Wildhorse, Young Scouts, Zotigh.

A New Beginning, 1894–1994: St. Michael's College [Sweet Grass 1994]

Lineup: Fly-In Eagle, Little Eagle, Stoney Park.

Northern Cree and Friends: Round Dance Songs Recorded "Live," Vol. 1 [Canyon 2002]

Lineup: Big River Cree, Blackstone, Eya-Hey-Nakoda, Fly-In Eagle, Little Island Cree, Logan Alexis, Gordon McGilvery, Northern Cree. Recorded on the Louis Bull Reserve, Alberta, March 3, 2002.

Northern Cree and Friends: Round Dance Songs Recorded "Live," Vol. 2 [Canyon 2003]

Lineup: Jack Bull, Eugene Cardinal, David McGilvery, Gordon McGilvery, Mountain Soul, Northern Cree, Arnold Pete, Melvin Stone, Norman Yellowbird.

Northern Gathering 1997 [SOAR 191 1998]

Omak Powwow 1980 [Canyon CR-6175]

Lineup: Eagle Star, Fraser Valley–Spotted Lake, Nespelem Valley Drummers, Nez Perce Nation, Spokane Bad Canyon Wellpinit, Treaty of 1855.

Onion Lake Powwow 1992 [Sunshine SSCT-4149]

Lineup: Blackfoot Crossing, Blacklodge, Pigeon Lake.

Powwow [Canyon CR-6088]

Lead singer John Knifechief. Recorded in 1971 during All Indian Days, Scottsdale, Arizona.

Powwow Songs: Music of the Northern Plains Indians [New World 1986; reissued by Arc Music 2001, United Kingdom]

Lineup: Jack Anquoe, Henry Collins, Bill Grass, James Kimble, Lionel Le Clair, Ed and Oliver Little Cook, Morris Lookout, the Los Angeles Northern, Adam Pratt, Joe Rush, Chris White. Recorded at the Kibekah Steh Powwow, Skiatook, Oklahoma, August 1975.

Powwow 2000 [Sunshine 2000]

Lineup: Blacklodge, Chi-Geezis, Chi Nodin, Cree Spirit, Eastern Eagle, Eyabay, Grassy Narrows, Little Otter, Logan Alexis, Moose Mountain, Northern Wind, Ojibway Travelers, Red Bull, Red Hawk, Silver Cloud, Smokey Town, Walking Wolf, Whitefish Bay, Whitefish Jrs., White Ridge.

Red Lake Nation [Turtle Island Music 1996]

Lineup: Battle River, Dakota Nation, Eyabay, Meskwaki Nation, Rose Hill.

Relentless Warrior [Gathering of Nations Records 2001]

Lineup: Arapaho Nation, Bear Creek, the Bucks, Red Horse, Southern Medicine, Southern Boys, Yellowhammer, Young Eagle.

Round Dance Songs, Vol. 2 [Arbor/ Native American Heritage Series 2003]

Lineup: Dakota Travels, Eagle Tail, Eyabay, Northern Wind, Pipestone, Red Tail, Sizzortail, Southern Boys, Spirit Sand, Thunderhorse, Young Spirit.

Schemitzun 2000: Hand Drum Songs [Sweet Grass 2001]

Lineup: Battle River, Blacklodge, The Boyz, Eagle Claw, Eyabay, Eya-Hey Nakoda, High Noon, Northern Cree, Red Bull, Walking Bull.

Schemitzun World Championship Round Dance Singing: Round Dance Singing [Turtle Island Music 2000]

Lineup: Battle River, Blacklodge, The Boyz, Eyabay, High Noon, Northern Cree, Red Bull.

Schemitzun World Championship 2000: Northern Style [Turtle Island Music 2001]

Lineup: Battle River, Eya-Hey Nakoda, High Noon, Red Bull, Star Blanket Jrs.

Schemitzun World Championship 2000: Round Dance Singing [Turtle Island Music 2001]

Lineup: Blacklodge, The Boyz, Eyabay, High Noon, Northern Cree, Red Bull.

Schemitzun World Championship 2000: Southern Style [Turtle Island Music 2001]

Lineup: Bad Medicine, Pawnee Yellowhorse, Silvercloud, Southern Boys.

SECC Earth Band [Sunshine 1998]

Lineup: Drum Circle, Red Hawk, Spring Creek, Turtle Island, Young Blood. Recorded at the Southeastern Cherokee Confederacy of Pennsylvania, Fifth Annual Cherokee Powwow.

Shake the Feathers: Live at Peguis Powwow '93 [Sunshine SSCT-4204]

Lineup: Chiniki Lake, Elk's Whistle, Hay Stack, High Rock Cree, Sioux Assiniboine, Whitefish Bay.

SIFC Annual Powwow [Sunshine SSCT-4168]

Lineup: Chiniki Lake, Cree Spirit, Fly-In Eagle, Starblanket Jrs., Stoney Eagle. Recorded live at the Fifteenth Annual Saskatchewan Indian Federated College Powwow.

SIFC Powwow Live '95 [SICC 1995]

Lineup: Eyabay, Nakoda Nation, Painted Horse, Pipestone Creek, Young Eagle Cree.

Sioux Favorites [Canyon 1968] Pine Ridge, Rosebud, Fort Thompson, and Cheyenne River, South Dakota

Songs from the Battleford Powwow [Canyon 1975]

Lineup: Alex Scalp Lock, Pat Kennedy, and Francis Green. Recorded in North Battleford, Saskatchewan.

Songs of the Blackfeet: Blackfeet Powwow Songs [Canyon 1974]

Lineup: Thomas NorRunner, Pat Kennedy, Edwin Calfrobe, Victor Surechief.

Songs of the Oglala Nation: Native American Powwow [Turtle Island Music 1998]

Lineup: Eagle Mountain, Kiyukaypi, Manderson, Porcupine, Pass Creek. Recorded at Porcupine, South Dakota

Songs of the Spirit: The Best of Sweet Grass [Sweet Grass/EMI 1995]

Lineup: Elk's Whistle, High Noon, Mandaree, Red Bull, Seekaskootch, Stoney Park, Sweet Grass, Whitefish Jrs.

The Sound of Champions [Sweet Grass 1994]

Lineup: Fly-In Eagle, High Noon, Red Bull, Stoney Park. Recorded live at Onion Lake, Saskatchewan.

Southern Gathering 1997 [SOAR 1998]

Spirit of the People [Sweet Grass/ EMI 1996]

Lineup: Crooked Lake Agency, Fly-In Eagle, Gray Boy, Parker School, Whitefish Jrs., Yellowmud Blanket; w/ Gord Tootoosis, MC.

Spirit of the Wolf [Turtle Island Music 1998]

Lineup: Battle River, The Boyz, Eyabay, Eya-Hey Nakoda, Fly-In Eagle, Pipestone Creek, Porcupine, Rose Hill, Star Blanket Jrs., White Swan, Yellowhammer.

Standing Our Ground [Turtle Island Music 1999]

Lineup: All Tribes, Fly-In Eagle, Littlewind, Mandaree, Mighty Few, Mystic River, Siksa Boyz, White Tail Cree, Yellowjacket.

Still the Eagle Flies, Vols. 1 and 2 [SICC 1995]

Lineup: Buffalo River Dene Drummers, Elk's Whistle, Eyabay, Fly-In Eagle, Onion Lake Hand Game, Red Bull, Southern Cree, Star Blanket Jrs., Whitefish Jrs., Young Eagle Cree.

37th Annual Milk River Indian Days Powwow Live at Fort Belknap, Montana [Sweet Grass 2003]

Lineup: Big Bear, Buffalo Stone, Chippewa-Cree, Dry Lake, Eagle Claw, Little Cree, Mandaree, Mountain Soul.

Thunder Bear Powwow [Sunshine SSCT-4188]

Lineup: First Nation, Northern Star, Northern Wind, Stoney Eagle, White Eagle, Whitefish Jrs. Recorded at the Thunder Bear Powwow, Winnipeg, Manitoba.

Thunderchild '98 [Turtle Island Music 1999]

Lineup: Battle Creek, Blackstone, Crooked Lake, Fly-In Eagle, High Noon, Little Island Cree, Mountain Soul, Red Bull, Spotted Eagle, Walking Buffalo, Wildhorse, Young Eagle Cree.

Thunder Drums, Vol. 1: *The Best of Arbor Records* [Arbor 2001]

Lineup: Battle River, Bear Creek, The Boyz, Burntside Lake, Cozad, Eyabay, Grey Fox, Lake of the Woods, Mandaree, Northern Wind, Red Tail, Sizzortail, Southern Boys, Spirit Mountain, Spirit Sand, Walkin Bull, White Lodge, Young Grey Horse.

Thunder Drums, Vol. 2: *The Best Powwow Songs from the World's Best Drums* [Arbor 2002]

Lineup: Battle River, Bear Creek, The Boyz, Crowe, Eastern Eagle, Eyabay, Northern Wind, Lake of the Woods, Little Otter, Mandaree, Red House, River Cree, Sizzortail, Southern Boys, Thunder Horse, Whitefish Bay, Whitelodge, Whitetail, Young Grey Horse, Young Spirit.

Thunder on the Lake [Arbor 2003]

Lineup: Bear Clan, the Bucks, Duck Creek, Gusto, Little Otter, Raining Thunder, Smokey Town, Wisconsin Dells. Recorded at the Indian Summer Festival, Milwaukee, Wisconsin.

Toronto Powwow [Sunshine 1998]

Lineup: Bear Clan, Big Stone, Blue Lake, Chi Nodin, Mystic River, Ramblers, Sasknorthern, Whistle Chant, Whitetail.

United Tribes International Powwow [Makoche 1995] two CDs

Lineup: Battle River, The Boyz, Chiniki Lake, Dakota Nation, Eagle Tail, Eyabay, Mandaree, Painted Horse, Porcupine, Red Bull, Sioux Assiniboine, Spirit Crossing, Star Blanket Jrs.

Voices from Thunderchild Powwow Songs [Turtle Island Music 2000]

Lineup: Bear Creek, Big Bear, Charging Buffalo, Fly-In Eagle, Red Bull, Sweet Grass, Whitefish Jrs. Recorded live at the 1999 Thunderchild Powwow, Saskatchewan.

White Earth 134th Annual Powwow Celebration [Arbor 2003]

Lineup: Black Bear Crossing, Cass Lake, Four Oaks, Grey Dog, Menomen Creek, Midnight Express, Ogli Daaki, Red Creek, Rez Riders, Woodland, Young Kingbird. Recorded live at White Earth, Minnesota, June 2003.

White Earth Powwow [Sunshine SSCT-4338]

Lineup: Chi Nodin, Chippewa Nation, Dakota Plains, Eyabay, Kingbird, Little Otter, Red Bull.

White Earth Powwow [Sunshine SSCT-4173]

Lineup: Anishnabe, Battle River, Cass Lake, Little Otter, Peace Maker, Young Eagle. Recorded live at White Earth, Minnesota, June 1993.

White Earth Powwow [Canyon CR-6171]

Lineup: American Indian, Eagle Butte, Joe Creek, Kingbird, Three Fires.

Whitefish Bay Powwow 1992 [Sunshine SSCT-4145]

Wisconsin Intertribal [Sunshine SSCT-4216]

Lineup: Cumberland, Eagle Mountain, Fon du Lac, Kingbird, Lac Courte Oreilles Badgers, Lakshore, Little Bear, Little Otter, Mississippi Ojibway, Summer Cloud, Wah'pe Kute, Wigwam Bay, Wisconsin Dells. Recorded live at Turtle Lake, Wisconsin.

Women's Fancy Dance Songs [Arbor/Native American Heritage Series 2003]

Lineup: Battle River, Bear Creek, Eastern Eagle, Eyabay, Lake Vermillion, Northern Wind, Red Tail, River Cree, Spirit Sand, Walkin Bull, Whitefish Bay, White Lodge, Young Grey Horse.

World Renowned Hand Drum Lead Singers, Vol. 1 [Sunshine 2000]

Lineup: Eugene Cardinal, Clayton Chief, Glen Lewis, Logan Alexis, Gordon McGilvery, Archie Moccasin, Arnold Pete, Edward Runaround, Melvin Stone, Gerald Waterhen, Norman Yellowbird.

World Renowned Hand Drum Lead Singers, Vol. 2 [Sunshine 2000]

Lineup: Eugene Cardinal, Clayton Chief, Glen Lewis, Logan Alexis, Gordon McGilvery, Archie Moccasin, Arnold Pete, Edward Runaround, Melvin Stone, Gerald Waterhen, Norman Yellowbird.

World's Best Chicken Dance Songs [Sunshine 2002] *See*: Nakoda Lodge

World's Best Crow Hop Songs [Sunshine 2001]

Lineup: Chi-Geezis, Chiniki Lake, Eagle Claw, Eyabay, Little Otter, Northern Wind, Red Bull, Walking Wolf, White Eagle, Whitefish Bay, Whitefish Jrs., Windy Rock, Young Blood.

World's Best Fancy Dance Songs, Vol. 1 [Sunshine 2000]

Lineup: Blacklodge, Chi-Geezis, Circle Strong, Dead Horse Creek, Drum Circle, Eyabay, Little Island Cree, Lone Creek, Northern Wind, Red Scaffold, Red Sons, Sioux Assiniboine, Smokey Valley, Two Feathers.

World's Best Fancy Dance Songs, Vol. 2 [Sunshine 2001]

Lineup: Blacklodge, Brown Eagle, Circle Strong, Eagle Claw, Echo Sky, Four Little Feathers, Grey Buffalo, Little Island Cree, Northern Wind, Red Scaffold, Red Hawk, Seekaskootch, Smokey Valley, Whitefish Bay, Ya-iyo-waza.

World's Best 49er Songs [Sunshine 2000] *See*: Walking Wolf Singers

World's Best Grass Dance [Sunshine 1998]

Lineup: Blacklodge, Eagle Singing, Grey Buffalo, Little Island Cree, Northern Wind, Red Hawk, Seekascootch, Smokey Town, Whirlwind, White Eagle, Whitefish Bay, Wisconsin Dells.

World's Best Intertribal Songs [Sunshine 2001]

Lineup: Blacklodge, Chi-Geezis, Chiniki Lake, Dead Horse Creek, Eyabay, Little Otter, Northern Wind, Red Hawk, Red Wind, Sioux Assiniboine, Smokey Town, Smokey Valley, Wandering Sound, Whitefish Bay.

World's Best Jingle Dress Songs [Sunshine 1998]

Lineup: Blacklodge, Chi-Geezis, Eagle Tail, Eastern Eagle, Hope Lake, Little Eagle, Little Otter, North Wind, Pigeon Lake, Sioux Assiniboine, Whitefish Bay, Whitefish Jrs.

World's Best Memorial Songs [Sunshine 2002]

Lineup: Blacklodge, Eagle Tail, Grassy Narrows, Hanisha, Northern Wind, Red Bull, Red Hawk, Smokey Valley, Two Feathers, Walking Wolf, Whirlwind, White Eagle, Whitefish Bay, Young Blood.

World's Best Powwow Drum Groups [Sunshine 2000]

Lineup: Blacklodge, Chi-Geezis, Eyabay, Little Otter, Logan Alexis, Moose Mountain, Northern Wind, Red Bull, Red Hawk, Smokey Town, Walking Wolf, Whitefish Bay.

World's Best Round Dance Songs [Sunshine 1997]

Lineup: Blacklodge, Chi-Geezis, Eyabay, Free Spirit, Little Otter, Logan Alexis, Northern Cree, Northern Wind, Red Bull, Seekaskootch, Silver Cloud, Sioux Assiniboine, Smokey Town, Stoney Eagle, Stoney Park, Whitefish Bay.

World's Best Round Dance Songs, Vol. 2 [Sunshine 2001]

Lineup: Blacklodge, Chi-Geezis, Dead Horse Creek, Free Spirit, Little Island, Logan Alexis, Mystic River, Northern Wind, Red Bull, Seekaskootch, Smokey Town, Stoney Eagle, Walking Wolf, Whitefish Bay, Whitespruce, Windy Rock.

World's Best Tiny Tot Songs [Sunshine 2000]

Lineup: Chi-Geezis, Eagle Claw, Eyabay, Little Thunderbirds, Red Bull, Red Hawk, Smokey Town, Smokey Valley, Stoney Eagle, Whirlwind.

World's Best Veteran Songs, Vol. 1 [Sunshine 2001]

Lineup: Blacklodge, Chi-Geezis, Eagle Tail, Grassy Narrows, Northern Wind, Pigeon Lake, Red Scaffold, Stoney Eagle, Thunder Mountain, White Eagle, Whitefish Bay, Willow Creek.

World's Best Women's Traditional Songs [Sunshine 2002]

Lineup: Eagle Tail, Eastern Eagle, Eyabay, Grassy Narrows, Lone Creek, Northern Wind, Red Bull, Red Iron, Red Sons, Seekascootch, Silver Cloud, Walking Wolf, Wandering Sound, Young Blood.

World's Leading Round Dance Songs [Sweet Grass 1996]

Lineup: Edmund Bull, Mervin Dreaver and Whitefish Jrs., Grey Eagle, McGilvery and Green, Mosquito, Red Bull, Songs of Bear Hills.

SECTION 7
Traditional/Archival Music
See: Arctic/Circumpolar; Peyote Ritual Music

Beginning in 1951, Phoenix-based Canyon Records released more than 250 single 78 rpm recordings of traditional Native groups and solo artists, which were then reissued on the twenty-volume Vintage series in the late 1990s.

Traditionally, songs are owned or kept by individuals, families, clans, and nations, depending on the song. Songs and dances come from nature and are the expressions of thanks for life and sustenance, as well as for healing, purification, reaffirmation, and a multitude of other reasons and purposes. Traditional music refers to a social order, territory, and organization; it also identifies gender. There is a song for everything, not just ceremony, but daily life and events as well; songs, prayers, and ceremonies can range from the simplest to the largest and most carefully organized gathering bound with intricate movements and patterns that are as highly evolved as the most complex mathematical equation. It is not my intent to offer description or detail of this music or activity.

The first commercial endeavor to record and market Native music began with the American Indian Sound Chiefs label, which was founded in the 1940s by the late Rev. Linn D. Pauahty (Kiowa), a Methodist minister from Carnegie, Oklahoma. He left an extensive recording legacy of material collected from the southern and northern plains.

Canyon Records founder Ray Boley *(left)* with Ed Lee Natay reviewing first test pressing, circa 1951. Photo courtesy Canyon Records.

By the 1950s, he had organized the recordings into styles and group; the collection has been reissued through Indian House Records.

Although millions of anthropological and ethnomusicological recordings are housed in numerous museums and university collections throughout the world, this section can only draw attention to their existence; no documentation as yet includes contemporary recordings (early to mid–twentieth century to the present) made by Native producers, researchers, and subjects. The ethnomusicologists mentioned herein are those few whose work has been reproduced and reissued by record labels.

The first documented use of mechanical recording equipment for ethnological research was by Jesse Walter Fewkes, an anthropologist with the Peabody Museum of Archeology and Ethnology at Harvard University. His work in 1890 included Passamaquoddy song and speech as well as Zuni and Hopi songs recorded on wax cylinder phonograph. His article "On the Use of the Phonograph in the Study of Languages of American Indians" was published in the *Journal of Science* 15 (May 2, 1890). Others who worked on similar projects include Benjamin Ives Gilman, who recorded *Kwakiutl Song and Speech* in 1893; Washington Matthews, who studied the Dineh in 1900; Herben J. Spinden, who studied the Nez Perce in 1907; and Roland Dixon, who wrote *California Indians and Mexican Pastores*, circa 1910. They produced hundreds of cylinders of recordings, 264 of which were transferred to tape (Library of Congress AFS 14,737–14,754) along with a Passamaquoddy field recording reproduced on vinyl LP (LBC-15) as part of the U.S. Library of Congress Folk Music in America series. In the Arctic/Circumpolar region, Christian Leden, Knud Rasmussen, and William Thalbitzer were among many who recorded traditional Inuit songs, circa 1904 to 1916 (*See*: Arctic/Circumpolar Compilations: *Traditional Greenlandic Music*).

After visiting Anishnabe communities in Ontario, Canada, Frances Theresa Densmore collected more than 2,500 songs between 1907 and 1941. In 1907, she began a fifty-year relationship with the Bureau of American Ethnology and authored more than twenty books and hundreds of articles. Her ten-year preparatory study began in 1893 at Minnesota's Oberlin College Conservatory of Music under the tutelage of Alice Cunningham Fletcher (1838–1923). Recognized as a pioneer in anthropology, Fletcher was most known for her fieldwork among the Omaha in Nebraska, and she coauthored *The Omaha Tribe* in 1911 with Francis La Flesche (Omaha; 1857–1932). La Flesche established a major collection of books, papers, and Omaha music and dance recordings (*See: Omaha Indian Music* comp).

Dr. Willard Rhodes of Columbia University, through the assistance of the Library of Congress and his employer, the Bureau of Indian Affairs (BIA), recorded the music of fifty different nations within a forty-year period. The Library of Congress archives contain material he collected from 1910 to 1952. Ten LP recordings based on the collection were released commercially to the public with the assistance of the BIA and the Indian Arts and Crafts Board; Dr. Rhodes also edited two albums for Smithsonian Folkways.

In his twelve years of fieldwork, Dr. Rhodes amassed more than 270 discs and 50 tapes, collectively known as *The Willard Rhodes Collection of Field Recordings of North American Indian Song 1940–1952*. The collection contains music of the Akimel O'odham, Apache, Arapaho, Arikara, Assiniboine, Blackfeet, Caddo, Cheehallis, Cherokee, Cheyenne, Choctaw, Clayoquot, Comanche, Creek, Crow, Delaware, Dineh, Havasupai, Hopi, Jemez, Kiowa, Kiowa-Apache, Klillam, Klamath, Kwakiutl, Laguna, Makah, Mandan, Nez Perce, Nitinat, Paiute, Pawnee, Potawa-tami, Quilente, Quinalt, San Ildefonso, San Juan Pueblo, Santa Clara Pueblo, Shawnee, Shoshone-Bannock, Shoshone, Sioux (Lakota, Dakota), Skokomish, Twana, Snuqualmie, Taos Pueblo, Tlingit, Ute, Walapai, Warm Springs, Washo, Wichita, Winnebago, Yakima, Zia, and Zuni. The collection, housed at the Canadian Museum of Civilization in Ottawa, contains music collections of Kickapoo, Huron, Wyandot, Algonkian, Iroquois, Shuswap, Lillooet, Salish, Tsimsyan, Haida, Tahltan, Carrier, and others.

Cuban-born Matilda Coxe Evans Stevenson was largely known for her work with the Zuni of the southwestern United States, beginning in 1881; Alexander Cringan recorded Haudenosaunee material in Canada in 1898; John Comfort Filmore (1843–1989) and Franz Boas (1858–1942), along with legions of other anthropologists, conducted major studies. However, their recordings are not commercially available and therefore are not listed in this volume.

Section 7-A
Traditional/ Archival Solo Recordings

Ahdunko, Donald—
(Delaware-Caddo)

Born 1926. Ahdunko grew up in Binger and Anadarko, Oklahoma, and is said to be the last known person to hold knowledge of the Delaware hand game and of the Washaneke and ghost dance songs of the Caddo.

The recordings were all homemade, with more than four hundred songs preserved on tape. No dates are available.

DISCOGRAPHY:
Turkey Dance of the Caddo [NDA]
Drum Dance [NDA]
Caddo Round Dance [NDA]
Caddo Washaneke and Delaware [NDA]
Woman Dance [NDA]
Social Dance Songs [NDA]
Ghost Dance/Delaware Hand Game [NDA]
Ghost Dance/Morning Dance [NDA]

Antiste, Mary—(Flathead)

DISCOGRAPHY:
Flathead Stick Game Songs [Canyon CR-8017]

Beaver Chief—(Lummi)

Lineup: Jorge Alfonso, flutes/drum; Lisa Brody, Ted Ryan, Fredrick Jameson, background vocals.

DISCOGRAPHY:
Red Cedar Medicine: Circle Songs [Lyrichord/Koch 1999]

Appearances:
Exiled in the Land of the Free [Columbia 1996] comp *See*: Contemporary Compilations

Begaye, Jay—(Dineh) *See*: Powwow Music: Cathedral Lake Singers

From Steamboat Canyon, Arizona. A multidisciplinary artist in both music and visual fields, as well as a former rodeo rider, Begaye first started singing powwow with the White Eagle Singers from 1982 to 1986. He moved to Canada in 1987 and formed the Cathedral Lake Singers in Keremeos, British Columbia. *Round Dance in Beauty* received an AFIM INDIE Award nomination and NAMA nominations in the categories of Best Male Artist and Best Traditional Recording in 2001.

DISCOGRAPHY:
Song of Colors [Canyon 2003]
Round Dance in Beauty [Canyon 2000]
Long Walk [Canyon 1999]
The Beauty Way [Canyon 1997]
Honoring Our Ways [SOAR 1995]

Appearances:
Cathedral Lake Singers:
Live at Window Rock [Canyon 1999]
American Powwow [SOAR 1993]
Powwow Songs, Vol. 3 [SOAR 1992]
Powwow Songs, Vol. 2 [SOAR 1991]
Powwow Songs, Vol. 1 [SOAR 1990]
Various:
Across Indian Lands [SOAR 1999] comp
    See: Powwow Compilations

Begay, Pauline M.—(Dineh)

Native American Music Award, Best Children's Album, 1999.

DISCOGRAPHY:
To All Our Precious Ones: Navajo Lullabies and Children's Songs [Cool Runnings 1998]
Stars in the Desert [SOAR 1993]

Appearances:
Soaring Hearts Tribal Peoples, Vol. 1
    [SOAR 1996] comp
Various Native American Artists: Solo
Flights Two, Vol. 2 [SOAR 1994] comp
    See: Contemporary Compilations

Benally, Jones—(Dineh) *See*: Contemporary Music: Blackfire

DISCOGRAPHY:
Navajo Reflections [Canyon CR-16275]

Appearances:
Blackfire:
One Nation Under [Tacoho [2001]
Blackfire [Tacoho 1998]
Blackfire [Tacoho 1994]
Various:
Geronimo, An American Legend [Walter Hill, 1993] sdtk *See*: Contemporary Soundtracks

Bennett, Kay—(Dineh)

DISCOGRAPHY:
Kaibah: Navajo Love Songs [Canyon CR-7167; reissued 1997]
Kaibah [Canyon CR-6667]

Bilagody, James—(Dineh) *See*: Contemporary Music: Robbie Robertson

DISCOGRAPHY:
Beauty Ways [SOAR 1994]

Appearances:
Robbie Robertson:
Contact from the Underworld of Redboy [Capitol 1998]
Various:
Various Native American Artists: Solo Flights Two, Vol. 2 [SOAR 1994] comp
    See: Contemporary Compilations
Various Native American Artists: Solo Flights, Vol. 1 [SOAR 1991] comp *See*: Contemporary Compilations

Bullhead, Earl—(Lakota) *See*: Powwow Music: Common Man Singers; Contemporary Music: Brule, Chante; Contemporary Spoken Word: Legends and Storytelling: Paul Goble

DISCOGRAPHY:
Father to Son [Arbor 2003]
Lakota Drum [SOAR 2002]
Touch the Heart [Rez Cue 2001]
Sacred Directions [SOAR 1997]
Keeper of the Drum [SOAR 1995]
Walking the Red Road [SOAR 1993]
Spirit of Song [Makoche 1991]

Appearances (listed alphabetically):
Brule:
Star People [SOAR 2001]
We the People [Natural Visions/SOAR 1995]
Chante:
Nightbird [Great Spirit 1994]
Common Man Singers:
Songs for the Common Man [SOAR 157]
Spirit of Song [Makoche 1995]
Signals from the Heart [SOAR 1992]
Bob Conti:
An Evening with Sitting Bull [Natural Visions/SOAR 1995] w/ Jose Feliciano
Paul Goble:
Love Flute [Dakotah/SOAR 1993]
Nicole LaRoche:
Passion Spirit [Natural Visions 2001]
Spirit of Song Singers:
Spirit of Song [Makoche 1991]
Various:
Across Indian Lands [SOAR 1999] comp *See*: Powwow Compilations
Soaring Hearts Tribal Peoples, Vol. 1 [SOAR 1996] comp
The Way West [American Experience/ Shanachie 1995] sdtk *See*: Contemporary Soundtracks

Cassa, Murphy—(Apache)

DISCOGRAPHY:
Remembering Murphy Cassa, Vol. 2 [Canyon CR-704, circa 1966]

Remembering Murphy Cassa, Vol. 1 [Canyon CR-703]

Cassadore, Patsy—(Apache)

DISCOGRAPHY:
I Build the Wickiup [Canyon CR-6102]

Appearances:
Sacred Souls [Manteca 2001, United Kingdom] comp *See*: Contemporary Compilations

Cassadore, Philip—(Apache)

DISCOGRAPHY:
Traditional Apache Songs [Canyon CR-6071, circa 1960]
Philip Cassadore Sings More Apache Songs [Canyon CR-6070]
Philip Cassadore Sings Apache Songs [Canyon CR-6056]
The Apache Day in Song [Apache Cultural History Project] two LPs

Appearances:
Sacred Souls [Manteca 2001, United Kingdom] comp *See*: Contemporary Compilations

Cody, Radmilla—(Dineh–African American)

Raised in Grand Falls, Arizona, Cody had an upbringing rich with traditional culture. A former Miss Navajo Nation (1997–98), Cody released her first project with the guidance of traditional elders and with the expectations of being a role model, but amid racial criticisms. She made her first recording while she was studying communications at Arizona State University. A percentage of album sales was earmarked for the Baahozho Foundation to support youth and culture.

DISCOGRAPHY:
Seed of Life: Traditional Songs of the Navajo [Canyon 2001]
Within the Four Directions: A Tribute to the Navajo Way of Life [Cool Runnings 2000]

Flying Bye, Joseph—(Lakota) *See*: Sissy Goodhouse

1917–2000
Born June 15, Standing Rock Sioux Reservation, North Dakota. A traditional medicine man, Flying Bye preserved the songs for future generations on two recordings.

DISCOGRAPHY:
Friend, Do It This Way: An Interpretation of the Pipe Filling Song [Center Records 2003]
The Night Is Sacred: Lakota Ceremonial Pipe Songs for Future Generations [Center Records 2001]

Fredlund, Rose—(Dene)

Born in Snare Lake, Northwest Territories, Fredlund learned the old ways of drum making, singing, and practicing medicine from her grandmother.

DISCOGRAPHY:
Maseecho [Sunshine 1997]

Goodhouse, Evelyn "Sissy"— (Lakota) *See*: Flute Music: Kevin Locke; Powwow Music: Common Man Singers

Educator, singer, activist, Goodhouse sings traditional Lakota songs, accompanied by nature sounds and the drum. Additional performers on her first release include Cedric Goodhouse Sr., Cedric Goodhouse Jr., J. D. Goodhouse, Bernice Goodhouse, Joe Many Bears, and Joe Flying Bye.

DISCOGRAPHY:
Tiwahe [Makoche 1997] w/ Kevin Locke
The Third Circle [Makoche 1994]
Spirit of Song [Makoche 1991]

Appearances:
Common Man Singers:
Songs for the Common Man [SOAR 157]
Spirit of Song [Makoche 1995]
Signals from the Heart [SOAR 1992]
Various:
Heartbeat 2: More Voices of First Nations Women [Smithsonian Folkways 1998] comp
Tribal Voices [Earth Beat! 1996] *See*: Contemporary Compilations

Haumpy, Bruce—(Kiowa)
DISCOGRAPHY:
Kiowa [Indian Records IR-655]
Kiowa [Indian Records IR-650] w/ Gertie Haumpy

Horncloud, William—(Lakota)

Born 1905, Medicine Root District, Pine Ridge, Potato Creek, South Dakota. Horncloud learned the traditional songs from Lakota elders throughout his life. He became well known on the powwow circuit as a singer and dancer, rodeo rider, orator, and interpreter of traditional songs and Lakota culture. In 1970, he conducted a number of workshops at Wesleyan University in Connecticut, teaching traditional music. A man known for his knowledge of culture and hospitality, Horncloud would host numerous guests, including Johnny Cash, who would spend time visiting and playing music.

DISCOGRAPHY:
Sioux Songs of War and Love [Canyon CR-6150]
Sings Sioux Rabbit Songs [Canyon 1971]
Sioux Love Song/Rabbit Dance Song [Can-

William Horncloud's 78-rpm single "Rabbit Dance Song" (circa 1952). Courtesy Canyon Records.

yon ARP 623, circa 1952] 78-rpm ten-inch vinyl

Appearances:
Enter Tribal [Canyon 2001] comp, w/ Cliff Sarde
Voices across the Canyon, Vol. 4 [Canyon 1999] comp *See*: Contemporary Compilations
Sioux Favorites [Canyon 1968] comp *See*: Powwow Music Complations
Authentic Music of the American Indian [Everest 3450/3, circa 1964] comp

Horne, Paula—(Dakota)

DISCOGRAPHY:
Heart Songs of Black Hills Woman [independent 1990]
Honor the Grandmothers [Kitchen Table Productions 1992] *See*: Contemporary Spoken Word: Miscellaneous

Horse, Roland, and Helen—(Kiowa)

DISCOGRAPHY:
Kiowa [Indian Records 656]

Hunting Horse, Billy—(Kiowa)

Recorded in Nashville, Tennessee, the album contains a collection of traditional Kiowa songs and 49ers.

DISCOGRAPHY:
Billy Hunting Horse Sings [Skylite Country Recordings SSC-7309]

Appearances:
Kiowa Gourd Dance, Vol. 2 [Indian House IH-2504] comp
Kiowa Gourd Dance, Vol. 1 [Indian House IH-2503] comp

Ironshell, James—(Lakota)

DISCOGRAPHY:
Lakota Sundance Songs [Cool Runnings 1998]

Ishi

Ishi was the last surviving member of the Yahi of northern California, who were hunted to extinction by white settlers in the late nineteenth to early twentieth centuries. He was found in 1911 and taken to the University of California Museum of Anthropology in San Francisco (now the Phoebe Hearst Museum, Berkeley, California), where he died of tuberculosis in 1916. These twelve tracks, culled from two hundred known recordings of Ishi's words and songs made by T. T. Waterman on Edison wax cylinder machines from 1911 to 1914, were remastered by Bernie Krause.

DISCOGRAPHY:
The Last Yahi [Wild Sanctuary 1992]

Jumper, Betty Mae—(Seminole) *See*: Contemporary Spoken Word: Legends and Storytelling

DISCOGRAPHY:

Appearances:

Crossroads, Southern Routes: Music of the American South [Smithsonian Folkways 1996] comp

Heartbeat: Voices of First Nations Women [Smithsonian/Folkways 1995] comp

Lame Deer—(Lakota Sioux)

Archie Fire Lame Deer sings traditional pipe and prayer songs; his father, John Fire Lame Deer, was recorded before his passing on December 14, 1976. Side two features two contemporary songs, "Wounded Knee" and "Medicine Man," written and performed by Paul Cypress, acoustic guitar, with John DeYoung, slide bass; recorded in Santa Barbara, California.

DISCOGRAPHY:

Medicine Man Chief of the Miniconju (Sioux) [Wambli Records 1980]

Looking Horse, Keith—(Lakota)

DISCOGRAPHY:

Sioux Songs [Indian Records IR-1173]

Mahone, Keith—(Hualapai)

DISCOGRAPHY:

Bird Songs of the Hualapai [Canyon 1996]

Appearances:

Sacred Souls [Manteca 2001, United Kingdom] *See*: Contemporary Compilations

Mahooty, Chester—(Zuni Pueblo)

See: Powwow Music: American Indian Dance Theater

Born 1928, Zuni Pueblo, New Mexico. A traditional song keeper, Mahooty established the Zuni Rainbow Dancers in the 1960s and worked with the American Indian Dance Theater in the 1980s.

Appearances:

American Indian Dance Theater:
American Indian Dance Theater [Broadway Limited Records 1984]

Various:
Spirit of the Native American Indians [ARC Music 1999, United Kingdom/Germany] comp

Between Father Sky and Mother Earth [Narada 1995] comp *See*: Contemporary Compilations

Talking Spirits [Music of the World 1992] comp

Traditional Global Voices [Music of the World MOW-146] comp

Michael, Sarah—(Mi'kmaq)

DISCOGRAPHY:

Mic Mac Songs [Sunshine SSCT-4163]

Mitchell, Davis—(Dineh)

DISCOGRAPHY:

Drummer Boy [SOAR 1996]

Songs from a Distant Drum [SOAR 137 1992]

A Good Year for the Rose [SOAR 1991]

The Navajo Kid Rides Again [SOAR 1990]

Navajo Singer Sings for You [SOAR 1988]

Appearances:

Soaring Hearts Tribal Peoples, Vol. 1 [SOAR 1996] comp

Various Native American Artists: Solo Flights, Vol. 1 [SOAR 1991] comp *See*: Contemporary Compilations

Moose, Warfield—(Lakota)

Words and interpretations of traditional songs of Black Elk sung by Warfield Moose Jr., Philomene Lakota, and Albert White Hat; Filomena Collins, associate producer.

DISCOGRAPHY:
Ben Black Elk Speaks [Yellow Spider Inc. 2002]

Morris, Ned—(Dineh)
DISCOGRAPHY:
Singing Navajo Songwriter [SOAR 1990]

Nanaba, Midge—(Dineh)
DISCOGRAPHY:
Traditional Navajo Songs [Canyon 1985]

Natay, Ed Lee—(Dineh)

Ed Lee Natay was the first singer to record for Canyon Records in 1951 and made two albums before his death in 1966.

DISCOGRAPHY:
Memories of Navajoland [Canyon CR-6057]
Natay: Navajo Singer [Canyon 1951]

Appearances:
The Rough Guide to Native American Music [Rough Guides 1998] comp

Nez, Billie—(Dineh) *See*: Peyote Music

Nez, D. J.—(Dineh)
DISCOGRAPHY:
Navajo in Paris [SOAR 1991]
My Heroes Have Always Been Indians [SOAR 1990]

Appearances:
Creation's Journey [Smithsonian/Folkways 1994] comp
Oyate [Nato 1990, France] comp *See*: Contemporary Compilations

Nightwalker, Roy—(Southern Cheyenne)

DISCOGRAPHY:
Southern Cheyenne Songs [Indian Records IR-322]
Southern Cheyenne Songs [Indian Records IR-320]
Southern Cheyenne [Indian Records IR-332A] w/ James Ola Mae
Southern Cheyenne [Indian Records IR-331A] w/ James Ola Mae

Obomsawin, Alanis—(Abenaki) *See*: Contemporary Music

Obomsawin recorded six traditional songs for radio broadcast to communities in northern Canada.

DISCOGRAPHY:
Indian Songs [CBC Northern Service QC-1406]

Quiltman—(Warm Springs Confederated Tribes) *See*: Contemporary Music: John Trudell

DISCOGRAPHY:
Three Sisters [Earth Beat! 1999]
Quiltman and Tewahnee: Traditional Songs [independent 1997] cass

Appearances:
Alcatraz Is Not an Island [James Fortier, 2002] score
Tribal Legends [Earth Beat! 2002] comp
Ravenous [Virgin 1999] sdtk
Tribal Fires [Earth Beat! 1997] comp

Running, Norbert—(Lakota)
DISCOGRAPHY:
Mitakuye Oyasin: Contemporary Lakota Sundance Songs [Red Road 1993]

Siwash, Claude—(Shoshone-Paiute)

DISCOGRAPHY:
36 Shoshone Paiute Songs [Indian Records IR-1161B]
36 Shoshone Paiute Songs [Indian Records IR-1161A]

Standing Deer; a.k.a. Pha-Quen-Nee-e—(Tiwa)

From Taos, New Mexico.

DISCOGRAPHY:
One Voice [White Wing 1993]

Tenakhongva, Clark—(Hopi)

Born at Keams Canyon, Arizona, 1957. He lived in Hotevilla, Third Mesa, Arizona.

DISCOGRAPHY:
Hear My Song, Hear My Prayer [Canyon 2003]

Thompson, Nick—(White Mountain Apache)

DISCOGRAPHY:
Cibecue Songs, Vol. 2 [Canyon CR-702] ten-inch 78-rpm vinyl
Cibecue Songs, Vol. 1 [Canyon CR-701]

Trejo, Judy—(Summit Lake Paiute)

Stick Game Songs of the Paiute received the NAMA for Best Historical Recording, 2000.

DISCOGRAPHY:
Stick Game Songs of the Paiute [Canyon 1999]
Circle Dance Songs of the Paiute and Shoshone [Canyon 1997]

Appearances:
Sacred Souls [Manteca 2001, United Kingdom] *See*: Contemporary Compilations

Tsinajinnie, Delphine—(Dineh) *See*: Contemporary Music: Keith Secola

Tsinajinnie (pronounced "sin-a-jinee") is a descendant of traditional Blessingway and Nightway medicine men of the Nihookaa Dineh. He has performed as part of Keith Secola's Wild Band of Indians.

DISCOGRAPHY:
Mother's Word [Canyon 2000]

Appearances:
Enter Tribal [Canyon 2001] comp; w/ Cliff Sarde

Tsosie Clark, Ned—(Dineh)

DISCOGRAPHY:
King of the Navajo Song and Dance [SOAR 107]

Wahpe Kute—(Dakota)

DISCOGRAPHY:
Dakota Songs [Featherstone FT-1002]

Walker, James

DISCOGRAPHY:
Omaha [Indian Records IR-827A]
Omaha [Indian Records IR-826A]

Washington, Joe—(Lummi)

Spiritual leader, lecturer, teacher, and counselor, Joe Washington made this recording with his wife, Martha, and son, Joseph Jr., along the banks of the Nooksack River on the Lummi Reservation, Washington.

DISCOGRAPHY:
Stick Game Songs [Canyon 1975]

Wathahine—(Mohawk) *See*:
Traditional/Archival Group:
Kanenhi:io

Traditional Mohawk social songs.

DISCOGRAPHY:
Journey [independent 1999]

Appearances:
*Native to Canada: Showcase of Aborigi-
nal Musicians at WOMEX 2000* [Canada
Council for the Arts 2001] comp *See*:
Contemporary Compilations

Videos:
Dahlia Wathahine [Raven Films/DMK/
Bravo!/FACTOR 1997]

Wettlin-Larsen, Georgia—
(Assiniboine-Nakota)

A trained singer and educator, Wettlin-
Larsen performed traditional songs and
stories for radio and television, including
Song of the Land, National Public Radio,
and *Northern Exposure* [CBS 1995].

DISCOGRAPHY:
*From the Sky: Native Stories in Song and
Sound* [Allies 1997]
Songs of the People [Featherstone FS-4003]

Appearances:
*Heartbeat 2: More Voices of First Nations
Women* [Smithsonian Folkways 1995]
comp
More Music from Northern Exposure [MCA
1994] sdtk *See*: Contemporary Soundtracks

Whiteman, Philip—(Cheyenne)

DISCOGRAPHY:
Northern Cheyenne Songs [Indian Records
IR-308B] w/ Jimmy Redcloud
Northern Cheyenne Songs [Indian Records
IR-308A] w/ Jimmy Redcloud
Northern Cheyenne Songs [Indian Records
IR-306]
Northern Cheyenne Songs [Indian Records
IR-305]

Wilson, Chesley Goseyun—(Apache)
See: Contemporary Music: Brent
Michael Davids

Historian-lecturer Chesley Goseyun Wilson preserved and revived the traditional
Apache violin, constructed from the agave
or century plant. Wilson was awarded the
National Heritage Fellowship given by
the Folk Arts Program of the National
Endowment for the Arts. His instrument
was used in performance with the Kronos
Quartet. He coauthored the book *When
the Earth Was Like New: Western Apache
Songs and Stories* [World Music Press 1994]
with Ruth Longcor Harnisch Wilson and
Bryan Burton.

DISCOGRAPHY:
When Earth Was Like New [World Music
Press 1994]

Appearances:
*Wood That Sings: Indian Fiddle Music of
the Americas* [Smithsonian/Folkways
1997] comp

Section 7-B
Traditional/ Archival Group Recordings

Allegheny Singers—(Seneca)

Lineup: Louis Castellano; Barney Clark; Bobby Cooper; Bill Crouse (*See*: Contemporary Music: Chief Rock); Dar, Kerwin, Kory, and Kyle Dowdy; Al George; Kevin Johnny-John; Steve Skye.

Their recorded collections contain many social dances including the stick dance, corn dance, smoke dance, cousin's dance, canoe dance, gartered dance. Recorded at Seneca, New York, February 29, 1996.

DISCOGRAPHY:
Earth Songs, Vol. 4 [independent 2002]
Earth Songs, Vol. 3 [independent 2002]
Earth Songs, Vol. 2 [independent 2002]
Earth Songs, Vol. 1 [independent 2002]

Beclabito Valley Singers—(Dineh)

Lineup: Daniel Van Lee, Willie Lee, John Blue Eyes, Henry Yabeny, Francis Morgan, Paul C. Benally, Dave Johnson, Harry Harrison, Jessie Smith, Rosemary Lee, May Lee, Helen Toglena.

DISCOGRAPHY:
Navajo Skip and Two-Step Dance Songs [Canyon CR-7151]
Skip and Two Step Dance Songs [Canyon CR-7150]

Big Mountain Singers—(Shoshone)

Lineup: Lenore, Lottie, Coleen, JoAnn, Linda, Maxine, Evalita, Emily, Helene, Wayland, and Dorothy Shoyo singing solo and as a group. Women singers and drummers of the Shoshone Nation in Nevada provided the audio portion for a book on Shoshone music by Judith Vander.

DISCOGRAPHY:
Songprints: The Musical Experience of Five Shoshone Women [University of Illinois Press 1988]

Bita Hochee Travellers—(Dineh)

Lineup: Ned Morris, Lee Begay, Ned Morris Jr., Gilbert Begay, Lee Begay Jr.

DISCOGRAPHY:
Two Step Songs [Canyon CR-8042]
Bita Hochee Travelers, Vol. 3 [Canyon CR-8041]
Bita Hochee Travelers, Vol. 2 [Canyon CR-8040]
Midnight Sweetheart [Canyon CR-6168] comp

Chinle Swingin' Echoes—(Dineh)

DISCOGRAPHY:
Voices from Canyon de Chelley [SOAR 110]

Chinle Valley Boys—(Dineh)

Lineup: Eddie Jones, Bonnie Begay, Jimmy Shorty, John Hardy, Gjermundson Yazzie, Harry Yellowhair, Danny Begay, Pat Ashley.

DISCOGRAPHY:
The Hearts of Navajoland, Vol. 2 [Canyon CR-7127]
Navajo Two Step and Skip Dance Songs, Vol. 1 [Canyon CR-7126]

Chinle Valley Singers—(Dineh)

Lineup: Elizabeth Davis, Elsie Deswood, Anita Davis, Esther Davis, Linda Teller, Geraldine Little.

DISCOGRAPHY:
Navajo Two Step, Skip Dance, and Double Time Songs [Canyon CR-7134]

Cove Nava Tune Singers—(Dineh)

Lineup: Ray, Rex, Tom, Reed, and Roger Lee; Gilbert Begay.

DISCOGRAPHY:
Navajo Two Step and Skip Dance Songs [Canyon CR-7131]

Dawnland Singers—(Abenaki)

Lineup: Joseph Bruchac (*See*: Contemporary Spoken Word: Legends and Storytelling); Jesse and Marge Bruchac; Awassos Sigan; Pablo Hurtado, flute. Recorded at Silver Fox Studios, Ballston Spa, New York.

DISCOGRAPHY:
Alnobak [Good Mind Records 1994]

Dene Singers—(Dene) Traditional Hand Drum

Lineup: Louie (Nambainnare), Modest (Denechzhe), and Alphonse (Gasayou). Three elders from Lac Brochet, Saskatchewan, made the first recording of traditional hand drum songs that originated from their area.

DISCOGRAPHY:
Denesuline Drum Songs [Sunshine 2002]

Dennehotso Swinging Wranglers—(Dineh)

Lineup: Wesley Gray, Harold Richards, Reeder Dee, Johnny Richards, Herbert Featherhat, Dickson Hoshnic, Tully Blackmountain.

DISCOGRAPHY:
Navajo Two Step and Skip Dance Songs [Canyon CR-7130]
Navajo Skip Dance Songs [Canyon CR-7129]
Swing with the Wranglers: Navajo Two Step and Skip Dance Songs [Canyon CR-7128]

Dine'Ba'Aliil of Navajoland, USA—
(Dineh)

Lineup: W. Dean Wilson, Roswell Bennett, Bill Sunrise, Paul Mason, Pearl Sunrise, Evelyn Becenti.

DISCOGRAPHY:
Navajo Songs and Dances [Canyon CR-6117]

Fisher, Burton, and George Fisher—(Northern Cheyenne)

DISCOGRAPHY:
Northern Cheyenne Songs [Indian Records IR-304]
Northern Cheyenne Songs [Indian Records IR-303]

Four Corners Singers of Teec Nos Pos

Lineup: Woody Johnson, David Jim, Clarence Weston, Tom Lowe, Robert Gould, Leo Johnson, and Calvin Weston.

DISCOGRAPHY:
Four Corners Singers, Vol. 5 [Canyon CR-8143]
Navajo Skip and Two Step Dance Songs [Canyon CR-8049]
Navajo Two Step Dance-Love Songs [Canyon CR-8048]
Navajo Skip Dance Songs [Canyon CR-8044]

Garcia, Peter, and the Garcia Brothers—(San Juan Pueblo) *See*: Oku Shareh

DISCOGRAPHY:
Songs of My People [Music of the World MOW-133]

Appearances:
Global Voices: Traditional [Music of the World MOW-146] comp

Turtle Dance Songs of the San Juan Pueblo [Indian House 1972] comp
Cloud Dance Songs of the San Juan Pueblo [Indian House 1971] comp

JJ Singers

DISCOGRAPHY:
Traditional Navajo Songs [Cool Runnings 1998]

Johnson, Art, and Lyle Anderson—
(Cayuga and Mohawk)

DISCOGRAPHY:
Iroquois Social Songs, Vol. 2 [OH-0028 2002]
Earth Songs, Vol. 1 [NFA-075 1998]

Kai-Spai Singers—(Blackfoot) *See*: Powwow Music

Wayne, Dean, and Theresa Plume; George and Georgina Whiteman; Domenic Cross Child; Joe and Wayne Beebe; Diana Bull Shields. Based in Alberta.

DISCOGRAPHY:
Songs of the Blood Reserve [Canyon 1975]

Kanenhi:io

Lineup: Lucia Sahanatien (Innu), Isabel Saez (Mapuche), Lorrie Leduc (Mohawk), Shirley Hay (Mohawk), Karen Peltier (Odawa), Wathahine (Mohawk), Anna Stock (Innu). Modern intertribal interpretations of Mohawk songs.

DISCOGRAPHY:
Kanenhi:io [independent 1999]

Klagetoh Maidens

Lineup: Joycetta, Rose, and Winnie Bonnie; Marie Brown; Bertha Johnson. Recorded in Klagetoh, Arizona, April 21, 1974; includes spin dance, walking dance, round dance, and two-step.

DISCOGRAPHY:
24 Social Dance Songs [Indian House 1975]

Klagetoh Swingers

1974 Lineup: Amos and Frank Begay, Ted Bonnie, Ned Clark, Ben Johnson, Joe Roanhorse. *1968 Lineup*: Boniface Bonnie, Autisdy Smith, Ben Johnson, Donald and Mary Deal, Stella and Winnie Bonnie, Nellie Curley. Recorded in Klagetoh, Arizona.

DISCOGRAPHY:
Navajo Songs about Love, Vol. 6 [Indian House 1982]
Navajo Songs about Love, Vol. 5 [Indian House 1981]
Navajo Songs about Love, Vol. 4 [Indian House 1978]
Navajo Songs about Love, Vol. 3 [Indian House 1978]
Navajo Songs about Love, Vol. 2 [Indian House 1976]
Navajo Songs about Love, Vol. 1 [Indian House 1975]
Navajo Corn Grinding and Shoe Game Songs [Indian House 1974]
Navajo Sway Songs [Indian House 1968]
Navajo Skip and Two Step Songs [Indian House 1968]
Navajo Round Dance [Indian House 1968]
Navajo Gift Songs and Round Dance Songs [Indian House 1968]
Night and Daylight Yeibichei [Indian House 1968] winter ceremony songs

Kontirennotatie—(Mohawk)

Lineup: Katiatant, Karonienhowe, Kaiatanoiron, Wenhni'tanoiron, Telohsera'hthe, Otsitsa'onwe Gaspe, Kahentiio'hstha Smith. From Kanehsatake, Quebec.

DISCOGRAPHY:
Kanehsatake Women Singers [independent 2000]

Koomsa Tribal Singers

Lineup: Bill Koomsa Sr., Billy Hunting Horse, Wilbur Kodaseet, Lonnie Tsotaddle, Georgia Dupoint, Bill Koomsa Jr., Ann and Martha Koomsa, Pearl Woodard.

DISCOGRAPHY:
Kiowa Scalp and Victory Dance Songs [Canyon CR-6166 1977]
Kiowa War, 49, and Horse Stealing Songs [Canyon CR-6145 1975]

Louie Traditional Singers—(Carrier)

Lineup: Martin, Zar, Veronica, Anita, Miriam, and Ozzie Louie; Bruce and Sadie Allen; Rose and Stan Luggi; Tanya Stump; Leonie Spurr. Recorded in Prince George, British Columbia.

DISCOGRAPHY:
Songs of the Carriers [independent 2000]

Lupton Valley Singers—(Dineh)
Women's Group

DISCOGRAPHY:
Summer Memories [SOAR 106]

Mesquakie Bear Singers

Lineup: Wayne and Adrian Pushetonequa, Alvin and Gaylord Bear, Mike Mitchell of the Mesquakie Red Earth People of Tama, Iowa.

DISCOGRAPHY:
War Dance Songs [Canyon CR-6090]

Molina and Valencia—(Yaqui)

DISCOGRAPHY:
Yaqui Pascola Music of Arizona [Canyon CR-7998]

Navajo Centennial Dance Team

DISCOGRAPHY:
Navajo Squaw Dance Songs [Canyon CR-6067] comp

Navajo Mountain Swingers

DISCOGRAPHY:
Traditional Skip and Two Step Songs [Cool Runnings 1999]

Oku Shareh

Lineup: Herman Agoyo; Anthony Archuleta; Cipriano, Peter, and Jerry Garcia; Steven Trujillo. Recorded at San Juan Pueblo, New Mexico, 1974.

DISCOGRAPHY:
Turtle Dance Songs of the San Juan Pueblo [New World Records 1979]

Red Shadow Singers

Lineup: Dave Courchene Jr., Dave Courchene III, Kyoki Iizuka, Rhonda and Dwyane McCorrister, Danny Quillet, Garnet and Stanley Stevenson, Adam Courchene, Shirley Guimond, Marie Mockers, Jenny Fontain, Michael Rundle, Lloyd and Darren Flett.

Proceeds from their recording were earmarked for the Mother Earth Spiritual Camp, where traditional teachings and lifestyles are shared. This collection of spiritual songs is intended for private use.

DISCOGRAPHY:
Red Shadow Singers [Sunshine SSCT-4165]

Riley and Endfield—(Apache)

DISCOGRAPHY:
Songs of the Arizona Apache [Canyon CR-705]

Rock Point Singers—(Dineh)

Lineup: Harry Tso Begay, Julius Begay, Glen Tsosie, Ken Woody Jr., Sam Woody. Formed in 1976; *Navajo Skip and Two Step Songs*, vols. 1 and 2, were recorded at Rock Point, Arizona, November 22, 1984.

DISCOGRAPHY:
Traditional Love Tunes [Canyon 1989]
Squaw Dance Love Songs, Vol. 3 [Canyon CR-7140]
Navajo Love Call, Vol. 2 [Canyon CR-8047]
Memory Love Songs, Vol. 1 [Canyon CR-8046]
Navajo Skip and Two Step Songs, Vol. 2 [Indian House IH-1532]
Navajo Skip and Two Step Songs, Vol. 1 [Indian House IH-1531]

Romero, Fred, and Taos Singers—(Taos Pueblo)

DISCOGRAPHY:
Taos Friendship Song/Taos Horse Tail Dance [Canyon ARP-154, circa 1952, 78-rpm ten-inch vinyl

Rosebud Sioux Singers—*See*: William Horncloud

DISCOGRAPHY:
Rosebud Omaha Song #2 / Rosebud Omaha Song #3 [Canyon ARP-673] 78-rpm ten-inch vinyl

San Juan Singers

Lineup: Thomas Blackhorse, Stan Benally Sr., Ken and Harry Benally, Tim Blackhorse, Jim Bitsilly, Paul Anderson, Jerry Jerome.

DISCOGRAPHY:
Navajo Traditional Two Step Songs [Canyon CR-7125]
Navajo Skip Dance Songs [Indian House 1979]

Selam and Hill—(Yakima)

DISCOGRAPHY:
Songs of a Yakima Encampment [Canyon CR-6129]

Sioux Singers

Sioux singers from Pine Ridge, Rosebud, Fort Thompson, and Cheyenne River.

DISCOGRAPHY:
Sioux Song/Rabbit Dance [Canyon ARP-613, circa 1953] 78-rpm ten-inch vinyl

Sioux Travelers

A selection that includes six Sioux war dances.

DISCOGRAPHY:
12 Sioux Songs [Indian Records IRC-1193]

Six Nations Singers—(Iroquois)

Lineup: Gordon Buck, Hubert Buck Sr., Hubert Buck Jr., Amos Keye Jr.

DISCOGRAPHY:
Iroquois Social Music [Music Gallery/ Woodland Indian Cultural Education Centre, circa 1974]

Six Nations Women Singers—

(Iroquois) *See*: Contemporary Music: Robbie Robertson, Russell Wallace

Lineup: Charlene Bomberry, Sadie Buck, Betsy Buck, Pat Hess, Janice Martin, Jaynane Burning.

DISCOGRAPHY:
We Will All Sing [SOAR 1996]

Appearances:
Gathering of Nations Pow-Wow 1995 [SOAR 1996] comp

Sons of Membertou—(Mi'kmaq) Trad/Folk

Lineup: Darrell Bernard; Graham Marshall; Victor, George, Mark, and Austin Christmas; Calvin Paul; Lincoln Gould; George Smith; Angelo Laporte; Rodney Bear; Dawn Isadore.

They combine spoken word and natural sounds with traditional Mi'kmaq music and contemporary instruments. They appeared with Nova Scotia–based singer John Gracie on his album *Identity*, which received a Juno nomination for Best Music of Aboriginal Canada, 2001.

DISCOGRAPHY:
Wapna'kik: The People of the Dawn [independent 1995]

Appearances:
John Gracie:
Identity [Tidemark 1999]

Sound Chief Singers—(Kiowa)

Lineup: James Anquoe, Nathan Doyebi, Ernest and Ruth Red Bird.

DISCOGRAPHY:
Kiowa Tribal Circle and Two-Step Songs [Sound Chiefs SC-266]
Kiowa Tribal Warrior Dances [Sound Chiefs SC-139]

Kiowa Warriors Dance Songs and Kiowa War Expedition Songs [Sound Chiefs SC-131]

Southern Maidens

Lineup: Lucy Bitsilly; Mary Chee; Irene, Marlene, Mary Lou, and Darlene Kinle-cheenie.

DISCOGRAPHY:
Navajo Skip and Two Step Songs [Indian House 1984]

Southwestern Singers—(Dineh)

Lineup: Bill and Annie McCabe, Danny and Helena Largo, Richard and Rita Begay.

DISCOGRAPHY:
Navajo Skip and Two Step Songs [Cool Runnings 1999]
Lexus [Canyon 1997]
Two-Step and Skip Dance Songs, Vol. 2 [Canyon 1996]
Two-Step and Skip Dance Songs, Vol. 1 [Canyon 1995]

Sweethearts of Navajoland

Lineup: Lillian Ashley, Darleen Juan, Pauline Hardie, Marleen Bengay, Linda Nez.

DISCOGRAPHY:
Traditional Value Songs [Canyon 1996]
Social Songs, Vol. 5 [Canyon 1995]
Social Songs, Vol. 4 [Canyon 1993]
Exploring Europe [Canyon 1992]
Traditional Two-Step Songs [Canyon 1991]
Traditional Two-Step Songs [Canyon 1990]

Takini *See: Amérique du Nord* comp

Lineup: Birgil Kills Straight and Kevin Locke, with Helga Lomosits and Alain Bray, producers.

DISCOGRAPHY:
Amérique du Nord: Music and Songs of the Lakota Sioux [Le Chant du Monde 1994/ 1998/1999, France]
Amérique du Nord: Music and Songs of the Lakota Sioux [Le Chant du Monde 1994, France]

Tatanka Oyate Singers—(Lakota)

Lineup: James Chase; Silas Drum; Tom Escarcega; Victor Fast Horse Sr.; Albert Foote Sr.; Bernard Youpee; Donald Iceman III; Anthony Bear Roberts; Chuck, Elwayne, and Lele and Spotted Bird. Recorded at Fort Peck, Montana.

DISCOGRAPHY:
Prayer and Sun Dance Songs Tatanka Oyate, Vol. 3 [Indian House 2000]
Prayer and Sun Dance Songs Tatanka Oyate, Vol. 2 [Indian House 2000]
Prayer and Sun Dance Songs Tatanka Oyate, Vol. 1 [Indian House 2000]

Tewa Women's Choir of San Juan Pueblo

The collection contains four original songs composed in the Tewa language for Catholic mass, Tewa versions of "Amazing Grace" and "How Great Thou Art," and three Ange-in (traditional San Juan Pueblo spiritual songs), accompanied by gourds, drum, turtle shells, and organ. Recorded in the church at San Juan Pueblo, New Mexico, April 26, 1994.

DISCOGRAPHY:
Songs from the Tewa Mass [Indian House TWC-1 1994]

Thunderbird Maidens—(Dineh)

Lineup: Tara, Terrilyn, and Therea Crank; Edie and Ziggy Baca; Keithryn Hyden; LaTanya Keams. Ranging in age from five to fourteen years, all singers attended the Tuba City Boarding School, Arizona. Songs composed by the school's language and cultural instructor Leo Begay; recorded by Allen Moore, March 26, 1995.

DISCOGRAPHY:
Young Voices of the Western Navajo [Canyon 1995]

Todi Neesh Zhee Singers

Original Lineup: Albert Nelson Jr.; Elliot, Elmer, and Alger Greyeyes; Paul Boone; Lonnie Yazzie; Ezra Greymountain; Everett Salt.
   Millennium Lineup: Albert Nelson; Alger, Herbert, Everett Jr., and Elmer Greyeyes; Albert Nelson Jr.; Paul Boone; Leander Seaton; Jerome and Harry Austin; Albert Nelson III; Jerome Cly; Gary Nelson; with Robert Tree Cody (*See*: Flute Music).

DISCOGRAPHY:
For All Eternity: Traditional Navajo Two-Step and Skip Dances [Canyon 2001]
Through the Old Eyes the Young Arise: Navajo Two-Step and Skip Dance Songs [Canyon 1995]
Dedicated to the Younger Generation: Navajo Two-Step and Skip Dance Songs [Canyon 1984]

Tsi Yi Tohi Singers; a.k.a. Woodspring Singers—(Dineh)

Lineup: Paul, Erin, and Ann Dokey; Miller and Mary Dedman; Vera Shirley.

DISCOGRAPHY:
Navajo Two-Step Songs, Vol. 3 [Canyon CR-7153]
Navajo Skip and Two Step Dance Songs [Canyon 1987]

Turtle Mountain Singers—(Dineh)

Lineup: John Comanche, Jimmie Castillo, Sam Harrison, John Dennison, Kee and Benson Trujillo, Ernest Chavez, Renzo Comanche. *Navajo Social Dance Songs* and *Navajo Songs Eastern Style* were recorded at Lybrook, New Mexico, March 14, 1987; *Welcome to Navajoland* was recorded at Lybrook, New Mexico, April 14, 1990; *Early This Morning* was recorded at Taos, New Mexico, June 23, 1990.

DISCOGRAPHY:
Early This Morning I Heard My Horse Calling [Indian House IH-1526]
Welcome to Navajoland [Indian House IH-1525]
Navajo Songs Eastern Style [Indian House IH-1524]
Navajo Social Dance Songs [Indian House IH-1523]

Tzo'kam *See*: Contemporary Music: Russell Wallace

Lineup: Flora Wallace, Joyce Fossella, Irma Rabang, Freda Wallace, Judy Wallace-Lemke, and Russell Wallace; cousin Maria Stiglich; and Flora's grandson Cyrus Point. Old and new songs from Mount Currie and Lillooet, British Columbia, in the Stalimx language (*See*: Compilations: *Hearts of the Nations*).

DISCOGRAPHY:
It'em "to Sing" [Red Planet Records 2000]

Appearances:
Under the Green Corn Moon [Silver Wave 1998] comp

Wind River Singers

DISCOGRAPHY:
Songs of the Arapaho Sun Dance [Canyon CR-6080]

Wood Brothers

DISCOGRAPHY:
Cree Stick Game Songs [Canyon CR-16228]

Woodland Singers

DISCOGRAPHY:
Traditional Mesquakie Songs [Canyon 1987]

Yakima Nation Singers

Status Longhouse Singers led by Gilbert Onepennee of Status, Washington.

DISCOGRAPHY:
Yakima Nation of Status Longhouse [Canyon CR-6126]

Section 7-C
Traditional/ Archival Compilation Recordings

Aboriginal Women's Voices in Concert [ANDPVA 1992] *See: Hearts of the Nations* comp

Lineup: Sadie Buck (Seneca) of the Six Nations Women Singers; Jacqui Lavalley (Anishnabekwe); Sandy Scofield (Metis; *See*: Contemporary Music); Honey Rose Ada White (Coast Salish–Umatilla); Margaret Mercredi (Anishnabekwe); Sharon King (Potawatomi); Kelly White (Coast Salish); Anita Anquoe George (Kiowa); Cornelia Bowannie (Zuni); Maggie Paul (Passamaquoddy); Marjorie Beaucage (Metis); Shelley Charles (Anishnabekwe). Recorded with support from the Association for Native Development in the Performing and Visual Arts and the Banff Centre for the Arts.

Across Indian Lands [SOAR 1999]

Lineup: Bryan Akipa (*See*: Flute Music); Earl Bullhead; Jack Anquoe; Eastern Canada Singers; Alexander Santos; Whitewind; Jay Begaye; Wil Numkena; Cornel Pewewardy (*See*: Flute Music); Yamparika; Paul Guy and Teddy Allen; Ken Scabby Robe and Blacklodge (*See*: Powwow Music).

All the Best from the American Indian: 26 Great Favorites [Madacy CLUC-CD51]

A Canadian bootleg recording of unaccredited songs from Apache, Arapaho, Arikira, Cheyenne, Crow, Dineh, Hopi, Kiowa, Omaha, Paiute, Pawnee, Ponca, Shawnee, Sioux, Taos Pueblo, Ute Zuni.

American Indian Ceremonial and War Dances [Tradition 2208]

Apache, Arapaho, Arikira, Cheyenne, Dineh, Kiowa, Ponca, Sioux, Taos Pueblo, Tohono O'odham, Ute.

American Indian Dances [Ethnic Folkways 1958]

Music of the Dineh, Sioux, Apache, San Ildefonso, Zuni, Flathead, Blackfoot. Designed as a teaching aid for scout troops and classrooms, featuring thirteen different dances with notes on arm and body movements, costumes, and steps compiled and collected by Ronnie and Stu Lipner.

American Indian Dances: Great Lakes Indians [ARC 1995, United Kingdom]

The collection is divided into two categories, Algonquin and Iroquois, and they are listed here as they were printed in the original liner notes: Wilson Roberts, Meskwaki of Tama, Iowa (1957); Fred Lacasse, Anishnabe of Lac du Flambeau, Wisconsin, with George Brown, Sam Link, and John Martin; Thomas Shalifoe, Anishnabe of Baraga, Michigan; Susan Shaonaby, (L'Arbre Croche), Michigan; David Kenosha, Odawa of Cross Village (L'Arbre Croche), Michigan; Whitney Albert (Blue Cloud), Odawa of Mikado, Michigan; Eli Thomas, Anishnabe of Isabella Reservation, Michigan; Percy Smoke, Onondaga, New York; Richard Buck, Cayuga-Tutelo of Six Nations Reserve, Ontario; Thomas Lewis, Onondaga, of Nedrow, New York; Huron Miller, Onondaga-Tuscarora of Six Nations Reserve, Ontario. Licensed from the Smithsonian Folkways recordings, 1996.

American Warriors: Songs for Indian Veterans [Ryko 1997] *See*: Powwow Music, various

Lineup: Blacklodge; Eniwube of Lac du Flambeau, Wisconsin, recorded by Frances Densmore, 1910; Edgar Red Cloud, 1972; Carnegie War Mothers Chapter Singers from the *Indians for Indians Hour* radio program on WNAD, University of Oklahoma broadcast during World War II; Win-nebago Sons; Smokeytown Singers; Fort Kipp Singers; the Sioux Valley Singers.

Amérique du Nord—(Lakota) *See*: Traditional/Archival Group: Takini

Takini Singers Lineup: Dean Rouillard, Ted Phelps, Branden McBride, Nathen Bennett, Jackie Rouillard, Tashina Sape Thunder Hawk, Bryan Akipa (*See*: Flute Music).

Eagle Mountain Singers Lineup: Dean Rouillard, Ted Phelps, Branden McBride, Nathen Bennett, Jackie Rouillard, Tashina Sape Thunder Hawk, Dusty Phelps, Lee Tenorio, Ben Iron Hawk, Austin Last Horse Jr., Matthew Phelps.

The recordings were developed through the Lakota Project of Pine Ridge, South Dakota, an exchange program with the assistance of the Working Group for Indigenous Peoples, United Nations, Geneva.

DISCOGRAPHY:
Takini: Musique et chants des Lakota Sioux, Vol. 2 [Le Chant du Monde 1998, France]
Takini: Musique et chants des Lakota Sioux [Le Chant du Monde 1994, France]

Anthology of North American Indian and Eskimo Music [Ethnic Folkways FE-4541] two LPs

Includes songs from the Assiniboine, Apache, Cayuga, Hopi, Inuit, Naskapi, Onandaga, Plains Cree, Sioux, Tuscarora, and others.

Apache [Library of Congress L42]

Lineup: Macklin Palmer; Sinew Riley; Clarence Peaches; Sam Haozous; James Humes. Crown dance songs, sunrise songs, Apache violin, girls' puberty rites songs, and others. Recorded by Willard Rhodes, 1940–52.

Apache [Canyon ARP-6053]

Brother and sister Philip and Patsy Cassadore (*See*: Traditional/Archival Solo) sing the songs handed down from their father, Broken Arrow; recorded 1966.

Apache Music of the American Indian [Library of Congress AFS L42]

Arapaho: Arapaho War Dance Songs and Round Dance Songs [Canyon 1972]
Arapaho: Social Songs of the Arapaho Sun Dance [Canyon 1970]

Lineup: Wind River Singers: Felix Groesbeck, Duane Tillman, Clark Trumbull Jr., Melvin Brown, Irma Groesbeck, Ambrosia Harris. Fort Washakie, Wyoming.

Authentic Music of the American Indian, Vol. 1: *War Dances and Honor Songs*
Authentic Music of the American Indian, Vol. 2: *Social Songs and Folk Songs*
Authentic Music of the American Indian, Vol. 3: *Ceremonial Songs and Chants* [Everest 3450/3, circa 1964] three-record set

Presents music and songs of the Akimel O'odham, Apache, Arikira, Cheyenne, Crow, Dineh, Hopi, Omaha, Paiute, Pawnee, Ponca, Sioux, Taos, Tewa, Tohono O'odham, Ute, Zuni. The original three-record set was accompanied by a hardcover book; now a deleted album collection, segments of the original recording have been bootlegged and reissued under numerous titles, including *Tribal Songs of the American Indian* [Prestige/Madacy 1995].
Original Lineup: Oglala Sioux Singers: William Horncloud (*See*: Traditional/Ar-

chival Solo), Ben Sitting Up and Frank Afraid Of His Horses; T. Night Walker and the White Skunk Singers (Cheyenne); Chief Spotted Back Hamilton and the Ponca Singers; White Shield Singers of North Dakota: Ralph Wells Jr., John Fox Sr., Chas Ross, Ralph Wells III, Tom Wells, Sam Howling Wolf; Morris Medicine, Pam Medicine, B. Pimpy (Cheyenne); Chief Spotted Back Hamilton and the Omaha Singers; Adam Trujillo and the Taos Singers; Dave Apakaun, William Koosma, and the Kiowa Singers; Reg Begay; Joe Lee; Roger McCabe (Dineh); Patsy and Philip Cassadore (Apache); Donald Deernose (Crow); Little Axe Singers; Rough Arrow and the Phoenix Plains Singers; Leo and Valentino Lecapa (Tewa); Mr. and Mrs. Bert Red, Eddie Box, James Mills (Ute); Dan Thomas and Paul Martin (Akimel O'odham); Fort Peck Sioux Singers; C. Hoffman and the San Carlos Apaches; Dick Young and the San Carlos Apaches; Northern Cheyenne Singers: Phil Whiteman, Tom Wooden Legs, Gilbert White Dirt, Harvey Whitman, Ross Teeth, James Red Cloud; Northern Arapaho Singers; Big Fields Villagers (Tohono O'odham); Mesa Verde Group Singers; Hopi Singers of Second Mesa; Wilbur Jack, Johnny Buffalo (Paiute).

Blackfeet Grass Dance and Owl Dance Songs [Sound Chiefs SC-104]

Lineup: Edward and Wilbur Morning Owl from Cardston, Alberta. Recorded 1962.

Blackfeet Grass Dance Songs [Sound Chiefs SC-100]

Lineup: Allen White Grass, Pat Kennedy, and Stanley Whiteman. Recorded Browning, Montana, July 2, 1960.

Blackfeet Hand Game Songs
[Canyon CR-6188]

Lineup: Thomas Big Spring and Floyd Henry Runner. Recorded 1986.

Caddo Tribal Dances [Sound Chiefs SC-300]

Lineup: Mr. and Mrs. Houston Edmonds, Mr. and Mrs. Lewis Edmonds, and Lowell Edmonds. Recorded Anadarko, Oklahoma, March 26, 1955. The recording features a variety of songs, including turkey dance, duck dance, green corn dance, bell dance, fish dance, stirrup dance.

The Canadian Blackfoot Indians
[Lyrichord 1982] *See*: Powwow Music: Scalp Lock Singers

Scalp Lock Singers Lineup: Alex Scalp Lock, Clarence Wolf Leg, Irvine, Arthur and Sheldon Scalp Lock.

Chants by the Cree [CBC Northern Service Broadcast Recording QCS-1458] Heritage Series

Recorded at Fort George, northern Quebec, with Joseph Rupert, George Pepabano, and William Kistenapo.

Chinle Valley Song and Dance Festival: Navajo Skip Dance Songs
[Canyon CR-7133]
Chinle Valley Song and Dance Festival: Navajo Two Step Songs
[Canyon CR-7132]

Lineup: Toh-Den-Nas-Shai Singers (Kayenta, Arizona); Twin Lakes Swingers (Twin Lakes, New Mexico); Smoke Signal Travelers (Smoke Signal, Arizona); Four Corners Singers (Shiprock, New Mexico);

Beclabito Valley Singers (Beclabito, New Mexico); Chinle Valley Boys (Chinle, Arizona). Recorded April 1986, Chinle, Arizona.

Chippewa-Cree Circle Dance [Sound Chiefs SC-200] *See*: Powwow Music: Rocky Boys

Rocky Boy Singers Lineup: Paul Eagleman, Charles Gopher, Bill Baker, John Gilbert Meyers, Windy Boy. Recorded Crow Agency, Montana, August 22, 1966.

Chippewa-Cree Grass Dance [Sound Chiefs SC-101] *See: Chippewa-Cree Circle Dance* comp

Cloud Dance Songs of the San Juan Pueblo [Indian House 1971] *See*: Traditional/Archival Group: Oku Shareh

Lineup: Joe Abeyta; Cipriano, Jerry, and Peter Garcia, Carpio and Ron Trujillo.

Creation's Journey [Smithsonian Folkways 1994]

Lineup: Blackfoot Crossing Singers; Comanche Singers; D. J. Nez; Tewa Drummers and Singers; Young Nation Singers; Lee Cremo; Kingfisher Trio. Yupik Singers: Elena Charles, Nicholas Charles Jr., and Joe Chief Jr. Kwakiutl Singers: Barb, Kevin, William, and Andrea Cranmer; Vera and Eva Dick; Henry Nelson; Ethel Scow; Henry Seaweed; Norine Charlie; Emma Tamlin; William Wasden Jr. Sata Kallta and Axawiri Imilla (Aymara); Zapotec Singers.

Crowdog's Paradise: Songs of the Sioux [Elektra 1971] *See*: Peyote Music: Crowdog

Lineup: Leonard and Henry Crowdog, w/ Al Running and Mary Crowdog; Peter Siegel, producer. Selected songs appear in the compilation *Sing Out! The Folk Song Magazine*, vol. 24, no. 5 [1975] comp.

Crow Grass and Owl Dance Songs [Sound Chiefs SC-116]

Lineup: Lloyd Old Coyote, Frank Backbone Sr., Robert Other Medicine, Lindsey Bad Bear. Recorded at the Crow Agency, Montana.

A Cry from the Earth [Ethnic Folkways 1979]

Thirty-three selections from twenty-four nations; edited by John Bierhorst.

Delaware, Cherokee, Choctaw, Creek [Library of Congress L37]

Delaware peyote songs, war dance songs, songs of the Delaware Big House; Cherokee lullaby, stomp dance, pumpkin dance, and Christian hymns; Choctaw Christian hymn; Creek lullaby, ball game songs, stomp dance, ribbons dance, and Christian hymns. Recorded by Willard Rhodes, 1940–52.

Ditch Cleaning and Picnic Songs of the Picuris Pueblo [Indian House 1971]

Ramos Duran. Recorded at Picuris Pueblo, New Mexico, September 11, 1966, and January 22, 1970.

Flathead Stick Game Songs [Canyon CR-8017]

Kootenai stick games songs led by Mary Antiste; recorded at the Arlee Powwow, Flathead Reservation, Montana, 1972.

Gourd Dances of the Kiowa [Canyon CR-6148]

Great Basin: Paiute, Washo, Ute, Bannock, Shoshone [Library of Congress L38]

Paiute coyote, mountain sheep, round dance songs; Washo round dance, girls' puberty songs; Ute bear dance, turkey dance, Peyote songs; Bannock warrior songs; Shoshone ghost dance songs; sun dance songs; hand game songs. Recorded by Willard Rhodes, 1940–52.

Haida: Indian Music of the Pacific Northwest [Folkways FE-4119] two LPs

Hand Game of the Kiowa, Kiowa Apache, and Comanche, Vol. 1 [Indian House IH-2501]
Hand Game of the Kiowa, Kiowa Apache, and Comanche, Vol. 2 [Indian House IH-2502]

Sung by two teams during a game, the Carnegie Roadrunners versus Billy Goat Hill, comprising more than sixty singers. Recorded live at Carnegie, Oklahoma, November 24, 1968.

Healing Songs of the American Indians [Ethnic Folkways FE-4251]

Nineteen songs from the Chippewa, Makah, Menominee, Northern Ute, Sioux,

Tohono O'odham, and Yuman; recorded by Frances Densmore.

Heartbeat: Voices of First Nations Women [Smithsonian Folkways 1995]

Lineup: Six Nations Women Singers (Iroquois); Joanne Shenandoah (Oneida; *See*: Contemporary Music); Lillian Rainer (Taos–San Carlos Apache; *See*: Flute Music); Georgia Wettlin-Larsen (Assiniboine-Nakota); Anita Anquoe George (Kiowa); Mary Ann Meanus and Verbena Green (Wasco and Warm Springs); Sweethearts of Navajoland; Nancy Richardson (Karuk-Shasta-Nahua); Betty Mae Jumper (Seminole; *See*: Contemporary Spoken Word: Legends and Storytelling); Geraldine Barney (Dineh; *See*: Contemporary Music and Flute Music); Poldine Carlo (Athabaskan); Cornelia Bowannie and Arliss Luna (Zuni; a.k.a. Zuni Olla Maidens); Tewa Women's Choir; Ulali (*See*: Contemporary Music); Crying Woman Singers (*See*: Powwow Music); Buffy Sainte-Marie (Cree; *See*: Contemporary Music).

Heartbeat 2: More Voices of First Nations Women [Smithsonian Folkways 1998]

Lineup: Bernice Toreez (Kashaya Pomo); Tzo'kam (Interior Salish); Mary Youngblood (Chugach Aluet-Seminole; *See*: Flute Music); Mary Stachelrodt and Elena Charles (Yupik); Jani Lauzon (Metis; *See*: Contemporary Music); Tudjaat (Inuit; *See*: Arctic/Circumpolar Contemporary); Wabanoag Singers (Wabanaki); Mary Ann Anquoe (Kiowa); Sissy Goodhouse (Lakota; *See*: Traditional/Archival Solo); Dorothy Whitehorse Delaune (Kiowa); Nellie Two Bulls (Lakota); Crying Woman Singers (Cree; *See*: Powwow Music); Laura Wallace (Dineh); Sharon Burch (Dineh; *See*: Contemporary Music); Judy Trejo (Paiute); Joy

Harjo and Poetic Justice (*See*: Contemporary Music).

Hearts of the Nations: Aboriginal Women's Voices . . . in the Studio 1997 [Banff Centre for the Arts/Sweet Grass 1997] *See*: Contemporary Music, various

Lineup: Sadie Buck (Seneca); Cornelia Bowannie (Zuni); Jani Lauzon (Metis); Jennifer Kreisbueg (Tuscarora); Olivia Tailfeathers (Blackfoot); Sharon King (Potawatomi); ElizaBeth Hill (Mohawk); Flora Wallace (Salish); Joyce Fossella (Salish); Soni Moreno (Mayan); Jerriann Buckskin (Blackfoot); Amber Weasel Head (Blackfoot); Cherokee Blood (Blackfoot); Melanie Printup Hope (Blackfoot). Juno Award nomination for Best Music of Aboriginal Canada Recording, 1999.

An Historical Album of Blackfoot Indian Music [Ethnic Folkways FE-34001]

Thirty selections of sacred and social songs recorded at the turn of the twentieth century, including pipe songs, sun dance songs, gambling songs, and others.

Hopi Butterfly [Canyon CR-6072]

A rare public recording of the butterfly dance, Third Mesa, Hotevilla, Arizona, 1967, by Ben Setima.

Hopi Katchina Songs and Six Songs by Hopi Chanters [Ethnic Folkways FE-4394 1964]

Seventeen songs recorded by Dr. Jesse Walter Fewkes (1850–1930) in 1924; edited by Charles Hofmann.

Hopi Social Songs, Vol. 1 [Canyon CR-6107] comp
Hopi Social Songs, Vol. 2 [Canyon CR-6108] comp

Lineup: Bernard Dawahoya; Riley and Alaric Polequaptewa; Loren Sakeva; Seymour Lomakema; Milland Lomakema Sr.; Milland Lomakema Jr.; Alde Qumyintewa; Patrick Lomawaima. From Shungopavi, Second Mesa, Arizona.

Indian Music of the Canadian Plains [Ethnic Folkways 1966]

Lineup: William Burnstick, George and Harry Nicotine, Antoine Lonesinger, William Peaychew, Alan Fox w/ Lawrence Kiskotagan, Elie Pooyak, Jim Low Horn, Adam Deleany, One Gun, Wilfred Calf Robe w/ Albert Scalp Lock.

Indian Music of the Pacific Northwest Coast [Ethnic Folkways FE-4523] two LPs

Indian Music of the Southwest [Folkways FE-8850]

Indian Songs of Today [Library of Congress L36]

Nineteen songs sung by children prior to 1951; Cherokee, Creek, Dineh, Kiowa, Picuris, Potawatomi, San Juan Pueblo, Seminole, Sioux, Tewa, Tlingit. Rcorded by Willard Rhodes 1940–52.

Indiani Yaquis: Musica e danze rituali [Arion 1979, Italy]

Iroquois Social Dance Songs, Vol. 1 [Iroqrafts 1969]
Iroquois Social Dance Songs, Vol. 2 [Iroqrafts 1969]
Iroquois Social Dance Songs, Vol. 3 [Iroqrafts 1969]

Lineup: George Buck, Raymond Spragge, Jacob E. Thomas, William Guy Spittal. Produced in Oshweken, Ontario, 1969.

Kiowa [Ethnic Folkways FE-4393]

Kiowa [Library of Congress L35]

George Hunt and Matthew Whitehorse, singers: sun dance, ghost dance, Setanke's death song, peyote songs, flag songs, Christian hymns, round dance, and others. Recorded by Willard Rhodes, 1941–51.

Kiowa Black Leggings Society Songs, War Mothers' Songs, Flag Song [Canyon CR-6167]

Lineup: Bill Kaulaity, Daniel and James Cozad, Georgia Dupoint, Roberta Toehay, Flora Weryackwe. Recorded Carnegie, Oklahoma, January 22, 1964.

Kiowa Church Songs, Vol. 1 [Indian House IH-2506]
Kiowa Church Songs, Vol. 2 [Indian House IH-2507]

Kiowa Christian church songs sung by David Apekaum, Ray Cozad, Harry Domebo, Walter Geionety, Tom and Nancy Tointigh, Ruby Bever, Kathleen Redbone, Joyce Robinson. Recorded Carnegie, Oklahoma, March 31, 1971.

Kiowa Circle and Two-Step Songs
[Sound Chiefs SC-278]

Lineup: Leonard Cozad, Jasper Sankadota, Oscar and Laura Tahlo. Recorded Carnegie, Oklahoma, January 22, 1964.

Kiowa 49 and Round Dance Songs
[Canyon CR-6087] *See: Kiowa Gourd Dance Songs* comp

Lineup: Mr. and Mrs. John Emhoolah Jr., Hershel Kaulaity, Mr. and Mrs. Billy Botone, Mr. and Mrs. Vincent Bointy, Mr. and Mrs. Bruce Haumpy, Ted Creeping Bear, Ray White Buffalo.

Kiowa 49: War Expedition Songs
[Indian House 1969]

Lineup: Bill Koomsa Sr.; Gregory Haumpy; Billy Hunting Horse (*See*: Traditional/Archival Solo); Ralph Kotay; Bill Koomsa Jr.; Barbara Ahhaitty; Pearl Kerchee; Angleine, Nan, and Wilda Koomsa; Wilbur Kodaseet; Georgia Dupoint; Pearl Woodard; Lonnie Tsotaddle; Ann Koomsa; Martha Koomsa Perez. Recorded at Carnegie, Oklahoma, April 29, 1969.

Kiowa Gourd Dance, Vol. 1 [Indian House IH-2503]
Kiowa Gourd Dance, Vol. 2 [Indian House IH-2504]

Lineup: Dan, Joe, Larry, and Velma Cozad; Leonard Cozad Sr.; Billy Hunting Horse; Adam Kaulity; Vince and Yale Spotted Bird; Barbara and Dobbin Ahhaitty Monoessy; Naomi Svital. Dancers: David Apekaum, Marty Autaubo, Richard Kauhquo, Elrod Monoessy, Curtis Toinigh. Recorded at Carnegie, Oklahoma, June 10, 1974.

Kiowa Gourd Dance Songs [Canyon CR-6103]

Lineup: Mr. and Mrs. John Emhoolah Jr., Hershel Kaulaity, Mr. and Mrs. Billy Botone, Mr. and Mrs. Vincent Bointy, Mr. and Mrs. Bruce Haumpy, Ted Creeping Bear, Ray White Buffalo.

Kiowa Songs and Dances [Ethnic Folkways FE-4393]

Twenty-six songs recorded in the early 1960s; Kenneth Anquoe, lead singer.

Kwakiutl: Indian Music of the Pacific Northwest [Ethnic Folkways FE-4122] two LPs

Twenty-five songs by Mungo Martin, Billy Assu, Tom Willie, and Stanley Hunt.

Lakota Pipe and Ceremonial Songs (Wahancanka) [Canyon 1998]

Rev. Joseph Shields Jr. (Dakota/Sicangu Lakota; *See*: Peyote Music).

Lakota Sundance Songs Taku Wakan [Red Road Recordings 1993]

Lineup: Lorenzo Eagle Road, Elmer Running, Roy Stone, Sam Wounded Head, Harold White Horse.

Lakota Thunder Veterans' Songs [Makoche 2000]

Lineup: Courtney and Dana Yellow Fat, Wyman Archambault, Frank and Kenny Bullhead, Reuben Fast Horse (*See*: Contemporary Music: Lunar Drive), John Gamio, Eddie Patterson, Carlos and Joe Picotte, Leo Standing Crow, Virgil Taken Alive, Kristian Theisz. The project was nominated for a Grammy Award in the Native music category established in 2001.

Lakota Yuwipi Songs, Taku Skanskan, Vol. 2 [Red Road Recordings 1993]

Lineup: Lorenzo Eagle Road, Elmer Running, Harold White Horse.

Lakota Yuwipi Songs, Tunkan Skanskan, Vol. 1 [Red Road Recordings 1992]

Lineup: Harold White Horse, Elmer Running, Lorenzo Eagle Road, Guildford Running.

Let's 49! [Indian Sounds IS-4901]

Forty songs from Oklahoma by ten male and fourteen female singers.

Lewis and Clark: Sounds of Discovery [Makoche 1998]

Lineup: Keith Bear, Mandaree, Nadine Vasquez (Shoshone), Len Weaskus (Nez Perce), Little Corner Singers (Blackfoot), Nellie Youpee (Mandan), Courtney Yellowfat (Lakota); David Swenson, producer.

Menominee and Winnebago Tribal Songs [American Indian Sound Chiefs 1956]

Lineup: John Awonohopay, Howard Raine, Winslow White Eagle.

Mississippi River of Song [Smithsonian Folkways 1997]

"Chippewa Powwow Song" is the only Native music track of a larger collection.

Music of the Algonkians, Woodland Indians, Cree, Montagnais, Naskapi [Ethnic Folkways FE-4253]

Music of the American Indians of the Southwest [Ethnic Folkways FE-4420]

Social and ceremonial songs of the Dineh, Havasupai, Hopi, San Ildefonso, Taos, Tohono O'odham, Walapai, Western Apache, Yuma, and Zuni. Notes by Dr. Willard Rhodes.

Music of the Native American Indians [ARC Music 1998, United Kingdom/Germany]

Lineup: "Butterfly Dance of the San Juan Pueblo": Herman Agoyo, Anthony S. Archuleta, Cipriano Garcia, Jerry Garcia, Peter Garcia, Steven Trujillo. "Seneca Alligator Dance": Leslie Bowen, Herbert Dowdy Sr., Avery, Johnson, and Marty Jimerson, Richard Johnny-John. "Northern Arapaho Eagle Dance": Los Angeles Northern Singers. "Creek Gar Dance" and "Cherokee Stomp Dance": Archie Sam, Jobie L. Fields, Van Johnson, Eli Sam, Cedo Screechowl, Robert Sumpka, Luman Wildcat, Squirrel Wildcat, Sonja Fields, Levana Jarjo, Evelyn Screechowl, Eliza Sumpka, Leona Wildcat. "Yurok Women's Brush Dance": Loren Bommelyn, Frank A. Douglas, Aileen Figueroa, Sam Lopez, Ella Vera Norris, Walter Richards Sr., Florence Shaughnessy, Hector Simms, Oscar Taylor. "Navajo Ribbon Dance": Frank Jishie Jr., Raymond Yazzie, Sam Yazzie Jr., Sam Yazzie Sr. "Southern Plains Oklahoma Two-Step": Jack Anquoe, Henry Collins, Bill Grass, James Kimble, Lionel Le Clair, Ed Little Cook, Oliver Little Cook, Morris Lookout, Adam Pratt, Joe Rush, E. R. Satepauhoodle, Harvey Ware, Chris White. All tracks recorded in 1975, licensed from New World Music.

Music of New Mexico: Native American Traditions [Smithsonian Folkways 1992] *See*: Contemporary Compilations

Includes songs from Dineh Nation, Picuris Pueblo, Taos Pueblo, Zuni Pueblo. John Rainer Jr., Fernando Cellicion, Geraldine Barney, A. Paul Ortega, and Sharon Burch (*See*: Contemporary Music). (*See*: Flute Music: Barney, Cellicion, Rainer.)

Music of the Nez Perce [Wild Sanctuary]

In the 1920s, twenty-six drummers and singers gathered to perform traditional songs. Five decades later, three survivors recorded their legacy.

Music of the Pascola and Deer Dance [Canyon CR-6099]

Music of the Pawnee [Ethnic Folkways FE-4334]

Forty-five songs sung by Mark Evarts; recorded by Dr. Gene Weltfish, 1935.

Music of the Plains Apache [Ethnic Folkways FE-4252]

Music of the Pueblos, Apache, and Navajo [Matrix KCMS 1204-5]

Taylor Museum of Colorado Springs Fine Arts Center.

Music of the Sioux and Navajo [Folkways FE-4401]

Recorded by Dr. Willard Rhodes.

My Beautiful Land [Canyon CR-6078]

Lineup: Danny Whitefeather Begay, Cindy Yazzie, Roger McCabe (all Dineh).

Native American Indian Chants and Dances: Overtunes [Sounds of the World 1998]

Navajo [Library of Congress L41]

Includes Yebechai, corn grinding, peyote songs; "Flag Raising at Iwo Jima," "Blessing Way," "Enemy Way," "Squaw Dance," and other social songs. Recorded by Willard Rhodes, 1940–52.

Navajo Social Songs [Canyon CR-6076]

Some of the oldest squaw dance songs performed by Robert Lee.

Navajo Songs from Canyon de Chelley [New World Records 1990]

Lineup: Kee Chee Jake, Sam Yazzie Sr., Lena D. Clark. Compiled by Charlotte Heth (Cherokee); recorded at Chinle and Canyon de Chelley, Arizona, September 1975.

Navajo: Songs of the Dine [Canyon CR-6055]

Lineup: Joe Lee, Mesa Verde Group Singers, Reg Begay, Natay, Laughing Boy, Tseyia Chee, Fort Defiance Yei-Be-Chai team.

Navajo Two-Step Songs, Vol. 1 [Canyon CR-7132]

1962 Dogrib Tea Dance [Dogrib Treaty 11 Council, Northwest Territories, Canada, 2000]

Tea dance (dancing in a circle without hand drums or frame drums), part of the Dene drum dance. Buckets of tea concocted from natural teas from the region, sometimes mixed with tobacco, or from imported black tea, is consumed during the breaks between dancing. Recorded at the annual Treaty Day ceremonies, July 1962, Rae, Northwest Territories, by June Helm from the University of Iowa and Nancy Lurie from the Milwaukee Public Museum.

Nootka Indian Music of the Pacific Northwest [Ethnic Folkways 1974] two LPs

Lineup: Peter Webster, George Clutesi, Mungo Martin, Fred Lewis, Ella Thompson, Joe Titian. A variety of social and ceremonial songs; recorded 1947–53 and 1965–72 at Alert Bay, Cape Mudge, and Port Alberni in Victoria and Vancouver, British Columbia.

Northern Cheyenne [Indian Records IR-303]

Philip Whiteman, John Whiteman, Burton Fisher, and George Fisher. Recorded in Lame Deer, Montana.

Northern Cheyenne Sun Dance Songs/Crow Tribal Sun Dance Songs [Sound Chiefs SC-700]

Cheyenne sun dance songs performed by Phillip Whiteman, Thomas Wooden Leg, and J. White Dirt; Crow sun dance songs performed by Pete Whiteman, Milton Yellow Mule, and Mrs. Yellow Mule.

Northern Cheyenne Warriors Dance/Crow Tribal Grass Dance Songs [Sound Chiefs SC-112]

Cheyenne warrior dance songs performed by Phillip Whiteman, Gilbert White Dirt, Thomas Wooden Leg, and James Red Cloud; Crow grass dance songs performed by Henry and Lloyd Old Coyote, Warren Bear Cloud, John Strong Enemy.

Northwest Puget Sound [AFS-L34 1954]

From the Archive of Folk Culture collected by Willard Rhodes, 1940–52, with songs from the Chinook, Klallam, Lummi, Makah, Quinalt, and Skagit.

Ojibway Music from Minnesota: A Century of Songs for Voice and Drum [MHS Press 1989/1997]

The book and recording feature singers including Swift Flying Feather, 1899; Kimiwun, 1910; Kingbird Singers (*See*: Powwow Music), 1988; Ponemah Ramblers, 1988; Whitefish Bay (*See*: Powwow Music), 1988; Leech Lake, 1988; Red Lake Singers, 1988; Fred Benjamin, 1988; James Littlewolf, 1971; Keith Secola (*See*: Contemporary Music), 1982 and 1985.

Old Time Navajo Songs [Canyon CR-6073]

Lineup: Kenneth and Edmund White.

Omaha Indian Music: Historic Recordings from the Fletcher/LaFlesche Collection [Folkways AFC L71, 1985]

The collection contains forty-four re-stored wax cylinder recordings collected by Francis La Flesche (Omaha, 1857–1932) and Alice Cunningham Fletcher (1838–1923) between 1895 and 1905. Cyde Sheridan III and the Tai Piah Singers were recorded in 1983 by Professor Roger Welsch, University of Nebraska.

Owicakeyakapo: Spirit of Song [Makoche 1991]

Lineup: Earl Bullhead; Frank Bullhead (guest); Tom Bullhead; Donald Ducheneaux; Ken Billingsley; Sissy Goodhouse (guest); Sissy Claymore; Marge Edwards; Salina Steele; Ronnie Allen; Cedric Goodhouse (guest); Betty Archambault; John Wells (guest); Dave Archambault; Jody Luger; Mike Kills Pretty Enemy. Recorded at Standing Rock College, Fort Yates, North Dakota.

Papago Dance Songs [Canyon CR-6098]

Aji-Kaij Mek Ne'etam Singers: Jose Pancho, Baptista, Mary, and Eva Lopez. Chelkona and Keihina dance songs recorded at Santa Rosa Village.

Plains: Comanche, Cheyenne, Kiowa, Caddo, Wichita, Pawnee [Library of Congress L39]

Comanche raiding song, 49s, round dance song, Christian hymn; Cheyenne lullaby, war dance, wolf song, "Story of the Bogey Man"; Kiowa love song, "Story of the Flute"; Caddo round dance, victory song, lullaby, "The Little Skunk's Dream";

Wichita deer dance, rain songs; Pawnee flag song, war song, ghost dance, hand game song, prayer song. Recorded by Willard Rhodes, 1940–52.

Ponca Tribal Songs [Sound Chiefs SC-119]

Lineup: Lamont Brown, Sylvester Warrior, Albert Waters, and Henry Snake. Recorded August 25–27, 1967. Includes veterans' song, memorial song, trot dance songs, war dance songs, and contest dance songs.

Ponca War Dances [Canyon 1974]

Ponca Indian Singers Lineup: Wilford Clark (Ponca-Omaha), Peewee Clark, Wilkie Eagle, Jim Kemble (Ponca-Creek).

Ponca Warriors Dance Songs and Pawnee Warrior Dance Songs [Sound Chiefs SC-118]

Lineup: Sylvester Warrior, Albert Waters, Francis Eagle (Ponca), Frank Murrie, Lamont Pratt, Phillip Jim, and Mrs. Jacob Leander (Pawnee).

Proud Heritage: A Celebration of Traditional American Indian Music [Indian House 1996]

Dineh, Kiowa, Lakota, Muscogee Creek, Picuris Pueblo, Ponca, San Juan Pueblo, Taos Pueblo. Carnegie Roadrunners (*See: Hand Game* and *Kiowa* comps); Tom Ware (*See*: Contemporary Music) and Kevin Locke (*See*: Flute Music); Badland Singers, Ironwood Singers, Southern Thunder (*See*: Powwow Music).

Pueblo Indian Songs from San Juan [Canyon CR-6065]

Lineup: Carpio Trujillo; Joe Abeyta; Peter, Juan, and Diego Aguino. Recorded live at the Forty-eighth Intertribal Indian Ceremonial, Gallup, New Mexico.

Pueblo Songs of the Southwest Recorded Live at the Gallup Ceremonial [Indian House IH-9502]

Hopi, Jemez Pueblo, Laguna Pueblo, San Juan Pueblo, Zuni Pueblo. Recorded at the Forty-eighth Intertribal Indian Ceremonial, Gallup, New Mexico, August 14–17, 1969.

Pueblo: Taos, San Ildefonso, Zuni, Hopi [Library of Congress L43]

Hopi, San Ildefonso, Taos Pueblo, Zuni Kachina dances. Recorded by Willard Rhodes, 1940–52.

Round Dance Songs of Taos Pueblo, Vol. 1 [Indian House IH-1002]
Round Dance Songs of Taos Pueblo, Vol. 2 [Indian House IH-1001]
See: Taos Pueblo Round Dance comp

Lineup: John C. Gomez, Orlando and Ralph Lujan, Bennie Mondragon, Ruben Romero, and Louis Sandoval. Recorded Taos Pueblo, New Mexico, November 12, 1966.

Sacred Music of the World: Ceremonial Songs and Dances from 30 Cultures [Arc 1999, United Kingdom] two CDs

Includes two tracks licensed from the Recorded Anthology of American Music Inc., New York, in 1998: San Juan Pueblo butterfly dance, recorded at San Juan Pueblo,

1975; Northern Arapaho eagle dance, recorded in Los Angeles, October 1975.

Scattered Corn: Mandan Women's Field Songs [North Dakota State Historical Society 1912]

Recorded by Frances Densmore on Edison Wax Cylinder; reissued on CD by Makoche Records, 1999.

Seminole Indians of Florida [Ethnic Folkways FE-4383]

Includes game, social, and history songs, the latter dealing with the removal to Oklahoma. Recorded on wax cylinder by Frances Densmore, 1931–33.

Seneca Social Dance Music [Ethnic Folkways FE-4072]

Songs by Avery and Fidelia Jimerson and seven women of the Allegheny Singing Society. recorded on the Allegheny Reservation, Cattaraugus County, New York, 1977–80.

Seneca Songs from Coldspring Longhouse [Library of Congress L17]

Traditional songs sung by Chauncey Johnny John and Albert Jones; recorded by William N. Fenton in New York State from 1941 to 1945.

Shaman, Jhankri, and Nele: Music Healers of Indigenous Cultures [Ellipsis Arts 1997] CD w/ book

Includes songs from Amazon, Anishnabe, Haiti, Huichol, Kuna, Maya, NAC, Panama, Peru, Tarahumara, Tuva, and others. Compiled by Pat Moffitt Cook.

Sing Out! The Folk Song Magazine, Vol. 24, no. 5 [1975] *See*: Contemporary Music: Peter LaFarge

Features music, writings, words, and songs from Rarihokwats (former editor of *Akwesasne Notes*), Greg Borst, Mary Crow Dog, Bob Onco, Roland Moussa, Richard Erdoes, Charles Morrow, Tony Isaacs, Fred Seibert, Martha Siegal, Paul Mintus, and David Baxter. The 33 rpm soundsheet contains: a "49 song," "Creek Stomp Dance" and" Flute Song" by Greg Borst, Bob Onco's "Wounded Knee Song," and the "AIM National Anthem"; w/ peyote songs by Mary Crow Dog, 1976 (*See: Crowdog's Paradise* comp).

Sioux [Folkways AFS L 40]

Recorded by Willard Rhodes, 1940–52.

Soaring Hearts Tribal Peoples, Vol. 1 [SOAR 1996]

Bryan Akipa (*See*: Flute Music), Tsa'ne Do'se, Cornel Pewewardy (*See*: Flute Music), Earl Bullhead, James Bilagody, P. M. Begay, Davis Mitchell, Arawak Mountain Singers (*See*: Powwow Music), Vince Two Eagles (*See*: Contemporary Music).

Social Songs from the Pima Indians [Canyon CR-6066]

Songs and Dances of the Eastern Indians from Medicine Spring and Allegheny [New World NW-337]

Ceremonial and social music from the eastern United States, with Cherokee songs recorded at Medicine Spring Ceremonial Ground, Sequoyah County, Oklahoma, and Seneca songs recorded at Salamanca, New York.

Songs and Dances of the Flathead Indians [Folkways FE-4445]

Nineteen medicine, social, and ceremonial songs recorded on the Flathead Reservation, Montana, in 1950.

Songs and Dances of Great Lakes Indians [Ethnic Folkways FE-4003]

Anishnabe and Haudenosaunee. Recorded by Gertrude Prokosch Kurath, 1956.

Songs from the Iroquois Longhouse [Library of Congress L6]

Eighteen songs recorded by William N. Fenton in New York and Ontario, 1941.

Songs from Laguna [Canyon CR-6058]

A series of dance songs from Laguna Pueblo, New Mexico, performed by Lynn Sheayea, Allen Martin, Edward Aragon, Victor and Albert Riley.

Songs from the Pima: Songs from the Swallow Series [Canyon 1970]

Lineup: Amos and Lydia Richards; Josiah and Jeanette King; David Lewis; Elizabeth Garcia. From Salt River, Arizona.

Songs of a Yakima Encampment [Canyon CR-6129]

Lineup: Leroy Selam (Yakima) and Fred Hill (Yakima-Umatilla).

Songs of the Caddo: Ceremonial and Social Dance Music, Vol. 1 [Canyon 1975/1999]
Songs of the Caddo: Ceremonial and Social Dance Music, Vol. 2 [Canyon 1975/1999]

Lineup: Lowell "Wimpy" Edmunds, Leon Carter, Houston Edmunds, Hubert Halfmoon, Irvin and Reuben Whitebead, Melford Williams. First public recordings of social and ceremonial songs of the Caddo of Hinton, Oklahoma.

Songs of the Chippewa [Library of Congress L22]

Thirty songs, including Midewin lodge songs, war songs, healing songs, love songs, and dream songs. Recorded by Frances Densmore between 1907 and 1910.

Songs of the Chippewa [Canyon 1978]

Lineup: Daniel, Antoine, and Joseph Ballanger; Ronnie Leith; Johnny Smith.

Songs of the Chippewa, Vol. 1: *Game and Social Dance Songs* [Folkways FE-4392]

Lineup: Jacob Redbird, Walter Drift, Ray Robinson, and August King. Recorded 1970–75.

Songs of Earth, Water, Fire, and Sky [New World NW-246]

Cherokee, Creek, Dineh, Northern Arapaho, Northern Plains, San Juan Pueblo, Seneca, Southern Plains, Yurok.

The Song of the Indian [Canyon CR-6050]

Acoma, Cheyenne, Dineh, Hopi, Sioux, Zuni.

Songs of the Lenape, Vol. 1 [Touching Leaves Indian Crafts 1980]
Songs of the Lenape, Vol. 2 [Touching Leaves Indian Crafts 1981]

Lineup: Freddie Washington, Bill Shawnee, Ray Elkhair, Jim Thompson, and John Falleaf. Recorded by Jim Rementer and Glenn McCartlin in Dewey, Oklahoma, between 1962 and 1973.

Songs of Love, Luck, Animals, and Music: Music of the Yurok and Tolowa Indians [New World Records 1977]

Twenty ceremonial, social, gambling, and love songs from the Yurok and Tolowa of northern California. Yurok singers: Frank Douglas, Aileen Figueroa, Ella Norris, Hector Simms, Oscar Taylor, and Florence Shaughnessy. Tolowa singers: Loren Bommelyn, Carl James, Sam Lopez, Walter Richards Sr., and Frederick Scott Jr. Yurok and Tolowa dancers: Carl James, Carole Korb, Casbara Ruud, Frederick Scott Jr., Sheryl Bommelyn Steinruck, and Lisa Sundberg.

Songs of the Menominee, Mandan, and Hidatsa [Library of Congress L33]

Recorded by Frances Densmore between 1915 and 1929, w/ twenty-three Menominee songs, three Hidatsa songs, and three Mandan songs of societal and medicine lodges. From the Smithsonian-Densmore Wax Cylinder Collection 1910–30.

Songs of the Muskogee Creek, Part 1 [Indian House IH-3001]
Songs of the Muskogee Creek, Part 2 [Indian House IH-3002]

Lineup: Harry Bell, James Deere, Netche Gray, Frank Jackson, Tema Tiger, David Wind, w/ shell shakers Frances and Stella Deere, Helen Tiger, Eliza Wind. Recorded at Seminole, Florida.

Songs of the Navajo [JVC 1994]

Lineup: Kee Kinlechene (Billie Rogers) and Yatza (Bella Rogers McCabe). Recorded in Albuquerque, New Mexico, December 11–12, 1993.

Songs of the Nootka and Quileute [Library of Congress L32]

Thirty songs recorded by Frances Densmore. From the Smithsonian-Densmore Wax Cylinder Collection 1910–30.

Songs of the Papago [Library of Congress L31]

Twenty-five social and spiritual songs recorded by Frances Densmore in 1925. From the Smithsonian-Densmore Wax Cylinder Collection 1910–30.

Songs of the Pawnee and Northern Ute [Library of Congress L25]

Seventeen Pawnee songs of the ghost dance, lance, and other ceremonial and social songs recorded in 1919 and 1920, and fourteen social and healing songs of the Ute recorded in 1914 and 1916 by Frances Densmore. From the Smithsonian-Densmore Wax Cylinder Collection 1910–30.

Songs of the Seminole Indians of Florida [Folkways FE 4383-1972]

Twenty-nine songs, including those from Cypress Swamp recorded by Francis Densmore, 1931–33, notes by Charles Hofmann.

Songs of the Sioux [Canyon CR-6062]

Songs of the Sioux [Library of Congress L23]

Recorded by Frances Densmore between 1911 and 1915 (Sitting Bull and Gabriel Renville), including honor songs, sun dance songs, grass dance, healing, and game songs. From the Smithsonian-Densmore Wax Cylinder Collection 1910–30.

Songs of the Warm Springs [Canyon 1975]

Lineup: Ellen Squiemphem, Susan Moses, Bernice Mitchell, Ada Sooksoit, and Adeline Miller.

Songs of the Warm Springs Indian Reservation [Canyon CR-6123]

Lineup: Susan Moses, Ellen Squiemphem, Bernice Mitchell, Ada Sooksoit, and Adeline Miller of the Northern Paiute, Wasco, and Warm Springs people who form the Warm Springs Confederated Tribes. Reissued on Canyon Record's Vintage Collection, the album contains songs not heard for more than fifty years prior to the making of this recording.

Songs of the White Mountain Apache [Canyon CR-6165]

Lineup: Alexander Holmes, Frank Gordon, George Gregg, Jimmy Tessay, Charles Henry Toney, Freda Goclaney, and Minnie Narcisco.

Songs of the Yuma, Cocopa, and Yaqui [Library of Congress L24]

Recorded in 1910 by Frances Densmore, including thirteen Yuman songs of healing, burial, and medicine; eleven songs of the Cocopa; and three Yaqui deer dance songs. From the Smithsonian-Densmore Wax Cylinder Collection 1910–30.

Sounds of Indian America Recorded Live at the Gallup Ceremonial [Indian House IH-9501]

Crow, Dineh, Hopi, Jemez Pueblo, Kiowa, Laguna Pueblo, Pawnee, Quecha, San Carlos Apache, San Juan Pueblo, Taos Pueblo, Ute, and Zuni. Recorded live at the Forty-Eighth Intertribal Indian Ceremonial, Gallup, New Mexico, August 14–17, 1969.

Southern Cheyenne Women's Songs [University of Oklahoma Press 1994]

Lineup: Joan Swallow, Wilma Blackowl Hamilton, Bertha Little Coyote, Mary Lou Stone Road Prairie Chief, Imogene Jones, Mary Armstrong, Rena Rose Young Bear, Mary Lou Birdshead Blackbear. Collected by Virginia Giglio, 1990–91.

Spirit of the Native American Indians: Songs and Dances of the Kiowa, Comanche, Navajo . . . [ARC Music 1999, United Kingdom/ Germany]

Lineup: Jones Benally Family (Dineh; *See*: Contemporary Music: Blackfire), Garcia Brothers (San Juan Pueblo), Chester Mahooty (Zuni), Cornel Pewewardy (Co-manche; *See*: Flute Music), Alliance West Singers (Kiowa), Cheyenne Group. Recorded at the Sixty-fifth Intertribal Indian Ceremonial, Gallup, New Mexico. Recordings licensed from Music of the World.

Spiritual Songs of the American Indian [Retro R2CD 40-31] bootleg *See: Authentic Music of the American Indian* comps

Stick Game Songs, Vol. 1 [Arbor 2003]

Lineup: Gloria, Robert Sr., Boss, Penny, and Stacy McGilvery. The stick game was played to create the exchange of goods for trade, and the songs themselves were said to possess powers that enabled the winning of the game. The stick game is part of a larger social event and sometimes takes place during powwows and other gatherings; contemporary stick games employ the use of modern currency as prize money. Two opposing teams can vary in size to limitless numbers. The rhythm of the singing sets the pace as a hidden object is passed from player to player, while the other side guesses at its whereabouts.

Stick Games Songs [Canyon CR-6105]

Stomp Dance, Vol. 1: *Muscogee, Seminole, Yuchi* [Indian House IH-3003]

Lineup: Jimmie Skeeter, Oscar Pigeon, Vernon Atkins, William Beaver, John McNac and Harry Bell; shell shakers: Linda Alexander, Frances Cosar, Edna Deere, Caroline Harry and Eliza Wind.

Stomp Dance, Vol. 2: *Muscogee, Seminole, Yuchi* [Indian House IH-3004]

Lineup: David Wind, Red Hicks, Joe Sulphur, Wade Buckrot Jr., Tony Hill, Tema Tiger. Recorded at Okemah, Oklahoma.

Summer Songs from Zuni [Canyon CR-6077]

Lineup: Leo Quetawki, Jimmie Awashu, Willie Lekeety, Hudson Ahiyite.

Talking Spirits [Music of the World 1992]

Music from New Mexico and Arizona featuring the Garcia Brothers (San Juan Pueblo); Chester Mahooty (Zuni); Roger Mase and the Second Mesa Singers (Hopi); Edward Battista (Laguna Pueblo); Zuni Olla Maidens. Recorded in 1986 at the Intertribal Ceremonial, Gallup, New Mexico.

Taos Pueblo Round Dance [Indian House IH-1005] *See: Round Dance Songs of Taos Pueblo* comp

Lineup: Jimmy Cordova, Orlando Lujan, Ernest Martinez, Ruben Romero. Recorded at Taos Pueblo, New Mexico, April 22, 1974.

Taos Pueblo Round Dance Songs, Vol. 1 [Indian House IH-1006]
Taos Pueblo Round Dance Songs, Vol. 2 [Indian House IH-1007]

Lineup: Joe Luis and John Mirabal, John Romero, Manuel Sandy, Jerry Lujan; recorded Taos Pueblo, New Mexico, May, 31, 1987.

Taos Pueblo Round Dance Songs, Vol. 3 [Indian House IH-1008]

Lineup: Joe Luis and John Mirabal, John Romero, Jerry Lujan and Curtis Sandova. Recorded Taos, New Mexico, October 30, 1999.

Taos Pueblo Tribal Songs [Sound Chiefs SC-205]

Lineup: Joe Trinidad Archuleta, George Archuleta, Joe Suazo. Recorded at Taos Pueblo, New Mexico, 1953.

Taos Round Dance, Part 1 [Indian House IH-1003]
Taos Round Dance, Part 2 [Indian House IH-1004]

Lineup: Steve Archuleta, Andy Lujan, Fredrick Lujan Jr., Hubert Lujan, Joseph Luis Mirabal, John Romero, Manuel Sandy. Recorded at Taos, Pueblo, August 11, 1969.

Traditional Global Voices [Music of the World MOW-146]

Lineup: Chester Mahooty, the Garcia Brothers.

Traditional Navajo Songs [Canyon 1969]

Lineup: Reg Begay, Roger McCabe, Natay, Mesa Verde Park Singers, Joe Lee Lukachuchai singers.

Traditional Papago Music [Canyon CR-6084]

An anthology of Tohono O'odham social and ceremonial songs recorded by J. Richard Haefer.

Traditional Pima Dance Songs [Canyon CR-8011]

Lineup: Leonard Carlos; Dorothy and Michael Lewis Russell Morgan; Oriole Singers: Blaine Pablo, Frank Kisto, and Eunice Antone.

Traditional Voices from the Eastern Door, Vol. 1 [independent no date]

Lineup: George, Joey, and Ivan Paul; James and Donna Augustine. Contemporary and traditional Mi'kmaq songs.

Tribal Gatherings [Music of the World MOW-154]

Lineup: Jones Benally (Dineh), Garcia Brothers (San Juan Pueblo), Red Eagle Wing (Dineh), Alliance West Singers (Kiowa).

Turtle Dance Songs of San Juan Pueblo [Indian House IH-1101] *See: Cloud Dance Songs of the San Juan Pueblo* comp; Traditional/Archival Group: Garcia Brothers, Oku Shareh.

Lineup: Joe Abeyta, Cipriano, Jerry and Peter Garcia, Carpio and John Trujillo. Recorded at San Juan Pueblo, New Mexico, February 13, 1972.

Turtle Mountain Music (North Dakota) [Folkways FE 4140] two LPs

Umatilla Tribal Songs [Canyon CR-6131]

Lineup: Lonnie Selam, Ronald J. Pond, Gabriel J. Selam, Alex Johnson.

Under the Green Corn Moon: Native American Lullabies [Silver Wave 1998]

Lineup: Lorain Fox (Aztec); Dorothy White Horse (Kiowa); Robert Mirabal (Taos Pueblo); Julia Begay (Dineh); Micki Pratt (Cheyenne); Joanne Shenandoah (Oneida; *See*: Contemporary Music); Alph Secakuku (Hopi); Mary Philbrook (Mi'kmaq); Tzo Kam (Stalimx); Dorothy Hunting Horse Gray (Kiowa); Tom Wasinger (Pawnee); Jerry Garrett (Oglala); Laughing Woman (Mashantucket Pequot); Ann Shadlow (Cheyenne); Kelly White (Salish).

Utes — Traditional Ute Songs: War, Bear, and Sun Dance Songs [Canyon 1974]

Lineup: Jim Box; Eddie Box Sr.; Gilbert, Lonnie, and Eddie Dutchie; Eddie Dutchie Jr.; Kenneth Frost; Gerald Ketchum. From Southern Ute Reservation at Ignacio, Colorado, and White Mesa, Utah. Reissued as Canyon Records Vintage Collection vol. 10 [Canyon 1998].

Voices of Forgotten Worlds [Ellipsis Arts 1993] two CDs w/ book

Includes singers from Dineh, Inuit, Kayapo, Maya, Northern Cree, Spokane, Tuva, and others; compiled by Brooke Wentz.

Wahancanka: Lakota Pipe and Ceremonial Songs [Canyon 1998]
See: Lakota Pipe and Ceremonial Songs comp

War Dance Songs of the Kiowa, Vol. 1 [Indian House IH-2508]
War Dance Songs of the Kiowa, Vol. 2 [Indian House IH-2509]

Lineup: Ralph and Mildred Kotay; Dixon Palmer; Rusty Wahkinney; Bill, Tom, and Truman Ware (*See*: Contemporary Music: Tom Ware); Mac Whitehorse; Maxine Wahkinney; Florene and Lucille Whitehorse. Songs of the O-ho-mah Warriors Society Lodge.

War Dance Songs of the Ponca, Vol. 1 [Indian House IH-2001]
War Dance Songs of the Ponca, Vol. 2 [Indian House IH-2002]

Ponca Hethoshka Lineup: Lamont Brown, Harry Buffalohead, Russell and Joe H. Rush, Sylvester Warrior, Albert Waters, Louis Yellowhorse, Alice Cook, Lucy Ribs, Stella Yellowhorse. Recorded in Ponca City, Oklahoma.

War Whoops and Medicine Songs [Folkways FE-4381]

Thirty-three songs from the Acoma, Chippewa, Sioux, Winnebago, and Zuni, from elders between the ages of sixty and eighty years old.

Warm Springs Confederated Tribes [Indian Records 1300]

Lineup: Sanders Heath, Ed Spino, Byton Patt, Nathan Jim, Duane Miller, and Rudy Clements. Recorded in Warm Springs, Oregon, March 29, 1973.

Winnebago Songs [Canyon 1974]

Hochungla Singers Lineup: Daniel White Eagle Sr. and Preston Thompson.

Wood That Sings: Indian Fiddle Music of the Americas [Smithsonian/Folkways 1997]

Lineup: Lee Cremo (*See*: Contemporary Music); Jimmie LaRocque, Turtle Mountain Chippewa, North Dakota; San Xavier Fiddle Band (*See*: Chicken Scratch); Chesley Goseyun Wilson; Georgia Wettlin-Larsen; Pahko'ola and Deer Singers (Yaqui), Arizona; Lawrence "Teddy Boy" Houle (Anishnabe), Manitoba, Canada; Bill Stevens (Gwich'in), Alaska; Nahua performers from Puebla, Yucatecan Maya, and Tancanhuitz, Tenek, Mexico; José Augustín Cruz and José Martín Cruz of Nahua, Mexico; Wirrarica (Huichol), Mexico; Francisco Barnet Astorga, Konkaak (Seri), Mexico; Mateo Mo Xal and Crisanto Coc, K'ekchi Maya, and Grupo Jolom Conob, Kanjobal Maya, Guatemala; Llacuari Pueblo, Peru; La Guanena Danubio Azul group, Columbia; Jose Enrique Benitez, Bolivia; Antonio Lorenzano, Warao, Venezuela; Gervasio Martinez and Mario Suilva, Mbya, Argentina. Edited by Charlotte Heth (Cherokee).

Yaqui Dances [Folkways FE-6957] ten-inch vinyl

Pascola dances recorded in Guaymas, Sonora, Mexico.

Yaqui Fiesta and Religious Music [Canyon CR-7999]

Historic recordings from Old Pascua Village, Arizona.

Yaqui Music of the Pascola and Deer Dance [Canyon 1973]

Recorded during the Tiniran Fiesta in Potam, Rio Yaqui, Sonora, Mexico.

Yaqui Pascola Music of Arizona [Canyon CR-7998]

Lineup: Francisco Molina, violin; Marcelino Valencia, harp.

Yaqui Ritual and Festive Music [Canyon 1976]

Deer, Pascola, and Matachini dances and folk songs from Pasua, Tucson, Arizona, and Rio Yaqui, Sonora, Mexico.

Yei-Be-Chai Songs [Canyon CR-6069]

Recorded in 1968 by the Yei-Be-Chai team (Dineh).

Zuni [Canyon 1972]

Lineup: Jimmie Awahau, William Leekey, Babalo, Willie Weahkee, Elijah Tekahe, Leo Quetawki, Shebaba Madlon, R. Gasper.

Zuni Fair—Live [Indian House 1971]

Harvest dances from Tekapo Village; Dineh songs and "Zuni Legend Song" by Zuni Olla Maidens; Hopi butterfly and Zuni butterfly dances by Pescado Village. Recorded live in Zuni, New Mexico.

Bibliography

Anderson, Edward F. *Peyote: The Divine Cactus.* Tucson: University of Arizona Press, 1987.

Bahr, Donald, Juan Gregorio, David Lopez, and Albert Alvarez. *Piman Shamanism and Staying Sickness.* Tucson: University of Arizona Press, 1981.

Brodzky, Anne, Rose Danesewich, and Nick Johnson, eds. *Stones, Bones, and Skin: Ritual and Shamanic Art.* Toronto: Society for Art, 1977.

Browner, Tara. *Heartbeat of the People.* Chicago: University of Illinois Press, 2002.

Burton, Bryan. *Moving within the Circle.* Danbury, Conn.: World Music Press, 1993.

Colombo, John Robert, ed. *Songs of the Indians.* 2 vols. Ottawa: Oberon, 1983.

Conklin, Abe. "Origin of the Powwow: The Ponca He-thus-ka Society Dance." *Native Amercian Expressive Culture* 11, nos. 3–4 (fall–winter 1994): 17–21.

Culin, Stewart. *Games of the North American Indians.* New York: Dover Press, 1975. First printed as *The Twenty-Fourth Annual Report of the Bureau of American Ethnology to the Smithsonian Institute.* Washington, D.C.: Government Printing Office, 1902–1903.

Densmore, Frances. *Teton Sioux Music and Culture.* Lincoln: University of Nebraska Press, Bison, 1992. First printed as *Teton Sioux Music.* Bulletin no. 61. Washington, D.C.: Bureau of American Ethnology, Smithsonian Institution, 1918.

Dyck, Paul. *Brule: The Sioux People of the Rosebud.* Flagstaff, Ariz.: Northland Press, 1971.

Gombert, Greg. *Native American Music Directory.* Fort Collins, Colo.: MultiCultural Publishing, Greg Gombert, 1994.

Hart, Mickey, with K. M. Kostyal. *Songcatchers: In Search of the World's Music.* Washington, D.C.: National Geographic, 2003.

Headington, Christopher. *The Illustrated Dictionary of Musical Terms.* New York: Harper and Row, 1980.

Heth, Charlotte. "This Precious Heritage." *Native Amercian Expressive Culture* 11, nos. 3–4 (fall–winter 1994): 31–37.

Hirschfelder, Arlene, with Martha Kreipe de Montano. *The Native American Almanac: A Portrait of Native America Today.* New York: Prentice Hall, 1993.

Howard, James H., with Willie Lena. *Oklahoma Seminoles Medicines, Magic, and Religion.* Norman: University of Oklahoma Press, 1984.

Hummelen, Remmelt, with Kathleen Hummelen. *Stories of Survival: Conversations with Native North Americans*. New York: Friendship Press, 1985.

Hungry Wolf, Adolf, and Beverley Hungry Wolf. *Powwow*. Vol. 1, *Photos and History for Dancers and Viewers*. Calgary: Good Medicine, 1983.

Johnston, Basil. *Ojibway Heritage*. Toronto: McLelland and Stewart, 1988.

Martin, Mick, with Marsha Porter. *Video and DVD Guide 2003*. New York: Ballantine, 2002.

Mohawk, John. "Drums and Turtle Rattles, Iroquois Music." *Native Amercian Expressive Culture* 11, nos. 3–4 (fall–winter 1994): 43–45.

Mooney, James. *The Ghost Dance Religion and Wounded Knee*. New York: Dover Press, 1973. First printed as *The Ghost Dance Religion and the Sioux Outbreak of 1890, of the Fourteenth Annual Report (Part 2) of the Bureau of American Ethnology to the Smithsonian Institute, 1892–1893*. Washington, D.C.: Government Printing Office, 1896.

Spier, Leslie. *Yuman Tribes of the Gila River*. Chicago: University of Chicago Press, 1933. Reprint, New York: Dover, 1978.

Students of Crazy Horse School, Wanblee, South Dakota, Pine Ridge Indian Reservation. *Pute Tiyospaye (Lip's Camp): The History and Culture of a Sioux Indian Village*. Albuquerque, N.M.: Sloves-Bunnell, 1978.

Taylor, Colin F. *The Plains Indians*. New York: Salamander, 1994.

Thomas, Bob, Mary Campbell, and Norm Goldstein. *The One and Only Bing*. New York: Associated Press, 1977.

Tooker, Elisabeth, ed. *Native North American Spirituality of the Eastern Woodlands*. Mahwah, N.J.: Paulist Press, 1979.

Vander, Judith. *Songprints*. Chicago: University of Illinois Press, 1988.

Viola, Herman J. *After Columbus: The Smithsonian Chronicle of the North American Indians*. New York: Orion, 1990.

Waldman, Carl, with Molly Braun. *Atlas of the North American Indian*. New York: Facts on File, 1985.

Wilson, Chesley Goseyun, Ruth Longcor Harnisch Wilson, and Bryan Burton. *When the Earth Was Like New*. Danbury, Conn.: World Music Press, 1994.

Index

About the Author

The professional career of Brian Wright-McLeod (Dakota-Anishnabe) has been as full and varied as his life experiences, which straddle two worlds. Raised with a deep awareness of his roots within an adopted family of mixed white and Metis heritage, he grew up around live music of all styles and developed a love for the arts. He began working as a music journalist in 1979 and has since interviewed numerous major recording artists, many of whom are featured in this volume. He has also traveled extensively throughout the world as a reporter for print and radio mediums.

His column *Dirty Words and Thoughts about Music* appears bimonthly in *News from Indian Country* (Hayward, Wisconsin); he is also a contributor to *Native Peoples* magazine (Albuquerque, New Mexico), the Smithsonian's National Museum of the American Indian quarterly publication *American Indian*, and *Spirit* magazine (Toronto, Ontario).

His activist work in Native rights took him to the airwaves on CKLN 88.1 FM (Toronto, Canada) in 1985, where he continues to produce and host *Renegade Radio*, a live two-hour weekly music and issues program. He freelanced as a Native music consultant for producers at CBC and BBC Radio and for the television series *Beyond Words* on APTN and BRAVO networks.

A former board member of the Native American Journalists Association, he holds degrees in graphic arts and journalism; he has served as a chair for the Best Native Music Recording category for the Juno Awards (CARAS). This encyclopedia is his first book.